*True spirituality – the authentic religious journey –
can never be an escape from life's problems....
Our spiritual journey...must be worked out now in a
global context in the midst of global crises and global
community.*

DR. PATRICIA MISCHE,
Co-founder of Global Education Associates,
in *Towards a Global Spirituality*

*In this new ecological age of developing global
community and interfaith dialogue, the world religions
face what is perhaps the greatest challenge that they
have ever encountered. Each is inspired by a unique
vision of the divine and has a distinct cultural identity.
At the same time, each perceives the divine as the source
of unity and peace. The challenge is to preserve their
religious and cultural uniqueness without letting it
operate as a cause of narrow and divisive sectarianism
that contradicts the vision of divine unity and peace.
It is a question whether the healing light of religious
vision will overcome the social and ideological issues
that underlie much of the conflict between religions.*

DR. STEVEN C. ROCKEFELLER,
in *Spirit and Nature*, p. 169

*All the religions and all the people of the world are
undergoing the most challenging transformation in
history, leading to the birth of a new consciousness.
Forces which have been at work for centuries are
drawing the human race into a global network, and the
religions of the world into a global spiritual community.*

DR. EWERT COUSINS,
in *Journal of Ecumenical Studies*

A SourceBook for Earth's Community of Religions

Revised Edition

Joel D. Beversluis, *Project Editor*

Co-published 1995 by

CoNexus Press, Grand Rapids, Michigan
&
Global Education Associates, New York

Revised Edition 1995
Revisions copyright ©1995 Joel Beversluis (ISBN 0-9637897-1-6)

First Edition 1993
Copyright © 1993 Council for a Parliament of the World's Religions
(ISBN 0-9637897-0-8)

The Revised Edition is published by:
    CoNexus Press
    P.O. Box 6902, Grand Rapids, MI 49516 USA
with
    Global Education Associates
    475 Riverside Dr., Suite 1848, New York, NY 10115 USA

Second printing, January 1966. Includes minor corrections and
new materials, especially on pp. 32–35.

PUBLISHER'S CATALOGING IN PUBLICATION

A Sourcebook for Earth's community of religions / Joel
Beversluis, project editor. – Rev. ed.   p.   cm.
Rev. ed. of: A sourcebook for the community of religions, 1993.
Includes bibliographical references and indexes.
Preassigned LCCN: 94-074622
ISBN 0-9637897-1-6

1. Religions. 2. Religions – Relations. I. Beversluis, Joel D. (Joel
Diederik) II. Council for a Parliament of the World's Religions.
III. Title: Source book for Earth's community of Religions.
IV. Title: Sourcebook for the community of religions.
V. Title: Source book for the community of religions.
BL80.2.S58 1995   291   QBI94-21310

CREDITS FOR THE REVISED EDITION:

Editing, design and typesetting by Joel Beversluis.
Cover photo: Scott Falls, Munising, Mich., by Joel Beversluis.
Proofreading by Robert F.Smith. First index by Nancy Freedom.
Printing by McNaughton and Gunn, Inc., Saline, Michigan.
The text is printed on J.B. Offset, a partially recycled paper.

SYMBOLS USED ON THE COVER:

Left column of symbols: *Right column:*
    Christianity   Sikhism
    Islam   Judaism
    Buddhism   Hinduism
    Wicca   Confucianism
    Zoroastrianism   Shintoism
    Jainism   Taoism
    Native American   Bahá'í faith

Most of the symbols used here were researched and compiled by
Frank Banko and Meribeth Krause for use on their poster
displaying the words "There will be peace on earth when there is
peace among the world's religions," in 18 languages. Copies of
this large and colorful poster are available for a small donation to
cover shipping and handling, from:
    Frank Banko, 452 Adaway SE, Grand Rapids, MI 49546 USA

ORDERING INFORMATION:

*Public libraries, bookstores, and those placing credit card
orders, contact:*
    **Atrium Publishers Group: (800) 275-2606
    or other fine distributors.**

Academic, religious, special sales, & mail orders, contact:
    **CoNexus Press
    PO Box 6902,
    Grand Rapids, MI 49516 USA**
    tel. (800) 452-7514 / fax 616 248-0943
$18.95 each plus $3.00 shipping & handling in the USA (book
rate); add $4.00 postage (surface mail) outside the USA.
Please pay in US$; make checks out to CoNexus Press.
Quantity discounts and billing are available for group orders,
events, and distribution by your store or organization; call or write
for terms.

Books are also available from:
    **Global Education Associates
    475 Riverside Drive, Suite 1848,
    New York, NY 10115 USA**
    tel. **(212) 870-3290** / fax **(212) 870-2729**
$18.95 plus $3.00 shipping & handling in USA (book rate);
add $4.00 postage (surface mail) outside USA.
Call or write for information on quantity discounts and billing.
Please pay in US$; make checks out to G.E.A.

*Distributors and stores outside the USA are invited to carry this
book.* Commercial outlets should contact Atrium. Institutions,
publishers and not-for profit organizations should contact
CoNexus Press for terms.

Contents

PART THREE:
Beyond Borders, 175

28: RELIGIONS AND GOOD GOVERNANCE

29: THE UNITED NATIONS AT 50

30: EARTH DAY, EVERY DAY

31: HUMAN RIGHTS AND RELIGIOUS FREEDOM

32: HUNGER

33: POPULATION

Acknowledgements

Grateful appreciation is due the following for use of their copyrighted and previously printed materials. (Some copyright notices, as well as sources for materials used, are printed with the articles, where appropriate.)

Albert Schweitzer Institute for the Humanities. Excerpts from "Framework for Preparation for the Year 2000," by Robert Muller, copyright 1994, used with permission.

American Humanist Association. *Humanist Manifesto II*. First printed in Volume 33, Number 5, September/October 1973, *The Humanist*. Reprinted with permission.

Beacon Press. Excerpts from *Spirit and Nature* by John C. Elder and Steven C. Rockefeller. Copyright 1992 by John C. Elder and Steven C. Rockefeller. Reprinted by permission of Beacon Press.

Campaign 1995 Committee, *New Beginnings* newsletter. Used with permission.
Excerpts from "A Call to Remembrance and Renewal."
"Steps to Abolish Nuclear Weapons."

Church World Service. "Myths and Realities," compiled by the Office on Global Education. Used with permission.

College Theology Society. "The Cosmology of Religions," by Thomas Berry, in *College Theology Annual Volume, #34,* edited by Dr. Paul Knitter. Used with permission.

Council for a Parliament of the World's Religions.
"Towards a Global Ethic (An Initial Declaration)." Copyright 1993. Used with Permission. P.O. Box 1630, Chicago, IL 60690-1630
Excerpts from the "Executive Summary." Copyright 1993
Council for a Parliament of the World's Religions.

Fox, Selena. "A Guide to Nature Spirituality Terms." Copyright 1994 Selena Fox. Used with permission.

GAIA Books Ltd. *The Gaia Atlas of First Peoples* by Julian Burger; A Gaia Original, copyright 1990 Gaia Books Ltd., 66 Charlotte Street, London W1P 1LR UK. Published in the US by Doubleday/Anchor. Used with permission.

Global Education Associates. Reprinted with permission.
"Religion and World Order," by Patricia Mische; "Project Global 2000," and "Guideline Questions" were printed in *Proceedings of the Symposium on Religion and Global Governance*. Copyright 1994.
"The Earth Covenant and an Earth Charter." Printed in *Breakthrough News,* Fall 1994.
"Toward a Global Spirituality," (excerpt) copyright 1982.
"To Set Our Leaders Free" (revised). First printed in *Breakthrough,* Fall '87, Spring '88.

International Committee for a Peace Council. Excerpts from "Peace Council," by Daniel Gomez-Ibanez. Copyright 1994. Reprinted with permission.

International Religious Foundation, Inc. "The One, the Other, the Divine, the Many in Zulu Traditional Religion of Southern Africa," by Lizo Doda Jafta, in *Dialogue and Alliance,* Summer 1992. Used with permission.

Inter Religious Federation for World Peace. Used with permission of IRFWP Newsletter editor, 4 W. 43rd St., New York, NY 10036.
"African Traditional Religion," by Darrol Bryant. The General Programme, IRFWP New Delhi Congress, 1993. Used with permission.
"The Human Problem and Evil," by Thomas G. Walsh. Printed in *IRFWP Newsletter,* Vol. II, Number 1, Spring 1994.
"Practical Responses to Evil," by Carl Becker. Printed in *IRFWP*

Newsletter, Vol. II, Number 1, Spring 1994.
"What Was Accomplished," by Thomas G. Walsh. Printed in *IRFWP Newsletter,* Vol. II, Number 1, Spring 1994.
"May the Light Dawn," by Paulos Mar Gregorios. Printed in *IRFWP Newsletter,* Vol. II, Number 1, Spring 1994.

IUCN/UNEP/WWF. Excerpts from *Caring for the Earth. A Strategy for Sustainable Living.* Copyright 1991, Gland, Switzerland. Used with permission.

Journal of Ecumenical Studies. "The Dialogue Decalogue," by Leonard Swidler. Reprinted with permission.

Kosei Publishing Company. "A Dual Awakening Process," by Dr. Ariyaratne, printed in *Dharma World,* July/August 1992; and the editorial by Kazumasa Osaka and other quotations from *Dharma World,* Jan./Feb. 1993. Used with permission.

LaChance, Albert. Excerpts from the Preface and Introduction to *Greenspirit: Twelve Steps in Ecological Spirituality,* published in the USA, 1991, by Element, Inc., 42 Broadway, Rockport, MA 01966; and in Great Britain in 1991 by Element Books Ltd., Longmead, Shaftesbury, Dorset. Used with permission.

Lucis Trust. "Testimony and Treasure" and "The Great Invocation." Used with permission Lucis Trust, 113 University Place, 11th Floor, New York, NY 10017-1888.

Millennium Institute. "The Role of the Faith Traditions," by Dr. Gerald O. Barney, Jane Blewett and Kristen Barney, from *Global 2000 Revisited.* Copyright 1993 Millennium Institute. Used with permission.

National Conference. "The World House," published Spring 1992. Chicago. Used with permission.

New Road Map Foundation. "A Declaration of Independence – from Overconsumption," by Vickie Robin. Copyright 1994. Used with permission.

Orbis Books. Excerpts from *The Desert is Fertile,* by Dom Helder Camara. Copyright 1983. Maryknoll, New York. Used with permission.

SCM Press Ltd., London, UK. Used with permission.
"Conclusions" of *Pilgrimage of Hope,* by Marcus Braybrooke. Copyright 1992 (US rights: Crossroad Publishing Co.).
Four excerpts from articles in *A Dictionary of Religious Education,* edited by John M. Sutcliffe. Copyright 1984.

The Tablet Publishing Co., Ltd. "The New Consciousness," by Bede Griffiths. Printed in the January 16, 1993 issue of *The Tablet,* edited by John Wilkins. London, UK. Used with permission.

United Nations. Declarations, conventions, materials from the Department of Public Information and other agency publications are not copyrighted.

World Conference on Religions and Peace. *Prayers from Religion for Peace: Proceedings of the Kyoto Conference on Religion and Peace,* edited by Dr. Homer Jack. Copyright WCRP 1973. Used with permission.

World Council of Churches. "We Will Not Hang our Harps on the Willows," by Barbel Von Wartenberg-Potter. Copyright 1987 WCC Publications, Geneva, Switzerland. Used with permission.

World Future Society. "Temples of Tomorrow," by Richard Kirby and Earl Brewer. Reprinted with permission from *The Futurist,* 7910 Woodmont Avenue, Suite 450, Bethesda, Maryland 20814; (301) 656-8274

World Happiness and Cooperation. "Decide to Network," articles and agendas previously printed by Robert Muller, reproduced by permission of Robert Muller; for more information, contact his publisher, World Happiness and Cooperation, P.O. Box 1153, Anacortes, WA 98221.

Note and Disclaimer

Introduction to the Revised Edition

Joel D. Beversluis

Project Editor, A SourceBook for Earth's Community of Religions; has worked in many areas of publishing; has served in peace, ecology, and interfaith movements; is completing graduate study in comparative religions at Western Michigan University; is self-employed as an editor and publisher.

*I*nitially created as a resource for participants in the 1993 Parliament of the World's Religions, this *SourceBook* is now substantially revised and enlarged. It is designed to serve all members of the world's religions and spiritual traditions as well as humanists, atheists and agnostics. Ultimately, its themes encompass the whole community of the Earth, a community which is facing increasingly severe challenges and crises of many kinds.

The pages of this *SourceBook* hold many convictions, including those of this Editor. Among them, this one is primary – that a critical task for all of the world's religions and spiritual traditions is to enrich the vision – and the reality – of the sense of community among us. Without this vision, as the Jewish prophet warned, we will perish. In fact, even now many of our brothers and sisters are victims of ethical, political and ecological chaos.

We are not, however, proposing the deliberate mixing or watering-down of traditions into a consensus or world religion. Rather, this book defends the integrity of diverse traditions and stands for the value of pluralism within our societies. Thus the agenda for Earth's community of religions is to respect our differences, embrace our similarities, define our common needs, and facilitate cooperative responses to critical local and global issues.

The contents

*T*his *SourceBook* is a unique anthology, bringing together elements characteristic of many different kinds of publications – religious studies and reference materials, public documents, inspirational reflections, prayers and scriptural texts, political and ecological analysis, directory information, and annotated resource guides. More than half of the contents were written for this book or are published here for the first time. The other contributions were previously printed in a wide variety of publications, from books and journals to flyers and newsletters.

This book deliberately crosses topical boundaries and links together items that are too often kept apart. It is, in short, a wholistic approach, what my Calvinist roots think of as a world-transforming, world-and-life view.

While the selection of the materials printed here inevitably reflects this Editor's values, the contents also showcase the distinctive beliefs, experience and knowledge of many hundreds of contributors. These members of different religions, professions, ages, and ethnic backgrounds do not always agree with each other; nevertheless, their inclusion here models an exciting interaction between diverse traditions, ethical considerations, and responses to issues. Out of this wide-ranging and challenging collage, each reader must draw out his or her own conclusions.

How to use the SourceBook

*A*lthough the book does follow a progression, you don't need to read it front to back. Indeed, it will be much more meaningful if you follow where your interests lead.

Here's a strategy to help you choose what to read and how to find what interests you.

1) Examine the table of Contents. There are Five Parts containing 44 thematically arranged chapters, plus an Epilogue and two indexes. Note that Part Five has extensive annotated Resource Guides to organizations, publications, and electronic media. There are also hundreds of listings "For more information," throughout parts one to four.

2) Examine the two indexes to see just how much information is packed into this book – and how to find what you want.

3) Read Chapter One for an overview. It includes introductory articles by this Editor and a Foreword by Dr. Robert Muller.

4) Focus on areas of special interest if you have them, or else browse among the hundreds of articles, essays, prayers, reflections, poems, quotations, and resource listings. Prepare to have your perceptions stretched.

A challenge

*D*ue in part to the media, to labor-saving devices, and to our uses of leisure time, we can very easily become spectators of life. Our scientific and liberal educations and even our religious lives are so colored by the inclination to observation and analysis that we grow accustomed to thinking that good thoughts and good reading – and even good entertainment – are nearly equivalent to good deeds.

This book is designed to nurture a process of reflection and action *combined*, in a transformative process. In presenting who we humans claim to be and hope to become, the *SourceBook* seeks to identify our tasks, acknowledge our strengths, and promote use of the many gifts among us. If the book helps readers move into more intriguing reflections on powerful ideas and beliefs, and then into responsible action, it will be accomplishing its goals. Now it is in your hands.

Foreword

Dr. David Ramage, Jr.

Chair of the Council for a Parliament of the World's Religions at the time of the Parliament; President of McCormick Theological Seminary (Emeritus); Chair of the Board of People for the American Way

*A*s we move into the global reality of interrelationships, interdependence and even, to some extent, shared social consciousness, the challenge is to find the ways in which we can come to understand each other's religious motivations and practices, cultural patterns, and realities. Therefore we must learn more about each other, talk to each other, work together for common goals, and refuse to allow differences to be exploited by others for political or material advantage. We cannot permit those who have extreme and rigid views to determine our behavior.

This is a demanding challenge, which all of humankind faces. History demonstrates how difficult the challenge is and will be. Current conflicts in the world and in our neighborhoods are not encouraging. Yet it is a challenge we must respond to if there is to be a hopeful and peaceful future for the peoples of the earth.

Fortunately, there are many who understand this and have initiated sharing and the search for mutual understanding. May that number increase to include us all!

The reality of a shrinking planet is all about us – in our neighborhoods, on TV, and in countless other ways. Let us find the ways to understand and appreciate our new neighbors, as well as the ways to work together for a peaceful, fruitful, safe, environmentally sound, and just common reality. It is already too late to wait.

This *SourceBook* is a major resource for continuing what happened so fruitfully at the Parliament – to deepen our understanding of each other and to encourage dialogue and cooperation.

May that which stirs our spiritual understanding motivate our action and responsibility.

Preface

Joel Beversluis

I am very grateful for the unique opportunity of compiling this *SourceBook*, the first edition for the Parliament and now this Revised Edition. Among the great rewards in a project like this is the interaction with committed authors and organizations; these have assisted by generously providing essays, articles, poems, permissions, and information. They have also offered friendly support and validation of the book's agenda.

In particular, I wish to express my appreciation to:

- Brother Wayne Teasdale, whose enthusiasm, ideas, and assistance have enriched the book and the process of making it;

- Board members, staff and trustees of the Council for a Parliament of the World's Religions, for their vision in creating the Parliament;

- Patricia and Gerald Mische of Global Education Associates, for their leadership, programs, and interest;

- my parents, Henry and Gertrude Beversluis, for a lifetime of intellectual and spiritual nurture;

- my children and their spouses and children, whose futures provide strong motivation for this work;

- Gwendolyn, my wife, whose encouragement, love and gardens are a blessing to me; and

- the creating and sustaining One.

*F*inally, but of great significance to me, is this observation: by participating in the creation of this book, the numerous and diverse contributors to it are themselves documenting the existence of – and potential for – Earth's emerging community of religions.

Making the Connections

Prologue

Joel Beversluis

An Overview of the title and contents

The lengthy title, *A SourceBook for Earth's Community of Religions,* does not roll easily off the tongue. Since a lot is packed into it as well as into the book itself, this overview should help the reader to better grasp their contents.

A SourceBook –

Its pages are brim full of beliefs, ideas, essays, prayers, scriptures, resource listings, organizational missions, wisdom, analyses, projects, visions, poems and strategies. Through its hundreds of contributions from members of the world's religions and spiritual traditions, the book also aims to reveal some things true about the Source of all, about the meanings and purposes of our lives, and about the challenges and opportunities in the contemporary world. This book is also a resource through which one may start to evaluate the uniquenesses and the commonalities of these beliefs and truths, which are expressed in many ways. Finally, this *SourceBook* provides resources that readers may use for further research and in expressing their ethical responses to our present and future world.

– for Earth's –

The word "Earth's" is difficult to pronounce. "Global" would have been easier and has many useful connotations – geography, politics, economics, communications, and so on; but it also has a mechanistic ring. The word "Earth" reinforces the *qualities* of life, relationship and value that this book seeks to address. The word also names our home, evoking an image of a wondrous blue and green planet in the mysterious cosmos.

The word "Earth's" is also usefully ambiguous in that it raises good questions: aren't many religions and spiritual traditions "other-worldly," having to do with the transcendent or eternity, with the Ultimate? and does the Earth "possess" us or do we own it?

Neither "owns" the other, of course. Yet, although we often don't appreciate our dependence on Earth, we are clearly part of its ecological community. Earth and its systems have given birth to us and nurtured us. Our personal and corporate experiences in the community of the Earth help to shape our values and beliefs, and these, in turn, directly influence the systems of the Earth.

– Community of Religions

This book affirms that the systems and laws of the Earth are partially expressed in the spiritual wisdom and truth of the ages. Furthermore, the interaction of Earth's systems and the truths of the ages together provide the essential matrix which binds the religions, spiritual traditions and world-views into what we have called "Earth's community of religions." Although this matrix has always been present and has been evident to some peoples, contemporary cultures are now in great need of the knowledge of its effects and of the obligations that these interaction place upon us.

Some who see the evidence of conflict between religions may view this alleged community as little more than a fantasy; clearly, the community of religions does have its dysfunctional aspects. Other observers, however, understand that naming the ideal provides a vision and hope for the future. And for many, including this writer, the concept of "Earth's community of religions" names an emerging reality: that we are becoming – and *must* become – community. Its emergence is proved in many ways, including by the analyses, activities, and values of those who are participants in this book.

The *SourceBook* is thus an attempt to reveal the character and purpose of individual and collective members of Earth's community of religions; it seeks to encourage the community's greater development, and it points to its beneficial effects, which are even now manifest in the ethics, organizations, and solidarity of countless human beings.

"My dear brothers and sisters:
we are already one,
but we imagine that we are not.
What we have to recover is our original unity.
What we have to become is what we already are."
THOMAS MERTON,
speaking to the First Spiritual Summit, in Calcutta,
sponsored by the Temple of Understanding

Foreword:
Preparing for the Next Millennium

Dr. Robert Muller

Former Assistant Secretary-General of the United Nations, and still active as Chancellor of the United Nations University for Peace in Costa Rica (Emeritus)

Dr. Muller is also author of numerous books, speeches and articles about global issues, the UN and education. In 1989 he was awarded the UNESCO Peace Education Prize and in 1993 the Albert Schweitzer International Prize for the Humanities. In 1994 he was recognized with the Eleanor Roosevelt Man of Vision Award.

*T*he centennial – and second – Parliament of the World's Religions in 1993 was a highly significant event taking place at the end of this century and millennium. The first edition of the *SourceBook,* prepared for the Parliament and the evolving community of religions, offered a substantial building block for the spiritual awakening we so desperately need. It is only in such a renaissance that we will find the fulfillment of humanity's extraordinary destiny in the unfathomable and mysterious universe. This second, expanded, and updated edition is an even stronger contribution – An Agenda for the Renaissance of World Spirituality!

A new self-consciousness

*C*elebrations and a rare date like the year 2000 provoke unusually deep thinking and taking stock, both in retrospection and envisioning the future. As preparation for the year 2000 and humanity's entrance into the next millennium, I was driven by curiosity to put together a list of major events which are taking place on this planet.* The result is amazing! It shows that, for the first time in history, humanity as a species is preparing itself *consciously* for entrance into a new century and age.

At the end of the last century, international commemorations of our entry into the 20th century were limited to the first World's Parliament of Religions in Chicago in 1893 – as part of a World's Fair celebrating progress – and the first international people's peace conference in the Hague in 1899. The only international organizations at that time were the Universal Postal Union and the International Telegraph Union, because mail and telegraph lines had to cross national borders.

Today we have a nearly universal United Nations of 184 member states and thirty-two international, specialized agencies and world programs covering every major global subject on earth and in outer space. We have a European Union of states between which all border and customs controls have been abolished. Fifteen other regional communities are in the making throughout the world.

Here are a few other international events leading into the 21st century – many of them expressed through the United Nations Organization – that illustrate this new, global self-consciousness:

1992

- The UN Secretary-General submits an unprecedented Agenda for World Peace to the Security Council meeting – for the first time at the level of heads of state – since the Cold War had now ended
- The Agenda for the 21st Century at the UN Conference on all major aspects of the world's environment and development, in Rio de Janeiro
- International Year of Outer Space

1993

- Second world conference on human rights and a program of action into the next century
- International Year of Indigenous People
- The international interfaith meeting in Bangalore commemorating the 1893 Parliament and planning for interfaith cooperation into the next century
- The centennial meeting of the Parliament of the World's Religions in Chicago, with a focus on critical issues and the next generations

1994

- International Year of the Family
- Third world conference on population
- International conference on education
- 50th anniversaries of the World Bank, the International Monetary Fund and the International Civil Aviation Org.
- 75th Anniversary of the International Labour Organization

1995

- 50th anniversary of the United Nations and of the Food and Agriculture Organization
- Fourth World Conference on Women
- World Summit on Social Development, including issues of poverty, unemployment and social integration
- International Year of Tolerance
- Report of the Independent Commission on Global Governance
- Report of the World Commission on Culture and Development
- Birth of the World Trade Organization

1996

- International Year for the Eradication of Poverty
- Second World Conference on Human Settlements
- 50th anniversaries of the World Health Organization, UNESCO, UNICEF, and the International Court of Justice.

The list goes on until the celebration of the year 2000, including in 1998 the fiftieth anniversary of the Universal Declaration of Human Rights, and, in 1999, the International Year of the Elderly and the centennial World Peace Conference in the Hague. The scope of this activity is unprecedented and full of hope for humanity.

In my view, from all perspectives – scientific, political, social, economic, and ideological – humanity finds itself in the pregnancy of an entirely new and promising age: the global, interdependent, universal age; a truly quantum jump; a cosmic event of the first importance that is perhaps unique in the universe: the birth of a global brain, heart, senses and soul to humanity, of a holistic consciousness of our place in the universe and on this planet, and of our role and destiny in them.

Much of this new consciousness is enhanced by the prodigious advances in sciences and technology. Yet most people, governments and institutions – including religions – are bewildered by this phenomenon. They have difficulty adapting to it with understanding and creativity; they were not educated for it. They see the future with anxiety. Many of them turn and cling to the past or look inwards to the nation, ethnic group or religion which they know and where they feel secure. As a result, the world seems at a loss and is badly equipped and organized globally and politically.

But we will make it. We are learning. Once aware of our problems and errors, we are beginning to correct them. The *Encyclopedia of World Problems and Human Potential,* published by the International Union of International Associations in Brussels, lists more than 11,400 world problems but even more potentials to solve them. One progress is happening after another: the decolonization of the planet in less than forty years; no world war in half a century; the end of the cold war; the end of apartheid; a substantial decrease in child mortality; the eradication of major epidemics; the increase in human longevity, both in poor and in rich countries; a universal organization of nations; one world conference after the other, attended by more and more heads of states (the first world conference on the environment in 1972 in Stockholm was attended by only two heads of states; the second conference twenty years later in Rio de Janeiro was attended by 140); the creation of free trade areas and regional communities; and I could go on with this list.

Yet there is infinitely more to do and it must be done much faster. That is why, on 11 July 1994, I began compiling a list of 2000 ideas – one for each day until the year 2000 – which can and must be implemented.

Why do I harbour such hope in the midst of prevalent pessimism? Because, when I look back at my forty years of world service at the United Nations, the house which gets every hopeless problem on Earth, I can hardly believe the changes I witnessed. Coming from war-torn and much disputed Alsace-Lorraine, I wonder if now I am dreaming! My grandfather knew three wars and had five nationalities in his lifetime, without leaving his village. My father knew two wars, was twice a French soldier and once a German soldier. I knew one war which made us twice refugees. Half of my cousins wore French uniforms, the other half German; we might have killed each other. Later, as I watched events from the UN, I was convinced on numerous occasions that another world war would break out. As a young official I was told that decolonization would take from 100 to 150 years. I was asked why I had joined the UN, and told that I would lose my job because it would not survive more than ten years.

Today, when there exists an international organization, conflicts have been substantially reduced: thanks to the UN, there are only three international conflicts left and they are contained; thanks to the International Labour Organization, in a world of much violence, there is no longer any labor violence, while at the end of the last century and the beginning of ours, labor violence was the order of the day. Now we have 69 internal, ethnic and religious conflicts around the world, which the United Nations for the first time has been asked to help solve. And it will succeed there too, with time, as it has succeeded with international conflicts. Today I am convinced that with all we have learned and continue to learn, there will be an acceleration in the solution of our world problems. There has to, because there are constantly new challenges and problems coming up! From being a pessimistic young man when I joined the UN, I have become its "Optimist-in-Residence."

A Missing Dimension

Nevertheless, one important dimension has been missing from this extraordinary journey of humanity in recent times, a dimension lamented by Secretaries-General Dag Hammarskjöld, U Thant and Javier Perez de Cuellar: the *spiritual* dimension, the highest, deepest, most common, universal and binding dimension of all. What science, politics, economics and sociology were trying to achieve, the religions knew long ago by virtue of transcendence, of elevated consciousness and union with the universe and time. This dimension is still missing, yet it is urgently needed in world affairs.

I too, through education in France, Germany and the US, had lost the spirituality given me by my parents and by my wonder, as a child, for the miracle of God's creation. My experience at the UN restored my spirituality. An astute Catholic sister once wrote to me:

> You were at the crossroads of all nations, at a center of the universal. You discovered that, you lived it and you became a universal, spiritual being. You had been cut from this source by your previous education and more limited interests. **

The crucial task of the world's religious and spiritual traditions, the Parliament and other interfaith organizations is restoring a sense of spirituality to all that we do. The common heritages and institutional authority of the religions, combined with an emerging global spirituality, can make enormous contributions to the challenges and details of creating a better world. Though an atheist, André Malraux has said that "the third millennium will be spiritual or there will be no third millennium." Dag Hammarskjöld, a rational economist and world observer whom the UN transformed into a mystic, said, " I see no hope for permanent world peace. We have tried and failed miserably. Unless the world has a spiritual rebirth, civilization is doomed."

The religions are still accused of hindering peace, human progress and brotherhood. How often have I heard, after one of my speeches, "Mr Muller, we agree with most of what you said, except one: forget about religions. They are one of the main troublemakers and dividing factors in the world." But I continue to preach about the spiritual and religious dimension. The new age we are entering will be an age of communities and of cooperation: it will be an age of family (celebrated by the UN in 1994), and of the family of nations. The family of religions cannot be absent; its absence could mean the retrocession and evanescence of religions, left behind by rapidly growing political, economic, scientific, ecological and sociological globalizations of the world.

The Parliament of the World's Religions has achieved several important objectives:

1) the Parliament has underlined the necessity that the world's religious and spiritual leaders must come to agreement about ways to continue interreligious collaboration for peace, the relief of suffering and the preservation of the planet;

2) the members of the Assembly agreed to bring plans and common projects to their communities and to their nations' leaders;

3) the Assembly adopted a world-renowned declaration, "Towards a Global Ethic," which has opened a chapter of upwelling preparations and drafting of ethical statements in many fields of human and planetary concern;

4) the Assembly asked the Council for a Parliament to study the question of an ongoing Parliament or Council of religious and spiritual leaders as a network of organizations devoted to finding solutions to the shared problems of the human community.

Regarding this last, still open question of a permanent institutional forum for interreligious cooperation, it is not a new idea. Now, however, the time seems ripe, on the eve of the year 2000 and the 21st century, for audacious thinking and proposals in this much-neglected field of human concern. It is not enough for religious leaders to meet once in a while in interreligious meetings. We must, together, create an agency within the UN and perhaps also an independent United Religions Secretariat. What an incredible challenge that would offer to the United Nations, and what untold good it would bring to humanity, which desperately needs a moral and spiritual Renaissance.

May I express my own overpowering conviction, born from five decades as a world servant? It is this:

At this crucial point of human history, on the eve of the third millennium, the main duty of the religions is not to propagate their dogmas and rituals or to try to increase their memberships. Their main *spiritual* duty is to give the world a desperately needed Renaissance from the extreme materialism and moral decay into which we have fallen. The issue is *not* whether we should pray standing or kneeling, our heads covered or uncovered; it is whether we will pray – period; whether we will be *good Samaritans* to those in need; whether we can give renewed hope to youth; whether we will revitalize the sacredness of life-giving, belief in the soul, marriage and fidelity. The main duty of religions must be to inspire love for all human brothers and sisters, especially the downtrodden, the poor, the handicapped, abandoned children, the homeless, the refugees, the innocent victims of violence.

We have five precious years before the year 2000. I hope to witness an unprecedented worldwide alliance of all religions against violence, misery, hopelessness and despair.

*M*ay the many fine contributions to this new edition of the *SourceBook* of religions become sources of hope and inspiration for a united human family.

May we enter the 21st century consciously choosing to live in love, togetherness and fulfillment on this beautiful and miraculous celestial body – endowed with life and perhaps unique in the fathomless and mysterious universe.

May the religions of the world help fulfill this dream of an old, faithful, and optimistic world servant:

My Dream 2000

I dream
That on 1 January 2000
The whole world will stand still
In prayer, awe and gratitude
For our beautiful, heavenly Earth
And for the miracle of human life.

I dream
That young and old, rich and poor,
Black and white,
Peoples from North and South,
From East and West,
From all beliefs and cultures
Will join their hands, minds and hearts
In an unprecedented, universal
Bimillennium Celebration of Life.

I dream
That the year 2000
Will be declared "World Year of Thanksgiving"
By the United Nations.

I dream
That during the year 2000
Innumerable celebrations and events
Will take place all over the globe
To gauge the long road covered by humanity
To study our mistakes
And to plan the feats
Still to be accomplished
For the full flowering of the human race
In peace, justice and happiness.

I dream
That the few remaining years
To the Bimillennium
Will be devoted by all humans, nations and institutions
To unparalleled thinking, action,
Inspiration, elevation,
Determination and love
To solve our remaining problems
And to achieve
A peaceful, united human family on Earth.

* *Framework for Preparation for the Year 2000, the 21st Century and the Third Millennium,* published by the Albert Schweitzer Institute, 515 Sherman Avenue, Hamden CT 06514. tel. 203 281-8925

**See *My Testament to the UN, A Contribution to the 50th Anniversary to the UN,* available from the UN Bookshop, Room GA-032A, tel. 212 963-7680

Dr. Muller's books and poems are also available from World Happiness and Cooperation, PO Box 1153, Anacortes, WA 98221 USA

The Global CoNexus

Seeking the True Meaning of Peace
through Spirituality, Ecology, and Good Governance

Joel Beversluis

*A*s we approach the year 2000 (in the Gregorian calendar), many of us are increasingly conscious of relentless change and mind-boggling crises. We seem to be at a point in time where circumstances created by numerous historical and cultural factors are converging into a nexus, a focal point where the energies are intense and swirling around us all. Although it is difficult to find our way through this unprecedented convergence of factors, we are learning that crises contain not only danger, but also opportunities – a better word is imperatives – for transforming the systems in which we live. What the future holds for us and our descendants will be determined in great part by how well we as a species use these opportunities to think and act in new ways.

We cannot easily escape the awareness that this mix of crises has the potential to cause enormous trauma and social conflict. Indeed, emergencies and disasters are already commonplace; the threats and warning signals that transcend national borders are so well known, in fact, that we are numbed to them and to our seeming powerlessness to respond adequately: poverty, hunger, disease, ethnic and regional wars, violence in our cities, unsustainable ecological and population patterns, ozone depletion and, though it has receded from our consciousness, nuclear war.

Many speakers and writers, including some in this book, claim that we live in a time of profound crisis and that the heart of the crisis is a moral or spiritual dilemma. Numerous conditions ranging from crimes of hate to the unethical dumping of toxic byproducts reveal that the human species and the world we inhabit are threatened most by humanity's own inner decay. Though we placed our trust in science and technology, it is increasingly clear that these tools cannot save us. We are realizing that, despite our material "progress," the human species is threatened most by moral ambiguity and inertia.

Seeking the true meaning of peace

*W*ithin most human hearts lies a strong desire for peace: we want harmony with our neighbors and we long for beautiful and healthy natural surroundings. Nevertheless, we will easily forfeit these when fear, greed, or even lofty goals seem more compelling. Our hearts also call out for justice for ourselves and, in principle, for others. Yet, for some, the pursuit of personal or group "justice" – in the form of revenge or self-interest – is another one of those compelling reasons to compromise the ideals of peace. Likewise, the crises mentioned above also have increasing power to disrupt the peacefulness of our daily lives, health, and security.

Aren't there more durable and persistent meanings of "peace" that can offer us the power to transcend those forces which disturb our peacefulness? Where shall we look for the true meaning of peace that can help us face the future with wisdom and effective action?

In this *SourceBook* we propose a closer look at the wisdom of the world's religions, spiritual traditions and venerable philosophies. Their diverse insights on peace and many other subjects are derived from many sources, including the experiences of life which have tested them and found them meaningful. The diversity of beliefs and analyses of the human condition found among the many claims is certainly a real factor, but it need not be problematic. Just as we need the genetic diversity of a rainforest, we now need to understand diverse perspectives both to validate our uniquenesses and to enrich our commonalities. In addition, the diversity itself offers a range of unique and tested perspectives that often have been overlooked by others.

We also propose a closer look at the commitments of those individuals and organizations who are advocating transformation and who are themselves participants in transformative responses to the critical issues. They bring analyses using the best of contemporary science and technology and they bring real-world tests of their visionary hypotheses. In a wide range of projects in the political and social cauldron of today's world, their statements and actions also reflect the wisdom of the ages.

The primary challenge and opportunity of this age is to identify the values, conditions, tasks and agents of peace – so that we can know what it is we seek and when we are finding it. When this pilgrimage bears fruit, the insights give us a place to stand and a vision of the future we want. The true meaning of peace provides a spiritual compass and a set of moral imperatives that can guide us through the nexus of our times.

Connecting ecology, governance, and spirituality

*B*eyond the deadly connections – between avarice and hunger, consumerism and ecological degradation, tribalism and suffering – are there also life-enhancing connections to help us define the tasks before us? Peace movements, Earth Day events, hunger concerts, UN commemorations and Parliaments of Religions will make a difference *only* as they bring *transformative* ideas into the public forum.

The idea that ecology, governance, and spirituality are indeed vitally connected is liberating and empowering. The policies and methods of governance at all levels have never had more influence on the global future than they do now. Implying much more than the term "politics," the concept of good governance incorporates the broad range of responses that must meet local, regional and global needs.

At the same time, each individual's responsibility for the whole must ensure that there is appropriate governance at all levels. This personal quality of universal responsibility, though innate, must be *activated* by religions, spiritual traditions, and world-views that generate compassion and personal commitment.

Along with the crises described above, transformative ideas and visions are also gathering in the global nexus, perhaps in response to the increased need. Operating something like a funnel or centrifuge that compresses the elements, the nexus is creating new "chemical reactions," breaking up old allegiances and revealing new connections. Among them is the evolving understanding of the idea of *interconnectedness* itself.

Thirty years ago ecology and environment were generally understood in terms of the interactions of the natural world and our impact on it. Now the terms are linked with the entire material and conceptual system in which we function, including economics, governance, sustainable development, peace and justice. This holistically-understood system now also encompasses world-views, the creation stories of both the sciences *and* religions, personal spirituality, and studies of the future. New mythologies, too, are arising as science and religions find unexpected bonds within the nexus.

The future, on the far side of the nexus, is, for the most part, unpredictable. Many things may happen there. Their shape will come through the convergence of very real crises with equally real opportunities for personal and global change. The prefix *Co-* in the word "CoNexus" reinforces the idea of the connectedness between crises, opportunities and an emerging global consciousness. *Co-* also suggests that we are engaged in an ongoing process, together.

Beyond the borders of self-interest

*I*t seems only common sense that in order for our species and earth's ecosystems to survive gracefully, we humans must change our ways. But, we may well ask: is there any hope? is it possible for the species to change so substantially? can *an emerging global consciousness buttressed by wisdom from the world's religious and*

spiritual traditions, as well as by the best contemporary knowledge, save us from ourselves? can an energetic community of religions empower their adherents to cooperate in changing our ways and reversing the threats?

Growing numbers of people worldwide do have these hopes and have committed themselves to assisting in the process. Others act because of a strong commitment to doing the right thing for future generations. Many people of all countries are busy acting locally, doing what they think needs to be done, working to recreate the world *as it should be*. The universal persistence of the "ideal" is itself a hope-engendering factor in the nexus; envisioning it is the first step in the process of creativity. As Goethe wrote, and many traditions affirm, the next step is to act boldly, for then the universe also acts *with* us.

Many necessary changes are possible simply because the opportunities and needs are found everywhere and call out to everyone to respond in very local and personal ways. Each person who acts for the well-being of others engages in a journey of personal growth, envisioning a future and acting locally in his or her own way. The teacher who recycles and the investor who chooses socially responsible funds are acting within a global context. Each student with a penpal across the planet, each man who plants a flower, and each child who cares for a pet is learning to think beyond the borders of self-interest. So it is that, through the little actions, momentous changes may evolve.

In this process of change, we can gain needed sustenance from the knowledge that we are not alone. Understanding the deadly connections and the scope of crises can be intimidating, but becoming familiar with helpful ideas and joining other motivated people is also highly energizing. The best energy in any transformative process is that which flows *through* us when we reflect on it, respond to it from our hearts and through our bodies, and then pass it on to others.

St. Francis sang, "Lord, make me an instrument of thy peace!" With the same prayer we may become instruments of the "CoNexus" – pioneers working the connections that link members of the world's religions and spiritual traditions into a community of peace, as fully responsible citizens of the larger community of the Earth.

The Age of Interspiritual Community

"*We are rapidly entering the age of interspiritual community. This new axial period will be characterized by the emergence of a profound sense of community among the world's religions and spiritual traditions; it will also draw them into deeper relationships with other areas of human culture, particularly the sciences, arts, economics, politics and media. The unfolding and expanding reality of this community will slowly dissipate the fears we have collected over the millennia, and it will reveal the precious gift of interspiritual wisdom.*

"In this age we will gain access to the treasures hidden in the depths of our own and other traditions of spirituality. These resources have the power to transform our attitudes and behavior toward one another, other species and the Earth itself. They will lead us into awareness of our larger communion with this sacred reality that is home for us all. The challenge for humankind is to actively participate in this process of transformation, while the task of the religions is to inspire in humanity the will to change and to summon up, within their own ranks, the courage to sustain it."

BROTHER WAYNE TEASDALE

Who Are We?

Major Religions, Spiritual Traditions and Philosophies of the World

Introduction

Joel Beversluis

*W*e – members of major religions, spiritual traditions, and philosophies of the world – are beyond counting and beyond comprehensive descriptions. Our local and individual variations cannot be circumscribed, in part because we are always in flux. We are influenced by each other, by our experiences in the world and by our own changing perceptions. So we are also beyond definition.

Nevertheless, we may describe some of our diverse characteristics and thus begin to develop a picture of the whole. One such image is that a sense of community is – and should be – emerging among the religions, spiritual traditions and philosophies, within the larger community of the Earth.

Those who read this *SourceBook* may conclude with its Editor that indeed there is a "community" and that, furthermore, one of its most significant characteristics is that this community has many wondrous yet under-utilized gifts within it. The sense of commitment engendered by the religions and spiritual philosophies, their organizational and motivational resources, the wisdom and insight in their heritages, and their practical experience with real life issues are all portions of a substantial cultural and spiritual legacy. These gifts must be given freedom and put to work!

*T*he authors of the essays in Part One have written not as official representatives, nor as disinterested specialists (though the majority of them are scholars), but, in most cases, as committed participants within the traditions they describe. In addition to the essays, most contributors also provided selections of scriptures, prayers and commentary valued by their traditions, and some even made original translations.

Most of the major religious and spiritual traditions of the earth – and some of their movements and branches – are portrayed here. Yet, since the traditions and their many manifestations are so numerous, this work must be seen as an introduction and survey. Much more detail is available in other works, some of which are noted in Chapter 43.

Despite enhancements in this *Revised Edition,* there remain imbalances. The alphabetical listing of so many traditions and movements side by side does not do justice to disproportions in the numbers of adherents, their global presence, and their complexity. The following criteria guided the choices made by the Editor: to include

1) religious and spiritual traditions that are historic and worldwide;

2) representative indigenous traditions;

3) spiritual and evolutionary philosophies;

4) influential new movements or branches;

5) groups that were accessible and whose members responded to the invitation to participate.

This last factor led to an emphasis on those groups with a substantial presence in North America; this emphasis is, of course, unfortunate in a book purporting to have a global outlook. It is also unfortunate because so many traditions have religious and cultural ties to the land itself – outside of North America. Yet, because the rich and increasingly pluralistic North American culture has adherents from so many traditions and lands of origin, we offer their beliefs and experience as a starting point.

*A*uthors of the *Portraits* were invited to write short essays and provide materials on:

1) origins, beliefs, and membership of their tradition;

2) approach to interreligious encounter and cooperation;

3) understanding of, and responses to, critical issues;

4) wisdom, scriptures, prayers, or commentary relating to the above.

Other articles offer insights into important aspects of a tradition or movement. The Editor has also selected previously printed articles, reflections, scriptures or prayers which provide further insight into the self-understanding of some members of a tradition. All materials are intended to add depth to our understanding and to provide insights about the challenges and opportunities we face in today's world.

African Traditional Religions

Zulu Traditional Religion of Southern Africa

Lizo Doda Jafta

Lecturer at the Federal Theological Seminary of Southern Africa, Natal

*O*ne of the basic human experiences is that a human being is a dependent creature; therefore, the contingency of being human demands that one should properly relate oneself to the environment upon which one depends. Thus the human sense of dependence becomes the root religion.

One becomes aware that one did not create the universe; one found the universe already created. This awe-inspiring universe with its boundless spaces and measureless forces occasions God-consciousness. Natural events in particular are occasions of God-consciousness among the Zulu people. The changes in the clouds, the highness of the heavens, the overflowing rivers, the frightening lightnings and thunderstorms side-by-side with religious ceremonies are all occasions of God-consciousness. In these events God is experienced as the One, the Other, the Divine and the Many. The key word is experience. [...]

The Zulu notion of God-consciousness ... says that God lives in, through and beyond everything and everyone, but that God is most clearly apprehended through those spirits who are always around, below, above, and in them .... When the Zulus see the Deity in every place and all the time, they are acknowledging the ubiquitous nature of God as well as their constant sojourn within the realm of the divine presence.

excerpted from
"The One, the Other, the Divine, the Many in Zulu Traditional Religion of Southern Africa" in *Dialogue and Alliance,* Summer 1992, pp.79–89.

An Introduction to African Traditional Religions

Rev. Dr. Abraham Akrong

Professor of Religion, McCormick Theological Seminary

The term "Africa"

*S*ince the time of Pliny the elder, who is reputed to have first used it, the term "Africa" has been a bone of contention because it means different things to different people – for many people Africa is essentially a racial group; for some, Africa is a geo-political entity carved up in the last century at the Berlin conference of 1884–85; for others, Africa is a linguistic-cultural entity that describes the life of the African peoples that belong to these communities: the Niger-Congo, the Nilo-Sahara, the Afro-Asiatic and the Khoisan linguistic groups.

Generally, today, we are conditioned to view Africa as a conglomeration of different ethnic groups bound together by the colonial divisions of Africa which still persist today in independent Africa.

The concept of African religion

Related to this geo-political and cultural view of Africa is the 19th-century classification based on the so-called evolutionary theory of culture and religion. This classification of religions based on belief systems puts African religion and culture on the lowest level of the evolutionary ladder, because, it was believed, African primitive culture can only produce the most elementary and primitive belief systems. Until recently, this treatment of African religions in the Western intellectual tradition has made it impossible for African traditional religion to speak for itself except in terms of 19th-century evolutionism or the Western anthropological theories of primitive religions and cultures.

From history to culture

Today the liberation from the classifications of the last century has given an intellectual autonomy to African religion and culture. They can now be understood as self-contained systems that are internally coherent without reference to any grand theories. This has allowed us to face up to the plurality of religions and cultures. Therefore in any discourse about African religion we must start from the perspective of the worshipers and devotees of African traditional religion.

African religion from within

A study of the beliefs and practices of the African peoples leads to the theological observation that African traditional religion is a religion of salvation and wholeness. A careful analysis shows an emphasis on this-worldly salvation and wholeness as the *raison d'etre* of African traditional religion. Because Africans believe that life is a complex web of relationships that may either enhance and preserve life or diminish and destroy it, the goal of religion is to maintain those relationships that protect and preserve life. For it is the harmony and stability provided by these relationships, both spiritual and material, that create the conditions for well-being and wholeness.

The threat to life both physical and spiritual is the premise of the quest for salvation. The threat is so near and real because, for the African, life is a continuum of power points that are transformed into being and life is constantly under threat from evil forces. This logic of the relationality of being and cosmic life gives rise to the view that all reality is inter-related like a family. This same relational metaphysics is what undergirds the life of the individual in community.

Individual in community

J. S. Mbiti captures this relational metaphysics succinctly in the dictum: "I am because we are and because we are therefore I am." The life of the individual comes into fruition through the social ritual of rites of passage. These rites are the process that can help the individual to attain to the goals of his or her destiny, given at birth by God. Those who successfully go through the rites of passage become candidates for ancestorhood—the goal of the ideal life. For the African, ancestors are much more than dead parents of the living. They are the embodiment of what it means to live the full life that is contained in one's destiny.

God, creation and cosmic life

God in Africa is a relational being who is known through various levels of relationship with creation. In relation to humanity, God is the great ancestor of the human race. Therefore, all over Africa God is portrayed more in terms of parent than as sovereign. In relation to the earth, God is a husband who stands behind the creative fecundity of the earth that sustains human life. God in relation to creation is the creator from whom life flows and is sustained. In relation to the divinities, God is their father who requires them to care for the cosmic processes.

Unity and diversity

The various elements of African religion that make what I call the transcendental structure of African religion are expressed differently by the various African peoples on the basis of their social organization and environment.

A definition

One can describe African religion as a this-worldly religion of salvation that promises well-being and wholeness here and now. It is a religion that affirms life and celebrates life in its fullness; this accounts for the lively and celebrative mood that characterizes African worship in all its manifestations.

Prayers and Religious Expression

Dr. Darrol Bryant

Professor of Religion, Waterloo University, and a Presiding Council Member, Inter Religious Federation for World Peace

*T*he expressions of African traditional religion are manifold. They have shaped the lives of African peoples from the dawn of history down to the present time. They have lived as oral traditions in the memory and practice of countless generations. The name of God varies across traditions as do the names of the divinities and the practices of the spiritual life. The Nuer of East Africa, for example, believe that prayer is appropriate at any time because "they like to speak to God when they are happy."

A typical Nuer prayer is:

Our Father, it is thy universe, it is thy will,
let us be at peace,
let the soul of thy people be cool.
Thou art our Father,
remove all evil from our path.

For African traditional religion there is a daily intercourse between the living and the dead, the ancestral spirits. The interaction with these realities is facilitated through prayers, rites, incantations and libations. Many of these practices involve elements of nature such as water, foodstuffs like cassava or nuts, or animals like chickens in sacrificial rites. Yoruba practices involve all types of foods and drinks in their offerings. A Yoruba chant cries out:

O God of heaven, O God of earth,
I pray thee uphold my hand,
My ancestors and ancestresses
Lean upon earth and succor me
That I may not quickly come to you.

This tradition celebrates the spirits present in the natural world and seeks to maintain proper relations between the living community and the living cosmos. Drums and dancing often figure prominently in its rites and practices. There is often a great concern for healing and health. Expressions of this tradition are too diverse to allow easy generalizations.

previously printed in the General Programme,
IRFWP New Delhi Congress, 1993

The Bahá'í Faith

A Portrait

Dr. Robert H. Stockman

Director of Research, Bahá'í National Center, Wilmette, Illinois

Gleanings from the Writings of Bahá'u'lláh

*"Be generous in prosperity,
and thankful in adversity.
Be worthy of the trust of thy neighbor,
and look upon him with a bright and
friendly face.
Be a treasure to the poor,
an admonisher to the rich,
an answerer of the cry of the needy,
a preserver of the sanctity of thy pledge.
Be fair in thy judgment,
and guarded in thy speech.
Be unjust to no man, and show all
meekness to all men.
Be as a lamp unto them that walk
in darkness, a joy to the sorrowful,
a sea for the thirsty,
a haven for the distressed,
an upholder and defender of the victim
of oppression.
Let integrity and uprightness distinguish
all thine acts.
Be a home for the stranger,
a balm to the suffering, a tower of
strength for the fugitive.
Be eyes to the blind, and a guiding
light unto the feet of the erring.
Be an ornament to the countenance of
truth, a crown to the brow of fidelity,
a pillar of the temple of righteousness,
a breath of life to the body of mankind,
an ensign of the hosts of justice,
a luminary above the horizon of virtue,
a dew to the soil of the human heart,
an ark on the ocean of knowledge,
a sun in the heaven of bounty,
a gem on the diadem of wisdom,
a shining light in the firmament
of thy generation,
a fruit upon the tree of humility."*

(p.285)

The Bahá'í Faith is an independent world religion now in the 150th year of its existence. According to the *Encyclopedia Britannica Yearbook* it is the second most widely spread religion in the world, with five million members residing in 232 countries and dependent territories, and national spiritual assemblies (national Bahá'í governing bodies) in 172.

The Bahá'í Faith began in Iran. Its history is intimately connected with the lives of its leading figures:

'Alí-Muhammad, titled *the Báb*. Born in southern Iran in 1819, in 1844 he announced that he was the promised one or Mahdi expected by Muslims. He wrote scriptures in which he promulgated a new calendar, new religious laws and new social norms. Opposed by Iran's Muslim clergy and ultimately by its government, thousands of the Báb's followers were killed; in 1850 the Báb himself was put to death.

Mírzá Husayn-'Alí, titled *Bahá'u'lláh*. Born in northern Iran in 1817, Bahá'u'lláh became a follower of the Báb in 1844 and was imprisoned for his beliefs. In 1853 he had a vision that he was the divine teacher the Báb had promised; he publicly declared himself as a messenger of God in 1863. He spent the rest of his life in exile and prison, where he wrote over 100 volumes of scripture.

'Abbas Effendi, titled *'Abdu'l-Bahá*. Son of Bahá'u'lláh, 'Abdu'l-Bahá was born in 1844 and accompanied his father on his exile to Palestine. Bahá'u'lláh appointed 'Abdu'l-Bahá his successor, the exemplar of his teachings, and the interpreter of his revelation. Under 'Abdu'l-Bahá the Bahá'í Faith spread beyond the Middle East, India, and Burma to Europe, the Americas, southern Africa and Australasia. He died in 1921.

Shoghi Effendi Rabbani. Grandson of 'Abdu'l-Bahá and his successor, Shoghi Effendi was born in Palestine in 1897 and received an Oxford education. As head of the Bahá'í Faith from 1921 until his death in 1957, Shoghi Effendi translated the most important of Bahá'u'lláh's scriptures into elegant English, wrote extensive interpretations and explanations of the Bahá'í teachings, built the Bahá'í organizational system and oversaw the spread of the Bahá'í Faith worldwide.

The Bahá'í scriptures constitute the books, essays and letters composed by Bahá'u'lláh, 'Abdu'l-Bahá, and Shoghi Effendi. Together they comprised nearly 60,000 letters, a significant portion of which are available in English; the content of this scriptural corpus is encyclopedic in nature. The Bahá'í teachings are those principles and values promulgated in the Bahá'í scriptures, and touch on nearly every aspect of human life.

Central Bahá'í teachings are: the *oneness of God*, that there is only one God and that God is actively concerned about the development of humanity; the *oneness of religion*, that God sends messengers such as Abraham, Moses, Zoroaster, Krishna, Buddha, Christ, Muhammad, the Báb and Bahá'u'lláh to humanity to educate it in morals and in social values; and the *oneness of humanity*, that all humans come from the same original stock and deserve equal opportunities and treatment.

The teachings also include: a detailed discussion of the spiritual nature of human beings, prayers and religious practices to foster spiritual growth, a strong emphasis on the importance of creating unified and loving families, and a prescription for solving the social ills of human society.

The *Bahá'í community* consists of those people who have accepted Bahá'u'lláh as God's messenger for this day and who are actively trying to live by, and promulgate, the Bahá'í teachings. The community has no clergy and a minimum of ritual. Independent investigation of truth, private prayer and collective discussion and action are the favored modes of religious action. Usually Bahá'í communities have no weekly worship service; rather, a monthly program called *feast* is held that includes worship, consultation on community business, and social activities.

Through a process that involves no campaigning and nominations, each local community elects annually by secret ballot a nine-member *local spiritual assembly*. The assembly coordinates community activities, enrolls new members, counsels and assists members in need, and conducts Bahá'í marriages and funerals. A nine-member *national spiritual assembly* is elected annually by locally elected delegates, and every five years the national spiritual assemblies meet together to elect the *Universal House of Justice,* the supreme international governing body of the Bahá'í Faith. Worldwide there are about 20,000 local spiritual assemblies; the United States has over 1,400 local spiritual assemblies and about 120,000 Bahá'ís.

The Bahá'í view of the challenges facing humanity

*T*he Bahá'í scriptures emphasize that the challenges facing humanity stem from two sources: age-old problems that could have been solved long ago had humanity accepted and acted on the moral and spiritual values given it by God's messengers; and new challenges stemming from the creation of a global society, which can be solved if the moral and spiritual principles enunciated by Bahá'u'lláh are accepted and followed. Chief among these principles are:

1. *Racial unity.* Racism retards the unfoldment of the boundless potentialities of its victims, corrupts its perpetrators and blights human progress. Bahá'u'lláh's call that all humans accept and internalize the principle of the oneness of humanity is partly directed at destroying racist attitudes.

2. *Emancipation of women.* The denial of equality to women perpetrates an injustice against one half of the world's population and promotes in men harmful attitudes and habits that are carried from the family to the workplace, to political life, and ultimately to international relations. Even though he lived in the 19th-century Middle East, Bahá'u'lláh called for the equality of women and enunciated their full rights to education and work.

3. *Economic justice.* The inordinate disparity between rich and poor is a source of acute suffering and keeps the world in a state of instability, virtually on the brink of war. Few societies have dealt effectively with this issue. The Bahá'í scriptures offer a fresh approach, including such features as a new perspective concerning money, profits, work and the poor; an understanding of the purpose of economic growth and the relationships between management and labor; and certain economic principles, such as profit sharing.

4. *Patriotism within a global perspective.* The Bahá'í scriptures state that citizens should be proud of their countries and of their national identities, but such pride should be subsumed within a wider loyalty to all of humanity and to global society.

5. *Universal education.* Historically, ignorance has been the principal reason for the decline and fall of peoples and the perpetuation of prejudice.

"*The essential purpose of the religion of God is to establish unity among mankind. The divine Manifestations were Founders of the means of fellowship and love. They did not come to create discord, strife and hatred in the world. The religion of God is the cause of love, but if it is made to be the source of enmity and bloodshed, surely its absence is preferable to its existence; for then it becomes satanic, detrimental and an obstacle to the human world."*
'ABDU'L-BAHÁ,
Promulgation of Universal Peace, p.202

"*Know thou of a certainty that Love is the secret of God's holy Dispensation, the manifestation of the All-Merciful, the fountain of spiritual outpourings. Love is heaven's kindly light, the Holy Spirit's eternal breath that vivifieth the human soul. Love is the cause of God's revelation unto man, the vital bond inherent, in accordance with the divine creation, in the realities of things. Love is the one means that ensureth true felicity both in this world and the next. Love is the light that guideth in darkness, the living link that uniteth God with man, that assureth the progress of every illumined soul. . .*

> "Love is the most great law that ruleth this mighty and heavenly cycle, the unique power that bindeth together the divers elements of this material world, the supreme magnetic force that directeth the movements of the spheres in the celestial realms. Love revealeth with unfailing and limitless power the mysteries latent in the universe. Love is the spirit of life unto the adorned body of mankind, the establisher of true civilization in this mortal world, and the shedder of imperishable glory upon every high-aiming race and nation."
>
> 'ABDU'L-BAHÁ,
> *Selections from the Writings of*
> *'Abdu'l- Bahá, p.27*

> "The unity of the human race, as envisaged by Bahá'u'lláh, implies the establishment of a world commonwealth in which all nations, races, creeds and classes are closely and permanently united, and in which the autonomy of its state members and the personal freedom and initiative of the individuals that compose them are definitely and completely safeguarded. This commonwealth must, as far as we can visualize it, consist of a world legislature, whose members will, as the trustees of the whole of mankind, ultimately control the entire resource of all the component nations, and will enact such laws as shall be required to regulate the life, satisfy the needs and adjust the relationships of all races and peoples.... In such a world society, science and religion, the two most potent forces in human life, will be reconciled, will cooperate, and will harmoniously develop."
>
> SHOGHI EFFENDI,
> *World Order of Bahá'u'lláh,*
> pp.203–204

The Bahá'í scriptures state that every human being has a fundamental right to an education, including the right to learn to read and write.

6. *A universal auxiliary language.* A major barrier to communication is the lack of a common language. Bahá'u'lláh urged humanity to choose one auxiliary tongue that would be taught in all schools in addition to the local native language, so that humans could understand each other anywhere they go on the planet.

7. *The environment and development.* The unrestrained exploitation of natural resources is a symptom of an overall sickness of the human spirit. Any solutions to the related crises of environmental destruction and economic development must be rooted in an approach that fosters spiritual balance and harmony within the individual, between individuals, and with the environment as a whole. Material development must serve not only the body, but the mind and spirit as well.

8. *A world federal system.* The Bahá'í scriptures emphatically state that for the first time in its history, humanity can and must create an international federation capable of coordinating the resources of, and solving the problems facing, the entire planet. A high priority needs to be given to the just resolution of regional and international conflicts; responding to urgent humanitarian crises brought on by war, famine or natural disasters; forging a unified approach to environmental degradation; and establishing the conditions where the free movement of goods, services and peoples across the globe becomes possible.

9. *Religious dialogue.* Religious strife has caused numerous wars, has been a major blight to progress, and is increasingly abhorrent to the people of all faiths and of no faith. The Bahá'í view that all religions come from God and thus constitute valid paths to the divine is a cornerstone of Bahá'í interfaith dialogue. Bahá'u'lláh calls on Bahá'ís to consort with the followers of all religions in love and harmony. Because Bahá'ís share with other religionists many common values and concerns, they frequently work with local interfaith organizations.

The Bahá'í response to the challenges facing humanity

*B*ahá'ís have responded to the challenges facing humanity in two ways: internally, by creating a Bahá'í community that reflects the principles listed above and that can serve as a model for others; and externally, to help heal the damage that inequality, injustice and ignorance have done to society.

The international Bahá'í community contains within it 2,100 ethnic groups speaking over 800 languages. In some nations minority groups make up a substantial fraction of the Bahá'í population; in the United States, for example, perhaps a third of the membership is African American, and Southeast Asians, Iranians, Hispanics and Native Americans make up another 20 percent. Racial integration of local Bahá'í communities has been the standard practice of the American Bahá'í community since about 1905. Women have played a major, if not central, role in the administration of local American Bahá'í communities, and of the national community, since 1910. American Bahá'ís have been involved in education, especially in the fostering of Bahá'í educational programs overseas, since 1909.

Worldwide, numerous Bahá'ís have become prominent in efforts to promote racial amity and equality, strengthen peace groups, extend the reach and effectiveness of educational systems, encourage ecological awareness and stewardship, develop new approaches to social and economic development, and promote the new field of conflict resolution. The Bahá'í Faith runs seven radio stations in less developed areas of the world that have pioneered new techniques for educating rural populations and fostering economic and cultural development. The Faith also conducts about 700 schools, primarily in the third world, as well as about 200 other literacy programs. Bahá'í communities sponsor 500 development projects, such as tree-planting, agricultural improvement, vocational training and rural health-care. The Bahá'í international community is particularly active at the United Nations and works closely with many international development agencies. Many national and local Bahá'í communities have been active in promoting interreligious understanding and cooperation.

PRAYER

O my God! O my God!
Unite the hearts of thy servants,
and reveal to them Thy great purpose.
May they follow Thy commandments and abide in Thy law.
Help them, O God, in their endeavor,
and grant them strength to serve Thee.
O God! Leave them not to themselves,
but guide their steps by the light of Thy knowledge,
and cheer their hearts by Thy love.
Verily, Thou art their Helper and their Lord.

BAHÁ'U'LLÁH,
Bahá'í Prayers, p.204

FOR MORE INFORMATION:

Bahá'í Community of the United Kingdom
27 Rutland Gate, London, SW7 1PD U.K.
(+71) 584-2566

The Bahá'í National Center of the U.S.A.
536 Sheridan Road, Wilmette, IL 60091
(708) 869-9039

The Bahá'í National Center of Canada
7200 Leslie St., Thornhill, Ontario L3T 6L8 Canada
(416) 889-8168

Bahá'í Publications Australia
P.O. Box 285, Mona Vale, NSW, 2103, Australia

Bahá'í Publishing Trust,
6 Mt. Pleasant, Oakham, Leics
LE15 6HU, United Kingdom

Bahá'í World Centre
P.O. Box 155
31001, Haifa, Israel

"The source of all learning is the knowledge of God, exalted be His glory, and this cannot be attained save through the knowledge of His Divine Manifestation. The essence of abasement is to pass out from under the shadow of the Merciful and seek the shelter of the Evil One.

The source of error is to disbelieve in the One true God, rely upon aught else but him, and flee from His Decree. True loss is for him whose days have been spent in utter ignorance of his self.

The essence of all that we have revealed for thee is Justice, is for man to free himself from idle fancy and imitation, discern with the eye of oneness His glorious handiwork, and look into all things with a searching eye.

Thus have We instructed thee, manifested unto thee Words of Wisdom, that thou mayest be thankful unto the Lord, thy God, and glory therein amidst all peoples."

BAHÁ'U'LLÁH

Buddhism

A Portrait

Dr. Geshe Sopa and Ven. Elvin W. Jones

"As the previous... Buddhas like a divine skillful wise horse, a great elephant, did what had to be done, accomplished all tasks, overcame all the burdens of the five aggregates controlled by delusion and karma, *fulfilled all their aspirations by relinquishing their attachments, by speaking immaculately divine words and liberating the minds of all from the bondage of subtle delusions' impression, and who possess great liberated transcendental wisdom, for the sake of all that lives, in order to benefit all, in order to prevent famine, in order to prevent mental and physical sicknesses, in order for living beings to complete a buddha's 37 realizations, and to receive the stage of fully completed buddhahood... I ... shall take the eight* Mahayana *precepts. . ."*

"One-Day *Mahayana* Vow Ritual," trans. Library of Tibetan Works and Archives

"Perfect Wisdom spreads her radiance... and is worthy of worship. Spotless, the whole world cannot stain her. . . . In her we may find refuge; her works are most excellent; she brings us safety under the sheltering wings of enlightenment. She brings light to the blind, that all fears and calamities may be dispelled... and she scatters the gloom and darkness of delusion. She leads those who have gone astray to the right path. She is omniscience; without beginning or end is Perfect Wisdom, who has emptiness as her characteristic mark; she is mother of the bodhisattvas *.... She cannot be struck down, the protector of the unprotected, ... the Perfect Wisdom of the Buddhas, she turns the Wheel of the Law.*

"Astasahasrika Prajnaparamita-sutra," *The Buddhist Tradition,* ed. by W.M. Theodore De Bary

Ven. Geshe Sopa, born in Tsang Province, Tibet, is Professor in the Department of South Asian Studies, University of Wisconsin-Madison. Elvin W. Jones is co-founder and associate director of Deer Buddhist Center, near Madison, Wisc.

*B*uddhism as we know it commenced in Northeast India about 500 BC through the teaching of Prince Siddartha Gautama, often known subsequent to his experience of "enlightenment" as Sakyamuni. Sakyamuni traveled around and taught in the Ganges basin until his death at the age of 84. From there Buddhism spread through much of India until its total disappearance from the land of its origin by the end of the 13th century. This disappearance occurred as a consequence of several centuries of foreign invasions leading ultimately to the conquest of India by successive waves of conquerors who had been unified under Islam.

By the time of its disappearance in India, Buddhism had spread through much of Asia where it has been a dominant faith in Southeast Asia in Sri Lanka, Thailand, Vietnam, Cambodia, Burma and Laos; in Central and East Asia in China, Korea, Japan, Tibet and Mongolia; and in numerous Himalayan areas such as Nepal, Sikkim, Butan and Ladak. It is estimated that today there are a little over 250 million Buddhists in the world. In the USA alone there are about five million, the majority of whom are Asian immigrants or their descendents. However, in recent years, numerous Americans of English and European descent have also adopted Buddhism.

From the start, the teaching of the Buddha was a middle way. In ethics it taught a middle way avoiding the two extremities of asceticism and hedonism. In philosophy it taught a middle way avoiding the two extremities of eternalism and of annihilation. The single most important and fundamental notion underpinning Buddhist thought was the idea of "contingent genesis" or "dependent origination" (*pratitya-amutpada*). Here the thought is that every birth or origination occurs in dependence on necessary causes and conditions; however, not everything so asserted can function as a cause – in particular, any kind of eternal or permanent whole. Consequently, the Buddhist idea of "contingent genesis" came to be characterized by three salient features, i.e., unpropelledness, impermanence and consistency. "Unpropelledness" signifies that origination or genesis is not propelled by an universal design such as the thought or will of a creator. "Impermanence" means that the cause of an effect is always something impermanent and never permanent. Finally, "consistency" requires that the genesis or effect will be consistent with and not exceed the creative power of the cause. For example, it is on the basis of the quality of consistency that the Buddhist denies that any kind of material body can provide a sufficient material cause for the production of a mind. Thus, on account of this primary philosophical underpinning of contingent genesis, Buddhism has produced a quite large etiological rather than theological literature.

Taking as his basis the idea of contingent genesis in general, Sakyamuni taught a specific theory of a twelvefold dependent genesis accounting for the particularized birth of a person or personality which naturally occurs in some kind of existence which is not free of various forms of suffering or ill. The spectrum of naturally occurring births which are characterized by ill is called the "round of transmigration" (*samsara*), and the force impelling this transmigration and unsatisfactory condition of attendant births was taught by Sakyamuni to be action under the sway of afflictors or afflicting elements such as nescience, attraction, aversion and so forth. In the language of Buddhism, this action is called *karma;* the afflictors are called *klesa;* and the resultant ills are called *dukha.* The Buddha called the reality of suffering (*dukha*) the truth of suffering, and called this action – conjoined with afflicting elements (*karma* and *klesa*) – the truth of the cause of suffering. These two truths constitute the first of the Four Noble Truths which were the principal teaching of Sakyamuni and the principle object of understanding of the Buddhist saint.

Sakyamuni also taught the possibility of freedom or emancipation from suffering or ill through its cessation. Likewise, he taught a path leading to this cessation. These two, cessation and path, constitute the third and fourth of the Four Noble Truths. Thus, we have suffering and its causes and the cessation of suffering and its causes; these are the Four Noble Truths of suffering, its causes, cessation and path. Through the cessation of suffering and its causes one obtains *nirvana* which is simply peace or quiescence, and the cause of the attainment of this peace is the path of purification eliminating action under the sway of the afflictors. The Buddha taught that of all the afflictors contaminating action, the chief is a perverse kind of nescience which apprehends a real or independent self existing in or outside of the various identifiable corporeal and mental elements which constitute a person or personality. Thus, the cultivation of the path of purification hinges on the reversal of this mistaken apprehension of a real soul or ego or selfhood. This Buddhist view that there is no real or enduring substratum to the personality is called *anatma.*

Sakyamuni's most precise and important articulation of the Four Noble Truths was his formulation of a twelvefold causal linkage generating each and every particular instance of birth of a person. This twelvefold causal nexus begins with nescience and ends with old age and death. This nescience is in particular the perverse ignorance which grasps a real selfhood. Conditioned by this kind of nescience, actions are performed which deposit inclinations and proclivities upon the unconscious mind. These proclivities are later ripened by other factors such as grasping and misappropriation and thereby bring about unsatisfactory results through birth and death. With, however, the correct seeing of the reality of no-self, this nescience may be stopped, and thereby the whole chain of causation leading to unsatisfactory birth is brought to an end. In this way the twelvefold causal linkage is not only a theory of the genesis of a personality but also a theory of its potential for deliverance from every kind of ill.

Thus it is said in Buddhist scripture:

"Gather up and cast away.
Enter to the Buddha's teaching.
Like a great elephant in a house of mud,
conquer the lord of death's battalions.

Whoever with great circumspection,
practices this discipline of the Law,
abandoning the wheel of births,
will make an end to suffering."

"Gather up and cast away" refers to the gathering together of virtuous or wholesome qualities and the abandonment of non-virtuous or unwholesome qualities in the personality. Thus the same scripture says:

"Not to do evil, to bring about the excellence of virtue,
completely to subdue the mind,
this is the teaching of the Buddha."

On his deathbed, the Buddha had exhorted his disciples to work on their own salvation with diligence; hence these teachings are sometimes characterized as a doctrine of individual emancipation.

About five to six hundred years after the passing away of the teacher Sakyamuni, another formulation of the Buddhist doctrine and practice gained a wide circulation in India. This later propagation is associated with the great Buddhist teacher Nagarjuna. Taking his stand on the fundamental Buddhist idea of contingent genesis, Nagarjuna argued that if every instance of genesis is a contingent genesis, then continued analysis will show that every kind of permanent and even impermanent cause proposed either by Buddhists or others will be non-absolute and non-ultimate; consequently, causality itself is in some sense illusory. In this sense even true phenomena like causality are just empty of any kind of ultimate nature. Nagarjuna carried his analysis to cover permanent non-originating phenomena like space as well. The nonexistence of all phenomena as ultimates or absolutes is the Buddhist idea of emptiness (*sunyata*), which provided a great impetus to another kind of religious aspiration aiming at the emancipation not only of one's own individual life-stream but that of all sentient life from the round of unsatisfactory birth and rebirth. He especially demonstrated the absence of any final or absolute difference between *samsara* and *nirvana*, even though phenomenally they are and will always remain opposites. Thereby, Nagarjuna opened wide the way for the pursuit of the non-attached *nirvana* taught to be achieved by the Buddhas along with numerous other sublime qualities of knowledge belonging to perfect enlightenment. From earliest times the Buddhist had already distinguished between the path of purification trodden by Sakyamuni himself, already known as the *Bodhisattva* path, and that taught and followed by numerous of his disciples. Now the Buddha's own path was encouraged for all. By its followers this later path was called *Mahayana,* or greater vehicle, whereas the former came to be called the *Hinayana,* or smaller vehicle. The *Mahayana* was synonymous with the path of a *Bodhisattva* or one who, moved by great compassion, developed the aspiration to perfect enlightenment for the sake of others. This aspiration was called *Bodhicitta,* or the mind to enlightenment, and provided the motivation for the cultivation of the *Mahayana* path. This *Mahayana* path was also taught extensively in the *Prajnaparamita-sutras* or *Perfection of Wisdom Scriptures* which also gained wide circulation in India through the efforts of Nagarjuna.

About 500 years later still another very important development occurred in Indian Buddhism. This development is associated with the brothers Asanga and Vasubandhu. This led to a great systematization of the *Mahayana* and in particular to another less radical interpretation of the meaning of the *Prajnaparamita-sutras* than that associated with Nagarjuna, whose school continued on and is generally called the *Madhyamika* or Middleist School; Asanga's is called the *Cittamatra* or Mind-only School.

Also around this time, a special kind of Buddhist esoteric scripture and practice gained wide currency. They constituted four classes or levels which moved from outer ritual action through inner meditative action to a full fledged esoteric path of spiritual attainment. These scriptures were known as the *tantras,* and their practice was called the diamond vehicle or the secret *mantra* vehicle. Espousing the practice of the *Mahayana,* they added many ritual methods together with numerous profound and difficult *yoga* or meditation practices and techniques. The *tantras* saw themselves as fulfilling the practice of the *Mahayana* as well as providing an accelerated path to its realization. The vehicle of the *tantras* is often called the vehicle of the effect because straightaway it envisages the final result of the path and imaginatively dwells upon and rehearses that until it becomes not an imagined but an accomplished result. The *Mahayana* being wisdom and method, the *tantras* add to the general wisdom and method of the *Mahayana* their own very special varieties.

Thus in India along with four classes of *tantras,* four main philosophical schools developed, each with a number of subschools, i.e. the *Vaibhasika, Sautrantika, Madhyamika* and the *Yogacara.* The former two are schools of the *Hinayana,* and the latter two are schools of the *Mahayana.* The *Vaibhasika* early developed 18 subschools, two of which are of particular importance – the *Sthaviravada,* which is the immediate ancestor of the *Theravada,* the principal Buddhism of Southeast Asia, and the *Sarvastivada,* which is the basis of monasticism in Tibet and the Tibetan community today. The *Madhyamika* provides the chief viewpoint of Tibetan Buddhism today, and the *Yogacara* has had profound and far reaching influences on the Buddhism of China, and through China on Korea and Japan. Some secret *mantra* practices were transmitted into China and from there to Japan where they survive today, and the practices of all four levels of *tantra* are still alive in the Tibetan community.

From India by way of Central Asia, Buddhism began its penetration into China around the first century CE. There it encountered the already developed systems of Confucianism and Taoism. The latter in particular provided the terminology and numerous seemingly analogous concepts for subsequent centuries of effort devoted to the translation of Buddhist scriptures into Chinese and the establishment of Buddhist practice in China. By the eighth century, Chinese Buddhism reached its mature form with its two main theoretical schools of *Tien-tai* and *Hua-yen,* together with its two popular schools of Pure Land and *Ch'an* (Japanese: Zen). These sinicized forms of Buddhism began their spread to Korea mainly from the fourth century on and commenced spreading from Korea to Japan from the middle of the sixth century.

Although some important Buddhist development occurred a century earlier, Buddhism began to be strongly cultivated in Tibet in the eighth century. In this century Indian and various Sinitic Buddhist developments collided in a debate held by the Tibetan king at Samyas, the first Buddhist monastery founded in Tibet. Tibetan history records that the Indian faction won this debate, and it is clear that afterwards Tibet looked to India throughout its prolonged subsequent period of importation of Buddhism. As a consequence, Tibet remains a great repository of a vast body of important literature which later perished in India itself. From Tibet, Buddhism was afterward spread into Mongolia and throughout the Himalayan region.

Now, in the aftermath of World War II and the collapse of Western colonial establishments in Asia, the modern efforts of numerous Asian countries to make a transition from agrarian to industrial societies has led and still leads often to the establishment of military dictatorships or to socialist totalitarian regimes. Buddhism has generally fallen upon difficult times particularly at the hands of Marxist-Leninist regimes, for whereas Buddhism does not see any natural conflict between itself and modern science, its middle way philosophy is staunchly opposed to dialectical materialism. In fact, two of the worst atrocities of nearly genocidal proportions to be perpetrated in modern times have taken place in two such countries, Cambodia and Tibet, the latter continuing – and this is hard to believe – for over 30 years.

Buddhist leadership nonetheless has continued to press for freedom and democracy, for peace and non-violence, as these will be the best safeguard for the natural human wish to avoid suffering. Here, it is particularly indicative to note that two recent Nobel Peace Prize winners have been Buddhists – His Holiness the 14th Dalai Lama of Tibet, and Daw Aung San Suu Kyi, of Burma.

"*For the last several years I have been looking at the world's problems, including our own problem, the Tibetan situation. I have been thinking about this and meeting with persons from different fields and in different countries. Basically all are the same. I come from the East; most of you are Westerners. If I look at you superficially, we are different, and if I put my emphasis on that level, we grow more distant. If I look on you as my own kind, as human beings like myself, with one nose, two eyes and so forth, then automatically that distance is gone. We are the same human flesh. I want happiness; you also want happiness. From that mutual recognition we can build respect and real trust for each other. From that can come cooperation and harmony, and from that we can stop many problems.*"

H. H. THE 14th DALAI LAMA OF TIBET

Buddhist Experience in North America

Ven. Mahinda Deegalle

Student of the History of Religions, University of Chicago, and member of the Sri Lankan Buddhist community

*T*he arrival of two leading Buddhists – Anagarika Dharmapala and Soyen Shaku – to attend the World's Parliament of Religions held in Chicago in 1893 was, and is, an important event for all Buddhists who are living in North America today. These two representatives are frequently named in tracing the birth of Buddhist traditions on this continent. In fact, however, Buddhism did not become a visible religious alternative to the Judeo-Christian tradition until the 1970s. Yet, as a minority tradition, its contribution to the religious life of Americans was quite apparent at the 1993 World's Parliament of Religions. This participation included very wide representation from Buddhist denominations which trace their affiliations to many different Asian countries.

Largely within the last three or four decades, a variety of Asian Buddhist traditions have found the United States a fertile land in which to establish their religious centers. As a result, Buddhist centers in all major American cities serve both Asian immigrants and non-immigrants who are interested in Buddhism. They provide facilities for meditation and educate Americans in the customs and cultural events of Asian countries. Like any other American religious group, American Buddhists are definitely a diverse group. In major cities such as Los Angeles, Chicago, San Francisco and Toronto there is a great deal of ethnic variety among the Buddhist denominations.

Nevertheless, Buddhist communities in these major cities seem to work very harmoniously together to spread the Buddha's teachings. For example, in Chicago, the members of The Buddhist Council of the Midwest celebrate Vesak – the birthday, the day of *samma sambodhi* (perfect awakening), and the passing away (*parinirvana*) of Gautama Buddha – jointly each year in May, with cultural festivals from Japan, China, Taiwan, Thailand, Vietnam, Cambodia, Burma and Laos. This unity among diverse denominations which trace their roots to different Asian nations is based on the understanding that, as Buddhists, they share certain fundamental doctrines in common, even while demonstrating cultural variety through their specific festivals and religious practices.

As members of immigrant communities and representatives of an alien religion, immigrant American Buddhists have to adapt to the cultural and religious setting of the United States and to deal with people who do not share their world view. It is important that Buddhists understand the way the people of other world religions think about the world and its problems.

Unlike Buddhists, for many Americans the notion of God is fundamental to life; all Judeo-Christian religious communities derive inspiration from a concept of 'God.' Also, American society is structured around individualism; there is a strong emphasis on the primacy of individuality rather than on the interests of the society or community as in Buddhist cultures. So Buddhists in general and Theravadins in particular have to struggle to understand these two world views. At the same time, since all Buddhist communities profess a doctrine of selflessness in one form or another, it is difficult for most Americans, who think mainly in terms of 'self' and 'individual,' to understand Buddhism.

With the development of an awareness of the earth, environment, plants and animals, American Buddhists seem to have embraced positive teachings of the Buddhist traditions with regard to plants and the environment. Rather than thinking that human beings are separate from nature and that human beings are rulers of the earth, people are starting to think of the entire universe as a 'whole,' of which humanity is only a 'part.' This sense of a global community sharing the resources of the earth harmoniously is a very

Zen

The Zen Center, San Francisco

*I*n the 6th century CE, Bodhidharma, the semi-legendary figure from whom all Zen schools trace their ancestry, brought to China that Buddhist practice which we call Zen. The word itself is a Japanese transliteration of a Chinese transliteration of a Sanskrit word meaning meditation. Thus, Zen is that school of Buddhism which emphasizes meditation (*zazen* = sitting meditation) as a primary practice for calming and clearing the mind and for directly perceiving reality. According to the texts the Zen that Bodhidharma taught and practiced can be summed up as:

> A special transmission outside the scriptures; no dependence upon words and letters; directly pointing at one's own nature; attaining Buddhahood.

Zen eventually reached Japan, where the Soto school was established by Eihei Dogen (1200–1255), who considered Zen not as a separate school but simply as Buddhism. In the early 1960s Shunryu Suzuki Roshi came to San Francisco to minister to the local Japanese congregation. Out of his contacts with Western students, Zen Center of San Francisco was born. Many other centers have since opened elsewhere in North America and in other countries.

positive development which has been encouraged during the last few decades, and is growing fast in the United States. This kind of a world view or consciousness of the environment and nature marks a shift in human thinking: human beings not as rulers of the earth but as a part of a larger global community.

In the development of an awareness of nature and the environment, Buddhist teachings, in particular the theories of co-dependent origination (*paticcasamuppada*) and interconnectedness, have a great deal to offer to Western thinkers. For example, the doctrine of co-dependent origination proposes an interdependence between nature and human beings. Furthermore, Buddhist teachings maintain that the nature of the human psyche affects the natural environment, while the natural environment in turn influences the shape of the human psyche positively or negatively. In particular, the doctrine of five laws *niyama dhammas* proposes that human beings and nature are bound together in a mutual causal relationship. The five laws are: physical, biological, psychological, moral, and causal. Among these five, the causal law operates within each of the first four; likewise, the physical law conditions biological growth, and all the laws influence human thought patterns, which eventually shape the moral standards of a society. These Buddhist doctrines and insights, which seem to appeal to modern Western thinking, attempt to suggest that human beings and the environment mutually condition and influence each other in the formation of the human psyche and of the nature of the world. The notions of interdependence and interconnectedness have become the centerpiece of the declaration, "Towards a Global Ethic," of the 1993 Parliament of the World's Religions.

Though some Buddhist communities have experienced resistance from certain segments of the American population, this does not reflect the attitude of the majority of Americans, whose pluralist tradition shows in their openness and willingness to help religious and ethnic minorities. However, some hostile elements are still present in certain sections of society and parts of this country; in the recent past, several temples have been burned or bombed, and some practitioners have even been murdered.

The most positive response towards Buddhism is found in the genuine interest of Americans from many parts of the country in knowing and practicing Buddhism. This positive tendency is quite evident in the curriculum of American colleges and universities. In several major universities, I have witnessed a genuine interest in learning about Buddhism, and private colleges and universities provide the facilities to do so. Every year, American universities produce a large number of academic specialists in diverse forms of Buddhism, such as Japanese, Chinese, Indian, Tibetan, Sri Lankan, Thai or Burmese.

While in many places Buddhism functions as a cultural resource and inspiration for Asian immigrant Buddhist communities, non-immigrant Caucasian converts are drawn to Buddhism for its contemplative and meditative aspects rather than because of its cultural specificity. One of the strengths which Buddhism offers to American practitioners of Zen, Theravadan or Tibetan meditation is its tradition of contemplative practice. The considerable growth of meditation centers shows that Buddhism is becoming a vital force in the pluralistic American society and is having an influential impact on it. The Buddhist experience in the United States highlights the ability of its practitioners to adapt to a completely different cultural and social environment and make remarkable progress in shaping the lives of others who encounter Buddhism. Since the establishment of Buddhism in the United States is still in progress, its impact and influence will become more clearly visible in the 21st century.

FOR MORE INFORMATION:

Buddha-Dhamma Meditation Center
8910 S. Kingery Highway, Hinsdale, IL 60521

Buddhist Churches of America
1710 Octavia St., San Francisco, CA 94109

Buddhist Peace Fellowships:

Box 368, Lismore, NSW 2480, Australia

ACFOD, GPO Box 2930, Bangkok, 10501, Thailand

c/o Aleda Erskine, 16 Upper Park Road, London NW3, UK

P.O. Box 4650, Berkeley, CA 94704 USA
(and their publication: *Turning Wheel*)

Buddhist Women's Network
50-62 47th St., Woodside, NY 11377

Dharma World Magazine (Risho Kosei-kai)
Kosei Publishing Company
2-7-1 Wada, Suginami-ku, Tokyo 166, Japan

Numata Center for Buddhist Translation and Research
2620 Warring St., Berkeley, CA 94704

Office of the Central Tibetan Administration, Thekchen Choeling,
McLeod Ganj, Dharamsala, H.P. 176219, India

Parallax Press
P.O. Box 7355, Berkeley, CA 94707

Risho Kosei-kai Buddhist Church
306 East 38 St., New York, NY 10016

Shambhala Publications, Inc.
Horticultural Hall, 300 Massachusetts Ave., Boston, MA 02115

Snow Lion Publications
P.O. Box 6483, Ithaca, NY 14851

Soka Gakkai International-USA, 525 Wilshire Boulevard,
Santa Monica, CA 90401-1427

South Asia Books
P.O. Box 502, Columbia, MO 65205

Tricycle: The Buddhist Review
163 West 22nd St., New York, NY 10011

Wisdom Publications
361 Newbury St., Boston, MA 02115

Won Buddhism of America
143-42 Cherry Ave., Flushing, NY 11355

World Fellowship of Buddhists
33 Sukhumvit Road, Bangkok 10110, Thailand

Christianity

Origins and Beliefs

The Rev. Thomas A. Baima, S.T.L.

Catholic Priest, Director of the Office for Ecumenical and Interreligious Affairs of the Archdiocese of Chicago, and Trustee of The Council for a Parliament of the World's Religions

Because the range of communities within Christianity is so wide, members of several distinct traditions have provided essays on specific topics. In the essay below, Father Baima introduces the origins and basic beliefs of Christianity and its approaches to interfaith relations.

*T*he origin of Christianity begins in the heart of God. The Divine nature is Love. Love is not something that comes from God. Love is God and God is love. If a Christian were to name the Divine in English, the best term would be simply "God-Love."

Within God-Love, before time, came an urge to create. This urge was not for pleasure, since God-Love is beyond such things. Rather it was, as Archbishop Joseph Raya says, for the multiplication of love. God created for this reason alone, that love might grow. Divine love by its very nature shares itself.

Made in the image and likeness of God-Love, humanity had the essential quality or condition that makes loving possible, free will. Some humans chose to reject the offer of close relationship with God-Love. This rejection, which we will call sin, entered human experience and remains a permanent part of it. Sin is separation or a false autonomy, false because it is not possible to be or exist independently of God. This false autonomy is the basis of human rejection of God-Love.

The separation between humanity and God-Love required divine action to overcome it. As a permanent part of human nature nothing we could do of our own power could heal the separation. A new offer of relationship by God-Love was required.

So God-Love selected one of the nations of the earth to be a sign and instrument of this divine action. That nation was the Hebrew people. Through a process of self-disclosure, God-Love guided Israel out of slavery into an experience of rescue. God-Love guided Israel through the naming of sin in the Ten Commandments and the calling to virtue through the commands to pray, celebrate sacred ritual and act with compassion.

The guiding and forming of Israel created a sign and instrument which could extend and express God-Love. Throughout almost 2,000 years of faithfulness and struggle, this one people, guided by prophets, priests and kings, was the light of God-Love among the nations.

Then God-Love chose to graft onto this one people all the nations. In a small village in the northern part of Palestine, a young woman became pregnant even though she was a virgin. Though no man had ever touched Mary, Life grew within her. Nine months later "a child was born, a son given, upon whom dominion rested. And the prophet had called him 'wonder-counselor, God-hero, Father forever and Prince of Peace.' " Mary named him Jesus – "God saves."

It is here that Christianity, which began eternally in the heart of God, is made visible in the person and event of Jesus. We who are his disciples have come to see the fullness of revelation from God-Love, of God-Love in him. For this reason we call him Lord, Son of God, Savior. And it is in the teaching of Jesus that we learned something new about the inner life of the one God. Within the Godhead there exist relationships of love – as Father, Son and Holy Spirit. God is personal, not merely as a way to relate to us, but in the very divine being. We would not know this about God had not the Son taken flesh in Jesus of Nazareth and revealed it to us.

In addition to this revelation of the inner life of God, the Lord Jesus taught a way of life that made it possible for God-Love to be experienced as a reality in the world. After his earthly ministry the Lord returned to his Father. He empowered and designated a few of the disciples to carry the teaching on. Thus it has come to us, handed on by living witnesses.

These living witnesses or apostles went out from Jerusalem and founded local assemblies of faith. Like Israel of old, these assemblies were the sign and instrument of the Lord Jesus in that place. It was by the example of love that others became attracted to Christianity. It was through prayer and life within the assemblies that the living witnesses were able to go forth and preach. And it was through incorporation into these assemblies that an individual came to know the Lord Jesus, receive formation in the Teaching, be sanctified in prayer and be guided in the Christian life.

Within these assemblies believers entered into worship of God – as Father, Son, and Holy Spirit. Through the singing of psalms, hymns and inspired songs, through the breaking of bread and the prayers, they met the Lord Jesus who sanctified their inner life. Through devotion to the teaching of the apostles, they came to know the revelation of God which Jesus had disclosed in himself.

The primary elements of the Teaching are:

There is one God who is almighty, whom Jesus called Father. This one God is the Creator of heaven and earth. Jesus is the divine and human, only Son of this Father, and as we call God Lord, we call Jesus Lord, for the Father is in him and he is in the Father. The miracle of Jesus' virgin birth attests to this. Jesus suffered at the hands of the Roman Governor, Pontius Pilate, giving his life in the process. He died and was buried as we all shall be. But he did not remain in the tomb, for God raised him up out of death. His suffering and death broke the chains of sin for all who died before his coming, again making God-Love available to them. He rose from the dead, making life with God now and forever our blessed hope. He ascended, returning into the presence of God-Love from which he came. He sent the Holy Spirit to create the assembly of believers and to be its constant guide in faith, hope and love. He will return to bring time to an end, to judge the living and the dead, and to complete creation with the inauguration of the eternal kingdom of, with, and in God-Love.

These assemblies of faith, formed and guided by the Spirit, also taught a way of conduct based not on law, but virtue. The Lord Jesus taught that all sin in life could be overcome and rooted out of human experience by the avoidance of negative behavior and the substitution of a corresponding virtue. These virtues are seen as active gifts of the Holy Spirit to the believer. Love, joy, peace, patience, kindness, goodness, faithfulness and self-control are the spiritual means to a Christian life.

This simple foundation of doctrine and virtue has been reflected on over the centuries in the development of our understanding. Through prayer, holy women and men have penetrated to the depths of these mysteries guided by the Holy Spirit of God-Love. The assemblies look to four sources for insights to develop the living faith carried in the mind of the whole people of Christ. These are the sources of theological reflection: Scripture, the Oral Tradition, Reason, and Experience.

1) Scripture includes the Hebrew Scriptures interpreted through the New Testament.

2) Tradition is the preaching, teaching and ritual which guide the assembly in prayer life, work and worship.

3) Reason is the application of disciplined thought to understand more fully the mystery.

4) Experience focuses on the changes within us which doctrine makes.

Faith is handed on through life in the assembly, sometimes through preaching and sometimes through sacred rites. Baptism and Eucharist are the signs and means of entrance into and nourishment of the assembly's life. Confession of sins and anointing with oil heal the spiritual and physical life of the body, while marriage and ordination create, lead, and guide the family and the assembly.

In Christianity today, almost 2,000 years after the ascension of the Lord Jesus, divisions exist. John Wesley, one of the great reformers in England, spoke of a fully balanced Christianity having the four components mentioned above – Scripture, Tradition, Reason and Experience – as the bases of religious knowledge. We could consider the divisions within Christianity to be a function of favoring one or more of these components over the others. Political, economic and other human considerations aside, the division in the Church has resulted from the development of different theological schools which emphasize the different components. For example, the Orthodox are known for their emphasis on Tradition and Experience; the Catholics on Tradition and Reason; the Protestants on Scripture and Reason; and Pentecostals on Scripture and Experience.

These differences in emphasis have led to differences in the formulation of doctrine, the number and status of the sacred rites or sacraments, and the authority of the ordered ministries. These emphases have brought each Christian community a deeper insight into faith but also have limited their fellowship with the rest of Christianity.

Interfaith relations

Christians also differ in their relation to non-Christians. These relations are characterized by three positions:

1) The **exclusive position** holds that a saving relationship with the Lord Jesus is the *only* way to salvation. In this perspective, those who lack this will suffer forever, excluded from God-Love.

2) The **pluralist position** sees Christianity as merely one path to God among other religions which also offer the possibility of salvation. This view sees salvation as universal and knowledge of God as relative to culture and tradition.

3) Between them is the **inclusive position.** While holding to the belief that the fullness of revelation came in the person of Jesus and that he is the ordinary way to right relationship with God, here it is believed that God-Love can work beyond this. Hence a Christian may esteem truth where he/she sees it, and we will know it is the truth when it agrees with Jesus and the teaching and example received from him. The revelation of God-Love is fully disclosed in Jesus.

This description of Christianity can in no way capture the breadth, height and depth of the religion. But it is our hope that this summary has presented a glimpse of our life.

Approximate Census of Christians Worldwide

- ROMAN CATHOLICS: 900 million
- ORTHODOX: 125 million
- PROTESTANTS AND PENTECOSTALS: 622 million

The Christian Family Tree

The Rev. Epke VanderBerg

Protestant minister, member of the Episcopal family and of the Grand Rapids Interfaith Dialogue Association

We present here short portraits of main families and communities within Christianity, particularly those in The Middle East, Europe, and North America. The descriptions provide some primary characteristics and a method of categorizing Christianity into fifteen families. A major resource for this summary was the work of J. Gordon Melton in *The Encyclopedia of American Religions* (Triumph Books, 1989, New York). Readers are encouraged to explore Melton's detailed and fascinating work.

*L*ooking back down the many branches of Christianity, we see a tree called Jesus the Christ. Beyond this trunk, Christianity is rooted in God's call to Abraham in the land of Ur. From the time of Jesus into the 20th century, the roots divided and multiplied, dipping into soils and water foreign to its beginning, affecting its color and character. Throughout its history, however, it never forgot its beginning, even though its memories of who Jesus was and what he taught, waxed and waned through time and place.

*W*estern Liturgical Family: The four oldest Christian families are the following: the Eastern Orthodox tradition, the non-Chalcedonian Orthodox tradition, the Western Catholic tradition and the Anglican tradition. A strong liturgical life characterizes these Christian families, along with true-creeds, sacraments, language and culture, which find their expression in their liturgy. Most of these families observe seven sacraments: baptism, eucharist, holy orders, unction, marriage, confirmation and penance. Two other characteristics mark these churches: allegiance to creeds, and belief in Apostolic succession. Even though these churches evolved from one common beginning, they unfolded into separate entities with Christianity's spread into other cultures.

The Eastern Orthodox family, its authority centered in the cities of Antioch, Alexandria and Constantinople, split from the Western Catholic tradition in 1054 AD. The Western Catholic tradition, based in Rome and entrenched in Western Europe, exercised strong political and religious authority. The Anglican tradition in England broke with Rome in the 16th century when Henry VIII saw opportunity for an independent church that would give him his desired divorce and financial freedom for battle. *The Thirty-nine Articles of Religion* and *The Book of Common Prayer* established it as a separate liturgical tradition. In the immigration to North America and after the American Revolutionary War, the Anglican Church became known, in 1787, as the Protestant Episcopal Church in the U.S.

*E*astern Liturgical Family: Political, cultural and doctrinal differences separated the Eastern Orthodox churches from the Roman churches in 1054. Thereafter, and not having a Pope, this family was governed by Patriarchs who have equal authority and are in communion with each other. Even though the family does not demand celibacy of its priests (as long as they are married before

their ordination), monks, who are celibate, are the only members who attain the office of bishop. This family does not recognize the authority of the Bishop in Rome, nor that part of the Chalcedonian Creed that says that the Holy Spirit proceeds from the Son.

A number of groups fall into this family:

Nestorians: This group, recognizing Christ's two natures, does not believe that Christ had two equal natures and that Mary bore only the human nature of Christ – she did not bear God [Mary is not *theotikos*].

Monophysites: This group believes that Christ is of one person (*mono*) and of one nature (*physis*); it rejects the two-nature position of the Nestorians.

The Armenians: Established in Armenia as a bishopric in 260, this group customarily celebrates Holy Communion only on Sunday, using pure wine [without water] and unleavened bread. Infants are served immediately after baptism. Under persecution by the Turks in 1890, many moved to North America. Controversy soon followed: would the pro-Soviet dominance of Armenia govern or would the Armenian nationalists?

Syrian Churches: under the leadership of Jacob Baradeus (followers were often called Jacobites), who was a monophysite, the Syrian churches spread throughout the Mediterranean region and beyond.

Coptic Churches of Egypt and Ethiopia: Formerly one of the largest Christian groups in the world, this group diminished through persecution. Today, found mainly in Egypt, its numbers are increasing. The Ethiopian Church differs from the Coptic on several points: 1) accepts Apocrypha as Scripture, 2) venerates the Sabbath along with Sunday, 3) recognizes Old Testament figures as saints, and 4) observes many Old Testament regulations on food and purification.

*L*utheran Family: Martin Luther, in cooperation with German princes, brought about the first successful breach with the Roman Catholic Church. Even though October 31, 1517, is often thought to be the start of the Lutheran Church, a more persuasive argument may be made for the year 1530, in which the Augsburg Confession was published. This confession became the standard that congregations used to justify their independent existence and distinguished the churches that used written confessions as "confessing churches." Luther taught that salvation is by grace through faith, rather than works and faith, and that the Bible is the rule of faith and sole authority for doctrine. Luther, in distinction from other Reformation churches, placed greater emphasis on the sacramental liturgy and understood the eucharist as consubstantiation (Christ present but elements not changed) in distinction from the Roman Catholic tradition of transubstantiation (elements changed into Christ's essence). Luther's translation of the Bible into the German vernacular (1532–34) became the standard for the German language and sparked the use of the vernacular in the

Lutheran liturgy. Through Luther, many new hymns came into use and changed the complexion of the liturgy.

Reformed-Presbyterian Family: The force behind this family is John Calvin, who established the Reformed church in Geneva, Switzerland, in the 1540s. The Reformed churches distinguish themselves from the other Christian families by their theology (Reformed) and the church government (Presbyterian). Calvin derived his Reformed theology from the major premise of God's sovereignty in creation and salvation. He taught that God predestined some to salvation and that atonement is limited to those whom God has elected. Today, a strict or lenient interpretation of predestination separates many Reformed churches. On the continent, the churches were known as Reformed; in the British Isles they came to be known as Presbyterian. The Reformed churches were one with other Protestant churches in adherence to the authority of the early Christian creeds and believing in the Trinity, salvation by grace through faith, and that the Bible is the sole authority for faith and doctrine (in opposition to the Roman Catholics' position of salvation by faith and works, and of authority in the Bible and tradition). These churches did not concern themselves with apostolic succession, but with the pure preaching of the Gospel (predominantly a teaching function) and in the pure administration of the sacraments (baptism and eucharist). In the eucharist, God, who is present, can be apprehended by faith; this is in opposition to the Lutherans and Roman Catholics who maintain God's special presence in the elements.

Pietist-Methodist Family: Three groups of churches fall under this category: the Moravian Church, the Swedish Evangelical churches and the Methodist (Wesleyan) churches. As a movement of pietism, these churches reacted to Protestantism as practiced in the late 17th century. They reacted to the rigidity and systematic doctrine of the scholastic Lutheran and Calvinist theologians. Not wishing to leave their established churches, they wanted a shift from scholasticism to spiritual experience. They advocated a Bible-centered faith, the experience of the Christian life, and giving free expression of faith in hymns, testimony and evangelical zeal. Through the early work of Philip Jacob Spener and August Hermann Francke, and using home studies, their work rejuvenated the Moravian Church in 1727, influenced John Wesley and helped establish the Swedish Evangelical Church. In their work they were open to traditional practices and beliefs and sought life within the forms of the traditional churches.

Methodists are characterized by their dissent from the Calvinist teachings on predestination and irresistible grace. In 1784, at a Christmas conference, the Methodists in America formed the Methodist Episcopal Church. Its history in North America reflects the history of other denominations, including their relationships to Old World governments, ecclesiastical affiliations, and changing North American political patterns.

Holiness Family: Through the influence of John Wesley's teaching of perfection, the holiness movement uses Matthew 5:48 as its theme: "Be ye perfect as my father is perfect." It is distinct from modern Wesleyism and other Protestant churches by how it understands the framework of holiness and perfection. These believers have traditionally separated themselves from Christians who did not strive high enough for perfection. Wesley, however, seeing the practical problems with perfection or sinlessness, then stressed love as the primary theme for Christians, while the holiness movement continued to stress sinlessness. Holiness, or the sanctification experience, is the end work of a process that starts with accepting Christ as one's personal savior (being "born again"). Having accepted Christ, one then grows in grace with the help of the Holy Spirit. The second work of grace comes when the Holy Spirit cleanses the heart of sin and provides the power for living the Christian life. Living the life of holiness results in banning certain forms of behavior as inappropriate for the Christian. This tendency resulted in the adoption of a strict set of codes of behavior. However, groups of churches, depending upon their understanding of holiness – whether it comes instantaneously or later – established their own independent churches.

Pentecostal Family: Today's Pentecostal family is usually traced back to the work of Rev. Charles Parham and his experience at Bethel Bible College in 1901. However, the movement has also had a long history replete with the experiences usually associated with it. What makes this family distinct from other Protestant churches is not their doctrinal differences; it is their form of religious experience and their practice of speaking in tongues – called glossolalia. Tongue speaking is a sign of baptism by the Holy Spirit, a baptism that often is accompanied by other forms of spiritual gifts such as healing, prophecy, wisdom, and discernment of spirits. Pentecostals seek the experience, interpret events from within it, and work to have others share in it. Those who do not manifest the experience are thought often to be less than "full of the Spirit." Pentecostal worship services appear to be more spontaneous than the traditional churches; however, Pentecostal services repeat a pattern of seeking the experience and showing the desire to talk about it. Because it is shaped by cultural forces, Pentecostalism appears in different forms, emphasizes different gifts, yet collects similar minds into its community. Neo-Pentecostalism, however, is a recent phenomenon, and has occurred predominantly in established churches that have found room for this movement.

European Free-Church Family: While Luther and Calvin advocated a fairly close relationship with the state, 16th century radical reformers from within the Roman Catholic Church advocated a complete break with the state church. Their doctrines resembled many of the Protestant doctrines, but their ecclesiology differed. They thought the visible Church to be a free-association of adults who had been baptized as believers (as opposed to being baptized as infants) and who avoided worldly ways. The free-church family is thought to have started on December 25, 1521, when one of the leaders celebrated the first Protestant communion service, a service format that is followed by much of Protestantism. From this group evolved the Mennonites, the Amish, the Brethren, the Quakers and the

Free Church of Brethren. Because many of them shunned allegiance to the government, they suffered persecution. Suffering persecution, many of them moved to North America and established congregations there.

Many members of these groups, particularly Quakers and Mennonites, are pacifists in their response to war; at the same time, they are highly active in their work to prevent war and in their relief efforts worldwide.

Baptist Family: As a free association of adult believers, Baptists make up the second largest religious family on the American landscape. Though they may also be related to the continental free-church family, American Baptists seem more related to British Puritanism. In general, they teach that the creeds have a secondary place to Scripture, that baptism is by immersion and administered only to believing and confessing adults, that the Lord's supper (not understood as a sacrament, but as an ordinance) is a memorial, that salvation is a gift of God's grace, and that people must exercise their free will to receive salvation. Even though they are a free association, they have organized themselves into various groupings, depending upon emphases of creed and the necessity for control, and at times by differences in theological perspectives due to the American phenomenon of regionalism (e.g., Southern and Northern Baptist conventions).

Independent Fundamentalist Family: Following the lead of Englishman John Nelson Darby (1800–1882), Independent Fundamental families distinguish themselves from Baptists by their belief in dispensationalism. The Fundamentalists believe the Bible is a history of God's actions with people in different periods. Because of apparent Biblical contradictions, they resolve those differences by assigning Biblical passages to different dispensations. By failing to meet God's commands, God's economy establishes new paths to follow, which in the present dispensation, leads to the final dispensation in which Christ is recognized as the supreme universal authority. This dispensational framework has resulted in much speculation about prophecy of the Last Times. Another distinguishing feature of this family is the belief that the Church is only a unity of the Spirit, and not of organization. The Fundamentalist family frequently uses the Scofield Reference Bible as a major source for doctrine.

Adventist Family: The feature that distinguishes the Adventist family from other Christian groups is their belief in the expectation or imminent return of Christ when Christ will replace the old order of the world with an order of joy and goodness. When Christ comes again, he will establish a millennial (a thousand-year) reign in which unbelievers will have a second chance to accept Christ's Lordship. Even though a belief in the imminent return has long roots, it was heightened with the work of William Miller, a poor New York farmer. He believed that Biblical chronology could be deciphered, a belief that prompted him to predict Christ's return between March 21, 1843, and March 21, 1844. The 50,000 people who followed these teachings, and who experienced the non-return, retrenched. Rather than seeing a literal return of Christ that failed, one group advocated a spiritualized return – following the teachings of Charles Taze Russell – in which the event is understood as a "heavenly or internal event." The Adventist Family shares many of the Baptist teachings, from which much of the family has its genesis. Some of the more distinctive teachings of the family (but not all) are the following: 1) the imminent return of Christ, 2) denial of a person's immortality, 3) Old Testament laws are effective, including the observance of the Sabbath (Saturday), 4) rejection of the belief in a Hell, 5) Christ's death counters the death penalty of Adam passed to his children by inheritance, 6) that the Church is the suffering body of Christ and offers a spiritual sacrifice of atonement to God, and 7) that God's name is Yahweh.

Some of the more well-known families that have evolved from the millennial expectation are the Seventh Day Adventists, Church of Jesus Christ of the Latter-Day Saints, the Jehovah's Witnesses, British Israel Movement, and the WorldWide Church of God.

Jehovah's Witnesses, who trace their roots to Charles Taze Russell, mentioned above, prefer to separate themselves from the Christendom that was founded nearly 300 years after Jesus' death, believing that its beliefs deviate greatly from what Jesus taught. For instance, they do not accept Christendom's belief in the doctrine of the Trinity, which teaches that Jesus *is* God, though he is identified as God's Son. They do not use the cross as a symbol; yet Jesus was the promised Messiah and did provide the legal means of rescuing mankind from the consequences of Adams's sin, thus fulfilling the requirements for the new covenant which would bring faithful people into the promised earthly Paradise. Today, Jehovah's Witnesses form a large international organization, well-known for its door-to-door evangelistic methods and its belief that many who are now living will survive when God's Kingdom brings an end to all present governments. Watch Tower, the denominational publishing company, provides Bible-study and educational materials.

The Liberal Family: Because yesterday's liberal may be today's conservative, the word "liberal" can be somewhat ambiguous. Most often, however, members of this family are identified as being against the mainstream theistic position of the dominant culture in Western society. The Liberal family, depending upon orientation, finds itself somewhere among the three positions of unitarianism, universalism and atheism. Unitarianists think that God is one, that the Trinity does not exist; the universalists think that all will be saved, that Hell does not exist; the atheists reject the idea of a transcendental God. Liberalism's American origins developed in reaction to New England's Calvinism. However, the genesis of Liberalism is most often thought to rest in the work of Michael Servetus, martyred by John Calvin in Geneva. Liberals have championed human rights, the need for education and the high worth of every person. By removing God from cosmic calculations, life's answers could only come from two other sources: human feelings – as in the position of Transcendentalists – and human reason – as in the Rationalist position. Early 18th century liberals advocated that people could improve the world through reason.

Nineteenth century liberalism, seeing the results of scientific thought, expanded the above with evolution, science and materialism, seen as necessary for uncovering the essential (monotheistic) laws of the universe.

Latter-Day Saints Family: Joseph Smith, in the fervor of revivalist movements sweeping New York in the early 19th century, received at the hands of an angel in 1827 gold plates written in what he described as a reformed Egyptian language. By means of two crystal-like stones, the *Urim* and *Thummim*, this translation has been become known as the *Book of Mormon*. The *Book of Mormon* claims to be the history of two tribes, the Jeredites and the Israelites. The Jeredites moved to North America after the Tower of Babel; the Israelites moved to North America after the destruction of Jerusalem in the 6th century BC. Joseph Smith published a number of other works including the *Book of Moses,* the *Book of Abraham* and the *Book of Commandments* (now called the *Doctrine and Covenants*). The early history of Mormonism includes persecution, schisms and violence, culminating in the murder of Joseph Smith in Carthage, Illinois, June 27, 1844. In the ensuing power struggle, Brigham Young moved his group to Salt Lake City, Utah, where he established the dominant branch of Mormonism. Another branch, which resides in Independence, Missouri, claiming Joseph Smith III as successor to his father, is known as the Reorganized Church of Jesus Christ of Latter-day Saints. Several major Mormon beliefs are the following: 1) affirmation of a trinitheism (not Christian trinity) of the Father, Jesus and Holy Spirit; 2) denial of original sin and the necessity of obedience to certain articles of faith for salvation; 3) a specific church hierarchy; 4) the Word of God consists of the Bible, the *Book of Mormon* and the *Pearl of Great Price;* 5) revelation is open and added to the *Doctrine and Covenants* when received; and 6) the future Kingdom of Zion will be established in North America – either in Independence, Missouri, or Salt Lake City, Utah.

Communal Family: Citing references to the early Christian Church, the communal family desires to share all its worldly possessions with other members of the group. Communalism made a serious start in the fourth century with the development of monasticism, a movement that thought the Western Catholic tradition brought everyone into the church rather than seeing the Church as the body of true believers. Monasticism thought the principle of equality could be achieved through poverty and renunciation of the world. Francis of Assisi, thinking that monasticism did not represent true poverty (monastic orders had become very wealthy), advocated poverty of use as a method of reform. The Roman Catholic Church did not accept his vision, but saw it as a threat. The Taborites and the Munsterites, shortly after the Reformation, set up several communities, but, for a variety of reasons, failed. After 1860, visionaries and reformists began the most active era in the building of communities. In North America, the most famous and successful of these is the Hutterite community. Having a similar background to Russian Mennonites, today these people have established and maintain well over 300 communities.

Christian Science-Metaphysical Family: Concerned with the role of the Mind in the healing process, the Christian Science and the New Thought movement drew on the metaphysical traditions of the 19th century that suggested the presence of spiritual powers operating on the mind and body. Swedenborg, a prolific writer, suggested the priority of the spiritual world over the material and that the material becomes real in its correspondence to the spiritual. The Christian Bible, he also taught, must be interpreted spiritually.

In the late 1800s, Mary Baker Eddy (the founder of Christian Science) and Emma Curtis Hopkins (the founder of New Thought) built on the methodology of Swedenborg. Disease, they taught, is the result of disharmony between mind and matter. New Thought, however, is distinct from Christian Science. New Thought governs itself through ordained ministers (most of whom are women), developed a decentralized movement, emphasized prosperity (poverty is as unreal as disease), and emphasized the universal position that all religions have value. Christian Science is a major religion founded on American soil over 100 years ago. Its primary text, *Science and Health with Key to the Scriptures*, has sold over eight million copies worldwide. Interestingly, Mary Baker Eddy was one of the few women who spoke at the 1893 World Parliament of Religions.

Unity School of Christianity: This is another religious organization with metaphysical inclinations. Founded more than 100 years ago and based on the teachings of Jesus Christ, Unity offers a practical approach to Christianity that helps people lead happier, healthier, more productive lives and find deeper spiritual meaning for their lives. Unity serves millions of people worldwide through its 24-hour prayer, publishing and education ministries. Through its publishing ministry, Unity produces a variety of inspirational resources for personal study and growth; *Unity* is a metaphysical journal and *Daily Word* is a devotional publication. Unity's educational ministry is designed to train and prepare Unity ministers and teachers for pastoral service and to foster personal spiritual growth.

FOR MORE INFORMATION

There are too many Christian, particularly Protestant, denominations and offices to list here. Many libraries have directories of denominational offices and services that provide specific addresses or other information; likewise, many cities have ecumenical offices which can provide information.

There are also numerous Christian publishers and thousands of Christian bookstores in North America alone. Only some Christian bookstores will stock a range of books dealing with issues of environment, social justice, peace, interfaith dialogue, human rights, population and so on. Most stores do, however, have publishers' catalogs and can help the inquirer find resources from a specific list or interest area. They can also look in data bases to order nearly any book if you provide the title or author.

Public libraries and many college and seminary libraries carry good selections of books, and one can always find additional titles from bibliographies printed in books on particular subjects of interest.

Christianity in the World Today

Dr. Dieter T. Hessel

This essay, addressing the critical issues and wisdom, is written by a Presbyterian minister and ethicist who directs the ecumenical Program on Ecology, Justice and Faith, and is editor of After Nature's Revolt (Fortress Press, 1992).[1]

The primary challenges and issues facing humanity

Among **perennial** challenges are the quest for meaningful human existence and the struggle for social justice and peace. Greater scientific and technological power over nature tempts humans to ignore creaturely limits and to make themselves the center of value. Human efforts to achieve inordinate security and comfort actually oppress and destroy other life, offending the Source of existence and warping right relationships in earth community. Today, the rich/poor gap has become harsher. More than a billion people lack enough to eat, while another billion misuse resources and overconsume. Militarization brings mass death to the "meek" even as it allows the militarily powerful to retain unjust advantage over the earth's resources for a wealthy few.

Pressing **new** issues face humanity, including the degradation of the environment on a global scale and the negative impact of exploding human population growth on social systems and other species. The world's religions and governments have also been surprised by a new public health crisis worsened by AIDS, and by the breakdown of public and private morality, as well as by the failures of common educational systems, in commodified societies. Meanwhile, counterrevolutionary forms of cultural/religious fundamentalism foster crusading intolerance of other faiths or ethnic groups and threaten minority rights. Mature religion and politics, to the contrary, will foster multicultural appreciation, religious tolerance, civil liberties, gender equality and racial justice.

How Christians respond to these issues

First, rethink and reinterpret faith for these times. Pertinent Christian faith expresses reverence for the Creator, Sustainer and Redeemer of the cosmos, and corresponding respect for all of the creatures whom God loves and enjoys. Such faith guides compassionate and courageous human living. The norm for spirited humanity is set by Jesus of Nazareth, "pioneer of faith" and "Son of God," whom Christians perceive as Reconciler of the world and Sovereign of life. His prophetic and healing public ministry inaugurates the Kingdom of God. Everyone is invited to enter this commonwealth, a community of *shalom* and sharing intended to encompass all known races, cultures, species, places. The church's role is to be the ecumenical social body of the crucified-risen Christ, celebrative of God's design, concerned for the well-being of all. Christian worship through word and sacrament and social witness in each locale visibly signify God's reign already operative but not yet fulfilled in history.

Secondly, embody an ethic of covenant faithfulness. A Christian ethics that is: a) based on the biblical story of God's love for creation and covenant with human creatures (*humus* = "from earth"), and b) responsive to the needs of the time, will foster and embody these values:

- love for human beings everywhere who are equally "created in the image of God," and respect for basic human rights,
- care for the well-being of near and distant neighbors, both human and otherkind, on this home planet,
- justice to the oppressed as well as generosity toward the deprived,

"The Lord said to Moses on Mount Sinai, 'Say to the people of Israel, When you come into the land which I give you, the land shall keep a sabbath to the Lord. Six years you shall sow your field, and six years you shall prune your vineyard, and gather in its fruits; but in the seventh year there shall be a sabbath of solemn rest for the land, a sabbath to the Lord; you shall not sow your field or prune your vineyard.' "

LEVITICUS 25: 1–4

"And he [Jesus] came to Nazareth, where he had been brought up; and he went to the synagogue, as his custom was, on the sabbath day. And he stood up to read; and there was given to him the book of the prophet Isaiah. He opened the book and found the place where it was written,

'The Spirit of the Lord is upon me, because he has anointed me to preach good news to the poor. He has sent me to proclaim release to the captives and recovering of sight to the blind, to set at liberty those who are oppressed, to proclaim the acceptable year of the Lord.' " LUKE 4: 16–21

"Blessed are you poor, for yours is the kingdom of God. Blessed are you that hunger now, for you shall be satisfied. Blessed are you that weep now, for you shall laugh. . . . But woe to you that are rich, for you have received your consolation. Woe to you that are full now, for you shall hunger. . . .

But I say to you that hear, love your enemies, do good to those who hate you, bless those who curse you, pray for those who abuse you. . . . And as you wish that men would do to you, do so to them. LUKE 6: 20–31
(Jesus' Sermon on the Mount)

- prophetic denunciation of sin toward neighbor and nature, and idolatry or corruption in personal life and public affairs,
- frugality of lifestyle – neither strictness nor laxity – so that there may be sustainable sufficiency for all,
- nonviolent action to resist exploitation, and cooperative habits of coping with social conflict,
- renewal of community life and cultivation of civil processes for the common good.

*T*hird, examine ambiguities of religious life.
Christianity in the late modern era has partially embodied but often contradicted its faith affirmations and moral imperatives. Transformative faith leading toward biophilic harmony has been obscured by domineering or distorting tendencies. Christians have proclaimed "the grace of our Lord Jesus Christ, the love of God and the communion of the Holy Spirit," while acquiescing to racist, sexist, classist, naturist and ecclesiastical practices of domination. The church's emphasis on human rights worldwide has fostered liberation of the oppressed, but is in fragmentary ways captive to individualism, ethnocentrism and popular moralism.

On every continent, Christian communions have been coopted by the forces of destructive nationalism, and even now the ecumenical church remains shamefully divided over issues of gender justice and reproductive rights, added to ancient divisions over faith and order. Moreover, most local congregations lack racial and class heterogeneity, or constructive relations with other faith communities and popular movements for social change.

Nations with Christian majorities have relied on military force much more than on peacemaking initiatives and cooperative development. Western economic ethics has favored democratic capitalism over policies and practices of social solidarity and ecological integrity. Newly awakened ecumenical concern for "integrity of creation" is still very anthropocentric and has just begun to explore intrinsic values in nature, or sacred dimensions of the evolutionary story.

Priestly celebrations of grace within nature will see earth, water and wind as sacramental, along with bread, wine and spirit. Prophetic responses to these times will seek "eco-justice" – social and economic equity coupled with ecological integrity and cooperative peacemaking for the sake of earth and people.

Ethical guidance in Christianity

*C*hristians characteristically ask *not:* "What is the good?" but: "What purposes and patterns of conduct are in keeping with being faithful *people of God*?" Since Pentecost, Christian communities have understood themselves to be people of "The Way" (Acts 4:32–35; 18:24–26). The Christian Way is viewed as consistent with the expectations of the Noachic and Sinai covenants. A Christian ethical spirituality – "Live your life in a manner worthy of the gospel of Christ" – is expressed in the communion meal and baptism, as well as in public preaching and social practice. The individualistic, bureaucratic and technocratic acids of modernity have corroded commitment to this way; intentional Christian communities, though often ignored by mainline churches, have been primary bearers of the tradition.

People of the Way have vision, values and virtues that are consistent with the basic themes, though not legal details, of the Hebrew *covenant* story. Today, Christians and Jews alike are rediscovering wisdom dimensions of covenant ethics, keyed to the rest-and-play Sabbath purpose of creation's seventh day. For example, Exodus 23, Leviticus 19 and 25, plus Deuteronomy 15 summarize covenant laws that contain the implicit ecological and social wisdom of herding tribes and primitive agrarians living close to the land. Faithful people give animals frequent "time off" and let the land lie fallow at least once every seven years. Neither neighbors nor nature are to be exploited. Earthkeeping humans are responsible for making sure that people, animals and the land have their times of rest, peace and restoration (Ex. 20:8–11; 23:10–12). It is a grand jubilee tradition (Lev. 25 & 26, Luke 4:16–22) with much contemporary relevance.

Covenant teaching fosters an ethic of environmental care coupled with social justice. Moral responsibility toward land and beasts must be matched by justice toward the poor. An appropriate response to poverty, therefore, involves more than alms-giving; it entails debt relief, gleaning opportunities, equitable redistribution of land, as well as care for "strangers, widows and orphans."

Yet, despite deep appreciation of nature and reverential descriptions in the Psalms, in Job, in Jesus' Sermon on the Mount, and despite Isaiah's hopeful vision of *shalom,* which includes a restored creation, scripture is punctuated with sad stories of land coveting and defilement. Some striking biblical examples of eco-injustice are the tale of Naboth's vineyard (I Kings 21), Solomon's order to cut down the beloved cedars of Lebanon to aggrandize Jerusalem (I Kings 5:6–11; Ps. 104:16), and the people's lament at becoming powerless tenant farmers after the return from exile (Neh. 5:3–5). Wherever human beings are unfaithful to the eco-social requirements of God's covenant, their idolatrous behavior has devastating consequences (Jer. 9:4–11); the land mourns, even the birds die (Hos. 4:3). Even so, there is hope for renewal of the covenant; God continually acts with justice and mercy to redeem creation.

Covenant ethics is concerned with right relationships within the whole web of created interdependency. It views Jesus Christ as the normative clue to faithful and fitting life. "Faithful" means loyal to the cause of God who makes covenant with creation after the flood, through the exodus, and at the incarnation. "Fitting" means practical human action consistent with the kingdom vision and covenant values. Responsible action "fits in" with everything that is going on and that is needed to solve problems.[2]

The *cross,* the central symbol in the new covenant story, signifies God grappling with human sin, accepting and overcoming life's persistent suffering and perpetual perishing, and ultimately creation's comprehensive renewal, including harmonious human living with myriad species of animals and plants (as envisioned by the prophet Hosea 2:18–22). That is not all it means, but Christians can perceive Jesus' crucifixion-resurrection as the deed that reconciles human beings to God, each other and the world of creation – *at-onement* with nature and society, *atunement* to what God is doing with us and all other creatures. The gracious, enabling work of Christ brings responsive communities of faith into right relation with God, other people and the larger ecological-social environment with its bio-diversity.

But "developed" and "developing" societies alike have yet to face the limits nature places on polluting economic growth and material consumption, and to adopt an ethic and practice of eco-justice that would keep the earth, achieve justice, build community. This ethic comes into sharp focus in terms of four norms: ecologically *sustainable* or environmentally fitting enterprise; socially *just participation* in obtaining sustenance and managing community life; *sufficiency* as an equitable standard of organized sharing that requires basic consumption floors and ceilings, and *solidarity* with other people and creatures—companions, victims and allies—in earth community. Observance of each ethical norm reinforces the others, serving the common eco-social good by joining what is socially just with what is ecologically right.

Enriching theological traditions

*T*he **covenant theology tradition**, going back to Augustine, and behind him to both testaments, has prominence in the preceding portrait of Christianity. But there are several other important Christian approaches, rooted in tradition, which can be viewed as having complementary rather than competing effects on Christian witness in the contemporary world.

One of these is the **wisdom tradition** of Job, the Psalms, Proverbs, Ecclesiastes, and the New Testament gospel and epistles of John. Practical folk wisdom among Christians carries on the tradition, which is also folded into Biblical covenant faith and ethics, as we have seen. Suffice it to add here that from the Wisdom perspective, Jesus is understood to be the incarnate Word of God, **logos** of life and reason—from the beginning to the end. The prologue to the book of *John* views the logos as involved immanently in the whole of God's creation, enlivening all living things while enlightening all that have such capacity.

Another approach is offered by **mature evangelical** Christianity (as distinct from crusading fundamentalism). It recognizes that to start and stay on a path of *sustainable sufficiency for all* requires spiritual conversion – change of heart and repentance moving toward sanctification that must be reinforced in a faithful, nurturing community. Saving grace is the joyous message so characteristic of 19th century Protestant hymnody. The crucial result of Christ's redemptive work is to restore human "mutability" – our ability to respond to God's call and to grow and change toward maturity. This is not possible by human willing alone. The gracious, saving work of Christ is necessary for the flourishing of responsible human activity.

Another Christian approach is the **sacramental tradition**, fostered by Catholic mystics, and supported in Anglican and Orthodox liturgy. It "ecstatically experiences the divine bodying forth in the cosmos, and beckons us into communion" (as Rosemary Radford Ruether writes in

Gaia & God, HarperCollins, 1992). "We must start thinking of reality as the connecting links of a dance in which each part is equally vital to the whole, rather than [using] the linear competitive model in which the above prospers by defeating and suppressing what is below." The resulting ethical spirituality knows the value and transcience of selves in relation to the great Self, the living interdependence of all things, and the joy of personal communion within the matrix of life – a sacred community.

Passionist Fr. Thomas Berry, a contemporary interpreter of the sacramental tradition, recently discussed the question, "What are the conditions for entering into a Viable Future?"

First condition: Recognize that the universe is a communion of subjects, not a collection of objects. (A theology of stewardship misses the point that communion – deep rapport – is the primary experience.) Earth community **is** the sacred society where we have complementary manifestations of the divine.

Second condition: Appreciate that the earth is primary; humans are derivative. So earth-healing comes first. All professions, business, education and religion must focus on the well-being of the whole community.

Third condition: Come to grips with the fact that in the future nothing much will happen that humans are not involved in, given our numbers and power. This requires human subjectivity in contact with the subjectivity of the world. "All human activities must be judged primarily by the extent to which they generate and foster a mutually enhancing human/earth relationship."

Adequate theological and ethical responses to the environmental challenge will encompass (in a wholistic way) both created reality **and** human subjectivity. William French of Loyola University, Chicago emphasizes the "need to move beyond dualistic thinking that suggests we must choose between focusing on subjectivity or creation, freedom or natural necessity, historical consciousness or ecological sensitivity" (in *Journal of Religion,* 1992). Just as subject-centered theology need not turn against creation, critical creation-centered theology need and should not reject the importance of human subjectivity or constructive historical projects.

Adequate theology and ethics will pay close attention to the "view from below" even as it also learns to listen to nature. The **feminist** or egalitarian insight is catching hold that

Domination of women has provided a key link, both socially and symbolically, to domination of earth; hence the tendency in patriarchal cultures to link women with earth, matter and nature, while identifying males with sky, intellect and transcendent spirit. . . . The work of eco-justice and the work of spirituality are interrelated, the outer and inner aspects of one process of conversion and transformation . . . [involving] a reordering to bring about just and loving interrelationships between men and women, between races and nations, between groups presently stratified into social classes, manifest in great disparities of access to the means of life.[3]

Knowing God Through Creation:
The Belgic Confession

Guido de Brés

First published 156 and revised 1566 and 1619, this *Confession* was used during and since the Reformation as a major teaching document in Protestant churches. A small part of it follows in the translation used in the *Psalter Hymnal* of the Christian Reformed Church.

ARTICLE1: The Only God

*We all believe in our hearts
and confess with our mouths
that there is a single
and simple
spiritual being,
whom we call God—
eternal, incomprehensible, invisible
unchangeable, infinite, almighty,
completely wise, just and good,
and the overflowing source of all good.*

ARTICLE2: The Means By Which We Know God

We know him by two means:

*First, by the creation, preservation,
and government of the universe,
since that universe is before our eyes
like a beautiful book in which all
creatures, great and small,
are as letters to make us ponder
the invisible things of God:
his eternal power
and his divinity.*

*As the apostle Paul says in Romans
1:20, 'All these things are enough to
convict men and to leave them without
excuse.'*

*Second, he makes himself known to
us more openly by his holy and divine
Word, as much as we need in this life,
for his glory
and the salvation of his own.*

Poor and indigenous communities of people who are most affected by economic exploitation and environmental destruction have important things to teach us about living in harmony with nature and caring for place. Such communities have priority justice claims on religious, educational, business and political organizations.

Finally, in response to modern physics, biology and ecology, we should note the maturing of a more philosophical and interdisciplinary style of Christian **process thought**, as fostered by John Cobb. His thought in *The Liberation of Life* (1981, with biologist Charles Birch) asserts the need for an organic or ecological view of God and reality that does not construe God as a substance isolated from the world. God is inherently related to the world, indwelling all eco-social systems, which by their nature are intrinsically interconnected communities. Rev. Carol Johnston, a student of Cobb, notes that,

> When relations are conceived as inherent, then the person is both influenced by relations with others and influences them. In this context, justice is a matter of the quality of relationships . . . characterized by freedom, participation and solidarity. Recognition of inherent relatedness establishes the need to take marginalized people and externalized ecosystems into account.... All entities have a right to be respected appropriate to their degree of intrinsic value and to their importance to the possibility of value in others.[4]

To cultivate a renewed spirituality that undergirds an ethic of care for earth community is the special obligation of religious leaders, clergy and lay, in these times. Otherwise, many more people will suffer from environmental degradation and social injustice, while numerous special places and wondrous otherkind will not be saved; sooner or later they also will fall to the utilitarian logic of the developers.

Authentic spirituality features awe, respect, humane pace, justice and generosity, **not** intensively efficient use of all being, as goes the instrumental logic of modern life and business. Authentic spirituality loves the suffering ones, aspires toward harmony with the wilderness, shows deep respect for the dignity of animals, plants, mountains and waters. Such religion celebrates spirit in creation, inculcates an ethic of genuine care for vulnerable people, creatures, eco-systems, as it appropriates the wisdom of nature and of long-standing communities.

In this web of life, religious people will praise and participate in the "economy of God" on this planetary home, foster loving deeds of eco-justice, build communities that model sufficiency, join with others to envision and move toward reverential, sustainable development (and foster corporate responsibility consistent with this goal). They will also explore urban and rural dimensions of ecology, encourage appropriate technologies at home and abroad, participate in community organizations that are working for environmental and economic justice, while they express integrity in both individual and institutional lifestyle, consistent with a spirituality of creation-justice-peace.

NOTES

1. Dieter Hessel also served the national staff of the Presbyterian Church (U.S.A.) for 25 years as coordinator of social education and of social policy development. His most recent book is *The Church's Public Role: Retrospect and Prospect;* Wm. B. Eerdmans, 1993.

2. See Charles McCoy, "Creation and Covenant: A Comprehensive Vision for Environmental Ethics," in *Covenant for a New Creation,* Carol S. Robb and Carl J. Casebolt, eds.; Orbis Books, 1991.

3. Ruether, *Gaia & God.*

4. "Economics, Eco-Justice, and the Doctrine of God," in Dieter T. Hessel, ed., *After Nature's Revolt;* Fortress Press, 1992. Also see Herman Daly and John B. Cobb, Jr., *For the Common Good: Redirecting the Economy toward Community, the Environment, and a Sustainable Future;* Beacon Press, rev. edition 1993.

African American Christianity

Dr. David D. Daniels

Associate Professor of Church History, McCormick Theological Seminary, Chicago, Illinois

African American Christianity is a religious community within global Christianity, located in the United States of America among the descendents of the African slaves who were violently transported to the Americas beginning in the 1500s. While it has always believed the common creeds of the Christian Church, the African American Christian community also recognizes that religion must be embodied in social structures and practices, and it demands correspondence between these social embodiments of faith in God with personal confessions and lives of faith.

The African American Church emerged in colonial British North America during the revolutionary fervor of the late 18th century. At that time, African Americans discerned the need for assuming responsibility for their religious lives within the Christian faith rather than totally entrusting their religious existence to their oppressors, the slaveholders of European national origins. The other major issue which promoted the emergence of African American Christianity was the institutional racism which shaped most American congregations. In these congregations, parishioners were segregated by race, and African Americans were denied the right to official religious leadership, including the office of minister.

Historically, the African American Church has struggled to create social space where a just system could be erected that affirms the human dignity of African Americans and their relationships with others. Currently, African American Christianity is an interdenominational movement with members in communions ranging from Roman Catholicism to Baptist and Pentecostal.

African American churches confess faith in God the Creator, accenting God's creation of all races from a common humanity. African Americans opened their congregations to all Christians regardless of race, and campaigned to end discrimination against persons because of race. During the late 19th and early 20th centuries, the African American Church buttressed its faith in God the Creator by confessing the essence of relationships as "The Fatherhood of God and the Brotherhood of Man." The Civil Rights Movement of the 1950s and 1960s, led by the Rev. Martin Luther King, Jr., communicated the strength of African American Christian faith and demonstrated its resolve to embody its faith within social structures. The congregations spearheaded a national interreligious campaign which struggled to reshape American society; its goal was to dismantle the system of legalized segregation which denied God as the creator of all races and the image of God in all humanity.

African American Christians, as other Christians, confess faith in the providence of God. During the eras of slavery and segregation, African Americans remained confident that God was acting in history to overthrow slavery and segregation. They held in creative tension a firm belief in both personal and social salvation. The African American Church is shaped by God's revelation in Jesus Christ. Jesus is worshipped in song, prayer and life as the revelation of God's solidarity with the poor and oppressed through the historical Jesus' identification with poor, the outcast, women and the oppressed of the first century CE.

The African American Church identifies racial injustice as the social impact of sin. The impact of slavery and segregation as forms of racism is evident in the structuring and legalizing of an inferior or less-than-human status of African Americans, beneath their God-given status and creation as human beings. The African American Church weds God's goodness to the African American practice of Christian love, along with strong demands for

"The spirit of the Lord is upon me for he has anointed me. He has sent me to announce Good News to the poor, to proclaim release for prisoners and recovery of sight for the blind; to let the broken victims go free, to proclaim the acceptable Year of the Lord." ISAIAH 61:1-3

"When you lift your hands outspread in prayer I will hide my eyes from you. Though you offer countless prayers, I will not listen. There is blood on your hands . . . cease to do evil, learn to do right, pursue justice and champion the oppressed, give the orphan his rights, plead the widow's cause." GOD, speaking in Isaiah 1:15–17

"Is not this what I require of you as a fast: to loose the fetters of injustice, to untie the knots of the yoke, to snap every yoke and set free those who have been crushed? Is it not sharing your food with the hungry, taking the homeless poor into your house, clothing the naked when you meet them and never evading a duty to your kinsfolk?" GOD, speaking in the Book of Isaiah

"Inasmuch as ye have done it to the least of these my brethren, ye have done it to me . . . . Inasmuch as ye have not done it to the least of these my brethren, ye have not done it to me." JESUS, in Matthew 25

justice; these are seen as keys to the social embodiment of faith in God the Creator and glimpses of the justice of God in society.

Racism, specifically slavery and segregation, is named as the curse of the earth, a violation of God's model of human interaction, a model which reflects God's justice and love which is to be reflected in human relationships. Racism is problematic because it reduces persons who are its victims to objects of labor. It arrogantly uncreates what God created – the humanity of its victims – thus blaspheming God. Racism violates creation by treating people as less than human. The issue goes beyond the denial of inalienable human rights, inhumane labor, restriction of freedoms or cruel treatment. At its core is the attempt to destroy the image of God in persons, annihilating the personhood of its victims. Ultimately, racism mars both the oppressed and the oppressor through its confusion of human authority with the prerogatives and authority of the Creator. Racism also undermines the bonds of human community and corrupts the religions and governments which sanction it.

Interreligious dimensions

*I*n addition to the interreligious dimension of the Civil Rights Movement, African American Christianity has indirectly created religious communities with Judaism and Islam through African Americans who adopted Jewish and Islamic beliefs and practices.

From African American Christianity there emerged in the 1890s a new movement which was led by converts to Judaism. While these converts borrowed heavily from Judaism, their core remained African American Christianity. Even the early names of their organizations within African American Judaism reflected Christian forms: Church of God and Saints of Christ; Church of the Living God. Other names, reflecting themes of identity were Ethiopian Hebrews and the Moorish Zionist Temple. During the late 20th century, dialogues with the world Jewish communities led African American Judaism to incorporate more aspects of Global Judaism.

In the 1910s there emerged a new movement within Islam led by converts from African American Christianity. Like African American Judaism, it relied on African American Christianity for its form, but borrowed heavily from Islam. This religious community is represented by such organizations as the Moorish Science Temple, the Nation of Islam and the American Muslim Mission.

The African American Church has provided an historic witness to the justice and sovereignty of God within the world community, identifying with many movements committed to the liberation of peoples from oppression. It has historically had dialogue with movements such as the Hindu-inspired decolonization campaign in India led by Gandhi and the Islam-inspired Palestinian liberation movement. Each endeavor worships God by bringing correspondence between the embodiment of faith in social structures and humane relationships, with personal confession and lives of faith.

Native American – Christian Worship

In North America, as in many countries, there has been a considerable range of interaction between Christians of many denominations and indigenous peoples from a variety of tribal communities. Some indigenous people are reclaiming parts of their heritage and combining them with the Christian message. The description which follows explains several elements which may be utilized in cross-cultural worship. One of the goals here is to appreciate the gifts, rituals, and meanings found in the traditions of "the other" – as the Native American believers themselves experience those meanings.

The Circle: For Native American people, and for their theology, the Circle is the symbol that expresses their unique identity as a people. It expresses the sense of wholeness, harmony, unity, and mutual interdependence that is at the heart of Native civilization. The Circle is a powerful metaphor for the special insights and gifts that Indian and Eskimo people bring into the Christian faith as part of their ancient cultural heritage.

The Drum: In Indian country, the term drum means more than just the physical instrument itself. It implies also the singers who are seen as an organic part of the music; they are also the instrument of the drum. The drum, a perfect representation of the Circle, embodies the heartbeat of the body of Christ.

The Four Sacred Directions: Within the Circle, the points of the spiritual compass indicate the four sacred directions of God's creation. These directions represent the eternal balance of the harmony and goodness of the world. They can be illustrated by different colors, depending on the tribal tradition.

Our Mother, the Earth: Here is a very precious part of Native American theology; it is one that must be accorded great respect. Speaking of the Earth is not done casually in Native worship; rather, the living Earth shows the nurturing, sustaining power of God in all its warmth and beauty.

Cedar, Sage, Sweet Grass and Tobacco: Many tribes have a form of incense to purify the place of prayer and worship. Any of these four can be used individually or collectively as incense during a service.

Native Hymns: A great many traditional Christian hymns have been translated into Native languages. One hymn, "Many and Great, O God, are Thy Works," is actually a Dakota hymn, translated into English, and a part of some hymnals.

Excerpted from the service booklet
for "A Celebration of Native American Survival,"
held at the National Cathedral on October 12, 1992.
(Derived from a longer article written by the Right Reverend Steve Charleston, a Native American, titled "Planning with Native Americans for a Shared Worship Experience," this explanation was previously printed in "Eco-Letter" of the NACRE, Fall-Winter 1992.)

A Call for Evangelical Renewal

Chicago Declaration II

In 1973 a group of evangelical Christians gathered in Chicago to offer a declaration of social concern. In November of 1993, evangelicals sharing the same concerns and convictions gathered again in Chicago to reconsider what they should do in the midst of a worsening social and moral crisis.

We give thanks

We give thanks for the Christian communities that are living out the sacrificial and compassionate demonstration of the reconciling love of God. Their faithfulness encourages us to follow Christ more closely in the power of the Holy Spirit. While we acknowledge our weaknesses and confess our failures, we take heart from the love of God at work in their lives and communities.

We weep and dream

We weep for those who do not know and confess Jesus Christ, the hope of the world. We dream of a missionary church that, by its witness and love, draws people into a living relationship with our Lord.

We weep over the persistence of racism, the broken relationships and the barriers that divide races and ethnic groups. We dream of churches that demonstrate the reconciling Gospel of Christ, uniting believers from every nation, tribe, and tongue.

We weep over the growing disparity between the rich and the poor, the scandal of hunger, and the growing number of people who live in oppressive conditions, insecurity, and danger. We dream of churches that work for education, economic empowerment and justice, both at the personal and structural levels, and that address the causes and the symptoms of poverty.

We weep over escalating violence, abuse, disregard for the sanctity of human life, and addiction to weapons – in both nations and neighborhoods – that destroy lives and breed fear. We dream of faith communities that model loving ways of resolving conflict, and seek to be peacemakers rather than passive spectators, calling the nations to justice and righteousness.

We weep over the brokenness expressed in relationships between generations, between men and women, in families, in distorted sexualities, and in cruel judgementalism. We dream of faith communities that honor and protect both our elders and our children, foster a genuine partnership and mutual submission between men and women, nourish healthy families, affirm celibate singleness, work for healing and compassion for all, and for the keeping of marriage covenants.

We weep over the spiritual emptiness and alienation of modern secular society. We dream of a redemptive church that restores personal identity, provides loving community, offers purpose in life, and brings transcendent values and moral conscience to the public square.

We weep over our exploitive practices and consumerist lifestyles that destroy God's good creation. We dream of a Church that leads in caring for creation and calls Christians to serve as faithful partners of God in renewing and sustaining God's handiwork.

In all of these, we have fallen so far short of God's glory and awesome holiness, yet we rejoice that in the incarnation, death and resurrection of Jesus Christ, and in the power of the Holy Spirit, we are called by God to the obedience than comes from faith.

We commit

Because of the hope we have in the Gospel, we dare to commit ourselves to the kingdom of God and oppose the demonic spiritual forces that seek to undermine the reign of God in this world. Because of our faith we dare to risk and seek the future that God has promised, and we give ourselves to works of love.

We recommit ourselves to grow in the knowledge and the love of God, drinking from the well of worship and praise, word and sacrament. We commit ourselves to sacrificial and loving engagement with God, with all other Christians, and with a needy world.

We commit ourselves to share the good news of Jesus Christ, by living and announcing the Gospel of the kingdom, so that all may come to know, love and serve God.

We repent of our complacency, our reliance on technique, and our complicity with the evils of the status quo. We repudiate the idolatries of nation and economic system, and zealously dedicate ourselves to Christ and his kingdom's values. We turn away from obsession with power, possessions, self-fulfillment, security, and safety, and willingly risk discomfort and conflict as we live our dreams.

In 1973, we called evangelicals to social engagement: this call still stands. We are thankful that more social engagement is emerging, yet tragically it has frequently divided us along ideological lines. Too often recent evangelical political engagement has been uncivil and polarizing, has demonized opponents, and has lacked careful analysis and biblical integrity. Faithfulness to the full authority of the Scriptures transcends traditional categories of left and right.

The Gospel is not divided – it embraces both the call to conversion and the summons to justice. Obedience to Jesus' teaching and example demands congregations that integrate prayer, worship, evangelism, and social transformation.

We Pray

In the face of such complex and unremitting problems, we claim the promise of God to give wisdom to those who ask. Therefore we ask: Oh God, Giver and Sustainer of life, Holy Redeemer and Lord, comforting and empowering Spirit, teach us your ways, show us your will, give us your presence and pour out your power. Amen. Come Lord Jesus.

FOR MORE INFORMATION:

Evangelicals for Social Action,
10 Lancaster Ave., Wynnewood, PA 19096

The Unitarian Universalist Church –
A History of Diversity and Openness

David A. Johnson

Pastor, First Parish in Brookline, Massachusetts

*T*he Unitarian Universalist Association is the modern institutional embodiment of two separate denominations that grew out of movements and faith traditions which extend back to the Christian reformation era (14–16th centuries CE) and well beyond. Universalist convictions are found as early as the church father Origen, who declared that all creation would ultimately be drawn back to its divine source and that nothing and no one would be ultimately and forever excluded. In its conviction that God is ultimately and absolutely One, Unitarian thought has been a recurring "heresy" within the established church since the first century of the Christian era.

The Roumanian-Transylvanian Unitarian Church, now more than four centuries old, stems originally from the sceptical and evangelical rationalist movements within the Roman Catholic Church and the openness engendered in the Reformation era. Its faith and struggle, and that of Socinianism in Poland and the low countries, became a fertile seeding ground for the beginnings of British Unitarian thought and structure. American Unitarianism has its own primary roots in the liberal Christian movement within New England's old Puritan establishment; a formal break with that tradition produced the American Unitarian Association in 1825.

Unitarian faith rejected Calvinist double predestination – the belief that original sin fatally flaws all human character – and the doctrine of the full and absolute personhood of each member of the Trinity. Instead, Unitarians affirmed the just and loving character of God, the God-given moral and reasoning capacity of all people, working out one's salvation through both diligence and God's grace, and, above all, one God.

Universalist institutional roots are in the Radical reformation, intertwined with the histories of several Anabaptist, Separatist and Pietist movements. The Universalists first organized separately in Britain as an offshoot of the Wesleyan Methodists. What was to become the Universalist Church of America was first gathered in September of 1793, making 1993 its 200th Anniversary. Universalism in this country found its supporters chiefly from Protestants disaffected by the bitter sectarian enthusiasms of much of American Protestantism, whose theologies condemned the great mass of humankind to eternal perdition. Many of those who could not believe that an everlasting fiery pit awaited all who lacked a proper faith and salvation experience joined the Universalists in the heady revival era of the late 18th and early 19th centuries.

Both the Unitarian and Universalist denominations were democratic in church polity and organizational structure. Both rejected absolute and binding statements of faith. Both affirmed freedom of personal belief within the disciplines of democratic community, as well as the freedom of each congregation to shape its own faith and worship, and choose its clergy. Both became clearly unitarian in theology long before the merger of the two associations of churches in 1961. The Unitarian Universalist Association has grown into an international association of churches in the last few years with congregations in several countries.

Because of its openness the Unitarian Universalist movement encompasses persons of liberal Christian, deist, theist, religious humanist and world religionist persuasions. When the first World Parliament of Religions gathered in Chicago in September of 1893, Rev. Jenkin Lloyd Jones (a Unitarian) was the secretary and general work horse of the planning committee. Rev. Augusta Chapin (a Universalist) was the chair of the womens' religion committee. Neither denomination was intimidated or feared contamination by the vigorous non-Christian world (as did so many others) there represented. Hundreds of Universalists and Unitarians participated in the Parliament as attendees, participants and speakers. Again in 1993 at the second Parliament, they were there to share, learn and inform their own faith.

Our ritual is as diverse as our congregations. While most congregations' worship shows its rootage in mainline protestantism, it is no surprise to find a tea ceremony, a Jewish high holy days service, a Hindu Festival of Lights, a Muslim prayer, or a Wiccan ritual in a Unitarian Universalist church.

Likewise, no single symbol has universal acceptance among us. For some the cross remains the central symbol, for others a grouping of world religious symbols centers worship, while for some no symbol is acceptable. In recent years the flaming chalice has become the most frequently used symbol. It originates in the movement that spread from the martyrdom of Jan Hus in the 13th century. The flame in the communion cup symbolized the enduring flame of his faith, burning up from the chalice, together forming the shape of a cross. Over time, the flaming chalice has been reshaped in many forms as congregations have used and adapted it; its most common meaning today is the light of knowledge and the search for truth.

Unitarian Universalists remain a small, vigorous and growing religious body loosely connected to protestant Christianity. Many members, however, see themselves as separate and different from that tradition.*

The UUA is a strong supporter of the International Association for Religious Freedom, an interfaith organization with 70 member groups in more than 25 nations, and is a member of a new coalition of Unitarian movements worldwide.

*Some readers will question placement of this article in this chapter, which may imply that UU churches are a branch of Christianity. A more appropriate image is of a new "tree," grown out of the roots of the Christian family tree, but fertilized by the search for truth and the rich compost from other religious trees. – Ed.

Confucianism

Dr. Douglas K. Chung

Professor, Grand Valley State University School of Social Work

Confucianism is a philosophy of a way of life, although many people also consider it a religion. The tradition derives its name from Kung Fu Tzu, or Confucius, (551–479 BC) who is renowned as a philosopher and educator. He is less known for his roles as a researcher, statesman, social planner, social innovator, and advocate. Confucius was a generalist with a universal vision. The philosophical method he developed offers a means to transform individuals, families, communities, and nations into a harmonious international society.

The overall goal of Confucianism is to educate people to be self-motivated, self-controlled and able to assume responsibilities; it has the dual aims of cultivating the individual self and contributing to the attainment of an ideal, harmonious society. Confucius based his method on the assumption that lawlessness and social problems result from the combination of unenlightened individuals and a social structure without norms.

The Confucian system is based on several principles:

1. In the beginning, there is nothing.

2. The Great Ultimate (*Tao*) exists in the *I* (change). The Great Ultimate is the cause of change and generates the two primary forms: the Great *Yang* (a great energy) and its counterforce, the Great *Yin* (a passive form). *Yang* and *Yin* symbolize the energy within any system of counterforces: positive and negative, day and night, male and female, rational and intuitive. *Yang* and *Yin* are complementary; in their interaction, everything – from quanta to galaxies – comes to be. Everything that exists – all systems – coexist in an interdependent network with all other systems.

3. The dynamic tension between *Yin* and *Yang* forces results in an endless process of change – of production and reproduction and the transformation of energy. This is a natural order, an order in which we can see basic moral values. Human nature is inherently good. If a human being goes along with the Great Ultimate and engages in rigorous self-discipline, that person will discover the real self (the nature of *Tao*) and enjoy the principle of change. And since all systems exist in an interdependent network, one who knows this truth also cares.

4. There are four principles of change:

a. Change is easy.

b. Change is a transforming process due to the dynamics between *Yin* and *Yang*. Any change in either part (*Yin* or *Yang*) will lead to a change in the system and related systems. This process has its own cycle of expansion and contraction.

c. Change carries with it the notion of changelessness; that there is change is a fact that is itself unchanging.

d. The best transformation promotes the growth and development of the individual and the whole simultaneously – it strives for excellence for all systems in the network.

5. Any search for change should consider the following :

a. The status of the object in the interdependent network – that is, what is the system and what are this object's role, position, rights and duties in the system?

b. Timing within the interrelated network – that is, is this the right time to initiate change?

c. The mean position or the Golden Path in the interrelated network situation; the mean position is regarded as the most strategic position from which one can deal with change. *Tao* (Truth) exists in the mean (*Chung*).

d. The respondence of *Yin* and *Yang* forces – that is, are the counterforces willing to dialogue or compromise?

e. The integration between the parts and the whole – that is, the system in its economic, political and cultural realms.

6. There is an interconnected network of individual existence, and this pattern of interdependent relationships exists in all levels of systems, from individual, through family and state, to the whole world. The whole is dependent upon the harmonious integration of all the parts, or subsystems, while the parts require the nurture of the whole. The ultimate unit within this framework is the universe itself. Self is a here-and-now link in a chain of existence stretching both into the past and into a future to be shaped by the way an individual performs his or her roles in daily life. One's humanity is achieved only with and through others.

Individual and social transformations are based on self-cultivation, the personal effort to search for truth and to become a life-giving person. Searching for and finding the truth will lead to originality, the creative ability to solve problems, and development. The process will also enable individuals and systems to be life-giving and life-sharing – to possess a *Jen* (love) personality. Wisdom, love and courage are inseparable concepts.

7. Organizational effectiveness and efficiency are reached when systematically interconnected individuals or subsystems find the truth – and stay with it. Existence consists of the interconnected whole. Methods that assume and take account of connections work better than methods that focus on isolated elements. Organizational effectiveness can be improved through a rearrangement of the relationships between the parts and the whole.

"The moral law begins in the relationship between man and woman, but ends in the vast reaches of the universe."
CONFUCIUS, *Doctrine of the Mean 12*

In other words, a balanced and harmonious development within the interdependent network is the most beneficial state for all. Self-actualizing and collective goals should always be integrated.

*T*hese principles of Confucian social transformation are drawn primarily from *I Ching, The Great Learning, Confucian Analects* and *The Doctrine of The Mean.* In contemporary terms, Confucianism can be defined as a school of social transformation that is research oriented and that employs a multidimensional, crosscultural, and comprehensive approach that is applicable to both micro and macro systems. It is a way of life – or an art of living – that aims to synchronize the systems of the universe to achieve both individual and collective fulfillment.

Two major schools of Neo-Confucianism eventually emerged: the rationalists, who emphasized the "inner world" (philosophy), and the idealists, who emphasized practical learning in the "outer world" (social science). The leading exponent of the rationalists was Chu Hsi (1033–1107 CE) and that of the idealists was Wang Yang-Ming (1472–1529 CE). The rationalists held that reason is inherent in nature and that the mind and reason are not the same thing. The idealists held that reason is not to be sought from without; it is nothing other than the mind itself. In ethical application, the rationalists considered the flesh to be a stumbling block to the soul. The idealists, on the other hand, considered the flesh to be as the soul makes it. Neo-Confucianism in Korea was led by Lee T'oegye (1501–1570), who taught a philosophy of inner life and moral subjectivity.

Confucianism in the world today

*C*onfucianism is a strong influence in China, Korea, Japan, and the countries of Southeast Asia as well as among people of Far Eastern descent living around the world. Western people are able to appreciate Confucianism through international contacts and through its literature.

Yet postindustrial social change has led to human crisis in social networks. Postindustrial Confucians today are carrying the vision forward by applying the Confucian model of social transformation to reach the goal of a Great Harmonious Society. The effects of this are seen in volunteerism, social support, social care, and the self-help movement.

In *Great Learning,* Confucius prescribed seven steps in a general strategy of social transformation to achieve the ideal society.

1. The investigation of things (variables). Find out the way things are and how they are related.

2. The completion of knowledge. Find out why things are the way they are; that is, why the dependent variable was related to other variables. This is the reality of things, the truth, *Tao.* And since everything exists in an inter-related network, discovering this truth empowers a person to transform his or her attitude.

3. The sincerity of thought. One should be sincere in wanting to change or to set goals that are a commitment to excellence and the truth, *Tao,* which is the source of

self-motivation, the root of self-actualization and the cornerstone of adequate I-Thou and I-Thing relationships. The most complete sincerity is the ability to foreknow.

4. The rectifying of the heart. The motivation for change must be the right one, good for the self as well as for the whole. It is a cultivation aimed at virtue, a moral self achieved through the intuitive integration of *Jen* (humanity, benevolence, perfect virtue, compassion, and love), *Yi* (righteousness), *Li* (politeness, respect), and wisdom (from steps 1, 2 & 3). Only such a self has real freedom – from evil, and to have moral courage and the ability to be good.

5. The cultivation of the person. There must be life-long integration between the "knowledge self" (steps 1 & 2) and the "moral self" (steps 3 & 4) through self-discipline (education) and self-improvement. This is the key to helping self and others.

6. The regulation of the family. One should use self-discipline within the family by honoring parents, respecting and caring for siblings, and loving children. One should understand the weaknesses of those one likes and appreciate the strength of those one dislikes to avoid prejudice and disharmony in the family.

7. The governance of the state. The state must provide public education, set policies to care for vulnerable people, root policies in public opinions, appoint and elect capable and moral persons as public officials, and apply management principles based on the mean and the Golden Path. This sort of public administration should lead to the harmonious state.

*T*he practice of these seven steps is a self-cultivated discipline that seeks the truth, *Tao,* as the practitioner enacts individual and social changes for an improved and more harmonious world. The most persistent form of the Confucian worldview sees the person as an integral part of a cosmos dominated by nature. Contentment and material success come only through acceptance of the rightness of the person adjusting himself or herself to the greater natural world to which that person belongs.

Under the impetus of a contemporary revitalization of Confucianism, Confucian ethics has become an important force for initiating social transformation and economic change in much of eastern Asia, including China, Japan, Hong Kong, Korea, Singapore and Taiwan.

Confucius described the ideal welfare state in *Li Chi* (*The Book of Rites*) as follows:

> When the Grand course was pursued, a public and common spirit ruled all under the sky; they chose people of talents, virtue, and ability; their words were sincere, and what they cultivated was harmony.

> Thus people did not love their parents only, nor treat as children only their own. An effective provision was secured for the aged till their death, employment for the able-bodied, and the means of growing up to the young.

> They showed kindness and compassion to widows/ers, orphans, childless people, and those who were disabled by disease, so that they were all sufficiently maintained. Males had their proper work, and females had their homes.

(They accumulated) articles (of value), disliking that they should be thrown away upon the ground, but not wishing to keep them for their own gratification.

(They labored) with their strength, disliking that it should not be exerted, but not exerting it (only) with a view to their own advantage.

In this way (selfish) scheming was repressed and found no development. Robbers, filchers and rebellious traitors did not show themselves, and hence the outer doors remained open, and were not shut. This was (the period of) what we call the Grand Union.   (pp.365–66)

Integration of Confucianism with Other Traditions

Dr. Douglas K. Chung

Chinese, Korean and Japanese philosophical systems have each synthesed elements from several traditions. The Chinese came in contact with Indian thought, in the form of Buddhism, around the first century CE. This event, comparable to the spread of Christianity in the West, was marked by three characteristics in particular:

First, the translation of the Buddhist *sutras* stimulated Chinese philosophers and led them to interpret the teachings of the Buddha in the light of their own philosophies. The impact of this study led to the establishment of the Hua-yen and Tien-tai schools of Buddhism in China and the Kegon school in Japan.

Second, under the influence of their familiar, pragmatic Confucian ways of thought, the Chinese creatively responded most to the practical aspects of Buddhism's spiritual discipline, which the Chinese called *Ch'an* (meditation). The *Ch'an* philosophy was eventually adopted by Japan around 1200 CE under the Japanese term Zen. Zen is thus a well-integrated blend of mystical Buddhism of India, the natural philosophy of Taoism, and the pragmatism of the Confucian mentality.

Third, traditional Chinese scholars, both Confucian and Taoist, felt that their cultural foundation had been shaken by the challenge of Buddhism. They reexamined their own philosophies and worked out a way to apply the *I-Ching* – and thus *Yin-Yang* theory – to integrate Buddhism into a new Chinese culture. The *I-Ching,* or *Book of Changes,* describes a universal ontology, the processes by which things evolve, principles of change, and guidelines for choosing among alternatives of change. This ancient book of omens and advice is the oldest of the Chinese classics. Confucius used it as an important text in instructing in methods of personal and social transformation.

Different interpretations of the *I-Ching* demonstrate how Buddhism, Taoism, and traditional Confucianism were blended into the Neo-Confucianism that profoundly affected the premodern Chinese, Korean, Japanese, and Vietnamese dynasties. These include interpretations by: Cheng Yi *(1050), I-Ching, the Tao of Organization;* Chih-hsu Ou-i (1599–1655), *The Buddhist I-Ching;* and Liu I-ming (1796), *The Taoist I-Ching: I-Ching Mandalas, A Program of Study for the Book of Changes,* translated by Cleary. Under the influence of the *I-Ching* the Chinese are equipped with a *both-and* mentality that seems to integrate religious diversity with less difficulty than the *either-or* tendency of Western mentality.

The Chinese Neo-Confucian school's synthesis of Confucianism, Buddhism, and Taoism culminated in the philosophy of Chu Hsi (1033–1107 CE), one of the greatest of all Chinese thinkers. It guides people to learn the truth *(Tao)* in order to solve problems, which leads one in turn to be harmonious with *Tao,* or truth (unification), the core of Confucianism and Taoism.

Both Confucianism and Taoism share the same ontology from the *I-Ching,* while Buddhism also came to use *I-Ching* to interpret Buddhist thought. The three philosophies use different approaches, however, to reach the unification with *Tao*/Brahman. Confucians emphasize a rational approach, Taoists focus on an intuitive approach and Buddhists favor a psychological approach. Confucianism favors education and the intellectual approach, while Taoism tends to look down on education in favor of intuitive insight into Nature. Buddhists are interested in changing human perception and thus stress detachment; each tends to participate in world affairs accordingly.

Huang Te-Hui (1644–1661 CE) of the Ching Dynasty integrated the three main belief systems of Confucianism, Taoism and Buddhism to form the Hsien-Tien-Tao. I-Kuan-Tao (Integrated *Tao)* evolved from the Hsien-Tien-Tao. Chang Tien-Jan was recognized as a master of I-Kuan-Tao in 1930. Various I-Kuan-Tao groups moved to Taiwan in 1946 and 1947, and today, I-Kuan-Tao priests preach an integrated religion drawn from Confucian, Buddhist, Taoist, Christian, and Islamic canons. The concept of oneness of all religions is the major theme, and its mission is to integrate all religions into one.

This group was among the first in contemporary society to start interfaith dialogue and interfaith integration. However, many people in Taiwan viewed the I-Kuan-Tao religion as a heresy, and it was banned for many years by the government. Since being granted official recognition in 1987, I-Kuan-Tao of Taiwan has expanded internationally. It now has organizations in South Korea, Japan, Singapore, Malaysia, Thailand, Indonesia, the Philippines, Australia, the United States, Canada, Brazil and Paraguay.

Building on the successful integration of Buddhism into Neo-Confucianism, many contemporary Confucians have issued a challenge for another religious integration among Buddhism, Christianity, Confucianism, Islam and Taoism. For this to come about, more Asians need to read the Bible and the *Qur'an,* and more Westerners need to know about the *I-Ching* and the *Qur'an.* Such a global dialogue would certainly help facilitate a new understanding of religions.

First Peoples and Native Traditions

The First Peoples in the Fourth World

Julian Burger explains (in *The Gaia Atlas Of First Peoples*) that there is no universally agreed name for the peoples he describes as "first peoples":

"... because their ancestors were the original inhabitants of the lands, since colonized by foreigners. Many territories continue to be so invaded. The book also calls them indigenous, a term widely accepted by the peoples themselves, and now adopted by the United Nations."

BURGER, p.16

" 'Fourth World' is a term used by the World Council of Indigenous Peoples to distinguish the way of life of indigenous peoples from those of the First (highly industrialized), Second (Socialist bloc) and Third (developing) worlds. The First, Second and Third Worlds believe that 'the land belongs to the people'; the Fourth World believes that 'the people belong to the land."

BURGER, p.18

A Portrait of the First Peoples

Some of what follows was written by representatives of indigenous peoples; some was provided by non-indigenous people. Texts and quotations identified with the citation *Burger* are from *The Gaia Atlas of First Peoples: A Future for the Indigenous World,* by Julian Burger with the assistance of campaigning groups and native peoples worldwide, some of whom are quoted below.

*F*irst peoples see existence as a living blend of spirits, nature and people. All are one, inseparable and interdependent – a holistic vision shared with mystics throughout the ages. The word for religion does not exist in many cultures, as it is so closely integrated into life itself. For many indigenous peoples spirits permeate matter – they animate it. This led the early anthropologists to refer to such beliefs as "animist." (Burger, p.64)

Myths that explain the origins of the world remind people of their place in the universe and of their connection with the past. Some are humorously ironic, others complex and esoteric. Some, notably Aboriginal Dreamtime, speak of the creation of the hills, rocks, hollows, and rivers formed by powerful ancestral spirits in the distant past. Others describe a dramatic split between the gods and humankind or the severance of the heavens and the Earth – as in the sudden separation of the Sky Father and Earth Mother in Maori legend. Others tell the story of how the earth was peopled, as in the sacred book of the Maya of Central America. Myths invest life with meaning. The rich symbolic associations found in the oral traditions of many indigenous cultures bring the sacred into everyday life – through a pipe, a feather, a rattle, a color even – and help individuals to keep in touch with both themselves and the spirit world. (Burger, p.66)

Indigenous peoples are strikingly diverse in their culture, religion, and social and economic organization. Yet, today as in the past, they are prey to stereotyping by the outside world. By some they are idealized as the embodiment of spiritual values; by others they are denigrated as an obstacle impeding economic progress. But they are neither: they are people who cherish their own distinct cultures, are the victims of past and present-day colonialism, and are determined to survive. Some live according to their traditions, some receive welfare, others work in factories, offices, or the professions. As well as their diversity, there are some shared values and experiences among indigenous cultures....

By understanding how they organize their societies, the wider society may learn to recognize that they are not at some primitive stage of development, but are thoughtful and skillful partners of the natural world, who can help all people to reflect on the way humanity treats the environment and our fellow creatures. (Burger, p. 15)

Voices of Indigenous Peoples

Earth

"Every part of the earth is sacred to my people. Every shining pine needle, every sandy shore, every mist in the dark woods, every clearing and humming insect is holy in the memory and experience of my people."

A DUWAMISH CHIEF (Burger)

"The Earth is the foundation of Indigenous Peoples; it is the seat of spirituality, the fountain from which our cultures and languages flourish. The Earth is our historian, the keeper of events, and the bones of our forefathers. Earth provides us with food, medicine, shelter, and clothing. It is the source of our independence, it is our Mother. We do not dominate her; we must harmonize with her." HAYDEN BURGESS, native Hawaiian (Burger)

"One has only to develop a relationship with a certain place, where the land knows you and experience that the trees, the Earth and Nature are extending their love and light to you to know there is so much we can receive from the Earth to fill our hearts and souls."

INTI MELASQUEZ, Inca (Burger)

"Man is an aspect of nature, and nature itself is a manifestation of primordial religion. Even the word 'religion' makes an unnecessary separation, and there is no word for it in the Indian tongues. Nature is the 'Great Mysterious,' the 'religion before religion,' the profound intuitive apprehension of the true nature of existence attained by sages of all epochs, everywhere on Earth; the whole universe is sacred, man is the whole universe, and the religious ceremony is life itself, the common acts of every day." PETER MATTHIESSEN, *Indian Country* (Burger)

"We Indian people are not supposed to say, 'This land is mine.' We only use it. It is the white man who buys land and puts a fence around it. Indians are not supposed to do that, because the land belongs to all Indians, it belongs to God, as you call it. The land is a part of our body, and we are a part of the land." BUFFALO TIGER, Miccosukee (Burger)

"When the last red man has vanished from the Earth, and the memory is only a shadow of a cloud moving across the prairie, these shores and forests will still hold the spirits of my people, for they love this Earth as the newborn loves its mother's heartbeat." SEALTH, a Duwamish chief (Burger)

"When Indians referred to animals as 'people' – just a different sort of person from Man – they were not being quaint. Nature to them was a community of such 'people' for whom they had a great deal of genuine regard and with whom they had a contractual relationship to protect one another's interests and to fulfill their mutual needs. Man and Nature, in short, was joined by compact – not by ethical ties – a compact predicated on mutual esteem. This was the essence of the traditional land relationship."

OJIBWAY MAGAZINE

"Our roots are deep in the lands where we live. We have a great love for our country, for our birthplace is here. The soil is rich from the bones of thousands of our generations. Each of us was created in these lands and it is our duty to take great care of them, because from these lands will spring the future generations of our peoples. We walk about with great respect, for the Earth is a very Sacred Place." Sioux, Navaho and Iroquois Declaration, 1978

Economy, wealth and a way of life

*T*he economic life of indigenous people is based not on competition but on cooperation, for survival is only possible when the community works

Partners toward a Sustainable Future

Maurice Strong

General Secretary of the United Nations Conference on Environment and Development, held in Rio de Janeiro in 1992

*A*s we awaken our consciousness that humankind and the rest of nature are inseparably linked, we will need to look to the world's more than 250 million indigenous peoples. They are the guardians of the extensive and fragile ecosystems that are vital to the wellbeing of the planet. Indigenous peoples have evolved over many centuries a judicious balance between their needs and those of nature. The notion of sustainability, now recognized as the framework for our future development, is an integral part of most indigenous cultures.

In the last decades, indigenous peoples have suffered from the consequences of some of the most destructive aspects of our development. They have been separated from their traditional lands and ways of life, deprived of their means of livelihood, and forced to fit into societies in which they feel like aliens. They have protested and resisted. Their call is for control over their own lives, the space to live, and the freedom to live their own ways. And it is a call not merely to save their own territories, but the Earth itself.

While no one would suggest that the remainder of the more than five billion people on our planet would live at the level of indigenous societies, it is equally clear that we cannot pursue our present course of development. Nor can we rely on technology to provide an easy answer. What modern civilization has gained in knowledge, it has perhaps lost in sagacity. The indigenous peoples of the world retain our collective evolutionary experience and insights which have slipped our grasp. Yet these hold critical lessons for our future. Indigenous peoples are thus indispensable partners as we try to make a successful transition to a more secure and sustainable future on our precious planet.

excerpted from the *Foreword* to
The Gaia Atlas of First Peoples, by Julian Burger

Native American Spirituality

Robert Staffanson

Executive Director, American Indian Institute

*N*ote a dictionary's definition of spirituality: "devotion to spiritual (i.e. metaphysical) things instead of worldly things." This definition does not apply to Native Americans because they do not recognize a dichotomy between "spiritual" and material things.

A simplistic definition of Native American spirituality would be that it is the opposite of pragmatism (i.e. short-term concern with "practical" results). While Native American spirituality is not easily defined, it has several defining characteristics:

a) **Recognition of the interconnectedness of all Creation**, and the responsibility of human beings to use their intelligence in protecting that inter-connectedness. That applies particularly to the lifegiving elements: water, air and soil.

b) **A belief that all life is equal**, and that the presence of the life spark implies a degree of spirituality whether in humans, animals or plants. In their view the species of animals and birds, as well as forests and other plant life, have as much "right" to existence as human beings, and should not be damaged or destroyed. That does not mean that they cannot be used but that use has limitations.

c) **Their primary concern is with the long-term welfare of life rather than with short-term expediency or comfort.** They consider all issues and actions in relationship to their long-term effect on all life, not just human life.

d) **Their spirituality is undergirded by thankfulness to the Creator.** Prayer, ceremonies, meditation and fasting are an important part of their lives. But they ask for nothing. They give thanks: for all forms of life and for all the elements that make life possible, and they are concerned with the continuation of that life and the ingredients upon which it depends.

Traditional Native Americans believe that any of their people who lack spirituality are no longer Indian. Traditional Native Americans do not see any spirituality in our "western" world. They believe that we have a kind of mindless materialism that is destroying both us and the world we live in.

together. Most small-scale indigenous societies have elaborate systems for sharing food, possessions, and ritualizing conflict. . . . Indigenous forms of economy cannot, of course, satisfy the needs of a burgeoning world population now nearing six billion. But the knowledge and, especially, the values of the peoples practicing them are vital. The scientific community has recently begun research into indigenous skills in resource management. But it is, above all, wisdom that is needed in Western culture – we all need to learn respect for the Earth, conservation of resources, equitable distribution of wealth, harmony, balance and modest cooperation. In 1928 Gandhi wrote:

> God forbid that India should ever take to industrialism after the manner of the West . . . It would strip the world bare like locusts.   (Burger, p.42)

"An Innu hunter's prestige comes not from the wealth he accumulates but from what he gives away. When a hunter kills caribou or other game he shares with everyone else in the camp."   DANIEL ASHINI, Innu (Burger)

War and peace, life and death

" 'Was it an awful war?'
'It was a terrible war.'
    'Were many people killed?'
'One man was killed.'
    'What did you do?'
'We decided that those of us who had done the killing should never meet again because we were not fit to meet one another.' "   SAN describing a war to Laurens van der Post (Burger)

In Papua New Guinea hostilities between groups are part of the cycle of events encompassing long periods of peace and enmity. War is just one aspect of cultural life. The idea of annihilating the other group is absent; indeed, the Tsembaga and Mae Enga are known as the peoples who marry their enemies. War is a means by which the individual and the group find their identity, and is largely ceremonial. . . even on the point of war there is always a ritual means of stepping back from open confrontation. Anger can be channelled into a "nothing fight," a competition of insults and shouting. Or else it may lead to a real fight, with blows exchanged and sometimes even serious casualties. After a war a lengthy process of peace-making begins. Gifts, ceremonies, and marriages establish links and obligations between the parties. (Burger, p.62)

"So live your life that the fear of death can never enter your heart. Trouble no one about his religion; respect others in their view, and demand that they respect yours. Love your life, perfect your life, beautify all things in your life. Seek to make your life long and its purpose in the service of your people. Prepare a noble death song for the day when you go over the great divide. Always give a word or a sign of salute when meeting or passing a friend, even a stranger, when in a lonely place. Show respect to all people and grovel to none.

"When you arise in the morning give thanks for the food and for the joy of living. If you see no reason for giving thanks, the fault lies only in yourself. Abuse no one and nothing, for abuse turns the wise ones to fools and robs the spirit of its vision. When it comes your time to die, be not like those whose hearts are filled with the fear of death, so that when their time comes they weep and pray for a little more time to live their lives over again in a different way. Sing your death song and die like a hero going home."   A teaching from TECUMSEH

Plastic Medicine Men

Resolution of the 5th Annual Meeting
of the Traditional Elders Circle

This resolution was made at the Meeting of the Elders Circle at Northern Cheyenne Nation, Two Moons Camp, Rosebud Creek, Montana, on October 5, 1980. It represents an early one of many responses by traditional elders as well as by the American Indian Movement and others to clarify that the Native American spiritual tradition is not for sale, is not legitimately sold, and that the components of the religion must be kept in balance by highly trained leaders who are legitimate representatives of the tribes. The elders feel that in many cases the appropriation of Native spirituality by non-Indians is another attempt by the dominant culture to take from the Indians, and shows considerable disrespect for the Native tradition and culture.

*I*t has been brought to the attention of the Elders and their representatives in council that various individuals are moving about this Great Turtle Island and across the great waters to foreign soil, purporting to be spiritual leaders. They carry pipes and other objects sacred to the Red Nations, the indigenous people of the western hemisphere.

These individuals are gathering non-Indian people as followers who believe they are receiving instructions of the original people. We the Elders and our representatives sitting in Council give warning to these non-Indian followers that it is our understanding that this is not a proper process and the authority to carry these sacred objects is given by the people, and the purpose and procedure is specific to time and the needs of the people.

The medicine people are chosen by the medicine, and long instruction and discipline are necessary before ceremonies and healing can be done. These procedures are always in the Native tongue; there are no exceptions and profit is not the motivation.

There are many Nations with many and varied procedures specifically for the welfare of their people. These processes and ceremonies are of the most Sacred Nature. The Council finds the open display of these ceremonies contrary to these Sacred instructions.

Therefore, be warned that these individuals are moving about preying upon the spiritual needs and ignorance of our non-Indian brothers and sisters. The value of these instructions and ceremonies is questionable, maybe meaningless, and hurtful to the individual carrying false messages. There are questions that should be asked of these individuals:

- What Nation do they represent?
- What is their Clan and Society?
- Who instructed them and where did they learn?
- What is their home address?

We concern ourselves only with those people who use spiritual ceremonies with non-Indian people for profit. There are many things to be shared with the Four Colors of humanity in our common destiny as one with our Mother the Earth. It is this sharing that must be considered with great care by the Elders and the medicine people who carry the Sacred Trusts, so that no harm may come to people through ignorance and misuse of these powerful forces.

Signed,
Austin Two Moons, Northern Cheyenne Nation; Larry Anderson, Navajo Nation; Thomas Banyacya, Hopi Independent Nation; Frank Cardinal, Sr., Chateh, Alberta; Phillip Deer, Muskogee (Creek) Nation; Walter Denny, Chippewa-Cree Nation; Chief Fools Crow, Lakota Nation; Peter O'Chiese, Entrance, Alberta; Izador Thorn, Washington; Tadadaho, Haudenassaunee; Tom Yellowtail, Wyola MT.

The Elders charged the American Indian Movement and others with responsibility for maintaining the integrity of the Indian traditions. AIM then made a resolution in 1984 naming some of those whom the Elders have in mind, and asserting, among other things, that "attempted theft of Indian ceremonies is a direct attack and theft from Indian people themselves." Some of those named are non-Indian authors and ritual leaders; others may be native Americans, but may also be distanced from their tribes and not designated as representatives of the people.

FOR MORE INFORMATION:

The Association on American Indian Affairs
245 Fifth Avenue, Suite 1801, New York, NY 10016-8728
tel. (212) 689-8720

American Indian Institute
P.O. Box 1388, Bozeman, MT 59715

American India Movement,
Sovereign Diné Nation, Window Rock, AZ

Cultural Survival
11 Divinity Avenue, Cambridge, MA 02138

Morningstar Foundation
403 10th St. SE, Washington, DC 20003

Native American Rights Fund
1506 Broadway, Boulder, CO 80302

World Council of Indigenous Peoples (International Secretariat)
555 King Edward Avenue, Ottawa, Ontario, Canada K1N 6NS

Quotations by Julian Burger and the indigenous peoples are used with permission of *The Gaia Atlas of First Peoples,* by Julian Burger with campaigning groups and native peoples worldwide; London: Gaia Books Ltd, 1990.

Hinduism

Wisdom from the Hindu Tradition

"We meditate upon that adorable holy Light of the resplendent Life-Giver Savitar. May He stimulate and inspire our intellects." Rig Veda, III-62-10

This is one of the most sacred of the *mantras,* prayers and chants that have played a dominant part in the religious history of the Hindus, as a part of their daily repeated prayers. All intellect, creativity and imagination is derived from God. He is the supreme Knowledge, pure Intelligence and Consciousness.

"I am firmly seated in the hearts of all. From Me comes knowledge and memory and the departing of doubts.
I am the Knower and Knowledge of the Vedas. *I am the author of* Vedanta *(the sacred* Upanishads *and their teachings, the means to spiritual salvation/liberation.)"* GOD (as Krishna) speaking, *Bhagavad-Gita* XV:15

"Then, in the beginning, there was neither non-being nor being (existence). Neither were there worlds, nor the sky, nor anything beyond... nor death, nor immortality was there, no knowing of night or day. That One (Ultimate) breathed by its own self-power, svadha, *without air. All was concealed in darkness.... That One became creative by self-power and the warmth of contemplation. There arose love and desire, the prime seed of the mind .... The gods appeared later than this original creative activity. Then, who knows wherefrom creation came into being? Who can know this truth? That One, who was supervising (the origins) from the highest heavens, indeed knows or knows not!"* Rig Veda X:129

In the above Hymn of Origins, several ultimate questions are raised:

HINDU WISDOM continues on next pages

A Portrait

Dr. T. K. Venkateswaran

Professor of Religious Studies (Emeritus), University of Detroit; former Research Scholar, Harvard University; member, International Advisory Council, The Council for a Parliament of the World's Religions; member, International Board of Advisors, The Temple of Understanding

Introduction

Hinduism is the oldest and perhaps the most complex of all the living, historical world religions. It has no one single identifiable founder. The actual names found for the religion in the Hindu scriptures are Vedic Religion, i.e. the Religion of the *Vedas* (Scriptures) and *Sangtana Dharma,* i.e. the Universal or Perennial Wisdom and Righteousness, the "Eternal Religion." Hinduism is not merely a religion, however. It encompasses an entire civilization and way of life, whose roots date back prior to 3000 BCE, beyond the peoples of Indus Valley culture. Yet, since the time of the *Vedas,* there is seen a remarkable continuity, a cultural and philosophical complexity and also a pattern of unity in diversity that evolved in the course of its history, also a demonstrated propensity for deep integration and assimilation of all new and external influences.

Main sources of religious knowledge

Scriptures: (1) The four *Vedas—Rig, Yajur, Sama* and *Atharva Vedas*—are seen as *Sruti,* "Heard," as Revelation and "not human-originated," though human beings, wise and holy sages, seers and prophets were the human channels of the revealed wisdom. They "heard" in their hearts the eternal messages and "saw" and symbolized various names and forms of the One, Sacred, Ultimate Reality, Truth, God from different perspectives and contexts. The Hindu gods and goddesses, worshipped with different names and forms and qualities are, in reality, many aspects, powers, functions, and symbols of the only One all-pervasive Supreme Being, without a second. The *Upanishads,* later portions in the *Vedas,* teach that salvation/liberation is achieved in an experiential way and that oneness with the supreme Reality, *Brahman,* is possible; the supreme goal, *Brahman,* is also the One Self, the higher Self found in all. The philosophy and spiritual practice is known as Vedanta.

(2) The *Agamas* (Further Scriptures) teach union with God as the Lord, the Highest Person, *Brahman* seen in the process of action.

Supplements to the Scriptures: (1) *Smritis* (works of Hindu Law, etc.). (2) The two epics: the *Ramayana* and the *Mahabharata* (along with the *Bhagavad Gita* in the latter, seen almost as an autonomous scripture) and the various *Puranas.*

Basic beliefs, values, paradigms and teachings

The one all-pervasive supreme Being is both immanent and transcendent, both supra-personal and highest person (God), who can be worshipped as both Father and/or Mother of the universe.

The universe undergoes endless cycles of creation, preservation and dissolution. All souls are evolving and progressing toward union with God and everyone will ultimately attain salvation/liberation.

Karma is the moral and physical law of cause and effect by which each individual creates one's own future destiny by accepting responsibility and accountability for one's own thoughts, words and deeds, individual and collective.

The individual soul reincarnates, evolving through many births and deaths, until all the *karmic* results, good and bad, are resolved. One can and should strive to attain liberation from this cycle of constant births and deaths in this very life, by pursuing one of the four spiritual paths to God-realization – the ways of Knowledge, Love and Devotion, Selfless Action, and Meditation.

Four aims or goals in life are arranged hierarchically: the *joy* cluster (sensual, sexual, artistic, aesthetic joys, compatible with ethics), the *economic and social fulfillment* cluster, the *morality* cluster (duties, obligations, right action, law, righteousness, general virtues, and supreme ethical values, etc.), and the *spiritual goal of salvation/liberation* (union and oneness with God). All the elements that are usually seen as exclusive or antagonistic in life are brought together in this holistic model, in which every goal has its own place.

Each individual passes through several stages in his/her journey through life toward the spiritual goal. The four classical stages in life are: (1) the student, (2) the house-holder, (3) retirement to the woods for spiritual pursuits and (4) renunciation (optional). Within each stage are specific goals which provide a practical model for the organization of life.

Divine aspects and elements of God, the "presence," are invoked through ritual symbolism and prayers in consecrated images and icons for purposes of worship. God also "descends," periodically, in incarnations and historical personalities such as Rama and Krishna.

All life is sacred and is to be loved and revered, through the practice of nonviolence, realizing that there is unity and inter-dependency among all forms of life and all aspects of the universe. Exemplary spiritual teachers (*Gurus*) who themselves are liberated in this life help the spiritual aspirants with their knowledge and compassion.

No particular religion (including Hinduism) teaches the only, exclusive way to God and salvation, above all others. All authentic, genuine religious paths and traditions lead to the One God and are facets of God's love and light, deserving proper respect, mutual tolerance, and right understanding.

Hindu sub-traditions (sampradayas)

*T*he One Brahman is conceived and symbolized according to divine functions as Brahma (the Creator), Vishnu (the Sustainer and Preserver) and Shiva (the Destroyer of evils and the Dissolver of the universe). This is referred to as the Hindu Trinity.

Within the Great Tradition of Hinduism are four main, living sub-traditions, called *sampradayas*: (1) Shaivites (2) Vaishnavites (3) Shaktas and (4) Smartas. The differences are based upon conceptions and worship of the central name, form, symbols, liturgies, mythologies and theologies of the One God, Lord and highest Person, as Vishnu, Shiva, Shakti (the Divine as Mother), etc. Smartas worship, equally, several personal manifestations of the supreme Reality and philosophically emphasize the ultimate identity-experience of the individual self with the supreme Self, which is also Brahman.

Hinduism has a vast network of sacred symbols. Some are drawn from sacred geography like the Ganges River, others are drawn from plant, bird and animal life; other symbols include profound polyvalent (multi-level meanings) symbols such as the sacred sound-syllable *Om* (also written as *AUM*) which contains all reality, and Shiva's icon as the "Cosmic Dancer," fulfilling all the divine functions.

Hindu wisdom, continued from preceding page

What is time? What is the nature of potency, *karma* (action-influence)? How to understand the mystery of division and differentiation through naming, language into being, non-being, death, immortality, and so forth? How to transcend the boundaries of conceptual thought?

Only the highest Spirit knows the full truth of the origins of creation and existence. The quest for the original undivided unifying "Field" and ground cannot be purely conceptual, but has to be experiential, through meditation and spiritual *yajna*. The hymn leads one to the farthest reaches of the frontiers of modern science and cosmology and shows the profundity of what lies beyond anything that can be conceived and spoken of.

"The Knowledge of Akshara, *the immutable unchanging ground of all relative existence and expressions, brings integrity, stability and fulfillment to the goals of life. One whose awareness is not opened up to realize that* Akshara, *what is the use of mere words and knowledge, scriptures, etc., to him?" Rig Veda I-164-39; also Svetasvatara Upanishad IV-1*

"Come together in unity. Speak in profound agreements. May your minds converge (in deep consensus). May your deliberations be uniform and united be your hearts. May you be firmly bound and united in your intentions and resolves." Rig Veda X-191, 2–4

"To one who aspires and is established in Rta, *the Cosmic and Moral Order and Harmony, sweet blow the winds. The rivers flow sweet. For us, who are rooted in* Rta, *may the herbs and plants be as sweet as also the nights and dawns. May the earth and its soil be full of sweetness. May our Father, may the Heaven be sweet. May the plants, the sun, and the cows (and animals) be full of sweetness in our life." Rig Veda I-90, 6–8*

*T*his beautiful hymn (above) is of profound value for environmental and ecological concerns and awareness. Such hymns in the *Vedas* link peace and sweetness, beauty and quality of life to the daily practice and experience of *Rta* in personal lives with sacred commitment. One of the oft-repeated definitions of God in the *Vedas* is *Rta*, which has several nuances of meanings: Cosmic and Moral Order, Balance, Harmony, the Divine Natural Law, and unified Life-giving Energy

Approaches to interfaith dialogue and cooperation

*T*here are several hymns in the *Vedas* and other scriptures which categorically declare that there are different approaches and perspectives to God and experience of God and ultimate reality. This also arises, necessarily, from different human contexts. The central teaching, constantly repeated, is: God is One, but names and forms are many; symbols and paths are many. Thus, there arose a rich theological and philosophical pluralism within Hinduism creating an internal "parliament of sub-traditions and sub-religions," but all grounded in the unity of the *Vedas* and One Brahman. Also, multiplicity is encouraged and thrives by means of the free choice and self-determined identification with one specially loved manifestation of God – Shiva, Krishna, Shakti, Rama, and so on – in pursuing the moral and spiritual path to salvation/liberation.

Because people are at different starting points and stations, Hindu scriptures affirm and accept variety in religious experiences as a necessity and psychological reality. This wisdom is extended to other non-Hindu religions as a spontaneous and logical outflow of the same ethos. There is no historical tradition or theological necessity in Hinduism for proselytization or conversion of non-Hindus to Hinduism. All authentic religions and traditions, all over the world, rising from different historical and cultural starting points and contexts, are to be respected, accepted, appreciated and cherished.

Multiplicity brings with it differences, which one cannot destroy or do away with. Yet, the deep commonalities in structures of religious experience and in the profound moral values found in all religions are to be constantly probed and appropriated for the development of a deeper spiritual and human solidarity and fellowship, transcending the cultural and other barriers. At the same time, the distinctive theological and core-symbol elements and central rites of all religions are to be respected in dialogue and interrelations, based on correct and accurate understandings and on mutual empathy. All should work together to eliminate, in the future, horrors that have been committed in the name of God and religion. Truth values are equally important to the values of religious satisfaction.

Primary challenges facing humanity at this time

*O*ur age has deteriorated to an age of quick fixes of meaning from sources such as science and the media; it has become an analgesic culture. Our contemporary metaphors, symbols and signals are mixed, confused and contradictory. Several examples can show that we live in a mosaic of fragmentation in consciousness, with nothing to hold the pieces together, nothing beneath to connect them and provide a meaningful substratum. We inhabit several historical ages simultaneously.

Social stability and participation in a common good have vastly eroded; we lack a broad consensus where an intricate web of mutual obligations and an accepted

---

WISDOM, continued

and Rhythm. *Rta* is also the fundamental norm of existence. Human greed, selfish power, transgression, and violation of *Rta* – individually and collectively – bring ecological and social disaster and destruction of the earth.

"May there be peace on earth, peace in the atmosphere and in the heavens. Peaceful be the waters, the herbs and plants. May the Divine bring us peace. May the holy prayers and invocations of peace-liturgies generate ultimate Peace and Happiness everywhere. With these meditations which resolve and dissolve harm, violence, and conflicts, we render peaceful whatever on earth is terrible, sinful, cruel, and violent. Let the earth become fully auspicious, let everything be beneficial to us."
　　　　　　　　　　　　　　　　　　　　Atharva-Veda, XIX-9

"Having entered into the earth with My Life-giving Energy, I support and uphold all the life-forms. Having become the life-giving nectar, I nourish all the herbs and plants."
　　　　　　　　　　　　　　　　　　　　Bhagavad-Gita XV-13

*I*n the above verse, God (speaking as Krishna) indicates that the healing and nourishing functions found in the herbs and plants is divine and of divine origin. The divinity cannot be segregated from Nature nor the latter exploited by human selfishness and greed.

"All this, whatsoever moves in this moving universe, is permeated and inhabited by God, enveloped by God. Therefore, you should enjoy (the world), only by first renouncing and disowning (the things of the world). Do not covet; whose indeed are (these) treasures (in the universe)? ... In darkness are they who worship only the world. In greater darkness are they who worship the Infinite alone. Those who accept both (seen in relationship), save themselves from death by the knowledge of the former and attain immortality by the knowledge of the latter. ... And one who sees all beings in his own Self, and his own Self in all beings, no more loathes and hates."
　　　　　　　　　　　　　　　　　　　　Isa Upanishad 1,6, 9–11

*T*he above verses teach non-possessive love and stewardship-enjoyment of things in the world.

"Everything here is verily Brahman (the supreme Sacred Divinity). Atman, the (higher) Self is Brahman. The Self has four grades (four states of consciousness). The first condition of the Self (state) is the waking life of outward cognition and consciousness (of subject-object, dualistic perception) .... The second state is the inward dream-state cognizing internal objects. The third condition is the deep sleep state, where there are no desires for objects nor any dream-objects, only

network of responsibilities uphold society. Family integrities are threatened.

Cultural and ecological balance and harmony in the universe are being depleted. Economic and technological progress has limits. It now seems unlikely that the wasteful affluence of the West can become available to all. Everyone should learn to endure more weal and woe equally, develop more patience, and pursue real quality of life on the planet, which is not found in the acquisitive amassing of material goods.

Uncontrolled population growth has become another global war, a war which must be won. Religious, cultural, and ethnic hatreds are on the increase; horrors of unprecedented scale, violence, and cruelty are being unleashed in different parts of the world. Group identities and ideologies are being sanctified and absolutized.

Holistic human development and the complete fulfillment of all needs – material, moral and spiritual – have been lost from view; physical and mental health and the quality of our lifestyles have deteriorated.

Depersonalization caused by mega-cities and technology continues to cheapen the richness and meaning of human joys and life. Computer simulations usurp relationships and are on the verge of providing the most intimate pleasures, on-line, providing virtual sex.

How do members of the Hindu community respond to these issues?

The responses of both the Hindu community and contemporary Hinduism are briefly summarized. Some of these responses are still modest.

There is a renewed and vigorous interest in restoring the rich, polyvalent Hindu myths and their moral, philosophical, and spiritual impact through new artforms, media ventures, etc. Of all the peoples, Hindus never abandoned their myths through excessive de-mythologization and heavy rationalization, as happened in the West. If the body needs a house and nourishing food, provided by latest technologies, the soul equally needs an abode in which to grow. In Hinduism, the religious myths built that house and provided a unified and integrated vision of life. One cannot live with values that are only contingent and ephemeral. Hindu art and myths save one from the one-sided, reductionistic understanding of reality. It should be carefully noted that myth is different from verbal dogma and ideology. They also help to raise the human consciousness to the highest levels and heal fragmentations.

The "four-fold goals" scheme and the "four-stages in life" paradigm, found in the Hindu *Dharma,* are both needed for holistic human development. These are now being carefully re-studied in their contemporary contexts with help and insight derived from the social sciences. Further relevant interpolations and applications are being generated, with universal implications. Too much emphasis on individual rights has somewhat torn the intricate and delicate network of obligations and duties that are necessary to sustain and uphold family integrity, restore a sense of community, and foster world-responsibilities. This

---

silent consciousness full of peace and bliss. The fourth (highest) grade of state of consciousness is the (complete) Self (God) in Its own pure state, the fully awakened (and integrated) life of supreme Consciousness. This (fourth) highest ineffable state of the Self is Peace, Love and Bliss, in which the fragmented world-perception disappears, which is the end of evolution, which is the One without a second and non-dual, which should be known, realized and experienced (in Life). In the oneness experience with Him (the Self) lies the ultimate proof of His reality. This Atman (Self) is (indicated, symbolized by) the eternal Word OM."

Mandukya Upanishad, (most of the verses)

"Oh Brahman Supreme! Formless and colorless are you. But in mystery, through your power you transform your light and radiance into many forms and colors in creation. You bring forth the creation and then withdraw them to yourself. Fill us with the grace of your auspicious thoughts and vision. . . . You are in the woman, in the man. You are in the young boy, in the youthful maiden. You are in the old man who walks with his staff... You are in the dark butterfly, in the green parrot with red eyes... You are without beginning, infinite, beyond time and space. All the worlds had their origins in you." Svetasvatara Upanishad, IV: 1–4

God reveals in silence through women, men, all life-forms. The above verses validate all the four stages of life and also tilt toward those usually neglected and abused – children, women, and the elderly – by specific scriptural mention. God is equally present in man and woman.

"They call and name the One, Indra, Mitra, Varuna, Agni and the beautiful Garutman. The Real is One, though wise sages (perceive in their minds) and name It variously."

Rig-Veda I-164-46

"The wise sages shape (and symbolize) the One, with their words and expressions into many forms and manifestations."

Rig-Veda X-114-5

The above and similar hymns categorically declare for the Hindu that God is One, but names and symbols are many, paths and perspectives are many, all to be respected and loved.

"In whatever way and path, humans worship Me, in that same path do I (meet) and fulfill their aspirations and grace them. It is always My Path that humans follow in all their different paths and journeys, on all sides."

Bhagavad-Gita IV:11

God's Way is the Way behind all paths and religions.

shredded fabric has thwarted the creation of abilities and energies needed to create new forms of consensus on the common good.

One of the central definitions of God (Brahman) found in the *Vedas* is *Rta*, which is manifested in the universe and also on planet Earth. *Rta* also has mystery and transcendental dimensions, with many meanings, including Order, Balance, Harmony, Law, Unified Life-Energy and the principle of Intelligence. The divine *Rta* is the foundational and fundamental norm of existence, the ground of cosmic and human morality and intelligence. To be fully and really rational is also to be fully moral. *Satya* (Truth) and *Rta* are two sides to the same Divine. Divinity should not be segregated from creation and the all-embracing presence should be constantly felt. This truth, a vital part of the Hindu tradition, is being researched and re-probed to formulate sound environmental and ecological policies and programs at the highest levels. The aim is to seek to restore cultural and ecological balance and harmony, including new population-management and family planning programs with a Hindu ethos, combined with the latest scientific help.

Preventive medicine as seen and practiced in the ancient Hindu medicine-texts and life-sciences such as *Ayurveda* and *yoga*-manuals, along with the already established and well-documented mind-body connections found in those ancient texts, have spurred vast new research and applications world-wide, with future relevance for all. Renewed interest in and use of ancient meditation-systems and techniques is supported by pioneering brain-studies, consciousness research and new mind-body behavior modifications techniques; together these are pointing toward renewed physical, mental, and spiritual health in humanity.

Conclusion

*T*he respect within Hinduism for other religions has been discussed in detail. Beyond that, Hindus everywhere are actively promoting and aggressively participating in interfaith dialogues and other interreligious projects. The constant message is: one should not delimit or circumscribe God by one's own concepts or by one's own religion or world-views.

"O Mother! Let all my speech be your prayer;
let all my crafts and technology be your worship
and be the mystic gestures of my hands, adoring you.
May all my movements become your devotional
circumambulations.
May everything I eat or drink be oblations to you.
Let my lying down in rest and sleep be prostrations to you.
Mother! Whatever I do, may all that become
a sacramental service and worship for you."

ADI SANKARA,
Hymn to the Divine Mother

*A*di Sankara of the eighth century CE here worships God as the Divine Mother, exemplifying the experience of Hindus who relate to God, the supreme Person, equally in male and female orientations, both as Father and as Mother. This has profound implications for the vision of equality towards and between the sexes.

"May there be welfare to all beings;
may there be fullness and wholeness to all people;
may there be constant good and auspicious life to everyone;
may there be peace everywhere....

May all be full of happiness and abundance;
may everyone in the world enjoy complete health,
free from diseases;
may all see and experience good things in their lives,
may not even a single person experience sorrow and misery.
Om!
Peace! Peace! Peace!"

Daily prayers of Hindus

*P*rayers like the ones above and below have been offered and recited daily since ancient times. It is to be noted that the word *sarve* (all, everyone) is constantly repeated. The prayers are universal, offered for all and in the name of all, not for one group, religion, nation or collectivity; they show the inter-dependence of the welfare of one with the welfare of all, treating the whole world as a single family.

"Lead us from the unreal to the Real,
from darkness to Light,
and from death to Immortality.
Om!
Peace, Peace, Peace."

from the *Upanishads*

On Yoga

Compiled by T.K. Venkateswaran

"Not even by deep learning and knowledge (alone) can the Self (Atman) be reached and realized, unless the evil ways are abandoned and there is discipline and rest in the senses and concentration and meditation practiced in one's mind."
                                                                    Katha Upanishad, Ch. II

"Yoga is the control and cessation of the constant fluctuations and modifications of the mind. Then, when the *citta* (mind-stuff) is ripple-less, the Subject (*Purusha,* Seer) is established in Its own real form (the original Self). By constant practice and detachment are these activities of the mind-stuff to be brought to stillness – or through deep meditation on the Supreme Spirit, the ultimate Lord who is the unique special Being, not vitiated by the afflictions, (selfish) works, resulting fruits of the impressions and desires thereof."
                                                                    The Yoga-Sutras, I Pada

"The eight limbs (and progressions) of Yoga are: self-restraint, moral rules and observances regulating one's life, postures of bodily restfulness, regulation and control of breath, inward withdrawal of the senses from the external field of objects, holding and fixing the mind on a spiritual symbol, profound continued meditation process (dhyana), and finally absorption and establishment of oneself in (union) and as the object of meditation.   The *Yoga-Sutras,* II Pada

"When one does not expect any selfish fruits even in meditation, (and when one) also has perfect knowledge and discernment and differentiation (between the real and the unreal), then the absorption (*samadhi*) also called the 'dharma-raining cloud' results (and is experienced). At that stage, all afflictions, sorrow, and selfish actions cease…. The blissful liberation of the soul (the individual self) is the Subject's (the Self's, God's) power established in its own true innate nature."
                                                                    The *Yoga-Sutras* IV Pada

*T*he above are excerpts from sage Patanjali's *Yoga-Sutras,* in the form of aphorisms. The whole work deals with the theory, guidance, and procedures for the practice of Yoga (meditation) leading to physical, moral, mental, and spiritual well-being and liberation. They can be fully and properly understood and practiced, under the instructions, guidance, and counseling, of a realized and accomplished spiritual *guru.*

There are several significant and "clinically" oriented commentaries on the *Yoga-Sutra,* including those of Vyasa, Bhoja, and Vacas-pati. The total corpus of these writings, many still untranslated from Sanskrit, are of great value in their contributions (some already made and many yet to be researched) to contemporary interdisciplinary studies of the mind-body continuum and the total understanding, cure, and care of the physical and mental health of the human person.

Yoga in the West

Joel Beversluis

Those who identify yoga primarily with bodily postures and breathing exercises for physical health may not recognize it in the texts provided by Dr. Venkateswaran. What many may have in mind is the teaching of *hatha* yoga as it has been adapted to accomodate the interests of Western cultures. It is more accurate to think of yoga as an ancient world-view and set of disciplines which aim for God- realization and union with the Divine.

Five approaches to Yoga:

1) *Hatha* Yoga focuses on concentration and physical well-being through attention to postures, breathing, and relaxation.

2) *Bhakti* Yoga is the way of devotion to personalized manifestations of God.

3) *Karma Yoga,* the way of selfless service, is for persons with an inclination to be active with interpersonal concerns and obligations.

4) *Jnana* Yoga names the path to God-realization through knowledge; it is particularly for aspirants with a strong intellectual inclination.

5) *Raja Yoga,* the path of meditation, is for those who choose an experimental and experiential approach.

*S*ome of the credit for the introduction of yoga to the West is attributed to Swami Vivekananda at the 1893 World's Parliament of Religions and during his subsequent tours throughout North America and Europe. Among his books is *Raja Yoga,* in which Vivekananda describes the goal of learning about God, our souls, and eternity through direct experience:

This is what Raja-yoga proposes to teach. The goal of all its teaching is to show how to concentrate the mind; then how to discover the innermost recesses of our own minds; then how to generalize their contents and form our own conclusions from them. It never asks what our belief is – whether we are deists, or atheists, whether Christians, Jews, or Buddhists. We are human beings, and that is sufficient. Every human being has the right and power to seek religion; every human being has the right to ask the reason why and to have his question answered by himself – if only he takes the trouble.

Vedanta, Ramakrishna, and Vivekananda

*V*edanta is a philosophy taught by the Vedas, the most ancient scriptures of India. Its basic teaching is that our real nature is divine. God, the underlying reality, exists in every being. Religion is therefore a search for self-knowledge, a search for God within ourselves.

"Find God. That is the only purpose in life."

RAMAKRISHNA

According to the words of a Sanskrit hymn, there are different approaches to God:

"As the different streams having their sources in different places all mingle their waters in the sea,

"So, O Lord, the different paths which men take through various tendencies, various though they appear, crooked or straight, all lead to thee."

Thus, Vedanta teaches respect for all religions.

Throughout the centuries, India has produced many great saints and illumined teachers. One of the greatest of these was Ramakrishna (1836-1886). His intense spirituality attracted a group of young disciples who, on his passing, formed a monastic community, later to be called the Ramakrishna Order of India.

One of the young monks, Swami Vivekananda, came to America as the representative of Hinduism at the World's Parliament of Religions held in Chicago in 1893. His success was so great that he was invited to remain. For three years he toured the United States lecturing and holding classes. With the help of some monks and nuns, Vedanta centers were started in America. Swami Vivekananda also had a profound influence throughout the world, spending time in England and Europe during his travels.

There are now 13 Vedanta Societies in the United States and 125 Centers in the world managed by the Ramakrishna Order. Over 1,000 more centers bear the names of Ramakrishna and Vivekananda.

FOR MORE INFORMATION:

What Religion Is, Self-Knowledge, the teachings of Ramakrishna and Vivekananda

Other publications: *The Bhagavad Gita; The Song of God; The Upanishads: Breath of the Eternal; Sermon on the Mount According to Vedanta; How to Know God*

Call (213) 465-7114, or write to Vedanta Press, 1946 Vedanta Pl., Hollywood, CA 90068

For a bibliography, write to the Vivekananda Foundation, PO Box 1351, Alameda, CA, 94501

Vivekananda speaks, from the 1893 Parliament

Personal spiritual growth

"Each soul is potentially divine. The goal is to manifest this divine within, by controlling nature external and Internal. Do this either by work, or worship, or psychic control or philosophy – by one or more, or all of these – and be free.

"This is the whole of religion. Doctrines or dogmas or rituals or books or temples or forms are but secondary details."

Peace and harmony

"I would ask mankind to recognize this maxim: DO NOT DESTROY! Break not, pull not anything down, but build. Help, if you can; if you cannot, fold your hands and stand by and see things go on.

"Do not injure if you cannot render help. Say not a word against any man's convictions so far as they are sincere.

"Secondly, take man where he stands and from there give him a lift... and at the centre where all the radii meet all our differences will cease."

Social justice

"My heart is too full to express my feeling: You know it, you can imagine it. So long as the millions live in hunger and ignorance I hold every man a 'traitor' who,

having been educated at their expense, pays not the least heed to them.

"...these men who strut about in their finery, having got all their money grinding the poor wretches, so long as they do not do anything for these millions, are no better than savages."

Faith, strength and women

"Ye are the Children of God, the sharers of immortal bliss, holy and perfect beings. Ye divinities on earth – sinners? It is a sin to call a man so; it is a standing libel on human nature. Come up, O lions, and shake off the delusion that you are sheep; you are souls immortal, spirits free, blest and eternal; ye are not matter, ye are not bodies; matter is your servant, not you the servant of matter....

"Let positive, strong, helpful thoughts enter into their brains from very childhood. Lay yourselves open to these thoughts, and not to weakening and paralyzing ones.

"Women must be in a position to solve their own problems in their own way. No one can or ought to do this for them. And our Indian women are as capable of doing it as any in the world."

The materials on this page were compiled by the Editor from brochures and commemorative materials provided by Vedanta societies

ISKCON; City of God; and Self-Realization Fellowship

International Society For Krishna Consciousness (Hare Krishna Movement)

*I*SKCON is a worldwide community of devotees practicing bhakti-yoga, the eternal science of loving service to God, which has been practiced in India for at least the last five thousand years. Its religious belief is monotheistic. Scriptures include the Vedas, particularly the Bhagavad-Gita and the Srimad-Bhagavatam. The Vedas deal with the process of devotional service to God as well as with different arts and sciences.

Basic beliefs include: everyone is a servant of God; belief in reincarnation (souls are reborn if necessary); a person is embodied at present, but the goal is to reconnect oneself with God; loving service is a method of reconnection; chanting of names of God (Hare Krishna) is a means of meeting God; God is one and has had many incarnations; four main laws of life include no meat, no intoxicants, no gambling, and no illicit sex.

The Hare Krishna movement was brought to the West in 1965 by A.C. Bhaktivedanta Swami Prabhupada. A very important figure in the history of the movement is the great saint Sri Caitanya Mahaprabhu, who lived in the sixteenth century. The Hare Krishna movement follows the disciplic succession named the Gaudia Vaishnava and is thus an authorized spiritual movement representing the ancient Vedic ideas.

Compiled by the Editor from information provided by:
ISKCON Centre
243 Avenue Road, Toronto, Ontario M5R 2J6, Canada
(416) 925-7092

City of God

*B*ased on the teachings of Lord Krishna, as understood by His Divine Grace Swami Bhaktipada, its founder, the City of God has its roots in the Krishna movement (ISKCON); however, as an interfaith city, City of God is now independent from ISKCON and serves people of all faiths from several centers throughout the world.

For more information, see entry in Chapter 42 or contact:
City of God, R.D. 1 Box 319, New Vrindaban, WV 26041
tel. (304) 845-9370

Self-Realization Fellowship

*S*elf-Realization Fellowship is an international religious organization founded in 1920 by Paramahansa Yogananda to disseminate his teachings worldwide. Those teachings – which provide in-depth guidance in all aspects of physical, mental, and spiritual development – center around the science of Kriya Yoga, an advanced system of meditation that leads to direct, personal experience of God. Yogananda's *Autobiography of a Yogi* provides a fascinating and comprehensive introduction to the science of yoga, and has remained a classic in its field since it was first published in 1946.

In the *Aims and Ideals of Self-Realization Fellowship,"* Paramahansa Yogananda set forth these principles:

- To liberate man from his threefold suffering: physical disease, mental inharmonies, and spiritual ignorance....
- To demonstrate the superiority of mind over body, of soul over mind....
- To serve mankind as one's larger self.

*F*rom the late 1930's until the early 50's, Sri Yogananda established several temples in southern California, Phoenix, AZ, and Washington DC. Each was christened as a "Self-Realization Fellowship Church of All Religions." The emphasis was on religious unity and dialogue with devotees of all faiths. SRF has participated in interfaith meetings and councils throughout the years, and has established several "world brotherhood colonies."

The Government of India paid tribute to the founder of Self-Realization Fellowship/Yogoda Satsanga Society of India on March 7,1977, the twenty-fifth anniversary of his passing: "The ideal of love for God and service to humanity found full expression in the life of Paramahansa Yogananda.... Though the major part of his life was spent outside India, still [he] takes his place among our great saints. His work continues to grow and shine ever more brightly, drawing people everywhere on the path of the pilgrimage of the Spirit." Compiled by the editor

For more information, call or write to:

Self-Realization Fellowship
3880 San Rafael Avenue, Los Angeles, CA 90065
tel. (213) 225-2471

FOR MORE INFORMATION:

The literature and organizations of Hinduism, Yoga and the many related topics are numerous even in North America. Here are a few places to begin looking for materials in addition to the organizations listed elsewhere in this chapter.

International Society of Divine Love,
400 Barsana Road, Austin TX 78737-9075

Gaytri Pariwar Chicago
(a Spiritual Institution Dedicated to Social Reconstruction)
8413 W. North Terr., Niles, IL 60714

Hinduism Today (an international newspaper published in many languages), **107 Kaholalele Road, Kapaa, HI 96746**

Integral Yoga Distribution
Satchidananda Ashram-Yogaville,
Buckingham, VA 23921

Reflections on Hinduism, published by the Hindu Host Committee for the Parliament of the World's Religions; 128 pages, large paperback, available for $10 plus $2.00 S&H from the CPWR.

South Asia Books
P.O. Box 502, Columbia, MO 65205

Vishwa Hindu Parishad of America
43 Valley Road, Needham, MA 02192

Yoga Journal, **2054 University Avenue, Berkeley, CA 94704-1082**

The Yoga Vedanta Science and Arts Center, Inc.
2414 West Oakland Park Blvd., Ft. Lauderdale, FL 33311

CHAPTER NINE

Humanism

One might not immediately classify Humanism among religions and spiritual traditions since it finds no evidence for – and therefore denies – claims of supernatural or transcendent realities. Humanist publications, furthermore, provide an ongoing and often appropriate critique of abuses by religions. On the other hand, there are those among humanists who label themselves *religious* humanists, and many others join societies and churches for fellowship and to affirm meaning and ethical commitments. The *Manifesto* itself describes humanism as "a living and growing faith." However one labels it – philosophical movement or worldview – humanism clearly reflects significant inclinations found in many modern and post-modern societies.

The document reprinted below is the second *Humanist Manifesto,* published in 1973. *Humanist Manifesto I,* published in 1933, was described by Raymond Bragg as

> ...designed to represent a developing point of view, not a new creed.... The importance of the document is that more than thirty men have come to general agreement on matters of final concern and that these men are undoubtedly representative of a large number who are forging a new philosophy out of the materials of the modern world.

That declaration is now superseded by *Humanist Manifesto II* which, like the first, represents a consensus statement on philosophy, ethics and social values.

Humanist Manifesto II

Introduction

*T*he next century can be and should be the humanistic century. Dramatic scientific, technological, and ever-accelerating social and political changes crowd our awareness. We have virtually conquered the planet, explored the moon, overcome the natural limits of travel and communication; we stand at the dawn of a new age, ready to move farther into space and perhaps inhabit other planets. Using technology wisely, we can control our environment, conquer poverty, markedly reduce disease, extend our lifespan, significantly modify our behavior, alter the course of human evolution and cultural development, unlock vast new powers, and provide humankind with unparalleled opportunity for achieving an abundant and meaningful life.

The future is, however, filled with dangers. In learning to apply the scientific method to nature and human life, we have opened the door to ecological damage, over-population, dehumanizing institutions, totalitarian repression, and nuclear and biochemical disaster. Faced with apocalyptic prophesies and doomsday scenarios, many flee in despair from reason and embrace irrational cults and theologies of withdrawal and retreat.

Traditional moral codes and newer irrational cults both fail to meet the pressing needs of today and tomorrow. False "theologies of hope" and messianic ideologies, substituting new dogmas for old, cannot cope with existing world realities. They separate rather than unite peoples.

Humanity, to survive, requires bold and daring measures. We need to extend the uses of scientific method, not renounce them, to fuse reason with compassion in order to build constructive social and moral values. Confronted by many possible futures, we must decide which to pursue. The ultimate goal should be the fulfillment of the potential for growth in each human personality – not for the favored few, but for all of humankind. Only a shared world and global measures will suffice.

A humanist outlook will tap the creativity of each human being and provide the vision and courage for us to work together. This outlook emphasizes the role human beings can play in their own spheres of action. The decades ahead call for dedicated, clear-minded men and women able to marshal the will, intelligence, and cooperative skills for shaping a desirable future. Humanism can provide the purpose and inspiration that so many seek; it can give personal meaning and significance to human life.

Many kinds of humanism exist in the contemporary world. The varieties and emphases of naturalistic humanism include "scientific," "ethical," "democratic," "religious," and "Marxist" humanism. Free thought, atheism, agnosticism, skepticism, deism, rationalism, ethical culture, and liberal religion all claim to be heir to the humanist tradition. Humanism traces its roots from ancient China, classical Greece and Rome, through the Renaissance and the Enlightenment, to the scientific revolution of the modern world. But views that merely reject theism are not equivalent to humanism. They lack commitment to the positive belief in the possibilities of human progress and to the values central to it. Many within religious groups, believing in the future of humanism, now claim humanist credentials. Humanism is an ethical process through which we all can move, above and beyond the divisive particulars, heroic personalities, dogmatic creeds, and ritual customs of past religions or their mere negation.

We affirm a set of common principles that can serve as a basis for united action – positive principles relevant to the present human condition. They are a design for a secular society on a planetary scale.

For these reasons, we submit this new *Humanist Manifesto* for the future of humankind; for us, it is a vision of hope, a direction for satisfying survival.

Religion

First: In the best sense, religion may inspire dedication to the highest ethical ideals. The cultivation of moral devotion and creative imagination is an expression of genuine "spiritual" experience and aspiration.

We believe, however, that traditional dogmatic or authoritarian religions that place revelation, God, ritual, or creed above human needs and experience do a disservice to the human species. Any account of nature should pass the tests of scientific evidence; in our judgment, the dogmas and myths of traditional religions do not do so. Even at this late date in human history, certain elementary facts based upon the critical use of scientific reason have to be restated. We find insufficient evidence for belief in the existence of a supernatural; it is either meaningless or irrelevant to the question of the survival and fulfillment of the human race. As nontheists, we begin with humans not God, nature not deity. Nature may indeed be broader and deeper than we now know; any new discoveries, however, will but enlarge our knowledge of the natural.

Some humanists believe we should reinterpret traditional religions and reinvest them with meanings appropriate to the current situation. Such redefinitions, however, often perpetuate old dependencies and escapisms; they easily become obscurantist, impeding the free use of the intellect. We need, instead, radically new human purposes and goals.

We appreciate the need to preserve the best ethical teachings in the religious traditions of humankind, many of which we share in common. But we reject those features of traditional religious morality that deny humans a full appreciation of their own potentialities and responsibilities. Traditional religions often offer solace to humans, but, as often, they inhibit humans from helping themselves or experiencing their full potentialities. Such institutions, creeds, and rituals often impede the will to serve others. Too often traditional faiths encourage dependence rather than independence, obedience rather than affirmation, fear rather than courage. More recently they have generated concerned social action, with many signs of relevance appearing in the wake of the "God Is Dead" theologies. But we can discover no divine purpose or providence for the human species. While there is much that we do not know, humans are responsible for what we are or will become. No deity will save us; we must save ourselves.

Second: Promises of immortal salvation or fear of eternal damnation are both illusory and harmful. They distract humans from present concerns, from self-actualization, and from rectifying social injustices. Modern science discredits such historic concepts as the "ghost in the machine" and the "separable soul." Rather, science affirms that the human species is an emergence from natural evolutionary forces. As far as we know, the total personality is a function of the biological organism transacting in a social and cultural context. There is no credible evidence that life survives the death of the body. We continue to exist in our progeny and in the way that our lives have influenced others in our culture.

Traditional religions are surely not the only obstacles to human progress. Other ideologies also impede human advance. Some forms of political doctrine, for instance, function religiously, reflecting the worst features of orthodoxy and authoritarianism, especially when they sacrifice individuals on the altar of Utopian promises. Purely economic and political viewpoints, whether capitalist or communist, often function as religious and ideological dogma. Although humans undoubtedly need economic and political goals, they also need creative values by which to live.

Ethics

Third: We affirm that moral values derive their source from human experience. Ethics is *autonomous* and *situational*, needing no theological or ideological sanction. Ethics stems from human need and interest. To deny this distorts the whole basis of life. Human life has meaning because we create and develop our futures. Happiness and the creative realization of human needs and desires, individually and in shared enjoyment, are continuous themes of humanism. We strive for the good life, here and now. The goal is to pursue life's enrichment despite debasing forces of vulgarization, commercialization, bureaucratization, and dehumanization.

Fourth: *Reason and intelligence* are the most effective instruments that humankind possesses. There is no substitute: neither faith nor passion suffices in itself. The controlled use of scientific methods, which have transformed the natural and social sciences since the Renaissance, must be extended further in the solution of human problems. But reason must be tempered by humility, since no group has a monopoly of wisdom or virtue. Nor is there any guarantee that all problems can be solved or all questions answered. Yet critical intelligence, infused by a sense of human caring, is the best method that humanity has for resolving problems. Reason should be balanced with compassion and empathy and the whole person fulfilled. Thus, we are not advocating the use of scientific intelligence independent of or in opposition to emotion, for we believe in the cultivation of feeling and love. As science pushes back the boundary of the known, man's sense of wonder is continually renewed, and art, poetry, and music find their places, along with religion and ethics.

The Individual

Fifth: *The preciousness and dignity of the individual person* is a central humanist value. Individuals should be encouraged to realize their own creative talents and desires. We reject all religious, ideological, or moral codes that denigrate the individual, suppress freedom, dull intellect, dehumanize personality. We believe in maximum individual autonomy consonant with social responsibility. Although science can account for the causes of behavior, the possibilities of individual freedom of choice exist in human life and should be increased.

Sixth: In the area of sexuality, we believe that intolerant attitudes, often cultivated by orthodox religions and puritanical cultures, unduly repress sexual conduct. The right to birth control, abortion, and divorce should be recognized. While we do not approve of exploitive, denigrating forms of sexual expression, neither do we wish to prohibit, by law or social sanction, sexual behavior between consenting adults. The many varieties of sexual exploration should not in themselves be considered "evil." Without countenancing mindless permissiveness or unbridled promiscuity, a civilized society should be a tolerant one. Short of harming others or compelling them to do likewise, individuals should be permitted to express their sexual proclivities and pursue their lifestyles as they desire. We wish to cultivate the development of a responsible attitude toward sexuality, in which humans are not exploited as sexual objects, and in which intimacy, sensitivity, respect, and honesty in interpersonal relations are encouraged. Moral education for children and adults is an important way of developing awareness and sexual maturity.

Democratic Society

Seventh: To enhance freedom and dignity the individual must experience a full range of *civil liberties* in all societies. This includes freedom of speech and the press, political democracy, the legal right of opposition to governmental policies, fair judicial process, religious liberty, freedom of association, and artistic, scientific, and cultural freedom. It also includes a recognition of an individual's right to die with dignity, euthanasia, and the right to suicide. We oppose the increasing invasion of privacy, by whatever means, in both totalitarian and democratic societies. We would safeguard, extend, and implement the principles of human freedom evolved from the *Magna Carta* to the *Bill of Rights*, the *Rights of Man*, and the *Universal Declaration of Human Rights*.

Eighth: We are committed to an open and democratic society. We must extend *participatory democracy* in its true sense to the economy, the school, the family, the workplace, and voluntary associations. Decision-making must be decentralized to include widespread involvement of people at all levels – social, political, and economic. All persons should have a voice in developing the values and goals that determine their lives. Institutions should be responsive to expressed desires and needs. The conditions of work, education, devotion, and play should be humanized. Alienating forces should be modified or eradicated and bureaucratic structures should be held to a minimum. People are more important than decalogues, rules, proscriptions, or regulations.

Ninth: *The separation of church and state and the separation of ideology and state are imperatives*. The state should encourage maximum freedom for different moral, political, religious, and social values in society. It should not favor any particular religious bodies through the use of public monies, nor espouse a single ideology and function thereby as an instrument of propaganda or oppression, particularly against dissenters.

Tenth: Humane societies should evaluate economic systems not by rhetoric or ideology, but by whether or not they *increase economic well-being* for all individuals and groups, minimize poverty and hardship, increase the sum of human satisfaction, and enhance the quality of life. Hence the door is open to alternative economic systems. We need to democratize the economy and judge it by its responsiveness to human needs, testing results in terms of the common good.

Eleventh: *The principle of moral equality* must be furthered through elimination of all discrimination based upon race, religion, sex, age, or national origin. This means equality of opportunity and recognition of talent and merit. Individuals should be encouraged to contribute to their own betterment. If unable, then society should provide means to satisfy their basic economic, health, and cultural needs, including, wherever resources make possible, a minimum guaranteed annual income. We are concerned for the welfare of the aged, the infirm, the disadvantaged, and also for the outcasts – the mentally retarded, abandoned or abused children, the handicapped, prisoners, and addicts – for all who are neglected or ignored by society. Practicing humanists should make it their vocation to humanize personal relations.

We believe in the *right to universal education*. Everyone has a right to the cultural opportunity to fulfill his or her unique capacities and talents. The schools should foster satisfying and productive living. They should be open at all levels to any and all; the achievement of excellence should be encouraged. Innovative and experimental forms of education are to be welcomed. The energy and idealism of the young deserve to be appreciated and channeled to constructive purposes.

We deplore racial, religious, ethnic, or class antagonisms. Although we believe in cultural diversity and encourage racial and ethnic pride, we reject separations which promote alienation and set people and groups against each other; we envision an integrated community where people have a maximum opportunity for free and voluntary association.

We are *critical of sexism or sexual chauvinism* – male or female. We believe in equal rights for both women and men to fulfill their unique careers and potentialities as they see fit, free of invidious discrimination.

World Community

Twelfth: We deplore the division of humankind on nationalistic grounds. We have reached a turning point in human history where the best option is to *transcend the limits of national sovereignty* and to move toward the building of a world community in which all sectors of the human family can participate. Thus we look to the development of a system of world law and a world order based upon transnational federal government. This would appreciate cultural pluralism and diversity. It would not exclude pride in national origins and accomplishments nor the handling of regional problems on a regional basis. Human progress, however, can no longer be achieved by focusing on one section of the world, Western or Eastern, developed or underdeveloped. For the first time in human history, no part of humankind can be isolated from any other. Each person's future is in some way linked to all. We thus reaffirm a commitment to the building of world community, at the same time recognizing that this commits us to some hard choices.

Thirteenth: This world community must *renounce the resort to violence and force* as a method of solving international disputes. We believe in the peaceful adjudication of differences by international courts and by the development of the arts of negotiation and compromise. War is obsolete. So is the use of nuclear, biological, and chemical weapons. It is a planetary imperative to reduce the level of military expenditures and turn these savings to peaceful and people-oriented uses.

Fourteenth: The world community must engage in *cooperative planning* concerning the use of rapidly depleting resources. The planet earth must be considered a single *ecosystem.* Ecological damage, resource depletion, and excessive population growth must be checked by international concord. The cultivation and conservation of nature is a moral value; we should perceive ourselves as integral to the sources of our being in nature. We must free our world from needless pollution and waste, responsibly guarding and creating wealth, both natural and human. Exploitation of natural resources, uncurbed by social conscience, must end.

Fifteenth: The problems of *economic growth and development* can no longer be resolved by one nation alone; they are worldwide in scope. It is the moral obligation of the developed nations to provide – through an international authority that safeguards human rights – massive technical, agricultural, medical, and economic assistance, including birth control techniques, to the developing portions of the globe. World poverty must cease. Hence extreme disproportions in wealth, income, and economic growth should be reduced on a worldwide basis.

Sixteenth: *Technology is a vital key* to human progress and development. We deplore any neo-romantic efforts to condemn indiscriminately all technology and science or to counsel retreat from its further extension and use for the good of humankind. We would resist any moves to censor basic scientific research on moral, political, or social grounds. Technology must, however, be carefully judged by the consequences of its use; harmful and destructive changes should be avoided. We are particularly disturbed when technology and bureaucracy control, manipulate, or modify human beings without their consent. Technological feasibility does not imply social or cultural desirability.

Seventeenth: We must expand communication and transportation across frontiers. Travel restrictions must cease. The world must be open to diverse political, ideological, and moral viewpoints and evolve a worldwide system of television and radio for information and education. We thus call for full international cooperation in culture, science, the arts, and technology *across ideological borders.* We must learn to live openly together or we shall perish together.

Humanity as a Whole

In closing: The world cannot wait for a reconciliation of competing political or economic systems to solve its problems. These are the times for men and women of goodwill to further the building of a peaceful and prosperous world. We urge that parochial loyalties and inflexible moral and religious ideologies be transcended. We urge recognition of the common humanity of all people. We further urge the use of reason and compassion to produce the kind of world we want – a world in which peace, prosperity, freedom, and happiness are widely shared. Let us not abandon that vision in despair or cowardice. We are responsible for what we are or will be. Let us work together for a humane world by means commensurate with humane ends. Destructive ideological differences among communism, capitalism, socialism, conservatism, liberalism, and radicalism should be overcome.

Let us call for an end to terror and hatred. We will survive and prosper only in a world of shared humane values. We can initiate new directions for humankind; ancient rivalries can be superseded by broad-based cooperative efforts. The commitment to tolerance, understanding, and peaceful negotiation does not necessitate acquiescence to the status quo nor the damming up of dynamic and revolutionary forces. The true revolution is occurring and can continue in countless nonviolent adjustments. But this entails the willingness to step forward onto new and expanding plateaus. At the present juncture of history, commitment to all humankind is the highest commitment of which we are capable; it transcends the narrow allegiances of church, state, party, class, or race in moving toward a wider vision of human potentiality. What more daring goal for humankind than for each person to become, in ideal as well as practice, a citizen of a world community. It is a classical vision; we can now give it new vitality. Humanism thus interpreted is a moral force that has time on its side. We believe that humankind has the potential intelligence, goodwill, and cooperative skill to implement this commitment in the decades ahead.

We, the undersigned, while not necessarily endorsing every detail of the above, pledge our general support to *Humanist Manifesto II* for the future of humankind. These affirmations are not a final credo or dogma but an expression of a living and growing faith. We invite others in all lands to join us in further developing and working for these goals.

Editor's Note: Thousands of names have been added to the list of signatories which followed the original Humanist Manifesto II, published in the September/October 1973 issue of *The Humanist* by the American Humanist Association, 7 Harwood Drive, P.O. Box 146, Amherst, NY 14226-0146; tel. (716) 839-5080.

Also, a Fellowship of Religious Humanists has formed "to promote and encourage the religious, ethical and philosophical thought and life of our members and society." For more information, contact: Fellowship of Religious Humanists, P.O. Box 597396, Chicago, IL 60659-7396; tel. (312) 338-5493.

Islam

A Portrait

Dr. Ghulam Haider Aasi

Associate Professor of Islamic Studies and the History of Religions, American Islamic College, Chicago; Trustee of the Council for a Parliament of the World's Religions

Islam

*I*slam is the proper name of religion which Allah, the Alone God, revealed to mankind through the series of human messengers-prophets in human history and completed in His final revelation of *Al-Quran al-Karim, Kalam-Allah* (the speech of God) sent down upon the Prophet Muhammad (570–632 CE) *Salla-Allahu alayhi wa Sallam* ("may Allah's blessings and peace be upon him"; this blessing on the names of honored prophets is sometimes abbreviated in print to SAAWS or SA). Within history, Islam is embodied in the *Qur'an* and in the *Sunnah* (the sayings, actions and approvals of the Prophet Muhammad) in its final and eternal form.

The term "Islam" derives from the root letters *s.l.m.* (*Ar. Sin, Lam, Mim*) which means "to be in peace," "to be secure" and "to be integral whole." Hence, Islam means one's conscious submission to the Will, Law, and Guidance of Allah, the Almighty Alone God and thus to be in peace with one's own self, with all creatures and with the Creator and Originator of all that exists. One who consciously surrenders one's whole being to God and commits oneself to pattern one's life on the divine guidance communicated and exemplified by the human messengers-prophets sent by God is called a "Muslim." The *Qur'an* describes Islam in two ways: 1) as the primordial or natural religion (*religio naturalis*) of the innate nature with which Allah created mankind (Q.30:30), and 2) as the religion which was completed and consummated in the *Qur'an*, the final and definitive Divine Writ from Allah.

Allah, the Exalted Almighty Alone God, declares in the *Qur'an* that all the universe and creation surrenders to Him either willingly or unwillingly and that all must return to him (Q.3:83). Whereas the universe surrenders to God's law by its innate nature and is endowed with order, humankind obeys the guidance of God through its divinely endowed moral choice and free will.

> Glorify the name of your Sustainer, the All-Highest, Who creates all that exists, then forms it in its best mold, determines its nature with the proper measure and guides it towards its fulfillment. (Q.87:1–3; tr.by M. Asad)

Allah created humanity, endowed them with an innate awareness of Him, empowered them with faculties of reason and cognition, and made them to inherit the earth, testing their free choice of good and evil by their obedience to or denial of Allah's universal guidance. *Qur'an* unequivocally declares the unity, uniqueness and universality of Allah, the unity and equality of all mankind, the universality of His guidance to all mankind through the human messengers-prophets, and the unity and indivisibility of the Truth. Allah created Adam, the first human being, made him and his progeny inheritors of the earth (*Khalifat-Allah fi al.Ard*), and endowed them with the requisite faculties to be His trustees on earth. His messengers-prophets, starting with Adam and culminating in the Prophet Muhammad (SAAWS), conveyed and exemplified His guidance to their communities.

Historical establishment

*M*uslims believe in the historical crystalization and establishment of Islam within the religious experience of the Prophet Muhammad (SAAWS). He actualized the Will of God as embodied in the *Qur'an* by his beautiful model, the *Sunnah*, and raised a society of true Muslims. His Companions, rightly guided *Caliphs* and *Imams*, carried out his tradition, transmitted it to the following generations and established it in history.

The Prophet Muhammad (SAAWS) was born at Makkah (Mecca) in what is now Saudi Arabia in 570 CE. From a very young age he came to be known as Al-Amin, the honest and trustworthy. At the age of 25 he married a righteous widow, Khadijah, who was 15 years his senior. When he was in his 40s, he was called upon by Allah to deliver His final guidance and message, the *Qur'an*, to mankind and to bring about the *Ummah Muslimah*, the community of submitters to Allah. The Prophet Muhammad received the first revelation sent down upon him through the agency of angel Jibrail (Gabriel) while he was meditating in the cave of Hira'. It reads in translation as follows:

> Read in the name of thy Sustainer, who has created. Created man out of a germ cell. Read, for thy Sustainer is the Most-Bountiful One. Who has taught man the use of the pen. Taught man what he did not know. Nay, verily, man becomes grossly overweening whenever he believes himself to be self-sufficient: for, behold, unto thy Sustainer all must return. (Q96:1–8; tr.by M. Asad)

In Makkah, the Prophet Muhammad called upon the

Arab idolaters of his time to believe in One Alone God, Allah (*Tawhid*), and not to ascribe divinity to aught beside Allah. As a result of the scathing criticism of the *Qur'an* against idolatry and its various forms of Associationism (*shirk*) the Makkan oligarchy turned to persecuting Muhammad and his followers. It became so harsh and harrying that the Prophet was commanded to migrate along with his Makkan followers to Yathrib.

This emigration of the Prophet Muhammad and his Makkan Muslims who since then were designated *Muhajirun* (migrants in the Cause of Allah) in 622 CE marked a watershed point in the history of mankind. The Muslims' religious calendar, known as *Hijri*, is based on this most meaningful and significant event. The city of Yathrib since then came to be known as Madinah (abbreviated from Madinat al-Nabi, city of the Prophet) and it was here that the Prophet was able to establish *Ummah Muslimah,* the religio-moral and socio-political community of Muslims, commonly known as the Islamic city state of Madinah.

Within a decade this nascent and model Muslim community was successful in establishing Islam in the whole of the Arabian Peninsula; in addition, the Prophet sent missions to all the surrounding rulers and empires including both the superpowers of the time, the Persian Sasanid and the Byzantian Roman Christian empires. Just months before his death, the Prophet Muhammad addressed all mankind during his Farewell Pilgrimage to Ka'bah, in Makkah and made the eternal message of Allah universally known and established. Some of the salient parts of this historic address are the following:

> O, mankind, listen to what I say: I do not know whether I will meet you ever at this place after this year. O, mankind, verily your lives, your honor and your property are inviolable and sacred like this day and this month until you meet your Sustainer. You will definitely meet your Sustainer and He will ask you of your deeds. … Whoever is entrusted with any trust, he must return the trust fully. Verily, all usury is abolished but you have your capital. Wrong not and you shall not be wronged. Allah has decreed that there is to be no usury. … You have rights over your women and they have rights over you.... Listen and understand, O, mankind, I am leaving with you the Divine writ, the Qur'an and the Sunnah of His Prophet. If you stick to it you will never go astray. This is a self-evident fact. You must know every Muslim is a brother to another Muslim. All Muslims constitute one brotherhood. One is only permitted to take from a brother what he gives willingly, so wrong not yourselves. O, Allah, be witness I have conveyed. (Ibn Hisham, *Sirat al-Rasul*)

*A*fter the death of the Prophet Muhammad in 10H/632 CE, the *Ummah* was first led by the four rightly-guided Caliphs (10–40H/632–661CE), followed by the dynastic rulers. Both the historical spread of Islam and unprecedented expansion of Muslim rule through all the continents known at the time, within less than a century after the death of the Prophet, changed not only the map of the world but also transformed the destiny of human history and world civilization. By 711 CE, Islam had crossed Gibraltar in the west, Caucasus in the north, Sudan in the south, and reached India and China in the east. Muslim *Caliphantes* ruled most of the world, from Al-Andalus, Spain (711–1492 CE) to Asia and Africa, at the period when Europe and the West were still in their dark and Middle ages. Islam made lasting contributions to human civilization and transformed ancient regional civilizations into a world civilization. The so-called Western civilization would never have emerged had there not been the integrating Islamic civilization across the European Dark and Middle ages and the Renaissance.

This *pax Islamica*, however, was never immune from internal disintegration or from external repulsions and reconquests. The Christian reconquest of Spain, the Inquisition and the Crusades set a course of historical conflict between the West and the Muslim world of which European Colonialism and Western Neo-imperialism have been the historical corollaries. Despite all these geo-political changes and socio-economic conflicts, Islam continued to spread, gaining adherents in all parts of the world. Today, Muslims total over a billion and their geographical spread is throughout all the continents. The historic spread of Islam has never been due to its early conquests alone; rather, its appeals are the egalitarian bonding of all believers into universal brotherhood (*Ummah*) and providing them with the spiritual truth of God-consciousness (*Tawhid* and *Taqwa*) that transforms their lives to be meaningful and purposeful.

Main sources

*F*or Muslims the essential sources for all aspects of life are: (a) the *Qur'an*, (b) the *Sunnah* and *Hadith*, (c) *Ijma* (traditional consensus of the Companions of the Prophet and teachings of the *Imams* for the Shi'ah), and (d) *Ijtihad* (reasoning and analogical deduction based on the *Qur'an* and *Hadith* to derive solutions for new problems).

(a) *The Qur'an.* Muslims believe in the *Qur'an* as verbatim revelation from Allah, sent down upon Muhammad through the agency of the angel Gabriel during Muhammad's prophethood, 610–632 CE. The whole *Qur'an* was sent down upon the Prophet piecemeal, was memorized, written and publicly transmitted upon its revelation. Its uniqueness as an inimitable miracle and the eternally definitive words of God, its historical preservation, regular and authentic transmission and dissemination are essential beliefs of Islam. It comprises 114 *surahs* (chapters) which are designated as Makkan or Madinan according to the place of their descent upon Muhammad.

(b) *Sunnah* and *Hadith*. The second universal source of Islam is the *Sunnah* which comprises sayings, actions and approvals of the Prophet Muhammad. Their reportage in narration is called *Hadith*. Six collections are recognized as authentic by the Sunni Muslims; the Shi'ah recognize Al-Kulini's collection, entitled "Al-Kafi," as earliest and authentic.

(c) *Ijma*. Sunni Muslims believe in the consensus of the

Muslim scholars and the community as the third source of Islamic law whereas the Shi'ah take the teachings and interpretations of the *Imams* as binding.

(d) *Ijtihad*. This names the total effort of a religious scholar to discover both the intent of the Islamic law and the correct answer to a new problem in light of the first two material sources called *Nass* (divine text), through a well-defined systematic procedure of *Qiyas* (analogical deduction).

Beliefs and observances

A. Articles of Faith (*Arkan al Iman*)

*M*uslims believe in six articles of faith which are derived from revealed sources, the *Qur'an* and the *Sunnah*. (Q.2:285; 4:136, 150–152)

(i) Belief in **One Alone God, Allah**. He is Unique, Infinite, Transcendent, Creator and Sustainer of all that exists. "Nothing is like unto Him." (Q.42:11) He Alone is worthy of worship. All else is His creature and servant. He is Unique both in his essence (*Dhat*) and in His attributes (*Sifat*). "His are the beautiful names (99 beautiful names described in the *Qur'an*) and all that is in the heavens and the earth glorify Him ...." (Q.59:24; 7:180; 17:110; 20:8)

(ii) Belief in the **eternal life of Hereafter** (*Al-Akhirah*). Muslims believe in the end of the world, in Resurrection, in the resurrection of whole person after death (*al-Ba'th*), in the Day of judgment (*Yawm al-Hisab*) and in eternal Hell and Paradise.

(iii) Belief in **angels**. Muslims believe in angels as creatures of Allah, eternally busy in His service, glorification and Praise: "... they never disobey God what he commanded them to do and do what they are ordered." (Q.66:6; 16:50)

(iv) Belief in **Revelations from God**, commonly known as belief in the Books from God. Muslims believe that Allah revealed His messages and guidance to different messengers at different times and places. These include the scrolls of Abraham, the *Torah* to Moses, Psalms to David, *Injil* to Jesus, culminating in the *Qur'an* to the Prophet Muhammad.

(v) Belief in **human messengers-prophets of God.** Muslims believe that Allah chose certain human beings as His prophets and messengers to convey His guidance and to exemplify it for their people. All peoples have a prophet from among themselves who conveyed the guidance and norms of God to them in their own language. Muslims believe that the series of prophets starts with Adam and includes Abraham, Noah, Moses, Jesus, and culminates in Muhammad, who is the Seal of the office of Prophethood. The office of Prophethood is indivisible. May God's blessing and peace be with all of them. (Q.10:47,14:4, 16:36, 21:25, 28:59, 33:40)

(vi) belief in the **Decree and Plan of God.** Muslims believe that all happens, good or evil, with the decree of God and nothing can fail His Plan. (*Qada wa Qadar*).

B. Pillars of Islam (*Arkan al Islam*)

(i) *Shahadah*: The statement of faith. A person becomes a Muslim when out of one's own will and conviction one bears witness to the fact that there is no deity but Allah and Muhammad is His messenger (and final prophet and servant).

(ii) *Salat*: Every male and female adult Muslim is obliged to offer five daily worship-prayers. (Q.4:103, 2:177)

(iii) *Sawm*: Fasting during the whole month of *Ramadan,* the ninth month of Muslims' lunar calendar and abstaining from food, drink, sex and all sorts of idle and immoral acts from dawn to sunset. (Q.2:183–187)

(iv) *Zakat*: Sharing wealth. Every Muslim who has his savings for a year is obligated to pay a fixed portion of it to the needy, the poor and those who are under debt. Wealth-sharing purifies the giver's wealth from greed and stinginess and reconciles the hearts of the recipients. (Q.9:60)

(v) *Hajj*: Pilgrimage. All Muslims who can afford the journey to Ka'bah, in Makkah, Saudi Arabia, both physically and financially, are obliged to perform the pilgrimage once in their lifetime; it is usually made during the first ten days of the last month of the Muslim *Hijri* Calendar, *Dhu-al. Hijjah*. Pilgrimage at other times is called *"Umrah."* (Q.2:189–179, 3:97)

Schools of law

*W*ith the developing needs of the Muslim *Ummah*, the expansion of the Muslim empire, and changing situations, there arose a need to derive laws from the revealed sources and to develop a systematic method for doing so. Though there were many legal opinions in the beginning, by the end of third century *Hijrah,* four schools of law were recognized as othodox among the Sunni Muslims: Hanafi, Maliki, Shafi'i and Hanbali. Among the Shi'ah, two became prominent: Ja'fariyah of the Twelver Shi'ahs of Iran and Zaydiyah (Fivers) of Yemen.

Theological schools

*A*t its earliest stage Muslim theological speculation emerged in response to internal political differences. The murder of Uthman (d.656 CE), the third Caliph, and subsequent civil wars raised important issues, including: Who is a true believer? what is the nature of faith (*Iman*) and its relation to Islam (submission to God's law)? what qualifies a person both to be the leader and member of a truly believing Community? Variant responses to these questions split the *Ummah* first into different political views and groups, then resulted in sects:

(i) *Khawarij*

The first explicit political and theological schism was of the Khawarij (Secessionists) who called for extreme piety and idealistic egalitarianism. They fought against all claimants of political rule. Some even rejected the need for any governing institution. Their pursuit of a pure society later led them to fanaticism and violence. Continuous rebellion against every goverment and ever-increasing internal dissension and disunity almost eliminated their role and existence. Those who survived took refuge in the rugged mountains of North Africa and Yemen.

(ii) *Shi'ah*

The second major schism represented, in its earliest phase, primarily a socio-political critique against the rulers; later it became a permanent sect or branch of Islam. The name "Shi'ah" was given to the partisans of 'Ali (d.661 CE), the son-in-law of the Prophet, the fourth rightly-guided *Caliph* of the Sunnis and the first *Imam* of the Shi'ah. They developed the doctrine of *Imamah* over and against the Sunni Khilafah. According to this view, the legitimate successor of the Prophet was 'Ali, their first *Imam,* whose succession then continued in his descendants who are thus political and religious leaders. These *Imams* are divinely inspired, infallible, and authoritative interpreters of the *Qur'an.* Later, debating the legitimacy of different Imams, Shi'ism split into numerous sects. Their main branches are:

a. *Ithna 'Ash'ariyyah* (Twelvers) believe in the 12 *Imams* and hold that a son, Muhammad al-Muntazar, was born to the 11th *Imam,* Hassan al-Askari (d.874) but went into concealment until he will reappear at the proper time to set the whole world in order. They subscribe to the legal school *Ja'fariyyah,* have been established in Iran since the *Safvid* period (1501), and are the largest branch of Shi'ah.

b. *Zaydiyah* consider Zayd b. Ali (d.740), the second grandson of Husayn, to be the fifth and final *Imam.* Zaydiyah follow the Zaydi school of Islamic law and are closer to Sunnis. They established themselves in Yemen.

c. *Isma'iliyah* take Ismail's (d.760) son Muhammad as the impending *Mahdi.* They split into many offshoots such as Fatimids, Qaramitah, Druz, Nizaris and Agha Khanis, continuing to present times.

(iii) *Sunnis*

The majority of Muslims – more than 90 percent of all Muslims in the world – identify themselves with the term *Ahl- al-Sunnah wa al-Jama'ah,* or People of the Tradition and the Community, commonly known as Sunni in distinction to non-orthodox sects and groups. Among them, two main theological schools and dispositions became permanent. In their classical terms, these are known as *Mu'tazilah* and *Ash'ariyah.* The first tendency represents rationalist philosophical theology while the second emphasizes the absolute primacy and total sufficiency of the revealed texts, the *Qur'an* and the *Sunnah.*

Contemporary movements

Most of the revivalist or reform movements – pejoratively called fundamentalist or neo-fundamentalist groups in the West – derive their thought and arguments from Ash'ariyah and its sister traditional theologies.

Feasts and festivals

*M*uslims observe a lunar calendar of 354 days. The two most important religious feasts celebrated by all, everywhere, are the two *Ids*:

(i) *Id al-Adha,* the feast of Sacrifice and *Hajj,* is celebrated on the tenth of *Dhu al-Hijjah,* the 12th month. Congregational worship prayer is offered in the open or in big *mosques.* Every household slaughters an animal, and meat of sacrifices is shared and distributed.

(ii) *Id al-Fitr* is celebrated on the first day of *Shawwal,* the tenth month, to give thanks for completion of the fasting of *Ramadan* and asking God's forgiveness. *Id-Salat* is offered in congregation in the open or in big *mosques.* On both *Ids,* charity is given, gifts are exchanged, open houses are maintained, visits are made to friends, neighbors, relatives and even to graveyards. Generosity, hospitality and caring are hallmarks of these feasts.

(iii) In addition to the two *'Ids* there are other optional small holidays or historical celebrations such as fasting on the tenth of the first month, vigil on *Laylat al-Qadr,* popularly on the 27th night of the fasting month of *Ramadan,* celebrating the birthday of the Prophet (Mawlid al-Nabi) on 12th of the third month and on first *Muharram,* as the *Hijri* new year day, etc. Shi'ah particularly commemorate the martyrdom of Husain (d.680), the grandson of the Prophet, during the first ten days of *Muharram.*

Sufism

*O*ne of the most enduring contributions of Islam to human spirituality is its mystical tradition and dimension generally known as Sufism, more correctly called *Tasawwuf.* It is unfortunate that, more often than not, Islam has been perceived as a political, legalistic, orthopraxic and this-worldly religion due to its distinctive emphasis on the Transcendence and complete otherness of Unique and Alone God. The historical fact, however, is that it is the Islamic spiritual reality rather than Muslim imperium or an Islamic state which made Islam a universal religion. This stream of spiritual experience has been carried on by Sufis who have been the mystics and scholars of traditional Islam up to the present. Sufism sees the essence of the human in his being "of God, in the world" rather than "of the world, for God." It sees humans innately bound with God due to the primordial covenant of their souls witnessing to the fact of God's lordship. (Q.7:172)

It is human forgetfulness of God and absorption in the material world that makes them alienated from their essence. (Q.59:18–19) Hence, to gain one's real self is to be in constant remembrance of God (*Dhikr*; Q.13:28) and to detach oneself from the transitory material world. True submission (*Islam*) is to make one's heart, not just head, the real throne of God where God manifests Himself both as Transcendent and Immanent. Realizing such presence of God requires one to experience the absolute love of God, by dying in Him and living in Him. Out of their religious experiences, Sufis derived the doctrines of *Fana* (dying in God or annihilation of the human self and attributes in God) and *Baqa* (living with God and acquiring divine attributes). They systematically developed and explained the different stations and states through which every genuine mystic has to tread on the path of spiritual experience of reality. While the primary requirement for a Muslim is to abide by the rules and regulation of the Islamic law and rituals (*Shari'ah*), that observance does not guarantee the spiritual experience of God and His vision.

By devoting and pledging oneself to God through the experienced guide, one can tread the path of spiritual reality (*Tariqah*). Within the variety of these religious-spiritual experiences, the mystics of Islam introduced their orders and provided institutions where adepts lead initiates to the experience of spiritual reality.

Islam and other religious traditions

*N*o other religious scripture addresses the issue of the religious diversity of mankind as directly as the *Qur'an*. It emphasizes the unity and universality of One Alone God, unity and equality of mankind, unity of the Truth and universality of God's guidance to all mankind through human messengers-prophets, starting from Adam and culminating in the Prophet Muhammad who is the final messenger and the mercy to all the worlds. (*Rahmatan lil'alamin*, Q.21:107; 7:158; 34:28; 33:40) The *Qur'an* declares that God created all mankind as one religio-moral community (*Ummah wahidah*). It was humanity's exercise of freedom of will and claim of self-sufficiency (Q.96:6-7) that led to differentiation and to deviation from the innate nature. Then God, out of His universal grace, raised among them messengers who conveyed God's guidance to them in their own languages. (Q.16:36; cf:35:23–25; 23:44; 10:47; 14:4 and more)

Whereas each community ought to have accepted the universality of God's messages and believed in His messengers-prophets, their mutual jealousy and attempts to appropriate God's favor turned them instead to splitting the one and true religion of God and dividing into sects and mutually exclusive communities. (Q.23:51–53; 21:92–94; 30:30–32) Yet even this religious diversity with different symbols and rituals is categorized by the *Qur'an* as God-willed reality so long as it does not fall into the worship of false deities (idolatry) and does not deny universal fundamental principles of truth and morality. (10:19; 11:117–119; 16:93; 42:8)

All mankind were once one single community; (then they began to differ) whereupon God raised up the prophets as heralds of glad tidings and as warners, and through them bestowed revelation from on high, setting forth the truth, so that it might decide between people with regard to all on which they had come to hold divergent views. Yet none other than the self-same people who had been granted this (revelation) began, out of mutual jealousy, to disagree about its meaning after all evidence of the truth had come unto them. But God guided the believers unto the truth about which, by His leave, they had disagreed: for God guides onto a straight way him that wills (to be guided). (Q.2:213; tr.by M. Asad)

And unto thee (O Prophet) have We vouchsafed this divine writ, setting forth the truth, confirming the truth of whatever there still remains of earlier revelations and determining what is true therein. Judge, then, between the followers of earlier revelation in accordance with what God has bestowed from on high, and do not follow their errant views, forsaking the truth that has come unto thee. Unto every one of you have We appointed a (different) law and way of life. And if God had so willed, He could surely have made you all one single community: but (He willed it otherwise) in order to test you by means of what He has vouchsafed unto you. Vie then with one another in doing good works! Unto God you all must return; and then He will make you truly understand all that on which you were wont to differ. (Q.5:48; tr. by M. Asad)

Qur'an rejects any claim of appropriating God's truth or favor. No person, race or nation is chosen of God. Any claim on God's unilateral covenant or saving grace by any atonement is vehemently rejected by the *Qur'an*. For God all humans are equal. What characterizes one as noble is one's God-consciousness (*Taqwa*) and carrying out His norms of universal ethics.

O' mankind, Behold, We have created you all from a male and a female and have made you into tribes and nations so that you might come to recognize one another as (interdependent and equal), verily noblest of you before God is one who is most conscious of Him, verily, God is all knowing, all aware. (Q.49:13; tr.by M.Asad)

Islam abolished and condemns all forms of racial, tribal or national prejudices which cause one to stand by one's own people in an unjust cause over and against truth and justice. (Q.5:2, 8)

The *Qur'an* reconfirms the fact of earlier revelations from God and hence it gives to the adherents of *Torah* and *Injil,* Jews and Christians, the appellation of *"Ahl-al-Kitab,"* the people of the revealed scriptures. Though the Qur'an explicitly identifies the Jews and Christians as *Ahl-al-Kitab,* the term in its general import and implicit *Qur'anic* allusions extends to all religious traditions which might concur with identifying their religious sources as derived from one and the same Divine source. Thus the Prophet also included Zoroastrians in this category. With the spread of Muslim rule over Asia, India, and Africa, some Muslim jurists later included both Hindus and Buddhists in the category of *Ahl-al-Dhimma* which, by extension, absorbed all non-Muslims who chose to be the subjects of the Muslim rule.

Islam does not identify people in terms of political, geographical, ethnic, racial, or national entities; rather, it categorizes them in terms of their religio-moral commitments and religious traditions. As Professor Dr. Syed Muhammad Naquib al-Attas, the Founder-Director of International Institute of Islamic Thought and Civilization, Kuala Lumpur, maintains:

We Muslims not only tolerated non-Muslims but also opened our doors of lands and houses even, our hearts and minds to make them feel at home amongst us.

But what made Muslims the pioneers of religious

coexistence was their recognition of non-Muslims as legal citizens based on rules derived from the teachings of the *Qur'an* and the *Sunnah*. And it was on these grounds that Muslims worked out the detailed legal rights and duties of non-Muslims vis-a-vis the Muslims as a part of Islamic law. Muslims were the first to recognize non-Muslims as *religio licita*, providing them legal religio-cultural autonomy. Every Muslim goverment or leader is obliged by the Prophetic command to safeguard the rights of non-Muslims with special care (*Dhimmat-Allah wa Rasulihi*).

The *Qur'an* categorically prohibits coercion in matters of religion, be it by sheer force or implicit deceptive ways. Muslims are obliged to call mankind toward submission to God by wisdom, good example, and sincere exhortation, not in argument, but with kind manner. (Q.2:257; 16:125) Such imperatives of the *Qur'an* provide Muslims with a clear call to humanity; Muslims repeat and try to live by the following guidelines in their interreligious dialogues and cooperations:

> Say, O followers of earlier revelation, come unto that tenet which we and you hold in common – that we shall not ascribe divinity to aught beside Him, and that we shall not take human beings for our lords beside God. (Q.3:64; tr.by M.Asad)

Cooperation, peace, justice and virtue

The main objective of every venture of interreligious dialogue and cooperation is to bring about justice, order and peace in the world. Cooperation in furthering virtue and justice and in ending evil and aggression is among the most distinctive imperatives of the *Qur'an*. (Q.5:2 & 8)

A personal plea

While I am writing these words early in July 1993, I cannot help but express my extreme disappointment in all world bodies and conferences, including religious organizations, with regard to the situation in Bosnia-Herzegovina. In his open letter addressed to: "All of Those Who Still Believe in Love and Divine Justice," my dear colleague and friend Dr. Mustafa Ceric, Supreme Head of Islamic Community in Bosnia-Herzegovina, writes:

> We, the Muslims of Bosnia, have been betrayed. All that remains to us is the hope that people who believe in love and justice, particularly the religious leaders of the world's major faiths, will stand with us.

> We call upon: all the Muslim *ulama* of the world in the name of Muslim altruism; on the leadership of all the Christian denominations – Catholic, Orthodox, Protestant and all others – in the name of Christian love and mercy; on the Jewish Rabbinate in the name of supreme justice; on every Buddhist leader in the name of Buddha's Compassion; on Hindus, Confucians, Taoists, Parsis, Bahá'ís, in sum, every religious leader as well as

secular humanists in the name of their principles, to help us....

> Let them voice love in the face of hatred, justice in the face of murder. And let them voice their religious vows here in Sarajevo, the city of mosques, churches, synagogues and temples where different faiths and traditions have always lived in peace . . . where today genocide of Bosnia's Muslims is carried out.

As I repeat this cry for justice and appeal to human conscience, my heart is rending with pain. Will the 1993 Parliament of the World's Religions in Chicago and other conferences of religious leaders stand to change the situation?

Islam and the Parliaments of the World's Religions

At the 1893 Parliament, Islam was not represented properly. Alexander Russell Webb, a singular American new Muslim, made a genuine effort to bring across the true teachings of Islam to the West, but to no avail. Since its historical inception to the present, Islam has been grossly misunderstood and distorted in the West. Most of the papers on Islam were read and written by Christian missionaries active in the Muslim world at the time. They not only explained away Islam, but also reasserted more stereotypes, a legacy which continues to the present. Whereas for centuries distortion of Islam and stereotypes of it were created and carried out by the missionaries and mercenary Orientalists, today this distortion continues by the Western media and by those who are antagonistic to Islam.

Muslims hope and pray that interfaith meetings such as the 1993 Parliament of the World's Religions at Chicago will lay the foundations of proper understanding of Islam in the West and America, and that the Western world will see in Islam the panacea rather than the threat to the needed just world order.

ACKNOWLEDGMENTS

First, all praise and thanks are due to Allah. I am also grateful to American Islamic College, both to its administration and community, for providing me with the time and facilities to work for the Parliament. For the preparation of this article, I am extremely thankful to International Institute of Islamic Thought and Civilization, Kuala Lumpur; to its Founder-Director, Dr. Prof. Syed Muhammad Naquib al-Attas; and to all its members for providing me with time and facilities. Special thanks are due to Ms. Nor Azimah for her typing.

Most of all, my heartfelt gratitude is due to my wife, Zubaida and to my children: Humaira, Sumaira, Irfan, Rummanah and Salman. Without their continous support and unceasing sacrifices I would have never been able to make contributions to these good causes.

Finally, I acknowledge Joel Beversluis, the Editor of this *SourceBook*, whose constant encouragement and unceasing forbearance brought this to publication.

May God Almighty bless all!

Islam in the World Today

Situations of Minority Conflict and the Ummah's Responsibilities

Syed Z. Abedin

Director of the Institute of Muslim Minority Affairs, Jeddah, Saudi Arabia, and London, U.K. (deceased May 1993)

Introduction

*T*he world situation with respect to Muslim minority communities around the globe is getting more complex day by day. No respite appears to be in sight. We at the Institute of Muslim Minority Affairs have at the moment no propositions either. In any case, we do not see ourselves as problem solvers. Most cases of conflict in present times which involve Muslims are of a political nature and their solution calls for political initiatives on the part of governments.

What we can do and have been doing over the past ten years, in our capacity as an independent research institute, is to formulate the right questions and to provide an accurate and objective database for possible answers. This helps to clarify the issues. And if there is will on the part of the contending parties, the Institute's input could facilitate the search for solutions.

One reason perhaps why viable solutions have not been forthcoming is that nobody is asking the right questions.

As is well known, there are at least half a dozen situations in various corners of the globe where Muslims are presently engaged in a desperate struggle. Imminent or potential conflict situations are many times this number.

Now in all these situations, live or latent, major or minor, the *Ummah* is urged to intervene. These calls for active intervention are made not only by those minority Muslims who are immediately affected but also by various constituents within the *Ummah*. Thus the pressure on the *Ummah* is both domestic and foreign, internal and external.

The *Ummah* is thus faced with a dilemma. The dilemma consists in that even if there were consensual will on issues of minority conflict on the part of all constituent members, resources are not inexhaustible. There is no way in which the *Ummah* could wage a determined, aggressive and successful campaign on all fronts where Muslims are presently engaged in conflict with others.

Let us not forget that even the United States not too long ago had to solicit material and manpower resources of over two dozen countries of the world in order to wage a successful campaign on one single front.

To make matters more complicated upholders of the Islamic cause inside the *Ummah* insist on making each occasion of conflict anywhere in the world, in which any number of Muslims are involved, a test case for the *Ummah's* Islamic commitment and its consciousness of accountability before God Almighty.

The *Ummah* has therefore before it two options: it could either choose to plunge into every quarrel anywhere in the world where Muslims in any number feel that they are being thwarted from getting whatever they want, and in consequence cease to be a credible world power; or it has to face the wrath of its own people, who see in the lack of alacrity on the part of the *Ummah* a sign of betrayal of Islam.

Verbal jihad

*T*he *Ummah's* record in the past indicates that to save face it has opted for a third alternative, which, for want of a better term, may be described as a verbal *jihad*. Every now and then, when the domestic pressures build up, various spokesmen of the *Ummah* come forward with passionate statements directed at the offending parties.

In these events, the statements could have constituted a clever, strategic compromise between the two options noted above. But these statements, pliable though they are, end up adding further fuel to a fire that should not have been started in the first place: they alienate the non-Muslims concerned from all the constituents of the *Ummah* (even from the faith they profess), and raise false hopes of *Ummah* support among the Muslim minorities. This leads to tragic consequences.

The Ummah concept

*O*ne possible way of resolving this dilemma could be to look at the *Ummah* as representing not a political but primarily a religious and spiritual concept. Realistically speaking, in present times there appears to be no other way of giving viable meaning to this concept. For, if the *Ummah* is projected as a political entity, then there is in truth no *Ummah*. There are indeed 50 or more sovereign Muslim states, but they are nation states, each with its own national goals and interests, but no *Ummah*.

If on the other hand the term *Ummah* is accepted as primarily reflecting a religious and spiritual concept, then in all situations of conflict the questions to ask would be: is this a religious conflict? *i.e.*, are Muslims being victimized because of their religion? are their rights to freedom of worship, belief, practice, and propagation being denied?

If the consensus among the constituents of the *Ummah* is that, yes, it is a religious conflict, then without doubt every effort should be made to resolve it to Muslim satisfaction.

But if our investigation reveals that the real cause of the conflict is not religious but ethnic, national, economic, strategic, or political and that religion is being used merely as a pretext, then like all secular conflicts it should be amenable to negotiations, accommodation, and compromise. The *Ummah's* responsibility would then be to use its good offices to facilitate such a resolution.

However, it is important to remember that the procedures adopted for doing so by the *Ummah* would be markedly different from those adopted in the case of a religious conflict. The hellfire and brimstone strategies most often employed in religious conflicts in our time are not likely to pay much in dividends in political conflicts.

Unfortunately, this important distinction has not always been maintained by even responsible spokesmen of the *Ummah*.

Furthermore, it has also to be considered that if a conflict is truly a religious conflict, then in all good conscience it has to be conducted as one. We cannot claim commitment to a cause and then go on to pursue the cause oblivious to its value limitations. Islam is not a racial, national, or ethnic concept. We are Muslims not because we all have kinship or language ties, or live in the same territory, or dress in the same way, or prefer the same cuisine. We are Muslims because we together believe in certain common values. These values color (or should color) everything we do. So that without being told who we are, anybody looking at us, from our appearance and behavior, could determine that these must be followers of the faith of Islam.

In Islam there is no concept of total war. In any case, we as a people were not raised to conquer the world for God. God is capable of doing so Himself. Didn't He say in the *Qur'an* that if He had wanted to He could have made the whole world Muslim? But He did not. (*Qur'an* 10:99) We were raised in order to be a witness (a model) unto what a God-conscious life of total surrender to His will is supposed to be lived like and look like.

Revenge or reconciliation?

In a situation of conflict between two groups, one Muslim and the other non-Muslim, in particular in the case of actual or potential conflict between Muslim minorities and non-Muslim majorities, the crucial question to determine at the very outset is: Is the primary concern of the *Ummah* to put a nation or a community or a religion in the dock before the international community, i.e., to determine culpability first?

Or, is it to provide urgent relief to the suffering millions engaged in conflict?

It should never be forgotten that however cheap Muslim life may have become in our time, causing its wanton loss for self-titillation or communal ego-boosting is still a cardinal sin.

It is also perhaps instructive to note here that however cynical and polarized, religiously or nationally, the world may have become, the conscience of the world community is still alive and well. Indeed, some of the most damaging indictments of government policies toward their Muslim minorities have come not from Muslims but from non-Muslims, both indigenous and foreign.

And herein lies our hope.

Let us build on this hope. Let not the forces of hatred and fanaticism drown our Islamic good sense. Let some people among us plumb the depths and resources of our moral and Islamic being and come up with ways of understanding and resolution.

Who knows what non-Muslim powers may also be waiting for such an opening. After all, they also well realize that, considering the present international order, the minorities that reside within their jurisdiction cannot be just wished away. In fact, looked at from the perspective of history, non-Muslim states such as Russia, China, India, and Bulgaria, which contain significant Muslim minorities, would not be what they are today if their national life had not been interwoven by the multiple and many-hued contributions of their minority constituents.

The people of conscience in these countries have given and are giving expression to their sense of outrage at the violation of human and civil rights perpetrated in these societies. Perhaps these people are also wishing for such a gesture on our part. They have already done *their* human duty. It is now *our* turn.

Let us put aside, for a while at least, our sense of umbrage as Muslims and take our Islamic courage in hand and be the first to break this impasse, this standoff between communities and states, between the governors and the governed.

Let the world community know that we come, not to condemn nor to aggravate an already sensitive and explosive situation, but that we desire only to understand and ameliorate. Whether it be Russia or China or India or the Philippines or Bulgaria or Cyprus or Burma, let the world know that we come, more in sorrow than in anger, to help find a workable arrangement that would put a stop to the bloodletting and the suffering and the humiliation and the loss of honor and dignity. And to help lift the burdens and the shackles that have oppressed the victims, and equally, the conscience of the perpetrators.

Is this too much to ask?

Islam in North America

Dr. Aminah B. McCloud

Professor of Islamic Studies in the Department of Religious Studies at DePaul University, Chicago

*I*slam first came to North America on the souls and tongues of African traders, and then in the hearts of many African slaves. Islam comes in a more noticeable garb with immigrants in the late 19th century and with a string of influence beginning with the 20th century. There is no monolithic Islamic expression among Muslims in America since it has all the diversity of the Muslim world. By 1960 Islam was definitely an American religion with its own institutions and several generations of indigenous Muslims. Muslim children could attend Muslim schools through the high school level in almost every major city in America by 1960. Since the 1960s the Muslim presence in the public space is also evident in the spread of the domed *masajid* and Arabic calligraphy signs.

The study of Islam in America is important for a variety of reasons. It is the fastest growing religion in America. Its basic practices and beliefs are obviously different from American Protestant Christianity. Since Muslims act in concert with other Americans in a wide assortment of tasks such as the practice of medicine, industry, education and even celebrations, some knowledge of those differences is crucial. To handle the needs of their community and to promote an understanding of Islam, Muslims have formed dozens of organizations – professional, social and educational. In spite of these efforts dialogue between Muslims and other religious communities has been sparse. While there are numerous texts on Muslim–Christian relations, there are almost no texts on encounters within the American context. It is only recently that Islam has come to be seen as a legitimate part of the American religious landscape by scholars, and most of this has come through a media focus.

In America, Muslims struggle to enact the obligations of their faith. The obligation to pray five times daily (*salat*) at certain times can be problematic in the American work-place or school. Often Muslims encounter the American resistance to the notion of prayer as an intimate part of one's self understanding. In the workplace, Muslims often trade breaks and/or lunch times to meet the obligations of daily prayer and the congregational prayer on Fridays (*Jum'ah*).

The work place can also provide challenging social encounters with regard to dress, lifestyles, holidays and professionalism. Most Muslim women have met numerous obstacles with reference to dress and their head scarves, while some Muslim men have the same problems with the length or presence of their beards. Muslim reluctance to participate in social gatherings where the main activity is drinking and dancing has led to difficulties. Differences have often led initially to hostility, later followed by understanding and in some cases accommodation. The celebration of holidays remains an issue since Islamic celebration days appear on very few calendars; most often, Muslims must take vacation or sick days in order to participate in the festivities. On Christian holidays, however, Muslims are forced to observe closed offices and the cessation of work.

Fasting (*sawm*) also provides some difficulty for the Muslim in America. The Islamic fast is one of abstinence from food, drink and certain behaviors from sunrise to sunset for 30 days. Alertness of mind and the ability to carry out tasks is somewhat compromised during the first few days of the fast, which can make the American work load difficult. Whether the Muslim is a student or a physician, this is indeed challenging. The other part of the tradition during this month of fasting where the believer tries to make extra prayers nightly in the *masjid* also puts a strain on the Muslim who has to be at work at 8 a.m. the next morning. Students often experience the most challenge in the public school systems where they may be questioned as to the legitimacy of this religious obligation.

Muslims fulfill the obligations of the giving of charity in several ways. *Zakat* (the formal giving of a specified amount of charity) is given to the local community for distribution to those in need at the end of the month of fasting. The more informal, day to day charitable response to misfortune or to assist in a positive venture is carried out on a person-to-person basis in and across communities.

Muslims in America have taken their diversity and in many ways have welded these cultural differences into one face of Islam. All communities are open for prayer and participation in social activities to everyone. Efforts in business and education express the variety of ethnicities and their social concerns. Muslims in America, without regard to ethnicity, remain tied to all parts of the Muslim world. Political issues emerging abroad have profound effects on Muslims in America at many levels. In many cases these communities are highlighted and sometimes maligned for political and religious differences. This is currently the fueling force for the necessity of dialogue.

The largest single contingent of Muslims in America is African American. At least 17 different communities evidence choices of Islamic philosophy and Islamic responses to American racism and theocentricity. As indigenous Americans and as ex-slaves, their move into the Islamic worldview has often been challenged as inauthentic. There remains an ongoing suspicion that these choices for Islam by up to four generations of African Americans continue to be a protest against the abuses of Christianity. While this may have been a primary impetus decades ago, it has long ceased to hold weight in current spiritual understandings and experience. African American Muslims, alongside their brothers and sisters from the Muslim world, have developed the necessary institutions and businesses for community in America.

The real need now is for greater attention to Islam in its American context. There is a critical need for awareness of the American Muslim position on American affairs as well as for dialogue on issues and concerns.

The Golden Words of a Sufi Sheikh

M. R. Bawa Muhaiyaddeen

Author of many books and pamphlets on the Sufi tradition; considered by many to have been a 20th century saint

*M*y son! This is a *hadith* of the *Rasulullah (Sal.)* about Islam:

Brothers in Islam! You who are *Iman-Islam!* You must not see differences between yourselves and your neighbors. You must not discriminate against any religion. You must not oppress or harm any man, no matter what religion or race he may be. Islam is one and Allah is one; just as we in Islam see Allah as one, we must see all mankind as one.

All the prophets brought the words of Allah, and all the words they brought are true. Allah sent His messages through each of the prophets, and they brought His commandments step by step. In the revelations contained in the Qur'an, Allah has given the entirety of His teaching. The Qur'an is the ultimate and final teaching, showing everything in its fullness.

All the children of Adam (*A.S.*) are brothers and sisters. They are not different. Although they may stand on different steps of the teachings brought by the prophets in their respective times, you must not discriminate against any of them. You must not harass their places of worship, their bodies, or their hearts. You must protect them as you would protect your own life.

To comfort the hunger of your neighbor, no matter who he is or what religion he belongs to, is Islam. When someone dies, to join together and give him a decent burial is Islam. To realize the pain and suffering of others and offer your hands in assistance, helping to alleviate their suffering, is Islam.

To see division is not Islam. To see other men as different is not Islam. In this world and the next, there must be no prejudice in our hearts, for all will come together on the Day of Reckoning and the Day of Judgement. All of us will come together in heaven. Therefore, we must not see any differences or create any divisions here. Where Allah does not see a difference, we must not see a difference. We must not despise anyone whom Allah loves – and Allah loves everyone. He belongs equally to everyone, just as Islam belongs equally to everyone. Islam is unity, not division.

Hurting another is not Islam. Failing to comfort the hunger of your neighbor is not Islam. The purity of Islam is to avoid hurting others; you must regard others as you regard yourself. You must accept Allah's word totally. There must be no discrimination in your heart against the children of Islam.

You who are Islam must understand what is *halal* and what is *haram,* what is permissible and what is forbidden. You must understand that there is only One worthy of worship. You must understand *Qiyamah*, the Day of Reckoning, and the Day of Judgment.

To understand this world and the next world is Islam. Because Islam is the wealth of grace, you must use that grace to wash and comfort the hearts of others. To truly understand this and see all lives as your own life, without any differences, is the way of Islam. To see your neighbor as yourself, to heal the suffering of others, to share food from the same plate in harmony and peace, to live unified in food and in prayer, in happiness and in sorrow, is the way of Islam. To live separated and divided is not Islam. You must reflect on this.

O you who have faith! Do not compare anything to Allah. Do not hold anything equal to Allah. Do not make distinctions between men; king and beggar must be equal in your sight. There must be no difference between rich and poor. No one is rejected by Islam. Islam is one. You must realize this.

This is what the *Rasulullah (Sal.)* has said. He has given countless *hadith* with his divine lips of grace, from the flower of his divine mouth, his mouth of faith, his mouth of Allah's grace, and his mouth of Allah's divine knowledge. O you who have received the wealth of faith! May you understand and act with the clarity of these teachings.

from *The Golden Words of a Sufi Sheikh,*by M. R. Bawa Muhaiyaddeen, (c) 1981 Fellowship Press, Philadelphia.

This book and others are available from Fellowship Press at 5820 Overbrook Avenue, Philadelphia, PA 19131; tel. (215) 879-8604

FOR MORE INFORMATION:

Since the Islamic world is so large and worldwide, it is possible to list only a fraction of its numerous associations, centers, publishers and educational institutions. North American inquirers may contact:

American Trust Publishers, Islamic Book Service
10900 W. Washington St. Indianapolis, IN 46231

Council of Masajids, 99 Woodview Dr., Old Bridge, NJ 08857

The Institute for Islamic Information and Education
P.O. Box 41129, Chicago, IL 60641-0129

International Institute of Islamic Thought
P.O. Box 669, Herndon, VA 22070

IQRA' International Educational Foundation
831 S. Laflin Ave., Chicago, IL 60607

Islamic Research Foundation for the Advancement of Knowledge,
7102 Shefford Lane, Louisville, KY 40242-6462

KAZI Publications, Inc. (Publisher and distributor of books, audio cassettes, videos and supplies on Islam and the Islamic world)
3023-27 W. Belmont Avenue, Chicago, IL 60618

"The Minaret," 434 South Vermont Avenue, Los Angeles, CA 90020

Muslim World League
1655 N. Fort Myer Dr., #700, Arlington, VA 22209

W. Deen Muhammad Publications, Inc.
P.O. Box 1944, Calumet City, IL 60409

***Periodica Islamica,* 22, Jalan Liku, 59100 Kuala Lumpur, Malaysia**

World Assembly of Muslim Youth
P.O. Box 10845, Riyadh 11443, Saudi Arabia

Jainism

A Portrait

Amar T. Salgia

Founding Member of Young Jains of America

*T*he religions of the world differ widely in their beliefs, faiths, and theories regarding good and evil, happiness and misery, and survival of death. A popular alternative to the doctrine of a kind and almighty creator who governs the universe is the theory of soulless, materialistic atheism which maintains that life and consciousness are the outcome of the activity of matter, to be dissipated upon death.

For those finding neither of these assertions satisfactory, there has been, since time immemorial, a system which neither denies the existence of the soul, nor starts with the presupposition of a creator. This system makes each individual the master of its own destiny, affirming the immortality of every soul and insisting upon the very highest rectitude of life, unto final perfection, as a necessary means to permanent happiness now and hereafter. In this modern era, it is commonly known as *Jainism.*

It is claimed of the ancient Jain spiritual teachers that they had purged themselves of the passions of anger, greed, ego and deceit, were free from all worldly attachments, and were therefore omniscient. The Jain scriptures are claimed to be the historical records of the lives and teachings of those omniscient spiritual leaders, and it is from these scriptures that the Jain doctrines are taken. These spiritual leaders lived in the flesh on earth, as human beings. They realized the true nature of worldly existence and taught the human race the path to Final Liberation.

Jainism begins with a serious concern for the human soul in its relationship with the laws governing existence in the universe, with other living beings, and to its own future state in eternity. First and foremost, it is a religion of the heart: the golden rule is *Ahimsa*, nonviolence by all faculties – mental, verbal, and physical. The whole of its structure is built upon compassion for all forms of life. Like an inner Japanese garden, with its profusion of inner worlds, restrained exuberance, and perfect orchestration, Jainism, too, emerges as a secret refuge for life, an artistic oasis; and its delicate balance spanning hope and despair does not brashly declare itself nor go in for theatrics.

Jainism offers a quiet, overwhelmingly serious way of life, a cultural insistence on compassion, a society of aesthetics that has dramatically changed the world and will continue to effect change. Jainism is a momentous example to all of us that there can exist a successful, ecologically responsible way of life which is abundantly nonviolent in thought, action, and deed. As a species, we might misread our history, go forward confusedly to perpetrate other follies, but we will do so knowing that there is a viable alternative.

Moreover, Jainism is unlike other systems of thought in that its theories of cognition, perception, and the nature of the cosmos are, to the utmost, accurate in the context of modern scientific thought and reasoning. They will bear the severest scrutiny of the intellect, and they give freedom to the individual. Jainism does not offer a deity for humanity to worship or but another means of obtaining its grace; beyond the rules of right conduct, which are based upon its understanding of reality and nature, it offers no commandments to obey or dogmas to accept unconditionally. It teaches that we – humans, animals, plants, angelics, or denizens of hell – are individually responsible to ourselves for our own condition, and for our conduct towards others. It ennobles the natural purity inherent in all souls, and allows one the freedom to perceive Truth as it truly is.

The "Jains" are, etymologically, the followers of the *Jinas.* "Jina" literally means "Conqueror." He who has conquered love and hate, pleasure and pain, attachment and aversion, and has thereby freed 'his' soul from the karmas obscuring knowledge, perception, truth, and ability, is a Jina. A Jina is omniscient and has realized the soul's innate qualities of Infinite Knowledge, Perception, Energy, and Bliss. Such a soul is also called an *Arihant* (Destroyer of Inner Enemies). The Jains refer to the Jina as God.

Time rolls along in an eternal cycle of rise and decline. An *Utsarpini* is a "rising" era in which human affairs and natural conditions improve and aggrandize over time. At the peak of the Utsarpini begins an Avasarpini, a "declining" era of the same length, in which the ultra-utopian which evolved gradually corrupts, weakens and becomes more difficult to endure. During every declining era are born twenty-four persons quite different from their contemporary societies. Upon realizing the nature of suffering, the cycle of misery, and the path to liberation from it, those twenty-four individuals renounce all ties to the world, mental and material. Those twenty-four, human like us, blaze a path to perfection. They are apostles of *Ahimsa,* born for the upliftment of all living things in the three worlds. The Jains refer to these individuals who become Jinas and teach mankind how to follow the noble path of *Enlightened Perception, Knowledge, and Conduct* the Twenty-four Crossing-Makers, or *Tirthankaras*. It is the ultimate goal of the Jain to follow in the footsteps of the Crossing-Makers by attaining freedom from the misery inherent in the material world while crossing the ocean of worldly existence.

*O*riginating on the Indian subcontinent, Jainism – or, more properly, the Jain Dharma – is one of the oldest religions of its homeland and indeed of the world. Having prehistoric origins before 3000 BCE, and before the propagation of Indo-Aryan culture, the Twenty-four Crossing-Makers guided its evolution and elaboration by first achieving, and then teaching. The first *Tirthankara* of the present declining era was Lord Rishabhanath, and the last was Lord Mahavira (599-527 BCE).

Jain religion is unique in that, during its existence of over 5,000 years, it has never compromised on the concept of nonviolence either in principle or practice. It upholds nonviolence as the supreme religion (*Ahimsa Paramo Dharmah*) and has insisted upon its observance in thought, word, and deed at the individual as well as social levels. Both in its philosophical essence as well as in its rituals, Jain religion invokes an intense and constant awareness of communion and understanding of not only all living beings but indeed all that exists. The holy text *Tattvartha Sutra* sums it up in the phrase *"Parasparopagraho Jivanam"* (all life is mutually supportive). Jain religion presents a truly enlightened perspective of *equality of souls,* irrespective of differing physical forms, ranging from human beings to animals and microscopic living organisms. Humans, alone among living beings, are endowed with all the six senses of seeing, hearing, tasting smelling, touching, and thinking; thus humans are enjoined upon to act responsibly towards all life by being compassionate, egoless, fearless, forgiving, rational, and therefore full of equanimity.

Jain religion has a clearly articulated scientific basis which elucidates the properties and qualities of animate and inanimate substances which make up the cosmos; their interrelationship is described in terms of evolution and growth of monads (like atoms), molecules, non-material continuums and souls. Jainism sets forth the existence of two fundamental categories of existing entities: *Jiva* and *Ajiva,* soul and non-soul. The non-soul "substances" are time, space, *pudgal* (the continuum of matter and energy), and the media of motion and rest. Genius lies in this cosmology. Elements of the Jain worldview, as taught for thousands of years before the Renaissance, include the atomic makeup of matter, the charged nature of elementary particles, the interconvertability of energy and matter, the conditions under which particles combine and dissociate, and dimensions of the universe comparable to those theorized by Einstein. Jiva and Ajiva are characterized as having distinct, immutable properties, but which undergo modification due to certain conditions. For the soul, those conditions are brought about as conscious and subconscious thought activity. Through the interworkings of passions and attachments, soul remains associated with non-soul, and persists in its cycle of material rise and decline, suffering and distress, delusion and wandering. Religious impulse is equated with the search for Truth, which begins with

thought activity along the lines of, "By soul alone I am governed" (*appanan anusasayi*), and, "Let karma not bind you." Dissociation from non-soul is brought about solely through the requisites of Enlightened Perception, Knowledge, and Conduct. Thus, the soul is no longer under the influence of that which it is not, and for the rest of eternity enjoys its natural attributes of Infinite Knowledge, Perception, Energy, and Bliss; thus the underlying theory translates directly into practice.

In short, the code of conduct is made up of the following five vows, and all of their logical conclusions: *Ahimsa, Satya* (truthfulness), *Asteya* (non-stealing), *Aparigraha* (non-possessiveness), and *Brahmacharya* (chastity). Jain religion focuses much attention on *Aparigraha,* non-possessiveness towards material things through self-control, self-imposed penance, abstinence from over-indulgence, voluntary curtailment of one's needs, and the consequent subsiding of the aggressive urge. The code of conduct prescribed for the Jain monastic order, made up of monks and nuns, is more rigorous than that prescribed for the laity.

Vegetarianism is a way of life for a Jain, taking its origin in the concept of compassion for living beings, *Jiva Daya.* The practice of vegetarianism is regarded as a potent instrument for the practice of nonviolence and peaceful, cooperative coexistence. Jains are strict vegetarians, consuming only one-sensed beings, primarily from the plant kingdom. While the Jain diet does, of course, involve harm to plants and microorganisms, it is regarded as a means of survival which involves the bare minimum amount of violence towards living beings. (Many forms of plant material, including roots and certain fruits, are also excluded from the Jain diet due to the greater number of living beings they contain owing to the environment in which they develop.)

Anekantavada, the doctrine of the multifaceted nature of Truth, is another basic principle of Jainism which offers systematic, logical, and nondogmatic algorithms for understanding the multifarious aspects of the truth behind

---

Ahimsa Parmo Dharma
Nonviolence is the Supreme Religion

*K*now other creatures' love for life, for they are like you.
Kill them not; save their life from fear and enmity.
All creatures desire to live, not to die.
Hence to kill is to sin.
A godly man does not kill.
Therefore, kill not yourself, consciously or
unconsciously, living organisms which move
or move not, nor cause slaughter of them.
He who looketh on the creatures of the earth, big and
small, as his own self, comprehendeth this immense
world.
Among the careless, he who restraineth self
is enlightened.

LORD MAHAVIRA

statements, human perceptions, knowledge, and the nature of the Self. As a very simple example, just as a father may also have the role of a husband, a brother, a boss, or a cousin to different persons, life cannot be understood if taken from one perspective that prejudices the individual against all others. Indeed, it is a doctrine rooted in *Ahimsa*.

Jainism has not only shown a spiritual way of life to its followers, but has inspired a distinct stream of culture which has enriched philosophy, literature, art, architecture, democratic living, and spiritual advancement in the land of India. Classical Jain literature is found in the Sanskrit, Prakrit, Hindi, Marathi, Gujarati, Kannada, and Tamil languages, and in varied forms of poetry, prose, drama, and story. Its influence has also been traced to other lands like Greece and Israel. In addition to compounding philosophical and spiritual treatises, the Jain ascetic-scholars were champions of secular learning in areas including astronomy, music theory, political science, linguistics and mathematics. The artistry and architecture of Jain temples all over the Indian subcontinent depict the magnificence of detachment, serenity, and the natural purity of the soul.

The followers of Jainism number around ten million. Jain societies are neither caste-ridden nor male-dominated.

Jainism is an eternal philosophy, whose benefits can be taken up by anyone willing to improve his or her life and rational conduct in situations of both stress and tranquility. Today, more than ever, when suspicion and distrust are vitiating the atmosphere of international peace, when the world is filled with fear and hate, we require a living philosophy which will help us discard those destructive qualities and recover ourselves. Such a living, wholesome philosophy, bearing a message of love and goodwill, *Ahimsa* and peace, personally as well as universally, is the Jain philosophy of life. This system of religion, thought and living stands for the highest and noblest human values, and offers a path guaranteeing eternal peace and happiness.

NOTES

Portions of this article have been adapted from Dr. N.P. Jain's article "A Portrait of Jainism."

BIBLIOGRAPHY

Jain, Jyoti Prasad, *Religion and Culture of the Jains*. Bharatiya Jnanpith, New Delhi: 1983.

Jaini, Padmanabh, *The Jain Path of Purification*. University of California Press, Berkeley, CA: 1979.

Tobias, Michael, *Life Force: The World of Jainism*. Asian Humanities Press, Berkeley, CA: 1991.

Warren, Herbert, *Jainism*. Shree Vallabhsuri Smarak Nidhi, Bombay: 1913.

Jain Prayers and Songs

1. May my thoughts and feeling be such that I may always act in a simple and straightforward manner.
May I ever, so far as I can, do good in this life to others.

2. May I never hurt and harm any living being; may I never speak a lie. May I never be greedy of wealth or the wife [spouse] of another. May I ever drink the nectar of contentment!

3. May I always have a friendly feeling towards all living beings of the world and may the stream of compassion always flow from my heart towards distressed and afflicted living beings.

4. May I never entertain an idea of egotism; nor may I be angry with anybody! May I never become jealous on seeing the worldly prosperity of other people.

5. May I never become fretful towards bad, cruel and wicked persons. May I keep tolerance towards them. May I be so disposed!

6. May I ever have the good company of learned ascetics and may I ever keep them in mind. May my heart be always engrossed and inclined to adopt the rules of conduct which they observe.

7. May my heart be overflowing with love at the sight of the virtuous, and may I be happy to serve them so far as possible.

8. May I never be ungrateful (towards anybody); nor may I revolt (against anybody). May I ever be appreciating the good qualities of other persons and may I never look at their faults.

9. May my mind neither be puffed up with joy, nor may it become nervous in pain and grief. May it never be frightened even if I am in a terrible forest or strange places of cremation or graveyards.

10. May my mind remain always steady and firm, unswerving and unshaken; may it become stronger every day. May I bear and endure with patience the deprivation of dear ones and occurrences of undesired evils.

11. May all living beings of the world be happy!
May nobody ever feel distressed! May the people of the world renounce enmity, sin, pride and sing the songs of joy every day.

12. May *Dharma* (truth) be the topic of house-talk in every home! May evil be scarce! May (people) increase their knowledge and conduct and thereby enjoy the blessed fruit of human birth.

13. May disease and pestilence never spread, may the people live in peace, may the highest religion of *Ahimsa* (non-injury) pervade the whole world and may it bring about universal good!

14. May universal love pervade the world and may ignorance of attachment remain far away. May nobody speak unkind, bitter, and harsh words!

15. May all become "heroes of the age" heartily and remain engaged in elevating the Cause of Righteousness. May all gain the sight of Truth called *Vastuswarupa* (Reality of substance) and may they bear, with pleasure, trouble and misfortunes!

AMEN

Nomokar Maha Mantra (The Universal Prayer)

Obeisance to the Arihantas – perfect souls – Godmen

I bow down to those who have reached omniscience in the flesh and teach the road to everlasting life in the liberated state.

Obeisance to the Siddhas – liberated bodiless souls

I bow down to those who have attained perfect knowledge and liberated their souls of all *karma*.

Obeisance to the masters – heads of congregations

I bow down to those who have experienced self-realization of their souls through self-control and self-sacrifice.

Obeisance to the teachers – ascetic teachers

I bow down to those who understand the true nature of soul and teach the importance of the spiritual over the material.

Obeisance to all the ascetic aspirants in the universe

I bow down to those who strictly follow the five great vows of conduct and inspire us to live a virtuous life.

This five-fold obeisance mantra

To these five types of great souls I offer my praise.

Destroys all demerit

Such praise will help diminish my sins.

And is the first and foremost of all

Giving this praise is most auspicious—

Auspicious recitations

So auspicious as to bring happiness and bliss.

From the Acharanga Sutra (1:4:1)

The Arhats and Bhagavats of the past, present and future all say thus, speak thus, declare thus, explain thus:

All breathing, existing, living, sentient creatures should not be slain, nor treated with violence, nor abused nor tormented, nor driven away.

This is the pure, unchangeable, eternal law, which the clever ones, who understand the world, have declared: among the zealous and the not zealous, among the faithful and the not faithful, among the not cruel and the cruel, among those who have worldly weakness and those who have not, among those who like social bonds and those who do not: 'that is the truth, that is so, that is proclaimed in this (creed).'

Prayer

Highly auspicious are the adorable ones
And so are the emancipated;
The saints too are the auspicious ones
And so is the speech divine.

Best in the world are the adorable ones
And so are the emancipated;
The saints too are the best in the world,
And so is the speech divine.

Refuge do I take in the adorable ones.
And also in the emancipated;
Saints are also the place of my refuge.
And so is the speech divine.

Thus do I pay homage and veneration
Unto the great Arihants every day
In devotion deep with the purity in mind,
In speech and in deed indeed.

The Immortal Song

1. May the sacred stream of amity flow forever in my heart. May the universe prosper – such is my cherished desire.

2. May my heart sing with ecstasy at the sight of the virtuous, and may my life be an offering at their feet.

3. May my heart bleed at the sight of the wretched, the cruel, the irreligious, and my tears of compassion flow from my eyes.

4. May I always be there to show the path to the pathless wanderers of life.
Yet if they should not hearken to me, may I bide in patience.

5. May the spirit of goodwill enter all our hearts.
May we all sing in chorus the immortal song of human concord.

Fight Against Desires

O man! Control thyself. Only then can you get salvation.
If you are to fight, fight against your own desires.
Nothing will be achieved by fighting against external enemies; if you miss this occasion, it will be lost forever.
One's own unconquered soul is one's greatest enemy.

The above prayers and songs are from
Jainism – Past and Present: Prayers, Articles and Short Stories,
published by Dr. Tansukh J. Salgia (1984, Parma, Ohio).
Available from the Brahmi Jain Society (see below).

FOR MORE INFORMATION:

Ahimsa Environment Award: Pankaj Shah
14 Dovedale Avenue, Kenton, Harrow, Middlesex HA3 ODX, U.K.

Brahmi Jain Society, 1884 Dorsetshire Rd, Columbus, OH 43229
USA; tel./fax. (614) 899-2678

Declaration on Nature (for the full document, contact):
Bhagwan Mahavir Memorial Samiti, 3 Benito Juarez Road,
New Delhi 110 021, India (or)

Federation of Jain Associations in North America (JAINA)
11820 Triple Crown Rd., Reston, VA 22091 USA

Institute of Jainology, 31 Lancaster Gate, London, W2 3LP, U.K.

International Mahavir Jain Mission (NGO)
65 Mud Pond Road, Blairstown, NJ 07825; tel. (908) 362- 9793

Jain Association Int'l., Brandweg 5 2091, Gartedt, Germany

Jain Bulletin Board Service (With a modem, dial: 919-469-0207; for
information *see Chapter 44 or call Pravin Shah, at 919-469-0956*)
Jain Study Center of North Carolina,
401 Farmstead Dr., Cary NC 27511

Jain International, 21 Saumya Apt., Ahmedabad 380 014 India
tel. 0272-465 129 / fax. 0272-445 945

Jain Meditation International Center (books, audio and video tapes)
Box 244 Ansonia Station, New York, NY 10023-0244
tel. (212) 362-6483

Jain Sangh of Kobe, 6-17 Yamamoto Dori, 1-Chome, Chico-ku,
Kobe 650, Japan

Jain Society of Sydney, 38 Ourimbah Road, Mosman, Sydney, NSW
2080, Australia

Judaism

THE WORTH OF WISDOM

*"With what shall I come before the LORD
And bow myself before God most high?
Shall I come before him with burnt-
    offerings, with calves a year old?
Will the LORD
be pleased with thousands of rams,
With myriads of streams of oil?
Shall I give my first born for my
    transgression,
The fruit of my body for the sin
of my soul?
You have been told, O man,
what is good,
And what the LORD requires of you:
    Only to do justice,
    and to love mercy,
    And to walk humbly with your God."*
                        MICAH 6:6–8

*"God shall judge between many peoples,
and shall decide for strong nations afar
off; and they shall beat their swords into
    plowshares,
and their spears into pruning hooks;
nation shall not lift up sword
against nation,
neither shall they learn war any more;
but they shall sit every man under his
    vine and under his fig tree,
and none shall make them afraid."*
                        MICAH 4:3–4

*"How happy is the one who finds
    wisdom,
The one who gains understanding!
For wisdom's income is better than
income of silver,
And her revenue than gold.
She is more precious than corals,
And none of your heart's desires can
    compare with her.*

WISDOM continues on following pages

A Portrait

Rabbi Herbert Bronstein

*Senior Rabbi, North Shore Congregation Israel, Glencoe, Illinois; member of the
Board of Trustees of the Council for a Parliament of the World's Religions*

"Hear O Israel,
the Lord Our God, the Lord is One."
And you shall love the Lord, your God,
with all your heart, with all your might, with all your soul.
And these words which I command you this day,
shall be upon your heart that you may remember,
do all my commandments
and be holy unto your God.

DEUTERONOMY (*D'Varim*) 6.4–9

*T*hough often spoken of as a "Western" religion and linked with Christianity (as in "Judeo-Christian tradition"), Judaism has its origins in the Middle East.

Judaism is a spirituality which indeed gave birth to Christianity, and later played a role during the emergence of Islam. But Judaism as we know it began almost 4,000 years ago among a pastoral/nomadic and later agricultural people, the ancient Hebrews.

The religion of the people Israel was and is the loving and faithful Covenant devotion to one God who revealed Divine Teaching through the mothers and fathers of the people of Israel (the Patriarchs and Matriarchs), through Moses and the Prophets and Sages whose spirituality is documented in the 22 books of the Hebrew Bible.

The goal of this Covenant consciousness in alliance with the Divine is clearly put in the ancient texts as:

A good life for all, through adherence to God's Teaching (*Torah*) and Commandments (*Mitzvot*), harmony on earth on the individual and social levels culminating in peace and well-being for all humanity.

Thus Judaism is characterized as a religion of deed, a "Way" by which human beings are capable of understanding and responding to God's teaching.

Because over the centuries every major power that entered the Middle East (namely Egypt, Assyria, Babylonia, Persia, Greece and Rome) coveted the land of Israel (a strategic joining point of Africa, Asia and Europe), the religion of Israel changed, not in central principles or institution, but in form, in response to the demands of changing conditions, including oppression and exile.

After the Roman destruction of the central Temple in Jerusalem and the end of Jewish independent existence in the Holy Land, Judaism was separated from the sacrificial cult, the priesthood disappeared, and Judaism became a religion of congregations all over the world in which worship, deeds of loving kindness, and the study of God's teaching replaced the central cult of the Temple in Jerusalem. Nevertheless, Jerusalem remained a central spiritual symbol of Jewry throughout the world linked with the vision of redemption of the Jewish people from exile and oppression, and peace for all the world (the Messianic vision).

In Judaism as it developed, prayer services emerged which recapitulated the main stories and themes of Judaism, from the universal *Creation* by the Universal God to the *Revelation* of God's Teaching to Moses and the people at Mount Sinai to the *Redemption* of Israel and all humanity. It is a way of life in which all Jews are equally responsible as "a Kingdom of Priests and a Holy People."

Over the centuries a vast body of teaching and lore has grown up, often taking the form of exegesis or interpretation of the ancient Biblical texts. This has included the elaboration of actual religious practice (the *Halacha* or "Way") and philosophical texts, stories, homilies, parable, and poetry (the *Aggadah*). The vast rabbinic text known as the *Talmud* (again, "Teaching"), is second only to the Bible in importance. There is also a continual mystical stream in Judaism embodied in the various texts known collectively as *Kabbalah* (the "received" tradition) such as the *Zohar* (the *Book of Splendor or Illumination*), which teach the emanation of the Godhead into the world, the experience of communion with God in transcendence of the self, and the maintenance of the cosmos through human action in Covenant with God. Again the basic mythos or narrative embodied in Judaic consciousness is *from* the universal God, Creator of all of existence *through* particular Jewish Covenant existence *to* the universal redemption of all Beings and all Being from bondage.

The basic symbol of Judaism is thus a seven-branched candelabrum which embodies cosmic images of all Time and Space. It is also a symbol of the Redemption which is the goal of human existence. This symbol is reducible to Light, which is expressed many times in Jewish observance: the kindling of the Sabbath and Festival lights in the home; the braided candle at the end of the Sabbath; the kindling of lights in the eight-day midwinter Festival of Lights (*Chanukah*), which commemorates the rededication of the holy Temple from pollution and therefore of the sacred from profanity; the memorial lights to remember the dead; and the Eternal Light over the Ark in the synagogue which contains the *Scroll of the Torah*.

Jews celebrate the recreation of the moral order of the world and the rebirth of the soul at the beginning of the religious year (*Rosh Hashanah* and the Day of Atonement, *Yom Kippur*) a ten day period of spiritual introspection and moral resolve. The home celebration or service which relives in story and song, ritual and prayer, the Exodus from Egypt at the Passover (*Pesach*) season is called a *Seder* celebration. Its themes reenergize Jewish social consciousness, Jewish hope and vision of a better day for all.

*J*ews are not divided into creedal denominations, strictly speaking, in the same manner as Christianity. There are "streams" of Jewish religious life which express varying responses to the encounter of Jews with the modern world. The most liberal of these is usually designated as **"Reform"** or **"Liberal"** Judaism, which has responded by adapting to more Western styles of worship. "Reform" leans toward the vernacular in worship and has modified considerably the forms of observance passed down by tradition.

Orthodox Judaism conceives of the entire corpus of Jewish observance, the received tradition, as equivalent to having been given by God at Sinai and therefore unchangeable except through procedures which were themselves given at Sinai.

Conservative Judaism finds its way between these two positions.

Reconstructionism is the most recent stream to emerge in modern Jewish life. It conceives of Jewish religious forms and observances as part of an historic Jewish culture or "civilization." Reconstructionism values this culture, linking its preservation with a naturalist theology. Reconstructionism has recently been hospitable to neo-mystical themes and observances.

However, this does not begin to describe the considerable varieties of Jewish religious life in all of its dimensions and degrees in our time. The

Long life is in her right hand,
In her left are riches and honor....
The LORD *by wisdom founded the*
earth,
By reason he established the heavens;
By his knowledge the depths are
broken up,
And the clouds drop down dew."
　　　THE BOOK OF PROVERBS

"The highest wisdom is kindness."
　　　BERAKOT, 17a

"Deeds of kindness are equal in weight
to all the commandments."
　　　T. J. PE'AH, 1:1

"'Thou shalt love thy neighbor as
thyself.' This is the great general rule
in Torah.*"*　　　T. J. NEDARIM, 9:4

"The beginning and the end thereof
[Torah] is the performance of
loving-kindness."　　　SOTAH, 14a

"If two men claim thy help, and one is
thy enemy, help him first."
　　　BABA METZIA, 32b,

"If the community is in trouble, a man
must not say, 'I will go to my house,
and eat and drink, and peace shall be
with thee, O my soul.' But a man must
share in the trouble of the community,
even as Moses did. He who shares in
its troubles is worthy to see its
consolation."　　　TA'ANIT, 11a

"The command to give charity weighs
as much as all the other
commandments put together.... He who
gives alms in secret is greater than
Moses."　　　BABA BATHRA, 9b

number of Jews is in the world is estimated at 12,807,000; the number of Jews in North American is estimated at 5,880,000.

Judaism and interfaith dialogue

*T*here is a profound religious and historic basis to the Jewish view on interfaith dialogue.

Jewish belief encompasses a dialectic between an all-embracing humane Universalism and deep commitment to a particular Jewish religious way of life and to the continuity of the Jewish people as a religious people. Between the two – namely, universal humane concern and Jewish particularism – there is, in the Judaic world view, no contradiction. And, in fact, the ideal Jewish position is integration of the two. On the one hand, the ideal Jew is deeply loyal to his own faith, way of life, and people. There is, at the same time, a firm commitment in Judaism to God's universal embrace, care, and love for all humanity, the ideal of loving one's fellow human being as oneself. The *Torah* teaches that all humanity is created in the image of God. In the Jewish myth of creation, one couple, Adam and Eve, are the parents of all humanity. In this view God speaks to all human beings and all human communities in various ways. All perceive the one God in their own way and take different paths to the service of the ultimate Godhead. Dialogue would therefore be an endeavor to understand, on the deepest level possible, the views and positions of the Other toward the goal of ultimate harmony between all human beings, which is the Judaic affirmation of the Sovereignty of God, harmony, peace, *Shalom*.

But over the centuries Jews, as a minority in the Christian world, were subject to persecution, degradation, impoverishment, rioting, and even mass death for their loyalty to their faith. "Interfaith" contact was all too often a staged disputation to prove the falsity of Jewish faith and a prelude to the burning of Jewish holy books, physical attacks, and even murder of Jews, sometimes in massive numbers. Jews often confronted the choice between conversion and martyrdom. Therefore, many Jews of traditional leaning, while willing and eager to work on ameliorative civil projects with all other groups, are leery of any theological dialogue that would tend to undermine the faith commitment of Jews as a minority community. However, throughout the modern period, but most particularly in the twentieth century and particularly in pluralistic North America, Jews have been partners in Christian/Jewish dialogue as well as with Muslims and Buddhists.

Today Jews join in that trend of dialogue which is moving toward an attempt to understand the *faith of the believer* rather than simply studying simplistically about the beliefs of other faiths.

"In that hour when the Egyptians died in the Red Sea, the ministers wished to sing the song of praise before the Holy One, but he rebuked them saying: 'My handiwork is drowning in the sea; would you utter a song before me in honor of that?' " SANHEDRIN, 98b

"In a city where there are both Jews and Gentiles, the collectors of alms collect both from Jews and Gentiles, and feed the poor of both, visit the sick of both, bury both, comfort the mourners whether they be Jews or Gentiles, and restore the lost goods of both." T. J. DEMAI, 6:6

"One man alone was brought forth at the time of Creation in order that thereafter none should have the right to say to another, 'My father was greater than your father.' " T. Y. SANHEDRIN, 4:5

"You must not pervert the justice due the resident alien or the orphan, nor take a widow's garment in pledge. You must remember that you were once a slave yourself in Egypt, and the LORD your God rescued you from there; that is why I am commanding you to do this.

When you reap your harvest in your field, and forget a sheaf in the field, you must not go back to get it; it is to go to the resident alien, the orphan and the widow, that the LORD your God may bless you in all your enterprises. When you beat your olive trees, you must not go over them a second time; that is to go to the resident alien, the orphan and the widow. When you pick the grapes of your vineyard, you must not go over it a second time; that is to go to the resident alien, the orphan and the widow. You must remember that you were once a slave yourself in the land of Egypt; that is why I am commanding you to do this." LEVITICUS 24:6–22

"When the Holy One created the first human beings, God led them around the Garden of Eden and said,
   'Look at My works.
   See how beautiful they are, how excellent!
   For your sake I created them all.
   See to it that you do not spoil or destroy My world –
   for if you do, there will be no one to repair it after you.' "
MIDRASH ECCLESIASTES RABBAH 7:13

PART ONE: WHO ARE WE?

On the Urgency of a Jewish Response to the Environmental Crisis

Issued by the Consultation on the Environment and Jewish Life, Washington, DC

March 10, 1992

*W*e, American Jews of every denomination, from diverse organizations and differing political perspectives, are united in deep concern that the quality of human life and the earth we inhabit are in danger, afflicted by rapidly increasing ecological threats. Among the most pressing of these threats are: depletion of the ozone layer, global warming, massive deforestation, the extinction of species and loss of biodiversity, poisonous deposits of toxic chemical and nuclear wastes, and exponential population growth. We here affirm our responsibility to address this planetary crisis in our personal and communal lives.

For Jews, the environmental crisis is a religious challenge. As heirs to a tradition of stewardship that goes back to Genesis and that teaches us to be partners in the ongoing work of Creation, we cannot accept the escalating destruction of our environment and its effect on human health and livelihood. Where we are despoiling our air, land and water, it is our sacred duty as Jews to acknowledge our God-given responsibility and take action to alleviate environmental degradation and the pain and suffering that it causes. We must reaffirm and bequeath the tradition we have inherited which calls upon us to safeguard humanity's home.

We have convened this unprecedented consultation in Washington, DC, to inaugurate a unified Jewish response to the environmental crisis. We pledge to carry to our homes, communities, congregations, organizations, and workplaces the urgent message that air, land, water, and living creatures are endangered. We will draw our people's attention to the timeless texts that speak to us of God's gifts and expectations. This Consultation represents a major step towards:

- mobilizing our community toward energy efficiency, the reduction and recycling of wastes, and other practices which promote environmental sustainability;

- initiating environmental education programs in settings where Jews gather to learn, particularly among young people;

- pressing for appropriate environmental legislation at every level of government and in international forums;

- convening business and labor leaders to explore specific opportunities for exercising environmental leadership;

- working closely in these endeavors with scientists, educators, representatives of environmental groups, Israelis and leaders from other religious communities.

*O*ur agenda is already overflowing. Israel's safety, the resettlement of Soviet Jewry, anti-semitism, the welfare of our people in many nations, the continuing problems of poverty, unemployment, hunger, health care, and education, as well as assimilation and intermarriage— all these and more have engaged us and engage us still.

But the ecological crisis hovers over all Jewish concerns, for the threat is global, advancing, and ultimately jeopardizes ecological balance and the quality of life. It is imperative, then, that environmental issues also become an immediate, ongoing, and pressing concern for our community.

FOR MORE INFORMATION:

Central Conference of American Rabbis
192 Lexington Ave., New York, NY 10016

Coalition of the Environment and Jewish Life
443 Park Avenue South, 11th Floor, New York, NY 10016-7322
tel. (212) 684-6950 (Especially see the Coalition's excellent *To Till and to Tend: A Guide to Jewish Environmental Study and Action,* published 1994 in conjunction with the National Religious Partnership on the Environment. In addition to articles and analysis for study, worship, and action, the book also lists resources both within and outside of the Jewish community.)

Council of Jewish Federations
1640 Rhode Island Ave., NW, Washington, DC 20002

Rabbinical Council of America
275 7th Ave., 15th Fl., New York, NY 10001

Religious Action Center of Reform Judaism (RAC)
2027 Massachusetts Ave., NW, Washington, DC 20036

Shalom Center, Dr. Arthur Waskow, 7316 Germantown Ave, Philadelphia, PA 19119-1790

Shomrei-Adamah/Keepers of the Earth, Ellen Bernstein, Exec. Dir., 5500 Wissahickon #804, Philadelphia, PA 19144

United Synagogues of Conservative Judaism
Sarae Crane, 155 Fifth Avenue, New York, NY 10010

"But ask the beasts, and they will teach you;
the birds of the sky, and they will tell you;
or speak to the earth and it will teach you;
the fish of the sea, they will inform you.
Who among all these does not know
that the hand of the Eternal has done this?"

JOB 12:7-9

Shinto

A Portrait

Naofusa Hirai

Professor at Kokugakuin University, Tokyo (Emeritus); assistance was graciously provided by Professor H. Byron Earhart of Western Michigan University

*"Then she commanded her August Grandchild, saying:
"This Reed-Plain-1500-autumns-fair-rice-ear Land is the region which my descendants shall be lords of.
Do thou, my August Grandchild, proceed thither and govern it.
Go! and may prosperity attend thy dynasty, and may it, like Heaven and Earth, endure for ever."*

from *The Divine Edict of Amaterasu Omikami to Her Grandson*, described in Japanese myth, when he descended from the Plain-of-High-Heaven to Japan with many deities. (Transl. by W. G. Aston, *Nihongi*, London, George Allen & Unwin, reprinted 1956, p.77)

This myth, blessing the eternality of the imperial line, is today interpreted by Shinto believers as a myth blessing the eternality of all humans including the Japanese people who have the imperial line as their center. Within Shinto we believe in the endless advance of descendants within this world, and we must work hard in order to realize this.

About Shinto

Shinto is the indigenous, national religion of Japan. It is more vividly observed in the social life of the people, or in personal motivations, than as a firmly established theology or philosophy; yet it has been closely connected with the value system and ways of thinking and acting of the Japanese people.

Modern Shinto can be roughly classified into three types: Shrine Shinto, Sectarian Shinto and Folk Shinto.

Shrine Shinto has been in existence from the prehistoric ages to the present and constitutes a main current of Shinto tradition. Until the end of 1945, it included State Shinto within its structure and even now has close relations with the emperor system.

Sectarian Shinto is a relatively new movement based on the Japanese religious tradition, and is represented by the 13 major sects which originated in Japan around the 19th century. Each of the 13 sects has either a founder or a systematizer who organized the religious body. New Shinto sects which appeared in Japan after World War II are conveniently included in this type.

Folk Shinto is an aspect of Japanese folk belief which is closely related to Shinto. It has neither a firmly organized religious body nor any doctrinal formulas, and includes small roadside images, agricultural rites of individual families, and so on. These three types of Shinto are interrelated: Folk Shinto exists as the substructure of Shinto faith, and a Sectarian Shinto follower is usually a parishioner of a certain shrine of Shrine Shinto at the same time.

The majority of Japanese people are simultaneously believers of both Shrine Shinto and Buddhism. The number of Sectarian Shintoists is about ten million. In North America, Shinto exists mainly among some people of Japanese descent.

The center of Japanese myths consists of tales about Amaterasu Omikami (usually translated as "Sun Goddess"), the ancestress of the Imperial Family, and tales of how her direct descendants unified the nation under her authority. At the beginning of Japanese mythology, a divine couple named Izanagi and Izanami, the parents of Amaterasu, gave birth to the Japanese islands as well as to the deities who became ancestors of various clans. Here we can see an ancient Japanese inclination to regard the nature around us as offspring from the same parents. This view of nature requires us to reflect on our conduct toward the pollution of the earth.

The same myth also tells us that if we trace our lineage to its roots, we find ourselves as descendants of *kami* (deities). In Shinto, it is common to say that "man is *kami's* child." This means that, as we see in the above mentioned myth, man has life given through *kami* and therefore his nature is sacred. Reinterpreting this myth more broadly in terms of our contemporary contacts with people of the world, we must revere the life and basic human rights of everyone, regardless of race, nationality, and creed, the same as our own.

At the core of Shinto are beliefs in the mysterious power of *kami* (*musuhi* – creating and harmonizing power) and in the way or will of *kami* (*makoto* –sincerity or true heart). Parishioners of a Shinto shrine believe in their tutelary *kami* as the source of human life and existence. Each *kami* is believed to have a divine personality and to respond to sincere prayers. Historically, the ancient tutelary *kami* of each local community played an important role in combining and harmonizing different elements and powers. After the Meiji Restoration (1868), Shinto was used as a means of spiritually unifying the people during the period of repeated wars. Since the end of World War II, the age-old desire for peace has been reemphasized.

Shinto in the world today

Since the Industrial Revolution, advanced countries including Japan have undergone rapid modernization in pursuit of material comforts and convenience. Unfortunately, these efforts have resulted in producing well-known critical global issues. To cope with such issues, Shinto leaders have begun to be aware of the necessity of international cooperation and mutual aid with other peoples. In this connection, there are several challenges facing Shinto.

1. Accumulation of experience in international life, which even today is not common in Japan.

2. Acquisition of new ethical standards to join a new spiritual and cultural world community, e.g. transforming the "in-group consciousness" which is one of the characteristics of the Japanese people. Today we need to care not only for the people within our own limited group, but also for unknown people outside our own group.

3. Changing the patterns of expression for international communication. As a cultural trait, Japanese people tend to express matters symbolically rather than logically. These efforts sometimes result in misunderstanding by others.

4. Cultivation of capable Shinto leaders equipped with a good command of foreign languages and cultures.

In spite of these difficulties, Shinto has the following merits for working positively with interfaith dialogue and cooperation.

1. Shinto's notion of *kami* emphasizes belief in many deities, and its doctrine does not reject other religions, so it is natural for Shinto to pay respect to other religions and objects of worship.

2. Within Shinto, it is thought that nature is the place where *kami* dwell, and we give thanks for the blessings of nature. This attitude toward nature may be of use to religious people considering environmental problems.

3. Within Japan, there is a tradition of carefully preserving and cultivating religions which originate in other countries. Within its boundaries, various religions have practiced cooperation and harmonious coexistence.

However, the emphasis of these three points is not suggesting that, at the present time, Shinto seeks a simple syncretism. Shinto leaders, while intent on the peaceful coexistence of all people, wish to preserve Shinto's distinctive features and strengthen its religious depths.

About 20 years ago, Shinto leaders, together with people of other religions, initiated various activities for the purpose of international religious dialogue and cooperation. Since the first assembly of The World Conference on Religion and Peace was opened in Kyoto in 1970, important figures within the Shinto world have participated both in Japan and abroad in the meetings of WCRP, IARF and others. Jinja Honcho, the Association of Shinto Shrines which includes about 99 percent of Shinto shrines, initiated in 1991 an International Department for the purpose of international exchange and cooperation.

One noteworthy movement in Japan is the "offer a meal movement." Supporters of this movement give up one meal (usually breakfast) at least once each month, and donate the equivalent expense through their religious organization. This money is used by the organization for international relief and other activities. This movement was begun in 1970s by the new religion Shoroku-Shinto-Yamatoyama; believers of Misogikyo (Sectarian Shinto) and Izumo Taisha (Shrine Shinto) have been doing the same for several years. Among Buddhists, Rissho Kosei-kai has actively advanced the same movement. While it is not easy to continue this practice, the participants have said "At first we thought this was for the sake of others, but actually we noticed this is the way to strengthen our own faith."

The following declaration was presented at the tenth anniversary of the founding of the Association of Shinto Shrines, and since that time has been recited at the beginning of many meetings of Shrine Shinto.

1) Let us be grateful for *kami's* grace
and ancestors' benevolence,
and with bright and pure *makoto* (sincerity or true heart)
perform religious services.

2) Let us work for people and the world,
and serve as representatives of the *kami*
to make the society firm and sound.

3) In accordance with the Emperor's will,
let us be harmonious and peaceful,
and pray for the nation's development
as well as the world's coexistence
and co-prosperity.

from *The General Principles of Shinto Life,*
proclaimed in 1956 by the Association of Shinto Shrines
(Transl. by Naofusa Hirai from the original declaration)

Sikhism

A Portrait

Dr. Rajwant Singh and Ms. Georgia Rangel

Dr. R. Singh is Secretary, The Guru Gobind Singh Foundation, Maryland, and a member of the Board of Directors of North American Interfaith Network; Georgia Rangel is a member of the Guru Gobind Singh Foundation.

*F*ounded only 500 years ago by Guru Nanak (1439–1539), Sikhism is one of the youngest world religions. After a revelatory experience at the age of about 38, Nanak began to teach that true religion consisted of being ever-mindful of God, meditating on God's Name, and reflecting it in all activities of daily life. He condemned superstition and discouraged ritual. He traveled throughout India, Ceylon, Tibet, and parts of the Arab world with followers of both Hindu and Muslim origin, discussing his revelation with those he met. His followers became known as Sikhs (from the Sanskrit word *shishya* – disciple.

Nanak and his nine successors are known as *gurus,* which is a very common term in all Indian traditions for a spiritual guide or teacher. In Sikhism, *"Guru"* means the voice of God speaking through someone. Sikh *gurus* were careful to prevent worship being offered to them. The last living *guru,* Guru Gobind Singh, who died in 1708, pronounced the end of the line of succession and declared that henceforth the function of the *guru* as teacher and final authority for faith and conduct was vested in the community and the Scriptures, the *Guru Granth Sahib.* It occupies the same place in Sikh veneration that was given to the living *gurus.*

The *Guru Granth Sahib* is at the heart of Sikh worship, and its presence lends sanctity to the Sikh place of worship, the *gurdwara.* This holy book contains devotional compositions written by the Sikh *gurus,* recorded during their lifetimes. It also contains hymns by Hindu and Muslim religious thinkers. Written in Sanskrit, Persian, Hindi, and Punjabi, the compositions are set in rhymed couplets. The *Guru Granth Sahib* is printed in *Gurmukhi* script, an alphabet adapted by the second *guru,* Guru Angad, for the Punjabi language. It has standardized pagination, all copies having 1,430 pages. The *Rehat Maryada* (Sikh Code of Conduct) published in 1945 by the SGPC of Amritsar, Punjab, India, regulates individual and corporate Sikh life.

Beliefs

*T*he seminal belief in Sikhism is found in the *Mool Mantra* with which the *Guru Granth Sahib* begins:

"There is One God.
  He

> Is the Supreme Truth
> Is without fear
> Is not vindictive
> Is Timeless, Eternal
> Is not born, so
> He does not die to be reborn.
> Self-illumined,
> By Guru's grace
> He is revealed to the human soul.

Truth was in the beginning,
and throughout the ages.
Truth is now and ever will be."

In Sikhism, time is cyclical, not linear, so Sikhism has no eschatological beliefs. Rather, just as time is seen as repeated sequences of creation and destruction, individual existence is believed to be a repeated sequence of birth, death, and rebirth as the soul seeks spiritual enlightenment.

Sikhs believe that greed, lust, pride, anger, and attachment to the passing values of earthly existence constitute *haumai* (self-centeredness). This is the source of all evil. It is a person's inclination to evil that produces the *karma* that leads to endless rebirth. *Haumai* separates human beings from God.

God is All-Pervading and is the Source of all life. Sikhism believes that human life is the opportunity for spiritual union with the Supreme Being – to merge with the Ultimate Reality as a drop of water merges with the ocean and becomes one with it. Thus is one released from the cycle of death and rebirth. By God's Grace, not by one's own merits, is achieved the level of spiritual self-knowledge necessary to reach this stage of enlightenment. Any person, of whatever intellectual or economic level, may become enlightened through a life of single-minded devotion to God. Enlightenment, not redemption, is the Sikh concept of salvation.

Life cycle events are recognized in Sikhism by naming of the newborn in the *gurdwar,* the marriage ceremony, and the funeral, following which the body is cremated. Any kind of funeral monument is forbidden.

Sikhism rejects asceticism and encourages full participation in family and workday life and responsibility as the framework within which to seek God. Sikhism is founded on the principle of equality of all persons. It rejects the caste system, and inculcates in its adherents an egalitarian attitude and practice toward men and women of all races, religions, and social classes.

Sikh names do not indicate gender. All Sikh men, therefore, take the additional name Singh (lion) and women take the name Kaur (princess). Guru Gobind Singh, the tenth *guru,* instructed his followers to drop their last names, which in India indicate one's caste. They are to use only Singh and Kaur to show their acceptance of the universal equality of all persons. Another symbol of the Sikhs' acceptance of universal equality is the *langar.* This is a meal which is eaten together by the congregation, shared food becoming a social leveler.

In adulthood, a Sikh is initiated into full membership by the *Amrit* ceremony which was originated by the last human *guru* in 1699. At this time, the initiate promises to follow the Sikh code of conduct as an integral part of the path toward God-realization. He or she vows at that time:

To abstain from the use of tobacco and/or other intoxicants.

Never to cut the hair on any part of the body.

Not to eat the meat of animals killed in a religious or sacrificial manner.

To refrain totally from any sexual contact outside of marriage.

To wear the five symbols of Sikhs.

After this ceremony, the initiate is considered a part of the *Khalsa* (belonging to God) brotherhood, and is enjoined to tithe both time and income and to pray and meditate daily. He or she must live a moral life of service to mankind, in humility and honesty. The five symbols worn by the initiated Sikh are:

1) unshorn hair, over which men wear a turban;
2) a comb; 3) a steel bracelet; 4) a short sword;

5) a type of knickers usually worn under a Sikh's outer clothes.

The symbols most often associated with Sikhs as a group are the characters which symbolize One God, and an arrangement of three swords (called *khanda*). (See the symbol on the book cover.)

Sikhs do not have a priestly order, nor monks, nor nuns. The Sikh "clergyman" is the *granthi,* who is encouraged to marry. Sikh congregations are autonomous. There is no ecclesiastic hierarchy. The *Akal Takhat* heads the five temporal seats of Sikh religious authority in India, which debates matters of concern to the Sikh community worldwide and issues edicts which are morally binding on Sikhs. These decisions are coordinated by the SGPC, which also manages Sikh shrines in India.

Formal Sikh worship consists mainly of singing of passages of the *Guru Granth Sahib* to the accompaniment of music. A passage of the *Guru Granth Sahib* is read aloud and expounded upon by the *granthi* at the conclusion of the religious service. The central prayer of Sikhs, *Ardas,* which simply means prayer, is recited by the *granthi* and the assembled congregation. This prayer gives a synopsis of Sikh history as well as being a supplication to God. Any Sikh with sufficient religious knowledge is permitted to conduct *gurdwara* worship in the absence of a *granthi.* All are welcome to religious services and to participate in the *langar* served after.

There are no denominations in Sikhism, but in the United States, in particular, there is grouping along language and cultural lines. The majority of Sikhs in the U.S. are immigrants of Indian origin, speak Punjabi, and have distinct customs and dress that originate in Punjab, India. Since the 1960s, however, there has existed a group, generally called American Sikhs, whose leader is Yogi Harbhajan Singh. American Sikhs are easily distinguished from others by their all white attire and by the fact that turbans are worn by both men and women. This group now numbers about 5,000. The majority of American Sikhs, who refer to their group as 3HO (Healthy, Happy, Holy Organization), know only limited Punjabi. Indian Sikhs and American Sikhs are mutually accepting and visit one another's *gurdwaras.* Sikhs of Indian origin number

---

Excerpts from *Guru Granth Sahib* (the Sikh scriptures):

Meditation

"Meditation on the Name (of God)
Quenches thirst of the Soul.
Let us drink together
The Nectar treasure of the Lord's Name."

"In the garden of the soul,
Plant the seed of the Word (Lord's Name).
Water the soil with love and humility
And reap the fruits of divinity."

Waheguru (Sikh name For God)

"You are the Creator of all.
You give the soul, the body, and life.
We are meritless, without virtue.
Bless us, O Merciful Lord."

"He creates the Universe and then reveals Himself
To us and in us. He made Himself manifest."

approximately a half million in North America and approximately 21 million throughout the world.

Interfaith dialogue

Interfaith dialogue and cooperation have been a part of Sikhism since the time of Guru Nanak, its founder. He did not attempt to convert the followers of other faiths but, rather, urged them to rediscover the internal significance of their beliefs and rituals, without forsaking their chosen paths. He indicated that because of human limitations, each group grasps only a narrow aspect of God's revelation. The Sikh *gurus* were opposed to any exclusive claim on truth which a particular religion might make.

Just as this indicates a pluralistic acceptance of the legitimacy of all faiths, and that all are valid, it indicates, too, an acceptance of all groups and individuals. Guru Arjan said:

> All are co-equal partners in the Commonwealth with none treated as alien. (*Guru Granth Sahib*, p.97)

Numerous examples show how this attitude has evidenced itself in Sikh history:

When compiling the manuscripts that would make up the *Guru Granth Sahib*, Guru Arjan included hymns written by both Hindu and Muslim religious thinkers. It is the only scripture which includes and sanctifies texts of people belonging to other faiths, whose spirit conformed to the spirit of Sikhism.

There are, in the *Guru Granth Sahib*, hymns written by persons considered by Hindus to be untouchables.

The holiest of Sikh shrines, the Golden Temple at Amritsar, has four doors, each facing a cardinal direction, to indicate that all are welcome. The cornerstone of the Golden Temple was laid by a Muslim holy man. The ninth *guru*, Guru Tegh Bahadur, died championing the rights of Hindus to practice their own religion.

In modern times, the lesson of equality that is taught by the *langar*, the meal eaten together by Sikh congregations, extends beyond caste-obliteration to the acceptance and toleration of people of all races, creeds, and nationalities. Sikhs do not disparage other faiths, nor claim sole possession of the truth. Sikhs do not attempt to convert adherents of other faiths.

In North America, Sikh congregations belong to local interfaith associations and participate fully in efforts such as environmental protection campaigns, issues affecting children, AIDS, food and other help for the homeless and displaced. In India, particularly, there are many free clinics operated by Sikhs which accept persons of all religions and castes as patients. In some North American cities, Sikhs have continued that tradition.

Since the intrinsic spirit of Sikhism is pluralistic, it has much to contribute towards interfaith and inter-community accommodation. It is a willing partner in the emergence of a pluralistic world community that preserves the rights of human dignity and freedom for all human beings. In witness of this attitude, the *Ardas* recited at the end of a Sikh religious service ends with the words "May the whole world be blessed by your grace."

Responses to social problems

Gender Equality: Sikhism recognizes each human being as a valuable creation of God, having a divine spark. Every human being has a right to live life free of religious, political, and economic exploitation. The Sikh *gurus* vehemently condemned the caste system in India which had divided the whole society into many hereditary castes and subcastes. The lowest caste, the untouchable, was the most exploited of all, even to the extent of being barred from temples, as were all women of all castes.

In the time of the *gurus*, as is true in many places even now, women of all social levels were treated as property and grossly exploited. Rejecting the idea of female inequality, Guru Nanak said:

> Man is nourished in the womb and born from a woman; he is betrothed and married to a woman. Friendship is made with women and civilization originates from a woman. When a wife dies, another wife is sought because family affairs depend upon a woman. Why call her bad, from whom are born kings? From a woman another woman is born; none is born without a woman.

Service

"By doing service one loses one's egoistic nature and thereby gets respect from the society."

"The Supreme Lord is realized only by those who indulge in selfless service."

"We should do active service within the world if we want to attain everlasting bliss."

Environment

"The world is a garden,
Waheguru (Sikh name for God) its gardener.

Cherishing all, none is neglected;
From all comes the fragrance put there by Waheguru –
By such fragrance is each known."

Caring and Human Rights

"Where the poor are cared for,
the rain of Your (God's) gracious glance falls, O Lord."

"The sign of a good man is that he always seeks the welfare of others."

Guru Nanak specifically forbade the practices of widow *sati* (self-immolation on the pyre of her husband). He encouraged the remarriage of widows, which was unheard of in his time. He was gravely concerned about the practice of female infanticide. Not only is it forbidden to Sikhs, but a Sikh cannot associate with anyone who kills his female children. In the name of equality, Guru Nanak abolished the custom of the bride's family giving the groom dowry, since this encourages men to think of women as commercial commodities.

In Sikh society, a woman occupies a position equal to men and is not prevented from fulfilling her potential through education, religion, or profession.

*E*nvironmental concerns: Conservation, preservation, restoration and enrichment of environment have become major global issues at all political, social, and ethical levels. Into his beautiful creation, God has placed man with the power to enhance or destroy. Modern technology and man's greed and unconcern have made the potential for destruction of species, of the fertility of the land, of the viability of our waters, indeed of the world itself, a very real possibility. The Sikh Scriptures say:

Air the vital force,
water like the father,
and earth like the great mother.
Day and night are like nurses
caring for the whole world in their lap.

If air is our vital force, it is a sin, as well as self-destructive, to pollute it. If we consider water to be our progenitor, dumping industrial wastes in it is unforgivable disrespect. As we destroy the ozone layer, the cycle that manufactures chlorophyll in green plants is damaged or interrupted; since plants are part of the air-producing cycle, we strangle ourselves.

Sikhism seeks to give to humankind a progressive and responsible philosophy as a guide to all of the world's concerns. Recognizing that there is a part of the divine in all that He created, we must recognize the interdependence of all generations, species and resources. We must preserve what was passed to us and pass it on in a healthy and robust condition.

*T*he Sikh Response to AIDS: During the time of Guru Arjan (1563-1606), leprosy was considered by most of the world's population, Indians included, to be a form of Divine retribution for a person's transgressions. Sikhs have, from the time of their founding, rejected the idea that God is vindictive, wreaking vengeance on humankind. To show his rejection of this concept, to show that lepers were not to be feared and that they deserve compassion and care, Guru Arjan set up a treatment area for lepers in the city of Lahore, and himself spent a year there serving them.

In this supposedly modern age, AIDS victims face the same kind of prejudice and fear. Sikhs follow the example of Guru Arjan and join in the care of those who are ill and dying of this terrible virus, as well as join in vocally pushing for more research to find a cure. Service and compassion characterize the Sikh approach to AIDS.

The Sikh scriptures say "...God dwells in you, unaffected, like the image in a mirror." Recognizing that God dwells in all, Sikhs reach out to those with AIDS, offering whatever service is needed.

Service to humanity

A cornerstone of the Sikh faith is the concept of *seva,* the selfless service of the community—not just the Sikh community, but the community of man. Bhai Gurdas, the early Sikh theologian, whose *Vars* (poems) are highly respected by Sikhs, says: "Service of one's fellows is a sign of divine worship." What one does in selfless service is considered to be real prayer. When one prays or meditates, it is often done for the good of one's own soul or to supplicate for one's own imagined needs. A Sikh who, with no thought of reward, serves others, performs the truest form of worship, whether he is feeding the homeless or bringing company and compassion to an AIDS sufferer.

Among the lowly, I am lowliest of the low.
My place is with them. What have I to do with the great?
(Guru Granth Sahib, p.15)

Sikhs are instructed to pray, before they eat, that a needy person will come and share their food. This attitude toward each person's role in achieving social justice motivates Sikhs to actively participate in ensuring that the poor in the world community, as well as in the local community, are fed, clothed and sheltered, and motivates them to be part of finding long-term solutions.

FOR MORE INFORMATION:

Guru Gobind Singh Foundation
1700 Pasture Brookway, Potomac, MD 20854

Guru Nanak (Sikh) Mission
506 Aspen Drive, Lombard, IL 60148 USA. (Also see *Outline of*

Sikh Religion: Beliefs and Practices of Sikhism), by Amarjit Singh, published 1993 for distribution at the Parliament of the World's Religions, available from the Mission.)

Sikh Dharma International
1620 Press Road, P.O. Box 351149, Los Angeles, CA 90035

Spiritual, Esoteric, and Evolutionary Philosophies

The several different philosophies and organizations represented in this chapter are only a sampling of numerous systems that might also have been included. While each of these has its own character, including differences of belief and practice from the others, the groups or philosophies represented here seem to this Editor to have the following elements in common:

1) belief in and encouraging the spiritual evolution of both individuals and the human race within a new civilization, as part of a larger cosmic scenario;

2) a focus on personal spiritual practice and experience, not on doctrines and dogma;

3) belief in the interpenetration of the material by the spiritual – thus they teach the spiritual or esoteric (hidden) meanings of experience, religions and scriptures;

4) a claim not to be a religion, though applauding the best ethics and wisdom from all religions; some encourage students to enrich their own traditions with insights derived from spiritual philosophy and from other religions;

5) paying particular attention to certain revealed or inspired sources of information and/or to charismatic figures who provide information, analysis and leadership – at the same time, encouraging personal independence;

6) tracing their roots back to "ageless wisdom" or ancient, perennial philosophy, though the organization or concepts taught have emerged in the past 125 years.

Anthroposophy: Toward a More Human Future

*E*choing the ancient Greek axiom, "Man, know thyself," Rudolf Steiner, the founder of anthroposophy, described it as "awareness of one's humanity." Nowhere is the need for such awareness greater than in relation to our fellow human beings, and to the life and work we share with them. It is this awareness that lies at the heart of the practical work fostered by the worldwide General Anthroposophical Society, which Steiner founded in 1923 as "an association of people who would foster the life of the soul, both in the individual and in human society, on the basis of a true knowledge of the spiritual world."

Rudolf Steiner (1861–1925) was born in Lower Austria and grew up with the clairvoyant certainty of a spiritual world. Recognizing the need to reconcile the experience of the supersensible realities with that of the material world, he schooled himself in modern science and philosophy, and developed anthroposophy as a "spiritual science." Steiner was active in the cultural and social life of his day, and shared the results of his spiritual research in over 6,000 lectures and 40 books. He is increasingly recognized as a seminal thinker of the 20th century and one of humanity's great spiritual teachers.

Anthroposophy embraces a spiritual view of the human being and the cosmos, but its emphasis is on knowing, not faith. It is a path in which the human heart and hand, and especially our capacity for thinking, are essential. It leads, in Steiner's words, "from the spirit in the human being to the spirit in the universe." Humanity (*anthropos*) has the inherent wisdom (*sophia*) to transform both itself and the world. Today, when many aspects of our culture are in crisis, and people are easily drawn into cynicism and despair, anthroposophy's vision of human potential is a source of hope and renewal.

Since Steiner's death in 1925, many people have sought to continue his research through study, reflection and meditation, and to apply it in many areas of human endeavor. The international center for this work is the School for Spiritual Science, at the Goetheanum in Dornach, Switzerland. The Society is entirely non-sectarian and non-political, but its activities range across many disciplines and interests, including the following:

- Waldorf Schools (500 worldwide) place as much emphasis on creativity and moral judgment as on intellectual growth, with reverence for beauty, goodness, truth, and freedom as the goals.
- Adult education balances study with inner development and creative work.
- Medical practice is holistic, treating body, soul, and spirit.
- Biodynamic agriculture relates to the earth as a living organism, utilizing sustainable and organic processes.
- Eurythmy translates the sounds, phrasing, and rhythms of speech and music into movement and gesture.
- Other work with the arts, cooperative projects, health products, and publishing demonstrate principles of anthroposophy.

"Anthroposophy intends to be a living presence; it wants to use words, concepts, and ideas so that something living may shine down from the spiritual world into the physical. Anthroposophy does not only want to impart knowledge, it seeks to awaken life."
— R. STEINER

Compiled by the Editor from brochures published by the Anthroposophical Society in North America: *Toward a More Human Future* and *Rudolf Steiner*

For more information, contact the Society at:
529 W. Grant Place, Chicago, IL 60614

The Arcane School

The Arcane School was established by Mrs. Alice A. Bailey in 1923 to help meet an obvious and growing demand for further teaching and training in the science of the soul. The School is one of many activities of the Lucis Trust (see Chapter 42 for more information).

The purpose of the esoteric training given in the Arcane School is to help the student grow spiritually toward acceptance of discipleship responsibility and to serve the Plan of the spiritual hierarchy by serving humanity. Esotericism is a practical way of life. The function of the School is to assist those at the end of the probationary path to move forward on to the path of discipleship, and to assist those already on that path to move on more quickly and to achieve greater effectiveness in service.

A disciple is one who, above all else, is pledged to do three things: (a) to serve humanity, (b) to cooperate with the Plan as he sees it and as best he may, and (c) to develop the powers of the soul, to expand his consciousness, and to follow the guidance of the higher self and not the dictates of his threefold lower self.

Discipleship is a word in constant use among aspirants in the world, both in the East and in the West. Discipleship could be defined as the final stage of the path of evolution. It is the stage in which a man knowingly pledges himself to impose the will of the soul (which is essentially the will of God) upon the lower nature. Upon this path he submits himself to a training process through a systematized and applied discipline, producing a more rapid unfoldment of the power and the life of the soul.

The training given in the Arcane School is based on three fundamental requirements – occult meditation, study, and service to humanity. The Arcane School is a place for hard work. The presentation of the teaching adapted to the rapidly emerging new civilisation includes the training of disciples in group formation and group meditation and study, helping to precipitate the ideas on which the new civilisation and culture will be founded. The work of the Arcane School all over the world is carried forward entirely by correspondence with one of three headquarters.

The Arcane School is non-sectarian, and respects the right of each student to hold his own view and beliefs. It does not rely upon an authoritarian presentation of any one line of thought or code of ethics. The knowledge, insight wisdom, and capacity to wield spiritual energy resulting from work and training with the Arcane School should be expressed and applied in daily living service in helping to materialize the Plan of God and to aid in solving the problems of humanity.

compiled by the Editor from materials provided by Lucis Trust

FOR FURTHER INFORMATION:

See the entry in Chapter 42 (Lucis Trust) or contact the schools at:

3 Whitehall Court, Suite 54, London SW1A 2EF, U.K.

113 University Place, 11th Floor, New York, N.Y. 10017-1888

1 Rue de Varembé (3e), Case Postale 31, 1211 Geneva 20, Switzerland

Testimony And Treasure

"In every race and nation, in every climate and part of the world, and throughout the endless reaches of time itself, back into the limitless past, men have found the Path to God; they have trodden it and accepted its conditions, endured its disciplines, rested back in confidence upon its realities, received its rewards and found their goal. Arrived there, they have "entered into the joy of the Lord," participated in the mysteries of the kingdom of heaven, dwelt in the glory of the divine Presence, and then returned to the ways of men, to serve. The testimony to the existence of this Path is the priceless treasure of all the great religions and its witnesses are those who have transcended all forms and all theologies, and have penetrated into the world of meaning which all symbols veil."
Alice A. Bailey,
The Externalization of the Hierarchy, p. 405

The Great Invocation

The Great Invocation is a world prayer translated into over fifty languages and dialects. It expresses certain central truths which all men innately and normally accept:

- That there exists a basic intelligence to whom we give the name of God.
- That there is a divine evolutionary Plan in the universe – the motivating power of which is love.
- That a great individuality called by Christians the Christ – the World Teacher – came to Earth and embodied that love so that we could understand that love and intelligence are effects of the purpose, and the will, and the Plan of God. Many religions believe in a World Teacher, knowing him under such names as the Lord Maitreya, the Imam Mahdi, and the Messiah.
- Only through humanity itself can the divine Plan work out.

From the point of Light within the Mind of God
Let light stream forth into the minds of men.
Let Light descend on Earth.

From the point of Love within the Heart of God
Let love stream forth into the hearts of men.
May Christ return to Earth.

From the center where the Will of God is known
Let purpose guide the little wills of men –
The purpose which the Masters know and serve.

From the center which we call the race of men
Let the Plan of Love and Light work out.
And may it seal the door where evil dwells.

Let Light and Love and Power
Restore the Plan on Earth.

The Evolutionary Philosophy of
Sri Aurobindo and the Mother

Sri Aurobindo

Sri Aurobindo is the highly respected author of 30 volumes of philosophy, poetry, political essays, and spiritual discourse. A scholar and political activist in India at the turn of this century, he withdrew to the reclusive, though prolific, life of a mystic following spiritual experiences he had while in prison. Sri Aurobindo's vision inspired the founding of the experimental community of Auroville in India (see article in Chapter 42).

"At once a first question arises – is this world an unchanging succession of the same phenomena always or is there in it an evolutionary urge, an evolutionary fact, a ladder of ascension somewhere from an original apparent Inconscience to a more and more developed consciousness, from each development still ascending, emerging on highest heights not yet within our normal reach? If so, what is the sense, the fundamental principle, the logical issue of that progression? Everything seems to point to such a progression as a fact – to a spiritual and not merely a physical evolution."

"This erring race of human beings dreams always of perfecting its environment by the machinery of Government and society, but it is only by the perfection of the soul within that the outer environment can be perfected. What thou art within, that outside thee thou shalt enjoy, no machinery can rescue thee from the law of thy being."

"Consciousness is a fundamental thing, the fundamental thing in existence – it is the energy, the motion, the movement of consciousness that creates the universe and all that is in it – not only the macrocosm but the microcosm is nothing but consciousness arranging itself. For instance, when consciousness in its movement or rather a certain stress of movement forgets itself in the action it becomes an apparently "unconscious" energy; when it forgets itself in the form it becomes the electron, the atom, the material object. In reality it is still consciousness that works in the energy and determines the form and the evolution of form. When it wants to liberate itself, slowly, evolutionarily, out of Matter, but still in the form, it emerges as life, as animal, as man and it can go on evolving itself still farther out of its involution and become something more than mere man."

The Mother

Sri Aurobindo's longtime student and companion, the Mother (Mirra Alfassa), continued his work, founding Auroville and helping to spread the vision worldwide. The Mother also wrote a 13-volume *Agenda* on her experiences and explorations in the expression of consciousness that resides within the body's cellular structure, as well as 12 volumes of collected conversations and writings.

"If we want to find a true solution to the confusion, the chaos and the misery of the world, we have to find it in the world itself. In fact, it is to be found only there: it exists latent, one has to bring it out. It is neither mystical nor imaginary, but altogether concrete, furnished by Nature herself, if we know how to observe her. For Nature's is an ascending movement; out of one form, one species, she brings forth a new one capable of manifesting something more of the universal consciousness. All go to prove that man is not the last step in terrestrial evolution. The human species will necessarily be succeeded by a new one which will be to man what man is to the animal; the present human consciousness will be replaced by a new consciousness, no more mental, but supramental....

"The time is come when this possibility... must become a reality lived upon earth."

These excerpts from the writings of Sri Aurobindo and the Mother are printed in a brochure, "Introduction to Auroville," available from Auroville International U.S.A., P.O. Box 162489, Sacramento, CA 95816; tel. (916) 452-4013. Used with permission.

Conscious Evolution:
A *Meta-Religio* for the 21st Century

Barbara Marx Hubbard

Futurist, author, speaker, social architect, and co-founder of the Foundation for Conscious Evolution.

*W*e are at the dawn of a radical new capability which can either destroy the world or create a future of immeasurable possibilities. I call this capacity *Conscious Evolution.* Up until our age evolution has proceeded without the conscious choice of any body. We are the first generation to be aware of the process of evolution and the first, therefore, to become responsible for guiding that process, on a planetary, then on a solar-systemic, and eventually on a galactic scale.

Conscious Evolution springs from three radically new conditions barely more than thirty to forty years old:

The *new cosmology,* which reveals that the universe has a history in time, as each of us does, and is still evolving through us and far beyond us. Everything we do affects the future. We are co-authors of creation.

The *new crises,* which for the first time in human history threaten our collective life support system and demand rapid change of behavior and consciousness on a species-wide scale if we are to survive.

Our *new capacities* in technology and social systems, such as molecular biology, the space programs, computers, cybernetics, robotics, artificial intelligence and nanotechnology, which give us the actual power to co-evolve with nature, to co-create new life forms and new worlds – or to destroy our world.

Conscious Evolution unfolds in three ways: *spiritually,* through inner attunement, resonance with Spirit, guidance; *socially,* through the desire to co-create humane, sustainable, compassionate, and creative social systems that liberate our full potential; and *technologically,* as we understand the design of evolution and learn to co-evolve with nature.

Conscious Evolution is, I believe, as profound an evolutionary step as was language and culture for the advent of Homo sapiens and as was the DNA, the genetically-coded intelligence, for the origin of life. Ultimately, if we learn Conscious Evolution, it means we tap into Universal Intelligence, the genius of the creative process which has organized form from the first sub-atomic particles, to billions upon billions of galaxies, to you and me. We are now just opening our young universal eyes to discover our place in the cosmos, our birth story as a planet, our requirement as members of this one body to coordinate ourselves as a whole. When we become mature universal humans we will be able to say: "We and Universal Intelligence are one."

But, quite clearly, there are as yet few schools for Conscious Evolution. We are young and inexperienced. Where can we go to learn how to be co-creators? No university in the world focuses upon how to evolve as a species. And, as Buckminster Fuller put it, "Spaceship Earth came without an operating manual." We can have compassion upon ourselves. This is a planetary first, perhaps as challenging as it was for the early, self-centered creature-humans to stand up in the animal world. We are among the first whole-centered, co-creative humans to arise in the world of a beleaguered and failing Homo sapiens.

The global crisis of danger/opportunity is calling forth from us the emergence of a mature humanity, a universal species, co-creative with nature, one another, and the Divine. Here is the challenge for the world's religions.

As Dr. Gerald O. Barney put it:

> In effect, we humans have become co-creators with the Divine of the future of the Earth....To my knowledge no faith tradition has prepared us for it. No faith anticipated the development of human power over Earth's future, this enormous responsibility. To my knowledge, no faith tradition has prepared us to know ourselves not as individuals but as a species. To my knowledge, no faith tradition has provided moral precepts to guide inter-species behavior, to decide which species should cease to exist, which new species shall be created through genetic engineering (and then patented), and to judge the alternative futures humans are considering for Earth. [1]

Yet this new Age of Conscious Evolution has in fact been foreseen and prepared for by a magnificent lineage of seers, mystics, scientists, and visionaries. The human precognition that we are approaching a quantum transformation is the original seed in many of the great faiths and cultures of the human race. Michael Grosso brilliantly traces this lineage in his book *The Millennium Myth.* [2]

The origin of the idea of Conscious Evolution is the faith that the "deep and radical regeneration of the human race is possible," and that we humans have a role to play in our own transformation. I believe that this faith was the intuition of the next stage of evolution, which we are beginning to experience in real time, in history.

*A*s Grosso points out, the seed-idea of Conscious Evolution cracked its shell with the Babylonian Creation Epic, the story of Gilgamesh, where Marduk creates a new world out of chaos. It sent its first green shoot upward with Zoroaster, the great Iranian mystic, who foresaw that death would be overcome, that bodily resurrection would occur, that spiritual equality was the way, that evil would be destroyed and all souls would be saved.

This "meme" or spiritual gene that guides human action and aspiration grew in the Hebrew prophets – in Daniel's faith in individual resurrection, in Enoch's vision of a new heaven, in Amos's concept of the Day of Yahweh, in Isaiah's vision that the wolf will lie down with the lamb, in the prophet Joel who saw there would be a time of radical collective transformation.

And it shall come to pass in the last days, saith God,
I will pour out of my Spirit upon all flesh:
and your sons and your daughters shall prophesy,
your old men shall dream dreams
and your young men shall see visions.
Even upon the manservants and maidservants in those
days, I will pour out my spirit. (Joel 2: 28, 29).

In the birth, teachings, crucifixion, resurrection and ascension of Jesus we find the transformed human embodied. The promise was made:

Truly, truly, I say to you, he who believes in me will also do the works that I do; and greater works than these will he do, because I go to the Father. (John 14:12)

As St. Paul put it:

Behold, I show you a mystery:
We shall not all sleep; but we shall all be changed.
In a moment, in the twinkling of an eye, at the last
trumpet. For the trumpet will sound, and the dead will be
raised imperishable, and we shall be changed....
Death is swallowed up in victory. O death, where *is* thy
sting? O grave, where *is* thy victory.
(1 Corinthians 15:51, 52, 54, 55.)

In The Book of Revelation we read:

Then I saw a new heaven and a new earth; for the first heaven and the first earth had passed away....
Behold, the dwelling of God is with them, and they shall be his people, and God himself will be with them;
and he will wipe away every tear from their eyes, and death shall be no more, neither shall there by mourning nor crying nor pain any more, for the former things have passed away." (Rev.21: 1,3,4).

As the dinosaur, the *Eohippus*, Neanderthal and millions of other species are passed away, so also will this stage of Homo sapiens pass away.

This seed of something new began to bud as a young tree of life in the 12th century with Joachim of Fiore. He saw the Trinity in a historical progression from the Age of the Father, to the Age of the Son, to the Age of the Holy Spirit. Grosso writes: "Christ was the juncture in human history where humanity began the process of assuming its likeness to God." Joachim revealed that we are to become a New People under the guidance of the Third Person of the Trinity.

This tree of new life grew through the Renaissance with such visionaries as Ficino and Pico della Mirandola, who drew from the concept, "And God said, let us make man in our own image and likeness." (Gen. 1:26).

It stretched its branches in the Enlightenment with such documents as the Declaration of Independence and the Bill of Rights. It went violently astray in the darkness of Hitler's perversion of the human craving for a super-humanity, and in Stalin's grotesque distortion of the desire of each of us to be part of a larger whole.

Yet this evolutionary idea would not die. It renewed itself in Teilhard de Chardin's vision of God manifesting in evolution, leading to a point of collective love – he called it the Christification of the Earth. Later Peter Russell was to describe the phenomenon in *A White Hole in Time*.[3]

Could it be that, in much the same way as the destiny of matter in a sufficiently massive star is to become a black hole in space, the destiny of a self-conscious species – should it be sufficiently full of love – is a 'spiritual supernova.' Is this what we are accelerating toward? A moment when the light of inner awakening radiates throughout the world? A white hole in time?

Our fear of our self-destructive power stresses us to the core. Hunger, violence, and pollution threaten our lives. Spiritual yearning rises en masse. Our new powers in science and technology give us the capacity for radical physical transformation or the destruction of life.

We cannot continue for many generations in our current consciousness and survive. Like a baby in the birth canal, we must be born. The only question is how. Will it be a gentle or a violent birth? Will we live and grow into a universal future, or will we be struggling for life, yet dying for lack of a vision and processes to nurture our emergence as divine humans, co-creators of new worlds?

Driven by our new crises as well as our new capacities, the seed idea of Conscious Evolution, the "millennium myth," seems to be coming to fruition in history, now, in the diverse flowering of the "new paradigm" in every field of human endeavor. The new cosmology has set the stage for conscious evolution and has given us the logic of hope – a multi-billion year trend line of ever greater freedom and consciousness through more synergistic order. Quantum physics reveals a co-creative, participatory, observer-created universe.

Theodore Roszak points out in *The Voice of the Earth* that the three concepts upon which scientific materialism was based – chance, materialism, and infinite time – are all but disappearing. Some scientists see an Anthropic Principle, a finely tuned universe designed to produce self-reflective life. As Roszak writes:

Our presence is based upon an astonishing number of delicately balanced physical coincidences.... The universe appears more and more as if it is grounded upon a nonphysical and ideational act of creation.[4]

Holistic health, transpersonal psychology, and other spiritual psychologies and therapies reveal our potential to be self-healing, self-regenerating, self-transcending beings. Molecular biology holds the promise of life extension, conscious reproduction, and life enhancement.

Nanotechnology gives us the potential power to release the obsolete industrial technologies and begin to build as nature does, atom by atom, with the ability to heal, regenerate, resurrect from DNA, clean the environment, live and work in outer space aesthetically and ecologically.

In the Gaia Hypothesis James Lovelock recognizes the whole Earth as an intelligent, self-regulating living system. We learn that ecology is not the study of an environment outside ourselves but is the awareness of the whole Earth including ourselves as one living body, in a universe that itself is a Whole System. We stretch our concept of Mother Earth to Mother Universe and stand in awe at the nature of our Mother and of ourselves maturing in the image of that universal Love-Intelligence that is creating us!

In *Metaman: the Merging of Humans and Machines into*

a *Global Super-organism,* Gregory Stock suggests that Gaia, combined with human culture, science, and technology, has created a super-organism of godlike capability.

To the ancients, unleashing a storm, healing, the sick, leveling a city, or foretelling the future would have been ample demonstrations of divinity. Now, having seen equivalent powers in Metaman, we might inquire how the 'miracles' were performed rather than falling to our knees. Flight, television, a corneal transplant that restores sight, even high explosives would have once been considered godlike. Now we take them for granted. Knowing more, seeing more, having greater powers than any who have gone before, we – through Metaman – have in a sense become as gods. And yet we are 'gods' only in the limited terms of early humans, because Metaman's emergence is giving us an awareness of the true enormity and power of the universe.... We can now contemplate the prospect of one day moving beyond the 'natural' conditions of hunger, disease, and perhaps even death itself.[5]

Beatrice Bruteau describes the entire story as the Theotokos Project.

The cosmos is a *Theotokos Project.* That is, it is an enterprise in which a finite system is developed by autopoiesis, through evolution, to the point where its complexity and consciousness make it capable of bearing the values of the Infinite Spirit whose expression it is. In a Catholic framework, this suggests the revelation of the incarnation conceived on a cosmic scale. The cosmos itself is the Godbearer. The cosmos itself is the embodied word of God.[6]

For me, the glory which shall be revealed is the creation of 'cosmogenitors.' We are co-creators. Based on the maturation of intellect and individuality, of science and spirituality we are gaining the power of "gods." We can use these powers to destroy or create. There is free will. We stand, mythologically, as new Eves and Adams at the Tree of Life, the tree of the gods, of immortality and the healing of the nations. We have been created in the image of God, and, finally, godlike we have become.

The destructive tendencies of the separated mind have now become lethal to Earth life. The only hope is our own capacity for maturation as universal, co-creative humans. This hope is buttressed by the fifteen-billion year tendency of nature to form beings of ever higher consciousness and freedom through more complex order. The great task of all religions now is to support the human race in conscious evolution.

Yet the magnum opus is the Person. The future of religion pulses as a seed of new life within our own hearts, ready to burst forth because planetary conditions are now ripe. This future is *ourselves* evolving, maturing as a species, growing up to our full potential as co-creators, conscious participants in the creation.

This dormant potential has been intuited and embodied by the great mystics, saints and seers of the world. Each religion was born out of the experience of one or more advanced humans. We can look upon them as the founders of the future. Each laid forth an aspect of the way toward our conscious evolution. In each tradition's vision is a template of our future which must now come to pass during the period of our "planetary birth" as a universal species.

When our potential is *fully* realized we can foresee that there will be no more "religion" as we know it. Each great faith will have served its purpose in the gestation of humanity as a species co-creative with the divine. It will be the fulfillment of Swedenborg's seminal insight that we are each equally imbued with the indwelling divine and are responsible for its manifestation. The future of religion will occur when the majority of us know and act on this awareness.

I believe that the new form of religion will be what Sidney Lanier calls the *sovereign person,* free-standing and responsible, freely joining with others in love to co-create a new world. Each of us will experience ourself as a unique expression of the Creative Intelligence, a vital member of the whole, expressing his or her creativity in unique vocations that evolve ourselves and our world. As whole persons, we will embody the Tao of Taoism, the unitive state of Hinduism, the enlightenment of the Buddha, the godlike capacities of Christ for love, healing, resurrection and ascension in new bodies. We will be advanced beings *ourselves,* as were the founders of each great religion.

What does Conscious Evolution mean to us?

*E*very person is needed, now. Each of us is being motivated from within to attune to his or her deeper life purpose. The mighty design of creation is calling us to our posts, for the crisis has come and the hour of our planetary birth is near.

We are to find life partners, co-creative teammates and dedicate ourselves to expressing our gifts as contributions to the world. We are to connect spiritually as a communion of pioneering souls, from every race, nation, and religion, until we can experience together the fact that we are members of one body, born into a universe of immeasurable potential, co-creative with one another, with nature, and with God.

We can create a Ground of the Whole and invite ourselves as members of each faith, each tradition, each discipline, each culture to enter that Ground, beyond all past labels and divisions, to give our gift to the conscious evolution of humanity.

NOTES:

See also Ms. Hubbard's new book, which lays out *Eight Steps Toward the Conscious Evolution of the World.*

1. Barney, G. in *A SourceBook for the Community of Religions,* CPWR, p.30.
2. Grosso, Michael: *The Millennium Myth,* (Quest) read by me in manuscript.
3. Russell, Peter: *A White Hole in Time,* Harper San Francisco, 1992, p.211.
4. Roszak, Theodore: *The Voice of the Earth,* Simon and Schuster, 1992
5. Stock, Gregory: *Metaman: the Merging of Humans and Machines into a Global Superorganism:* Simon and Schuster, 1993, p. 244.
6. Bruteau, B.: *Embracing Earth: Catholic Approaches to Ecology,* Orbis, 1994

Copyright 1994 Barbara Marx Hubbard

FOR MORE INFORMATION:

Foundation for Conscious Evolution
P.O. Box 6397, San Rafael, CA 94903-0397 USA

A Portrait of Theosophy

Dr. John Algeo

President of the Theosophical Society in America

About Theosophy

*T*he modern Theosophical movement dates from the founding of the Theosophical Society in New York City in 1875 by Helena Petrovna Blavatsky, Henry Steel Olcott, William Quan Judge, and others. The movement, however, views itself as a contemporary expression of a tradition going back to the Neo-Platonists of Classical antiquity (hence the name) and earlier. Primary concepts are:

(1) the fundamental unity of all existence, so that all dichotomies – matter and spirit, the human and the divine, I and thou – are seen as transitory and relative distinctions of an underlying absolute Oneness;

(2) the regularity of universal law, cyclically producing universes out of the absolute ground of being; and

(3) the progress of consciousness developing through the cycles of life to an ever-increasing realization of Unity.

Theosophy is nondogmatic, but many Theosophists believe in: reincarnation; *karma* (or moral justice); the existence of worlds of experience beyond the physical; the presence of life and consciousness in all matter; the evolution of spirit and intelligence as well as matter; the possibility of conscious participation in evolution; the power of thought to affect one's self and surroundings; free will and self-responsibility; the duty of altruism, a concern for the welfare of others.

*T*hese beliefs often lead to such practices as meditation, vegetarianism and care for animal welfare, active support of women's and minority rights, and a concern for ecology. Knowledge of such ideas and practices derives from the traditions of cultures spread over the world from antiquity to the present in a "perennial philosophy" or "ancient wisdom," held to be fundamentally identical in all cultures. But it also derives from the experiences of individuals through the practice of meditation and the development of insight. No Theosophist is asked to accept any opinion or adopt any practice that does not appeal to the inner sense of reason and morality.

Theosophy has no developed rituals. Meetings typically consist of talks and discussion or the study of a book, although they may be opened and closed by brief meditations or the recitation of short texts. There are no privileged symbols in Theosophy, but various symbols from the religious traditions of the world are used, such as the interlaced triangles and the ankh.

Today there are three main Theosophical organizations. Membership statistics are not available for all of them, but the American section of the society with international headquarters in Madras, India, has a membership of about 5,000. There are associated groups in about 50 countries.

Theosophy in the world today

*T*he first object of the Theosophical Society is (in one wording), "To form a nucleus of the Universal Brotherhood of Humanity without distinction of race, creed, sex, caste, or color"; and the second is, "To encourage the study of comparative religion, philosophy and science." As those objects indicate, Theosophy is dedicated to increasing cooperation among human beings and understanding among their cultures and religions.

Theosophy holds that all religions are expressions of humanity's effort to relate to one another, to the universe around us, and to the ultimate ground of being. Particular religions differ from one another because they are expressions of that effort adapted to particular times, places, cultures, and needs. Theosophy is not itself a religion, although it is religious, in being concerned with the effort to relate. Individual Theosophists profess various of the world's religions – Christian, Jewish, Moslem, Zoroastrian, Hindu, Buddhist; others have no religious affiliation.

The Theosophical Society has, from the time of its founding, promoted dialogue and cooperation among the religious traditions of humanity, since we regard them all as varying expressions of a basic human need and impulse. The Society itself is an expression of the faith that human beings, however diverse their backgrounds, can communicate and cooperate.

Wisdom in the Theosophical Tradition

"It is well known that the first rule of the society is to carry out the object of forming the nucleus of a universal brotherhood. The practical working of this rule was explained by those who laid it down, to the following effect:

"He who does not practice altruism; he who is not prepared to share his last morsel with a weaker or poorer than himself; he who neglects to help his brother man, of whatever race, nation or creed, whenever and wherever he meets suffering, and who turns a deaf ear to the cry of human misery; he who hears an innocent person slandered, whether a brother Theosophist or not, and does not undertake his defense as he would undertake his own – is no Theosophist."   H. P. BLAVATSKY,
"Let Every Man Prove His Own Work," 1887, *CW* 8:170–71

"There is but one way of ever ameliorating human life and it is by the love of one's fellow man for his own sake and not for personal gratification. The greatest Theosophist – he who loves divine truth under all its forms – is the one who works for and with the poor."

H. P. BLAVATSKY, "Misconceptions," 1887, *CW* 8:77

PART ONE: WHO ARE WE?

Primary challenges and issues facing humanity

*H*umanity is faced by a range of seemingly insuperable problems: uncontrolled population growth, diminishing resources, exploitation of one group by another, ancient animosities, passion for revenge, racial antagonism, religious prejudice, territorial ambition, destructive use of the environment, oppression of women, disregard of the rights of others, greed for wealth and power, and so on. In the Theosophical view, all these are secondary or derivative problems – the symptoms of a disease. The primary, original problem, the cause of the disease, is the illusion of separateness, the notion that we are unconnected, independent beings whose particular welfare can be achieved at the expense of the general good.

The primary challenge facing humanity is therefore to recognize the unity of our species and in turn our ultimate unity with all life in the universe. Despite the superficial cultural and genetic differences that divide humanity, we are a remarkably homogeneous species – physically, psychologically, intellectually, and spiritually. Biologically, we are a single human gene pool, with only minor local variations. Psychologically and intellectually, we respond to stimuli in fundamentally the same way. Linguistically, behind the surface variations of the world's tongues, our underlying language ability is remarkably uniform. Spiritually, we have a common origin and a common destiny.

Neither is the human species isolated from the rest of life in the universe. We are part and parcel of the totality of existence stretching from this planet Earth to the farthest reaches of the cosmos in every conceivable dimension. When we realize our integral connection with all other human beings, with all other life forms, with the most distant reaches of space, we will realize that we cannot either harm or help another without harming or helping ourselves. We are all one, not as metaphor, but as fact.

Individual Theosophists engage in social, political, and charitable action as they are moved by their consciences and sense of duty to become so engaged. They are urged by the Theosophical tradition to realize the concept of Unity in practical responses to the challenges we face. Collectively and as Theosophists, however, we do not regard it as our special calling to be social, political, or charitable activists. Theosophy addresses the cause rather than the symptoms of the human disease. Theosophy seeks to make humanity aware – intellectually, affectively, and experientially – of our unity with one another and with the whole universe. From such awareness will flow naturally and inevitably a respect for differences, a wise use of the environment, the fair treatment of others, a sympathy with the afflictions of our neighbors, and the will to respond to those afflictions helpfully and lovingly.

"Help Nature and work on with her; and Nature will regard thee as one of her creators and make obeisance."
[sl. 66]

"To live to benefit mankind is the first step." [sl. 144]
H. P. BLAVATSKY, *The Voice of the Silence*, 1889

"There is a road, steep and thorny, beset with perils of every kind, but yet a road, and it leads to the very heart of the Universe: I can tell you how to find those who will show you the secret gateway that opens inward only, and closes fast behind the neophyte for evermore. There is no danger that dauntless courage cannot conquer; there is no trial that spotless purity cannot pass through; there is no difficulty that strong intellect cannot surmount. For those who win onwards, there is reward past all telling – the power to bless and save humanity; for those who fail, there are other lives in which success may come."
H. P. BLAVATSKY, 1891, *CW* 13:219

"O hidden Life,
  vibrant in every atom,
O hidden Light,
  shining in every creature,
O hidden Love,
  embracing all in oneness,
May all who feel themselves
  as one with thee
Know they are therefore one
  with every other."
ANNIE BESANT

"The Society was founded to teach no new and easy paths to the acquisition of "powers"; . . . its only mission is to re-kindle the torch of truth, so long extinguished for all but the very few, and to keep that truth alive by the formation of a fraternal union of mankind, the only soil in which the good seed can grow."
H. P. BLAVATSKY, "Spiritual Progress," 1885, *CW* 6:333

"The path of right progress should include the amelioration of the individual, the nation, the race, and humanity; and ever keeping in view the last and grandest object, the perfecting of man, should reject all apparent bettering of the individual at the expense of his neighbor."
H. P. BLAVATSKY, "The Struggle for Existence," 1889, *CW* 11:151–52

FOR MORE INFORMATION:

Theosophical Society, International Headquarters Adyar, Madras, India 600020

Theosophical Society in America *(and Quest Books)* PO Box 270, Wheaton, IL 60189

The Theosophical Society *(and Theosophical University Press)* PO Box C, Pasadena, CA 91109

United Lodge of Theosophists 245 W. 33rd St., Los Angeles, CA 90007

The Emergence of Maitreya, the World Teacher

Monte Leach

Editor for "Share Magazine" and "Emergence Quarterly"
These two publications come from Share International and the Tara Foundation, non-profit organizations that provide information about the teachings and emergence of Maitreya, the World Teacher. While some of their philosophy is aligned with the teachings of Alice Bailey and some Theosophical traditions, this movement's message goes beyond the others in claiming that Maitreya is now on the planet in human form. Much of the information about Maitreya is revealed to Benjamin Creme, an esotericist, who receives it through "telepathic communications from a Master of Wisdom."

*F*rom very ancient times a body of spiritual teachings known as the Ageless Wisdom, or esoteric philosophy, has been passed from generation to generation, usually by word of mouth, from teacher to pupil. It has been the well-spring for the arts and sciences of countless civilizations, as well as the common foundation of all the world's religions.

According to the Ageless Wisdom teachings, humanity has advanced primarily through the influence of a succession of enlightened teachers who inspire humanity at the beginning of every new cosmic cycle or age. The wisdom and spiritual power of these teachers have been so far above the norm that followers have built religions around Them to spread Their teachings. We know some of these teachers as Krishna, Confucius, Zoroaster, the Buddha, the Christ, and Mohammed.

The scriptures of every major religion promise further revelations with the return of a great spiritual teacher. Today, Christians hope for the return of Christ, Jews await the Messiah, Moslems look for the Imam Mahdi or Messiah, Hindus expect Krishna, and Buddhists anticipate the Fifth (Maitreya) Buddha. Students of the Ageless Wisdom teachings know all these as different names for the same individual, the World Teacher, Maitreya.

At the dawn of the Aquarian Age, many people believe that Maitreya, the World Teacher, is now living in the world.

A gradual emergence

*I*n recent years, information about Maitreya's emergence has come primarily from Benjamin Creme, a British artist and author who has been speaking and writing about this event since 1974. According to Creme, Maitreya descended in July 1977 from His ancient retreat in the Himalayas and took up residence in the Indian-Pakistani community of London. He has been living and working there, seemingly as an ordinary man, His true status known to relatively few. He has been emerging gradually into full public view so as not to infringe on humanity's free will.

Preferring to be known simply as the Teacher, Maitreya has not come as a religious leader, or to found a new religion, but as a teacher and guide for people of every religion and those of no religion.

As a modern man concerned with today's problems, Maitreya has worked on many levels since 1977 to prepare humanity for His outward presence. From behind the scenes, the outpouring of His extraordinary energy has been the stimulus for dramatic changes on many fronts, including the fall of communism in the Soviet Union, the collapse of apartheid in South Africa, the rapprochement between East and West, the growing power of the people's voice, and a worldwide focus on preserving the environment.

Since 1988 Maitreya has appeared miraculously throughout the world, mainly to orthodox religious groups, presenting in the simplest terms the great spiritual laws governing our lives. And, through steadily increasing signs and spiritual manifestations, widely reported in the media, He has touched the hearts of millions, preparing them for His imminent appearance.

Day of Declaration

*A*t the earliest possible moment, Maitreya will demonstrate His true identity. On the Day of Declaration, the international radio and television networks will be linked together, and Maitreya will be invited to speak to the world. We will see His face on television, but each of us will hear His words telepathically in our own language as Maitreya simultaneously impresses the minds of all humanity. Even those who are not watching Him on television or listening to the radio will have this experience. At the same time, hundreds of thousands of spontaneous healings will take place throughout the world. In this way we will know that this man is truly the World Teacher for all humanity.

Maitreya, working openly in the world, will inspire humanity to see itself as one family, and create a civilization based on sharing, economic and social justice, and global cooperation. He will launch a call to action to save the millions of people who starve to death every year in a world of plenty. Among Maitreya's recommendations will be a shift in social priorities so that adequate food, housing, clothing, education, and medical care become universal rights.

Under Maitreya's inspiration, humanity itself will make the required changes and create a saner and more just world for all.

FOR MORE INFORMATION:

Share International, PO Box 41877, 1009 DB Amsterdam, Holland

Tara Center, P.O. Box 6001, North Hollywood, CA 91603; tel. 818-785-6300.

On the Internet, go to the Share International gopher (shareintl.org 7004). On CompuServe, go to the New Age Forum (go newage). Enter Lib12. Find file si0101.txt.

Taoism

A Portrait

Dr. Douglas K. Chung

Professor at Grand Valley State University School of Social Work, Grand Rapids, Michigan

Li Erh (6th century BCE) commonly known as Lao Tzu (the Old Master), was a contemporary of Confucius. He was the keeper of the imperial library, but in his old age he disappeared to the west, leaving behind him the *Tao Te Ching* (*Book of Tao and Virtue*).

Taoism derived its name from this profoundly wise book, only about 5,000 words in length. It can be used as a guide to the cultivation of the self as well as a political manual for social transformation at both the micro and macro levels. The philosophy of Taoism and its belief in immortals can be traced back to the Yellow Emperor, Huang-Ti. That is why Taoism is often called the "Huang-Lao" philosophy.

Taoism believes *Tao* to be the cosmic, mysterious, and ultimate principle underlying form, substance, being, and change. *Tao* encompasses everything. It can be used to understand the universe and nature as well as the human body. For example, "*Tao* gives birth to the One, the One gives birth to Two, and from Two emerges Three, Three gives birth to all the things. All things carry the *Yin* and the *Yang,* deriving their vital harmony from the proper blending of the two vital forces." (*Tao Te Ching*, ch. 42)

Tao is the cause of change and the source of all nature, including humanity. Everything from quanta to solar systems consists of two primary elements of existence, *Yin* and *Yang* forces, which represent all opposites. These two forces are complementary elements in any system and result in the harmony or balance of the system. All systems coexist in an interdependent network. The dynamic tension between *Yin* and *Yang* forces in all systems results in an endless process of change: production and reproduction and the transformation of energy. This is the natural order.

Tao and virtue are said to be the same coin with different sides. The very title *Tao Te Ching* means the canon of *Tao* and Virtue. Lao Tzu says, "The Highest Virtue is achieved through non-action. It does not require effort," because virtue is natural to people. This is what is meant by "Tao creates and Virtue sustains" (ch. 51).

Taoists believe that *Tao* has appeared in the form of sages and teachers of humankind, as, for example, Fu Hsi, the giver of the Pa Qua (eight trigrams) and the arts of divination to reveal the principles of *Tao*. The *Pa Qua* is the foundation of the *I Ching* and represents the eight directions of the compass associated with the forces of nature that make up the universe. There are two forms of the *Pa Qua*: the *Pa Qua* of the Earlier Heaven (the *Ho To*), which describes the ideal state of existence, and the

Pa Qua of Later Heaven (*Lo Shu*), which describes a state of disharmonious existence. The path of the Return to the *Tao* is the process of transforming Later Heaven into Earlier Heaven. In other words, it is the process of a reunification with *Tao*, of being transformed from a conflicting mode to a harmonious mode.

The conflicting mode is the destructive or waning cycle of the Five Elements (metal, wood, earth, water and fire). The destructive cycle consists of metal destroying wood (axes cutting trees); wood dominating earth as the roots of the trees dig into the ground (power domination); earth mastering water and preventing the flood (anti-nature forces); water destroying fire (anti-nature causes pollution that destroys the beauty of the world); and fire melting metals (pollution).

Taoists believe that through both personal and social transformation we can convert the destructive cycle of the Five Elements into a creative cycle of the Five Elements – to change from a conflicting mode of life into a supportive way of living. The creative cycle of the Five Elements is this: metal in the veins of the earth nourishes the underground waters (purification); water gives life to vegetation and creates wood (nourishment); wood feeds fire to create ashes forming earth (nature recycling). The cycle is completed when metal is formed in the veins of the earth. The path of the Return to the *Tao* is clearly needed in light of today's concerns about energy and environment.

Taoism believes in the value of life. Taoists do not focus on life after death, but rather emphasize practical methods of cultivating health to achieve longevity. Therefore, Taoism teaches people to enhance their health and longevity by minimizing their desires and centering themselves on stillness. Taoists firmly believe that human lives are in our control. For example, Lao Tzu promotes *Chi Kung* (breathing exercise) to enhance life (ch. 5, 20, 52). He offers three methods of life enhancement: 1) keeping original "oneness," that is, to integrate energy, *chi*, and spirit; 2) maintaining one's vital energy in order to retain the flexibility and adaptability a newborn baby has; 3) persisting in practice for longevity (ch. 10, 52, 59). To practice *Chi Kung* is to practice the path of the Return to the *Tao* on an individual level to integrate physical, emotional, and spiritual development for health and longevity.

Taoism advocates nonaggressive, nonviolent, peaceful coexistence of states. For example, Lao Tzu describes an ideal state as one in which people love their own country and lifestyle so much that, even though the next country is so close the citizens can hear its roosters crowing and its dogs barking, they are content to die of old age without ever having gone to see it (ch. 80). Lao Tzu regards weapons as the tools of violence; all decent people detest them. He recommends that the proper demeanor after a military victory should be the same as that at a funeral (ch. 31).

Taoism advocates a minimum of goverment intervention, relying instead on individual development to reach a natural harmony under *Tao*'s leading. To concentrate on individual development is to practice the path of the Return to the *Tao* on a macro level. Lao Tzu writes:

The Tao never does anything, yet through it all things are done. (ch. 37)

If you want to be a great leader, you must learn to follow the Tao. Stop trying to control. Let go of fixed plans and concepts, and the world will govern itself. The more prohibitions you have, the less virtuous people will be. The more weapons you have, the less secure people will be. The more subsidies you have, the less self-reliant people will be. (ch. 57).

Act without doing, work without effort. Think of the small as large and the few as many. Confront the difficult while it is still easy; accomplish the great task by a series of small acts. The Master never reaches for the great; thus achieves greatness. (ch. 63)

Prevent trouble before it arises. Put things in order before they exist. The giant pine tree grows from a tiny sprout. The journey of a thousand miles starts from your first step. (ch. 64)

Lao Tzu's view of social distribution is this:

Tao adjusts excess and deficiency so that there is perfect balance. It takes from what is too much and gives to what isn't enough. Those who try to control, who use force to protect their power, go against the direction of the Tao. They take from those who don't have enough and give to those who have far too much. (ch. 77)

Basically, Taoists promote a way of life that exhibits six characteristics (Ho, 1988): (1) determining and working with the Tao when making changes; (2) basing one's life on the *laissez faire* principle – let nature follow its own course as its guideline for change; (3) modeling one's life on the sage, on nature, and thus on the *Tao*; (4) emphasizing the *Tao*'s strategy of reversal transformation; (5) focusing on simplicity and originality; (6) looking for intuitive awareness and insight and deemphasizing rational and intellectual efforts. These characteristics are the essential Taoist guidelines for personal and social development.

Taoism in the world today

*T*he people of the world today are confronted with the problems of environmental pollution, fragmentation, competition, dehumanization, and no common agreement on what constitutes an ideal society. In this world of conflict and unrest, a world that is nevertheless interdependent, Taoists still search to provide natural ways of solving problems. They gain the strength to transform their own lives and thereby to fulfill their mission. They try to help individuals as well as societies to transform from a way of life based on conflict to a harmonious way of life.

The practitioners of Taoism and those who are influenced by its philosophy include environmentalists, naturalists, libertarians, wildlife protectors, natural food advocates or vegetarians, and many physicists. More and more Westerners are able to appreciate Taoism through international contacts and Taoist literature.

Dr. Eva Wong, the director of studies at Fung Loy Kok Taoist Temple, is a member of the state of Colorado's Interfaith Advisory Council to the governor. She translated *Cultivating Stillness: A Taoist Manual for Transforming Body and Mind* (1992). She also offers graduate-level courses on Taoist and Buddhist philosophy at the University of Denver. Fung Loy Kok Taoist Temple has two branch temples in the United States and four temples in Canada. These temples offer various activities, including scripture study, lectures, meditation, classes in chi-kung, cooking, retreats, *kung-fu*, and training in traditional Lion Dance.

Chungliang A. Huang formed the Living Tao Foundation to promote Tao sports and to publish various books related to Tao. Many people practice *chi-kung*, *Tai-chi chuan* and acupuncture daily even without knowing that they are practicing Taoism.

"Trees and animals, humans and insects, flowers and birds: these are active images of the subtle energies that flow from the stars throughout the universe. Meeting and combining with each other and the elements of the Earth, they give rise to all living things. The superior person understands this, and understands that her own energies play a part in it. Understanding these things, she respects the Earth as her mother, the heavens as her father, and all living things as her brothers and sisters."

"Those who want to know the truth of the universe should practice...reverence for all life; this manifests as unconditional love and respect for oneself and all other beings."

LAO TZU (translated by Brian Walker)

FOR MORE INFORMATION:

Fung Loy Kok Taoist Temple
47 W. 11th Avenue, Denver, CO 80204

BOOKS:

Capra, F. (1991). *The Tao of Physics*. Boston: Shambhala.

Chang, P. T. (1986). *The Inner Teachings of Taoism*. Boston: Shambhala.

Cheng Yi (11th century). *I Ching The Tao of Organization*, trans. T. Cleary (1988). Boston: Shambhala.

Cleary, T., trans. (1990). *The Tao of Politics*. Boston: Shambhala.

Cleary, T., trans. (1989). *The Book of Balance and Harmony*. San Francisco: North Point Press.

Cleary, T., trans. (1989). *I Ching Mandalas: A Program of Study for The Book of Changes*. Boston: Shambhala.

Graham, A. C. (1989). *Disputers of the Tao Philosophical Argument in Ancient China*. La Salle, Ill.: Open Court.

Ho, J. Y. (1988). *Lao Tzu's Taoism*. Taipei: Wu Nan Publishing Co.

Huang, C. A. & Lynch J. (1992).

Thinking Body, Dancing Mind. New York: Bantam Books.

I-Ching Mandalas: A Program of Study for The Book of Changes, trans. T. Cleary (1989). Boston: Shambhala.

Kongtrul, J., trans. (1987). *The Great Path of Awakening*. Boston: Shambhala.

Lao Tzu (5th century BC). *Tao Te Ching*, trans. S. Mitchell (1988). New York: Harper & Row Publishers.

Liu I-ming (1796). *The Taoist I-Ching*, trans. T. Cleary (1986). Boston: Shambhala.

Min, C. (1988). *Yen Hsin Scientific Chi Kong*. Hong Kong: China Books Press.

Watts, A. (1976). *Tao: The Watercourse Way*. London: Jonathan Cape.

Wong, E. (1989). *Fung Loy Kok Week, 1988*. The Taoist Tai Chi Society of Colorado.

Wong, E., trans. (1992). *Cultivating Stillness: A Taoist Manual for Transforming Body and Mind*. Boston: Shambhala.

Wong, E., trans. (1990). *Seven Taoist Masters: A Folk Novel of China*. Boston: Shambhala.

The Unification Church

A Portrait

Dr. Frank Kaufmann

Executive Director, Inter Religious Federation for World Peace, which arranges interfaith meetings and publications

*T*he Unification Church is best understood in the context of the larger work of Reverend Moon and Mrs. Moon. In addition to heading the Unification Church, Reverend Moon and Mrs. Moon have founded and support dozens of initiatives for world peace in all spheres of human endeavor. Of special note are the Inter-Religious Federation for World Peace, The International Federation for World Peace and the Women's Federation for World Peace. These are surounded by a constellation of cultural, educational, relief, and humanitarian projects. Two important elements must be considered in order to develop an accurate grasp of the Unification Church: (1) the teachings which guide the Unification community, namely the *Divine Principle;* and (2) the status of Reverend and Mrs. Moon.

Reverend Moon was born in what is now North Korea, January 6, 1920, during the period of brutal Japanese occupation. The fifth of eight children, Sun Myung Moon came from a family well respected for its great hospitality and who were referred to as "those who could live without law," a Korean phrase indicating people who were capable of guiding themselves by conscience alone. Reverend Moon's religious foundations combined the ancient traditions of Korea with the message of Christian missionaries. According to Reverend Moon, Jesus appeared to him while deep in prayer on a Korean mountainside, on Easter Sunday, 1936. Jesus asked him to complete the responsibility left unfinished since the origin of humankind. From that point the life of Sun Myung Moon changed dramatically. For nine years Sun Myung Moon researched the Bible, the natural world and the spiritual world to produce what is known today as the *Divine Principle*.

The *Divine Principle* is divided into three sections – Creation, Fall and Restoration. It teaches that God's original ideal is expressed in "the three great blessings" found in the Genesis account of human origins. To "be fruitful" is understood as the commission for each person to perfect his or her unique individuality by uniting mind and body and being in full union with God. These perfected individuals, man and woman, were to "multiply," forming families born of the unconditional love of a husband for his wife, of a wife for her husband. It is taught that the original human couple were thus to become "True Parents." This ever-expanding family should "have dominion," namely establish a perfect ecological relationship with the natural universe. This ideal was not achieved by the first human ancestors, who instead violated God's commandment "not to eat the forbidden fruit," by engaging in physical love without receiving God's blessing to do so. This act of disobedience, in which the Archangel Lucifer participated, created the personage of Satan and bound the first human ancestors with him. Satan participates in human affairs through the perpetuation of impure love and lineage.

Salvation providence reveals God's work to re-create the conditions for: 1) the fulfillment of the original three great blessings, and 2) to liberate the descendants of Adam and Eve from their bondage to Satan. This task constitutes the mission of the Messiah, who by the fulfillment of his own responsibility obeys the commandment and fulfills the purpose of creation. Thus Jesus came both as "Adam" and as the Savior to fulfill the three blessings and to liberate all of humankind. The faithlessness of those around Jesus led to his crucifixion, thus preventing him from his opportunity to fulfill the three great blessings. The divine love of Jesus, however, preserved the mission of Savior, allowing Jesus to provide spiritual salvation to those who believe in him and follow his teachings. Jesus promised the "second coming of Christ," knowing that the original will of God, the three blessings, remained unfulfilled despite his own ministry. It is this original mission that Jesus asked Sun Myung Moon to fulfill in 1936.

In the 20th century Sun Myung Moon came as the return of Christ (at the end of WWII, in 1945), but, like Jesus, he was rejected. When this failure occurred, Reverend Moon was forced to establish a religious community which could carry out the mission of Christianity and serve as the Bride of Christ. This community became known as the Unification Church, founded in 1954. In 1960 Reverend Moon married Hak Ja Han Moon, thus fulfilling for the first time in human history the original mission of True Parents. Unification Church members and members of other religions have their marriages "blessed" by Reverend and Mrs. Moon, whereby they inherit the potential to themselves become true parents.

The mission of the True Parents and Savior is to all people in all religions. The Unification "Church" does not desire to be an enduring religious body. Long before the Unification Church appeared each world religion was already instructed to await and receive the one who will end evil history and restore an unbroken relationship between God and all humanity. The Unification Church exists to teach the Divine Principle and support the effort of the True Parents freely to give the blessing.

Wicca and Nature Spirituality

A Portrait of Wicca

H. Ps. Phyllis W. Curott, J.D.

President Emerita, Covenant of the Goddess (COG)
COG is one of the largest and oldest Wiccan religious organizations, with members in North America, Europe and Australia.

*W*icca is a vital, contemporary spiritual path reviving the ancient, pre-Christian indigenous religion of Europe. It is a life-affirming Earth religion which is both old and new, "traditional," and vibrantly creative. Wiccans experience the Divine as immanent, as embodied in the Universe, the world in all its aspects and in humanity, as well as transcendent. Therefore all of life is perceived as sacred and interconnected. Modern Wicca incorporates ancient and modern liturgy, ritual and shamanic practices by which people attune themselves to the natural rhythms of the Earth and the Universe, enabling them to experience communion with the embodied Divine. Wiccans honor nature as a profound spiritual teacher and devote themselves to the contemplation and integration of the spiritual wisdom inherent in the Earth's cycles of seasonal transformation.

Wicca – also known as the Old Religion, Witchcraft, or the Craft – is derived from the old Anglo-Saxon word *wicce,* pronounced "witche," giving rise to the commonly used but frequently misunderstood term Witchcraft. *Wicce* meant a practitioner of the Old Religion, and reflects the influence of the Old Norse word *vitke,* meaning a priestess, seer or shaman. The word pagan is from the Latin *paganus,* a country dweller. *Heathen,* another related term also misinterpreted as a pejorative, meant one who dwelt on the heath. All were European peoples who, like Native Americans and other indigenous groups, lived close to the Earth and respected their relationship to nature as sacred.

Wicca is non-dogmatic. There is no single leader or prophet, nor is there a Wiccan bible or literature of revealed and absolute truth. Rather, Wicca is a dynamic and accessible system of techniques, the mastery of which enables each individual to experience the Divine personally. Most Wiccans consider their practice a priest/esshood involving years of training and passage through life-transforming initiatory rituals. Priestesses and priests are respected as Elders and teachers of these techniques, for it is a basic Wiccan precept that each individual has the capacity and the responsibility to experience the sacred mystery that gives life true meaning.

It is a Wiccan tenet that spiritual insight is achieved through living in harmony with the Earth. Like the spiritual worldview and practices of Native Americans, Taoists and many indigenous Earth religions, Wiccan spiritual practices are intended to attune humanity to the natural rhythms and cycles of nature. Rituals therefore coincide with the phases of the moon, which are particularly significant for women, and the seasonal changes. Wiccans seek to live in a balanced way with nature and to practice their spirituality not only in sacred rituals but in the way they live each day. Thus the Divine is experienced not only in prayer, meditation, ritual, and shamanic work, but in gardening, preparing a meal, recycling trash, making love, giving birth, and growing old. Divine presence is felt in the air we breathe, the water we drink, the food upon our tables, the creatures and plants with which we share this beautiful planet, and the sacred Earth that nourishes and sustains us.

Our reverence for the Earth expresses our reverence for the Divine which it embodies and reflects a deep ecological concern which is more than pragmatic. As an embodiment of the Divine, the Earth is not treated as a utilitarian object, to be exploited, polluted and destroyed for man's short-term greed. Rather it is inherently sacred in its value. This fundamental respect for the Earth as sacred has drawn many people to the practice of Wicca and, like other indigenous religions, may be one of its greatest contributions to a world imperiled by ecological crisis.

The Divine is also perceived and experienced anthropomorphically as well, though there is great diversity among Wiccans as to whether they characterize the Divine as exclusively feminine or as a multiplicity or dyad of feminine and masculine forms and metaphors. In contrast to most of the world's religions, Wicca acknowledges the Divine as feminine as well as masculine. The Goddess, who is seen as both transcendent and immanent, is an essential aspect of Wiccan worship. She may be worshipped as the nameless single Goddess, or as any of the many aspects and names by which She has always been known. Personified as the Triple Goddess, the Great Mother, Isis, Gaia, Demeter, Cerridwen, Brigid, Oestara, Innana, Ishtar, Shekinah, Shakti, Kali, Amaterasu, and many others, the Divine feminine is also experienced in the energies of the Universe, the mysteries of the moon, the blessings of the Earth, and the wonders of our own bodies, which like the Earth itself are held to be sacred. This honoring of the Divine in its feminine aspect, as well as the genuine respect for women as spiritual leaders, wise women and healers, has been a primary reason for the rapid growth in popularity of Wicca among women. According to the Institute for the Study of American Religion (U.C. at Santa Barbara), Goddess spirituality, to which Wicca is a venerable contributor, is the fastest growing religion in America.

Wiccans have one fundamental ethical precept: *An* (if) *it harm none, do what you will.* This honors the great freedom that each individual has to ascertain truth, to experience the Divine directly, and to determine how to best live her or his own life. With that freedom, however, comes a profound responsibility that none may be harmed by one's choices and actions. As in many religions, individual Wiccans reach different conclusions when applying these fundamental precepts to such issues as vegetarianism, abortion, or participation in war.

Wiccan spiritual practices, often referred to as "magic," are in fact ancient techniques for changing consciousness at will in order to better perceive and participate in Divine reality. A primary purpose of Wiccan techniques is the transformation of the self to fully develop one's gifts and capacities to live a full, joyful, and spiritual life. In this sense, they are also used for practical ends such as healing, divination, purification, blessing, and the raising of energy to achieve positive life goals such as fulfilling work and relationships. All of these techniques, which may include prayer, meditation, ritual, drumming, singing, chanting, dancing, journeying, trance, and others, require and engender wisdom, maturity, patience, passion, and an abiding commitment to the sacred.

The "casting of a spell," frequently misunderstood as a means of having power over people or nature by the use of supernatural forces, is actually a form of ritual and meditation which is very similar to prayer in other religions, except that, instead of beseeching the aid or intervention of an external deity, the indwelling Divine energy is drawn outward into manifestation in the world through harmonious interaction with the Divine presence already present. The idea of controlling and having dominion over nature or others is alien to Wiccan cosmology. Wiccans do not work with supernatural powers nor do they seek to have "power over." The essence of Wiccan spirituality is respect for and attunement with the natural energies of the Earth and the Universe as a means of attuning oneself with the sacred. It is unethical to engage in any form of spiritual work which seeks to control, manipulate or have power over others. While work may be done on behalf of another, such as healing which is an important and ancient aspect of Wicca, even this is never done without the knowledge and consent of the person who is being assisted.

There are many different traditions or denominations within the Old Religion. Some reflect the particular practices of certain ethnic groups such as Celtic, Norse, Welsh, Greek, Italian, Finno-Ugric, Lithuanian, etc. Some are part of the initiatory traditions made public by such practitioners as Gerald Gardner. Still other practice with the guidance of liturgical works published and taught by contemporary Wiccans. Some practitioners search within themselves for inspiration and direction or work creatively in groups in a mutually agreed upon group structure. Some traditions are practiced by women only, others by men only, and many include both women and men. Some traditions may date back for hundreds of years or more, and others have been in existence for only a few years.

Whether carrying on the spiritual vocabulary of an ancient lineage or drawing forth the highest creative and spontaneous expression of a single individual, the great strength of Wicca lies in its diversity and vitality – it is a living, growing religious tradition.

The Charge of the Goddess

*L*isten to the words of the Great Mother, she who was of old also called Artemis, Astarte, Athene, Dione, Melusine, Cerridwen, Arianrhod and many other names:

"Whenever you have need of anything, once in the month, and better it be when the moon is full, then shall you assemble in some secret place and adore my spirit, which is Mother of all creation. There shall you assemble, who are fain to learn all mystery, yet have not won the deepest secrets; to you shall I teach things that are yet unknown. And you shall be free from slavery; and as a sign that you are truly free, you shall be naked in your rites, and you shall dance, sing, feast, make music, and love all in my praise. For mine is the ecstasy of the spirit and mine also is joy on earth, for my law is love unto all beings. Keep pure your highest ideal; strive ever towards it; let naught stop you nor turn you aside. For mine is the secret door which opens upon the Land of Youth, and mine is the cup of the wine of life, the Cauldron of Cerridwen, which is the Holy Grail of immortality. I am the gracious Goddess, who gives the gift of joy unto the hearts of humanity. Upon earth I give knowledge of the spirit eternal and beyond death I give peace, and freedom and reunion with those who have gone before. Nor do I demand aught in sacrifice, for behold, I am the Mother of all living and my love is poured out upon the earth.

*H*ear the words of the Star Goddess: she in the dust of whose feet are the hosts of heaven, and whose body encircles the universe:

"I am the beauty of the green earth, and the white moon among the stars and the mystery of the waters, and the desire of the hearts of humanity. I call unto thy soul – arise, and come unto me. For I am the soul of nature, who gives life to the universe. From me all things proceed, and unto me all things must return. Before my face, beloved of Gods and humanity, let thine innermost divine self be enfolded in the rapture of the infinite. Let my worship be within the heart that rejoices, for behold, all acts of love and pleasure are my rituals. And therefore, let there be beauty and strength, power and compassion, honor and humility, mirth and reverence, within you. And you who think to seek for me, know your seeking and yearning shall avail you not unless you know the mystery: that if that which you seek you find not within you, you will never find it without. For behold, I have been with you from the beginning, and I am that which is attained at the end of desire."

Composed by Doreen Valiente and
Gerald Gardner from inspiration and traditional sources

A Guide to
Nature Spirituality Terms

Selena Fox

Founder and leader of Circle Sanctuary, an internationally-linked Nature Spirituality resource center and Shamanic Wiccan church based in Mt. Horeb, Wisconsin

Animism: ancient philosophy that views everything in Nature as having an indwelling spirit/soul, including the plants, rocks, waters, winds, fires, animals, humans, and other life forms. Animism is the foundation of shamanism and has been considered the earliest form of human religion on planet Earth.

Earth-centered Spirituality: honoring the spiritual interconnectedness of life on planet Earth, often as Mother Earth or Gaia, but sometimes as a gender neutral Earth Spirit. Sometimes called *Earth religion* and *Gaian (Gaean) religion.* Related EcoChristian form is Creation-Centered Spirituality.

Ecofeminism: feminist environmental philosophy that draws parallels between the oppression of women and the oppression of Nature by patriarchy and which advocates the spiritual and political liberation of both.

Goddess Spirituality: revering Nature and honoring the Great Goddess in one or more of Her many forms. Usually polytheistic and sometimes multicultural in practice. Usually incorporates feminist perspectives.

Heathen: Another name for Pagan. Many contemporary practitioners of Teutonic Nature religions prefer this term for themselves and their spirituality.

Nature Religions: religions that include an honoring of the Divine as immanent in Nature. May be pre-modern, modern, or post-modern in philosophical orientation. Usually polytheistic, animistic, and pantheistic. Include traditional ways of various native peoples of the Americas, Africa, Asia, Australia, Polynesia, Europe, and elsewhere; religions of ancient Pagan cultures, such as Egyptian, Greek, Roman, Minoan, Assyrian, Celtic, Teutonic, and others; and contemporary Paganism.

Nature Spirituality: honoring the spiritual interconnectedness of life not only on Planet Earth but throughout the Universe/Cosmos; more encompassing term than Earth-centered Spirituality because it also includes Celestial religions; used by some as synonymous with contemporary Paganism and by others as also including interfaith blends, such as those that combine Paganism with EcoChristianity or EcoBuddhism.

NeoPagan: Contemporary Pagan.

Pagan: pertains to a Nature religion or a practitioner of an ancient and/or contemporary Nature religion; also used to refer to a Nature Spirituality, Earth-centered Spirituality, and/or Goddess Spirituality group or practitioner.

Pantheism: the Divine as immanent, the Divine is in everything and everything has a Divine aspect.

Panentheism: Pantheism that also includes a transcendent component conceptualized as the Sacred Whole or Divine Unity.

Polytheism: honoring Divinity in two or more forms. Can be belief in/worship of multiple aspects of a particular deity; of the Divine as Goddess and God; or of many Goddesses, Gods, Nature Spirits, and/or other Divine forms. Some, but not all, polytheistic Nature religions acknowledge an all-encompassing Divine Unity.

Shaman: an adept who serves as healer and spirit world communicator for her/his tribe or community. Sometimes known as a *Medicine* person. This role is tribal culture/community defined.

Shamanic Practitioner: someone learning and working with shamanistic healing practices for self-development, and in some cases, also for helping others. Sometimes known as a *Medicine worker.* This role is self-defined.

Shamanism: animistic spiritual healing practices usually involving ecstatic trance and spirit world journeys by adepts. Forms of shamanism include *Traditional,* which are rooted in specific indigenous tribal people's cultures, and *Multicultural,* which are contemporary forms that integrate old and new spirit wisdom ways from more than one culture.

Wiccan Spirituality: contemporary paths rooted in one or more Nature folk religions of old Europe. Also known as the *Old Religion, the Craft, Wicca, Wicce, Ways of the Wise, NeoPagan Witchcraft,* and *Benevolent Witchcraft.*

Witch: Some Wiccan practitioners use the word "Witch" for themselves in connection with their spirituality to bring back its pre-Inquisition use in Europe as a term of honor and respect, meaning "medicine person/medicine worker," "shaman/shamanic practitioner," "wise woman/man," "priestess/priest of the Old Religion." Other Wiccans refuse to use the word "Witch" because of later negative definitions of the word which led to its use as a tool of Pagan genocide and religious oppression in Europe and North America for hundreds of years. During the "Burning Times" of the Middle Ages, bigots in power changed its definition, making it a term linked with evil, and used it as a brand to mark and exterminate folk healers, those who refused to convert to state-sanctioned forms of Christianity, political rivals, and others. Contemporary usage of the word "Witch" by non-Wiccans is diverse but in recent years has been changing in academia and elsewhere to reflect the growing public awareness and understanding of Wiccan Spirituality's reclaiming of the word.

FOR MORE INFORMATION:

Circle Sanctuary Inc.
P.O. Box 219, Mt. Horeb, WI 53572
tel. (608) 924-2216 / fax. (608) 924-5961

Covenant of the Goddess
P.O. Box 1226, Berkeley, CA 94701

EarthSpirit Community,
PO Box 365-P, Medford, MA 02155

Zoroastrianism

A Portrait

Dr. Pallan R. Ichaporia

Chair of the Research and Preservation Committee of the Federation of Zoroastrian Associations of North America

The Opening Prayer

"In humble adoration, with hands outstretched,
I pray to Thee, O Lord, Invisible benevolent Spirit:
Vouchsafe to me in this hour of joy,
All righteousness of action, all wisdom of the Good Mind,
That I may thereby bring joy to the Soul of Creation."

Yasna 28.I, from the *Gathas*

An ancient monotheistic religion

Zoroastrianism is the first revealed monotheistic religion of the world. The date of its founding is lost in antiquity, but general consensus places it between 2000 to 1800 BCE . Its founder, Zarathushtra or Zoroaster (as called by the Greeks), flourished on the East Iranian Plateau. Zarathushtra saw the God (Ahura Mazda – the Wise Lord), felt conscious of His presence, and heard His words, which are recorded in the five Songs or Poems he composed. These are called the *Gathas*. One easily understands Zarathushtra by seeing the Prophet's zeal in the *Gathas* and the visible manifestation of his meeting the God.

Primary beliefs

Zoroastrians believe in the One Supreme, Omnipotent, Omniscient God, called Ahura Mazda. He is to be understood through his six divine attributes: *Vohu Mana* (Good Mind), *Asha* (Truth, Righteousness), *Spenta Armaity* (Correct Thinking, Piety), *Xsthra Vairya* (Divine Domain), *Haurvatat* (Perfection, Integrity), and *Ameratat* (Immortality). His attributes are also found in each and every human being who must work as a co-worker of God to defeat evil and bring the world to perfection. This can be achieved by good thoughts, good words, and good deeds.

Angels, known as the *Yazatas,* work endlessly to aid humans in bringing the world to perfection. All the natural elements like air, water, and lands are to be kept pure. Their pollutions are to be prevented at all cost. This makes Zoroastrianism the first true ecological religion of the world. After death, the immortal soul of the departed person is judged according to all the good deeds done by him or her in this world; the soul then enjoys the pleasures of paradise or undergoes the tortures of hell.

There is also belief in the appearance of the last savior, called Sosayant, and of the final day of judgment with the resurrections of all who have died (these last two are later beliefs).

Main sources of religious knowledge

The primary source is the *Gathas of the Prophet*; this is followed by *Hapatan Haiti*, the seven chapters written by the Prophet's disciples. These scriptures are called *Old Avesta* as their language differs from the later scriptures, called the *Younger Avesta*. Together they are known as the *Avestan*. The *Younger Avesta* consists of the *Yasna* (without the *Gathas*, containing 72 chapters), *Vispered*, *Vendidad* and the *Yasts*. The original *Avestan* scriptures were written in 21 books called *the Nasks*, from which only one complete *Nask – Vandidad* – has survived the ravages of time. The *Gathas* and the rest of the scriptures survived because they formed part of the long *Yasna* liturgical ceremony, which was passed from generation to generation by oral tradition.

Rituals

The most important ritual which every Zoroastrian has to undergo is the *Navzote* or *Sudraposhi Ceremony*, which is for new initiates (ages 7 to 15 years) entering the Religion. Generally the rituals are divided into two classes: (1) those like the *Yasna* ceremony, to be performed in the Zoroastrian Fire-Temples; and (2) those to be performed anywhere outside the Zoroastrian Temples, like *Jashan* (thanksgiving) ceremony.

The word *fire temple* is a misnomer as the Zoroastrians do not worship the fire. The fire is kept as a symbol of purity, acting as the focal point (like the *Kebla* of the religion of Islam) for prayers.

A minority religion

The Zoroastrians are the smallest minority of all religions, having undergone the severest persecutions for centuries in Iran at the hands of its conquerors, after the fall of the last Sassanian Zoroastrian Empire. At one time the number of the community ran into millions (650 CE). A small band of the community migrated to India (between the ninth and tenth centuries CE) to avoid harassment and persecution; called the Parsees, these now number fewer than 60,000 in India and 2,500 in Pakistan. Still fewer have survived in Iran (10,000), and some have settled in the West, mostly in North America (12,000) and in Europe (7,000); there may be 3,000 in other parts of the world. With such a small total number of the community there are no fixed denominations as such, although the Iranian Zoroastrians and the Parsees have different cultures and mother tongues, which developed due to long separation.

Zoroastrianism in the World Today

Dr. Jehan Bagli

Founding member of the Zoroastrian Association of Quebec, Editor of Gavashni and first Editor of FEZANA Journal

*T*hroughout its long history, the Zarathustrian tradition has experienced numerous social environments shaped by various ruling dynasties, in different eras in early Iran. Consequently, from early times the adherents have learned to coexist with people of different beliefs. This has built within the tradition a strong sense of tolerance for other faiths and other religious viewpoints, an attribute which is firmly intertwined with the teachings of the first revealed religion of mankind.

The basic tenets of the faith proclaim respect for creation of nature and of equality for all human beings; these are the fundamental cornerstones of the tradition. With these axioms in focus, Zarathustrians consistently make a concerted effort to learn and comprehend the nature and beliefs of other faiths. The migration of Zarathustrians from Iran to India around 936 CE put them within the milieu of the Hindu society. Here they emerged as the most intellectual, honest and hard-working minority of the world. Despite imbibing the knowledge and customs of other faiths, they have for the past 3,500 years maintained the integrity and identity of their faith with glowing success.

*A*t this time the major challenge for humanity to overcome in the world is a breakdown in true respect and tolerance for other human beings. Much of this is motivated by materialism and greed, but conflicts are frequently perpetrated in the name of religion, under false pretenses. The understanding that all humans emerge from the same creating force has been totally overshadowed by dogmatic and egotistic endeavors, without regard for the needs of others.

The other major issue in our highly technocratic society is the lack of regard for the elements of creation. In the interest of bettering living conditions, the relationship between humanity and the creation has reached an all-time low. The concept of the preservation of the creation, with humans as its stewards and as co-workers with the creator, promoted by various religious traditions, has totally disappeared. Exploitation of our non-renewable resources, pollution of our waters with chemical wastes, and excessive deforestation are some of the most serious infractions by the human society towards the elements of creation.

*T*here is a great renaissance of spiritual awareness among the Zarathustrian community. Attempts are being made to disseminate the message of the prophet to the youth and to adults to make them aware of these injustices that are perpetrated in the name of religion. The Federation of Zoroastrian Associations of North America (FEZANA) is making all efforts to spread awareness of the Zarathustrian religion through interfaith dialogue with other religious groups and to make our sentiments known.

"O Ahura Mazda, and O Spirit of Truth:
Do you grant me and my followers
such strength and ruling power,
that with the help of the Benevolent Mind,
we may bring to the world,
restful joy and happiness,
of which, Thou, O Lord,
art indeed the first Possessor."

Yasna 29.10, from the second chapter of the *Gathas;* passages from the *Gathas,* here and above, are from "Understanding the Gathas, the Hymns of Zarathustra," by Dinshan J. Irani

Contributions to Western Thought

Rohinton M. Rivetna

President of the Federation of Zoroastrian Associations of North America, and Trustee of the CPWR

*Z*oroastrian ideas have played a vital role in the development of Western religious thought. Some theological concepts shared by Zoroastrianism with Judaism and Christianity are:

- Belief in one supreme and loving God
- Heaven and Hell, resurrection, and final judgement
- Ultimate triumph of good over evil
- A strict moral and ethical code
- The Messiah to come for the final restoration
- The words *satan, paradise,* and *amen* are of Zoroastrian origin

The interchange of Zoroastrian thought with Judaeo-Christian ideology first took place when Cyrus the Great defeated the Assyrians and released the Jews from Babylonian captivity. They heralded Cyrus as their messiah, as prophesied two centuries earlier in Isaiah 45:1–3. The Old Testament is replete with references to the Persian emperors Darius, Cyrus, and Xerxes, all of whom were Zoroastrians. [...]

*Z*oroastrian rituals and prayers are solemnized in the presence of a flame. Scrupulously tended with sandalwood and frankincense, a flame is kept burning in the inner sanctum of every Zoroastrian temple, and often in Zoroastrian homes. Fire is revered as a visible symbol of the inner light that burns within each person. It is a physical representation of the Illumined Mind, Light, and Truth, all highly regarded in the Zoroastrian doctrine. Despite its prehistoric origins, Zoroastrianism has vehemently denounced idolatry in any shape or form.

The *Fravashi* or *Farohar* is the presence of *Ahura Mazda* in every human being. It is the Divinity in Humanity. It is the conscience. The *Fravashi* is immortal and does not die with the person, but lives on forever. The *Fravashi* is ever present to guide and protect the person. It is the duty of a person, in making the choice between good and evil, to seek guidance from his *Fravashi.*

from *Followers of an Ancient Faith in a Modern World*, published by the Federation of Zoroastrian Associations of North America

FOR MORE INFORMATION:

Federation of Zoroastrian Associations of North America, 5750 S. Jackson St., Hindsdale, IL 60521 USA

Becoming a Community of Religions

"[The moral person] accepts as being good:
    to preserve life, to promote life, to raise to its highest value
    life which is capable of development;
and as being evil:
    to destroy life, to injure life,
    to repress life which is capable of development.
This is the absolute fundamental principle of the moral.

A man is ethical only when life, as such, is sacred...,
that of plants and animals as well as that of his fellow man,
and when he devotes himself helpfully to all life
that is in need of help."

ALBERT SCHWEITZER,
Out of My Life and Thought: An Autobiography, trans. C. T. Campion, p.158

"A number of philosophers and social scientists have pointed out
that the history of human morals is a story of a developing sense of
community that begins with the family and tribe
 and then gradually extends outward embracing the region,
 the nation, the race, all members of a world religion,
 and then all humanity. The sense of community involves an
awareness of kinship, identity, interdependence, participation in a
shared destiny, relationships to a common good.
It gives rise to the moral feelings of respect
and sympathy, leading to a sense of moral obligation...."

STEVEN C. ROCKEFELLER
from *Spirit and Nature*, p.144

Joining the Sacred Community

Who Lives in the "Global Village?"

Donella H. Meadows

Principal author of the influential (9 million in print, in 29 languages) The Limits to Growth *(1972). That book's reassessment and sequel,* Beyond the Limits, *was published in 1992.*

If the world were a village of 1,000 people, it would include:

- 584 Asians
- 124 Africans
- 95 East and West Europeans
- 84 Latin Americans
- 55 Soviets (including for the moment Lithuanians, Latvians, Estonians and other national groups)
- 52 North Americans
- 6 Australians and New Zealanders

The people of the village have considerable difficulty in communicating:

- 165 people speak Mandarin
- 86 English
- 83 Hindi/Urdu
- 64 Spanish
- 58 Russian
- 37 Arabic

That list accounts for the mother tongues of only half the villagers. The other half speak (in descending order of frequency) Bengali, Portuguese, Indonesian, Japanese, German, French and 200 other languages.

In this village of 1,000 there are:

- 329 Christians (among them 187 Catholics, 84 Protestants, 31 Orthodox)
- 178 Moslems
- 167 "non-religious"
- 132 Hindus
- 60 Buddhists
- 45 atheists
- 3 Jews
- 86 all other religions
- One-third (330) of the 1,000 people in

the world village are children and only 60 are over the age of 65. Half the children are immunized against preventable infectious diseases such as measles and polio.

- Just under half of the married women in the village have access to and use modern contraceptives.
- This year 28 babies will be born. Ten people will die, 3 of them for lack of food, 1 from cancer, 2 of the deaths are of babies born within the year. One person of the 1,000 is infected with the HIV virus; that person most likely has not yet developed a full-blown case of AIDS.
- With the 28 births and 10 deaths, the population of the village next year will be 1,018.
- In this 1,000-person community, 200 people receive 75 percent of the income; another 200 receive only 2 percent of the income.
- Only 70 people of the 1,000 own an automobile (although some of the 70 own more than one automobile).
- About one-third have access to clean, safe drinking water.
- Of the 670 adults in the village, half are illiterate.

The village has six acres of land per person, 6,000 acres in all, of which

- 700 acres are cropland
- 1,400 acres pasture
- 1,900 acres woodland
- 2,000 acres desert, tundra, pavement and other wasteland
- The woodland is declining rapidly; the wasteland is increasing. The other land categories are roughly stable.

The village allocates 83 percent of its fertilizer to 40 percent of its cropland – that owned by the richest and best-fed 270 people. Excess fertilizer running off this land causes pollution in lakes and wells. The remaining 60 percent of the

land, with its 17 percent of the fertilizer, produces 28 percent of the food grains and feeds for 73 percent of the people. The average grain yield on that land is one-third the harvest achieved by the richer villagers.

In the village of 1,000 people, there are:

- 5 soldiers
- 7 teachers
- 1 doctor
- 3 refugees driven from home by war or drought

The village has a total budget each year, public and private, of over $3 million – $3,000 per person if it is distributed evenly (which, we have already seen, it isn't).

Of the total $3 million:

- $181,000 goes to weapons and warfare
- $159,000 for education
- $132,000 for health care

The village has buried beneath it enough explosive power in nuclear weapons to blow itself to smithereens many times over. These weapons are under the control of just 100 of the people. The other 900 people are watching them with deep anxiety, wondering whether they can learn to get along together; and if they do, whether they might set off the weapons anyway through inattention or technical bungling; and, if they ever decide to dismantle the weapons, where in the world village they would dispose of the radioactive materials of which the weapons are made.

The preceding text was previously printed as most of one side of a large poster published for the Earth Summit in Rio de Janeiro, in June 1992. (The other side bears a photo portrait of the earth in full color against black space. The *Value Earth* poster, 27"x 39", is $7 postpaid from Value Earth, c/o David Copeland, 707 White Horse Pike, C-2, Absecon, NJ 08201. Used with permission.

The Cosmology of Religions

Dr. Thomas Berry

Eco-theologian, anthropologist, philosopher, Catholic monk and scholar of Teilhard de Chardin

Father Thomas Berry's books and vision challenge the religions and our culture as well to consider a new story of the universe and of our place in it.

*T*he universe is the primary sacred community; all human religions are participants in the religious aspect of the universe itself. With this recognition, we are moving from the theology and anthropology of religions to the cosmology of religions. In the past 50 years in America there has been intense interest in the sociology and psychology of religions, and even more interest in the history of religions, yet these all fall within the general designation of the anthropology of religions.

Because none of these have been able to deal effectively with the evolutionary story of the universe or with the ecological crisis, we are led on to the cosmological dimension of the religious issue both from our efforts at understanding and from our concerns for survival.

What is new about this sense of the universe's religious mode of being is that the universe itself is now experienced as an irreversible time-developmental process, not simply as an abiding season-renewing universe. Not so much cosmos as cosmogenesis.

Our recent knowledge of the universe comes primarily through the empirical, observational sciences rather than from intuitive processes. We are listening to the earth tell its story through the signals that it sends to us from outer space, through the light that comes to us from the stars, through the geological formations of the earth and through a vast number of other evidences of itself that the universe manifests to us.

In its every aspect the human is a participatory reality. We are members of the great universe community. We participate in its life. We are nourished, instructed, and healed by this community. In and through this community we enter into communion with that numinous mystery on which all things depend for their existence and activity. If this is true for the universe entire, it is also true in our relations with the earth.

From its own evidences we now know the story of the universe as an emergent process in its fourfold sequential story: the galactic, the earth, the life, and the human story. These constitute for us the primordial sacred story of the universe.

The original flaring forth of the universe carried the present within its fantastic energies as the present expresses those original energies in their articulated form. This includes all those spiritual developments that have occurred in the course of the centuries. In its sequence of transformations, the universe carries within itself the comprehensive meaning of the phenomenal world. In recent secular times this meaning was perceived only in its physical expression. Now we perceive that the universe is a spiritual as well as a physical reality from the beginning.

This sacred dimension is especially evident in those stupendous moments of transformation through which the universe has passed in these 15 billion years of its existence. These transformations include moments of great spiritual as well as physical significance—the privileged moments in the Great Story. The numinous mystery of the universe now reveals itself in a developmental mode of expression, a mode never before available to human consciousness through observational processes.

Yet all this means little to our modern western theologians who have shown little concern for the natural world as the primary bearer of religious consciousness. This is one of the basic reasons why both the physical and spiritual survival of the planet have become imperilled.

Presently we in the West think of ourselves as passing into another historical period or undergoing another cultural modification. If we think that the changes taking place in our times are simply another in the series of historical changes we are missing the real order of magnitude of the events taking place. We are at the end of an entire biological era in Earth history. We are now in a religious-civilizational period. In virtue of our new knowledge we are changing our most basic relations to the world about us. These changes are of a unique order of magnitude.

Our new acquaintance with the universe as irreversible developmental process is the most significant religious, spiritual, and scientific event since the beginning of the more complex civilizations some five thousand years ago. But we are bringing about the greatest devastation the earth has ever experienced in the four and a half billion years of its formation. Norman Myers, a specialist in the biosystems of the planet, estimates that we are causing an extinction spasm that is liable to result in the greatest setback to the abundance and variety of life on earth since the first flickerings of life some four billion years ago.

We are changing the chemistry of the planet, disturbing the biosystems, altering the geological structure and functioning of the planet – all of which took billions of years of development. In this process of closing down the life systems of the planet we are devastating a sacred world, making the earth a wasteland, not realizing that as we lose the more gorgeous species, we thereby lose modes of divine presence, the very basis of our religious experience.

Because we are unable to enter effectively into the new mystique of the emergent universe available to us through our new modes of understanding we are unable to prevent the disintegration of the life systems of the planet taking place through the misuse of that same scientific vision. Western religion and theology have not yet addressed these issues or established their identity in this context. Nor have other religious traditions done so. The main religious traditions have simply restated their beliefs and their spiritual disciplines. This new experience of the religious being of the universe and of the planet earth is not yet perceived on any widespread scale within academic, theological, or religious circles.

We cannot resolve the difficulties we face in this new situation by setting aside the scientific venture. Nor can we assume an attitude of indifference toward this new context of earthly existence because it is too powerful in its effects. We must find a new way of interpreting the process itself, because, properly interpreted, the scientific venture might even become one of the most significant spiritual disciplines of these times. This task is particularly urgent just now because this new mode of understanding has such powerful consequences on the very structure of the planet Earth. We must learn to respond to its deepest spiritual content or we will be forced to submit to the devastation that lies before us.

The assertions of our traditions cannot by themselves bring these forces under control. We are involved in the future of the planet in its geological and biological survival and functioning as well as in the future of our human and spiritual well-being. We will bring about the physical and spiritual well-being of the entire planet or there will be neither physical nor spiritual well-being for any of our earthly forms of being.

The traditional religions have not dealt effectively with these issues or with our modern cosmological experience because they were not designed for such a universe. Traditional religions have been shaped within a predominantly spatial mode of consciousness. The biblical religions, although they have a historical developmental perspective in dealing with the human spiritual process, perceive the universe itself from a spatial mode of consciousness. Biblical religions only marginally provide for the progress of the divine kingdom within an established universe that participates in the historical process. They seem to have as much difficulty as any other tradition in dealing with the developmental character of the universe.

Although the antagonism toward the idea of an evolutionary universe has significantly diminished, our limitations as theologians in speaking the language of this new cosmology is everywhere evident. Much has been done in process theology in terms of our conceptions of the divine and the relations of the divine to the phenomenal world, but little has been done in the empirical study of the cosmos itself as religious expression.

To envisage the universe in its religious dimension requires that we speak of the religious aspect of the original flaming forth of the universe, the religious role of the elements, the religious functioning of the earth and all its components. Since our religious capacities emerge from this cosmological process, the universe itself may be considered the primary bearer of religious experience.

Thinking about the emergent universe in this way provides a context for the future development of religious traditions. Indeed all the various peoples of the world, insofar as they are being educated in a modern context, are coming to identify themselves in time and space in terms of the universe as described by our modern sciences, even though none of us have learned the more profound spiritual and religious meaning indicated by this new sense of the universe.

> *"It will be proved, I know not when or where, that the human soul stands even in this life in indissoluble connection with all immaterial natures in the spirit world, that it reciprocally acts upon these and receives impressions and help from them."*
>
> IMMANUEL KANT

This story of the universe is at once scientific, mythic, and mystical. Most elaborate in its scientific statement, it is nevertheless among the simplest of creation stories and, significantly, the story that the universe tells about itself. We are finally overcoming our isolation from the universe and beginning to listen to it in some depth. In this we have an additional context for the religious understanding of every tradition. Through listening to the universe we also gain additional depth of spiritual understanding that was not available through our traditional insights. Just as we can no longer live simply within the physical universe of Newton so we can no longer live spiritually within the limits of our earlier traditions.

The first great contribution this new perspective on the universe makes to religious consciousness is the sense of participating in the creation process itself. We bear within us the impress of every transformation through which the universe and the planet earth have passed. The elements out of which we are composed were shaped in the supernova implosions. We passed through the period of stardust dispersion resulting from this implosion-explosion of the first generation of stars. We were integral with the attractive forces that brought those particles together in the original shaping of the earth. Especially in the rounded form of the planet we felt the gathering of the components of the earthly community and we experienced the self-organizing spontaneities within the megamolecules out of which came the earliest manifestations of the life process and the transition to cellular and organic living forms. These same forces that brought forth the genetic codings of all the various species were guiding the movement of life on toward its latest expression in human consciousness.

This sacred journey of the universe is also the personal journey of each individual. We cannot but marvel at this amazing sequence of transformations. Our reflexive consciousness, which allows us to appreciate and to celebrate this story, is the supreme achievement of our present period of history. The universe is the larger self of each person since the entire sequence of events that has transpired since the beginning of the universe has been required to establish each of us in the precise structure of our own being and in the larger community context in which we function.

Earlier periods and traditions have also experienced their intimacy with the universe, especially in those moments of cosmic renewal that took place periodically, particularly in the springtime of each year. Through these grand rituals powerful energies flowed into the world. Yet it was the *renewal* of the world or the sustaining of an abiding universe, not the irreversible and non-repeatable *original* emergence of the world that was taking place. Only such an irreversible self-organizing world such as that in which we live could provide this special mode of participation in the emergent creation itself. This irreversible sequence of transformations is taking shape through our own activities as well as through the activities of the multitude of component members of the universe community.

It is not a straight line sequence, however; the component elements of the universe move in pulsations, in successions of integration-disintegration, in spiral or circular patterns, especially on earth in its seasonal expressions. On earth, in particular, the basic tendencies of the universe seem to explode in an overwhelming display of geological, biological, and human modes of expression, from the tiniest particles of matter and their movement to the vast movements of the seas and continents, with the clash and rifting of tectonic plates, the immense hydrological cycles, the spinning of the earth on its own axis, its circling of the sun, and the bursting forth of the millionfold variety of living forms.

Throughout this confused, disorderly, even chaotic process, we witness an enormous creativity. The quintessence of this great journey of the universe is the balance between equilibrium and disequilibrium. Although so much of the disequilibrium falls in its reaching toward a new and greater integration, the only way to consistent creativity is through the breakdown of existing unities. That disturbed periods of history are the creative periods can be seen in the Dark Ages of Europe as well as in the period of breakdown in imperial order in China at the end of the Han Dynasty around the year 200 CE.

So too religiously, the grand creativity is found in the stressful moments. It was in a period of spiritual confusion that Buddha appeared to establish a new spiritual discipline. The prophets appeared in the disastrous moments of Israel. Christianity established itself in the social and religious restlessness of the late Roman Empire. Now we find ourselves in the greatest period of disturbance that the earth has ever known, a period when the continued existence of both the human and the natural worlds are severely threatened. The identity of our human fate with the destiny of the planet itself was never more clear.

In terms of liturgy, a new sequence of celebrations is needed based on those stupendous moments when the great cosmological transformations took place. These moments of cosmic transformation must be considered as sacred moments even more than the great moments of seasonal renewal. Only by a proper celebration of these moments can our own human spiritual development take place in an integral manner. Indeed these were the decisive moments in the shaping of human consciousness as well as in the shaping of our physical being.

First among these cosmic celebrations might be that of the emergent moment of the universe itself as a spiritual as well as a physical event. This was the beginning of religion just as it was the beginning of the world. The human mind and all its spiritual capacities began with this first shaping of what was to become the universe as we know it. A supremely sacred moment, it carries within it the high destinies of the universe in its intellectual and spiritual capacities as well as in its physical shaping and living expression.

Also of special import is the rate of emergence of the universe and the curvature of space, whereby all things hold together. The rate of emergence in those first instants had to be precise to the hundred billionth of a fraction. Otherwise the universe would have exploded or collapsed. The rate of emergence was such that the consequent curvature of the universe was sufficiently closed to hold the universe together within its gravitational bondings and yet open enough so that the creative process could continue through these billions of years, providing the guidance and the energies we need as we move through the dangers of the present into a more creative and perhaps more secure future.

This bonding of the universe whereby every reality attracts and is attracted to every other being in the universe was the condition for the rise of human affection. It was the beginning and most comprehensive expression of the divine bonding that pervades the universe and enables its creative processes to continue.

It might be appropriate then if this beginning moment of the universe were the context for religious celebration, perhaps even for a special liturgy; it should be available, in a diversity of expressions, to all the peoples of the planet as we begin to sense our identity in terms of the evolutionary story of the universe rather than in purely physical terms or in mythic modes of expression. Although it seems difficult, at first, to appreciate that these are supreme spiritual moments, these and other transformative moments did help establish both the spiritual and the physical contours of the further development of the entire world.

Among these supreme moments we might list the supernova explosions that took place as the first generation of stars collapsed into themselves in some trillions of degrees of heat; this process generated the heavier elements out of the original hydrogen and helium atoms, and then exploded into the stardust with which our own solar system and planet shaped themselves. New levels of subjectivity came into being, new modalities of bonding, new possibilities for those inner spontaneities whereby the universe carries out its self-organization. Along with all this came a magnificent array of differentiated elements and intricate associations. The earth, in all its spiritual as well as its physical aspects, became a possibility.

To ritualize this moment would provide a depth of appreciation for ourselves and for the entire creative process. Such depth is needed because the entire earthly process has become trivialized, leaving us with no established way of entering into the spiritual dimension of the story that the universe is telling us about itself.

The human is precisely that being in whom this total process reflects on and celebrates itself and its numinous origins in a special mode of conscious self-awareness. At our highest moments we fulfill this role through the association of our liturgies with the supreme *liturgy* of the universe itself. Since the earliest times of which we have information, the human community has been aware that the universe itself is the primary liturgy. Human personality and community have always sought to insert themselves into space and time through this integration with the great movement of the heavens and the cycles of the seasons, which were seen as celebratory events with profound numinous significance. What is needed now is integration with a new sequence of liturgies related to the irreversible transformation sequence whereby the world as we know it has come into being.

We could continue through the entire range of events whereby the universe took shape, inquiring about the religious meaning and celebrating a great many of the mysteries of the earth. The invention of photosynthesis is especially important in this context. Then the coming of the trees, later the coming of the flowers, one hundred million years ago; and finally the birth of the human species.

Only such a selective sequence of religious celebrations could enable the cosmology of religions to come into being. If the sacred history of the biblical world is recounted with such reverence, how much more the recounting of the sacred history of the universe and of the entire planet Earth.

We find this difficult because we are not accustomed to think of ourselves as integral with, or subject to, the universe, to the planet Earth, or to the community of living beings; especially not in our religious or spiritual lives which identify the sacred precisely as that which is atemporal and unchanging even though it is experienced within the temporal and the changing. We think of ourselves as the primary referent and the universe as participatory in our own achievements. Only the present threats to the viability of the human as a species and to the life systems of the Earth are finally causing us to reconsider our situation.

This leads us to a final question in our consideration of the various religious traditions, the question of the religious role of the human as species. History is being made now in every aspect of the human endeavor, not within or between nations, or ethnic groups, or cultures, but between humans as a species and the larger Earth community. We have been too concerned with ourselves as nations, ethnic groups, cultures, religions. We are presently in need of a species and interspecies orientation in law, economics, politics, education, medicine, religion, and whatever else concerns the human.

If until recently we could be unconcerned with the species level of human activities, this is no longer the situation. We now need a species economy that will relate the human as species to the community of species on the planet, and that will ultimately be an integral Earth economy. Already the awareness is beginning to dawn that the human is overwhelming the entire productivity of the

We have been too concerned with ourselves as nations, ethnic groups, cultures, religions. We are presently in need of a species and interspecies orientation in law, economics, politics, education, medicine, religion, and whatever else concerns the human. THOMAS BERRY

"Only when the cosmos is acknowledged as the matrix of all value will we be able to solve the ecological crisis and arrive at a more comprehensive view of who we are in the community of the Earth." THOMAS BERRY

Earth with its excessive demands, using up some 40 percent of the entire productivity of the Earth. This leaves an inadequate resource base for the larger community of life. The cycle of renewal is overburdened, to such an extent that even the renewable life systems are being extinguished.

We could say the same thing for medicine; the issue of species health has come into view and beyond that the health of the planet. Since human health on a toxic planet is a con- tradiction, the primary objective of the medical profession must be to foster the integral health of the earth itself. Only then can human health be adequately attended to.

We can in a corresponding manner outline the need for a species, interspecies, and even planetary legal system as the only viable system that can be functionally effective in the present situation. As in economics and medicine, the planet itself constitutes the normative reference. There already exists a comprehensive participatory governance of the planet. Every member of the Earth community rules and is ruled by the other members of the community in such a remarkable manner that the community as a whole and its individual members have prospered over the centuries and millennia. The proper role for the human is to articulate its own governance within this planetary governance.

What remains is the concept of a religion of the human as species in the larger Earth and universe communities. This concept implies a prior sense of the religious dimension of the natural world within the cosmos. Just as we can see the Earth in economic, biological, and legal modes of being, so might we think of the earth as having a religious mode of being. Although this concept is yet to be articulated effectively in the context of our present understanding of the great story of the universe, the ideas seem to be explicit in many of the scriptures of the world.

In general, however, we have thought of the Earth as joining in the religious expression of the human rather than the human joining in the religious expression of the Earth. This has caused difficulties in most spheres of human activity. We have consistently thought of the human as primary and the earth as derivative; in the future, and in a cosmology of religions, we must understand that the Earth is primary and the human is derivative. Only when the cosmos is acknowledged as the matrix of all value will we be able to solve the ecological crisis and arrive at a more comprehensive view of who we are in the community of the Earth.

Previously published in *Pluralism and Oppression: Theology in a World Perspective*, ed. Paul Knitter, Annual Volume #34, published by College Theology Society, pp. 99–113

Sacred Community
at the Dawn of the Second Axial Age

Brother Wayne Teasdale

A Christian sannyasi (monk) in the lineage of Father Bede Griffiths, a writer, lecturer and Trustee of the Council for a Parliament of the World's Religions

*W*e are rapidly entering an axial time, a new age which may well be decisive for humanity and the Earth. It will be an age unlike any other in the issues it will resolve, in the direction it assumes, in the consciousness that guides it, and in the truly global civilization it will fashion. Nationalism and fanaticism will evaporate before the human family's discovery of a more universal identity. Humankind will come of age, and will outgrow these forms of association as doubtful luxuries no longer desirable or affordable.

Curiously, it is the religions that are playing a central role in leading the world into this new age. It was Mahatma Gandhi who first observed so prophetically that there would never be peace on Earth unless there was first peace among the religions. Hans Küng has reiterated this truth in our time, particularly at the Parliament of the World's Religions. A subtle shift is occurring in how the religions relate to one another. Often antagonists in the past, their rivalry produced tens of thousands of wars throughout recorded history. Suspicion, competition, and conflict have characterized their relationship. Their cultures developed in splendid isolation, occasionally influencing one another. Now, a new paradigm of relationship is emerging as the barriers dividing the world's religions collapse. Faced with the same critical issues threatening all of us – the ecological crisis, escalating violence, economic instability, hunger, poverty, disease, the population explosion, racism – the religions have found a new mode for cooperation, and through collaboration, the possibility of genuine community among the traditions.

Living in community was always a potential because of the deeper reality out of which we have all come, but the dark forces of fear, insecurity, and ignorance led us into patterns of competition and bloody conflict. When we see this tragic history in the light of our profound and primordial unity, then these conflicts resemble the petty squabbles of children on a playground where cruelty and mean-spiritedness take over.

The cultural transformations that are occurring are global in scope, comprehensive in extent – affecting everything – and radical in their depth. A new awareness of our interconnectedness but also of our fragility and the fragility of the Earth is changing how we look at the planet and one another. The media are an important tool in breaking down the old exclusivistic attitudes that each society, culture, and religion has followed. It was television that brought us the breathtaking image of the Earth from Apollo. In that precious image more like some ethereal jewel, a new consciousness was born, the fruit of an enlightening revelation that compelled us to confront our essential interdependence and our inescapable fragility. It is this realization that is the basis of the new age we are now entering.

This approaching period, which is singularly important to the survival and well-being of our planet and its species, has the character of an axial event. Thus far in human history only one other Axial Age has been identified. This term was popularized by the German philosopher Karl Jaspers to designate the time frame from 1,000 BCE up to and including the time of Christ. This millennium is called the *Axial Age* because it was the golden age of so many spiritual geniuses whose insights became the foundations of all the great ancient civilizations, and which are enduring even into our century. These figures include Mahavira, the Jain saint, Gautama the Buddha, Zoroaster, Socrates and Plato in Greece, Lao-Tzu and Confucius in China, Elijah, Isaiah and Jeremiah in Israel, and numerous sages in India who inspired the Vedas and Upanishads. These extraordinary beings provided the axis of our cultures up until the present, and their influence will continue till the end of time because of the perennial nature of their wisdom.

Now, the radical changes taking place around the globe are propelling us quickly into what can be called the Second Axial Age. Like the first period, the second will provide the foundation for culture, but this culture will be universal in scope. The coming age will never dispense with the spiritual, psychological, and moral wisdom of the First Axial Age. It will build on the experience, wisdom, and insight of the great sages of the first period of humankind's awakening.

The latter half of the 20th century has witnessed at least

In a Dream I Get a Peek

into the future.
I look in terror
as I see the destruction.

The earth looks like
it's been burnt to a crisp

with hardly any vegetation
left to see. And there's no sign

of life whatsoever, and
no atmosphere at all.

With a large explosion,
it is the end of the world

as a line of fire goes blazing across the whole earth.

JEFF MARCHAND, 8th grade

three revolutionary religious/cultural events: the Second Vatican Council (1962-1965), the arrival of Tibetan Buddhism and the Dalai Lama on the world stage, and the Parliament of the World's Religions.

The first two events will impact life and culture for centuries and both have implications for the new axial period; indeed, they are part of it. The third event, the Parliament of the World's Religions, is so radically significant as to be a catalyst into the next age. This is where a shift in relationships among the great world religions and smaller ones became explicit.

What happened at the Parliament of the World's Religions was singular and miraculous. Some 8,700 people representing 125 religions, along with a large number of groups standing for various causes came from around the world. They participated in the grandest display of diversity and creativity ever recorded, even more diverse than the Rio Earth Summit of June 1991. The Parliament was a transcendent moment in history animated by a spirit of genuine openness, mutual listening, and respect. Aside from a few minor exceptions greatly exaggerated by the media, it was as if there had never been any religious wars and other struggles. During those momentous days at the end of summer 1993, a revelation was given to humanity. The veil was parted for the brief period of eight days, and a new awareness became evident among the participants, those with and without a religious tradition or a spirituality. This extraordinary awareness revealed some of the attributes we will need for our planet to survive and flourish. These skills include: dialogue, sustainable economic and social life, conflict resolution, a Global Ethic, a Universal Spirituality, a willingness to share, mutual openness, trust, respect, and the capacity for profound listening to others, to ourselves and to the planet itself.

These attributes also encompass the values and practices we need in order to actualize the deeper, more inclusive type of community which was glimpsed during the second Parliament. The Parliament gave us a vision of sacred community that includes all religions, nations, groups, organizations, species, the Earth with the entire cosmos. If we want this dream to be, then we must exercise these skills. We must always be willing to dialogue or communicate in an authentic manner; no one should be excluded! Our economic and social life has to be in harmony with the natural world; sustainability with the Earth and with one another demands genuine justice: for the planet itself (eco-justice), for other species, and for members of our own species. How we utilize resources affects justice and peace. There can be no actual peace unless there is true justice which is both ecological, that is, towards the Earth, and social, or within our communities. More and more this will be the case, so it is imperative that we embrace the practice of sharing our resources. Sharing will create the conditions for justice and will contribute to a sustainable economics.

The ecological crisis has emerged as the most pressing of the critical issues and the chief moral concern of the coming age. The Earth has become the matrix of interfaith dialogue just as it is the medium in and through which we

"All ethics so far evolved rest on a single premise: that the individual is a member of a community of interdependent parts....

The land ethic simply enlarges the boundaries of the community to include soils, waters, plants, and animals, or collectively: the land.... In short, a land ethic changes the role of Homo sapiens from the conqueror of the land-community to plain member and citizen of it. It implies respect for his fellow-members, and also respect for the community as such."

ALDO LEOPOLD,
from *A Sand County Almanac*, pp. 239, 240

live. For far too long we have abused the natural world unaware of what we were doing. Now we neglect it to our own peril. We need a whole new vision of human life as part of and in harmonious interaction with the natural world and the cosmos.

The Second Axial Age is also the Ecozoic Age, the shift away from an exclusively anthropocentric culture to a geocentric and cosmocentric one. Such a momentous and radical alteration of culture, and the evolution of a global society or civilization that is friend to the Earth, requires the active participation of the religions. For just as there can be no world peace unless there is first peace between and among the religions, there can be no new vision of life, culture, and the human family's relationship to nature unless all the religious traditions support it and realize its critical necessity.

Because there already exists a community of the faith traditions within the larger identity of the Earth Community, spiritual interdependence is a growing insight, and with this realization is the further creative possibility of interspiritual wisdom. These truths are also explicit developments from the consciousness of the Parliament event. They are now integral to the process of self-awareness and vision of the Parliament as it continues

Last Night a Frog Spirit Spoke to Me

Last night a frog spirit spoke to me.
He did not speak through words
but through thoughts. Nor did I speak.
He spoke only good – no bad,
for his soul would not let it.
Nor was he the leader of frogs
he was a messenger.

He spoke of the future and of the past
but none of the present
for he was a foreseer.

He spoke of many dreams
only a few of which could
or would come true.

JOSH CLAYTON, 7th grade

its self-defining and self-reflection. The notes of interfaith community, spiritual interdependence, and interspiritual wisdom are equally axial in significance. They represent good news for the planet as a whole in all its glorious variety.

The document signed by most of the 250 members of the Assembly of Religious and Spiritual Leaders at the Parliament is entitled *Towards A Global Ethic (An Initial Declaration)*. This kind of document represents the first indication of a consensus on ethics among the religious and spiritual traditions. The Global Ethic contains general norms of behavior which are universally acceptable and applicable. It is one thing, however, to recognize and outline these norms and quite another to implement them around the world. Something further is required to inspire humankind to live this more mature expression of moral life, and to actualize fully the human adventure in contemplative consciousness. What is needed is an understanding of a universal spirituality. (See *Elements of a Universal Spirituality* in Chapter 25.)

The great religions, indeed all the religions and all organizations concerned in any way with human responsibility, must work together in forging such a vision. Collectively, the spiritual heritage of humankind is deposited among the traditions. This heritage belongs to each one of us and is accessible to all in differing degrees. The religions possess enormous psychological, moral,

educational, and spiritual resources. These may now be marshalled in the olympian task of creating and expressing the new vision; it can and will happen eventually. The Global Ethic and a tentative, emerging knowledge of universal spirituality are but two examples of what can be achieved by drawing on these vast inner resources, the treasures of humanity's religious consciousness.

The members of the community of religions have a sacred responsibility to create the conditions for formulating, spreading and implementing the new vision. They have been groping forward now for more than a century, since the first Parliament of 1893. The second Parliament, possessing the necessary awareness and consensus, has the duty to help create the permanent platform for the religions in collaboration with the other international interfaith organizations, like the World Conference on Religion and Peace, the Temple of Understanding, the Fellowship of Reconciliation, the World Congress of Faiths, and many other groups. This new global community will only be achieved if the world's religions and other organizations and groups accept together their universal responsibility for the planet. Together, however, we can inaugurate the vehicle that will inspire a new global culture and civilization, one that will be a mature expression of humankind's collective wisdom: a civilization, a society, and a spirituality with a heart!

The Mysterious Flower

In a dream a bat
appeared in front of me
and told me that a single rose
is a real mysterious,
dark, loving flower,
and that we should teach
each other how to love
one another like
a bushel of roses.

ANDREA SWANSON, 6th grade

"All [humans] are caught in an inescapable network of mutuality, tied in a single garment of destiny. Whatever affects one directly, affects all indirectly. I can never be what I ought to be until you are what you ought to be, and you can never be what you ought to be until I am what I ought to be."

MARTIN LUTHER KING, JR.

Legacies of the Parliaments

Responses to the 1893 World's Parliament of Religions

Compiled by Dr. Homer A. Jack, a founder of the World Conference on Religion and Peace (WCRP) and, at his death in 1993, its Secretary-General Emeritus. He was also a member of the Board of the U.S. Committee of the International Association for Religious Freedom (IARF), and was well-known as a peace activist, writer and organizer. These materials are part of a larger paper and packet of materials he gathered for organizers of interfaith activities.

Reactions of participants and contemporaries

"I am in full sympathy with the proposed World's Religious Convention. The idea seems to me an inspiration.... In my 84th year, and in very feeble health, I can do but little in aid of this great work. May God bless thee in the noble work assigned thee."

JOHN GREENLEAF WHITTIER,
the Quaker poet

"I deem the movement you are engaged in promoting worthy of all encouragement and praise.... If conducted with moderation and good will, such a Congress may result, by the blessing of Divine Providence, in benefits far more far-reaching than the most sanguine could dare hope for."

JAMES CARDINAL GIBBONS,
Baltimore

"The very conception of a Parliament of Religions... is in itself a sign of the times in which we live, and is worthy of the great nation from which it emanates."

ALI BILGRAMI,
Deccan, India

"The project is an admirable one, and it ought to receive the encouragement of all who really love truth and charity and who wish to further their reign among mankind."

BISHOP JOHN J. KEANE, Rector,
The Catholic University of Washington

"I trust that your largest hopes concerning the Parliament may be fully realized. I am not surprised that narrow-minded men, in our own church even, should oppose it. There are some good bigots who imagine that God will not cease working until he has made all men Presbyterians...."

S. J. NICHOLLS, formerly Moderator
of the General Assembly of the Presbyterian Church

"I am impressed with the momentous consequences of your undertaking, in its relation to Christian missions....

I foresee as its result a great enlightenment of missionary sentiment at home and a grand reform of mission methods on the field."

REV. GEORGE T. CANDLIN,
Tientsin, China

"I accept with pleasure the honor of my nomination to the Council . . . sympathizing heartily with the principles of the Parliament of Religions."

SIR EDWIN ARNOLD,
author of the epic poem, "The Light of Asia"

"You have my most cordial sympathy in the great work of bringing together, on a common humanitarian platform, the representatives of all important moral creeds. I regard your program as marking an epoch in the history of religious development."

JUSTICE AMEER ALI,
Calcutta

"It is the greatest event so far in the history of the world, and it has been held on American soil."

DR. ALFRED W. MOMERIE,
professor at King's College, London

"We take hence with us in parting the richest treasures of religious instruction ever laid before man."

RABBI EMIL C. HIRSCH,
Sinai Temple, Chicago

"This Parliament of Religion is the most remarkable event in history."

RT. REV. R. SHIBATA,
Shintoist

"We believe your next step will be toward the ideal goal of this Parliament, the realization of international justice."

KINZA RIUGE M. HIRAI,
Buddhist

"For once in history all religions have made their peace, all nations have called each other brothers."

P. C. MAZUMDAR,
Hindu

"The great battle of the future will not be the Fatherhood of God, nor that we need a redeemer, mediator, or a model man between God and man, but it is to acknowledge the Brotherhood of Man practically."

BISHOP B. W. ARNETT,
African Methodist Episcopal Church

"People have been entertaining views and expectations of the most opposite character concerning this most unique religious gathering and its probable results. Some have thought it an injury done to the Christian religion.... Others have regarded it as almost the end of religious differences.... Both of these views are extremes and therefore erroneous.... I am confident that the net result will be for the good of religion.... The Parliament has been a long stride toward the much desired reunion of Christendom, and, with that end in view, the oftener such gatherings are held, the better."

BISHOP JOHN J. KEANE

"There are few things which I so truly regret having missed as the great Parliament of Religions, held in Chicago as a part of the Columbian Exposition. Who would have thought that what was announced as simply an auxiliary branch of that exhibition could have developed into what it was; could have become the most important part of that immense undertaking; could have become the greatest success of the past year, and I do not hesitate to say, could now take its place as one of the most memorable events in the history of the world? Even in America, where people have not fully lost the faculty of admiring, and of giving hearty expression to their admiration, the greatness of that event seems to me not yet fully appreciated."   PROFESSOR F. MAX MULLER
of Oxford University,
and editor of *Sacred Books of the East*

"Few persons today realize how great a thing that first Chicago Parliament of Religions was, and fewer still how wide-reaching and important have been the results following it. It is probably not an exaggeration to represent it as marking an epoch, if not in the religious history, at least in the religious progress of the world. It was something absolutely new, unique, unprecedented; mankind had never seen anything like it.... In that great Chicago Parliament, for absolutely the first time in human history, eminent representatives of all the important religious faiths of mankind came together in a great world assemblage, and what was more, came in the spirit of equality and mutual respect; came not to antagonize or criticize but to fellowship; came not even for debate, but for thoughtful and brotherly conference over the great world-wide problems and interests of religion, each to present for the consideration of the rest of the world, an affirmative statement, a constructive interpretation of the central truths, aims, and ideals of the faith which he represented, as understood not by its enemies but by its friends."   JABEZ T. SUNDERLAND
(attended both the Parliament in 1893 and the Assembly
of the World Fellowship of Faiths in 1933 at the
1933 Chicago World's Fair)

Evaluations by modern scholars

"Because the Parliament stimulated a considerable amount of religious irenicism and a recognition of the goodwill of the proponents of other religions, it can and ought to be regarded as a hesitant step on the road to the present ecumenical age."   JAMES F. CLEARY,
The Catholic Historical Review, January 1970, 585-609

"The World's Parliament of Religions called forth a great variety of interpretations. It was, in fact, a kind of religious Rorschach test. It was denounced as a betrayal of Christ, praised as a forum to demonstrate Christian superiority, encouraged as a movement toward world peace, urged as an opportunity for the study of comparative religion, sneered at as an exercise in futility. Most liberals saw it as a death-blow to bigotry and a demonstration of the religious unity of mankind. Despite its universalistic pretensions, it was, in fact, an inter-denominational gathering of Americans in the Judaeo-Christian tradition, with slightly more than a token representation of European and Asian guests...."
THOMAS GRAHAM,
Collegium Proceedings, 1978-79, 61-81

"The 1893 Parliament of Religions provides a point... to study the nineteenth-century American discovery of Asian religion. In the years since Emerson had hailed the East, a series of events and movements had pushed the Asian religions into growing prominence. The Parliament was in many respects the culmination. Several writers would argue that such a congress, in which represent- atives of all religious viewpoints met on a common platform to present their distinctive doctrines, could not have taken place in any other country at any other time. An exaggeration perhaps, yet it does seem that the United States offered a peculiarly hospitable site for the Parliament. If the Parliament of Religions marked a culmination of preceding developments, it also pointed to the future. The appearance of Asians at the Parliament heralded the twentieth-century situation in which Asian spokesmen and Asian movements have increasingly taken the lead in bringing Oriental religion to Americans. In this sense, the Parliament of Religions marked the closing of one era but also the opening of another."
CARL T. JACKSON,
The Oriental Religions and American Thought

"The most elaborate display of religious cosmopolitanism yet seen on the continent."   MARTIN E. MARTY,
Modern American Religion. Vol. 1. *The Irony of It All, 1893-1919*

"As a symbolic event, the Parliament can undoubtedly be called a significant watershed in American religious life.... After the Parliament, there were many new ways to be religious.... America had gone into the Parliament claiming to be a cosmopolitan nation and had come out having to live up to the claim. There was no going back."   RICHARD HUGHES SEAGER,
Editor of *The Dawn of Religious Pluralism*

"A milestone in the history of interreligious dialogue, the study of world's religions, and the impact of Eastern religious traditions on American culture.... A pioneering ecumenical event, international in scope."
ROBERT S. ELLWOOD, "World's Parliament of Religions,"
The Encyclopedia of Religion

The Vision Beckons:
From Parliament of Religions to Global Concourse of Religions

Dr. Paulos Mar Gregorios

Metropolitan of Delhi (the Orthodox Syrian Church of the East), and former President for Asia, World Council of Churches

Widely respected throughout the world for his insights and leadership over several decades in interreligious organizations and conferences, Dr. Gregorios was invited by the Council for a Parliament of the World's Religions to deliver this Address at the Inaugural Ceremonies for the Centennial, held at Rockefeller Chapel, Chicago, in November of 1989.

*F*or me this is a great privilege indeed, to inaugurate the centenary celebrations of the World's Parliament of Religions. The World's Parliament of Religions, convened in this historic city of Chicago a century ago, held aloft a torch which helped us see a vision. We are far today from having realized it; but to renew that vision is the purpose of my few words this evening.

It is a perennial yearning of the human race to find its own unity. To this, I believe, the 1893 Parliament responded. Of course, the Columbian Exposition was there with all the glory of the technology which had just come into being in the last two decades of the last century. But along with all that urban/industrial, scientific/technological progress, in the mind of humanity there was another yearning – the yearning for that which binds humanity together, the unity of humanity on a spiritual basis and not just on the basis of a mere technological/industrial civilization. That is the vision before us today. Technology and modern civilization are not that which will unite us ultimately. That civilization has made it possible for us to come together, to communicate with each other, but that civilization cannot, alas, provide the necessary foundation for the spiritual unity of mankind. It is in search of that foundation that we – a hundred years late – begin these celebrations.

1. Religions and the secular world

*I*n 1893, perhaps the purpose was to fight irreligion. Today, that cannot be our purpose. We do not want to fight. Religions have done their share of fighting in the past. We shall not fight wars, but wage peace. Because a thousand million secular people without belief are also human beings, we are not going to fight them. Religions should never gang up against something called irreligion. No, that shall not be our purpose. Our purpose shall be to provide a multi-faceted foundation on which, in mutual respect, the cultures of the world can come together and live in a global concourse of religions.

And we shall *not* take the Golden Rule as our uniting principle as they did a hundred years ago. That was in fashion at the end of the last century, when American liberal Christianity had lost its spiritual moorings and could only find this little plank of the Golden Rule to hold on to. That is not what is before us. What is before us is a rich, deep, penetrating, respectful understanding of each other's religions. Not a common religion which puts everything into one pot; we do not want a religion which unites all religions. What we want is a Global Concourse of All Religions, to which the unbeliever shall not be a stranger, but shall be wholly welcome. That is the vision we need to recreate.

You know, in the Soviet Union, which was supposed to be the most anti-religious expression of secular forces, today the accent is totally different. Marxists have recognized that the values which shall unite humanity and shall make it possible for nations to live together in peace cannot come out of a secular ideology, but will have to come from a moral vision of humanity as a global phenomenon. And, as a result of that, they are now openly apologizing for their attitude towards religion in the past.

"We meet on the mountain height of absolute respect for the religious convictions of each other; and an earnest desire for better knowledge of the consolations which other forms of faith than our own offer to their devotees. The very basis of our convocation is the idea that the representatives of each religion sincerely believe it is the truest and the best of all; and that they will, therefore, hear with perfect candor and without fear the convictions of other sincere souls on the great questions of the immortal life."

HON. CHARLES CARROLL BONNEY,
Opening Address at the World's Parliament of Religions,
September 11, 1893

"'Buddhists are not looking for a convergence of religions.'

Quoting the well known edict of the Buddhist Emperor, Asoka, Ven. Vajiragnana continued,

'Let us be prepared to accept our crucial differences without trying to throw a threadbare rope between them. Rather, let us build bridges of better understanding, tolerance for diverse views, plus encouragement for morality and ethical culture. This is where harmony is to be found.'"

VEN. PANDITH M. VAJIRAGNANA
at the 1988 WCF Conference,
described in *Pilgrimage of Hope* by Marcus Braybrooke, p.79

Last August [1989] the Central Committee of the World Council of Churches met in Moscow. Two hundred people were invited to the Kremlin for a reception. At that reception, the Prime Minister of the Soviet Union, Mr. Ryzhkov, made a 20-minute address in which he openly stated that the Party and government in the Soviet Union were wrong in their attitude towards religious people in the past, and asked us, literally, to forgive them.

That is the world in which we live, where even secular people are turning towards religion to find meaning and hope. The unfortunate part of it is that religions are not quite ready to face that challenge, because the kind of exclusivistic traditional religion on which most of us have been nurtured is not able to cope with the crying need of humanity for meaning.

2. A global concourse of religions

And that is the fundamental purpose of a permanent Parliament of Religions which will come out of these celebrations which we inaugurate this evening. I call it a "Global Concourse of Religions." You may later on agree to call it a Parliament; I would not quarrel. Parliament literally means *a talking shop*. That is all right. But what I would like to see is a *concourse* – a flowing together, a running together – of all religions: active, dynamic, without losing their identity, but in relation to each other, understanding each other, with mutual respect, and moving toward certain specific goals.

Let me say something now which I hope can be understood: so long as Western civilization or Western Christianity dominate the World Parliament or Concourse, it will not work, because the identities of the other religions bear strong hostility toward both Western Christianity and Western civilization for their aggression against the cultures of the world. Western civilization has been a largely one-way mission, in which both the civilization and the church claimed to know the truth and refused to listen to aspects of truth in the experience of the rest of humanity. And, therefore, I want to say this from the heart: I love my Western brothers and sisters; I love my Western *Christian* brothers and sisters also. But where they dominate, an impasse prevails which does not allow the other cultures of the world to function. They are helplessly dominant. Men or women, they cannot do anything but dominate. And, therefore, the most important thing for a Global Concourse of Religions is for the Western civilization and Western Christianity to be humble and courteous enough to take a back seat.

The West has contributions to make, of course. Especially, their capacity to organize is unparalleled – even by the Japanese! And so we will need your help in the organization of such a Global Concourse of Religions. But can you do it without dominating, quietly, and let others be free to do it their way? Try! Then we might be able to use your God-given capacity in our common work, not as a leader, but in a more modest way. Otherwise, we would find the rest of the cultures of the world still inhibited by fear that they would be steam-rolled by Western civilization, Western Christianity and their values and approaches. This is a very fundamental thing that I wanted to say on this occasion.

3. Justice, peace and environment

A second fundamental thing that I wanted to say is that this Global Concourse of Religions must be committed not just to dialogue with each other, but to the future of humanity as a whole. If religions cannot get into that question of the welfare of all humanity, those great values to which they bear witness will not make much sense to vast millions of the people of this world. On the one hand, all religions have to develop a deep spiritual commitment, the re-creation of the deepest levels of meaning for human existence in a personal and communal spirituality. But equally important is the other pole: the commitment to the welfare of humanity, the commitment to justice, the commitment to peace, the commitment to an environment that promotes life rather than threatens to extinguish it, the commitment to eliminate toxic drugs and nuclear weapons. Three foci for such a Global Concourse are: justice, peace, and the environment. Those must be three overarching goals of any global concourse that we shall set up. If it is not so, then most of the people of the world will say, "Well, another organization of religious people to talk among themselves about things which are interesting to them, but not of immediate concern to us."

I would say that the cry for justice is the most heart-rending cry of humanity, and if religion is not relevant to justice in the world, religion is not worth having. If religion is an escape from the struggle for justice, then it's not worth much for most of the people in this world. Many would rather do away with religion altogether. And to touch on the issue of justice is also to touch on the fact that, among perpetrators of injustice, the religious people have more often been on the side of the oppressor than standing with the oppressed. This is what has made religion repulsive to many people. The reason why the secular humanist movement had to arise in the West was because the Christian religion lost its humanist vision. Because religion supported the cause of the oppressor, the slave owner, the exploiter, therefore a rival secular morality had to arise in this civilization. That is why we don't need to fight secularism, but rather should learn from it. We need to learn those great human values to which all people of good will stand committed, values which come out of our various religious heritages, but which the religions are not practicing today. If that doesn't happen, if this is going to be simply a talking-shop for old-style religion, then the Global Concourse may not make much sense to most people.

We all can talk about peace. Christians will say, "Christ is the Prince of Peace." Hindus can say, "*Shanti, shanti, shanti.*" Jews can say, "*Shalom.*" Muslims can say, "*Salaam.*" All mean peace. Wonderful. But until recently, most of the wars in the world came out of religious conflicts. The last two world wars were, perhaps, not like that, but in the history of humanity religion has too often been the cause of war while talking about peace. And, therefore, we will have to shift our emphasis from talking to action for peace.

In each religion there are two levels. One level is exclusivistic and expansionist. That is to say, each religion says, we have the truth and if you want to have the truth, join us. That is the exclusivist, expansionist, lower type of religion. All religions have that lower type.

But in religions there is also a higher type, a type which is universal in its orientation, which is all-embracing in its love, which is non-discriminating between members of its own community and those outside. That good, humanistic, open tendency in all religions will have to be brought to the top. It is there. It only needs to be emphasized further. Only that way will we promote Peace on Earth.

4. Three concerns: a supranational spirit, security and science

Let me mention some of the areas where I think this Global Concourse of Religions will have to put some emphasis. First of all, ailing and alienated humanity is desperately in need of transcending national loyalties. For the last 200 years, the nation has often been our identity, and our loyalties have been to one's own nation's interests over against the interests of other nations. We will have to move out of this kind of identity. History is pushing us to move out of national parochialism into a universal humanism. That global perspective is in every country just beginning to break out, but the governments are not able to embody that principle. Governments still give higher priority to national interests than to human interests. There is where religion has to play a major role, in changing the very attitude of governments so that they no longer think of national interests except in the context of universal human interests. Religion must help each nation and people to move beyond national, tribal, regional parochialisms, to give priority to their global humanity over nation and region and race.

A second thing to which humanity is aspiring is called *comprehensive global common security – C.G.C.S.* This is a concept which the religions have to pick up and develop in the world. What does this mean? This means, first, security without weapons, security based on trust. We must move in that direction. We cannot go on arming ourselves to the teeth and destroying and wasting our resources in a blinding and senseless militarism, which pervades all nations in the world, including my own country, India. We must move out of the concept that it is behind the guns and rockets that one finds national security. We must move internationally towards that same kind of mutual trust by which people within one nation today trust each other and do not have to be pointing guns at each other in order to live in security. We must learn to trust each other, and to live in a global community as responsible citizens. Again, this means a fundamental shift in the way human beings think. I believe religion has a responsibility in moving the human race out of national

patriotism to patriotism of the globe – the love of humanity, planetary patriotism.

Let me say a third fundamental thing and then I shall stop. The hardest job that religions have is in liberating science and technology from being inhibiting factors and destructive factors. You know, in the medieval times, we black-robed clergymen had the final authority, at least in Europe. When there was a dispute, it was the clergy who gave the final verdict. That's gone, those days when one could say, *"Roma locuta est, causa finita est,"* "Rome has spoken, the cause is finished." Today it seems that the role of the black-robed clergy is assumed by the white-robed scientist at his computer or in his laboratory, so that today the phrase is, *"Scientia locuta est, causa finita est";* "Science has said the last word, nothing further can be discussed." I think just as the clerical dictatorship of the medieval ages was overthrown, science's doctrinaire authoritarianism will have to be overthrown. But science itself cannot be abandoned. Science itself is the best tool that has come the way of man. Unfortunately, science and technology are now prisoners – prisoners of either profit-minded large corporations or destruction-minded defense establishments. They are the ones who finance science today, and they control research, and research is oriented either towards making a fast buck in business or the most effective way of exterminating people. Those are the two directions in which scientific research is now moving: making money for the corporations, or killing people. That is where the urban/technological culture we celebrated once has now led us.

We must emancipate science, both from its authoritarianism and from its orientation toward profit and war. And there, again, I believe religions have a major role to play. But religions shall not attack science, only show science its limitations and its enslavement and try to emancipate it from its limitations, so that the same science and technology can now be applied to finding bread for the hungry, shelter for the homeless, clothing for the naked, transportation, communication—the basic needs of humanity. And in that process, science itself will become an ally of religion, not the hostile enemy of religion. And religion also will not have to regard science as an enemy, but as an ally. That is the kind of orientation that I would like to see for a Global Concourse of Religions. But it shall not abandon its primary role, which the *Upanishad* spoke about: *"Tamaso ma jyotirgamaya, asato ma sadgamaya, mrityormamritam gamaya."* That is,

From darkness to light,
from untruth to truth,
from death to life.

That is our primary orientation, but along with that, these three other orientations would have to be kept, and to that kind of vision, I beseech you, my beloved brothers and sisters, to give your commitment to act and your committed prayer.

May God bless you!

A Pilgrimage of Hope

The Rev. Marcus Braybrooke

Formerly Executive Director of the Council of Christians and Jews and currently Chairman of the World Congress of Faiths

Since the 1893 Parliament, numerous interfaith dialogues, shared worship services and joint responses to a variety of issues have served as bridges to interreligious harmony. No one has charted that activity better than Rev. Braybrooke. This essay is the concluding chapter of *Pilgrimage of Hope*, his history of 100 years of the interfaith movement.

*T*he interaction of people of different faiths has increased enormously in the last century. Partly, this is for technological reasons. Far more people travel to other countries, whilst television gives us easy access to information about other cultures. Large numbers of people have been uprooted from one country to another, either as refugees or immigrants.

This human interaction, which may be very personal as in the case of marriages between people of different faiths, has been accompanied by a growing desire to know about other people's religion and way of life. The study of religions has become more common in colleges and schools, and books about world religions are now plentiful. By contrast, 150 years ago, very few of the religious classics of Asia had been translated into European languages and often Asians themselves were unfamiliar with their scriptures. At the same time, partly through the missionary efforts of the churches, some knowledge of Christian teaching is widespread. There are also Christian communities, often very small, in most countries of Asia, and now Muslim, Sikh, Hindu, and Buddhist centers are to be found throughout Europe and America.

Too often, the interaction is negative, hostile, and violent. The recent revival of religious enthusiasm in some areas of the world has been accompanied by an increase in religious extremism and intolerance. In parts of the Muslim world, for example, the revival of Islam has led to the persecution of Bahá'ís and other religious minorities. Many minority groups, in countries across the world, feel that they suffer from discrimination. Religious differences also continue to enflame other causes of division, for example in the Punjab, in Israel and the West Bank, in Northern Ireland, and in Sri Lanka.

Yet the ever-growing interaction of people of different religions has also been accompanied by the growing desire that this should be friendly and creative. I have been astonished, in my research, to discover how many groups in so many different places are seeking interreligious understanding and cooperation. Only the larger groups have been mentioned [in *Pilgrimage of Hope*] and not all of them. They are matched by numerous local groups and by the efforts of people of goodwill, who belong to no particular interfaith organization. I think of ministers of religion who proclaim their faith without adverse comments on the beliefs of others, or of teachers who treat with proper respect the different religions of their pupils, or television producers who convey with integrity the beliefs

and practices of people of another faith, or of all who work for good community relations or who support the great variety of bodies which work for peace, justice, international understanding and the relief of human need. These efforts seldom attract media reports, but they need to be set in the balance when there are much-publicized accounts of interreligious conflict.

Meanings of dialogue

*T*he wide range of such efforts points to the considerable variety of what may be described, rather generally, as interreligious dialogue. Professor Diana Eck, who is Moderator of the World Council of Churches' Sub-Unit for Dialogue, has distinguished six forms of dialogue. The first is parliamentary-style dialogue. She traces this back to the 1893 World's Parliament of Religions and sees it carried forward by the international interfaith organizations, although, as we have seen, their way of working is now very different from the approach of the World's Parliament. Secondly, there is institutional dialogue, such as the regular meetings between representatives of the Vatican and the International Jewish Committee for Inter-religious Consultation. Thirdly, there is theological dialogue, which takes seriously the questions and challenges posed by people of other faiths. Fourthly, dialogue in community or the dialogue of life is the search for good relationships in ordinary life. Fifthly, spiritual dialogue is the attempt to learn from other traditions of prayer and meditation. Lastly, there is inner dialogue, which is "that conversation that goes on within ourselves in any other form of dialogue."[1]

There are various levels of dialogue and it is a process of growth. An initial requirement is an openness to and acceptance of the other. It takes time to build trust and to deepen relationships. This is why some continuity in a dialogue group is helpful and why patience and time are necessary – all of which are particularly difficult to ensure at an international level. Too easily, we find ourselves imposing our presuppositions on the conversation. Christians, for example, often assume that Muslims really adopt a critical attitude to the *Qur'an* similar to that common amongst Christians in their reading of the Bible. We have to learn to enter another world that may seem alien and which has different presuppositions. We have to allow our deepest convictions to be questioned. Some Buddhists, for example, will question deeply held Christian assumptions about God and the self. It is important for those venturing into dialogue to be secure in their own faith. They need to beware of becoming marginalized in or alienated from their own religious tradition. Dialogue needs also to be of equals, that is to say of those with similar levels of scholarship and study.

At its deepest, dialogue will raise questions of truth. Rabbi Dr. Norman Solomon, Director of the Centre for the Study of Judaism and Jewish/Christian Relations at Selly

Oak, Birmingham, said in his inaugural lecture, "Dialogue admits of degrees: there is dialogue which is of value though it does not reach deep. Much of the dialogue between Jews and Christians is a matter of simply learning to be nice to each other, trying a little to understand what the other is doing, cooperating in social endeavor.... Many ordinary Jews or Christians lack the skills necessary to engage in a deeper, theological dialogue, and are rightly wary of setting their faith at risk in a confusing enterprise. Yet the heart of dialogue is in talk together of theologians of both faiths, for it is they whose concern is with the meaning of life at its deepest level and it is they who translate from the doctrinal formula to the underlying reality."[2]

Dialogue does not necessarily produce agreement and, if it is a search for truth, there is no desire for easy compromise. Sometimes it makes clearer where essential differences lie, exposing the various presuppositions or views of the world with which partners in dialogue are operating. Sometimes it can be painful. The American Jewish writer, Dr. Eugene Borrowitz, has said, "Only by directly confronting our deepest differences can we come to know one another fully. Despite risks, interreligious discussion needs at times to be interreligious debate. That is one way it shows its conviction that truth is ultimately one."[3]

The distinctive character of interfaith organizations

With the growth of dialogue, the vocation of interfaith organizations needs to be distinguished, on the one hand from bodies which may be described as "universalist movements for spiritual unity"[4] and, on the other hand, from the agencies for interreligious relations of a particular religion, such as the Pontifical Council for Inter-Religious Dialogue. The work of interfaith organizations needs also to be distinguished from centers and bodies devoted to the academic study of religions.

The interfaith organizations all accept the multiplicity and particularity of the world religions. As Dr. Francis Clark puts it in his *Interfaith Directory,* "the majority of those who are involved in the worldwide interfaith movement... see the rich multiformity of the world's religious traditions as a positive value to be treasured and developed, and take it as a basic datum in their quest for interreligious understanding and cooperation."[5] It has been repeatedly said that no one participating in the organizations is expected to compromise their own faith commitment – the only requirement is that a person should show the same respect to the faiths of other people as he or she would hope that others would show to his or her religion. Members of interfaith organizations hold a variety of views about the relationship of religions to each other. The question of the relationship of religions to each other is very much a matter of debate within several of the world religions.

The universalist movements for spiritual unity, by contrast, are likely to presuppose or to proclaim a particular view of the relationship of religions. Because of their fear that members of the major religions will call them syncretistic, interfaith organizations have kept rather aloof from universalist movements. If, however, the distinction is acknowledged, there could in the future be a closer cooperation in some areas of work between interfaith and universalist bodies. It is perhaps particularly important that interfaith organizations enter into greater dialogue with New Age movements and also the so-called "new religions." It is understandable that whilst the interfaith organizations were themselves viewed with suspicion by the major religious communities, they were careful not to increase that suspicion by keeping company with "strange bedfellows." Now that the major interfaith organizations have an established record of achievement and a proven integrity, they may feel greater confidence in entering into dialogue with New Age and universalist groups, not least because of the gap between those who share these spiritual aspirations and many members of more traditional religious communities.

If interfaith organizations respect the integrity of the world religions, equally they do not offer a preferential position to any one religious group. This is why they are all concerned to ensure a broad range of representation, drawn from many faiths, on their controlling body and to ensure that their funding comes from a variety of sources. This also distinguishes them from agencies for interreligious relations of a particular religious community. Such agencies have to reconcile their search for good

---

Sarva Dharma Sammelana

One of the major international centennial observations of the 1893 World's Parliament of Religions, Sarva Dharma Sammelana (Religious People Meeting Together), was held in Bangalore, India, from 19-22 August 1993. More than 600 persons from 28 countries came together for four days with the goal of promoting understanding and cooperation among members of different religious communities. This event was sponsored by the International Interfaith Organizations Coordinating Committee (IIOCC), an ad hoc committee of four organizations chaired by Marcus Braybrooke: the International Association for Religious Freedom (IARF), the Temple of Understanding (ToU), the World Congress of Faiths (WCF), and the World Conference on Religion and Peace (WCRP).

Three programs were offered to participants:
1) recommendations for future interfaith work;
2) visiting religious centers in Bangalore to learn more about the spiritual traditions of India; and
3) workshops on topics such as communalism, education for understanding, towards a global ethic, and religious contributions to peacemaking.

The book *Visions of an Interfaith Future,* by Celia and David Storey, contains the proceedings of the Conference. It is available from the new International Interfaith Centre, 2 Market St., Oxford OX1 3EF, United Kingdom.

relations with other religious groups with their traditional claims to an exclusive or privileged knowledge of truth. For such agencies and their parent religions, questions of the relationship of dialogue and mission and of the truth claims of their religion are very important. Certainly members of these agencies may enter into the fullest and most open dialogue with people of other faiths, but they have to interpret their position to their fellow believers. Members of interfaith organizations, who are themselves believers, have, of course, the same questions with which to wrestle and the same task of interpretation. Yet this is not the responsibility of the interfaith organizations themselves. As the religions have seen the importance of dialogue, the number of their agencies for dialogue have increased.

In recent years, there has been a growing partnership between the interfaith organizations and these agencies, as both recognize their particular tasks. In preparation for the World Day of Prayer for Peace at Assisi, the Vatican Secretariat for Non-Christians enlisted the help of World Conference on Religion and Peace, so that those of other faiths would feel that the invitation to participate had no hidden implications. Similarly, it is the interfaith organizations which rightly can sponsor The Year of Interreligious Understanding and Cooperation, although the support of the agencies for dialogue will be vital.

Differences of emphasis in interfaith work

Amongst the interfaith organizations themselves, differences of emphasis can be recognized. There are those which have concentrated on building up understanding and friendship and those who feel that such understanding will grow as people of different religions cooperate in tackling the urgent problems of the world. The latter have been less concerned to discuss the theoretical relationship of religions to each other.

Those interfaith organizations, such as World Congress of Faiths and the Temple of Understanding, which have seen the building up of a fellowship of faiths as their primary task, have grappled with the question of the relationship of religions. They tend to assume a pluralist position, in which the independent validity of the world religions is acknowledged. No one religion is assumed to

be superior. Rather, it is assumed that each has a contribution to make to the fuller awareness of truth. For some, the pluralist position is based on an "impelling awareness of the historico-cultural limitation of all knowledge and religious beliefs, and the difficulty, if not impossibility, of judging the truth claims of another culture or religion on the basis of one's own."[6] Such a view was particularly associated, in a previous generation, with the German theologian Ernst Troeltsch[7] and today with the British theologian and philosopher John Hick. Others put the emphasis on the infinity and ineffability of the Divine Mystery, to which all religions point. This is a view that echoes the *neti-neti* tradition of Hinduism. The Divine transcends our human thought and language and this involves a recognition of the relativity of all religious language and symbols. This "forbids any one religion from having the 'only' or 'final' word."[8] Dr. Radhakrishnan was an eloquent exponent of this position, which has also been expounded by Professor Wilfred Cantwell Smith of Harvard University. For Professor Raimon Panikkar, pluralism implies a pluralism of truth. For others, such as R. E. Whitson,[9] there is the suggestion that through dialogue there may be a growing convergence of religions in deeper understanding of the Divine—and this is one reason for seeing the interfaith movement as a "pilgrimage of hope."

The other hope that inspires the interfaith movement is that together people of all faiths may work for peace and justice and the protection of the environment. "Economic, political and especially nuclear liberation is too big a job for any one nation, or culture, or religion," writes Paul Knitter of Xavier University, Cincinnati. "A worldwide liberation movement needs a worldwide interreligious dialogue."[10] This emphasis has characterized WCRP and also organizations, which are multireligious in character, which campaign on specific issues, such as the Global Forum or the World Wide Fund for Nature.

One interfaith organization?

Would it be helpful for the various interfaith organizations to come together in one body? Such a suggestion was made at the first Ammerdown Conference as they began to get to know each other better, but on

---

"Some years ago, a meeting such as this would have been unthinkable. And, let us admit, even today, each one of us is aware of the difficulties he has to face within his own congregation.

"The important fact is the miracle accomplished by the Lord: we are here. We respect each other. None of us is prompted by proselytizing motives. Each one has come with an open heart, ready to understand and love his brethren.... Above all, we are anxious to find effective ways of coming into agreement with a view to help Humanity face its immense problems....

"A real meeting requires each one to come out of his shell and overcome his selfishness. A real meeting requires that each one, while remaining loyal to his own conscience and to his own conviction, should aim at discovering whatever may unite us, without measuring sacrifices, and at whatever may make it possible, tomorrow, to work together for the greater glory of God and the well-being of mankind."

DOM HELDER CAMARA
in *Religion for Peace: Proceedings of the Kyoto Conference on Religion and Peace*

fuller acquaintance, there has come the recognition that each has its own constituency and its own special vocation. Yet, easily, the organizations could become competitive for resources. Already certain world religious leaders are in great demand to attend international interreligious conferences. Rather than creating one organization, it may be more valuable to strengthen the mechanisms for coordination and cooperation, both between interfaith organizations themselves and between such organizations and the agencies for dialogue of the religious communities. Planning for the Year of Interreligious Understanding and Cooperation in 1993 is already an occasion for greater liaison. More permanent and effective structures for coordination will be necessary in the future. The interfaith networks established in the United Kingdom and in North America may provide models.

What has been achieved?

As of all efforts to change attitudes, it is hard to estimate what has been achieved in 100 years of the interfaith movement. There has been an ever-widening circle of those involved in interfaith encounter. As it is a personal journey, each individual has to make the discoveries for herself or himself. Dialogue, therefore, involves a continuing process of learning and re-education. This suggests that the struggle against prejudice and intolerance is also a continuing process. At one time, I hoped that tolerance would gradually spread as people of different faiths got to know each other better. It seems, however, that certain forms of religious experience and loyalty breed intolerance, which too easily is exploited by political leaders, and that constant vigilance is necessary to curb religious extremism. Tolerance itself has its own limits and the search for interreligious cooperation means opposition to those who use religion to bolster fanaticism and to those who use religion as a cloak for power, prejudice, and injustice.

Those who have entered deeply into dialogue all speak of the personal enrichment, both in terms of new friendships and of a deeper appreciation of other faiths and of their own. Many have had to sense a feeling of alienation within their own religious communities. Today, however, the religious communities have begun to appreciate the importance of interreligious dialogue and are encouraging their adherents to take part in it. This, one hopes, will bring to the religious communities the enrichment that individuals have already discovered.

In terms of the struggle for peace and a world community, the interfaith movement has done much to break down prejudice, both by encouraging personal meeting and by public education. The skills necessary to make effective contributions to conflict resolution have yet to be adequately developed. Together members of all religions need to give increasing attention to the search for shared moral values, which undergird human rights, and which can give an ethical basis to the emerging world society.[11]

When he addressed the Global Forum on Human Survival in Moscow in 1990, President Mikhail Gorbachev acknowledged that it was the alarm voiced by some scientists, which was taken up by some members of the public and then by the media, which had forced the politicians to take notice and to act. The beginnings of change lie with a few visionary individuals and a creative minority. An example of this is the way that the suggestion of international arbitration to settle disputes, made in some small peace groups in the middle of the last century, has been adopted by the nations. The prayer and work for peace in the eighties of this century seems to have created a new international atmosphere to which the politicians have responded. Increasingly members of all religions speak of the need for understanding and cooperation, rather than of the conquest of the world by a single religion. Change is possible and it is made possible by the vision and creative energies of dedicated people, but continuing vigilance is necessary to ensure that changes for the better are not eroded. The interfaith movement has been a creative energy, building friendship between people of different religions and enabling them to work together for a better world. Its hopes are far from realized. It has been said that the next century will be a spiritual century or it will not be. Interfaith pilgrims need still to discover for themselves that the One God of many names is a Lover of all nations and they need to share that discovery with others so that we all may know, in our hearts, in our homes, in our nations and in our world, the "peace of God's will, the peace of our need."[12]

NOTES

1. Diana L. Eck, "What Do We Mean by 'Dialogue?' " *Current Dialogue,* WCC, Geneva, 1987, pp. 5ff.

2. Norman Solomon, "Jewish/Christian Dialogue. The State of the Art," *Studies in Jewish/Christian Relations,* No. 1, Selly Oak, Birmingham, 1984, p. 8

3. Eugene R. Borrowitz, *Contemporary Christologies: A Jewish Response,* Paulist Press, 1980, p.19.

4. Francis Clark (ed.), *Interfaith Directory,* New Era, New York, 1987, p. viii.

5. *Ibid.,* p. v.

6. Paul Knitter, Preface to *The Myth of Christian Uniqueness,* ed. John Hick and Paul F. Knitter, SCM Press and Orbis Books, 1988, p. ix.

7. E. Troeltsch, "The Place of Christianity among the World's Religions" in *Christian Thought,* 1923. See my *Together to the Truth,* CLS, Madras, 1971, pp. 112–113.

8. Knitter (n.6), p. x.

9. Robert Edward Whitson, *The Coming Convergence of World Religions,* Newman Press, Westminster, MD 1971.

10. Knitter (n. 6), p. xi.

11. See for example: *The Ethics of World Religions and Human Rights,* ed. Hans Küng and Jürgen Moltmann, SCM Press, 1990; my chapter, "Seeking Community" in *Belonging to Britain,* ed. Roger Hooker, The Council of Churches of Britain and Ireland, 1991; R. Traer, *Faith in Human Rights,* Georgetown University Press, Washington, DC 1990; and Hans Küng, *Global Responsibility,* SCM Press and Crossroad Publishing, New York, 1991.

12. I echo the prayer, "O God of many names" by George Appleton, used by the Week of Prayer for World Peace. I recognize, of course, that some Buddhists and others are uneasy with the use of the term "God."

The 1993 Parliament of the World's Religions

Executive Summary

The materials presented below are excerpted from the "Executive Summary" of the Council for a Parliament of the World's Religions (CPWR). Issued in November 1993, the "Summary" provides basic information about the intent, results, and future of the Parliament, which was held August 28 through September 5, 1993, at the Palmer House Hilton Hotel in Chicago. Not itemized here but undergirding the whole effort was the time and commitment of an "army" of volunteers, a few of whom worked for up to 6 years to create the Parliament; some of these are still involved.

History

*I*n 1893, the world turned its attention to Chicago when the city hosted the World's Columbian Exposition. During the Exposition, congresses were held in the areas of government, jurisprudence, finance, science, literature, and religion "to bring about a real fraternity of nations and unite the enlightened people of the whole earth in a general cooperation for the attainment of the great ends for which humanity is organized." Many other congresses eventually were organized under thirteen departments.

The World's Parliament of Religions was the centerpiece and the most remarkable of the many congresses that were held as part of the Exposition. To prepare for the event, a steering committee composed of sixteen Christian and Jewish leaders from the Chicago area sent over ten thousand letters of invitation to religious leaders throughout the world. The Parliament brought together some four hundred men and women representing forty-one denominations and religious traditions. It lasted for seventeen days in September of 1893. Of all the congresses, the Parliament of Religions was by far the most popular with the public and the press. Audiences of four thousand or more attended each of the daily sessions.

The Parliament was the first formal public meeting of representatives of the major religions in the history of the world. It has been called a watershed event in American history. It saw the assertion of Catholicism and Judaism as mainstream American religions, and recognized both African Americans and women as religious leaders. It marked the beginning of interfaith dialogue in the modern world.

Non-Western religions also have recognized its importance. Several, such as Hinduism and Buddhism, trace their beginnings in the West to their participation in the 1893 World's Parliament of Religions. As one contemporary described the event, "It was, perhaps, the most important religious gathering which has ever assembled." According to another, the Parliament marked "a new era in the evolution of religious life for the world."

The first Parliament left Chicago with both a legacy of interfaith dialogue and an unfinished agenda for greater cooperation and understanding. Thus, in 1988, a group of people of different faiths began meeting to plan a centenary celebration of the Parliament in 1993. The Council for a Parliament of the World's Religions was incorporated as a nonprofit organization dedicated to celebrating and furthering this legacy.

Mission statement

*T*he Council for a Parliament of the World's Religions was formed in the spring of 1988 to prepare for a centennial celebration of the World's Parliament of

---

Statements from Co-sponsors of the 1993 Parliament

From the Bahá'í International Community, National Assembly of the Bahá'ís of the United States, and the Spiritual Assembly of the Bahá'ís of Chicago:

At the 1893 World's Parliament of Religions in Chicago the name of Baháu'llah, prophet-founder of the Bahá'í Faith, was first mentioned on the continent of North America.... The Bahá'í Faith has as its central tenets the oneness of humanity and the essential unity of all religions. Bahá'ís support ardently the Year of Inter-religious Understanding and Cooperation. "So bright is the light of unity," wrote Baha'u'llah, "that it can illuminate the whole earth."

From Rev. Dr. Joan B. Campbell, General Secretary, National Council Churches of Christ, USA:

The NCCC has for a number of years been engaged in the slow process of building interfaith relationships of mutual trust and commitment to justice with our Jewish and Muslim sisters and brothers; we are just beginning to work on developing ties with other religious communities here in the US. The events of 1993, we hope, will enable all of us to move forward together on this path.

From Archbishop Khajag Barsamanian, Primate of the Diocese, Armenian Church of America:

Who among us would not offer his blessing to a project whose objective is "Interreligious Understanding and Cooperation?" Armenian Christians have suffered terrible cruelties at the hands of those for whom such ideals held no value, and such tribulation continues even today for our brothers and sisters in Karabagh. If such understanding and cooperation offer even a glimmer of tranquillity to our troubled world, then we as people of faith and goodwill are obliged to pursue it. But let us never forget that these virtues are simply means to a greater end, and that the peaceable kingdom we seek to create would not be worth having if it meant sacrificing our dedication to the truth. Understanding, cooperation, ecumenism, friendship: all of these point beyond themselves to an even greater peace, which passeth human understanding, and which can only be found in the humble contemplation of God.

From Prevez P. Patel, Priest, Zoroastrian Association of Greater New York:

The Zoroastrian community, followers of Prophet Zarathushtra of ancient Iran, have practiced their religion for centuries in the Middle East and in India, and now a significant number of Zoroastrians live in the United States and Canada.... As a tiny minority religious community, we pray to Ahura Mazda (the Great Light) that we are guided in our attempts to seek communication and understanding with peoples of all faiths, and we pray for this Parliament, whose success will only be seen in how well we can all make peace and not war in the century that will soon be upon us.

From Brahma Kumaris World Spiritual University:

Respect, understanding and tolerance enable us to celebrate life in all its diversity. Living by these values develops a deeper spirituality in our vision towards each other. Sharing these values establishes the common ground on which we all live as one human family. It is our sense that God's vision and desire will move the events of the year. It is our delight to be a part of the 1993 celebrations and deliberations.

Religions held in Chicago in 1893. Itself a group bringing together people of many faiths, the Council had the following objectives:

- To convene a Parliament of the World's Religions in Chicago in 1993.
- To promote understanding and cooperation among religious communities and institutions.
- To encourage the spirit of harmony and to celebrate, with openness and mutual respect, the rich diversity of religions.
- To assess and to renew the role of the religions of the world in relation to personal spiritual growth and the challenges facing the global community.
- To promote and sponsor conferences, workshops, and studies, interfaith encounters, conversations, and exchanges; publications; exhibits and festivals of religious art, music, dance, and ritual; and other appropriate activities, in anticipation of and preparation for the 1993 Parliament.
- To develop and encourage interfaith groups and programs which will carry the spirit of the Parliament into the twenty-first century.

Co-sponsors

*I*n accordance with the by-laws of CPWR, Article III section 2, co-sponsors were sought and approved by set procedures. "Co-sponsors shall be religious or other institutions or organizations which subscribe to the purpose of the Council and agree to contribute actively to the accomplishment of its objectives. Candidates for co-sponsorship must be proposed by at least three co-sponsors or by at least three Trustees and be approved by the Trustees. Representatives of the co-sponsors shall review the work of the Council and are welcome to make recommendations to the Trustees." The cosponsorship committee of the Board of Trustees screened potential candidates for recommendation to the full Board.

There were 198 co-sponsors accepted by the opening of the 1993 Parliament of the World's Religions. Five groups withdrew their support during the course of the Parliament: American Jewish Committee, American Jewish Congress, Anti-Defamation League of B'nai B'rith, Greek Orthodox Diocese of Chicago, and the Jewish Community Relations Council. The 193 remaining groups represent most of the world's religions, multiple civic and humanitarian interests from around the world.

While a large majority of co-sponsors listed United States addresses (180), there was representation from Africa, Asia, and Europe. Co-sponsors listed addresses in Bangladesh, Canada, France, Germany, Hong Kong, India, Ireland, Korea, Malaysia, Saudi Arabia, Sri Lanka, Switzerland, Thailand, Uganda, United Kingdom, and United States. Many organizations maintained offices in the United States which acted as liaison with CPWR.

Representation of co-sponsors was well distributed across religious and civic lines. Predominant religious groups were distributed as follows: 3 Bahá'í, 20 Buddhist, 51 Christian, 15 Hindu, 6 Islam, 4 Jain, 6 Jewish, 2 neo-Pagan, 6 Sikh, 1 Taoist, 5 Unitarian Universalist, 2 Wiccan and 1 Zoroastrian. There were many organizational co-sponsors which did not fit easily into sectarian affiliations, including: 8 academic; 11 civic; 27 ecumenical, interfaith, and inter-religious; 6 humanist; 3 publishing; and 1 spiritual healing.

Host committees

*D*uring the 15 months leading up to the 1993 Parliament, there was a concerted effort on the part of the various religious and spiritual communities of metropolitan Chicago to play a significant role in the event. Their primary goal was to present "the living face" of various religious and spiritual traditions to the world.

In order to facilitate the participation of these local communities in the Parliament, Host Committees were formed in 14 traditions: Bahá'í, Buddhist, Christian (Anglican, Roman Catholic, Orthodox, Protestant and African-American Protestant), Hindu, Jain, Jewish, Muslim, Native American, Sikh and Zoroastrian.

Among the many tasks undertaken by Host Committees were fundraising, publicity, and encouraging registrations for the event. Most importantly, the Council looked to these Committees to represent their particular religious and spiritual traditions to the Parliament and, through the Parliament, to the world.

The work and presence of these Host Committees had a profound impact on the Parliament, for several reasons.

First, they embodied the acknowledgment that the living expression of a particular religious or spiritual tradition is its highest expression.

Second, they provided the practical assistance of making contact with the speakers and planning the programs, workshops, and cultural presentations that would best represent their tradition in the Parliament forum.

Finally, these Host Committees provide the basis for the future of interreligious dialogue and cooperation in this community. Metropolitan Chicago is one of the only cities of its size in North America that does not have an active, metropolitan-wide, constituency-based interreligious forum. For such a forum to emerge from these Host Committees, by which the collective religious and spiritual community could have a greater voice in matters of moral and social concern at the local level, would be a tremendous legacy from the Parliament.

Registration

*I*t was a resplendent sight to see the many hued and traditionally attired people attending the 1993 Parliament of the World's Religions! Many, many people attended in a variety of capacities. Some individuals attended the entire eight days; others were only able to come on a daily basis, either registering each day or for a three-day registration.

Displays of faith traditions of all types were on view in the exhibit hall. Many organizations had representatives working in their respective booths, handing out literature and discussing the philosophy or spiritual views of their religion or faith tradition to curious persons.

Presenters from all theological and social leanings conversed before and after their presentations, oftentimes carrying forward ideas and views expressed during their respective sessions.

There were approximately 8,100 registrations in nine separate registration categories. These registration categories were Board of Trustees, Assembly of Religious and Spiritual Leaders, Parliament Staff, Press, Presenters, Full Conference, Three Day and One Day Registrations, and Exhibitors.

About 9% of individuals were registered in two or more registration categories (some registered to attend and also were registered as a presenter, for example). A little more than 16% of the registrants did not attend the Parliament. This figure is consistent with most registration statistics at conferences such as the Parliament.

Taking into account the no-shows and the people registered in more than one registration category, there were approximately 6500 people, including Assembly and Board of Trustee members, Presenters, and Parliament Staff and Volunteers, who attended the Parliament over the eight days. Of this total, there were 857 registrations for the press. Most of these registrations came during the Parliament and account for the largest number of people registered in more than one registration category. Over 600 people came to work in the many exhibit booths over the course of the Parliament. Again, many of these individuals were also registered to attend the Parliament.

Fifty-seven percent of the people who registered came from the United States. All of the states, except Alaska, were represented. Illinois had the most number of attendees followed by California and New York. Canada was well represented with two percent coming from all of its provinces. Internationally, the attendees came from 55 countries: from Albania to the West Indies, from Cambodia to South Korea, from Australia to Uzebekistan.

All of the major religions and most of the world's faith traditions were represented. As people wrote their religion in the space provided on the registration form, many indicated (besides the major religions and commonly

From Imam Dawud Assad, President, The Council of Masajid of USA:

According to Islam, God created all people as one community, emanating from one origin and sharing the same end. Though we differ in race, color, tongue and nationality, these differences should not clash with the principle of unity of mankind or be the cause of conflict, but rather acquaintance with each other should foster mutual friendship, tolerance, and understanding, and bring harmony with nature and the Almighty Creator.

From the Temple of Understanding, New York City:

The Temple of Understanding, America's oldest international interfaith organization, is pleased to be listed among the co-sponsors of the 1993 Parliament of the World's Religions, and to join in this effort to proclaim 1993 as a "Year of Inter-religious Understanding and Cooperation." The Temple of Understanding is one of four international interfaith organizations that have pooled their resources to create a parallel centenary event in Bangalore, India – working in the spirit of cooperation that we hope will become the standard for people throughout the world.

From Rabbi Marshall T. Meyer, Congregation B'nai Jeshrun, New York:

When institutionalized religions engage in violent conflict, or by commission or by omission are responsible for the spread of injustice, they blaspheme the Living God. Let us unite in brother- and sisterhood to eradicate prejudice, racism and bigotry from our midst as we respect each other's uniqueness.

From Mrs. Norma Levitt, World Union for Progressive Judaism:

Significant experience underlies my personal conviction that religion can be important for peacemaking. As a Jewish woman, I have been involved with multi-religious cooperation for peace for over two decades. Religious representatives need to cooperate to mobilize their resources in the service of peacemaking.

From the National Conference:

Sixty-five years of promoting understanding through interfaith dialogue have taught us that open and honest encounter among people of faith is indeed one of the things that make for peace.

From the Ramakrishna Order of India and its Centers in America

The Parliament of Religions held in Chicago in 1893 envisioned the harmony of religions and unity of humankind. One hundred years have passed, yet the dream of unity and harmony continues to prove elusive.... The acts of hatred and violence, committed in the name of God and religion, are disgraces of human history.... we recall the words spoken at the Parliament by Swami Vivekananda: "Upon the banner of every religion will soon be written, in spite of resistance: 'Help and not Fight,' 'Assimilation and not Destruction', 'Harmony and Peace and not Dissension.'"

From Rev. Chung Ok Lee, General Secretary, International Won Buddhism

We have to build mutual understanding and cooperation among religions in order to promote world peace. In the coming new era, we cannot practice our own religious life without some understanding of other religions because we are part of a single world. Building a peaceful world through inter-religious dialog in the world community is the new mission of religious people in these days. We believe that you are sending a positive signal to the global community. We pray for your success.

**A note from one who could not attend:
P. V. Narasimha Rao,
Prime Minister of India:**

I regret that I will not be able to join you at this commemoration, but I wish you and your colleagues success in organizing meaningful and productive discussions. All of us need a sense of community and receptivity to each other's concerns and beliefs as much and more, now, as a hundred years ago. I hope that in trying to capture the imaginative spirit of enquiry in the Parliament of 1993, we may rediscover the humane and tolerant core of all religions.

known faith traditions) that they were "Catholic Quaker," "blends of many," "atheist," "Celtic," "eclectic," "Hindu Theosophy," and "interreligious," among many other forms of belief. A number of people simply indicated they were "Christian," for example, without specifying a particular denomination. The same was true of persons indicating Buddhism, Hinduism, or Islam; they did not specify a form of their religion. The largest religious representation was among the Christian faiths, followed by the Hindus. These were followed by the Buddhists, Bahá'ís, and Muslims.

The Parliament program

*T*he 1993 Parliament program began each morning at 7:00 a.m. with special meditations. Each evening, as late as 11:00 p.m., the program would conclude with a thematic plenary. These programs were held at the Palmer House Hilton Hotel located in Chicago. Other programs were held at various sites throughout the city. For the final three days of the event, the Assembly of Religious and Spiritual Leaders was held in the afternoons at the Art Institute of Chicago.

The Opening Plenary was a celebratory pageant of music from East and West, an interfaith processional, welcomes, blessings, and invocations. The Closing Plenary included a keynote address by H.H. the Dalai Lama, invocations from the Parliament Presidents, concluding remarks, performance by a multi-cultural dance company, and a rousing final concert by Walter Whitman and the 200-voice Soul Children of Chicago Choir.

Preceding the Closing Plenary was a concert in Grant Park. Arlo Guthrie, Stephen Halpern, a specially formed band of Rastafarian musicians, Tibetan monks performing their timeless chants, and superstar Kenny Loggins all graciously contributed their talents to create a spirit that could not have been bought at any price.

The thematic plenaries – "Interfaith Understanding," "What Shall We Do?", "Visions of Paradise and Possibility," "Voices of the Dispossessed," "Voices of Spirit and Tradition," "From Vision to Action: Celebrating Dialogue," "The Inner Life," "Life in the Community," and "The Next Generation" – were full-scale productions of live performance, multi-media showmanship, stimulating commentary, and heart-moving personal sharing. A capacity audience attended and responded with eager enthusiasm.

During the week, over 500 major presentations, seminars, lectures and workshops on faith teachings and critical issues proceeded very smoothly. One professional critic on conference structure reported:

> ...The Chicago event was exceedingly complex... the softbound book of 152 pages amounted to a "street map" through which the three-dimensional space-time maze of the event could be navigated... an excellent program.

Major independent symposia on Science, Religion and Violence, Business, Media, and Pluralism were offered as micro-conferences over the full course of the program. A thematically ordered, guest-moderated academic component was also offered daily. Movement, meditation, exercise and wellness workshops were also available to participants.

A major fine arts exhibit drew crowds in the upper exhibition hall, and a special viewing room harbored a Film/video Festival throughout the week. A preview of the feature film *Baraka* attracted almost 1,000 people at its Art Institute screening. The Festival of Sacred Performing Arts intrigued its audience with dance, song, music, poetry, ceremonies, and drama for more than four hours. The Empire Room hosted international performances in all media for four full days.

The TogetherNet computer network seminar ran from morning through evening each day Many participants signed on and were grateful that this resource had been made available.

The Parliament of the People, held during the lunch hour for four days, successfully established a sense of community among this highly diverse group, ultimately producing a set of twelve communal newsletters entitled,

"Your Voice." Issue #12 of this effort was a detailed report by the Facilitation Team of the discussions that took place during the Assembly.

The scope and richness of the Parliament program has been noted as "unprecedented" in the experience of many conference-goers. Of course, the event in its entirety was a sterling experience for so many.

Critical issues

*E*arly in the planning process, it was agreed that one of the major dimensions of the 1993 Parliament program should be focus on the encounter of the world's religions with the critical issues which challenge the human community at the threshold of the 21st century. Three years ago, the CPWR Board entered into a partnership agreement with the Institute for 21st Century Studies (now the Millennium Institute) and its Executive Director, Dr. Gerald O. Barney, to collaborate on the development of this phase of the event. That collaboration proved extremely fruitful in several ways:

- The Institute aided the Program Committee and staff in securing the active participation of a significant number of "issue-oriented" organizations and individuals who brought their expertise on a wide range of topics and concerns which might be addressed. Several of these organizations became co-sponsors.
- Dr. Barney was responsible for the design and implementation of the Plenary Session, "What Shall We Do?"
- Over one-third of the major presentations, seminars, and lectures offered during the event addressed the relationship between religion and the critical issues. The Critical Issues programs were among the best attended of the week.

The CPWR may consider future efforts along these lines, and the possibility of further cooperation with the Millennium Institute.

Assembly of Religious and Spiritual Leaders

*P*erhaps one of the most significant aspects of the Parliament of the World's Religions was the convening of the Assembly of Religious and Spiritual Leaders and their discussion of issues and challenges that face the global community. The Assembly affirmed the process of developing a framework within which there would be a broad and common understanding for how people behave in relation to one another, for shared behaviors which are acceptable and unacceptable across religious and spiritual traditions. The Assembly, as a consultative body, also affirmed the ongoing process of articulation and debate, discussion, and scholarly critiques as means by which the declaration could "take root."

The Council will decide how to reorganize, if at all, to assist in conflict resolution, to encourage interfaith dialogue and discussion, and to encourage people to work together. The consultative Assembly requested that the Council review possible options toward sustaining this work internationally. This "international initiative," with the help of the Assembly Presidents, a special task force, and existing interfaith organizations, is to be broadly inclusive to ensure that smaller traditions and parts of the world not adequately represented at the Parliament may participate.

Metropolitan Assembly

A significant event in the development of a lasting legacy of the 1993 Parliament was the Metropolitan Assembly of Religious, Spiritual and Civic Leaders, held on August 31, 1993, at St. James Episcopal Cathedral in downtown Chicago.

One hundred and thirty persons attended, representing the diversity of the Chicago metropolitan area. Presentations were made on the opportunities and challenges presented by the cultural, religious, and spiritual diversity of metropolitan Chicago. The Assembly was presented with background information and perspectives gathered from the networking and planning process of CPWR. In small group discussions, the Assembly considered a strategic development process for a future interreligious organization.

The high point of the gathering was the signing of a statement entitled "Our Commitment to Interreligious Dialogue and Cooperation." In it, the assembled leaders pledged to "respect, understand, learn, and benefit from the religious, spiritual and cultural traditions of [our] neighbors." They further pledged to strive together to build a more interactive and interdependent metropolitan community. They vowed to draw upon the spiritual teachings of their religious and spiritual traditions and apply them to the deep wounds and tragic injustices that afflict their neighbors and themselves, so that together they might "defeat racism and sexism, alleviate poverty, reduce hostilities and tensions, empower the disenfranchised, preserve and nurture the Earth."

Finally, the CPWR process for a future organization received a series of endorsements representing the range of metropolitan Chicago's religious and spiritual communities including the Roman Catholic Archdiocese, the Northern Illinois Conference of the United Methodist Church, the Brahma Kumaris World Spiritual University, DePaul University, and African-American Protestant, Hindu and Muslim Host Committees.

The Metropolitan Assembly concluded, with ringing affirmation from those participating, to join together to make this commitment to interreligious dialogue and cooperation a living reality in metropolitan Chicago. The work will now be carried on by the Metropolitan Interreligious Initiative Task Force of CPWR. [...]

"Towards a Global Ethic (An Initial Declaration)"

*O*ne of the key outcomes of the 1993 Parliament of the World's Religions was the endorsement by the Assembly of Religious and Spiritual Leaders of "Towards a Global Ethic, An Initial Declaration." This remarkable document stands as a permanent contribution of the Parliament to the global conversation on how human beings should live together with each other and the planet. [...] [The Declaration and a description of its drafting and reception are presented in the next chapter.]

International Initiative

*C*alls to create an ongoing international organization began to emerge strongly during the Opening Plenary of the 1993 Parliament. In the first keynote address, Dr.

Robert Muller, former Assistant Secretary-General of the United Nations, forcefully stated,

> You must create a permanent institution. What is needed is a place where you have a good number of people from various nations, from various nations, from various races, from both sexes, from various beliefs, from various languages, work together on a daily basis. This is the miracle I have seen at the United Nations.

Dr. Muller went on to urge

> that a preparatory committee be established to come up with the proposal of a world spiritual institution which would then be approved by another Parliament in a few years from now, and I would very much like to have this done by 1995, the fiftieth anniversary of the UN.

Likewise, Dr. Gerald Barney, in his articulation of some of the most critical issues facing our generation, called for future collaborative efforts by religious leaders working together. These ideas echoed throughout the hallways for the remainder of the week.... [See articles in Chapter 24.]

During the period of open discussion in the final session of the Assembly, Dr. L. M. Singhvi put forth a resolution that called upon the Board of Trustees of the Council for a Parliament of the World's Religions to organize a planning process to prepare the way for the establishment in due course of a permanent international organization. The resolution, which was supported by an overwhelming majority of the participants, called for the participation of Assembly Presidents, and for the involvement of existing international interfaith organizations in discussions designed to bring a suitable agency into existence:

> that there be established an international, interfaith organization to continue and enlarge the work begun by the Parliament of the World's Religions; an organizing committee be formed to explore the options for the creations of such a body; that this committee send representatives to visit a number of countries and religious communities to seek trustees, participants and financial support.

> We want a continuing spiritual council of religions encouraged by all faiths with authority from religious leaders in order that such an interfaith council would be able to influence events.

Finally, a number of invitations and suggestions were received for the Parliament to reconvene the Assembly of Religious and Spiritual Leaders in conjunction with the various significant international events between now and the year 2000. The occurrence of these meetings could provide important opportunities to launch such initiatives.

Media coverage

*I*nternational media at the 1993 Parliament of the World's Religions included journalists from Australia, Hong Kong, England, Canada, Germany, Japan, and India. Print coverage from international papers is not fully tabulated, but US print coverage of the Parliament of the World's Religions contained approximately 4,000 articles. These articles were from neighborhood, city, and national newspapers including the Associated Press, the *New York Times* and the *Wall Street Journal*. Other print journalists present to cover the events were from several magazines including *Mirabella, Esquire* and *Time*.

There were over 850 press registrations. Coverage of this historic event was not limited to the print media. In addition, several video and audio crews attended in order to capture Parliament proceedings for archival and educational purposes. Electronic media such as the BBC, Voice of America, CNN and National Public Radio, to name a few, came to the Parliament to conduct on-camera interviews with Parliament dignitaries and to tape Parliament proceedings for worldwide broadcast. A documentary crew from CBS, as well as from the Chicago Broadcast Ministries, prepared a one-half-hour and a one-hour video compilation, respectively, of interviews and Parliament highlights.

With the above mentioned coverage, millions of people read about, saw or heard about the 1993 Parliament [...]

The Archives

*I*n November, 1993, the Council for a Parliament of the World's Religions designated DePaul University as the repository of the Archives. [... See Chapter 43.]

Where Do We Go from Here?

*T*he Council for a Parliament of the World's Religions now has the task of preserving a history that will propel it into the future of interfaith dialogue. The 1993 Parliament is not only an event that was held in Chicago, but a milestone in the history of interfaith dialogue. The current task of the CPWR Board of Trustees is to articulate, publicize and frame the continuing work of the Parliament through asking the question: "What was realized in Chicago and what continuing hope comes out of the Parliament?" [...]

Some key staff and trustees for the Parliament

Dr. Daniel Gómez-Ibáñez, *Executive Director*
Dr. Nelvia Brady, *Chief Operating Officer*
Ms. Barbara Bernstein, *Director of Program*
Rev. Dirk Ficca, (current) *Director, Metropolitan Task Force*
Mr. Haik L. Muradian, *Host Committee Coordinator*
Ms. Jacqueline Trussell, (current) *Office Coordinator*
Ms. Melinda Weaver, *Director of Logistics*

Dr. David Ramage, *Chair of the Board of Trustees (emeritus)*
Dr. Howard Sulkin, (current) *Chair of the Board of Trustees*
Ms. Maria Svolos Gebhard, *Vice Chair, Public Information*
Mr. Jim Kenney, *Vice-Chair, Program*
Mrs. Betty Reneker, *Vice-Chair*
Ms. Yael Wurmfeld, *Vice Chair and Secretary*
Father Thomas Baima and Dr.David Breed, *Treasurers*

Compiled by the Editor with appreciation also to numerous others who contributed enormously to the success of the Parliament: host committees, program, logistics, fundraising, publicity, registration, and more.

The Role of the Faith Traditions

Dr. Gerald O. Barney, Jane Blewett and Kristen R. Barney

As part of the preparation for the Parliament of the World's Religions, staff of the Millennium Institute prepared a book on the critical issues of the 21st century. Titled *Global 2000 Revisited: What Shall We Do?*, the book's contents identify and analyze a number of issues in detail; its scientifically derived projections, based on extensive research and consultation, compel us to take these issues seriously. In addition, the authors raise fundamental questions and perspectives about the role of faith traditions in both the origin and resolution of these global concerns. These excerpts present some of the challenges addressed to religious and spiritual leaders and their congregations.

*W*e humans have begun asking questions about "sustainable development." This is an important question, but it does not go deep enough. We must also begin asking questions about "sustainable faith."

Is there a faith tradition in existence today that is practicing a way of life that provides "progress" for the whole community of life, not just the human species? Is there a faith tradition such that if everyone on earth suddenly adopted it, the human future on Earth would be assured? . . .

Sir Shridath Ramphal, former secretary general of the Commonwealth and foreign minister of Guyana, has implicitly raised this same question in the context of the "holy texts of many religions." He writes as follows in the official report prepared for the opening of the United Nations Conference on Environment and Development:

In the language of the Independent Commission on International Humanitarian Issues. . . , the holy texts of many religions, not to mention legal traditions, philosophies and customs ". . . abound in moral injunctions that imply an ethic of human solidarity. . . . For centuries, the great religious texts have taught the essential oneness of the human race." What scriptures have not always taught is that nature is the loom on which is woven life's seamless fabric of which humanity is a significant, but not unduly dominant, part.[64]

The God I know is still speaking, and there have been at least four new revelations.

First, it has been revealed that among the most destructive forces on Earth today is hatred between the followers of different faith traditions. Of the almost 50 armed conflicts in progress currently, the vast majority are motivated in significant part by hatred of the followers of one faith for the followers of another faith.[65] The arms industry – the largest industry in the world, larger even than illegal drugs and oil – is supported in significant part by the hatred of the followers of one faith for the followers of another faith.

Examples of the destructiveness of interreligious hatred are found almost daily in all major newspapers. . . . What faith is now *not* involved in acts of hatred and violence in one or more of the ethnic and religious wars currently in progress?[67]

The second new revelation comes from a 1,500-year meditation on Earth, a meditation we usually call "science." From this meditation we know that Earth is the product of a 15-billion-year journey from the first burst of creative energy. We know that we humans and all other life on Earth are intimately connected through a single, integral, and continuing creation journey, and that we humans are related genetically to everything that contains the DNA molecule: to eagles, apes, snakes, frogs, trees, grasses, molds, bacteria.... We are all cousins, and we all depend on each other through the complex bio-geo-chemical cycles of Earth. Earth is not just our home; we are Earth. Our entire physical being is made up of bits and pieces of Earth – water, air, rice, potatoes, etc. – and we, collectively, are an important part of the consciousness of Earth.[68]

The third revelation is that five billion of us individual humans, both poor and affluent, are acting today in ways that are destroying the life-sustaining capabilities of Earth and thereby destroying our own prospects. Nothing survives now – no person, no species, no lake, no river, no ocean, no forest, no soil, no mountain, not even the atmosphere – unless we humans will it so.

The fourth revelation is that we humans – not as individuals, but as a species – will exercise an enormous influence on the future of Earth. There is little question that we can destroy our species and many others with us. We can create an Earth future without humans. We might also create an Earth future in which there is a rich and mutually enhancing Earth-human relationship. In effect, we humans have become co-creators with the Divine of the future of the Earth.

This fourth revelation is of some considerable import, but to my knowledge, no faith tradition has prepared us for it. No faith anticipated the development of human power over Earth's future, this enormous responsibility. To my knowledge, no faith tradition has prepared us to know ourselves not as individuals but as a species. To my knowledge, no faith tradition has provided moral precepts to guide inter-species behavior, to decide which species should cease to exist, which new species shall be created through genetic engineering (and then patented), and to judge the alternative futures humans are considering for Earth.[69]

Where can we turn with questions that deal with matters of ultimate meaning and direction, with cherished beliefs, with fears and insecurities about the future? Where can we turn to learn to act responsibly as a species? Where can we turn for insights into what possibilities there might be for a mutually enhancing human-Earth relationship in the future? Where can we turn for insights into what the original creative energy might desire our species – humans collectively – to make of Earth?

These are fundamentally spiritual questions, and they are being raised openly today in many communities, by scientists and economists, by philsophers and theologians, by historians and anthropologists, by religious and secular leaders alike.[70] Such questions are in the hearts of ordinary men and women who wonder about the future for all life and wonder how to answer their children's questions.

The questions being raised are unique to the experience and consciousness of peoples of our time, peoples who have looked into the farthest reaches of space, seen back in time to the very origins of the cosmos, have come to know Earth to be a relatively small planet in a galaxy of billions of stars and planets in a cosmos of billions of galaxies; people who have probed the core of the atom, lived with the prospect of nuclear annihilation, and now face the possibility of ecological annihilation. The questions are welling up from the human spirit struggling to be faithful to the moment. So, in hope and trust, we turn to you, the carriers of our spiritual wisdom, with our questions.

Questions for our spiritual leaders

What are the traditional teachings – and the range of other opinions – within your faith on how to meet the legitimate needs of the growing human community without destroying the ability of Earth to support the community of all life?

- What does your faith tradition teach about how the needs of the poor are to be met as human numbers continue to grow? What is the cause of human poverty?

- How are the needs and wants of humans to be weighed relative to the survival of other forms of life?

What are the traditional teachings – and the range of other opinions – within your faith on the meaning of "progress" and how it is to be achieved?

- What does your faith tradition teach about human destiny? Is human destiny separable from that of the Earth?

- What is your destiny, the destiny of the followers of your faith tradition? What does your faith tradition teach concerning the followers of other traditions?

- How are we to measure "progress?" Can there be progress for the human community without progress for the whole community of life?

What are the traditional teachings – and the range of other opinions – within your faith tradition concerning a proper relationship with those who differ in race or gender (conditions one cannot change), and culture, politics, or faith?

- Much hatred and violence are carried out in the name of religion. What teachings of your faith tradition have been used – correctly or not in an attempt to justify such practices?

- Discrimination and even destructive behavior of men toward women are often justified in the name of religion. Which, if any, of the teachings of your faith have been used – correctly or incorrectly – in this way?

- How does your faith tradition characterize the teachings and followers of other faiths? Do some adherents of your tradition hold that the teachings and followers of other faiths are evil, dangerous, misguided? Is there any possibility that your faith tradition can derive wisdom, truth, or insight from the teachings of another faith?

What are the traditional teachings – and the range of other opinions – within your faith on the possibility of new revelation, new understanding, new interpretation, new wisdom, and new truth concerning human activity affecting the future of Earth?

- Does your faith tradition envision and provide for the criticism, correction, reinterpretation, and even rejection of ancient traditional assumptions and "truth" in light of new understandings or revelations?

NOTES

64. Ramphal, Shridath. 1992. *Our Country, The Planet: Forging a Partnership for Survival.* Washington, DC: Island Press. pp. 202-203

65. Binder, D. and Crossette, B. "As Ethnic Wars Multiply, U.S. Strives for a Policy." *The New York Times.* February 7, 1993. p.A1

. . .

67. For a list of the 48 religious and ethnic wars now in progress on every continent, see: Binder, D. and Crossette, B. "As Ethnic Wars Multiply, U.S. Strives for a Policy." *The New York Times.* February 7, 1993. p.A1

68. See Swimme, Brian and Berry, Thomas. 1992 *The Universe Story;* Cloud, Preston. *Oasis in Space: A History of the Planet from the Beginning.* Cambridge University Press; Capra, Fritjof, and Steindle-Rast, David. *Belonging to the Universe.* HarperCollins. 1991; and Wilson, E.O. *The Discovery of Life.* Belknap-Harvard.

69. While no faith tradition has gone very far in developing inter-species ethics and morality, a few individuals have made significant steps in this direction. See, for example: Engel, Ronald J., and Engel, Joan Gibb, eds. 1992. *Ethics of Environment and Development: Global Challenge and International Response.* University of Arizona Press.

70. For examples of questions being raised by others, see: Forrester, J.W. 1971. "Churches at the Transition Between Growth and World Equilibrium." In: Forrester, J.W. 1975. *Collected Papers of Jay W. Forrester.* Cambridge, MA: The M.I.T. Press. pp. 255–269; Shiva, V. 1989. *Staying Alive: Women, Ecology, and Development.* London: Zed Books; Spretnak, C. 1991. *States of Grace: The Recovery of Meaning in the Postmodern Age.* San Francisco: HarperCollins; Hardin, G. 1963. "A Second Sermon on the Mount." *Perspectives in Biology and Medicine.* vol. vi, no. 3, Spring 1963; Hardin, G. 1968. "The Tragedy of the Commons." *Science,* vol. 162, December 13, 1968. pp.1243–1248; Vickers, G. 1970. *Freedom in a Rocking Boat: Changing Values in an Unstable Society.* Middlesex, England: Pelican Books.

The above excerpts are from *Global 2000 Revisited.* Copyright © 1993 Millennium Institute. Used with permission.

FOR MORE INFORMATION:

Millennium Institute
1611 North Kent Street, Suite 204, Arlington, VA 22209-2111 USA
tel. (703) 841-0048 / fax. (703) 841-0050

To purchase books, contact:

Public Interest Publications
P.O. Box 229, Arlington, VA 22210 USA
tel. (800) 537-9359 (US, Canada and Mexico)
(703) 243-2252 (elsewhere) / fax. (703) 243-2489

A Parliament Retrospective

Joel Beversluis

Editor of A SourceBook for Earth's Community of Religions

Surveying the Parliament of the World's Religions from sixteen months later, can we find any lasting significance in it? Or will the 1993 Parliament seem to fade and leave imprecise markings on the course of religions and history, as seemed to happen following the 1893 event? Then, the dominant North American religious communities mostly ignored the World's Parliament of Religions despite its now apparent impact on the study of world religions and on the interfaith movement. On the other hand, the impact of the 1893 event was much more widely remembered in India and Japan than in North America; among other effects, 1893 marked the beginning of the missionary journeys from eastern religions to the West and greatly enhanced Western fascination with those traditions. Will there be comparable, long-lasting effects from this Parliament, and is there any way it can be considered a watershed event?

It seems to me that the Parliament's lasting significance resides in its vision that the religions of the world – through their spiritual and ethical values, their institutions and their potential influence on personal behavior – can and must play a positive role in the increasingly challenging matrix of our planetary life. The Parliament was both symbolic of this vision and a major step towards its fulfillment. Religious leaders from all traditions, members of numerous planning and host committees, and trustees and staff from the Parliament all broadcast one aspect or another of this inspiring message: Despite the problems caused by religions, in the face of increasing secularization, and contradicting the assumptions of scientism and reductionistic technique, the people of the Parliament affirmed that the wholistic nature of religious and spiritual experience, in its noblest forms, guarantees religion's ongoing relevance to life, peace, and wellbeing.

Conspiracy or CoNexus?

Some fearful observers, particularly those who picketed the event from the sidewalk outside Chicago's Palmer House Hotel, were concerned that the Parliament's underlying significance was its pursuit of a convergence of beliefs into one world religion. Other conspiracy theorists tied the Parliament and one world religion to the spectre of one world government, via the United Nations. These concerns fly in the face of the evidence. Both the intentions of the organizers and the actions of most participants indicated a healthy respect for the uniquenesses and diversity of religions; indeed, most participants would not have been there if their religious identities were being threatened in any way.

Although some religions and many individuals do affirm the convergence of religions or believe in a common spiritual destiny, the presentation of these concepts was neither a goal of the Parliament nor a dominant voice.

Organizers took pains to avoid the appearance of that agenda, and the interfaith movement in general is clearly leaning towards the understanding and appreciation of diversity. Likewise, while issues of global policies and responsibilities were quite apparent, many people also affirmed the greater effectiveness of local and regional efforts in the resolution of those problems.

My perception of the Parliament is not of a conspiracy leading to any significant structural or doctrinal unity. Rather, my image portrays a gathering of members of the religious and spiritual traditions into an historic nexus – a focal point or convergence of a sometimes overwhelming assortment of factors – world views, critical issues, information, wisdom, and experience. An important quality of a nexus is that the future – beyond the nexus – is open to numerous possibilities which are determined by the choices people make as they proceed through the focal point. As I see it, the Parliament's participants recognized that the time had come to acknowledge the scope of this nexus and to help the world move through it, cooperatively. In my use of the word *conexus*, I mean to suggest the cooperation and interconnectedness we can find at the points where we interact with the nexus.

Our task was to acknowledge the critical issues and the sometimes harsh realities of a pluralistic world, but we also chose to look beyond the differences so that we could focus on the changes in attitude that are necessary if we are to meet our common challenges and aspirations. In short, Parliament participants arranged to meet "at the conexus" and to begin responding together in whatever ways were appropriate to us as individuals, out of our personal commitments to our religiously-based ethics.

Six lessons for the community of religions

A closer look at the Parliament and the context in which it was held suggests the following lessons about its significance to the wider community of religions.

1) The Parliament gave eloquent witness to assertions of religious identity and diversity. The Palmer House and the streets of Chicago were filled with the costumes, languages and accents, ritual smells and sounds, and the goodwill of more than 6,500 participants (some estimates claim up to 10,000 due to shared registrations) from 56 countries and most of the world's organized religions. During an intense 8 days, participants encountered the richness of the religious and cultural experience of those whom we met in the lobbies, elevators, bathrooms, and meeting halls. Although an impressive 43% of the participants live outside of the United States, by no means did all the diversity leave town after the final sessions. The world's religions and cultures have moved permanently and in large numbers into Chicago and across North America. The lesson is that we don't need to look or travel very far to see the increasing need for new modes of interreligious encounter and understanding.

In response to these needs, new grassroots interfaith groups are putting on conferences and promoting dialogue in places as varied as Grand Rapids, Toronto, Delhi, and Rio de Janeiro. There are new interfaith centers and revitalized chapters of international organizations in the U.K., the Middle East, and Asian countries, among others. New publications about the world's religions, about interfaith and inter-ideological dialogue, and for use in religious education — including within public school systems – are supporting these grassroots efforts to encourage understanding of religious identity and diversity.

2) Current environmental disasters and more serious prognoses of ecological crises as well as interreligious conflicts are, ironically, drawing the religions together into new alliances with each other and with secular institutions. The lesson from the Parliament's focus on the critical issues is the growing consensus that these crises are, essentially, matters of the human heart and will; furthermore, religious and spiritual traditions have much to offer in motivations and techniques for personal changes of heart. Since we all will face these ecological challenges, either cooperatively or competitively, we were invited to learn from the wisdom and ecological experience of traditions other than our own. For instance, an understanding of indigenous people's sustainable relationships with the earth can help inform our own responses to these issues and re-sensitize us to the wisdom within our own traditions.

Parliament participants acknowledged the ugly realities of religiously-sanctioned violence, but we also noted the religiously-based ideals which can ameliorate it. The Parliament also presented the needs of suffering and dispossessed brothers and sisters, and asserted that we share responsibility for meeting those needs with others of goodwill, beyond the parameters of our own traditions and institutions.

3) The declaration "Towards a Global Ethic" defines the context and principles for a minimum global ethic. A consensus document derived from core values in all the major religious and spiritual traditions, this effort of the Parliament is unprecedented in its scope and intent. The declaration and principles were drafted by Hans Küng and members of the Parliament's organizing Council, in consultation with hundreds of others. It was signed (provisionally, as "An Initial Declaration") by more than 200 of the 240 members of the Assembly of Religious and Spiritual Leaders. It has since been presented to wider audiences at several conferences and through substantial media coverage, and may be revised after wider consultations within and among religious bodies. Its primary value and lesson lies in the explicitly interreligious consensus on ethical principles and responsibilities – necessary ingredients in the development of any community. Having this consensus in written form provides us with a tool for increased understanding and self-criticism within religious traditions throughout the world. Furthermore, because the "Ethic" is grounded in humanity's common wisdom and experience rather than in any specific scriptures or claims of transcendence, it is also useful to non-religious persons.

Many people are searching for ways to facilitate the social and personal changes that seem necessary if humans are to sustain the ecological and cultural systems on which we and our heirs depend. Religious and government leaders, scientists, the business community, educators, advocates, and the public, whether secular or religious, are uged to use "Towards a Global Ethic" for discussion and as a standard for self-analysis. It is worth testing whether this statement of a common ethic can provide a useful and authoritative catalyst for appropriate change.

4) The Parliament was as much an experience of the heart as of the head; many participants were deeply moved by the experience. For these, the Parliament offered an alternative to the insular and competitive approach common to many religious and spiritual traditions. It would be a mistake, however, to think that the Parliament affected only the registrants. Far beyond North America, interest in the 1993 Parliament and in other centennial commemorations of the 1893 Parliament was high, reflecting a shifting of attitudes towards other religions.

At least some of the participants at the Parliament and those they influence in their communities are, I believe, part of a much larger movement which can be described as spiritual awakenings. One characteristic of this movement among practicing members of diverse religious traditions is the rediscovery of the genius at the heart of their own traditions. It is also noteworthy that for many people, the awakening includes revitalized faith in divine intervention, despite the contrary effects of secularization and scientific educations. Worldwide, there is a growing sense, expressed through many different religious perceptions, that a "divine orchestration," emanating from divine love and compassion, is assisting us in responding to our crises.

Another element in this movement is the individual's desire to clarify ethical, religious, and spiritual commonalities *and* differences. While some people believe that the doctrinal differences between religions should be resolved and perhaps erased, many others believe that religious identities and distinctions will be preserved even while our hearts and hands reach across such boundaries. In either case, this clarification of ethics and spiritual meaning meets very personal, existential needs of searching individuals. The answers provide a place for people to stand, from which they can identify purpose and generate hope, even in hard times. Significantly, the clarification of ethical commonalities also serves the very pragmatic desire to galvanize the spiritual and institutional resources of the world's religions into cooperative action.

These shifting attitudes indicate that the resurgence of fundamentalisms is not the only contemporary religious feature to watch. Both movements are responses to pluralism in our cultures, to turmoil and to portents of crisis. Each of these movements is naming its perception of the dangers, and each develops its best defensive maneuvers. One movement feels the need to guard the gates, to focus on the truth and well-being of those within and to open the gates only when its disciples are bringing that truth to those outside. The other movement identifies common threats and common aspirations on both sides of the walls; its best defensive strategy calls for a unified response, which it does with an openness to mysteries, to the experiences of other persons and to their perceptions of the Other. The lesson is that the "opening of the gates" in this movement allows participation in a wider community of religions and enables collaborative responses on behalf of the larger community of the earth.

5) Although we might enjoy this vision of a community of religions, we cannot ignore that there was also a great range of goals and participation at the Parliament. As in any village or city, the Parliament's community was not always harmonious. Some members did not carry their share; some never came to the interfaith table, or withdrew; some were not respectful of others, and some were angry; some expressed their pain. Yet, many needs were met, new connections were joined, new voices were heard, and numerous members of the community were enriched. The observations which follow demonstrate some of this range in more detail.

The uses of God-language during plenary sessions was problematic for some, particularly for Buddhists; yet the absence of references to God or Allah in the declaration "Towards a Global Ethic" was problematic for others, particularly Muslims and Christians. Some major speakers assumed or declared universalistic beliefs, without acknowledging those who disagree. Some minority religions and movements got extensive recogniton and media attention, to the dismay of others. Members of some religions concluded that they could not associate with others with whom they had major differences of culture or doctrine. Religious and ethnic traditions which were not present or substantially represented in 1893, including African-Americans, Native Americans, Bahá'ís, Sikhs, and Zoroastrians, to name a few, made important contributions to this Parliament. At the same time, some of these also revealed their great pain and, in the process, raised real-world tensions. Hindus and Buddhists had a very substantial presence commensurate with the significance they attach to the 1893 Parliament (comparable to Christian sentiments about Paul's missionary visit to Mars Hill). Muslims, almost completely absent in 1893, were present at this Parliament in substantial numbers. This time, though still a minority at plenary session podiums, women were much more present within the organization, making presentations, and among the registrants. Western Christian participants did not dominate the Parliament as in 1893, and they were not out to "Christianize" the world; perhaps because of the agreement by cosponsors to refrain from proselytizing, conservative white evangelical Christians were notably under-represented. On the other hand, many Chicago-area African-American churches and young people participated with enthusiasm.

The lesson is that, despite the tensions and range of participation, the vast majority of the members of the community of religions at the Parliament was able to show a remarkable degree of harmony, respect and appreciation for others.

6) The number of interreligious encounters has increased geometrically during the past fifty years. Organizations such as the International Association for Religious

Freedom, World Conference on Religion and Peace, Temple of Understanding, World Fellowship of Religions, the Interreligious Federation for World Peace, Global Forum of Spiritual and Parliamentary Leaders, World Congress of Faiths, and the International Conference (formerly of Christians and Jews) have been sponsoring a wide variety of interfaith programs. Though it was a major event, the 1993 Parliament was only one of many activities which took place last year throughout the world. The year 1993 had been designated as the Year of Interreligious Understanding and Cooperation by a coalition of international, interfaith organizations, whose own substantial centennial commemoration was held in Bangalore, India. Numerous other local, regional and international meetings have been held since the Parliament – including one in Delhi, India – which attracted more than one hundred thousand participants.

The continuing growth of this movement is both necessary and inevitable. As we commemorate the 50th anniversary of the United Nations and look ahead to numerous events and projects associated with the year 2000, even more interfaith meetings lie in store. A recurrence of religious concern and engagement is afoot across the planet, with potential for both good and ill. The recent U.N. population conference in Cairo is new evidence that the challenges of global governance cannot be met without consulting the values and power of the religions, whether or not we personally agree with their stances. Likewise, it is becoming apparent that statecraft, international policies, and remedial actions will have limited success unless they collaborate in strategic ways with the values and influence of the world's religions. The lesson and challenge to the community of religions is to use the interfaith movement to shape relationships and to influence structures that will evoke the best that religions can offer.

I conclude these lessons from the Parliament and the larger interfaith context with this paraphrase of a statement made by Charlene Spretnak in *States of Grace*:

> We seek engagement; we join the effort to cross lines of fragmentation and compartmentalization that have become habitual in the modern age. We challenge the widespread assumption that religions or spiritualities have nothing to do with the pragmatic concerns of modernity.

Restructuring the CPWR

*T*he work of the Parliament is not finished. The Council for a Parliament of the World's Religions (CPWR) continues shifting gears from its focus on creating the 1993 event. Since the commemoration of the centennial had never been the Council's only objective, a wide array of new challenges and opportunities is appearing. Under the leadership of Dr. Howard Sulkin, President of Spertus College, the CPWR is refining new initiatives and structures, identifying new sources of funds, and clarifying its relationships with other interfaith organizations.

The Metropolitan Council

*E*ven in the late 1980's, many CPWR trustees wanted to establish a permanent interfaith organization that would carry the vision of the Parliament forward within metropolitan Chicago long after the centennial events. That dream is now taking form in the Metropolitan Interreligious Initiative. Its director, the Rev. Dirk Ficca, notes that the constituents of this emerging network will include the congregations of numerous religious and cultural communities from across the metropolitan Chicago area as well as the region's many seminaries and schools of religion. During 1994–1995 the taskforce charged with implementing this Initiative is conducting more than 400 interviews with religious leaders to identify the objectives and concerns of those who will be served by the network. Startup funding is committed, and a series of interreligious forums and pilot projects has been launched.

The International Initiative

*T*he most challenging of the Parliament's new ventures is the shaping of a new Initiative in response to calls for an ongoing international presence and activity. Proposals have included the establishment of a permanent, international interreligious body – a United Religions – or a permanent Assembly of Religious and Spiritual Leaders.

To assess the available resources and directions to be taken, a one-year anniversary celebration and consultation of Assembly members was held in September 1994. At this meeting, many voices suggested that the CPWR should *not* pursue efforts to establish a new international organization. Some opponents of this vision pointed to the enormous difficulty of establishing an equitable representational structure among structurally diverse religions; others felt that the religious and spiritual leaders affiliated with the Assembly should not engage in the lobbying efforts typical of international affairs. In addition, financial and organizational resources have not been identified to support such an effort, and there were legitimate concerns that such an effort might compete with the work of other international interfaith organizations.

Alternative emphases at this advisory session encouraged the CPWR to provide leadership through programs which develop the numerous resources already gathered via the Parliament. Projects mentioned include the publication of Parliament presentations, better networking and communications with cosponsors and grassroots efforts, and the development of educational resources. Some members of the CPWR are also exploring and developing a Religious Conflict Resolution program.

The Report of the Ad-Hoc International Advisory Committee

December 1994

*B*ased on the results of the September consultation, CPWR Chair Dr. Howard Sulkin invited a group of leaders from around the world to meet on November 18-19 to develop concrete recommendations for the International

Inititiative. Its *Report* and recommendations indicate numerous opportunities for the CPWR as well as for many others in collaboration with the Council. Below are this author's condensation of some recommendations from the *Report*:

"Towards a Global Ethic"

Understanding that the document is in no way a final work but rather part of a larger process of discussion, reflection, and movement "towards a global ethic," the Committee recommended that the document be more widely disseminated and discussed. A supplement should be developed including explanatory notes and commentary, critiques, and study guidelines. Cooperative relationships should be established with other individuals and organizations who are likewise promoting understanding of the ethical common ground of the world's religions.

Periodic parliaments and assemblies

The CPWR should explore ways of supporting the movement and spirit of the 1993 Parliament by encouraging future Parliaments, held every five years in appropriate locations throughout the world. A new Assembly of Religious and Spiritual Leaders should be convened three years before each Parliament to identify the locations and agendas for future Parliaments and to carry the message back to their communties. CPWR should encourage regional "chapters" to focus on issues of concern.

Projects 2000

The Committee recommended that CPWR identify and implement one or more projects in cooperation with the proposal of the Millennium Institute, which suggested that the occasion of the millennium be used to inspire individuals, groups, nations, and faith traditions to make strategic "millennial threshold gifts." Gifts would be non-sectarian and must involve concrete outreach and service. CPWR should work closely with the Host Committees and Co-sponsors of the Parliament in promoting and adopting projects.

A world interreligious academy

The Committee considered and appointed a sub-committee to evaluate the recommendation that CPWR help create a World Interreligious Academy, to serve as a center (or centers) for interreligious study, dialogue, cooperation, and the development of resources.

UN50 commemorations

The Council will cooperate in interfaith services and forums which will be held at the UN50 events in San Francisco in June and in New York in October.

A "United Religions Organization"

While the majority of the committee did not feel inclined to pursue this proposal, a minority did urge the establishment of a permanent institution. The Committee recommended that CPWR establish a study group to continue examining the feasibility of the creation of such an institution and to recommend possible approaches.

Funding and Infrastructure

Like many organizations comprised of volunteers and seeking a clear mission, the CPWR does not have a solid funding base. The Committee urged that funding be developed to provide startup costs to cover the above initiatives. The Committee also encouraged the Council to broaden its base of support by increasing international representation on the CPWR.

Moving through the CoNexus

*T*he proposals and projects noted above demonstrate that there is much that can be done to enhance the lasting significance of the Parliament, but it is clear that the momentum cannot and should not come only from the CPWR's base in Chicago. This writer's opinion is that if it is to continue to have an impact, the CPWR must become a flexible and collaborative service organization. Since its Board and limited staff cannot do all of the organizational work, it must find ways to encourage and support – but not control – self-supporting, independent projects which will provide those services. When it meets specific needs of the movement and is identified with new and successful projects, CPWR's efforts will be rewarded.

Other self-directed individuals and organizations must be empowered not by an organization but by the vision and energy which inspired the numerous individuals who created the Parliament. In addition to the Trustees, the paid staff, the Host Committees, and the co-sponsors, there were also hundreds of staff volunteers, and more than 1000 individuals who participated in presenting the extensive program. This energy and commitment must have its own expressions far beyond Chicago and the CPWR.

This *SourceBook* provides documentation that there is no shortage of projects and committed people around the world who are serving a similar vision. Members of the more established international interfaith organizations, as well as those serving religious non-governmental agencies, religious and spiritual communities, and national and international agencies are themselves contributing substantial new initiatives and projects to the larger movement.

*T*he vision of the Parliament is not about building an institution. It is about individuals joining a movement which links the larger community of religions and spiritual traditions with the needs and opportunities of the future. Those who are seeking ways of working through these challenges – and even those who aren't – must be served!

The legacies of the Parliaments – both 1893 and 1993 – will be significant to the extent that they have contributed to a world where the community of religions is more inclined to live in harmony and to the extent that the religions contribute to an equitable and sustainable life for all in the community of the earth.

What Was Accomplished?

Dr. Thomas G. Walsh

Editor of the Newsletter of the Inter-religious Federation for World Peace

*O*ne basic question that conferences or conventions like the Parliament raise is, "What was accomplished?" There are several accomplishments that can be identified. First of all, there is the accomplishment of reconnecting to and/or meeting many friends and contacts working in the field of interfaith. That is, connections are made and networks are formed. Secondly, consciousness is raised. In particular, groups that are not well known or which suffer from media misrepresentations and distortions have the opportunity to present themselves as they are. This helps others base their judgments on direct encounter, rather than on mass media caricatures. Also, in this way, religious persons and groups can also cultivate a more appreciative, rather than suspicious or hostile attitude toward other traditions. Religions have often welcomed the denigration of rival religious traditions, in the same way that politicians enjoy the criticisms, even when unfair, of their rivals. Thirdly, out of such conferences there emerge publications and pronouncements that can be used as educational tools in the future. The Parliament, for example, drafted a declaration for a global ethic.

The most fruitful outcome of the deliberations that have taken place during this interfaith year [1993 was declared the Year of Interfaith Understanding and Cooperation] would be the emergence of a progressive new stage in the evolution of interfaith. In this new stage, close identification with a particular religious tradition should in no way serve to prevent anyone from receiving full acceptance as a contributor in the ongoing, inter-religious quest for having truth and peace fully manifest in our world. The quest for inter-religious peace can and must be a religious quest, and one that takes its life precisely from being grounded within a tradition. At the same time, this new stage of interfaith would have those deeply rooted in particular traditions opening and offering themselves up to an encounter with those they've heretofore been either unaware of or averse to.

This coming into openness must occur not only among the religiously rigid, but also among the religious liberal and the humanist who find the beliefs and practices of the religiously conservative both alien and distasteful. Interfaith activists need to do more to create a context hospitable to conservative Christians, Jews, Muslims, Hindus, and others; otherwise we stand to create institutions in which the voices of a few, boldly but not rightly, claim to speak on behalf of the whole. The Chicago Parliament, in many respects, represented a significant step toward a new stage of interfaith. But much work remains to be done.

from the IRFWP Newsletter, Vol. II, Number 1, Spring 1994

A Global Ethic

Moving towards a Global Ethic

Dr. Daniel Gómez-Ibáñez

Executive Director of the Parliament of the World's Religions (Emeritus)

Dr. Gómez-Ibáñez first presented this essay to the Fifth National Conference on Ethics in America, held in Long Beach, California, in March of 1994. In it he describes the context and drafting process behind the declaration *Towards a Global Ethic,* as well as some critiques of it. The author played a key role in the preparation of this highly significant document. From his perspective, "A major achievement of *Towards A Global Ethic* is that an agreement could be found at all. In a world which sometimes seems drenched with the blood of inter-religious wars, such [ethical] consensus amongst religions is perhaps even more significant than the details of the document itself."

Introduction

I begin with a story that takes place in New York a year ago. I was at the United Nations for a meeting on another matter, when the subject of the Global Ethic came up. A diplomat asked me whether the text could be made public. I said, "No, it was still being revised and would not be ready until the 1993 Parliament of Religions met several months later." She frowned, "I wish we could take it to Vienna this week for the UN Conference on Human Rights. It would be so useful."

You will recall that the Conference on Human Rights was nearly torn apart by disagreement between two points of view. Representatives of several countries argued that human rights are not absolute, but instead are conditioned by culture, and that the Western countries' assumption that there might be such a thing as universal human rights was just another example of neo-colonial domination. They asserted that human rights are relative, and must be variously interpreted according to the culture of each country. Any attempt to impose a foreign notion of right and wrong on a country, they said, was inadmissible.

Towards A Global Ethic, the document we were discussing, was one of the most significant results of the 1993 Parliament of the World's Religions. More than 200 scholars and theologians from the world's religions had been consulted during a two-year period of preparation, and at the Parliament, the declaration was signed by more than a hundred religious and spiritual leaders from all over the world. *Towards A Global Ethic* clearly states that human rights are not relative, and that the requirement to treat all persons humanely, without exceptions, is fundamental to the religious faiths of all the world's peoples. The diplomat in New York knew that such an

unequivocal statement might have been very helpful in the debates which opened the Vienna Conference on Human Rights. That discussion at the United Nations is significant because it underscored what I believe is a widespread hunger not only for moral and ethical road maps, but also for harmony and agreement on the most fundamental issues of human life and conduct. A major achievement of *Towards A Global Ethic* is that an agreement could be found at all. In a world which sometimes seems drenched with the blood of inter-religious wars, such consensus amongst religions is perhaps even more significant than the details of the document itself.

Every religion teaches peace, but religion was claimed as a justification for more than half of the more than 50 wars and armed conflicts which raged in various nations during the last year.[1] Religious hatred and intolerance resulted in death and destruction in almost every part of the globe. Faith inspires extraordinary allegiance: religions are among the very few causes for which people are willing to die and kill. It is no wonder that religion has been condemned by many as the cause of much of the world's strife and suffering. Moreover, it is not simply a matter of demagogues exploiting religious fervor for their own purposes. The seeds of intolerance and hatred can be found in some of the teachings of many faiths, for example those which assert the exclusiveness of the faith, or the superiority of the faithful, the "saved," or the "chosen," over the infidel, the heathens, or simply those who are different. Religious teachings also are used to justify socially destructive practices within communities, especially with regard to the proper roles for women and men. Organized religion tends too often to be a force for conservatism, clinging to old ways, opposed to change, avoiding self-criticism.

Some religious communities – especially in the West – have been silent on many of the critical issues which we face as we prepare to enter the third millennium, fueling criticism that they are aloof and unconcerned with the world. There has not been enough Christian outrage at the violence in Bosnia, Northern Ireland, or Armenia, for example. Too few Hindu leaders have renounced the communalism which led to the destruction of the Babri Mosque at Ayodhya, or have been critical of Tamil violence in Sri Lanka. Not enough Muslim voices have been raised against religious repression in the Sudan, Pakistan, or Saudi Arabia. Similar observations could be made about many other places and other religious communities. None is purely a victim.

So this historic declaration is important, and in this talk I want to discuss some of the questions which it raises. I should also say that I do not intend to summarize the ethic in this talk. The document can speak for itself! [The full Declaration immediately follows this introduction.] To put the questions about the ethic in context, though, let me raise them while I tell you some of the story of how *Towards A Global Ethic* came into existence.

The 1993 Parliament of the World's Religions

*T*he seeds of the present document were planted in 1988 and 1989 in separate developments in Europe and North America. In 1988 the Council for a Parliament of the World's Religions (CPWR) was formed in Chicago to organize a centennial celebration of the epochal 1893 World's Parliament of Religions. That event, held in conjunction with the 1893 World's Fair (World's Columbian Exposition) in Chicago, was the first formal public meeting of representatives of the major religions in the history of the world. Authoritative representatives of many of the Asian religions were heard in the West for the first time, and today Buddhists, Hindus, Confucians, Jains, Zoroastrians, and Taoists trace their beginnings in North America to having sent someone to represent them at the 1893 Parliament. It marked the beginning of modern efforts for inter-religious cooperation and understanding.

The centennial would be celebrated all over the world. In Chicago, we decided to focus on the encounter of religion and the critical issues. By these we meant the grave and widespread threats to the global environment; the grotesque extremes of affluence and poverty; the divisions of racism, inter-religious hatred, gender discrimination, tribalism, and xenophobia that wound our human family; and the prevalence of war, violence, oppression, and injustice.

We saw these primarily as spiritual problems, and we knew that these critical issues are knotted together. Hatred and war, selfishness and injustice, environmental damage and poverty – it is not possible to disentangle cause from effect, or isolate one sort of problem from the others. They all are parts of our single problem: how to live together justly and sustainably, caring for one another and for the planet that nourishes the community of all life.

These problems – this problem – cannot be solved simply by better technology or even by better political or economic strategies, although all these will help. At its heart, the kind of future we make for our children is a question of values, a question, really, of our individual and collective wisdom. We wanted religious and spiritual people to come to grips with their responsibilities in the face of these most serious threats.

Hans Küng and Projekt Weltethos

*A*t the same time, at the University of Tübingen in Germany, Professor Hans Küng began working on a striking manifesto which appeared in 1990 as *Projekt Weltethos*.[2] His book was preceded by talks he gave at a colloquium convened by UNESCO in Paris in 1989, and at Toronto and Chicago later in the same year. *Projekt*

Weltethos was translated and appeared in English in 1991 as *Global Responsibility; In Search of a New World Ethic*.[3]

Küng's search for an ethic also was grounded in the critical issues of the world. His book opens with these stark words:

Every *minute,* the nations of the world spend $1.8 million on military armaments. Every *hour,* 1500 children die of hunger-related causes. Every *day,* a species becomes extinct. Every *week* during the 1980s, more people were detained, tortured, assassinated, made refugee, or in other ways violated by acts of repressive regimes than at any other time in history. Every *month,* the world's economic system adds over $7.5 billion to the catastrophically unbearable debt burden of more than $1,500 billion now resting on the shoulders of third world peoples. Every *year,* an area of tropical forest three-quarters the size of Korea is destroyed and lost. Every *decade,* if present global warming trends continue, the temperature of the earth's atmosphere could rise dramatically (between 1.5 and 4.5 degrees Celsius) with a resultant rise in sea levels that would have disastrous consequences, particularly for coastal areas of all earth's land masses.

The heart of Küng's concern was expressed in his introduction:

It has become increasingly clear to me in recent years that the one world in which we live has a chance for survival only if there is no longer any room in it for spheres of differing, contradictory, and even antagonistic ethics. This one world needs one basic ethic. This one world society certainly does not need a unitary religion and a unitary ideology, but it does need some norms, values, ideals and goals to bring it together and to be binding on it.

Küng agrees to collaborate with the CPWR

*K*üng and the Parliament organizers first met when he came to speak about his concerns at the University of Chicago in 1989. After a subsequent exchange of letters, Küng agreed that the 1993 Parliament would be the ideal launch for a global ethic which might be endorsed by many of the world's best known religious and spiritual leaders. Küng, however, never supposed he would be involved in drafting the ethic. During the next two years, his book, *Global Responsibility,* was widely noticed, and a number of attempts were made to draft the ethic he had called for, most notably by Professor Leonard Swidler of Temple University. Swidler, a close colleague of Küng's, is also editor of the *Journal of Ecumenical Studies.* In 1990 and 1991 Swidler and Küng circulated Swidler's appeal for the creation of a "Universal Declaration of Global Ethos." The appeal was signed by a number of prominent scholars and theologians and published in 1991.[4]

The growing interest in an ethic was reflected in the publication in 1992 of *Stepping Stones to a Global Ethic* by Rev. Marcus Braybrooke, President of the World Congress of Faiths (London).[5] Braybrooke has spent a lifetime in the service of interfaith understanding and cooperation, and knows the field first-hand. In his book he cited nearly four dozen international and interfaith declarations made since World War II which clearly are attempts to find common ethical ground.

In February, 1992, I went to visit Hans Küng in Tübingen to persuade him to draft the ethic himself. No one, I thought, would be in a better position to begin the work. I remember discussing the project with Georgia, my wife, before leaving on the trip. An ethic for the world, she said, should be clear, strong, and simple, like a prayer, something even a child could understand and memorize easily. (We remembered attending a public lecture by the Dalai Lama a few years earlier. Someone asked him to summarize the meaning of Buddhism and Buddhist teaching. His reply came, with a smile, in only two words: "Be kind!") Küng was hesitant at first, keenly aware of the difficulties. But in the end he agreed, and we discussed at length what an ethic should include and how it should be presented.

How specific can the ethic be? We talked about Georgia's criteria for a good ethic: short, clear, strong, and simple. But Küng could not imagine that anything so brief could be specific enough to be challenging. And it was clear that we must challenge the world with the ethic. It could not be so general or so simple that people would tend to assume they were in compliance without thought for the implications. ("Be good," it might say. "Yes, of course," we would respond easily, "yes, I'm good.") To be useful, the ethic should make it clear that those who accepted its guidance would find themselves challenged by thorny questions. The ethic should at least suggest questions about all aspects of the daily lives of individuals and about the conduct of nations, corporations, and communities. At the same time, we could not produce a document which would be so detailed and so explicit as to make consensus impossible. We did not want to write an ethic about which, for example, it would be argued whether or not we should have included a reference to ozone depletion, or to the situation in Kashmir. After all, we did want a statement which many religious and spiritual leaders could endorse. It must be capable of securing a consensus. Küng would have to set a course deftly between an ethic so brief that anyone[6] could easily dismiss it as irrelevant, and an ethic so excessively specific that no one would endorse it.

The ethic should focus on problems and issues, not on dogma or theology. We were talking about finding an ethic for the world in the teachings of the world's faiths: a single ethic that all faiths could accept as authentic. But we were not interested in reconciling the differences between the religions. We were *not* trying to synthesize a single, unitary faith, or combination of faiths. And we certainly did not want to promote one faith over the others. One way to avoid these traps was to avoid references to dogma or theology. These have no place in an ethic, which has a much more straightforward aim: to set down simple rules for living on which the world's faith traditions can agree — a minimum basic consensus on values and norms. The

differences between the religions are real and they must be acknowledged, but they must not be allowed to obscure common concerns. The ethic must be concrete, and it must focus on the practical realities of daily life on Earth. Without such consensus, Küng had written, "no human society worth living in is possible in either a smaller or a larger community."[7]

The ethic should raise the level of ethical standards and expectations. At the same time, we agreed that the ethic should push humanity forward to higher levels of ethical behavior. Progress in the human condition is not only possible, it is an historic fact. (I am talking here about ethical and moral progress, not material progress.) As examples: (1) Beginning two hundred years ago, the ideals of freedom and democracy took root in the Americas and in Europe, and have since spread over the globe, an achievement which should not be overlooked even though its realization is far from perfect. (2) Slavery is no longer accepted in the world (that is, it is no longer legal, even though it still occurs.) It was accepted, widespread, and legal in many places as recently as 150 years ago. (3) State-sanctioned capital punishment for crimes has been outlawed in most countries. (4) Although we still have a long way to go, it is true that we have greatly increased our knowledge and awareness of the adverse social and environmental consequences of the modern economy.

The ethic should raise moral standards and expectations. It should demand not only tolerance, but respect for and acceptance of difference; not only freedom and equality, but also justice; not only coexistence, but also peace and non-violence. It should call for equal partnership between women and men. It should teach that we humans must not be deluded by our material progress into thinking that we are masters of Earth, but must live and act in a spirit of interdependence and harmony with all of nature.[8]

The ethic should be meaningful to religious and non-religious persons alike. The ethic would be a declaration by religious and spiritual leaders, and it would have its foundations in religious teachings. At the same time it should be based on principles which non-religious persons would recognize as valid. A year after my visit to Tübingen to talk with Küng, I discussed the ethic with His Holiness the Dalai Lama. He insisted on the same point: an ethic – even though it were interfaith – would be useless and no help to the world if it were not meaningful for non-religious persons as well as religious persons.

This requirement meshed well with the need to keep the document free from sectarian dogma or theology, and the need to avoid emphasizing one religion over another. The ethic has no quotes from scriptures, and makes no references to God. This later provoked criticism of the document from some religious persons, who would have preferred an ethic based on divine authority or scriptural commandments. But if we had succumbed to the temptation to utilize scriptural references there would have been no end of squabbling over which scriptural passages to include, and which to omit, and about balance and appropriateness. And any reference to God would have been totally inappropriate in an interfaith declaration. Not all religions are theistic – Buddhism being the best-known example.

After it was written, a few persons criticized the ethic for being "too religious." But we did not want to produce a merely secular declaration, something which would have been more appropriate for the world of jurisprudence, laws, and rights. The United Nations' Universal Declaration of Human Rights, for example, is such a document.[9] The global ethic is not about rights. It is about responsibilities. The values, standards, and attitudes expressed in the ethic are not intended to be negotiable or the subject of legislation or litigation. They are statements intended to resonate in the hearts of individuals.

How would the ethic be drafted? Finally, Dr. Küng and I agreed that the ethic should come from a single pen, not a committee, although it would be necessary to consult widely and honestly with scholars from all the world's major religious traditions. Küng would have to submerge his own predilections and outlook to produce a true interfaith statement, but it required a single author, we thought, to ensure coherence.

Küng decided then and there to scrap plans he had already made for his seminar during the summer semester of 1992, and instead devote the seminar to an interdisciplinary colloquium on the global ethic. The seminar would explore common ethical principles which might be found in the world's religions.

We agreed on a timetable. A first draft would be ready to circulate to a worldwide network of scholars and theologians during the fall of 1992. After one or two rounds of revision, we would circulate the declaration to key religious leaders for comment early in 1993. The aim was to secure their endorsements and publish the signed document well in advance of the 1993 Parliament, which would open on August 28. At the Parliament the ethic would receive additional signatures and be proclaimed at the closing plenary on September 4, 1993.

As it turned out, Küng met this ambitious schedule, but the trustees of the Council for a Parliament of the World's Religions did not. Prolonged discussion of Küng's draft in Chicago during the winter and spring of 1993 meant that we were not able to secure the leaders' signatures for the final document before the Parliament. In fact the ethic was completed in late July. A few leaders signed in August, before the Parliament, but most signed in Chicago.

In February, 1992, Küng's greatest worries about agreeing to draft the ethic had more to do with its tone and style than with its content. We both saw it as potentially one of the most significant statements of the modern era. What *needed* to be said seemed relatively clear. But how much of this *could* be said, and how forcefully? And how should it be expressed? The language needed to be generally understandable and accessible as well as inspiring, authoritative yet simple. The ethic must flow from the best, the strongest, and the most profound traditions of the faiths; yet – because of the need to acknowledge the sometimes harmful roles of religion in the modern world – the document must also be self-critical.

An ethic for the world

*A*s he worked on the document (aided by his own and the Council's networks, which eventually came to include more than 200 scholars and theologians from the world's faiths), Küng slowly moved towards resolving the concerns which had been left unanswered in our discussion in February.

Küng and the network of others who collected around the effort came to the conclusion that the ethic, even though it could be seen as a prescription, must avoid moralizing or sermonizing or, as he called it, "finger wagging." It could not be a political declaration. Nor could it be an enthusiastic religious or mystical proclamation. Nor should it be a philosophical treatise.[10] It should simply present rules for living – insights that come from the heart of human experience.

He began the text of the ethic with a recitation of the agonies of the modern world, and with the call for a new – or perhaps I should say renewed – ethical vision for Earth. The next two sections constitute the specific teachings of *Towards A Global Ethic.*

Küng discovered that the ethic itself could be based principally on an ancient precept found in religious teachings everywhere, "What you do not wish done to yourself, do not do to others." Or in positive terms: "What you wish done to yourself, do to others!"[11] Whence the fundamental demand of the global ethic:

Every human being must be treated humanely.

From this principle could be drawn at least four standards of behavior which are held firmly by faiths the world over. *Towards A Global Ethic* calls them "irrevocable directives." They are:
1) Do not kill; have respect for life!
2) Do not steal; deal honestly and fairly!
3) Do not lie; speak and act truthfully.
4) Do not commit sexual immorality; respect and love one another!

The implications of these ancient commandments (and related precepts) are developed in four corresponding sections.

The closing section speaks of the necessity for a transformation of individual and collective consciousness. It acknowledges the limitations of *Towards A Global Ethic* and the need for much more meditation on specific ethical issues which could not be addressed in such a general document. The last paragraph pledges the signers to work for "better mutual understanding . . . socially beneficial, peace-fostering, and Earth-friendly ways of life."

The role of the CPWR

*H*ans Küng had consulted with a network of more than 100 scholars and theologians representing the world's religions.[12] He had discussed the progress of the ethic at numerous conferences throughout the world. He now felt ready to send the draft to us in Chicago. Professor Leonard Swidler translated Küng's German text into English by the end of October, 1992.

We of course had our own equally large network of

scholars and spiritual leaders, and we were just as anxious as Küng to present a declaration that could both secure a broad and impressive consensus and be a challenging and significant statement for a world sorely in need of ethical guidance. We began circulating the draft. The process took months, not only because we had to allow time for study and comments by persons located all over the world, but also because we had to secure the formal approval of a large board of trustees, most of whom had no experience or academic training in ethics, not to mention inter-religious ethics.

The trustees realized that this document would become perhaps the most significant product of the Parliament. We approached its approval very cautiously, and we created several committees to review and revise Küng's draft. The Council's comments were returned to Küng only in June, 1993. He quickly revised his text. Swidler made another translation, and in Chicago I made the last revisions to the final text – making very few substantive changes – mostly smoothing Swidler's translation. Finally, Rev. Thomas A. Baima of the Roman Catholic Archdiocese of Chicago and I (working with a small ad-hoc committee of fellow trustees) wrote an introductory summary for the declaration in July. The global ethic was approved by the Council's trustees in late July, 1993.

The Council's "Declaration:" Rediscovering ancient truths

In its final form, the global ethic has two main parts. The second part is the text written by Küng and the network of scholars. We gave it the title "Principles of a Global Ethic." The first part, which we called "The Declaration of a Global Ethic," was written by Rev. Baima and me for the Council.[13] We wrote it because we thought that the ethic needed a brief summary. This "Declaration," however, while mainly serving to summarize the "Principles," emphasized two ideas which were less prominent in the text drafted by Hans Küng.

The first idea is that the global ethic represents nothing new. It is an affirmation of a common set of core values which are found in the teachings of the world's religions. The truth of the ethic, in other words, is already known the world over, "but yet to be lived in heart and action."

We affirm that there is an irrevocable, unconditional norm for all areas of life, for families and communities, for races, nations, and religions. There already exist ancient guidelines for human behavior which are found in the teachings of the religions of the world and which are the condition for a sustainable world order.

It is this collective affirmation and its endorsement by hundreds of revered spiritual leaders from all the world's major faith traditions which is the unprecedented and important contribution of *Towards A Global Ethic.*

Interdependence and universal responsibility

The second idea emphasized in the "Declaration" perhaps amounts to a different conception of the logic of the ethic than that which is found in the text of the "Principles" section.

You can imagine that as I was working on the ethic, I was also meditating on its meaning, and some of the questions I asked myself ran something like this:

Why is it that we find a common set of ethical principles no matter where we are in the world of women and men? What is it that makes nearly everyone on earth acknowledge the inherent goodness of such ideals as kindness, generosity, honesty, selflessness (non-selfishness), respect for others, and respect for life? Is there some transcendent fact in the universe which leads inexorably to these moral conclusions?

My answer was, "yes, there is such a fact. It is the fact of interdependence. Everything is related to everything else: the critical issues, living beings, the physical systems of the universe and of the ecosphere, our communities, institutions, even cultures and ideas, all are linked in a complete and simultaneous whole." Interdependence is not simply a philosophical premise or an assertion; it is a fact, supported by the observations of scientists as well as by our own experiences.[14] But its implications often are ignored.

What we do in one area affects all other areas. It is difficult to deal with one problem without inadvertently causing other problems. We often act without much thought for the many ways in which our actions have consequences. Most of us will be able to think of everyday examples of this. When we are not aware of our interdependence we easily make mistakes. But when we know how things work together we may discover that one wise action brings benefits in many places.

The obvious ethical consequence of the fact of interdependence is what might be called "universal responsibility." (The Dalai Lama uses this term.) If I am linked in some way to all that is, however tenuous the links may seem, then I am in some respect responsible for the welfare of all that is, also. I am responsible for the common good. That realization, it seemed to me, might be the foundation for all ethics, including, of course, the golden rule. I put this realization into the opening words of the Declaration.

We are interdependent. Each of us depends on the well-being of the whole, and so we have respect for the community of living beings, for people, animals, and plants, and for the preservation of Earth, the air, water and soil.

We take individual responsibility for all we do. All our decisions, actions, and failures to act have consequences.

We must treat others as we wish others to treat us...

The Assembly of Religious and Spiritual Leaders

The first formal presentation of the *Declaration of a Global Ethic,* as it was then called, was to the approximately 150 world religious and spiritual leaders who had come to the 1993 Parliament of the World's Religions in Chicago. Part of that event (which attracted about 8,000 participants) was a separate meeting of the leaders on September 2, 3, and 4, 1993. We invited them to sign the ethic. Most did, but not without much discussion.

The most frequent objection to the ethic did not concern the need for such a statement, or even its general principles, but rather our decision not to allow any modifications to a text which had been so painstakingly developed over the preceding two years. We knew that the ethic was a bona-fide interfaith creation, in that eminently qualified persons of many faiths had participated actively in its drafting. But most of the members of the Assembly of Religious and Spiritual Leaders at the Parliament had not been part of the drafting, and they were uncomfortable with our presenting them with a *fait accompli* on such a vital subject – essentially telling them, "take-it-or-leave-it." (We never doubted the competence of the Assembly members, of course. But we were convinced that inviting modifications from a three-day gathering of 150 persons was simply unworkable.)

At the same time, the leaders did want to sign the document, because, as they said repeatedly, the world desperately needed this evidence of ethical consensus. No one, even those who objected strongly to some detail of the text, wanted to be put in the position of not signing the Declaration. The compromise reached by the Assembly was to change the title of the document from *Declaration of a Global Ethic* to *Towards A Global Ethic (An Initial Declaration)*. That done, most signed willingly. And of course, we and Hans Küng would be the first to acknowledge the accuracy of the new title!

Criticism of
Towards A Global Ethic

*I*n addition to the procedural objections raised at the Assembly, reviewers and signers of the ethic raised a number of significant substantive questions. One criticism, heard from a number of persons, is that the ethic is too anthropocentric, too little concerned with the welfare of the ecosphere as a whole, on which, of course, human welfare ultimately depends. This seems to me to be a valid point, especially in view of Küng's and my goal of increasing the level of ethical standards. Two points may be made in defense of the document, however. The first is that environmental issues and a concern for all life (not just human life) are not ignored in *Towards A Global Ethic*,

although these points are not strongly emphasized. A concern for all life is found in the references to "Earth," – without the article, as if she were a being incorporating all creation – and in various explicit references to our environmental responsibilities which are scattered through the text, but found most notably in section III (1) (d). The second (more depressing) point is that the text probably fairly represents the present consensus on how much emphasis should be given to the environment in such a document.

Another objection, heard mainly from North American and European (liberal) Christian reviewers, was that it was inappropriate to condemn "sexual immorality" (in the *Declaration*). They wanted to know exactly what we meant by the term! Some feared it might be used as an excuse for condemning minority sexual practices, such as homosexuality or plural marriages. The response is that the traditions do in fact condemn sexual immorality, whatever that may mean to them. Further clarification of the ethics of particular sexual practices is certainly an obligation of each community, one which we thought could be guided by the principles expressed throughout the global ethic. In section III (4), the ethic's view of sexual issues is put very positively, I think: respect and love one another.

The ethic's firm stand for an equal partnership between women and men made a few religious leaders uncomfortable. But no one was willing publicly to voice an objection!

Another objection was that the text was in various ways "too Western," the structure "too Cartesian." (I think most of these objections came from Westerners.) This criticism may be valid; the final drafting, after all, was done by Westerners. In defense of what we wrote, I can only tell a story. A few days before the Parliament opened, Maha Ghosananda, the senior-most monk and supreme patriarch of Cambodian Buddhism, was sitting in my room at the Palmer House Hotel, reading the global ethic for the first time. Suddenly he broke away from his concentration and looked at me, his faced beaming, "This is wonderful!" he said, "I will be honored to sign it. It sounds like Lord Buddha himself is speaking!"

The objections to the ethic's stance
on non-violence

Towards A Global Ethic takes a strong stand on non-killing. This ancient directive, *ahimsa* in Sanskrit, is rarely qualified or watered-down in the traditional

---

"You can imagine that as I was working on the ethic, I was also meditating on its meaning, and some of the questions I asked myself ran something like this:

"Why is it that we find a common set of ethical principles no matter where we are in the world of women and men? What is it that makes nearly everyone on earth acknowledge the inherent goodness of such ideals as kindness, generosity, honesty, selflessness (non-selfishness), respect for others, and respect for life? Is

there some transcendent fact in the universe which leads inexorably to these moral conclusions?

"My answer was, 'yes, there is such a fact. It is the fact of interdependence. Everything is related to everything else: the critical issues, living beings, the physical systems of the universe and of the ecosphere, our communities, institutions, even cultures and ideas, all are linked in a complete and simultaneous whole.'"

DANIEL GÓMEZ-IBÁÑEZ

---

sources.[15] But some persons at the Parliament – especially Muslims – were distressed that the ethic seemed so strict in its call for non-violence as to prohibit self-defense. This would be contrary to the teachings of Islam and contrary to interpretations in some other religious traditions. Forgiveness and returning good for evil are taught by the Koran.[16] But prevailing interpretations of the Koran allow war in self-defense. And the Koran allows punishment of wrongdoers equal to the injury they have caused.[17]

I think that a careful reading of *Towards a Global Ethic* produces a more ambiguous interpretation, though strongly advocating non-violence as the ideal. Section III (1) (a) says, "No one has the right physically or psychically to torture, injure, much less kill, any other human being." But section III (1) (b) states, for example,

> Of course, wherever there are humans there will be conflicts. Such conflicts, however, should be resolved without violence within a framework of justice. This is true for states as well as for individuals. Persons who hold political power must work within the framework of a just order and commit themselves to the most non-violent, peaceful solutions possible. And they should work for this within an international order of peace which itself has need of protection and defense against perpetrators of violence. Armament is a mistaken path; disarmament is the commandment of the times. Let no one be deceived: there is no survival for humanity without global peace!

Again, from the section on justice:

> Wherever those ruling threaten to repress those ruled, wherever institutions threaten persons, and wherever might oppresses right, we are obligated to resist – whenever possible non-violently. [Section III (2) (d)].

What next?

These criticisms, and others that certainly can be raised, ensure that *Towards a Global Ethic* will be a living text: it will be transformed and augmented by thoughtful debate around the world. It will always need revision! Specific ethical questions on which the global ethic is silent will need answers, for example questions relating to bio- and medical-ethics on abortion, euthanasia, genetic manipulation, or transplants. There is nothing in the document on these, not only because it was intended to be a text capable of securing a consensus, but also because it was conceived as a set of minimum binding norms and values which might provide a basic ethical framework for humankind.

Perhaps it falls short even in that regard. Perhaps we should have been much bolder. For example, I would have preferred stronger statements on generosity and sharing, and on the renunciation of materialism. I think these will be necessary if Earth is to continue to provide a humane and fulfilling future for all its inhabitants. *Towards A Global Ethic* is not silent on these matters, but perhaps we should have stated them more forcefully.

In the final analysis, it will have succeeded as an ethic insofar as it succeeds in inspiring or provoking people to think, and to think again, about their values, attitudes, and behavior. We offer it to everyone, hoping it will be, not a monument standing firm, but a river: ever moving, changing, nourishing, carrying away debris, and with the possibility of leading people of all cultures and beliefs to a better, kinder world.

NOTES

1. See Stockholm International Peace Research Institute (SIPRI): World Armaments and Disarmament Yearbook (published annually); and D. Binder and B. Crossette, "As Ethnic Wars Multiply, U.S. Strives For A Policy," The New York Times, February 7, 1993, pp. A1 & A14.

2. Published by R. Piper GmbH & Co. KG, Munich, 1990.

3. Published by The Crossroad Publishing Company, New York, 1991.

4. See Journal of Ecumenical Studies, 28.1, editorial, and Suddeutsche Zeitung, November 16-17, 1991. Dr. Hans Küng's account of the global ethic can be found in Hans Küng & Karl-Josef Kuschel, *A Global Ethic; The Declaration of the Parliament of the World's Religions* (New York, Continuum, 1993).

5. Marcus Braybrooke, *Stepping Stones to a Global Ethic* (London, SCM Press, 1992). Braybrooke also is the author of the best history of the interfaith movement: *Pilgrimage of Hope: One Hundred Years of Interfaith Dialogue* (London, SCM Press, 1992).

6. Any thoughtful and responsible person should be able to derive all ethical behavior from even the simplest precept, like the Dalai Lama's "Be kind!" But in the real world, alas, most of us need more instructions!

7. Global Responsibility, p. 28.

8. Compare *Global Responsibility*, pp. 67-69.

9. Adopted by the United Nations General Assembly on 10 December, 1948.

10. See Küng & Kuschel, *A Global Ethic*, pp. 55-57.

11. Westerners know this as the "golden rule." As examples: "What you yourself do not want, do not do to another person." (Confucius, c. 551-489 BCE, *Sayings*, 15.23 [Confucianism]); "Do not do to others what you would not want them to do to you." (Rabbi Hillel, 60 BCE to 10 CE, *Shabbat*, 31a [Judaism]); "Whatever you want people to do to you, do also to them." (Jesus of Nazareth, *Matthew 7.12, Luke 6.31* [Christianity]); "None of you is a believer as long as he does not wish his brother what he wishes himself." (an-Nawawi, *Forty Hadith* 13 [Islam]); "Human beings should be indifferent to worldly things and treat all creatures in the world as they would want to be treated themselves." (Sutrakritanga I, 11, 33 [Jainism]); "A state which is not pleasant or enjoyable for me will also not be so for him; and how can I impose on another a state which is not pleasant or enjoyable for me?" (*Samyutta Nikaya V, 353.35-342.2* [Buddhism]); "One should not behave towards others in a way which is unpleasant for oneself: that is the essence of morality." (*Mahabharata XIII 114,8* [Hinduism]). These are cited by Küng on pp. 71-72 of Küng & Kuschel, *A Global Ethic*.

12. See Küng's acknowledgments on pp. 45-52 of Küng & Kuschel, *A Global Ethic*.

13. The first part of the "Declaration..." which begins "The world is in agony," was written principally by Rev. Baima. The second part, beginning "We Declare:" was written principally by me. Both parts were reviewed by a small subcommittee of the Board of Trustees of the Council for a Parliament of the World's Religions. 14. Of course I do not claim that I discovered anything new, either! Buddhists will recognize here the principle of "dependent co-arising." Scientists will think of recent contributions to the fields of physics, ecology, cosmology, mathematics, and the emerging field of chaos theory.

15. It is the first of the last five (ethical) commandments of the decalogue (Exodus, 20.13); the first of the five restraints (*yama*) cited by Patanjali (Yoga Sutras, II, 30 & 35), and the first of the five Buddhist precepts. It is the principal ethic of the Jain religion.

16. Koran (Surah 42, 37).

17. Koran (Surah 22, 39-40).

Towards a Global Ethic

(An Initial Declaration)

This interfaith declaration is the result of a two-year consultation among approximately two hundred scholars and theologians from many of the world's communities of faith. On September 2-4, 1993, the document was discussed by an assembly of religious and spiritual leaders meeting as part of the 1993 Parliament of the World's Religions in Chicago. Respected leaders from all the world's major faiths signed the *Declaration*, agreeing that it represents an initial effort – a point of beginning for a world sorely in need of ethical consensus. The Council for a Parliament of the World's Religions and those who have endorsed this text offer it to the world as an initial statement of the rules for living on which the world's religions can agree.

The Declaration of a Global Ethic

The world is in agony. The agony is so pervasive and urgent that we are compelled to name its manifestations so that the depth of this pain may be made clear.

Peace eludes us ... the planet is being destroyed ... neighbors live in fear ... women and men are estranged from each other ... children die!

This is abhorrent!

We condemn the abuses of Earth's ecosystems.

We condemn the poverty that stifles life's potential; the hunger that weakens the human body; the economic disparities that threaten so many families with ruin.

We condemn the social disarray of the nations; the disregard for justice which pushes citizens to the margin; the anarchy overtaking our communities; and the insane death of children from violence. In particular we condemn aggression and hatred in the name of religion.

But this agony need not be.

It need not be because the basis for an ethic already exists. This ethic offers the possibility of a better individual and global order, and leads individuals away from despair and societies away from chaos.

We are women and men who have embraced the precepts and practices of the world's religions:

We affirm that a common set of core values is found in the teachings of the religions, and that these form the basis of a global ethic.

We affirm that this truth is already known, but yet to be lived in heart and action.

We affirm that there is an irrevocable, unconditional norm for all areas of life, for families and communities, for races, nations, and religions. There already exist ancient guidelines for human behavior which are found in the teachings of the religions of the world and which are the condition for a sustainable world order.

We Declare:

*W*e are interdependent. Each of us depends on the well-being of the whole, and so we have respect for the community of living beings, for people, animals, and plants, and for the preservation of Earth, the air, water and soil.

We take individual responsibility for all we do. All our decisions, actions, and failures to act have consequences.

We must treat others as we wish others to treat us. We make a commitment to respect life and dignity, individuality and diversity, so that every person is treated humanely, without exception. We must have patience and acceptance. We must be able to forgive, learning from the past but never allowing ourselves to be enslaved by memories of hate. Opening our hearts to one another, we must sink our narrow differences for the cause of the world community, practicing a culture of solidarity and relatedness.

We consider humankind our family. We must strive to be kind and generous. We must not live for ourselves alone, but should also serve others, never forgetting the children, the aged, the poor, the suffering, the disabled, the refugees, and the lonely. No person should ever be considered or treated as a second-class citizen, or be exploited in any way whatsoever. There should be equal partnership between men and women. We must not commit any kind of sexual immorality. We must put behind us all forms of domination or abuse.

We commit ourselves to a culture of non-violence, respect, justice, and peace. We shall not oppress, injure, torture, or kill other human beings, forsaking violence as a means of settling differences.

We must strive for a just social and economic order, in which everyone has an equal chance to reach full potential as a human being. We must speak and act truthfully and with compassion, dealing fairly with all, and avoiding prejudice and hatred. We must not steal. We must move beyond the dominance of greed for power, prestige, money, and consumption to make a just and peaceful world.

Earth cannot be changed for the better unless the consciousness of individuals is changed first. We pledge to increase our awareness by disciplining our minds, by meditation, by prayer, or by positive thinking. Without risk and a readiness to sacrifice there can be no fundamental change in our situation. Therefore we commit ourselves to this global ethic, to understanding one another, and to socially beneficial, peace-fostering, and nature-friendly ways of life.

We invite all people,
whether religious or not,
to do the same.

The Principles of a Global Ethic

*O*ur world is experiencing a fundamental crisis: a crisis in global economy, global ecology, and global politics. The lack of a grand vision, the tangle of unresolved problems, political paralysis, mediocre political leadership with little insight or foresight, and in general too little sense for the commonweal are seen everywhere: too many old answers to new challenges.

Hundreds of millions of human beings on our planet increasingly suffer from unemployment, poverty, hunger, and the destruction of their families. Hope for a lasting peace among nations slips away from us. There are tensions between the sexes and generations. Children die, kill, and are killed. More and more countries are shaken by corruption in politics and business. It is increasingly difficult to live together peacefully in our cities because of social, racial, and ethnic conflicts, the abuse of drugs, organized crime, and even anarchy. Even neighbors often live in fear of one another. Our planet continues to be ruthlessly plundered. A collapse of the ecosystem threatens us.

Time and again we see leaders and members of religions incite aggression, fanaticism, hate, and xenophobia – even inspire and legitimize violent and bloody conflicts. Religion often is misused for purely power-political goals, including war. We are filled with disgust.

We condemn these blights and declare that they need not be. An ethic already exists within the religious teachings of the world which can counter the global distress. Of course this ethic provides no direct solution for all the immense problems of the world, but it does supply the moral foundation for a better individual and global order: a vision which can lead women and men away from despair, and society away from chaos.

We are persons who have committed ourselves to the precepts and practices of the world's religions. We confirm that there is already a consensus among the religions which can be the basis for a global ethic – a minimal *fundamental consensus* concerning binding *values,* irrevocable *standards,* and fundamental *moral attitudes.*

I. No new global order without a new global ethic!

*W*e women and men of various religions and regions of Earth therefore address all people, religious and non-religious. We wish to express the following convictions which we hold in common:

- We all have a responsibility for a better global order.
- Our involvement for the sake of human rights, freedom, justice, peace, and the preservation of Earth is absolutely necessary.
- Our different religious and cultural traditions must not prevent our common involvement in opposing all forms of inhumanity and working for greater humaneness.
- The principles expressed in this global ethic can be affirmed by all persons with ethical convictions, whether religiously grounded or not.
- As religious and spiritual persons we base our lives on an Ultimate Reality, and draw spiritual power and hope therefrom, in trust, in prayer or meditation, in word or silence. We have a special responsibility for the welfare of all humanity and care for the planet Earth. We do not consider ourselves better than other women and men, but we trust that the ancient wisdom of our religions can point the way for the future.

After two world wars and the end of the cold war, the collapse of fascism and nazism, the shaking to the foundations of communism and colonialism, humanity has entered a new phase of its history. Today we possess sufficient economic, cultural, and spiritual resources to introduce a better global order. But old and new ethnic, national, social, economic, and religious tensions threaten the peaceful building of a better world. We have experienced greater technological progress than ever before, yet we see that worldwide poverty, hunger, death of children, unemployment, misery, and the destruction of nature have not diminished but rather have increased. Many peoples are threatened with economic ruin, social disarray, political marginalization, ecological catastrophe, and national collapse.

In such a dramatic global situation humanity needs a vision of peoples living peacefully together, of ethnic and ethical groupings and of religions sharing responsibility for the care of Earth. A vision rests on hopes, goals, ideals, standards. But all over the world these have slipped from our hands. Yet we are convinced that, despite their frequent abuses and failures, it is the communities of faith who bear a responsibility to demonstrate that such hopes, ideals, and standards can be guarded, grounded, and lived. This is especially true in the modern state. Guarantees of freedom of conscience and religion are necessary but they do not substitute for binding values, convictions, and norms which are valid for all humans regardless of their social origin, sex, skin color, language, or religion.

We are convinced of the fundamental unity of the human family on Earth. We recall the 1948 Universal Declaration of Human Rights of the United Nations. What it formally proclaimed on the level of rights we wish to confirm and deepen here from the perspective of an ethic: the full realization of the intrinsic dignity of the human person, the inalienable freedom and equality in principle of all humans, and the necessary solidarity and interdependence of all humans with each other.

On the basis of personal experiences and the burdensome history of our planet we have learned

- that a better global order cannot be created or enforced by laws, prescriptions, and conventions alone;
- that the realization of peace, justice, and the protection of Earth depends on the insight and readiness of men and women to act justly;
- that action in favor of rights and freedoms presumes a consciousness of responsibility and duty, and that

therefore both the minds and hearts of women and men must be addressed;

- that rights without morality cannot long endure, and that *there will be no better global order without a global ethic.*

By a global ethic we do not mean a global ideology or a single unified religion beyond all existing religions, and certainly not the domination of one religion over all others. By a global ethic we mean a fundamental consensus on binding values, irrevocable standards, and personal attitudes. Without such a fundamental consensus on an ethic, sooner or later every community will be threatened by chaos or dictatorship, and individuals will despair.

II. A fundamental demand: every human being must be treated humanely.

*W*e all are fallible, imperfect men and women with limitations and defects. We know the reality of evil. Precisely because of this, we feel compelled for the sake of global welfare to express what the fundamental elements of a global ethic should be – for individuals as well as for communities and organizations, for states as well as for the religions themselves. We trust that our often millennia-old religious and ethical traditions provide an ethic which is convincing and practicable for all women and men of good will, religious and non-religious.

At the same time we know that our various religious and ethical traditions often offer very different bases for what is helpful and what is unhelpful for men and women, what is right and what is wrong, what is good and what is evil. We do not wish to gloss over or ignore the serious differences among the individual religions. However, they should not hinder us from proclaiming publicly those things which we already hold in common and which we jointly affirm, each on the basis of our own religious or ethical grounds.

We know that religions cannot solve the environmental, economic, political, and social problems of Earth. However they can provide what obviously cannot be attained by economic plans, political programs, or legal regulations alone: a change in the inner orientation, the whole mentality, the "hearts" of people, and a conversion from a false path to a new orientation for life. Humankind urgently needs social and ecological reforms, but it needs spiritual renewal just as urgently. As religious or spiritual persons we commit ourselves to this task. The spiritual powers of the religions can offer a fundamental sense of trust, a ground of meaning, ultimate standards, and a spiritual home. Of course religions are credible only when they eliminate those conflicts which spring from the religions themselves, dismantling mutual arrogance, mistrust, prejudice, and even hostile images, and thus demonstrating respect for the traditions, holy places, feasts, and rituals of people who believe differently.

Now as before, women and men are treated inhumanely all over the world. They are robbed of their opportunities and their freedom; their human rights are trampled underfoot; their dignity is disregarded. But might does not make right! In the face of all inhumanity our religious and

ethical convictions demand that *every human being must be treated humanely!*

This means that every human being without distinction of age, sex, race, skin color, physical or mental ability, language, religion, political view, or national or social origin possesses an inalienable and untouchable dignity, and everyone, the individual as well as the state, is therefore obliged to honor this dignity and protect it. Humans must always be the subjects of rights, must be ends, never mere means, never objects of commercialization and industrialization in economics, politics and media, in research institutes, and industrial corporations. No one stands "above good and evil " – no human being, no social class, no influential interest group, no cartel, no police apparatus, no army, and no state. On the contrary: possessed of reason and conscience, every human is obliged to behave in a genuinely human fashion, to do good and avoid evil!

It is the intention of this global ethic to clarify what this means. In it we wish to recall irrevocable, unconditional ethical norms. These should not be bonds and chains, but helps and supports for people to find and realize once again their lives' direction, values, orientations, and meaning.

There is a principle which is found and has persisted in many religious and ethical traditions of humankind for thousands of years: *What you do not wish done to yourself, do not do to others.* Or in positive terms: *What you wish done to yourself, do to others!* This should be the irrevocable, unconditional norm for all areas of life, for families and communities, for races, nations, and religions.

Every form of egoism should be rejected: all selfishness, whether individual or collective, whether in the form of class thinking, racism, nationalism, or sexism. We condemn these because they prevent humans from being authentically human. Self-determination and self-realization are thoroughly legitimate so long as they are not separated from human self-responsibility and global responsibility, that is, from responsibility for fellow humans and for the planet Earth.

This principle implies very concrete standards to which we humans should hold firm. From it arise four broad, ancient guidelines for human behavior which are found in most of the religions of the world.

III. Irrevocable directives.

1. Commitment to a culture of non-violence and respect for life

Numberless women and men of all regions and religions strive to lead lives not determined by egoism but by commitment to their fellow humans and to the world around them. Nevertheless, all over the world we find endless hatred, envy, jealousy, and violence, not only between individuals but also between social and ethnic groups, between classes, races, nations, and religions. The use of violence, drug trafficking and organized crime, often equipped with new technical possibilities, has reached global proportions. Many places still are ruled by terror "from above;" dictators oppress their own people, and institutional violence is widespread. Even in some countries where laws exist to protect individual freedoms, prisoners are tortured, men and women are mutilated, hostages are killed.

a) In the great ancient religious and ethical traditions of humankind we find the directive: *You shall not kill!* Or in positive terms: *Have respect for life!* Let us reflect anew on the consequences of this ancient directive: All people have a right to life, safety, and the free development of personality insofar as they do not injure the rights of others. No one has the right physically or psychically to torture, injure, much less kill, any other human being. And no people, no state, no race, no religion has the right to hate, to discriminate against, to "cleanse," to exile, much less to liquidate a "foreign" minority which is different in behavior or holds different beliefs.

b) Of course, wherever there are humans there will be conflicts. Such conflicts, however, should be resolved without violence within a framework of justice. This is true for states as well as for individuals. Persons who hold political power must work within the framework of a just order and commit themselves to the most nonviolent, peaceful solutions possible. And they should work for this within an international order of peace which itself has need of protection and defense against perpetrators of violence. Armament is a mistaken path; disarmament is the commandment of the times. Let no one be deceived: There is no survival for humanity without global peace!

c) Young people must learn at home and in school that violence may not be a means of settling differences with others. Only thus can a culture of nonviolence be created.

d) A human person is infinitely precious and must be unconditionally protected. But likewise the lives of animals and plants which inhabit this planet with us deserve protection, preservation, and care. Limitless exploitation of the natural foundations of life, ruthless destruction of the biosphere, and militarization of the cosmos are all outrages. As human beings we have a special responsibility – especially with a view to future generations – for Earth and the cosmos, for the air, water, and soil. We are all intertwined together in this cosmos and we are all dependent on each other. Each one of us depends on the welfare of all. Therefore the dominance of humanity over nature and the cosmos must not be encouraged. Instead we must cultivate living in harmony with nature and the cosmos.

e) To be authentically human in the spirit of our great religious and ethical traditions means that in public as well as in private life we must be concerned for others and ready to help. We must never be ruthless and brutal. Every people, every race, every religion must show tolerance and respect – indeed high appreciation – for every other. Minorities need protection and support, whether they be racial, ethnic, or religious.

2. Commitment to a culture of solidarity and a just economic order

Numberless men and women of all regions and religions strive to live their lives in solidarity with one another and to work for authentic fulfillment of their vocations. Nevertheless, all over the world we find endless hunger, deficiency, and need. Not only individuals, but especially unjust institutions and structures are responsible for these tragedies. Millions of people are without work; millions are exploited by poor wages, forced to the edges of society, with their possibilities for the future destroyed. In many lands the gap between the poor and the rich, between the powerful and the powerless is immense. We live in a world in which totalitarian state socialism as well as unbridled capitalism have hollowed out and destroyed many ethical and spiritual values. A materialistic mentality breeds greed for unlimited profit and a grasping for endless plunder. These demands claim more and more of the community's resources without obliging the individual to contribute more. The cancerous social evil of corruption thrives in the developing countries and in the developed countries alike.

a) In the great ancient religious and ethical traditions of humankind we find the directive: *You shall not steal!* Or in positive terms: *Deal honestly and fairly!* Let us reflect anew on the consequences of this ancient directive: no one has the right to rob or dispossess in any way whatsoever any other person or the commonweal. Further, no one has the right to use her or his possessions without concern for the needs of society and Earth.

b) Where extreme poverty reigns, helplessness and despair spread, and theft occurs again and again for the sake of survival. Where power and wealth are accumulated ruthlessly, feelings of envy, resentment, and deadly hatred and rebellion inevitably well up in the disadvantaged and marginalized. This leads to a vicious circle of violence and counter-violence. Let no one be deceived: there is no global peace without global justice!

c) Young people must learn at home and in school that property, limited though it may be, carries with it an obligation, and that its uses should at the same time serve the common good. Only thus can a just economic order be built up.

d) If the plight of the poorest billions of humans on this planet, particularly women and children, is to be improved, the world economy must be structured more justly. Individual good deeds, and assistance projects, indispensable though they be, are insufficient. The participation of all states and the authority of international organizations are needed to build just economic institutions.

A solution which can be supported by all sides must be sought for the debt crisis and the poverty of the dissolving second world, and even more the third world. Of course conflicts of interest are unavoidable. In the developed countries, a distinction must be made between necessary and limitless consumption, between socially beneficial and non-beneficial uses of property, between justified and unjustified uses of natural resources, and between a profit-only and a socially beneficial and ecologically oriented market economy. Even the developing nations must search their national consciences.

Wherever those ruling threaten to repress those ruled, wherever institutions threaten persons, and wherever might oppresses right, we are obligated to resist – whenever possible non-violently.

e) To be authentically human in the spirit of our great religious and ethical traditions means the following:

- We must utilize economic and political power for service to humanity instead of misusing it in ruthless battles for domination. We must develop a spirit of compassion with those who suffer, with special care for the children, the aged, the poor, the disabled, the refugees, and the lonely.

- We must cultivate mutual respect and consideration, so as to reach a reasonable balance of interests, instead of thinking only of unlimited power and unavoidable competitive struggles.

- We must value a sense of moderation and modesty instead of an unquenchable greed for money, prestige, and consumption. In greed humans lose their "souls," their freedom, their composure, their inner peace, and thus that which makes them human.

3. Commitment to a culture of tolerance and a life of truthfulness

Numberless women and men of all regions and religions strive to lead lives of honesty and truthfulness. Nevertheless, all over the world we find endless lies and deceit, swindling and hypocrisy, ideology and demagoguery:

- Politicians and business people who use lies as a means to success;

- Mass media which spread ideological propaganda instead of accurate reporting, misinformation instead of information, cynical commercial interest instead of loyalty to the truth;

- Scientists and researchers who give themselves over to morally questionable ideological or political programs or to economic interest groups, or who justify research which violates fundamental ethical values;

- Representatives of religions who dismiss other religions as of little value and who preach fanaticism and intolerance instead of respect and understanding.

a) In the great ancient religious and ethical traditions of humankind we find the directive: *You shall not lie!* Or in positive terms: *Speak and act truthfully!* Let us reflect anew on the consequences of this ancient directive: No woman or man, no institution, no state or church or religious community has the right to speak lies to other humans.

b) This is especially true

- for those who work in the mass media, to whom we entrust the freedom to report for the sake of truth and to whom we thus grant the office of guardian – they do not stand above morality but have the obligation to respect human dignity, human rights, and fundamental values; they are duty-bound to objectivity, fairness, and the preservation of human dignity; they have no right to intrude into individuals' private spheres, to manipulate public opinion, or to distort reality;

- for artists, writers, and scientists, to whom we entrust

artistic and academic freedom; they are not exempt from general ethical standards and must serve the truth;

- for the leaders of countries, politicians, and political parties, to whom we entrust our own freedoms – when they lie in the faces of their people, when they manipulate the truth, or when they are guilty of venality or ruthlessness in domestic or foreign affairs, they forsake their credibility and deserve to lose their offices and their voters; conversely, public opinion should support those politicians who dare to speak the truth to the people at all times;

- finally, for representatives of religion – when they stir up prejudice, hatred, and enmity towards those of different belief, or even incite or legitimize religious wars, they deserve the condemnation of humankind and the loss of their adherents.

Let no one be deceived: there is no global justice without truthfulness and humaneness!

c) Young people must learn at home and in school to think, speak, and act truthfully. They have a right to information and education to be able to make the decisions that will form their lives. Without an ethical formation they will hardly be able to distinguish the important from the unimportant. In the daily flood of information, ethical standards will help them discern when opinions are portrayed as facts, interests veiled, tendencies exaggerated, and facts twisted.

d) To be authentically human in the spirit of our great religious and ethical traditions means the following:

- We must not confuse freedom with arbitrariness or pluralism with indifference to truth.

- We must cultivate truthfulness in all our relationships instead of dishonesty, dissembling, and opportunism.

- We must constantly seek truth and incorruptible sincerity instead of spreading ideological or partisan half-truths.

- We must courageously serve the truth and we must remain constant and trustworthy, instead of yielding to opportunistic accommodation to life.

4. Commitment to a culture of equal rights and partnership between men and women

Numberless men and women of all regions and religions strive to live their lives in a spirit of partnership and responsible action in the areas of love, sexuality, and family. Nevertheless, all over the world there are condemnable forms of patriarchy, domination of one sex over the other, exploitation of women, sexual misuse of children, and forced prostitution. Too frequently, social inequities force women and even children into prostitution as a means of survival, particularly in less developed countries.

a) In the great ancient religious and ethical traditions of humankind we find the directive: *You shall not commit sexual immorality!* Or in positive terms: *Respect and love one another!* Let us reflect anew on the consequences of this ancient directive: no one has the right to degrade others to mere sex objects, to lead them into or hold them in sexual dependency.

b) We condemn sexual exploitation and sexual discrimination as one of the worst forms of human degradation. We have the duty to resist wherever the domination of one sex over the other is preached – even in the name of religious conviction; wherever sexual exploitation is tolerated, wherever prostitution is fostered or children are misused. Let no one be deceived: There is no authentic humaneness without a living together in partnership!

c) Young people must learn at home and in school that sexuality is not a negative, destructive, or exploitative force, but creative and affirmative. Sexuality as a life-affirming shaper of community can only be effective when partners accept the responsibilities of caring for one another's happiness.

d) The relationship between women and men should be characterized not by patronizing behavior or exploitation, but by love, partnership, and trustworthiness. Human fulfillment is not identical with sexual pleasure. Sexuality should express and reinforce a loving relationship lived by equal partners.

Some religious traditions know the ideal of a voluntary renunciation of the full use of sexuality. Voluntary renunciation also can be an expression of identity and meaningful fulfillment.

e) The social institution of marriage, despite all its cultural and religious variety, is characterized by love, loyalty, and permanence. It aims at and should guarantee security and mutual support to husband, wife, and child. It should secure the rights of all family members.

All lands and cultures should develop economic and social relationships which will enable marriage and family life worthy of human beings, especially for older people. Children have a right of access to education. Parents should not exploit children, nor children parents. Their relationships should reflect mutual respect, appreciation, and concern.

f) To be authentically human in the spirit of our great religious and ethical traditions means the following:

- We need mutual respect, partnership, and understanding, instead of patriarchal domination and degradation, which are expressions of violence and engender counter-violence.

- We need mutual concern, tolerance, readiness for reconciliation, and love, instead of any form of possessive lust or sexual misuse.

Only what has already been experienced in personal and familial relationships can be practiced on the level of nations and religions.

IV. A transformation of consciousness!

*H*istorical experience demonstrates the following: Earth cannot be changed for the better unless we achieve a transformation in the consciousness of individuals and in public life. The possibilities for transformation have already been glimpsed in areas such as war and peace, economy, and ecology, where in recent decades fundamental changes have taken place. This transformation must also be achieved in the area of ethics and values!

Every individual has intrinsic dignity and inalienable rights, and each also has an inescapable responsibility for what she or he does and does not do. All our decisions and deeds, even our omissions and failures, have consequences.

Keeping this sense of responsibility alive, deepening it and passing it on to future generations, is the special task of religions.

We are realistic about what we have achieved in this consensus, and so we urge that the following be observed:

1. A universal consensus on many disputed ethical questions (from bio- and sexual ethics through mass media and scientific ethics to economic and political ethics) will be difficult to attain. Nevertheless, even for many controversial questions, suitable solutions should be attainable in the spirit of the fundamental principles we have jointly developed here.

2. In many areas of life a new consciousness of ethical responsibility has already arisen. Therefore we would be pleased if as many professions as possible, such as those of physicians, scientists, business people, journalists, and politicians, would develop up-to-date codes of ethics which would provide specific guidelines for the vexing questions of these particular professions.

3. Above all, we urge the various communities of faith to formulate their very specific ethics: what does each faith tradition have to say, for example, about the meaning of life and death, the enduring of suffering and the forgiveness of guilt, about selfless sacrifice and the necessity of renunciation, about compassion and joy? These will deepen, and make more specific, the already discernible global ethic.

*I*n conclusion, we appeal to all the inhabitants of this planet. Earth cannot be changed for the better unless the consciousness of individuals is changed. We pledge to work for such transformation in individual and collective consciousness, for the awakening of our spiritual powers through reflection, meditation, prayer, or positive thinking, for a conversion of the heart. Together we can move mountains! Without a willingness to take risks and a readiness to sacrifice there can be no fundamental change in our situation! Therefore we commit ourselves to a common global ethic, to better mutual understanding, as well as to socially beneficial, peace-fostering, and Earth-friendly ways of life.

We invite all men and women,
whether religious or not,
to do the same.

Members of the Assembly who signed this Initial Declaration at the Parliament

Tan Sri Dato' Seri Ahmad Sarji bin Abdul-Hamid (Muslim, Malaysia)
Prof. Masao Abe (Buddhist, Japan)
Dr. Thelma Adair (Christian, USA)
H.R.H. Oseijeman Adefunmi I (Indigenous, USA)
Dr. Hamid Ahmed (Muslim, India)
Mrs. Mazhar Ahmed (Muslim, India)
Pravrajika Amalaprana (Hindu, India)
Dastoor Dr. Kersey Antia (Zoroastrian, USA)
Mme. Nana Apeadu (Indigenous, Ghana)
Dr. M. Aram (Hindu, India)
Rev. Wesley Ariarajah (Christian, Switzerland)
Dr. A. T. Ariyaratne (Buddhist, Sri Lanka)
Imam Dawud Assad (Muslim, USA)
Jayashree Athavale-Talwarkar (Hindu, India)
H.H. Shri Atmanandji (Jain, India)
H.I.G. Bambi Baaba (Indigenous, Uganda)
Rev. Thomas A. Baima (Christian, USA)
Dr. Gerald O. Barney (Christian, USA)
H.Em. Joseph Cardinal Bernardin (Christian, USA)
Mr. Karl Berolzheimer (Jewish, USA)
Père Pierre-François de Béthune (Christian, Belgium)
Dr. Nelvia M. Brady (Christian, USA)
Rev. Marcus Braybrooke (Christian, UK)
Dr. David Breed (Christian, USA)
Rabbi Herbert Bronstein (Jewish, USA)
Rev. John Buchanan (Christian, USA)
Mrs. Radha Burnier (Theosophist, India)
Rev. Baroness Cara-Marguerite-Drusilla, L.P.H. (Neo-Pagan, USA)
Mr. Blouke Carus (Christian, USA)
Mr. Peter V. Catches (Native American, USA)
Sister Joan M. Chatfield, M.M. (Christian, USA)
H.H. Swami Chidananda Saraswati (Hindu, India)
Swami Chidananda Saraswati Muniji (Hindu, USA)
Ms. Juana Conrad (Bahá'í, USA)
H.H. The Dalai Lama (Buddhist, India)
Swami Dayananda Saraswati (Hindu, USA)
Counsellor Jacqueline Delahunt (Bahá'í, USA)
Dr. Yvonne Delk (Christian, USA)
Sister Pratima Desai (Brahma Kumaris, USA)
Dr. Homi Dhalla (Zoroastrian, India)
Very Rev. R. Sheldon Duecker (Christian, USA)
Prof. Diana L. Eck (Christian, USA)
Dr. Wilma Ellis (Bahá'í, USA)
Hon. Louis Farrakhan (Muslim, USA)
Dr. Leon D. Finney, Jr (Christian, USA)
Rev. Dr. James A. Forbes Jr. (Christian, USA)
Dr. Rashmikant Gardi (Jain, USA)
Mr. Dipchand S. Gardi (Jain, India)
Mrs. Maria Svolos Gebhard (Christian, USA)
Preah Maha Ghosananda (Buddhist, Cambodia)
Dr. Daniel Gómez-Ibáñez (Interfaith, USA)
Dr. Hamid Abdul Hai (Muslim, USA)
Dr. Mohammad Hamidullah (Muslim, Uganda)
B.K. Jagdish Chander Hassija (Brahma Kumaris, India)
Rev. Theodore M. Hesburgh, C.S.C. (Christian, USA)
Prof. Susannah Heschel (Jewish, USA)
Dr. Aziza al-Hibri (Muslim, USA)
Mr. Chungliang Al Huang (Taoist, USA)
Dr. Asad Husain (Muslim, USA)
Dato' Dr. Haji Ismail bin Ibrahim (Muslim, Malaysia)
Prof. Ephraim Isaac (Jewish, USA)
Hon. Narendra P. Jain (Jain, India)
Dastoor Dr. Kaikhusroo Minocher JamaspAsa (Zoroastrian, India)
Very Rev. Frederick C. James (Christian, USA)
Ma Jaya Bhagavati (Interfaith, USA)
Ajahn Phra Maha Surasak Jvnando (Buddhist, USA)
Dr. Chatsumarn Kabilsingh (Buddhist, Thailand)
Abbot Timothy Kelly OSB (Christian, USA)
Mr. Jim Kenney (Christian, USA)
Sadguru Sant Keshavadas (Hindu, India)

Siri Singh Sahib Bhai Sahib Harbhajan Singh Khalsa Yogiji (Sikh, USA)
Dr. Irfan Ahmad Khan (Muslim, USA)
Dr. Qadir Husain Khan (Muslim, India)
Mr. P.V. Krishnayya (Hindu, USA)
Dr. Lakshmi Kumari (Hindu, India)
Prof. Dr. Hans Küng (Christian, Germany)
Mr. Peter Laurence (Jewish, USA)
Ms. Dolores Leakey (Christian, USA)
Rev. Chung Ok Lee (Buddhist, USA)
Mrs. Norma U. Levitt (Jewish, USA)
Rev. Deborah Ann Light (Neo-Pagan, USA)
Mr. Amrish Mahajan (Hindu, USA)
Sister Joan Monica McGuire, O.P. (Christian, USA)
Imam Warith Deen Mohammed (Muslim, USA)
Very Rev. James Parks Morton (Christian, USA)
Mr. Archie Mosay (Native American, USA)
Dr. Robert Muller (Christian, Costa Rica)
Rev. Albert Nambiaparambil, CMI (Christian, India)
Prof. Seyyed Hossein Nasr (Muslim, USA)
Prof. James Nelson (Christian, USA)
Mr. Charles Nolley (Bahá'í, USA)
Rev. Koshin Ogui, Sensei (Buddhist, USA)
Dastoor Jehangir Oshidari (Zoroastrian, Iran)
Dr Abdel Rahman Osman (Muslim, USA)
Luang Poh Panyananda (Buddhist, Thailand)
Ven. Achahn Dr. Chuen Phangcham (Buddhist, USA)
Pravrajika Prabuddhaprana (Hindu, India)
B.K. Dadi Prakashmani (Brahma Kumaris, India)
Mr. Burton Pretty On Top (Native American, USA)
Rev. Dr. David Ramage, Jr. (Christian, USA)
Ven. Dr. Havanpola Ratanasara (Buddhist, USA)
Dr. Krishna Reddy (Hindu, USA)
Prof. V. Madhusudan Reddy (Hindu, INDIA)
Mrs. Robert Reneker (Christian, USA)
Rev. Dr. Syngman Rhee (Christian, USA)
Mr. Rohinton Rivetna (Zoroastrian, USA)
Lady Olivia Robertson (Neo-Pagan, Eire)
Most Rev. Placido Rodriguez (Christian, USA)
Most Rev. Willy Romélus (Christian, Haiti)
Ven. Seung Sahn (Buddhist, USA)
Swami Satchidananda (Hindu, USA)
Ms. Dorothy Savage (Christian, USA)
Rabbi Herman Schaalman (Jewish, USA)
Hon. Syed Shahabuddin (Muslim, India)
Bhai Mohinder Singh (Sikh, USA)
Dr. Karan Singh (Hindu, India)
Dr. Mehervan Singh (Sikh, Singapore)
Mr. Hardial Singh (Sikh, India)
Mr. Indarjit Singh (Sikh, UK)
Singh Sahib Jathedar Manjit Singh (Sikh, India)
Dr. Balwant Singh Hansra (Sikh, USA)
H.E. Dr. L. M. Singhvi (Jain, UK)
Ms. R. Leilani Smith (Bahá'í, USA)
Ms. Helen Spector (Jewish, USA)
Brother David Steindl-Rast, OSB (Christian, USA)
H.H. Satguru Sivaya Subramuniyaswami (Hindu, USA)
Dr. Howard A. Sulkin (Jewish, USA)
Ven. Samu Sunim (Buddhist, USA)
Hon. Homi Taleyarkhan (Zoroastrian, India)
Mr. John B. Taylor (Christian, Switzerland)
Brother Wayne Teasdale (Christian, USA)
Rev. Margaret Orr Thomas (Christian, USA)
Rev. Robert Traer (Unitarian, UK)
Dr. William F. Vendley (Christian, USA)
Pravrajika Vivekaprana (Hindu, India)
Prof. Henry Wilson (Christian, Switzerland)
Ven. Dr. Mapalagama Wipulasara Maha Thero (Buddhist, Sri Lanka)
Ms. Yael Wurmfeld (Bahá'í, USA)
Rev. Addie Wyatt (Christian, USA)
H.H. Dr. Bala Siva Yogindra Maharaj (Hindu, India)
Baba Metahochi Kofi Zannu (Indigenous, Nigeria)
Dastoor Kobad Zarolia (Zoroastrian, Canada)
Dastoor Mehraban Zarthosty (Zoroastrian, Canada)

The Oneness of the Human Family

Bahá'í:

"Blessed is he who preferreth his brother before himself."

Baha'u'llah, Tablets of Baha'u'llah, 71

Buddhism:

"Hurt not others in ways that you yourself would find hurtful."   Udana-Varga, 5:18

Christianity:

"All things whatsoever ye would that men should do to you, do ye even so to them."

Matthew 7:12

Confucianism:

"Do not unto others what you would not have them do unto you."   Analects 15:23

Hinduism:

"This is the sum of duty: do naught unto others which would cause you pain if done to you."   Mahabharata 5:1517

Islam:

"No one of you is a believer until he desires for his brother that which he desires for himself."   Sunnah

Jainism:

"In happiness and suffering, in joy and grief, we should regard all creatures as we regard our own self."

Lord Mahavira, 24th Tirthankara

Judaism:

"What is hateful to you, do not to your fellow man. That is the law: all the rest is commentary."   Talmud, Shabbat 31a

Native American:

"Respect for all life is the foundation."

The Great Law of Peace

Sikhism:

"Don't create enmity with anyone as God is within everyone."   Guru Arjan Devji 259, Guru Granth Sahib

Zoroastrianism:

"That nature only is good when it shall not do unto another whatever is not good for its own self."   Dadistan-i-Dinik, 94:5

Compiled by the Temple of Understanding, a global interfaith organization

How to Read the Declaration
Towards a Global Ethic

The Rev. Thomas A. Baima

Director, Office of Ecumenical & Interreligious Affairs, Archdiocese of Chicago, and Trustee of the Council for a Parliament of the World's Religions

*T*he Declaration states:

We affirm that there is an irrevocable, unconditional norm for all areas of life: for families and communities; for races, nations and religions; there already exist ancient guidelines for human behavior which are found in the teachings of the religions of the world and which are the condition for a sustainable world order.

The vision of the Declaration is quite simple. It says "No" to the modern claim that, because of the diversity of cultures and religions, we cannot find an agreement on human behavior. Instead, it offers a vision that the points of agreement which already exist between the historic religions are the place to start if we hope to find a universally applicable ethic.

All parts of the text emerged out of a process of interreligious dialogue – a process by which the historic religions of the world were already engaged in conversation about ethical norms. More than 200 theologians, scholars of religions, and religious leaders critiqued the basic paper which Dr. Küng drafted such that every paragraph of the original paper was altered.

The final document, then, represents a preliminary consensus among the historic religions that we have not previously seen in history. Furthermore, it is part of a work in progress, affirmed and endorsed by nearly 200 members of the Assembly of Religious and Spiritual Leaders who called for wider consultations to continue to develop a true consensus document.

This ultimately will be the test for this document:

If someone brings it to me and I read it and see that my deeply held beliefs are reflected in it, then I already possess the motivation to agree with it *as a Christian*. If the same document is given to my Jewish friend who reads it and sees that his deeply held beliefs about Judaism are reflected in the document, then he also has the motivation to practice it.

Though of different religions, we are joined in this ethic precisely because of our faith in our own religion. I do not have to be persuaded to the truth of the Global Ethic because my Christian faith already grounds it.

The Ethic, therefore, is not some kind of negotiated agreement between religions but is a discovery and proclamation of agreements that already exist.

Translations and editions of *Towards a Global Ethic*

*S*ince the Parliament, the Declaration has appeared in many editions and translations of the book by Hans Küng and Karl-Josef Kuschel, as follows: *American:* Continuum, New York; *English:* SCM Press, London; *Italian:* Rizzoli, Milano; *Spanish:* Trotta, Madrid; *Finnish:* Arator, Helsinki; and *French:* Du Cerf, Paris. Further translations, especially Chinese, Japanese and Turkish, are also likely to appear.

Hans Küng and Karl-Josef Kuschel will also publish a book of responses to the Declaration by more than 35 world-known personalities from many religions and countries. It will appear in Fall of 1995 for the fiftieth anniversary of the United Nations (most likely by some of the same publishers who have published the Declaration).

Religions United?

The Promise of a
Permanent United Religions Organization

Dr. Robert Muller

Former Assistant Secretary-General of the United Nations, Chancellor (Emeritus) of the University for Peace in Costa Rica, and author of many books and speeches on global education and critical issues

While delivering a keynote address to the Parliament of the World's Religions, Dr. Muller challenged the Parliament and its Assembly of Religious and Spiritual Leaders to create an ongoing international organization. Many others have echoed his proposal during and since the Parliament.

In response, the Council for a Parliament of the World's Religions created an International Initiative Committee which has worked hard to evaluate and test the support for this proposal. It has concluded, however, that the CPWR does not now have the resources or mandate to address the enormous task or to itself create such an institution. Nevertheless, there remains a great deal of interest in the idea in Chicago and worldwide.

Following this excerpt from Dr. Muller's speech to the Parliament in 1993 are some of his current observations.

"What is needed is a place where you have a good number of people from various nations, from various races, from various sexes, from various beliefs, from various languages, working together on a daily basis. This is the miracle I have seen at the United Nations."

*O*n the still open question of creating a permanent institutional forum for inter-religious cooperation, the following can be reported:

- The United Nations has held preparatory meetings to the 1995 World Social Summit in Copenhagen, including a meeting on the role of spirituality and the religions in alleviating human misery. This initiative was highly applauded now that the Eastern European countries are no longer opposed to such views. [See Chapter 34.]

- In his proposed redraft of the United Nations Charter, Harold Stassen, the last living member of the US delegation to the Commission which drafted the Charter in San Francisco, proposes a yearly world-wide conference of religions to be convened by the United Nations

   "…in recognition that future interrelationships in the world and within member states of people of different religious faiths and beliefs will be one important factor affecting the prospects of peace or war, progress or catastrophe, and influencing the degree to which the objective of the United Nations can be fulfilled."

- On the occasion of the 25th anniversary of the UN on 24 October, 1975, I endorsed the proposal made at the meeting of spiritual leaders that the United Nations create "an agency that would bring the much-needed resources and inspirations of the spiritual traditions to the solution of world problems."

- At the 1993 Bangalore meeting of interfaith organizations commemorating the centennial of the 1893 Parliament, I submitted my vision of "The State of the World in 2013," twenty years after the important sessions of 1993. It deals with the role of a United Nations World Spiritual Agency.*

- There is currently an effort in San Francisco to evaluate the process and objectives of creating a United Religions institution; it hopes to build upon the commemoration of the 50th anniversary of the United Nations, particularly the events in San Francisco and the interfaith service at Grace Cathedral in June 1995, to take concrete steps toward forming a United Religions organization.

*I*t is not enough for religious leaders to meet once in a while at interreligious meetings, not even to meet regularly every year. Why? Because once they get home, they are reabsorbed by their own problems, by their own constituencies, by their losses of membership and decline in faith, by the recruitment of new leaders and clergy, and a host of other *immediate* problems. They forget about world religious cooperation, the need for a planetary spirituality and the resolutions at the interfaith meetings they attended.

This preoccupation with the tasks at hand is not unusual; we have exactly the same problems with heads of states who administer the lands and people of this planet. But there is a difference: the heads of state now have a United Nations and several functional agencies in which 50,000 of their nationals do work together from morning to evening, day after day, week after week, year after year as international civil servants who take the oath to be first of all servants of humanity. It is on these servants that governments rely to give them an overall view of the world and its problems, to prevent conflicts, to make peace, to help the poor, to defend human rights, to obtain the equality of races and sexes, to face new problems, to form new policies of cooperation, to come up with ideas and visions for a better world.

Likewise, what the world needs above all at this stage is a United Religions organization with a strong interreligious secretariat similar to the UN's international Secretariat, beginning at least with a few hundred religiously affiliated world servants. These too would work together from morning to evening, day after day, year after year on the resolution of religious conflicts and on the restoration in the world of the great moral concepts proclaimed by all religious founders and prophets: love, peace, hope, faith, compassion, charity, forgiveness, sanctity, purity, sacredness, communion with Creation and eternity, belief in life and afterlife, and many other concepts which are common to most religions but often absent from international relations.

What an incredible challenge to the United Nations that would be, and what untold good it would bring to humanity that desperately needs a moral and spiritual renaissance. Please, I beg you: on the occasion of the 50th anniversary of the United Nations, make this miracle happen! And do not worry if not all religions will join the United Religions organization. Many nations did not join the UN at its beginning, but later regretted it and made every effort to join. It was the same with the European Community and it will be the case with the world's religions because whoever stays out or aloof will sooner or later regret it.

We have still five precious years before the year 2000. If we put together our energies, our minds, our hearts and our souls, keeping always before our eyes the images of the poorest, most suffering, down-trodden brothers and sisters on this planet, we can make the creation of a United Religions of the World organization the most significant, hope-engendering event taking place at the end of this millennium.

* See my book *Most of All, They Taught Me Happiness*, pages 199-201

Towards a United Religions Organization

Richard Kirby and Earl D.C. Brewer

Richard Kirby is chief executive officer of the World Network of Religious Futurists, has served as consultant with several branches of the United Nations and is co-author of *Temples of Tomorrow: World Religions and the Future*, with Earl D.C. Brewer, deceased, who was chair of the Network. Among their proposals is a United Religions Organization, modeled on the United Nations; it might include, among other services, a computerized "world heart," which recalls past conceptions of a world brain.

*T*he world's religions are on the move, reaching out to new territories and new peoples. They are on the move intellectually, changing their theologies and learning more about their histories. They are on the move toward each other, in interfaith meetings and associations.

And the religions of the world are also moving into the future, learning how to take up important places in the design of the shape of things to come. Religions are now headed toward what may eventually form a United Religions Organization (URO), structured in much the same way as the United Nations and sharing similar goals.

As theologian Francis Clark describes this vision, the URO would be a forum for representatives of the main faiths to meet and deliberate. It would bring together professional theologians and their societies with interfaith associations to encourage the highest standards of intellectual progress and accuracy. This colony of creative thinkers could also include artists, monks, psycho-therapists, mystics, and futurists.

Building a moral parliament

*T*he URO, as we envision it, would gather representatives of the world religions in perpetual spiritual-parliamentary session in order to advance the knowledge of God or the Transcendent for the whole human family. It would inquire – by religious, spiritual, and theological colloquy and research – into the human predicament and its counterbalancing opportunities. And it would inspire the religions, old and new, to go speedily to the rescue of suffering creatures everywhere and at all times, to succor them with both the divine message and its accompanying grace and with the resources to save them from death, illness, degradation, and torment and to equip them for such living as may be a blessing to the whole human community.

The URO must be guided by new concepts of parliament suited to its sacred purposes. Many religious thinkers are familiar with existing secular models and examples of parliament, senate, and congress. However, these houses of debate and deliberation operate in accordance with outmoded political philosophies. Other concepts of parliament are available to the modern world; the URO could test at least one such alternative model – the model of sacred, scientific speech (parliament) in a collaborative rather than adversarial setting. Its major premise would be that politics advances not by conflict but by love. In Buddhist thought, right speech is a precondition for the attainment of Nirvana. In sacred scientific parliament, sacred speech is the means to success. Brevity, honesty, and accuracy in speech, the habit of respectful attention to others, and partnership rather than prominence in plenary sessions are the keys to moral success in parliament.

The founders of the United Religions Organization will find it helpful to look at the work done by each branch of the United Nations and consider whether the URO needs an equivalent. For example, what in the URO might function as the counterpart of the UN Secretariat, the Security Council, UNICEF, or UNESCO? For the URO secretariat, there may need to be permanent "civil servants" trained in ethics of management, information, spirituality, collaboration, and science. As in the United Nations, there would need to be dedicated chambers or rooms – perhaps dedicated to spirituality-theology-mysticism, mission, science, liturgy (worship), history, scriptures, ministry, temples, congregations, communities, and dialogue.

Addressing the world's problems

The URO would address civic problems, such as disaster relief, as well as specifically religious issues, such as women and religion (the goddess motif), the spiritual path, and New Age thought. But perhaps most importantly, the URO would address areas of concern in which civic and religious issues overlap.

Issues that the URO would research and develop solutions for include:

- **Human degradation.** Famine, drought, tempests, and wars decimate whole populations in many lands. What can the United Religions Organization do to help? What untapped resources of the human spirit can be called into compassionate action? This should be a standing question for the organization.

Crisis-intervention task forces will, we hope, one day stand on permanent alert in the "World Heart" computer rooms of the URO, but we should raise our consciousness and compassion to a sufficient degree to sense that any loss of life, any illness or loneliness, is a "crisis."

On the positive side, the URO should not only succor the needy, but create a positive new spiritual and just world culture. Examples frequently cited include sustainable growth, a just economics, bioregionalism, and a true democracy in every land. Such principles should also apply to space colonies and other "far future" human activities.

- **Environmental ethic.** The Green Movement offers one of many possible environmental ethics. The world religions in the URO can debate the other possibilities for human values expressed in environmental ethics so as to maximize freedom, cooperation, and beauty.

- **War and peace.** Just as war galvanizes science and technology in the search for victory, so could the search for peace galvanize the URO to focus its scientific studies. Futurists Parker Rossman and Takeshi Utsumi,

in their essay "Waging Peace with Globally Interconnected Computers" in *Challenges and Opportunities* (World Future Society, 1986), described the potential for super-computers to bring together a powerful collective intelligence to practice world peace research.

The URO, as the sole world organization aiming to integrate science, religion, and politics, would have a major responsibility to bring together computer manufacturers with peace/war academics and United Nations officers. Unlike war games, which must of necessity be kept secret, peace gaming would be public and could be at the center of a global university's curriculum on international affairs. Most important, it would embody a peaceful use of science and technology.

A new covenant

These suggestions and programs amount to a kind of theological revolution that recalls the prophets of Israel. Those prophets engendered new relationships with God, and in the fullness of time a new covenant. Now, in planetary crisis, that new covenant between God and humankind needs urgently to be extended to science, politics, government, and technology. The URO, perhaps over decades of research and discussion, will discern the nature of that covenant, and with it the responsibilities, rather than the rights, of planetary citizenship.

The case for a United Religions Organization, in summary, is that it provides a conduit for divine power to bring healing and inspiration to Earth. The URO should also enlarge the religious vision of the human race as a whole and, hence, human decency. To be sure, religions have caused great distress on Earth and have been hindrances to many kinds of progress, but they have also authored many blessings. By coming together, religions may minimize the evil and maximize the good. They may inspire and sometimes challenge each other to bring their best elements to bear upon the human predicament.

reprinted by permission of The Futurist

FOR MORE INFORMATION:

The Temples of Tomorrow. World Religions and the Future (Gray Seal Books, 1993), is available from the Futurist Bookstore for $35 ($29.50 for Society members)

For more information about the World Network of Religious Futurists, contact: Reverend William A. Heins, PO. Box 998, Eau Claire, WI 54702; tel. 1-800-554-3467

Interactive, Electronic Global Ecumenism

Bruce Schuman

Creator of an Internet archive called "ORIGIN" and listowner of The Bridge Across Consciousness, an online forum dedicated to storage of and access to a great diversity of materials relating to the religions and interfaith processes.

The author argues that an ongoing "electronic parliament of world religions" is feasible, desirable, and might well serve the communication needs of a united religions organization.

*T*he recently concluded Parliament brought together religious leaders from all over the world, representing every tradition, into a "common marketplace" of religious ideas and dialogue. But a religious conference cannot truly address and begin to resolve the enormously complex and challenging issues that face the world religious community. And indeed, the emphasis today, as it was at the 1893 Parliament, tends to be on "diversity" rather than "unity," on the vast variety among the world's religious traditions, rather than on the underlying similarities and common factors which some visionaries believe all religions share.

At the 1893 World Parliament of Religions, the influential Hindu Swami Vivekananda, chief disciple of Ramakrishna, and founder of the Vedanta Society in America, strongly advocated such a vision of unity among the world religions. In his article on Vivekananda's vision in the July/August 1993 issue of "Yoga International," author Richard Kenyon quotes Vivekananda as saying

> Sectarianism, bigotry, and its horrible descendant, fanaticism, have long possessed this beautiful earth. They have filled the earth with violence, drenched it often with human blood, destroyed civilizations, and sent whole nations to despair. Had it not been for these horrible demons, human society would be far more advanced than it is now. But their time has come, and I fervently hope that the bell that tolled this morning in honor of this convention may be the death knell of all fanaticism, of all persecutions with the sword or with the pen, and of all uncharitable feelings between persons wending their way to the same goal.

Vivekananda's hopes have not yet been realized; sectarian and ethnic strife today is fueling warfare in Europe, Asia, and Africa. In this climate, it seems clear that an ongoing dialogue, conducted 24 hours a day every day, is not only highly desirable, but probably essential to world harmony and peace.

The 1993 Parliament of the World's Religions was a successful step forward, but when the Parliament was concluded, the dialogue necessarily came to an end, and the relationships between religious leaders were based on only a few days of face-to-face personal contact. As important as this contact is, it does not even begin to address the fundamental questions which divide the world's religious communities. These multi-faceted and highly abstract issues cannot be adequately considered in a social context involving just a few hours of personal meetings and discussions. While the "chemistry" of a personal face-to-face meeting may be very advantageous, little more than token statements of friendship and intention can be exchanged in such a context; underlying issues can scarcely be addressed at all.

An electronic parliament

*F*or these reasons, and given the explosive growth of Internet communications, it seems clear and obvious that an ongoing "electronic parliament of religions" is not only technically feasible, but highly desirable. In an expandable electronic forum, the many complex and challenging issues which divide religious groups can be articulated in detail, every aspect and question stated precisely, and detailed documentation introduced.

At almost no expense, religious leaders or their representatives can interact through our global electronic environment, laying the groundwork for high level face-to-face meetings and building detailed agreements on aspects of interreligious cooperation and vision. Scientific studies pertaining to religious ideas can be developed and discussed, an elaborate database of scriptural sources created, and related issues involving politics, economics, and the environment may be brought into play. The entire discussion can be conducted 24 hours a day, and it can become a permanent feature of the world's intellectual and spiritual environment.

Such a communications forum can be quite inexpensive; the major cost involved is the time and effort of the participants. The Internet today is almost entirely "free," and low-cost access is available to many persons. The Bridge Across Consciousness and The Online Cathedral are but one set of tools in this rapidly growing environment. There are many others, including a wide variety of related mailing lists, conference formats and networks, and a variety of databases and file archives. Through integrated addressing schemes such as "gopher," it will soon be possible to compile a wide range of these resources into a single integrated format; soon, any person with an Internet terminal will be able to consider this vast array of "globally distributed" materials as though it were stored in their own personal computer.

This discussion can reach out across the entire planet, engaging anyone with an interest in this work – including religious leaders in specialized conferences. This forum can compile into a single facility a comprehensive spectrum of ideas, visions, negotiations, dialogues, and resources. Over time, and with continuing investment and vision, it will be possible to integrate an enormous range of interactions, establishing direct contact with and among the most influential religious personalities in the world.

FOR MORE INFORMATION:

See Ch. 44, *A Global Brain.*
Contact the author via E-Mail at: origin@rain.org
On the WWW: http://rain.org/~origin/

Peace Council

Dr. Daniel Gómez-Ibáñez

Executive Director (Emeritus) of the Parliament of the World's Religions

The following materials are excerpted from Dr. Gómez-Ibáñez' description of an initiative he is developing with a core group of religious and spiritual leaders in response to the needs expressed at the Parliament and elsewhere.

*T*he peoples of the earth need to rediscover a way of living based on a genuine understanding and wholehearted acceptance of the interdependence of all life and our universal responsibility for the well-being of all. Without this we are lost. This transformative insight, which is the shared legacy of the great faith traditions, must guide the lives of individuals, communities, organizations, corporations, and nations. The urgency is undeniable. Now is the time to act. [...]

We propose the Peace Council as an answer to the many calls at the 1993 Parliament of the World's Religions for an organization or network concerned with the critical issues of the 21st century and committed to effective action.

What is the Peace Council?

*W*e envisage a Peace Council of 12–25 spiritual leaders: men and women who live the ways of peace – ways which would be admired anywhere. Theirs are lives of kindness, simplicity, generosity, understanding, and compassion. They are grounded in the traditional wisdom of their faiths. At the same time they are aware of, and they participate fully in, the world of today. Each has found ways to serve the needs of others in her or his own community.

We seek persons of great moral standing in their communities and beyond, actively engaged in social action, often evidencing exceptional strength and courage. They are respected for what they do and stand for and how they live, not because they hold high offices (although some also may serve in that way.)

We seek spiritual leaders who are convinced that they can accomplish much together. They are committed to sharing their knowledge, networks, and influence. They are willing to speak forcefully and collectively on issues which transcend cultural and religious boundaries. [...]

Our goals in proposing a Peace Council are:

1. To promote peaceful, ethical and sustainable living.

2. To increase awareness of the interdependence of all life, and to promote the values of universal responsibility.

3. To influence values and behavior on a broad scale.

4. To provide a voice of conscience for the world, emphasizing the links between peace and social, economic, and ecological responsibility.

5. To bring an end to inter-religious conflict and warfare.

6. To increase understanding, respect, and cooperation between people who differ in religion, culture, nationality, race, or economic status.

7. To provide a framework for spiritual leaders to work together. [...]

Activities and initiatives

We suggest the following activities for consideration by the Peace Council:

A forum for spiritual leaders

- Periodic meetings at which members of the Peace Council can work together, get to know one another as friends and colleagues, and establish networks and initiatives.

A voice for peace

- Reevaluation of religious teachings or interpretations that appear to condone or inspire mistrust or hatred. Rejection of violent extremism and of the misuse of sacred teachings.

- Clear statements on the importance of interfaith harmony and acceptance.

Peacemaking

- Dramatic and well-publicized instances of dialogue and collaboration between members of different religious communities.

- Repeated, insistent, and collective calls for peace, for economic and social justice, and for wise environmental stewardship. These include inspiring and symbolic actions by leaders of religious communities whose members are in conflict.

- Where conflicts are in progress, close cooperation with local groups to encourage religious leaders (whose followers are justifying their violence on religious grounds) to meet, to engage in dialogue, and to call on their followers to renounce violence.

- Interfaith "pilgrimages" or missions of spiritual leaders to places or regions in need, in close cooperation with local groups in those places.

- Collaboration in conflict mediation – making the "good offices" of religion available to existing international (intergovernmental) organizations and quasi-public conflict mediation groups.

- Private mediation, where practicable, between groups in conflict.

- Public or private search for workable alternatives to conflict.

- Quiet diplomacy, including confidential (non-publicized)

message-carrying between the leaders of warring factions (or between parties that find themselves close to blows) who are willing to participate in this quiet diplomacy.

- A Peace Yearbook which would include an audit of conflicts and potential conflicts – not only wars but also other threats to the community of living beings – and a record of peace initiatives. It would profile winners of international peace awards.

[...]

Dialogues on critical issues

- Promotion of interfaith dialogue on the critical issues of living together in the world such as the relief of suffering; peaceful alternatives to conflict; economic and social justice; the links between violence, poverty, hunger, environmental damage, social justice, and values; and ways to preserve the community of all life on Earth.
- Encouragement of groups organizing grassroots dialogues on peaceful living.
- Promotion by individual Council members of dialogue within their own religious communities – intra-faith dialogue – on these issues, and dialogue between religion and science, government, business, and other professions.

[...]

Cooperation with existing organizations

The Peace Council we propose would support and complement the activities of the many existing interfaith and peace organizations and programs, and it will be structured in consultation with them. It can assist in the exchange of information about successful initiatives.

In general, the Council's own programs and activities would be implemented by collaborating and by establishing partnerships with and among existing organizations: peace groups, other issue-oriented organizations, religious organizations, governments, and NGOs.

Example of collaboration –
The Millennium Gifts to the Earth Project

The Millennium Institute of Arlington, Virginia, USA, has proposed that governments, organizations, corporations, communities, and individuals mark the entry of the Earth into a new millennium by making gifts that will benefit Earth, especially gifts that will keep on benefitting the Earth as the new millennium progresses. This project of the Millennium Institute will focus the energies that are inspired by the beginning of the new millennium in the year 2000. People all over the world – even those whose faiths use different calendars – will want to celebrate this milestone on what has become the commercial world's most widespread calendar.

The role for spiritual leaders, and specifically for the Peace Council, would be to give the project an ethical and spiritual context, and to inspire persons and institutions to make gifts to the Earth. A ceremony for heads of state is envisaged at which governments would make their gifts and pledges. Spiritual leaders also would bring gifts and would serve as witnesses to the governments' pledges.

Example of collaboration –
Mediation of inter-religious conflict

Many individuals and groups are engaged in conflict mediation. A few specialize in quiet diplomacy, including non-publicized message-carrying between the leaders of warring factions willing to participate in such quiet diplomacy. For example, Quaker Peace & Service, a department of the London and Ireland Yearly Meetings of the Religious Society of Friends, has established an impressive record of peace-making by carrying messages between leaders of parties in conflict. At present, Quaker Peace & Service is able to field only about a dozen persons in this activity. The Council could augment the experience and expertise of groups such as Quaker Peace & Service by increasing the people and money available for this work.

[...]   *Copyright 1994 International Committee for the Peace Council*

"The religious community has the saving vision. It is the ancient prophetic vision of human unity, now become an urgent, pragmatic necessity. . . . Human unity is not something we are called upon to create, only to recognize and make manifest."

WILLIAM SLOANE COFFIN,
A Passion for the Possible

FOR MORE INFORMATION:

International Committee for the Peace Council,
W9643 Rucks Road,
Cambridge, WI 53523 USA

tel. (608) 423-4066 / fax. (608) 423-4966

Toward Spiritual Concord

Elements of a Universal Spirituality

Brother Wayne Teasdale

Christian monk, author, lecturer, sannyasi in the tradition of Dom Bede Griffiths, and Trustee of the Council for a Parliament of the World's Religions

*T*he declaration *Towards a Global Ethic*, prepared for the Parliament and signed by most of the 250 members of the Assembly of Religious and Spiritual Leaders, is the first explicit expression of a consensus on ethics among the religions. The declaration contains general norms of behavior and responsibility which are universally acceptable and applicable. It is one thing, however, to recognize and outline these norms, but quite another to implement them around the world. Something further is required to inspire humankind and give it the capacity to *live* this more mature expression of moral life, as the Global Ethic itself suggests in its last paragraphs (p.136). What is needed is a universal spirituality which enables humankind to actualize its potential for the inner, transformative experience, to achieve the fruition of the human adventure in contemplative consciousness.

A global or universal spirituality does not mean a super-spirituality. The aim of describing a global spiritual life is not the reduction of the rich variety of humanity's inner life to one common form or generic type. That would be neither possible nor desirable. There are literally thousands of forms of spirituality; indeed it can be said that each person has his or her own kind of spirituality.

Yet we can describe common elements; just as there is a consensus on ethics among religions, there can also be a consensus on the essential elements of a global spirituality. Likewise, just as the goal of a global ethic is to identify common standards for the transformation of consciousness, so all authentic spirituality is itself transformative. True spirituality, in its social dimension, is a deep and personal appropriation of the moral life, and makes each of us better than we were before.

There is a spiritual interdependence among the various religions in the same way as there is a metaphysical interconnectedness to all reality. Each religious tradition and each form of spirituality develops in relation to actual life. Spirituality is a personal response and commitment to reality in its deepest sense. It is the source of self-knowledge that sees our human condition with all its woundedness, but which also offers us the possibility of real growth toward becoming an integrated person, one who is alive, holy, and wise. It gives us a sensitivity to life in all its variety.

Spirituality is an inner stand in relation to the Divine or Ultimate Reality that calls us to higher realization. Spirituality embodies our profoundest and purest desire, our passionate yearning for the Divine itself. It is a longing for union and communion with God, with Ultimate Reality. Characterized by this passionate commitment to the Ultimate, all spirituality takes the form of embracing the spiritual journey, the road to inner transformation and growth. Each kind of spirituality awakens us to reality as it is and to our own condition. Spirituality itself, as the deepest dimension of life and being, is common to all religions.

In identifying the essential elements of a global spirituality – those elements that will be part of any viable tradition – seven are clearly discernable:

    1) a capacity to live morally;
    2) deep nonviolence;
    3) a sense of spiritual solidarity with others, including other species and the Earth;
    4) a spiritual practice and comprehensive self-knowledge;
    5) simplicity of lifestyle;
    6) selfless service; and
    7) prophetic action.

Moral capacity and commitment

The capacity to live morally or ethically is the indispensable foundation of the spiritual life in any tradition. One who is on the spiritual journey is always a morally committed individual. A universal spirituality would easily adopt the code of the *Global Ethic*, and spirituality would provide the inner motivation for implementing its norms in one's life, or in the life of a community.

Deep nonviolence

A deeply-rooted attitude of nonviolence is also an important aspect of spirituality. As one becomes more awake within, one also becomes gentle and sensitive without – that is, in relations with others. Not just nonviolence, but *deep nonviolence* must be emphasized because of the growing problem of violence all over the world. Deep nonviolence means a non-harming that is the fruit of wisdom and compassion; it is really a form of love, and it is also a way to spread peace: by living nonviolently! If we truly wish to teach peace, we must live nonviolently!

Spiritual solidarity

Every person who follows the call of the inner life knows there is a deep bond of human and spiritual solidarity that unites us all. It emanates from the unity of reality itself, and because of this oneness, there is also a spiritual oneness, the basis of our interdependence. That means actually that reality has degrees of subtlety and unity – subtlety-in-unity. Spirituality has a high degree of unity that can be seen as solidarity on the human level. Practically speaking it implies a responsibility to assist and guide any seeker on the spiritual journey who asks for our aid. Thus, a spiritual solidarity exists in life, and we receive what we need, while the journey provides what is required for us.

At the same time, we have a spiritual solidarity with the other species and with the Earth in a special way. It manifests in the possibility of harmony and communion with them both. This harmony and communion is not as rare as we might imagine; it is common to many very advanced in holiness who also have a highly evolved sensitivity towards the created order. Examples include St. Francis of Assisi, the nature mystics and poets and certain monastics, as well as some unusual lay persons.

Spiritual practice and self-knowledge

All genuine spirituality has a spiritual practice, the heart of spirituality which brings about the process of inner change. Without it, spirituality is not authentic nor viable. Spiritual practice may consist of some form of mature prayer, meditation, or interiority, a discipline of contemplation, spiritual reading, reflection, study, work, or a simple resting in the Divine. Spiritual practice often involves all or most of these activities. It also may involve liturgy or some kind of ritual. The only rule is that spiritual practice must be transformative. It must initiate, follow through and sustain fundamental, indeed radical change in the aspirant. Spiritual practice, with the aid of grace, initiates a four-fold transformation: of consciousness, of will, of character, and of action. This four-fold transformation has self-knowledge as its basis, and, again, all genuine spirituality requires a comprehensive self-knowledge.

One's consciousness grows by addition of greater knowledge and awareness. Perception of reality becomes more profound and all-embracing. This includes an awareness of the three primary worlds: the material, the psychological, and the spiritual dimensions of all reality, life, and being. The person becomes proficient in spiritual wisdom as his or her consciousness becomes more and more subtle. The individual acquires a progressively deeper understanding of hidden motives and unconscious emotional programs originating from infancy. Eventually these give way to spiritual maturity. The person's will, like the mind, is transformed; it no longer seeks selfish ends, and becomes more other-centered. It seeks the permanent in the midst of what is passing away, and pursues harmony with the divine will and with the totality of life. Similarly, the human character knows a far-reaching transformation whereby the person becomes more and more grounded in virtue, grace, and holiness. Saintliness of character emerges as the person submits to love and is shaped by this into a loving, wise, compassionate being. One's behavior is altered as selfish patterns give way to altruistic actions governed by love, kindness, compassion, mercy, and wisdom.

Simplicity

The fifth element of a universal spirituality is simplicity of life or lifestyle. Its power and truth are eloquently expressed in the admonition: "Live simply so that others may simply live!" Simplicity in style of life, in the use of the Earth's goods, has for millennia in every tradition been a requirement and a sign of the genuine nature of one's spiritual witness. In monasticism and other forms of religious life the vow of poverty is meant basically to emphasize the need for simplicity in living. Simplicity also has a direct bearing on the cultivation of detachment, and detachment facilitates growth in our spiritual lives, especially in holiness and our attachment to the Eternal – that is, to God.

"Live simply so others may simply live," refers, of course, to the poor in its original social context, but it also has a direct bearing on the Earth. Our self-indulgent consumer society has caused and continues to cause a serious deficit to the planet itself. Simplification of life means above all using only what we need of resources and nothing beyond. This principle of spirituality thus translates into a benefit for the Earth and all its inhabitants, and indicates the eminently practical nature of spirituality itself. As Gandhi recognized, we don't need much to live and be happy; he often remarked that the Earth has sufficient resources for humankind's needs, but not for its greeds.

Selfless service

The sixth principle or guideline in a universal spirituality is selfless service. The transformation of the person living an intense inner life, especially the radical change in character and will, leads spontaneously to the development of a sensitivity to the needs of others. One's relationship with others is grounded on compassion, kindness, love, and the possibility of service or compassionate action. One becomes capable of thinking and acting beyond self-interest, able to discern among the needs of others what is required, based upon justice and charity. This pattern of behavior is found in every valid expression of the spiritual life and is one of the infallible signs of its genuineness. These enduring fruits of enlightened awareness unfold in the spiritual journey.

Prophetic action

A seventh and final element of a universal spirituality is the freedom to exercise prophetic action calling for change; it may mean taking a courageous stand for others in matters relating to justice, peacemaking, economic policy, refugees, hunger, poverty, women, the elderly, children, the unemployed, the homeless, AIDS and other diseases, and the whole critical issue of the environment. Prophetic action requires spiritual leadership and the courage to take a stand that may have political implications and consequences.

The issue of Tibet, for instance, is one that cries out for an effective voice. For nearly five decades now the Tibetan people have endured immense suffering, oppressed by the Chinese who have carried out physical and cultural genocide against them, inflicting on them unspeakable forms of torture and numerous other indignities. The world has stood by in utter silence. The United Nations has ignored the whole question, and the religious leaders of the world, with the notable exception of Buddhists, have been equally reticent. Can they not sense the extreme anguish and pain of the Tibetan people? Genuine spirituality demands prophetic speech and action in such cases.

Another example is the plight of indigenous peoples. We have not dealt adequately with their complaints nor have we been sensitive to their intense pain over the centuries, a suffering for which we bear a certain historical responsibility. Healing must take place between native peoples and the Europeans who have oppressed and nearly destroyed indigenous tribes in the Western Hemisphere and Australia. The indigenous population in Guatemala is nearly 75% of the total, yet they are still treated as a minority in their own country; their rights are systematically denied them by the 25% of European descent who rule Guatemala. Authentic spirituality demands a prophetic response.

In this age of spiritual interdependence, when we have finally discovered the profoundly rich bonds of sacred community that unite us, our global spiritual tradition must possess the ability to speak out when the occasion requires it. Such moral leadership is yet another fruit of a genuine spiritual life, and in our age it is much more. It is an essential demand and function of a global culture.

A universal order of sannyasa

*F*inally, I offer one last vision: the creation of a universal "order" of *sannyasa,* an order of mystics or contemplatives coming from all the great world religions that possess a mystical life and teaching. This would not be a new form of elitism, for it would be open to all who have the desire and the potential for spiritual development within and, perhaps, beyond their traditions and to those who are open to integrating insights and experiences from other traditions.

In the Sanskrit of the Hindu tradition, *sannyasa* means renunciation: of desire, wealth, power, sex, and oneself. The purpose of this great renunciation that the renunciate, monk, or nun makes is to be free to go in quest of the Absolute. In an essential way, the *sannyasi* stands beyond all formal religion while still being loyal to and rooted in his or her own tradition. In this usage, "beyond" religion means that the *sannyasi* knows interiorly that Ultimate Reality cannot be circumscribed by theological formulations. In the inner awareness he or she transcends the limits of understanding. So, in this essential way, the *sannyasi* is "beyond."

Since the 17th century there has been a Christian form of *sannyasa* and it has been growing steadily in India during the course of this century. This proposal suggests the extension of *sannyasa* to the other traditions as a spiritually uniting medium, though not a formally synthetic act of integration. Its primary purpose would be to promote peace among the members of the community of religions, not confusion or syncretism. A universal order of *sannyasa* could, thus, be profoundly beneficial to interreligious dialogue and reconciliation, and thus to the realization of universal spiritual concord.

Declaration on the Oneness of the Human Family

*Adopted by the Temple of Understanding
at the Spiritual Summit Conference VI in 1984*

A convergence of world religions towards a "Global Spirituality" might suggest the following points in common:

1. the oneness of the human family, irrespective of color, sex, creed, nation or any other distinctive characteristics.

2. The harmonious place of the individual person in the total order of things, as a unique entity of divine origin, with a basic relationship to the universe and eternity.

3. The importance of spiritual exercises, meditation, prayer, contemplation, and the inner search as links between human life and the universe.

4. The existence of an incipient conscience at the heart of humanity which speaks for what is good and against what is bad for the human family; which advocates and fosters understanding, cooperation and altruism instead of division, struggle and indifference among nations.

5. The value of dedicated service to others, with a compassionate response to human suffering, with special attention to the oppressed and the poor, the handicapped and the elderly, the rejected and the lonely.

6. The duty to give thanks and express gratitude for the abundance of life which has been given to humanity, an abundance not to be selfishly possessed or accumulated, but to be shared and given generously to those who are in need, with a respect for human dignity and a sense of social justice.

7. The need for ecumenical agencies and world religious organizations to foster dialogue and collaborative arrangements, and to bring the resources and inspirations of the religions to bear upon the solution of world problems.

8. A rejection of violence as being contrary to the sanctity and uniqueness of life and a total acceptance of the precept "Thou shalt not kill."

9. An affiliation of the law of love and compassion as the great transcending force which alone can break the nemesis of war and establish a planet of peace.

10. The evolutionary task of human life and society to move through the eternal stream of time towards interdependence, communion, and an ever-expanding realization of divinity.

FOR MORE INFORMATION:

Temple of Understanding , Cathedral of St. John the Divine, 1047 Amsterdam Ave. at 112th St. , New York, NY 10025 USA

Also see Temple of Understanding in Chapter 42

Guidelines for Interreligious Understanding:
Points of Agreement or Similarity

Father Thomas Keating, O.S.C.O.

Convener of the Snowmass Conference and member of Monastic Interfaith Dialogue

A report on an experience of on-going interreligious dialogue might be helpful at this point. In 1984 I invited a group of spiritual teachers from a variety of the world religions – Buddhist, Tibetan Buddhist, Hindu, Jewish, Islamic, Native American, Russian Orthodox, Protestant, and Roman Catholic – to gather at St. Benedict's Monastery, Snowmass, Colorado, to meditate together in silence and to share our personal spiritual journeys, especially those elements in our respective traditions that have proved most helpful to us along the way.

*W*e kept no record and published no papers. As our trust and friendship grew, we felt moved to investigate various points that we seemed to agree on. The original points of agreement were worked over during the course of subsequent meetings as we continued to meet, for a week or so each year. Our most recent list consists of the following eight points:

1. The world religions bear witness to the experience of Ultimate Reality to which they give various names: Brahman, Allah, Absolute, God, Great Spirit.

2. Ultimate Reality cannot be limited by any name or concept.

3. Ultimate Reality is the ground of infinite potentiality and actualization.

4. Faith is opening, accepting and responding to Ultimate Reality. Faith in this sense precedes every belief system.

5. The potential for human wholeness – or in other frames of reference, enlightenment, salvation, transformation, blessedness, *nirvana* – is present in every human person.

6. Ultimate Reality may be experienced not only through religious practices but also through nature, art, human relationships, and service of others.

7. As long as the human condition is experienced as separate from Ultimate Reality, it is subject to ignorance and illusion, weakness and suffering.

8. Disciplined practice is essential to the spiritual life; yet spiritual attainment is not the result of one's own efforts, but the result of the experience of oneness with Ultimate Reality.

*A*t the annual Conference in May 1986, we came up with additional points of agreement of a practical nature:

A. Some examples of disciplined practice, common to us all:

1. Practice of compassion

2. Service to others

3. Practicing moral precepts and virtues

4. Training in meditation techniques and regularity of practice

5. Attention to diet and exercise

6. Fasting and abstinence

7. The use of music and chanting and sacred symbols

8. Practice in awareness (recollection, mindfulness) and living in the present moment

9. Pilgrimage

10. Study of scriptural texts and scriptures

And in some traditions:

11. Relationship with a qualified teacher

12. Repetition of sacred words (mantra, japa)

13. Observing periods of silence and solitude

14. Movement and dance

15. Formative community

B. It is essential to extend our formal practice of awareness into all the aspects of our life.

C. Humility, gratitude, and a sense of humor are indispensable in the spiritual life.

D. Prayer is communion with Ultimate Reality, whether it is regarded as personal, impersonal, or beyond them both.

*W*e were surprised and delighted to find so many points of similarity and convergence in our respective paths. Like most people of our time, we originally expected that we would find practically nothing in common. In the years that followed we spontaneously and somewhat hesitatingly began to take a closer look at certain points of disagreement until these became our main focus of attention. We found that discussing our points of disagreement increased the bonding of the group even more than discovering our points of agreement. We became more honest in stating frankly what we believed and why, without at the same time making any effort to convince others of our own position. We simply presented our understanding as a gift to the group.

"In the next generation the question may not be which religion one belongs to, but whether religion itself is of value. Those who have had some experience of transcendence must find some way to communicate the fact that the experience of the Ultimate Mystery is open to *every human person who chooses to pursue the search for truth and embark on the spiritual journey – a journey which is literally without end."* THOMAS KEATING,
from "One Voice," p.127, in
Speaking of Silence, edited by Susan Walker

Interfaith Dialogue

A Study Guide for Interreligious Cooperation and Understanding

Rev. Marcus Braybrooke

Vicar of Marsh Baldon, Chair of the World Congress of Faiths, Trustee of the International Interfaith Centre (Oxford), and author

Marcus Braybrooke has been involved in the interfaith movement for over 25 years. For much of this time he has been an officer of the World Congress of Faiths and was for many years Editor of *World Faith Insight,* predecessor of the journal *World Faiths Encounter.* He has participated in conferences of IARF, the Temple of Understanding, WCRP, the Parliament and other interfaith bodies. As a factual foundation to this study we highly recommend Rev. Braybrooke's book, *Pilgrimage of Hope,* which provides a full account of the history of the interfaith movement. He has also written *Time to Meet: Children of God,* and *Stepping Stones to a Global Ethic.*

The aim of this *Study Guide* is to help readers and study groups become more aware of the growth of the interfaith movement during this century and to see how their own experiences relate to these developments. This guide was first published for use in connection with *1993: A Year of Interreligious Understanding and Cooperation,* a year-long commemoration promoted by the *ad hoc* International Interfaith Organizations Coordinating Committee. The *Study* was published with help from members of the World Congress of Faiths. It may now serve groups or individuals in a variety of interfaith considerations.

(The *Study* may be reproduced for group use, with acknowledgements: Copyright Marcus Braybrooke 1992.)

Interfaith cooperation: achievements and possibilities

*T*he year 1993 marked the hundredth anniversary of the interfaith movement, which dates from the World's Parliament of Religions held in Chicago in 1893. This *Study Guide* summarizes its development into a world-wide movement involving people from all religions.

The story of the Chicago World's Parliament and of the growth of the main international interfaith organizations is outlined and questions raised about the relation of religions to each other, their influence on war and peace and about the successes and failures of the interfaith movement. Pointing to what the interfaith movement hopes to achieve, the guide is a quick introduction to this inspiring endeavor and provides a good basis for discussion by one-faith and interfaith groups; study questions are also provided.

1. Rivalry or cooperation?

*T*he hope of the interfaith movement is that religious differences can be enriching and that each religious tradition will make its distinctive contribution to the welfare of humankind. Sadly, religious differences have often been a cause of conflict.

In some societies, one religious tradition has been dominant and upheld by the ruling authorities. Sometimes, the practices of other religious communities were forbidden. Those who engaged in them risked punishment and even death. Elsewhere, other religions were allowed, but their followers were treated as "second-class citizens," with various civil disabilities.

Sometimes, members of different religious communities have been rivals. When allied with opposing political powers, there has been active hostility and warfare – "religious wars." Elsewhere, the rivalry has been competition for adherents.

At times, the rivalry and hostility has been more hidden, where religious differences have reinforced racial, national, ethnic, or class differences. Religious teaching has been exploited to foster prejudice, discrimination, and communalism. Sometimes it has belittled those of another faith.

Elsewhere, people of different religious traditions may occupy the same geographical space, but with very little human meeting. There may be some commercial dealings, but each faith has its own schools and welfare institutions. People only marry within their own community. Each community may speak a different language.

In some societies, often described as "pluralist," there are several religious groupings and none has a preferential position. If the government is religiously neutral, it may be described as "secular." Other governments are clearly opposed to all religious practices.

This century has seen large-scale migrations of people. Vastly improved means of communication and international travel have become available for some people. Many members of a religious tradition are now more aware of the existence of other religious traditions. There is more personal meeting.

Members of the interfaith movement believe that this encounter has creative possibilities. Indeed, peace between religious communities is essential, if there is to be peace in the world.

FOR REFLECTION AND GROUP DISCUSSION

Q. How would you characterize the religious situation of your society: (Good, Tolerable or Bad)

    a. locally?

    b. nationally?

Q. What is it that makes religious communities competitive?

Q. What is it that best produces cooperation? For what reason?

---

2. Chicago, 1893

More than 100 years ago, a World Parliament of Religions was held at Chicago. This is now seen to be the beginning of the interfaith movement.

Isolated figures such as the Buddhist Emperor Asoka or the Mogul Emperor Akbar or the mediaeval Cardinal Nicholas of Cusa had advocated religious tolerance. There had also been some earlier interreligious debates and disputations. The World Parliament was new in attempting to bring together in a conference leaders of the world's religious traditions.

Held in Chicago in connection with its Columbian Exposition, the majority of the participants were Protestants from North America, although American Roman Catholics and Jews played a significant role both in the preparations and the Parliament itself.

Twelve Buddhists came from Asia, including Anagarika Dharmapala from Sri Lanka, who founded the Maha Bodhi Society, and Shaku Soyen from Japan, who was to introduce Dr. D. T. Suzuki to the West. There were several Hindus, including B. B. Nagarkar and P. C. Mozoomdar of the Brahmo Samaj, and Swami Vivekananda, a follower of Sri Ramakrishna. Swami Vivekananda was one of the most colorful figures of the Parliament and his plea for universal tolerance won much sympathy. The only Muslim representative was an American convert. There do not appear to have been any Sikhs present. The Parliament was the first occasion when a reference to Bahá'í religious teaching was made at a public meeting in the West.

Lectures were given both on the teachings of the different religious traditions and on social problems of the day. There was much discussion about the relationship of different traditions to each other. Some claimed that their religion would ultimately become the one religion of the world – perhaps by adapting and incorporating aspects of other religions. Others hoped that a new, more universal religion would emerge from the coming together of the world religious traditions. Others expected that the great religions would retain their distinct identity, although they hoped that the relations between them would reflect friendliness and charity.

Despite different views about the relationship of religions, most participants hoped that religious communities could work together to promote the peace of the world. In his opening address, Charles Bonney, who was the President of the Parliament, voiced this longing: "When the religious faiths of the world recognize each other as brothers, children of one Father whom all profess to love and serve, then, and not till then, will the nations of the earth yield to the spirit of concord and learn war no more."

The three key organizers of the Parliament each had a different purpose for it. This suggests that even if people have different philosophical presuppositions they can still work together for interreligious cooperation and understanding.

Charles Bonney hoped the Parliament would "unite all Religion against all irreligion;" and that it would "make the Golden Rule the basis of this union; (and) present to the world... the substantial unity of many religions in the good deeds of the religious life."

John Henry Barrows, a Presbyterian minister, whose hard work and charm as Chairman did much to ensure the success of the Parliament, believed that Christianity, by drawing on the insights of other great religious traditions, could grow into the universal faith.

Jenkin Lloyd Jones, a Unitarian minister and the Secretary, looked forward to a universal faith dedicated to the inquiring spirit of progress: "Let us build a temple of universal religion dedicated to the inquiring spirit of progress, to the helpful service of love."

There are groups today who hope for a future universal religion or believe that all religions are essentially the same. Some of their members share in interfaith work, but all interfaith organizations affirm and value the distinctiveness of the world religions.

FOR REFLECTION AND GROUP DISCUSSION

Q. Which of the three purposes, declared by the three organizers, would come nearest to your own?

Q. What did you hope might come out of interfaith meetings, when you first took part?

Q. Have your hopes changed during your participation in interfaith activities? What do you now hope for?

Q. Does it matter if people in the same organization have rather different motivations?

Q. Might the "Golden Rule" have a potentially significant role as a basis for cooperation?

3. What unites us?

Despite the difference of belief and practice between and within the great religious traditions, a growing number of people seek a bond between religious believers.

There are now many local and national interfaith gatherings. Four organizations, particularly, try to link this global activity. Three of them are described below and the fourth, The World Conference on Religion and Peace, is described in the next section. [These and many other organizations are described in more detail in Chapter 42.]

The **International Association for Religious Freedom** (IARF) was founded in 1900 by some of those who attended the World's Parliament of Religions. Initially most of its members were religious liberals, drawn from Unitarian churches in Britain, Hungary, and North America, free Christian churches in Western Europe, the Brahmo Samaj in India, and the Japan Free Religious Association. As membership has increased, the spectrum of religious groups and nationalities taking part has grown enormously. The IARF now has more than 70 member groups in 25 countries.

There are many differences among members of the International Association for Religious Freedom, but all are united by a commitment to religious freedom and truthful living. IARF Congresses are held every three years and include personal sharing, worship services in the tradition of each member group, and programs on religious, ethical, political, and theological issues. The IARF supports social service projects through its member groups in Eastern Europe, India, Bangladesh, the Philippines, and Africa. It has representatives at the United Nations, in both New York and Geneva, and IARF members support religious freedom by writing to government officials on behalf of oppressed communities of faith.

The **World Congress of Faiths** (WCF) was founded in 1936 by Sir Francis Younghusband. In 1903, in Lhasa, Tibet, he had a decisive spiritual experience of an underlying unity of all beings. His hope was that, through WCF, members of all religious traditions would become aware of this universal experience and that "the roots of fellowship would strike down deep to the Central Source of all spiritual loveliness." The WCF, which is based in Britain, has arranged a wide variety of conferences, helping people to learn about other faiths and to rethink traditional attitudes of opposition and hostility. It has encouraged members to appreciate one another's spiritual practices and on occasion to pray together. Rather than build up its own international organization, WCF has developed links with like-minded groups across the world and stimulated the growth of an interfaith movement, which is larger than any organization. Its journal, *World Faiths Encounter,* has facilitated the growth of the interfaith movement.

The **Temple of Understanding** (ToU), now based in New York, was founded in 1960 by Judith Hollister. The hope, as yet unfulfilled, has been to build a "temple" that would symbolize the shared spiritual quest of all religious traditions. Meanwhile the organization has fostered the spirit of understanding. The ToU has held a series of Summit Conferences in different parts of the world and has had an international influence through contacts with delegates to the United Nations. It helped to give birth to the Global Forum on Human Survival which brings together religious leaders, politicians, and scientists to try to save life on this planet. Thomas Merton, at the First Spiritual Summit Conference, said, "We are already one, but we imagine that we are not. What we have to recover is our original unity." The Temple has affirmed "The Oneness of the Human Family, irrespective of color, sex, creed, nation or any other distinctive characteristic and also the harmonious place of the individual person in the total order of things, as a unique entity of Divine Origin, with a basic relationship to the Universe and Eternity."

Does interfaith activity encourage syncretism?

These four international interfaith organizations all reject "syncretism," which implies an artificial mixing of religious beliefs and practices; they also reject "indifferentism," which suggests that it does not matter what you believe. None of these four organizations are trying to create one new world religion, although some other groups have that hope.

The interfaith organizations assume that most of their members will be loyal and committed members of their own faith communities. Respect for the integrity of other people's faith commitment and religious practices is essential. A few members of interfaith organizations may have no specific allegiance and describe themselves as "seekers."

Aware of the distinctiveness of the world religious traditions, members of interfaith organizations yet hope that some basis of unity exists or may be discovered. For some people, this rests upon our common humanity; for others, there is a mystical unity; still others hope that through dialogue people of different religious traditions will come closer together and grow in their understanding of the divine mystery; some stress the need of religious people to work together for peace and justice and the relief of human suffering; for others, it is enough that there should be tolerance and respect, without bothering about questions of "truth."

All these shades of opinion and many more are reflected within the interfaith organizations. For them, the search for understanding and cooperation is urgent in itself.

FOR REFLECTION AND GROUP DISCUSSION

Q. How do religious practices and beliefs agree and differ?

Q. How do you assess the ways religious people come together? What are your experiences and evaluations?

- Socially – to meet as friends
- To work together for good community relations and peace
- In a shared project of social service

- To try to understand each other's beliefs and practices
- To seek agreement on religious belief
- To learn about each other's ways of prayer and meditation

- To pray or to meditate together

Q. Do you belong to any of the interfaith organizations mentioned above or to other interfaith groups?

4. The religious search for peace

Whilst all efforts for interfaith understanding promote a climate of peace, some interfaith organizations, especially the World Conference on Religion and Peace (WCRP), have concentrated on encouraging religious people to be active in peace work.

Attempts to bring together people of different religious traditions to promote peace date back to the early part of this century. The first Assembly of the World Conference on Religion and Peace, however, did not meet until 1970. Members were aware that often religious communities had aggravated conflict. Yet it was seen to be important that leaders of the world's religious communities should affirm together their concern for peace and human dignity and that religious people should be more aware of the major issues facing humankind, especially as they are reflected in the concerns of the United Nations. The World Conference on Religion and Peace now has chapters in many countries and there are regional as well as international gatherings. Assemblies have been held in Asia, Europe, North America, Africa, and Australia. A carefully thought out structure tries to ensure a proper balance between different religious communities and nations.

There are also peace-groups within many religious communities and denominations. Increasingly these are working together and building up interfaith contacts.

It is difficult to assess the impact that religious people

can have on political processes, especially as politicians seldom acknowledge those who have influenced them. Modern communications have given added weight to popular opinion. Religious leaders may play an important role in forming public opinion. They can insist on the relevance of spiritual and moral considerations. They have helped to maintain public alarm at the enormous stockpile of nuclear weapons and other means of mass destruction. They have voiced public outrage at the starvation of millions of people, as a result of hunger, war, injustice, and an unfair pattern of international trade. They have upheld human dignity and protested against torture and racism. They have supported efforts to develop internationally agreed standards of human rights and have helped to monitor their application. Interreligious conferences have been among the first to warn of threats to the environment.

In local areas of conflict, religious people have often maintained contact across boundaries and despite divisions. Sometimes they have been agents of reconciliation and conflict-resolution. They have taken a lead in relief work. Sometimes, they have encouraged acts of repentance in an effort to heal deeply rooted bitterness. Yet often, too, religious people have used religious loyalties to inflame conflict and have allowed particular interests to outweigh common human and religious moral values. Some

The World Conference on Religion and Peace speaks on:

PEACE AND DEVELOPMENT

"Delegates from Asia, Africa, and Latin America have given us all a new perspective on the arms race, as seen through the eyes of the poor. For the poor, survival is not primarily a question of the future in a nuclear world, but an urgent question of the present in a world beset with hunger, drought, and disease. Our common commitment to peace is based upon the clear interrelatedness between disarmament and development."

WCRP Nairobi Declaration, 1984

CONFLICT RESOLUTION

"Whatever conscientious religious people decide in respect to the use of violence, we urge religious leaders everywhere to work ceaselessly, in the first instance, for the reduction of the level of violence in all social struggles with the final elimination of violence in favor of peaceful solutions as their firm objective. To respond to violence with violence without first seeking to eliminate its cause is to embark upon the course of unending escalation."

WCRP Leuven Declaration, 1974

DISARMAMENT

"We express our profound concern over the massive increase in military spending, which has rocketed. It seems a cruel irony that, while millions sleep with hungry stomachs, nations and their governments devote a great part of their resources to armaments, ignoring the demands of social justice. We therefore appeal to the members and leaders of our respective communities to use every political and moral influence to urge a substantial reduction in the current military expenditures of their own nations and the utilization of the funds thus saved for development around the world."

WCRP Princeton Declaration, 1979

ENVIRONMENT AND ECONOMICS

"Economic systems must be measured by ethical criteria, by how justly they provide for the well-being of all members of society, and by how they respect and use the environmental base that sustains all life."

WCRP Melbourne Declaration, 1989

extremists stir up religious passions to gain support for their concerns.

FOR REFLECTION AND GROUP DISCUSSION

Q. Can you think of areas of conflict in your society where religious people have helped or are helping to solve them? List these and then share them with others.

Q. Internationally, consider areas where religious loyalties inflame conflict.

Where is religious faith a power for peace?

Q. Should religious communities get involved in comment on the following issues: human rights? armaments? torture? poverty? environment?

Q. Is there anything that all religious people can say together on these subjects?

Q. How should we respond to those in our own religious tradition who seem to us to espouse extremism and fanaticism?

---

5. Religious communities in dialogue

*O*ften those who have pioneered the search for good relations between religious communities have faced misunderstanding and even hostility in their own faith community. They have been accused of compromising or "watering down" the distinctive beliefs of their own religious traditions. In fact, however, many have found that learning about other religious traditions has helped them appreciate their own more deeply.

Slowly the benefits of interfaith dialogue have become more widely recognized. Many religious and denominational bodies now have agencies to encourage such dialogue. There are some official discussions between religious organizations. For example, the Jewish world, through The International Jewish Committee on Interreligious Consultations (IJCIC), has held formal discussions with the Roman Catholic and with other churches. The Vatican has a Pontifical Council for Interreligious Dialogue and the World Council of Churches has a Unit for Dialogue with People of Living Faiths, which has arranged various consultations. Muslim groups,

including the Islamic Conference of Jeddah and the World Muslim Congress, have engaged in dialogue. Buddhist organizations also take part: the Dalai Lama and several Japanese Buddhist groups, especially Rissho Kosei Kai founded by Rev. Nikkyo Niwano, have been active in encouraging interreligious understanding and in work for peace. Hindu movements have also sponsored interreligious gatherings. Many smaller groups have also taken initiatives. The Unification Church, through the Council for World Religions and other organizations, has arranged a number of interfaith consultations.

Clearly, official dialogue has a character of its own. Participants have some representative role. Much of the work is to remove misunderstanding and build up good relations, as well as to encourage practical cooperation on moral issues and social concerns. More speculative discussion about questions of "truth" may be inappropriate. Further, whilst most organizations fully respect the freedom of all who participate in consultations, the host organization may have its own agenda. This means that official interreligious discussions need to be distinguished from "interfaith" organizations, where ultimate control rests with a board or executive which is itself multifaith in composition and where funding comes from several religious communities. The growth of interreligious discussions is, however, a sign that the importance of harmony between religious communities is now seen as urgent and this is in part due to the pioneering work of interfaith organizations.

As in the family, where at times two members want to talk by themselves, so there are occasions when members of just two religious traditions wish to engage in dialogue. A particular example of this is Jewish–Christian dialogue, and a major international organization, the International Council of Christians and Jews, was formed in 1975 to foster good relations between the two faith communities. There is also growing Christian–Muslim dialogue and some Muslim–Jewish dialogue. There is considerable Christian–Buddhist dialogue both in North America and in Japan. Christians and Hindus have engaged in debate and discussion for nearly two centuries and there is some Sikh–Christian dialogue. There are now many study and conference centers in different parts of the world which promote dialogue between members of two or three religious communities.

HUMAN RIGHTS

"Peace is imperiled by. . . the tragic violation of human rights all over the world. . . . Religions in their historical manifestations have not always been respectful of human rights themselves and have on some occasions purported to justify violations of human rights on religious grounds."
WCRP Kyoto Declaration, 1970

PEACE EDUCATION

"We pledge ourselves to stressing and raising to public consciousness the foundations of peacemaking within our own religious traditions, through education in temples, churches, mosques, synagogues and homes. . . . As religious people of action, we must deliberately link our personal lives and daily choices to our wider work as peacemakers."
WCRP Nairobi Declaration, 1984

CHILDREN AND YOUTH

• WCRP convened the three-day international conference "The World's Religions for the World's Children" at Princeton University in July 1990.

See Chapter 37 for details of the conference on children.
See also the article on WCRP in Chapter 42

6. Education

This century has seen an enormous increase in knowledge about world religious communities. Books, films and videos are widely available. Many universities have departments for the study of religion, and others are providing materials for schools. [See Chapter 43.]

This study has helped to provide accurate information about the religious traditions of the world. Even so, much ignorance and prejudice still exist. It has been debated whether the study should actively encourage religious tolerance or whether it should be neutral. It is also debated whether a person who is not a member of a religion can teach about it accurately and sympathetically.

There have been many debates about the pattern of religious education for children and young people. Many believers are keen that their children should be nurtured in their faith. In some countries, at least some schools have a religious foundation, where there is both instruction in a particular religion or denomination and worship according to its traditions and rites. This helps young people to grow up in a community of faith. It may, however, emphasize communal and religious divisions in a society, although a deep reverence for one's own faith should encourage respect for the faith of others.

In other schools, attempts are made to help pupils learn about the teachings of all the main religious traditions. This may encourage understanding and tolerance, but may not help pupils to grow in their own faith. In some countries, this "nurture" in one's own faith is the responsibility of parents, church, synagogue, mosque, temple, or *gurdwara* and not the task of the school. In other countries, there is no religious instruction in schools, and in some places even religious teaching at home or by the faith community is forbidden. Sometimes, minority groups have difficulty in providing religious education for their members.

If members of several different religious communities attend the same school, sometimes all are given the same course on world religions and sometimes they are divided into groups for instruction in their own religious tradition. In some countries, schools provide acts of worship or "assemblies." The question then arises whether people of different faith traditions may pray together.

Knowledge may not of itself create sympathy. Opportunities for personal meeting and friendship are important to dispel prejudice and to encourage real understanding. Many interfaith groups attach much importance to providing opportunities for young people to meet. Often they discover that they face similar problems and that in every society many young people are questioning all religious traditions and teachings. They may also discover how much people of all faiths can do together to work for a better world.

7. Praying together

People of different religious traditions coming together in prayer and meditation can be one way that understanding may emerge amidst the diversity of experience.

In October 1986, Pope John Paul II invited other religious leaders to join him at Assisi in Italy, the home town of St. Francis, to pray together for peace. Members of each religious community represented at the gathering offered prayers for peace, drawn from their own tradition, in the presence of those of other faiths. Similar occasions have been arranged at Mt. Hiei in Japan and at Mornington Beach in Australia.

Many similar local gatherings have been held, especially during the **Week of Prayer for World Peace.** Many people regularly pray the Universal Prayer for Peace:

> Lead me from Death to Life
> From Falsehood to Truth
> Lead me from Despair to Hope
> from Fear to Trust
> Lead me from Hate to Love
> from War to Peace
> Let Peace fill our Heart,
> our World, our Universe.

At the 1893 World's Parliament of Religions, each morning began with silence and prayer and the opening and closing sessions included some hymns. Subsequent international interreligious conferences have included times of prayer. The International Association for Religious Freedom invites participants in its programs to take part, to whatever extent they wish, in the worship conducted by its different religious member groups. Mahatma Gandhi at his ashram included hymns and readings from many traditions in the evening prayer-time. Various groups, such as the Brahmo Samaj, the Bahá'ís, the Unitarians and the Universalists, include readings from the scriptures of the world in their services. The World Congress of Faiths and Temple of Understanding have arranged, on special occasions, public gatherings for people of all faiths to pray together.

Such gatherings for prayer sharply focus the question of the relationship of religious traditions. How do we balance recognition of religious diversity with acknowledgment of some common bonds? Joint gatherings are not intended to replace the regular prayer of any faith community, but are for special occasions which stress our shared humanity and recognition of a sacred dimension to life.

Many people have found one of the best ways of learning about another religious group is to be present at times of worship, prayer and meditation. Attempts have also been made to help members of one faith tradition begin to experience the spiritual practices and traditions of another religion. A pioneer of this approach, Swami Abhishiktananda, spoke of it as a "meeting in the cave of the heart." The Quaker, Douglas Steere, spoke of "mutual irradiation." Sufis, Universalist groups, and some members of "New Age" movements and others who emphasize the mystical approach to religion have also encouraged opportunities for people of different faith traditions to meditate and pray together.

There are personal occasions too when people of different religious traditions wish to meet together in prayer. Two people of different religious traditions may marry and want a blessing from each tradition, even though most faith communities do not encourage intermarriage. At a funeral, mourners may belong to more than one religious community.

These are areas on which there is no agreement, but in a fast changing world, new situations arise about which we need to think together.

FOR REFLECTION AND GROUP DISCUSSION

Q. Have there been any occasions when you have prayed with people of other faith traditions?

Q. Were there difficulties? Was there also enrichment?

Q. What effect do you think prayer has?

Q. Have you attended places of worship belonging to religious groups other than your own?

Q. Do you think there are occasions when it is helpful for people of different religious traditions to come together to pray? If so, when?

Q. Do you know of marriages in which the partners belong to different religious traditions? Discuss the possibilities and any problems there may be.

8. 1993 and beyond

A century after the first World's Parliament of Religions, it is hoped that the religions have a growing awareness of our shared global humanity. In recent years there has been a rapid and widespread growth of interfaith dialogue, although there has also been renewed religious extremism and fanaticism. Many different interfaith initiatives have been taken across the world, and attempts have been made to link them, especially by the International Association for Religious Freedom, the World Congress of Faiths, the Temple of Understanding, and the World Conference on Religion and Peace, discussed above.

A meeting was held at Ammerdown, near Bath in England, in 1985 to see whether interfaith organizations could relate more closely to each other. It was eventually agreed to concentrate on plans to mark 1993, the centenary of the World's Parliament of Religions in Chicago, as a "Year of Interreligious Understanding and Cooperation." The four international interfaith organizations also jointly sponsored a four-day program in Bangalore, India, entitled "Religious People Meeting Together," or Sarva-Dharma-Sammelana" in August of 1993.

During that year and as an ongoing process, we are seeking agreement about the present situation. What are the achievements of the interfaith movement? What are its weaknesses? What should it now seek to achieve?

This means considering the basis for interreligious cooperation as well as how to overcome prejudice and rivalry. It suggests that religious people need to consider more urgently what they can do together to promote peace and justice, to uphold human rights, to relieve suffering and to preserve the planet.

These are questions to each of us as individuals, as members of a particular religious tradition, and as members of interfaith organizations. Interfaith organizations need to consider how they can be more effective. Each has its own distinct tradition and area of work, but perhaps they would achieve more through greater cooperation. Some people have suggested a World Council of Religions [or a United Religions]; other people think this might be bureaucratic and that we should think more in terms of a movement, with close networking between different groups, instead of an organization.

What of the relations of religious communities toward each other? Many people would like to see religious leaders stress the values that they hold in common and be a more effective voice for justice and peace. Others believe that the only hope for the future is a renewal of spiritual values and an appreciation of the oneness of humanity.

FOR REFLECTION AND GROUP DISCUSSION

Q. How do you think interfaith organizations can be more effective?

Q. What do you think should be the priorities for interfaith work in the next century?

Q. What is your vision for the world in the next century?

A Grassroots Model:
The Grand Rapids Interfaith Dialogue Association

Dr. Lillian Sigal

Professor of Humanities, organizer of interfaith dialogue

For those thinking about initiating interfaith dialogue meetings or a local organization, here is a model based on the experience of people in Grand Rapids, Michigan.

Introduction

*T*he Interfaith Dialogue Association in Grand Rapids began as the brainchild of two women – Rev. Marchiene Rienstra, a Christian, and myself, a Jew. Marchiene and my late husband, Rabbi Phillip Sigal (a New Testament scholar), met at Calvin College, where they frequently dialogued about Judaism and Christianity. Phillip dreamt of establishing a Jewish-Christian ecumenical center. After he died, Marchiene and I determined to make his dream a reality; however, we decided to broaden its scope to include all the world religions. The seed for the Interfaith Dialogue Association (IDA) was planted in 1988; it flowered as a chartered, non-profit organization in 1990; and in 1994 it is still a fledgling plant needing consistent nurturance, but betokening greater growth and outreach to fulfill its mission.

Based on my experience as co-president of IDA, I offer below suggestions for organizing, dialoguing, and developing programs for an association such as ours.

Forming a dialogue organization

*W*e began the process of establishing IDA by first brainstorming with a cross section of leaders from the religious and academic community – both lay and clergy – to determine whether our community needed such an organization. These people strongly endorsed our concept, and many of them became members of our Board of Directors, providing us with ideas, contacts, and resources to fulfill our objectives.

Subsequently, we met with a core group to create bylaws and appoint an executive committee consisting of two co-presidents, a secretary and a treasurer. We established membership dues (with option of reduced rate or no fee, depending upon financial status), a quarterly newsletter, and a brochure stating our goals and activities.

Ideas for dialogue groups

- If possible, have two groups meeting monthly on different nights to accommodate different peoples' schedules. Ideally, discussion thrives in a group of 9–12 people. However, realistically, the mailing list should be 15–18, because of absenteeism.
- Encourage members to put the dates of the monthly meetings on their calendars and to be committed to them.
- Strive to make the group as religiously and ideologically diverse and balanced as possible, and include humanists.
- Meet in members' homes to enhance development of

personal relationships, opportunities to see and experience the cultural milieu of different members – their food, art, ritual objects, etc.

- Begin with a prayer or ritual led by a member of a different religion each time who explains its meaning.
- Discuss various festivals at seasons when they are observed.
- Generate ideas from members for a text to read in advance of each meeting. This should be done at the beginning of the year. Huston Smith's *The World Religions* was an excellent choice one year.
- Begin the first meeting with a discussion of the Dialogue Decalogue [see p.158] to establish guidelines for meaningful and sensitive dialogue.
- Appoint a group coordinator who sends reminders of meetings.
- Appoint a group leader for each session to keep the discussion focused, to encourage full participation, to avoid monopolization of the discussion by a few members, and to faithfully follow the guidelines of the Dialogue Decalogue.
- Make one person responsible for summarizing or providing historical background for the reading material.
- Occasionally, invite an outside speaker, especially on a subject in which no group member has any expertise.
- Use the comparative method, i.e., when a theme is discussed in one religion elicit responses from members of the other religions on that theme.
- Allow time for announcements of events, religious festivals, or news of interfaith activities in the community.
- Occasionally, share a potluck to provide opportunities for personal friendships to develop.
- Ask members for feedback on how things are going.

Major programs

- Have an annual membership meeting with a program and a social hour to bring together the dialoguers and people on our mailing list who support us, but do not attend dialogue groups. Open these programs to the public to help advertise the organization and gain new members. The best source of members, nevertheless, is the members themselves – their friends and acquaintances.
- Offer an annual conference with an outstanding leader who has contributed to interfaith dialogue. So far, we've invited Leonard Swidler, director of the Interreligious-Interideological Institute at Temple University, and Huston Smith, author of *The World's Religions*; our third conference featured Muslim feminist Riffat Hassan, chair of Religious Studies at the University of Louisville, KY. These conferences included an interfaith panel of respondents to the keynoter and conference themes, and offered small discussion groups of those attending the conference, facilitated by members of our organization.
- Our fourth annual conference followed a more academic model, offering more than 30 papers and presentations with respondents. The Keynote address was given by Dr. David

Ramage, Jr., Chair of the Council for a Parliament of the World's Religions (Emeritus).

- Some funding for these conferences has been provided by three local colleges who served as cosponsors.

Goals of IDA

1. *To eliminate prejudice* that creates tension between members of different religious traditions and ideologies.

2. *To advance understanding of religions and ideologies* by study, dialogue, and sharing of religious experiences.

3. *To foster appreciation for the richness of diverse ideologies and religions.*

4. *To identify commonalities and differences among religions and ideologies* to enhance personal growth and transformation.

5. *To promote friendship and trust* among people of diverse ideologies and religions.

Conclusion

I have discovered that interfaith dialogue that is serious and not superficial involves challenges and risks, but also opportunities for personal growth and spiritual enrichment. Bahá'ís compare humanity to a rose garden. A garden where all the roses are white or red would be boring – the beauty of the garden resides in its variety of colors. Grassroots interfaith activity enables us to join the growing momentum – evidenced in the Parliament of the World's Religions – for global bonding to displace the hostility that religious differences have unfortunately created. Indeed, as Hans Küng has noted, "There will be peace on earth when there is peace among the world religions."

Code of the Inter Faith Network of the United Kingdom

The Inter Faith Network links nearly 70 organizations, including representative bodies of all Britain's major faith communities. This code was produced and endorsed by its affiliated organizations in 1993. The Network hopes this code of conduct will become the basis for discussion and will help towards building good relations between people of different faiths in Britain and elsewhere.

In Britain today, people of many different faiths and beliefs live side by side. The opportunity lies before us to work together to build a society rooted in the values we treasure. But this society can only be built on a sure foundation of mutual respect, openness, and trust. This means finding ways to live our lives of faith with integrity, and allowing others to do so, too. Our different religious traditions offer us many resources for this and teach us the importance of good relationships characterized by honesty, compassion, and generosity of spirit. The Inter Faith Network offers the following code of conduct for encouraging and strengthening these relationships.

As members of the human family, we should show each other respect and courtesy. In our dealings with people of other faiths and beliefs this means exercising goodwill and:

- Respecting other people's freedom within the law to express their beliefs and convictions;
- Learning to understand what others actually believe and value, and letting them express this in their own terms;
- Respecting the convictions of others about food, dress, and social etiquette and not behaving in ways which cause needless offence;
- Recognising that all of us at times fall short of the ideals of our own traditions and never comparing our own ideals with other people's practices;
- Working to prevent disagreement from leading to conflict;
- Always seeking to avoid violence in our relationships.

When we talk about matters of faith with one another, we need to do so with sensitivity, honesty, and straight-forwardness. This means:

- Recognizing that listening as well as speaking is necessary for a genuine conversation;
- Being honest about our beliefs and religious allegiances;
- Not misrepresenting or disparaging other people's beliefs and practices;
- Correcting misunderstanding or misrepresentations, not only of our own, but also of other faiths whenever we come across them;
- Being straightforward about our intentions;
- Accepting that in formal inter faith meetings there is a particular responsibility to ensure that the religious commitment of all those who are present will be respected.

All of us want others to understand and respect our views. Some people will also want to persuade others to join their faith. In a multi-faith society where this is permitted, the attempt should always be characterized by self-restraint and a concern for the other's freedom and dignity. This means:

- Respecting another person's expressed wish to be left alone;
- Avoiding imposing ourselves and our views on individuals or communities who are in vulnerable situations in ways which exploit these;
- Being sensitive and courteous;
- Avoiding violent action or language, threats, manipulation, improper inducements, or the misuse of any kind of power;
- Respecting the right of others to disagree with us.

Living and working together is not always easy. Religion harnesses deep emotions which can sometimes take destructive forms. Where this happens, we must draw on our faith to bring about reconciliation and understanding. The truest fruits of religion are healing and positive. We have a great deal to learn from one another which can enrich us without undermining our own identities. Together, listening and responding with openness and respect, we can move forward to work in ways that acknowledge genuine differences but build on shared hopes and values.

Inter Faith Network, 5-7 Tavistock Place, London WC1H 9SS, U.K.

The Dialogue Decalogue:
Ground Rules for Interreligious, Interideological Dialogue

Dr. Leonard Swidler

Editor of the Journal of Ecumenical Studies and Professor of Catholic Thought and Interreligious Dialogue at Temple University

*D*ialogue is a conversation on a common subject between two or more persons with differing views, the primary purpose of which is for each participant to learn from the other so that he or she can change and grow. This very definition of dialogue embodies the first commandment of dialogue.

In the religious-ideological sphere in the past, we came together for discussion with those differing with us – for example, Catholics with Protestants – either to defeat an opponent, or to learn about an opponent so as to deal more effectively with him or her, or at best to negotiate with him or her. If we faced each other at all, it was in confrontation – sometimes more openly polemically, sometimes more subtly so, but always with the ultimate goal of defeating the other, because we were convinced that we alone had the absolute truth.

But dialogue is not debate. In dialogue each partner must listen to the other as openly and sympathetically as he or she can in an attempt to understand the other's position as precisely and, as it were, as much from within, as possible. Such an attitude automatically includes the assumption that at any point we might find the partner's position so persuasive that, if we would act with integrity, we would have to change, and change can be disturbing.

We are here, of course, speaking of a specific kind of dialogue, an interreligious, interideological dialogue. To have such, it is not sufficient that the dialogue partners discuss a religious-ideological subject, that is, the meaning of life and how to live accordingly. Rather, they must come to the dialogue as persons somehow significantly identified with a religious or ideological community. If I were neither a Christian nor a Marxist, for example, I could not participate as a "partner' in Christian-Marxist dialogue, though I might listen in, ask some questions for information, and make some helpful comments.

It is obvious that interreligious, interideological dialogue is something new under the sun. We could not conceive of it, let alone do it in the past. How, then, can we effectively engage in this new thing? The following are some basic ground rules, or "commandments," of interreligious, interideological dialogue that must be observed if dialogue is actually to take place. These are not theoretical rules, or commandments given from "on high," but ones that have been learned from hard experience.

FIRST COMMANDMENT:

The primary purpose of dialogue is to learn, that is, to change and grow in the perception and understanding of reality, and then to act accordingly. Minimally, the very fact that I learn that my dialogue partner believes "this" rather than "that" proportionally changes my attitude toward her; and a change in my attitude is a significant

change in me. We enter into dialogue so that we can learn, change, and grow, not so we can force change on the other, as one hopes to do in debate – a hope realized in inverse proportion to the frequency and ferocity with which debate is entered into. On the other hand, because in dialogue each partner comes with the intention of learning and changing herself, one's partner in fact will also change. Thus the goal of debate, and much more, is accomplished far more effectively by dialogue.

SECOND COMMANDMENT:

Interreligious, interideological dialogue must be a two-sided project within each religious or ideological community and between religious or ideological communities. Because of the "corporate" nature of interreligious dialogue, and since the primary goal of dialogue is that each partner learn and change himself, it is also necessary that each participant enter into dialogue not only with his partner across the faith line – the Lutheran with the Anglican, for example – but also with his co-religionists, with his fellow Lutherans, to share with them the fruits of the interreligious dialogue. Only thus can the whole community eventually learn and change, moving toward an ever more perceptive insight into reality.

THIRD COMMANDMENT:

Each participant must come to the dialogue with complete honesty and sincerity. It should be made clear in what direction the major and minor thrusts of the tradition move, what the future shifts might be, and, if necessary, where the participant has difficulties with her own tradition. No false fronts have any place in dialogue.

Conversely each participant must assume a similar complete honesty and sincerity in the other partners. Not only will the absence of sincerity prevent dialogue from happening, but the absence of the assumption of the partner's sincerity will do so as well. In brief – no trust, no dialogue.

FOURTH COMMANDMENT:

In interreligious, interideological dialogue, we must not compare our ideals with our partner's practice, but rather our ideals with our partner's ideals, our practice with our partner's practice.

FIFTH COMMANDMENT:

Each participant must define himself. Only the Jew, for example, can define what it means to be a Jew. The rest can only describe what it looks like from the outside. Moreover, because dialogue is a dynamic medium, as each participant learns, he will change and hence continually deepen, expand, and modify his self-definition as a Jew – being careful to remain in constant dialogue with fellow Jews. Thus it is mandatory that each dialogue partner define what it means to be an authentic member of his own tradition.

Conversely – the one interpreted must be able to

recognize herself in the interpretation. This is the golden rule of interreligious hermeneutics, as has been often reiterated by the "apostle of interreligious dialogue," Raimundo Panikkar. For the sake of understanding, each dialogue participant will naturally attempt to express for herself what she thinks is the meaning of the partner's statement; the partner must be able to recognize herself in that expression. The advocate of "a world theology," Wilfred Cantwell Smith, would add that the expression must also be verifiable by critical observers who are not involved.

SIXTH COMMANDMENT:

Each participant must come to the dialogue with no hard-and-fast assumptions as to where the points of disagreement are. Rather, each partner should not only listen to the other partner with openness and sympathy but also attempt to agree with the dialogue partner as far as is possible while still maintaining integrity with his own tradition; where he absolutely can agree no further without violating his own integrity, precisely there is the real point of disagreement – which most often turns out to be different from the point of disagreement that was falsely assumed ahead of time.

SEVENTH COMMANDMENT:

Dialogue can take place only between equals, or *par cum pari*, as Vatican II put it. Both must come to learn from each other. Therefore, if, for example, the Muslim views Hinduism as inferior, or if the Hindu views Islam as inferior, there will be no dialogue. If authentic interreligious, interideological dialogue between Muslims and Hindus is to occur, then both the Muslim and the Hindu must come mainly to learn from each other; only then will it be "equal with equal." This rule also indicates that there can be no such thing as a one-way dialogue. For example, Jewish-Christian discussions begun in the 1960's were mainly only prolegomena to interreligious dialogue. Understandably and properly, the Jews came to these exchanges only to teach Christians, although the Christians came mainly to learn. But, if authentic interreligious dialogue between Christians and Jews is to occur, then the Jews must also come mainly to learn; only will it then too be *par cum pari*.

EIGHTH COMMANDMENT:

Dialogue can take place only on the basis of mutual trust. Although interreligious, interideological dialogue must occur with some kind of "corporate" dimension, that is, the participants must be involved as members of a religious or ideological community – for instance, as Marxists or Taoists – it is also fundamentally true that it is only persons who can enter into dialogue. But a dialogue among persons can be built only on personal trust. Hence it is wise not to tackle the most difficult problems in the beginning, but rather to approach first those issues most likely to provide some common ground, thereby establishing the basis of human trust. Then, gradually, as this personal trust deepens and expands, the more thorny matters can be undertaken. Thus, as in learning we move from the known to the unknown, so in dialogue we proceed from commonly held matters – which, given our mutual ignorance resulting from centuries of hostility, will take us

quite some time to discover fully – to discuss matters of disagreement.

NINTH COMMANDMENT:

Persons entering into interreligious, interideological dialogue must be at least minimally self-critical of both themselves and their own religious or ideological traditions. A lack of such self-criticism implies that one's own tradition already has all the correct answers. Such an attitude makes dialogue not only unnecessary, but even impossible, since we enter into dialogue primarily so *we* can learn – which obviously is impossible if our tradition has never made a misstep, if it has all the right answers. To be sure, in interreligious, interideological dialogue one must stand within a religious or ideological tradition with integrity and conviction, but such integrity and conviction must include, not exclude, a healthy self-criticism. Without it there can be no dialogue – and, indeed, no integrity.

TENTH COMMANDMENT:

Each participant eventually must attempt to experience the partner's religion or ideology "from within;" for a religion or ideology is not merely something of the head, but also of the spirit, heart, and " whole being," individual and communal. John Dunne here speaks of 'passing over' into another's religious or ideological experience and then coming back enlightened, broadened, and deepened. As Raimundo Panikkar notes, "To know what a religion says, we must understand what it says, but for this we must somehow believe in what it says": for example, "A Christian will never fully understand Hinduism if he is not, in one way or another, converted to Hinduism. Nor will a Hindu ever fully understand Christianity unless he, in one way or another, becomes Christian."

Interreligious, interideological dialogue operates in three areas: the practical, where we collaborate to help humanity; the depth or "spiritual" dimension, where we attempt to experience the partner's religion or ideology "from within"; the cognitive, where we seek understanding and truth. Interreligious, interideological dialogue also has three phases. In the first phase we unlearn misinformation about each other and begin to know each other as we truly are. In phase two we begin to discern values in the partner's tradition and wish to appropriate them into our own tradition. For example, in the Buddhist-Christian dialogue Christians might learn a greater appreciation of the meditative tradition, and Buddhists might learn a greater appreciation of the prophetic, social justice tradition – both values traditionally strongly, though not exclusively, associated with the other's community. If we are serious, persistent, and sensitive enough in the dialogue, we may at times enter into phase three. Here we together begin to explore new areas of reality, of meaning, and of truth, of which neither of us had even been aware before. We are brought face to face with this new, as-yet-unknown-to-us dimension of reality only because of questions, insights, probings produced in the dialogue. We may thus dare to say that patiently pursued dialogue can become an instrument of new "re-velation," a further "un-veiling" of reality – on which we must then act.

There is something radically different about phase one on

the one hand and phases two and three on the other. In the latter we do not simply add on quantitatively another "truth" or value from the partner's tradition. Instead, as we assimilate it within our own religious self-understanding, it will proportionately transform our self-understanding. Since our dialogue partner will be in a similar position, we will then be able to witness authentically to those elements of deep value in our own tradition that our partner's tradition may well be able to assimilate with self-transforming profit. All this of course will have to be done with complete integrity on each side, each partner remaining authentically true to the vital core of his/her own religious tradition. However, in significant ways that vital core will be perceived and experienced differently under the influence of the dialogue, but, if the dialogue is carried on with both integrity and openness, the result will be that, for example,

the Jew will be authentically Jewish and the Christian will be authentically Christian, not despite the fact that Judaism and/or Christianity have been profoundly "Buddhized," but because of it. And the same is true of a Judaized and/or Christianized Buddhism. There can be no talk of a syncretism here, for syncretism means amalgamating various elements of different religions into some kind of a (con)fused whole without concern for the integrity of the religions involved – which is not the case with authentic dialogue.

Previously published in *Journal of Ecumenical Studies,* Vol. 20:1, Winter 1983 (September, 1984, revision).

The *Journal of Ecumenical Studies* and copies of "The Dialogue Decalogue" are available from J.E.S., Temple University (022-38), Philadelphia, PA 19122.

The Rio de Janeiro Interfaith Network

Andre Porto

An organizer of the Rio Interfaith Network and a staff member of the Interfaith Fund Against Hunger and for Life

Andre Porto co-produced the video "One Day for the Earth" (about the interreligious vigil at the Earth Summit), and directed and produced the video "The Interfaith Message of the Parliament of the World's Religions" from the 1993 gathering in Chicago. (See Chapter 43.) This article describes a particularly good example of interfaith *cooperative activities* generated around ethical and critical issues of our time.

*T*hat was a great recipe you gave me last meeting!" comments an Evangelical priest to a Hare Krishna monk. Nearby an Afro-Brazilian "saint mother" tries on an Indian sari given to her by a member of a Hindu group. Scenes like this are becoming very frequent at gatherings of the Rio Interfaith Network, an informal community of some 30 faith traditions that has been working together for over two years. Members are proud and enthusiastic about the interchange, tolerance, and respect they feel for each other, but it hasn't been easy to come to this point.

Everything started three months before the United Nations "Earth Summit" held in Rio in June, 1992. The Institute for Religious Studies (ISER), a large non-profit organization based in Rio, got permission to organize an all-night vigil at the Global Forum park. The Global Forum was a parallel "people's event" during the two weeks of the Earth Summit. The idea was to gather as many religious groups as possible to celebrate the sacredness of the earth, during an entire night.

Eight planning meetings brought 25 religions and spiritual paths together to work in such a way that every group could participate without feeling disrespected. Throughout the large bayside park, each group was assigned a meeting tent where members would do their own practices throughout the night – be it an hourly mass

by the Catholics or chanting by the Hari Krishnas. Joint opening and closing ceremonies, including major personalities like the Dalai Lama, were planned for a large outdoor auditorium. At the first planning meetings, participants felt nervous and cold, but everyone warmed up as the planning continued.

In the end, some 25,000 people attended the vigil that became a lively, inspiring all-night festival of art, music, sharing, and spiritual communion. It was the first time ever that such a number of people from different religious communities joined together in common celebration. The Brazilian and the international media covered the "One Day for the Earth" vigil as a major event of the Earth Summit. The religious leaders brought attention to the spiritual side of the ecological crisis, bringing up the concept of inner ecology. "Without a balanced, healthy relationship with our inner nature, we will not be able to have a healthy relationship with the environment," was an often-echoed comment.

The interfaith vigil had a tremendous effect on Rio's religious community. In the following weeks, ISER received many calls and letters asking for more interfaith gatherings. An opportunity for this came three months later, on September 7th, Brazil's Independence Day. This second vigil centered around the theme, "For Ethics in Politics," and occurred during a major crisis in Brazilian government when the President, proven corrupt, was being tried for impeachment.

This gathering was organized along similar lines as the first. People from all faiths were happy to have the chance to express their opinions about ethics and corruption at this critical point in Brazilian history. At the press conference, one reporter asked if the religions had come together only to pray. A Lutheran minister answered that he felt religions have an important role to play in politics, and that together, their voice is louder. In fact, this was true: a collective declaration on ethics in politics written during the event and signed by all faiths, was published in many of the major newspapers. If each faith had written its own opinion, probably none of them would have been published.

After this second gathering, ISER decided formally to start the Rio Interfaith Network. Staff members produced a video on the two vigils and began work on a book about the gatherings and their significance. Beginning in March 1993, they began a program of monthly celebrations that continues today. Each faith takes a turn to host a celebration based on its own tradition: Buddha's Birthday, Easter, or the Chinese New Year, for example. The event is held at ISER's center and all the other groups are invited to promote interchange and respect. Each month, at least 100 people attend, from all different groups. These people have developed strong friendships and realized they have more in common that they had imagined. They have accepted the concept of unity in diversity and felt the importance of breaking down prejudice and misunderstanding.

Two other large public events were organized in 1993, one against hunger and poverty, and another for peace. Both involved concerts with famous Brazilian musicians and received major attention from the press which has come to accept the Rio Interfaith Network as an established movement.

In fact, at the end of 1993, Brazil's president, Itamar Franco, asked ISER to produce an interfaith New Year's message to be shown on all the TV stations. Previously, only a Catholic message had been broadcast. But this time, the highest leaders of seven different religions were chosen, including Afro-Brazilian and Hindu, and the message was edited in three different, highly professional versions, that were shown frequently throughout the New Year's season to a very positive response. This TV exposure led to an invitation from the largest Rio radio station. The broadcasters invited the Rio Interfaith Network to produce a ten-minute weekly journal each Saturday. This station has the largest audience in Brazil, with millions of listeners. So, since March, 1994, two or three representatives of different paths dialogue on spiritual and social issues, on air, and news and other information is presented.

While everything had been going well, still some groups felt that they could do more together, and expressed a desire for a collective social service outlet. All the energy generated through so many gatherings created the desire to do something more concrete. So some of the groups, along with ISER, created an interfaith fund to support projects working with street children, slum dwellers, homeless people, and concerns of education and health care for poor communities. A board of seven advisors, from seven different faiths, and a paid staff of six people now form the core of the Interfaith Fund Against Hunger and for Life, which has been in operation since November, 1993. The principle mission of this group is to collect funds from various corporations and funding sources and channel that money to needed social projects. In Brazil, such a fund, with religious leadership, has special importance, as many people fear giving money due to the corruption rampant in both private and public organizations.

The biggest success of the Fund has been through an announcement sent out by the electric company with their bills. In two months, this campaign garnered $450,000. The Fund worked hard in research and outreach and finally chose 65 projects to receive the money. Along with basic necessities such as clinics and pre-schools, many of the funded projects were those that generated jobs to bring money to poor communities, such as bakeries for a teen home and a small furniture factory for an ex-addict center. Now the Fund is promoting interchange between these projects, and working on new funding sources.

All of these interfaith activities have been a source of inspiration and enthusiasm for the people in Rio de Janeiro and all of Brazil. The desire and success of people of faith to join efforts towards common goals have proved that there is a lot of hope for humanity's future.

FOR MORE INFORMATION:

Rio Interfaith Network, Av. Rio Branco, 125 /.13 Andar Centro, Rio de Janeiro, RJ Brazil tel. 55-21-232-8213 / fax. 55-21-205-8035

See the Resource Guides, especially Chapters 42 and 43, for addresses and annotated listings of many national and international interfaith organizations, books, videos and other useful information.

"As we allow ourselves to be known by that which we know, our capacity for knowledge grows broader and deeper. The knower who advances most rapidly toward the heart of truth is one who not only asks 'What is out there?' in each encounter with the world, but one who also asks 'What does this encounter reveal about me?'

"Only as we allow ourselves to be known – and thus cleansed of the prejudices and self-interests that distort the community of truth – can we begin to truly know."

PARKER J. PALMER
from *To Know as We Are Known: A Spirituality of Education,* p. 60

Facing Intolerance, Violence, and Other Evils

The Human Problem and Evil

Dr. Thomas G. Walsh

Editor of the Newsletter of the International Religious Federation for World Peace *and of the interfaith journal* Dialogue and Alliance

Written as an editorial for the Newsletter which featured IRFWP's Spring 1994 Seoul Congress, this article introduces the need to look at the nature of the human problem, particularly the problem of evil, and to respond to specific evils within our own traditions.

The question of the human problem is a central dimension of all the world's religious traditions. All religions share a common hope that humankind will advance toward greater understanding of the Ultimate, and, based on this, move toward higher levels of goodness. Religions have also had to address the question of evil, that which places obstacles in front of human beings as they seek to achieve ultimate goodness. Buddhism speaks of suffering or *dukkha;* Hinduism of *samsara;* Judaism speaks of the Fall of Adam and Eve; Christianity of original sin. No religion fails to attend to aspects of the human condition which stand in contrast to goodness, enlightenment, or unity with the divine reality.

Without an understanding of evil – its origin, its essential nature, its characteristics, and its means of proliferation – the pursuit of religious ideals is futile. As IRFWP President, Paulos Mar Gregorios, has said, "In our work for the unity of humanity, we have to face the problem of evil, because evil is the great obstacle to true unity." In the words of IRFWP President, Chung Hwan Kwak, "Our premise is simply that world peace cannot be properly pursued without some clear understanding of the true nature of our problem, its roots and its means for self-perpetuation." Recognition of the power, tenacity, and, often, sovereignty of evil in our world is imperative for those committed to world peace through inter-religious dialogue.

Perhaps it is only a caricature, but some view inter-religious dialogue with skepticism, as a task fit only for those who see the harmony, the bridges, and the goodness of the other, but who cannot adequately comprehend the enormity of our world's disharmony, the chasms, and the evil that lurks in every human heart and mind. Certainly there are so-called realists who know the territory of evil well and who use such knowledge as an excuse for cynicism. Such cynicism reasons that dialogue is an ineffective counterforce to evil and so not worth pursuing.

A realistic vision

*I*nter-religious dialogue is in need of a realistic vision, one which attracts not only the tenderhearted lover of harmony, but also those tempted to cynicism who see most clearly the problems we must confront. Moreover, this realistic vision must vigilantly guard against politicization or any version of what has at times been referred to in the United States as "political correctness." The success of evil is seen precisely as its ability to emerge universally, and with a certain degree of absolute equality.

> "Religions!
>
> "How many bitter historical memories does this word evoke! Religions have caused some of the most cruel and savage wars in history, leaving on the face of humanity the most hideous scars, to the shame of our race. Alas, that is not only past history, ancient or medieval: almost all the situations of serious tension on our earth in the present day still have a religious colouring.
>
> "We must of course recognize that those so-called "wars of religion," both today and in the past, have usually had, and still have, motives which are less religious than political, ethnic, economic, ideological, or of other origin. Nevertheless, strictly religious factors have indeed been operative in some of those painful conflicts. But it is more than time to put an end to all that troubled past. We have an acute and common awareness of the urgency of this need; it is that which is the theme of our meeting here today.
>
> BISHOP BOUTROS MOUALLEM,
> Eparch of the Melkite (Greek-Catholic) Church
> in Brazil, speaking at the Seoul Congress
> of the IRFWP

One of evil's great accomplishments has been its ability to infiltrate our religious traditions, often undetected. Any religion's inability to recognize the enemy within its own inner sanctum can be a fatal error. The same applies to the morally conscientious, for evil cleverly infiltrates morality, again often undetected. Moralists, both religious and secularist, representing one cause or another, fail to see how, in their own highminded protest or crusade, they too have been coopted even as they blush from the accolades poured out by admirers. Yes, the pursuit of peace too stands tainted. After all, it is precisely in the interest of evil to manifest itself as a good, the peacemaker, the moralist, the reformer.

By focusing on evil, IRFWP shows leadership in two important ways. First of all, it encourages scholars and religious leaders to explore together the nature of the human problem. In this way, there is hope of both recovery and innovation in the effort to illuminate, on the theoretical level, the problem of evil. Secondly, IRFWP shows a willingness to engage – as any authentic exploration of evil must – in not only other-critical reflection, but self-critical reflection as well.

Practical Responses to Evil

Compiled by Dr. Carl Becker

A report on one of the group discussions at the 1994 Seoul Congress of the Inter Religious Federation for World Peace, this article demonstrates an interfaith dialogue on a difficult and global issue.

Group A of Section Two consisted of nine members representing four continents and five major religious traditions. Our concerns were to address what humans could do to address the problems of evil, loosely defined as unchosen suffering. How can we, who have burned much fuel and energy to arrive here, justify our consumption of this fuel and energy to those whom we deprive of its use, by what we say or do here? Only if our consumption can directly or indirectly alleviate at least as much suffering as it will have caused. Our group produced countless gems of wisdom and pithy platitudes, all terribly sincere, but few that healed any pain other than the utterer's. This report cannot hope to represent everyone's papers and standpoints equally, but will try to give some of the stream of thought as well as conclusions reached.

Biblical and Islamic traditions

Morality, order, and communication are essential to human society. People of many traditions appeal to their scriptural traditions to justify their approaches to contemporary ethical problems. Our discussion began with a review of biblical and Islamic traditions. Biblical authors were concerned to prevent disorder of their community, seen as violation of the order prescribed by God. This disorder was to be avoided by following strict rules which God prescribed through the priests and prophets. The longstanding rules of Middle Eastern religions do not necessarily speak to the problems of the modern world. But rejection of rules is not a clear solution. Our group recognized the need for new values and rules to protect the integrity of the new and internationalizing society.

Some in our group believed in an inherent natural order, which can be identified by studying the natural and human world, and are identified already by more enlightened thinkers. Others rejected altogether the notion of an inherent order or its discernibility, and proposed that the intermingling of cultures and the borderlessness of world trade and pollution require redefinition of values to approach a new and sustainable order on a more global scale. All expressed concern that order be balanced with limits on the enforcers of order, lest their own imposition of order turn into oppression. Aside from the idea of the fall away from divine good, ignorance and organic imbalance were cited as Indian and East Asian ideas of the origins of evil.

Our African representatives spoke out against corruption, partially attributing it to Christianization, alias modernization. Others defended that the faith itself was not to blame, but people who used the faith for personal ends. And we constantly see the discrepancy between that which people profess and that which they do, whether religious, political, or social. We recognized that "universal" religions have often destroyed the native customs and worldviews, replacing valuing of family, hierarchy, or social obligation with valuing of money or material goods. This, combined with the impersonalization of urban societies, has enabled deceit, theft, and corruption to multiply in societies where they were previously virtually unknown. But we failed to come up with specific ideas of how world religions might respond to this breakdown in traditional values. The center of worldviews is moving from community and family concerns to self-concerns, from respect of age and wisdom to respect of youth and physical power, from respect of etiquette and morality to respect of money and material status symbols.

Personalized evil

Some religions feel evil as more personalized (as Satan in Unificationism), while others as more endemic to the material condition (as in Buddhism). Those who believed in personalized evil seemed to feel more threatened and therefore possibly more concerned to fight evil in their own lives, although those who do not hold the personal devil view were not all persuaded by this analysis.

In sum, religions that believe in a "Good, Creator God" face a problem in explaining why such a God permits evil in the world. Over many centuries, they developed explanations such as:

1) Evil is a test of our faith and helps us grow spiritually;

2) Evil adds to the variety of the world, helps us appreciate good;

3) Evil is to be borne now to bring greater blessings later;

4) Evil is God's will, but humans cannot know why they are afflicted;

5) Evil is all perspective; it's not evil in a changed standpoint.

Now all of these "explanations" may help people retain their faith in God and help them deal psychologically with suffering, but it does not remove the brutal facts of poverty, sickness, and suffering. Even those who do not feel the theological problem that suffering threatens their faith in a good God still face tremendous suffering from their role in the human condition.

The reality of suffering

Our African members especially emphasized that suffering is not mere theological theory, but involves malnutrition, sickness, and uncared-for elderly. In traditional religions, people could not address God or gods directly, but had to go through the ancestors, elders, or priests to address them. This fostered a sense of one's place in community and respect for elders. But in the monotheistic teachings of Christianity and Islam, the ability of the individual to "speak directly to his/her Maker" has contributed to a loss of roles of and respect for the elderly. Independence from the elderly also has led to a cutting of the elderly loose from family support and further fragmentation of the family.

Many voiced concerns about overpopulation. The world's population has grown beyond the ability of the society and the earth to provide for it. There is a serious need for religions to contribute not only to responsible family planning, but to educating people in lifestyles that will keep them from debilitating and expensive illnesses such as lung cancer, diabetes, and hardened arteries. So religions have a role and opportunity in re-educating their societies to caring for their resources and society by not overpopulating or overconsuming.

Materialism prevails

Traditional religious ideals of the family and honoring people have given way to materialist values. Indeed, one teaching basic to the great religions is that we should respect human hearts and souls more than money or possessions. This teaching needs to be further believed and practiced. But how can it be made more attractive to consume less? Only if clean air and water, happy families, crime-free neighborhoods, etc., are made more attractive, visible, and prestigious to invest in than are conspicuous consumption and materialism. It is within the interest as well as the teaching of the great religions to spearhead such a lifestyle trend and re-education. Ultimately, environmental problems may provide a spur to rethinking our relationship with nature, but our need for spiritual growth will not stop even if environmental problems are overcome. The great religions have the staff and facilities with which they could conduct significant reform and welfare programs, but the priests and religious leaders themselves need to be trained or educated to be able to reach out and effectively manage educational, medical, and social services. [...]

Social shame

Most societies of the world use the social sanction of shame to condemn undesirable behaviors. By contrast, Americans not only have no sense of social shame, but exalt criminality and deviance by giving it great publicity and putting convicts on TV talk shows. But when life gets tough in America, even Americans fall back on their faith for something to live by. Those from more traditional societies voiced the hope that their teachings of sin and shame could be preserved, not only to protect their society, but to encourage proper relations between humans and the universe.

While hoping that religions will contribute to tolerance, we recognize and regret that religious intolerance continues to be a cause of suffering in many countries represented. In the end, we turned our attention to specific things we hope religions can do to respond to evil, such as:

1) Bringing the family to pray together daily, and teaching them moral responses to the challenges of the times.

2) Mobilizing the collective consciousness of the believers, through sermons and publicity, to their responsibility (= ability to respond to the plight) of the elderly and delinquent.

3) Encouraging youth from each religion to interact in work projects with youth groups from other religions, youth groups such as the Religious Youth Service (of IRFWP).

4) Training of religious leaders must include social work and social responsibility, over ritual and rank.

5) Rethinking religion as not human-centered, but as universe-centered, caring for the welfare not only of the human population, but also of the variety of species.

6) Influencing mass media, both by contact with its operators, and by influencing the viewing patterns of its community.

7) Identifying and eliminating textbooks and trade books that foster hatred, prejudice, or misunderstanding of other religions. Such a project could identify the misstatements of books and films and lobby for the elimination of prejudice.

8) Soul-searching by each religion to repent and to start over from basic principles.

9) Recognizing saintly or religious people, either living or recently departed, through biography, awards or film depictions, to provide moral models for the youth to admire.

10) We all recognize that the ultimate responsibility lies in the heart of each religious person, and that we must act out and live our beliefs in practical and visible ways in order to alleviate pain and suffering in a sustainable world.

All wish to reiterate our thanks to IRFWP for making this kind of dialogue possible.

May the Light Dawn

Dr. Paulos Mar Gregorios

Bishop of the Syrian Othodox (Christian) Church in India, and a President of Inter-Religious Federation for World Peace

The following address was presented at the Opening Plenary of the 1993 IRFWP Congress in New Delhi, India, in February 1993, shortly after the militant Hindu Kar Sevaks had destroyed the Muslim mosque at Ayodhya. The author identifies elements of evil in religious violence but also in the scientism, secularism and corporate fascism that characterize our urban-technological societies.

*T*oday, as I welcome you to this first global celebration of the centenary year of the Chicago Parliament of Religions and to this New Delhi Congress of the Inter-Religious Federation of World Peace on Global Harmony through Inter-Religious Action, I do so with sadness in my heart. My land to this day moans with pain at what took place in Ayodhya on December 6th last year, and in the whole country in the aftermath.

This land of the Vedas and the Upanishads, the Gita and the Guru Granth Saheb, of Gautama Buddha and Ashoka Priyadarshin, of Jaina Mahavira and Kabir, of Ramakrishna Paramanhansa and Swami Vivekananda, of Nizamuddin and Sri Aurobindo, of Rabindranath Tagore and Maulana Abu'al Kalam Azad, of Sri Ramana and Mahatma Gandhi, of Sadhu Sundar Singh and Sirdi Sai Baba; this land of Dharma and Ahimsa; this unique land where people of many religions have for two and a half millennia lived together in peace and harmony; this land of the rishis and sages weeps today because religion has been highjacked by some politicians and prostituted by a few religious leaders. Political parties abuse and pervert religion as a mere means to get votes, even at the expense of hurting the feelings of other communities or of destroying the places of worship of other religions! Neither these political leaders nor these religious dignitaries show any compassionate concern about what happens to people or the nation in the process.

Pity on religious fanatics

*S*wami Vivekananda, in an address to the Shakespeare Club in Pasadena, California, January 27, 1900, said that in India, "even if you want to set up a gang of robbers, the leader will have to preach some sort of religion." The Swami used his statement to show that in India, in all things, religion has to be uppermost. But what he said in his address to the concluding session of the World Parliament of Religions in Chicago in 1893, exactly a hundred years ago, is more significant and memorable:

If the Parliament of Religions has shown anything to the world it is this: it has proved to the world that holiness, purity, and charity are not the exclusive possessions of any church in the world, and that every system has produced men and women of the most exalted character. In the face of this evidence, if anybody dreams of the exclusive survival of his own religion and the

destruction of others, I pity him front the bottom of my heart.

Well, sisters and brothers in the Spirit, who have come to us from all regions and religions of the world, Swami Vivekananda meant by that pity for the fanatic Christian missionaries whom he had encountered. Now there are people of my country also who think along the lines Swami Vivekananda condemned, who deserve to be pitied from the bottom of your hearts. But give us a little more than your pity. Give us also your generous understanding and kind compassion.

This nation and our great neighhor, Pakistan, both bear the trauma of being born in the midst of violence and hatred in 1947; we were drawn, even through all that murder and bloodshed, by two different pious hopes: India's "Tryst with Destiny," understood as a secular liberal democratic paradise where Hindu and Muslim, Christian and Sikh, Buddhist and Jaina, Jew and Parsi, Adivasi and people of no specific religious faith could all live and work together in peace with mutual respect, where justice would rule, where no one religion would dominate, and where the poor and the downtrodden would flourish in dignity and freedom; and Pakistan's fond dream of a perfect Islamic society where all would be equal and free from what they see as the arrogant and godless culture of the West, to live by the noble shariyah, worshipping Allah, in a nation where the lofty ideals of the Qur'an would become a social-historical reality.

Now both dreams have gone sour. Please forgive us for behaving irrationally. We are not in our best elements. We are a bit confused. That goes for all of us, Christians and Sikhs, Hindus and Muslims. Even our intellectuals are not at their best. Bear with us. We will come around to our senses, we promise you. [...]

The question today is: shall religion still look to the technological civilization as its patron and censor, as it did a hundred years ago? Shall it meekly accept the insignificant corner in the margin allotted to it by a secular and earth-bound culture dominated by the dazzle of modern science/technology, which was beating its drums of triumph at the Columbian Exposition a hundred years ago? Shall we continue to pin our hopes on a secular culture which has not been able to provide us with inter-religious and inter-ethnic harmony within a nation, not to speak of global harmony? Or shall all religions go back to their own sources in conversation with other religious traditions, to seek renewal and gain a new self-understanding, so that we can develop again the spiritual depth and the cultural creativity necessary for functioning as humanity's true guides and advocates?

The human race first needs to be rescued from the adolescent hubris of an unreflective secularism and scientism on the one hand, and from the meaning-distorting and soul-destroying urban-technological civilization developed by the white West and their allies on the other hand. That is only part of the mammoth task facing humanity.

The secularism we want to be rescued from is the one that glibly assumes that the world open to our senses is the chief part of reality; that meaning can be found without reference to anything transcending that world; that religion is a matter of private individual choice (free enterprise religion, I suppose), to be banished from the public sphere, in such a way that the main human activities like economic activity, politics, education, and health care can be undertaken without any transcendent reference.

The scientism from which we seek liberation is the one that assumes that modern empirical science is the chief way to get hold of reality, and that scientific knowledge is the higher kind of human knowledge. Our purpose in this civilization shaped by scientism-technologism seems to be to make reality too our colony, so that we can have a domineering, imperialist, exploiting grip on reality through our technology. We want to make reality our slave and our hoard.

[This attitude] looks like the same imperialist-fascist greed that drives rioting mobs to loot and arson, rape and plunder in Ayodhya or Bombay. The only difference between the industrial-urban-technological civilization and the rioting mobs seems to be one of style and scale and sophistication. Corporate and brutal violence exercised by the many over the few (the essence of fascism), monumental, heartless injustice with no concern for the victim, and plunder and looting, with or without sophistication, seem to be common to both.

Different versions of the same are taking place everywhere – in former Yugoslavia, in Somalia, in the Middle East, and elsewhere. Adherents of religions are fully involved in the arson and plunder, in the torture and persecution, in the corporate violence of groups and governments which perpetrate injustice with impunity. [...]

Declaration of Mutual Acceptance
by the Community of Religions

This declaration was drafted by Brother Wayne Teasdale for Monastic Interreligious Dialogue, and was presented at the Parliament of the World's Religions.

*O*ur common awareness and our collective wisdom have brought us to this realization:

We proclaim for our time and the ages to come, a mutual tolerance, acceptance, and respect among all the religions of the world. The countless wars in history and even today, rooted in ignorance, intolerance, and an appalling lack of acceptance, show the compelling need for this statement of commitment.

Human intolerance comes from fear of differences in language, customs, rites, and symbols. Ultimately, all external fears are driven by our own self-fear of the contradictions within each one of us. All fear disturbs our sense of security; thus we reject differences in order to maintain an intellectual security and contentment. Here lies the basis of all religious conflict.

"The friendly study of all religions is the sacred duty of every individual."
                                                    MAHATMA GANDHI

"Nonviolence is to violence what light is to darkness."
                                                    ARUN GANDHI,
                        M. Gandhi Institute for Nonviolence

Acceptance of others begins with self-acceptance, and self-acceptance requires genuine self-knowledge. It means confronting our fears and weaknesses, and integrating our contradictions. Mutual acceptance between and among religious traditions must begin with this self-acceptance in its members, particularly in its leaders.

Each faith tradition possesses a special, even mystical knowledge of our deep unity and interdependence. Now, that precious wisdom must be applied toward the transformation of past attitudes of intolerance and hatred which have produced so many terrible wars.

We recognize that the world's religions are no longer simply isolated traditions competing with one another, but belong to a greater community of religions. In this commonwealth, each religion preserves and celebrates its uniqueness while collaborating with the others in the work of building a new civilization with a heart!

We rejoice in our rich diversity of expression, a brilliant tapestry of experience, insight, and creativity, joyfully accepting each and every religion. We commit ourselves to teach this value and skill of openness. In another application of the Golden Rule, we declare: let us accept others with sincerity and enthusiasm, just as we wish for ourselves.

This quality of acceptance grows through the practice of dialogue. It evolves from mere tolerance to open acceptance, to fondness and love, and, finally, into communion. It is this gift of communion – the fruit of mutual knowledge and trust – that is the goal of the Community of Religions and of a civilization with a heart. We call upon all peoples everywhere to embrace this value of living dialogue and acceptance with us.

Declaration on the Elimination of All Forms of Intolerance and of Discrimination Based on Religion or Belief

United Nations

Introduction

One of the basic purposes of the United Nations, as set forth in its Charter, is the promotion and encouragement of respect for human rights and fundamental freedoms for all without distinction as to race, sex, language, or religion.

Freedom of belief is one of the rights proclaimed in the Universal Declaration of Human Rights, adopted by the General Assembly in 1948, and in the International Covenant on Civil and Political Rights, adopted in 1966.

The Preamble to the Universal Declaration of Human Rights states that "the advent of a world in which human beings shall enjoy freedom of speech and belief and freedom from fear and want has been proclaimed as the highest aspiration of the common people."

Article 2 declares that: "Everyone is entitled to all the rights and freedoms set forth in this Declaration, without distinction of any kind, such as race, colour, sex, language, religion, political or other opinion, national or social origin, property, birth or other status."

Article 18 of the Universal Declaration of Human Rights states that: "Everyone has the right to freedom of thought, conscience and religion; this right includes freedom to change his religion or belief, and freedom, either alone or in community with others and in public or private, to manifest his religion or belief in teaching, practice, worship, and observance." [The full text is printed on pp. 223-3.]

This right was transformed into a legal obligation for ratifying States in article 18 of the International Covenant on Civil and Political Rights, which states that:

"1. Everyone shall have the right to freedom of thought, conscience and religion. This right shall include freedom to have or to adopt a religion or belief of his choice, and freedom, either individually or in community with others and in public or private, to manifest his religion or belief in worship, observance, practice and teaching.

"2. No one shall be subject to coercion which would impair his freedom to have or to adopt a religion or belief of his choice.

"3. Freedom to manifest one's religion or beliefs may be subject only to such limitations as are prescribed by law and are necessary to protect public safety, order, health, or morals or the fundamental rights and freedoms of others.

"4. The States party to the present Covenant undertake to have respect for the liberty of parents and, when applicable, legal guardians to ensure the religious and moral education of their children in conformity with their own convictions."

Preparation of a draft declaration on the elimination of all forms of intolerance and of discrimination based on religion and belief originated in 1962, when the idea of a United Nations instrument on this issue was first approved by the General Assembly. Two distinct documents were then envisaged: a declaration and an international convention.

In 1972 the General Assembly decided to accord priority to the completion of the Declaration before resuming consideration of the draft International Convention. At the Assembly's request, the question of a draft Declaration was considered by the Commission on Human Rights at each of its annual sessions from 1974 to 1981. In March 1981, the Commission adopted the text of a draft Declaration, which was submitted, through the Economic and Social Council, to the General Assembly at its regular session later that year.

On 25 November 1981, the General Assembly proclaimed the Declaration on the Elimination of All Forms of Intolerance and of Discrimination Based on Religion and Belief, stating that it considered it essential "to promote understanding, tolerance, and respect in matters relating to freedom of religion and belief" and that it was resolved "to adopt all necessary measures for the speedy elimination of such intolerance in all its forms and manifestations and to prevent and combat discrimination on the grounds of religion or belief."

The full text of the Declaration follows.

The Declaration

Adopted by the General Assembly of the United Nations on 25 November 1981 (resolution 36155)

The General Assembly,

Considering that one of the basic principles of the Charter of the United Nations is that of the dignity and equality inherent in all human beings, and that all Member States have pledged themselves to take joint and separate action in co-operation with the Organization to promote and encourage universal respect for and observance of human rights and fundamental freedoms for all, without distinction as to race, sex, language or religion,

Considering that the Universal Declaration of Human Rights and the International Covenants on Human Rights proclaim the principles of nondiscrimination and equality before the law and the right to freedom of thought, conscience, religion and belief,

Considering that the disregard and infringement of human rights and fundamental freedoms, in particular of the right to freedom of thought, conscience, religion or whatever belief, have brought, directly or indirectly, wars and great suffering to mankind, especially where they serve as a means of foreign interference in the internal affairs of other States and amount to kindling hatred between peoples and nations,

Considering that religion or belief, for anyone who professes either, is one of the fundamental elements in his conception of life and that freedom of religion or belief should be fully respected and guaranteed,

Considering that it is essential to promote understanding, tolerance and respect in matters relating to freedom of religion and belief and to ensure that the use of religion or belief for ends inconsistent with the Charter, other relevant instruments of the United Nations and the purposes and principles of the present Declaration is inadmissible,

Convinced that freedom of religion and belief should also contribute to the attainment of the goals of world peace, social justice and friendship among peoples and to the elimination of ideologies or practices of colonialism and racial discrimination,

Noting with satisfaction the adoption of several, and the coming into force of some, conventions, under the aegis of the United Nations and of the specialized agencies, for the elimination of various forms of discrimination,

Concerned by manifestations of intolerance and by the existence of discrimination in matters of religion or belief still in evidence in some areas of the world,

Resolved to adopt all necessary measures for the speedy elimination of such intolerance in all its forms and manifestations and to prevent and combat discrimination on the grounds of religion or belief,

Proclaims this Declaration on the Elimination of All Forms of Intolerance and of Discrimination Based on Religion or Belief:

Article 1

1. Everyone shall have the right to freedom of thought, conscience and religion. This right shall include freedom to have a religion or whatever belief of his choice, and freedom, either individually or in community with others and in public or private, to manifest his religion or belief in worship, observance, practice and teaching.

2. No one shall be subject to coercion which would impair his freedom to have a religion or belief of his choice.

3. Freedom to manifest one's religion or beliefs may be subject only to such limitations as are prescribed by law and are necessary to protect public safety, order, health or morals or the fundamental rights and freedoms of others.

Article 2

1. No one shall be subject to discrimination by any State, institution, group of persons or person on the grounds of religion or other beliefs.

2. For the purposes of the present Declaration, the expression "intolerance and discrimination based on religion or belief" means any distinction, exclusion, restriction or preference based on religion or belief and having as its purpose or as its effect nullification or impairment of the recognition, enjoyment or exercise of human rights and fundamental freedoms on an equal basis.

Article 3

Discrimination between human beings on the grounds of religion or belief constitutes an affront to human dignity and a disavowal of the principles of the Charter of the United Nations, and shall be condemned as a violation of the human rights and fundamental freedoms proclaimed in the Universal Declaration of Human Rights and enunciated in detail in the International Covenants on Human Rights, and as an obstacle to friendly and peaceful relations between nations.

Article 4

1. All States shall take effective measures to prevent and eliminate discrimination on the grounds of religion or belief in the recognition, exercise and enjoyment of human rights and fundamental freedoms in all fields of civil, economic, political, social and cultural life.

2. All States shall make all efforts to enact or rescind legislation where necessary to prohibit any such discrimination, and to take all appropriate measures to combat intolerance on the grounds of religion or other beliefs in this matter.

Article 5

1. The parents or, as the case may be, the legal guardians of the child have the right to organize the life within the family in accordance with their religion or belief and bearing in mind the moral education in which they believe the child should be brought up.

2. Every child shall enjoy the right to have access to education in the matter of religion or belief in accordance with the wishes of his parents or, as the case may be, legal guardians, and shall not be compelled to receive teaching on religion or belief against the wishes of his parents or legal guardians, the best interests of the child being the guiding principle.

3. The child shall be protected from any form of discrimination on the grounds of religion or belief. He shall be brought up in a spirit of understanding, tolerance, friendship among peoples, peace and universal brotherhood, respect for freedom of religion or belief of others, and in full consciousness that his energy and talents should be devoted to the service of his fellow men.

4. In the case of a child who is not under the care either of his parents or of legal guardians, due account shall be taken of their expressed wishes or of any other proof of their wishes in the matter of religion or belief, the best interests of the child being the guiding principle.

5. Practices of a religion or beliefs in which a child is brought up must not be injurious to his physical or mental health or to his full development, taking into account article 1, paragraph 3, of the present Declaration.

Article 6

In accordance with article 1 of the present Declaration, and subject to the provisions of article 1, paragraph 3, the right to freedom of thought, conscience, religion or belief shall include, *inter alia,* the following freedoms:

(a) To worship or assemble in connection with a religion or belief, and to establish and maintain places for these purposes;

(b) To establish and maintain appropriate charitable or humanitarian institutions;

(c) To make, acquire and use to an adequate extent the necessary articles and materials related to the rites or customs of a religion or belief;

(d) To write, issue and disseminate relevant publications in these areas; (e) To teach a religion or belief in places suitable for these purposes;

(f) To solicit and receive voluntary financial and other contributions from individuals and institutions;

(g) To train, appoint, elect or designate by succession appropriate leaders called for by the requirements and standards of any religion or belief;

(h) To observe days of rest and to celebrate holidays and ceremonies in accordance with the precepts of one's religion or belief;

(I) To establish and maintain communications with individuals and communities in matters of religion and belief at the national and international levels.

Article 7

The rights and freedoms set forth in the present Declaration shall be accorded in national legislations in such a manner that everyone shall be able to avail himself of such rights and freedoms in practice.

Article 8

Nothing in the present Declaration shall be construed as restricting or derogating from any right defined in the Universal Declaration of Human Rights and the International Covenants on Human Rights.

United Nations Department of Public Information, document DPI/714-84-33131

FOR MORE INFORMATION:

NGO Committee on Freedom of Religion or Belief, 546 East 11th St., Apartment 4-A, New York, NY 10009 USA tel. (212) 687-2163 / fax. (212) 808-5480

American Indian Freedom of Religion

Joseph Grant

Formerly Director of the Anawim Center, an interfaith spiritual center for American Indians in Chicago; now working as an advocate for homeless people in Louisville, Kentucky

*I*n the US, freedom of religion (rights of practice, belief, and affiliation) is considered a fundamental principle of human rights and guaranteed protection by the First Amendment of the U.S. Constitution. This specific freedom and element of individual liberty has, however, been systematically denied to America's First Nations. There has been a long and well-documented history of religious persecution and suppression of American Indian sacred ways by Federal Government authorities in collaboration with various Christian churches.

In the past this has involved the forced separation of Native children from their families and their relocation to Christian boarding schools, the outlawing of traditional ceremonies, the destruction of religious objects, and the desecration of sacred places of worship and gravesites. Aware that spiritual traditions are the cohesive force which preserves the integrity of Native communities, some Christian and Government authorities directly targeted traditional religious practices in their assimilation policies. As a result, some American Indian religious practices have been completely lost and others forced into secret practice.

On August 11, 1978 President Carter signed Public Law 95-341, the American Indian Religious Freedom Act (AIRFA), as a first attempt to recognize and afford a measure of protection to the religious traditions of American Indian people. Recent Supreme Court decisions have made clear that such protection is entirely inadequate. In 1994 attempts were made by members of Congress to address the inadequacies of AIRFA by introducing the Religious Freedom Restoration Act; the legislative battle continues to seek for American Indians the basic freedom which is considered the birthright of all US citizens.

Meanwhile, many sacred sites across the country are still not recognized; access is denied to Native people while mining, logging, or construction in such areas continues. The sacramental use of peyote cactus in Native American Church ceremonies remains outlawed in some states. American Indian inmates in many federal and state penitentiaries are denied access to their spiritual leaders, and the sacred objects and burial remains of Native people continue to be placed on public display in museums throughout the nation.

The struggle to secure greater recognition for American Indian religious ways promises to be long and arduous. Prior attempts have been defeated by powerful alliances between federal land agencies, mining, timber, and oil companies. A general lack of understanding imbued with prejudicial stereotypes about American Indian people and their religious ways continues to hinder progress.

Fortunately, many religious and spiritual communities are rallying to the cause of Native American religious freedom, while mainline Christian churches are seeking to redress their history of religious persecution. A renewed appreciation for the validity of American Indian spiritual tradition is clearly evidenced by the prominent role which Native spiritual leaders were given at the 1993 Parliament of the World's Religions in Chicago. What is becoming clear among the diverse religious communities of the US is that the denial of religious freedom to one group affects the religious liberty of all believers.

previously printed in the *CPWR Journal*, September 1994

FOR MORE INFORMATION:

Indian Treaty Rights Committee
4554 N. Broadway, Suite 258
Chicago, IL 60640 USA tel. (312) 561-6155

Anawim Center
4554 N. Broadway, Suite 258
Chicago, IL 60640 USA tel. (312) 561-6155

See also articles in Chapter 42 on related organizations.

Lutherans and Judaism – A New Possibility

Dr. Stephen A. Schmidt

Professor of Pastoral Studies, Loyola University, Chicago

Among the steps needed to transcend religious discrimination and intolerance is theological and cultural recognition of the errors of the past. This article presents one recent attempt to rectify those errors and the tragedies they helped to create.

The Evangelical Lutheran Church in America (ELCA) has taken a dramatic step to heal centuries of distrust between Lutherans and Jewish Americans. That healing process happened because Lutherans are taking both their Scripture studies and their Gospel seriously. They are attending to matters of political history, and their new awareness of past experiences of anti-Semitism. They now are able to acknowledge that such bigotry was a denial of the Gospel and to face many other issues of social justice and compassion.

Last April 18, The Church Council of the ELCA adopted a sensitive statement on Lutheran-Jewish relations (below). What this "Declaration" announces is a beginning of new relationships between the two religious traditions. It begins with a straightforward confession of past social sins by the worldwide community of Lutherans. It particularizes the terrible actions of Lutheran Christians in relationship to the Nazi Holocaust. It names the sin and the sinner. It explicitly acknowledges Luther's "anti Judaic diatribes and violent recommendations in his later writings against the Jews." It makes public confession and it asks for reconciliation with the (American) Jewish Community. All this in mutual words of prayer for the "continued blessing of the Blessed One," Yahweh/God for both communities.

On November 13, Chicago Lutherans with representatives from the larger American church met at Grace Lutheran Church in River Forest, Illinois, for evening prayer of public confession and repentance. After this service of repentance and confession the assembly walked to West Suburban Temple Har Zion for words of healing and reconciliation. A public presentation of the "Declaration" was given to the Jewish community, and a first step toward a modest future of dialogue and new possibilities for trust and healing has begun.

This action could not have transpired if Lutherans were not serious about their theological traditions. This was an event more about confession and absolution than about face-saving or guilt. It was possible, I think, because for this time in this small but important event Lutherans are taking the Gospel seriously, and acting out of their own sin and the clear understanding of the need for repentance and absolution. It is an event that took history seriously, in this case the history of a religious tradition. And it was an event that cared about acts that denied God's justice in a particular time and place, in a very political setting.

So Lutherans did what they will continue to do if they take the core of the Gospel seriously. They will cease attempting justification by action or by some kind of public gesture. They can confess and they can begin renewal because they know they are judged and loved by a God who calls them to justice and love in return. They kept covenant. They theologized out of historical reality. They prayed and ritualized the event around word and sacrament and they turned a page to a new horizon for Jewish-Lutheran dialogue. They participated in a little process of creating public documents that in some small measure contributes to the public paideia. A small step, faithfully taken. And I am glad.

Declaration of the ELCA to the Jewish Community

In the long history of Christianity there exists no more tragic development than the treatment accorded the Jewish people on the part of Christian believers. Very few Christian communities of faith were able to escape the contagion of anti-Judaism and its modern successor, anti-Semitism. Lutherans belonging to the Lutheran World Federation and the Evangelical Lutheran Church in America feel a special burden in this regard because of certain elements in the legacy of the reformer Martin Luther and the catastrophes, including the Holocaust of the twentieth century, suffered by Jews in places where the Lutheran churches were strongly represented.

The Lutheran communion of faith is linked by name and heritage to the memory of Martin Luther, teacher and reformer. Honoring his name in our own, we recall his bold stand for truth, his earthy and sublime words of wisdom, and above all his witness to God's saving Word. Luther proclaimed a gospel for people as we really are, bidding us to trust a grace sufficient to reach our deepest shames and address the most tragic truths.

In the spirit of that truth-telling, we who bear his name and heritage must with pain acknowledge also Luther's anti-Judaic diatribes and the violent recommendations of his later writings against the Jews. As did many of Luther's own companions in the sixteenth century, we reject this violent invective, and yet more do we express our deep and abiding sorrow over its tragic effects on subsequent generations. In concert with the Lutheran World Federation, we particularly deplore the appropriation of Luther's words by modern anti-Semites for the teaching of hatred toward Judaism or toward the Jewish people in our day.

Grieving the complicity of our own tradition within this history of hatred, moreover, we express our urgent desire to live out our faith in Jesus Christ with love and respect for the Jewish people. We recognize in anti-Semitism a contradiction and an affront to the Gospel, a violation of our hope and calling, and we pledge this church to oppose the deadly working of such bigotry, both within our own circles and in the society around us. Finally, we pray for the continued blessing of the Blessed One upon the increasing cooperation and understanding between Lutheran Christians and the Jewish community.

Universal Declaration on Nonviolence:
The Incompatibility of Religion and War

*T*his document is an attempt to set forth a vision of nonviolence within the context of an emerging global civilization in which all forms of violence, especially war, are totally unacceptable as means to settle disputes between and among nations, groups, and persons. This new vision of civilization is global in scope, universal in culture, and based on love and compassion, the highest moral/spiritual principles of the various historical religions. Its universal nature acknowledges the essential fact of modern life: the interdependence of nations, economies, cultures, and religious traditions.

As members of religious groups throughout the world, we are increasingly aware of our responsibility to promote peace in our age and in the ages to come. Nevertheless, we recognize that in the history of the human family, people of various religions, acting officially in the name of their respective traditions, have either initiated or collaborated in organized and systematic violence or war. These actions have at times been directed against other religious traditions, groups, and nations, as well as within particular religious traditions. This pattern of behavior is totally inappropriate for spiritual persons and communities. Therefore, as members of world religions, we declare before the human family, that:

Religion can no longer be an accomplice to war, to terrorism or to any other forms of violence, organized or spontaneous, against any member of the human family. Because this family is one, global, and interrelated, our actions must be consistent with this identity. We recognize the right and duty of governments to defend the security of their people and to relieve those afflicted by exploitation and persecution. Nevertheless, we declare that religion must not permit itself to be used by any state, group or organization for the purpose of supporting aggression for nationalistic gain. We have an obligation to promote a new vision of society, one in which war has no place in resolving disputes between and among states, organizations, and religions.

In making this declaration, we the signatories commit ourselves to this new vision. We call upon all the members of our respective traditions to embrace this vision. We urge our members and all peoples to use every moral means to dissuade their governments from promoting war or terrorism. We strongly encourage the United Nations organization to employ all available resources toward the development of peaceful methods of resolving conflicts among nations.

Our declaration is meant to promote such a new global society, one in which nonviolence is preeminent as a value in all human relations. We offer this vision of peace, mindful of the words of Pope Paul VI to the United Nations in October 1965: "No more war: war never again!"

*S*ignatories: *Thomas Keating, Johanna Becker, Wayne Teasdale, Dom Bede Griffiths, Raimundo Panikkar, Katherine Howard, Pascaline Coff, Theophane Boyd, Ruth Fox, Timothy Kelley,* and other members of the North American Board for East-West Dialogue;
and *His Holiness the Dalai Lama*

Promulgated and signed on April 2, 1991, at Santa Fe, NM, USA

Resolution on Tibet

Monastic Interreligious Dialogue

While there are many troubled spots in the world deserving the attention and resolve of the religious community, and which therefore might be included in this book, the Tibetan struggle for justice stands out as a model of *nonviolent* moral resistance. As the world community – both religious and secular – pursues a culture of peace and condemns injustice, it must identify and support nonviolent responses to situations of conflict wherever they occur.

*W*e have observed the intense suffering of the Tibetan people that has been inflicted on them for more than four decades. It is with concern, empathy, a deep sense of responsibility and solidarity that we express our collective outrage at the brutal and callous actions of the People's Republic of China in Tibet. These actions include cultural genocide, torture, forced abortion, sterilization, and systematic violation of the human rights of the Tibetan People, as well as deforestation and dumping of nuclear waste in Tibet. Above all, the massive transfer of Chinese immigrants into Tibet which has already transformed the Tibetans into an insignificant minority in their own country, threatens the very existence of the Tibetan national and cultural identity. Such actions are thoroughly reprehensible and morally repugnant to all people within the religions, and even to those with no religion.

*T*herefore, considering the seriousness of the situation in Tibet, we call for the complete and immediate restoration of the legitimate rights of the Tibetan people, and urge the international community to address the issue of Tibet at various world forums, in particular at the United Nations.

Nonviolent Response to Violence

Joel Beversluis

Editor of A SourceBook for Earth's Community of Religions

*R*eaders of this *SourceBook* are probably distraught over the warfare and continuing violence in many countries. We are equally upset over the failures of international diplomacy and threats of military intervention, neither of which is restoring peace in the former Yugoslavia. The United Nations' goal of peacekeeping is being sorely tested here as well as in other troubled spots – the Middle East, Cambodia, Rwanda, Sudan, and Somalia, to name a few. Yet that goal must be reinforced; casualties and failures notwithstanding, the United Nations must preserve its peacekeeping function.

Are current political and media responses a betrayal of those who are being violated? Dr. Mustafa Ceric, Supreme Head of the Islamic Community in Bosnia-Herzegovina, provides one answer within the *Islam* article in Chapter 10 of this book. In the former Yugoslavia as well as in other places, international inaction and disengagement from the issues, especially at early stages when nonviolent intervention can be most effective, are clearly a betrayal of suffering humans. Inaction also betrays our standards of good and evil and our proclamations regarding human rights.

Interreligious conflict

*W*ars like the ones in Bosnia-Herzegovinia have numerous subtle and interrelated causes and factors, including tribal or racial, economic, and political. Like most other human interactions, conflicts are holistic in that they engage many interconnected aspects of individuals and societies. It is therefore not accurate to suggest, as some do, that in this modern era the religions are a primary source of conflict, that they are dividing people and causing wars. On the other hand, religions *do* often contribute greatly to conflicts by *sanctifying* the causes. Thus violence not only is justified in the name of religion, but often is made 'holy.'

Is there room midst this common and unholy alliance between religions and violence for a religious response that serves a culture of peace? Despite the contributions of religions to conflict, the most persistent voice for nonviolence also comes from the religions. Jainism is one of the oldest sources of nonviolence through its insistence on *ahimsa*. Many other traditions also have peacemaking and pacifist inclinations. We may wonder, however, whether human rights and justice can be restored through *nonviolent* means.

Citizen witnesses

*N*ational and international diplomacy, whether successful or not, should not blind us to other possibilities of nonviolent action originating in popular and religious movements. Growing numbers of citizens from many countries and religions are discovering the simple truth that diplomacy for peace and intervention for human rights are the right and responsibility of the people, and not the domain only of nation-states and international agencies. More and more committed citizens are engaged in peacemaking, ecological preservation, disaster relief, and solidarity movements. These activities operate independently of the nation-states and sometimes even stand in opposition to their policies, as with the Witness for Peace program of intervention and public disclosure in Central America. Non-governmental organizations and citizens' movements are also developing creative strategies for conflict resolution, the pursuit of justice, and approaches to sustainable development.

The motivations for these autonomous actions are often spiritual as well as ethical, and their members are often based in religious organizations, embodying religious responses to humanitarian, political, and ecological crises. These groups are, in fact, modeling strategies for the development of a culture of peace.

Media and the religions

*T*he media do not pay much attention to these citizens' activities. Instead of seeing them as pioneering attempts to implement the highest values of religious and political will, they often dismiss them as fringe protests, out of touch with mainstream thought. In fact, however, mainstream thought is changing, in part because of the success of these efforts as well as because military methods are always expensive and often fail. Now, international agencies, governments, and military departments are exploring and utilizing conflict resolution techniques and peace teams to defuse tensions.

While those efforts are commendable, it is time to modify the common perception that the power and influence for good resides primarily in the politicized diplomatic and military responses of the nation-states. Organized religions and the establishment media should also learn how to support and participate in these nonviolent and idealistic challenges to the destructive impulses of humans that have such power within our societies.

Prophetic nonviolence

*T*rue nonviolent responses are not passive, and do not shy away from analyzing and speaking the truth in the face of the abuses of power, as Gandhi demonstrated. This is, in fact, a prophetic task, consistent with that of the righteous prophets of ancient Judaism, Christianity, and Islam. Furthermore, those who work for peace without taking sides, who risk their lives in solidarity with those who are suffering, and who are making injustice visible are expressing the power of nonviolence. They are, at the same time, embodying some fundamental truths of the religions of the world. They require our support.

Peace Teams:
Their Time Has Come

Father Peter Dougherty

Catholic priest, longtime peace activist and nonviolence trainer

SOME TIME IN THE FUTURE . . .
NEWS FLASH, DECEMBER 25:

*T*hree weeks ago the U.S. government announced plans for air strikes against the country of Iraq because Saddham Hussein's forces the previous week took over a 20-square-mile section of Turkey, claiming it as Iraq's own, historically. Turkey had called on its ally, the USA, for military intervention.

20,000 nonviolent peacemakers from North America, Europe, Central and South America, Asia and Africa, came to Iraq and the tiny disputed section of Turkey. They were welcomed by those governments. The peacemakers took no public stand on Iraq's action in Turkey, but called for just negotiations rather than a military "solution" of the problem. Thousands camped outside or stayed in homes of Iraqi people in all major cities and towns of the country, and were present at all utility and power plants that comprised the country's infrastructure.

Witnesses have been amazed at the discipline, skill, and democratic organization of the venture. It was obvious that all had undergone nonviolence training and had pledged to adhere to the nonviolent discipline. The international coordinating committee informed Washington of the exact sites where all peacemakers were – all the probable targets of U.S. missiles and bombers. About 500 peacemakers were prepared to stay for six months or longer, as long-term delegates, while all the rest were to stay from two to four weeks, with others lined up to replace them in a continuous rotation plan.

After three weeks, when it was apparent to Washington that the peacemakers had the commitment, person-power, and logistics to continue the nonviolent campaign indefinitely, the U.S. government announced it had arrived at a diplomatic solution to the problem with the Iraqi and Turkish governments.

Looking back to the future

*T*hat type of scenario was not just drummed up today in someone's head. Mahatma Gandhi articulated it before the 1920s, and began the formation of the *Shanti Sena* (Peace Brigades) in India. He wanted to utilize such a nonviolent army to quell riots between Hindus and Muslims in his country and to counter a feared Japanese invasion there during World War II. He said it was "blasphemy" to say it would not work among nations.

In the 1960s, Martin Luther King, Jr., and James M. Lawson, Jr., drew up plans for a "ten thousand-person nonviolent army" to serve in the civil rights struggle. We know the results. In the 1980s, new developments gave the idea new life. A *Shanti Sena* was formed in India in the

spirit of Gandhi. Witness For Peace (WFP) began its peace team presence in Central America. Peace Brigades International (PBI) began in Central America and Sri Lanka. By the end of the decade Christian Peacemaker Teams (CPT) formed and began to send out teams. The Global Peace Service (GPS) was born as a movement to create structures and prepare large numbers of nonviolent peacemakers for such a worldwide service.

Experiences out in the field

*S*omeone has said that today we are about where Marconi and Edison were soon after the discovery of electricity. We have this awesome power, and have hardly begun to utilize it – the power of nonviolent action in conflict and war zones.

The "experiment in truth" with peace teams up to now has been primarily on a small scale. In the early 1980s a delegation of U.S. citizens stood with the Nicaraguan citizens of Jalapa in protest against the U.S.-armed Contras. A Nicaraguan said, "Because you've been here this week, the Contras haven't attacked." Thus, WFP was born. For eleven years now it has sent delegations to Central America, most often composed of a handful to perhaps a dozen peacemakers. They have found that unarmed international nonviolent peacemakers cut down violence, provide support and advocacy for oppressed people, document human rights abuses, and come home on fire to change U.S. military policy and educate citizens about the issues.

Ernesto Cardinal, Nicaraguan Minister of Culture during the Contra war, said of WFP and other peacemakers: "We need more of these groups and we need them quickly. Wherever they have been there has been no violence."

One form of peace team work is accompaniment. Thousands of Guatemalans had been driven from their homes by the brutal Guatemalan army. The refugees fled to southern Mexico. They have been returning home accompanied by many groups of peacemakers as a protection against military brutality.

Peace Brigades International (PBI) began with the big vision of large peace teams in war zones, but its mission evolved into being a protection for individuals targeted by death squads. Even Nazi-like military and paramilitary groups do not want the world watching them kill such peacemakers. With PBI delegates as "bodyguards," targeted peasant organizers, church workers, human rights lawyers, etc., are not attacked.

Christian Peacemaker Teams has had a continuous presence for over a year in the city of Jeremie, Haiti. Perhaps from three to a dozen peacemakers have been there at any given time. Just this past October, the Chief of Police of the city said of them: "I am ashamed and embarrassed that those foreigners in St. Helens have been doing the work of keeping the people secure for the past year."

The problems of numbers

I was part of the Mir Sada peace team effort in Bosnia in August of 1993. Perhaps as many as 2,500 peacemakers came from all over Europe and North America (plus four from Mexico) to caravan into Sarajevo, which was being shelled by Bosnian Serbs at the time. Thousands of families of the city were inviting us to live for those two weeks in their homes. We quickly found out that many of those coming had not been trained in nonviolence and did not adhere to the structure and discipline required for being part of the project. Organizational structure broke down, and in the heat of war the organizers called off the project. We never got to Sarajevo.

One thing that was clear to me was that there was no lack of courage, ingenuity, and willingness to put up with hardship in a war zone by the majority who were there. I learned that it will take more work to ground individuals in nonviolence and skills, screen applicants, and have a system of deciding who may not go. It will also take more planning to work out the logistics for large groups in a war zone: food, water, communications systems, medical teams and equipment, reconnaissance expertise, etc. One huge problem is that of money: how do you get the funds to organize and maintain such a nonviolent army in a war zone? (How about the $263 billion dollar Pentagon budget?)

Should we use existing structures?

*T*he Global Peace Service (GPS) believes the United Nations should be an integral part of the creation of large peace team ventures. It has structures, money, expertise, connections and global influence. Some think peace teams could evolve out of the peacekeeping structures of the UN. Frank O'Donnell, Chief of the Humanitarian Relief Unit of the U.N. Volunteers, is already setting up the organizational structure to field peace team projects in Bosnia, Burundi, and the Caucasus. Some also urge the involvement of the nongovernmental organizations accredited to the United Nations.

Many in the peace movement, such as myself, do not want to hand over the task to the United Nations. We believe the United Nations is steered by political and economic decisions, mainly for the advantage of the First World nations. The Gulf War is a recent obscene example of that. I believe that citizen peacemaker groups have to create the reality. When there are obvious success stories, the United Nations might imitate it because it works; but citizens must never turn peace team peacemaking over to the United Nations. We need to learn from the United Nations, militaries, and other such groups how to create the logistics to make it possible. We must also find the best ways to fund it all. We don't have those answers – yet.

Goran Backstrand of the Red Cross and Red Crescent Liaison Office at the United Nations said we should use the Red Cross in this peacemaking capacity. He said at the 1993 GPS Consultation: "I think the time has come that this Red Cross/Red Crescent movement shall be more used

... to prevent war.... You should look upon these Red Cross members, the 110 million around the world, as a sleeping giant." What a powerful thing that would be – if the 110 million would become peacemakers as well as humanitarian aid workers.

Domestic peace teams

*D*aniel Alejandrez of Barrios Unidos in Santa Cruz told us at that Global Peace Service Consultation:

Is the GPS important? It's very important right here. It's very important in Watts, Chicago, Santa Cruz, East L.A., Omaha. In all these areas there is violence happening, and we need you. In California we have a war.

In the future a large peace team could be fielded when a serious civil disorder breaks out in an urban area, instead of waiting for a governor to send in the National Guard. [...]

There is one thing I have come to know. Developing a nonviolent heart and learning skills in one area, such as ending neighborhood violence, applies in other areas, such as peace team ventures in overseas war zones. Many individuals could go on short-term delegations in domestic or overseas war zones, utilizing nonviolence skills they learned in the peace movement, neighborhood and school conflict resolution programs, or elsewhere. The dream is great. It is realizable. It will take a lot of work. It is taking shape. And it is exciting!

Previously printed in Synapse,
Winter 1994

FOR MORE INFORMATION:

Following are addresses for some of those who are creating peacemaking organizations and are currently staffing teams to conflicted areas, including Haiti, Guatemala, and the former Yugoslavia:

Christian Peacemaker Teams, PO Box 6508, Chicago, IL 60680-6508

Global Peace Service, c/o Mary Evelen Jagen, 701 East Columbia Ave, Cincinatti, OH 45215

Peace Brigades USA, 343 Dolores St. #228, San Francisco, CA 94110

Peace Brigades Canada, 192 Spadina Ave., Suite 304, Toronto, ON M5T 2C2, Canada

Peace Brigades Europe, 88 rue d'Albanie, B-1060, Bruxelles, Belgium

Peaceworkers, c/o David Hartsough, 721 Shrader St., San Francisco, CA 94117

Witness for Peace, 2201 P St. NW, Rm. 109, Washington, DC 20037

World PeaceMakers, c/o Bill and Betty Price, 11427 Scottsbury Terrace, Germantown, MD 20876

Beyond Borders

Toward a Culture of Peace, Justice, and Sustainability

"Reason, justice and compassion are small cards to play in the world of politics, whether international, national, or tribal, but someone has to go on playing them. If you hold on to your belief in reason and compassion despite all political maneuvering, your efforts may in the end produce results.

"A determined effort to do what seems objectively right may sometimes eventually transcend the vicissitudes of politics."

SIR BRIAN URQUHART
A Life in Peace and War, Widenfeld and Nicholson, 1987, p. 196

"Is there anywhere in the world free from injustice, inequality, and division? Is there anywhere where injustice is not the primary violence breeding all other violence? Where violent protest against injustice, taking to the streets, does not threaten public order and the security of the state? And where it does not meet with violent repression by the authorities?

"...There are also many who want a juster and more humane world but do not believe that force and armed violence are the best way of getting it. Those who choose active nonviolence – the violence of the peaceful – do not need religion or ideology to see that the earth is ruled today by powerful combines, economic, political, technocratic, and military alliances. How would it be possible to beat these lords of the earth in armed combat when they have as their allies arms manufacturers and warmongers?

"...The essential thing is this marvelous discovery: that all over the world, among all races, languages, religions, ideologies, there are men and women born to serve their neighbor, ready for any sacrifice if it helps to build at last a really juster and more humane world. They belong in their own environment but they feel themselves to be members of the human family."

DOM HELDER CAMARA,
The Desert is Fertile,
excerpted from pp.1, 2 and 5

Religions and Good Governance

Religion and World Order

Dr. Patricia M. Mische

Co-founder of Global Education Associates, coordinator of the Religion Council of Project Global 2000, and author of numerous works, including Toward a Human World Order *(with Gerald Mische) and "Toward a Global Spirituality"*

The essay which follows is from the introduction to *Religion and World Order: Proceedings of the Symposium on Religion and Global Governance,* which was held February 4, 1994 in Washington DC.

*I*t is now commonplace to speak of a new world order. But there is not yet a shared vision of what that new world order should be. We live in a transformative moment, but how deep will that transformation go? The task of shaping a new world order has yet to be undertaken. It beckons to us on the road ahead as a challenge and opportunity to create the not yet but possible future.

Thus, the question now before us is not *whether* there will be a new world order, but *what kind* of world order? Based on what values? With what underlying vision and spirit? Guided by what kind of ethical principles and policies? By what systems and structures? Who will shape this new world order? For whose benefit? Will the 21st century see a repeat of the violence, ethnic cleansings, apartheids, genocides, and ecocides of the 20th? Or will we who live on the cusp between two centuries use the openness of this historical moment to develop a more humane, just, peaceful, and ecologically sustainable world order? Can we shape a world order that benefits not only some of us, but all of us; not only those of us living now, but also those yet to come who will inherit the world we create?

These are some of the questions being addressed in Project Global 2000 (PG2000), a partnership of 4 UN agencies and 13 nongovernmental organizations that are collaborating to expand public discourse and action for more humane and ecologically sustainable global systems. People from different walks of life who want to participate in this process can do so through the Project's six program councils: Business, Communications, Education, Health, Youth, and Religion.... *[See sidebar below].*

The need

*T*he 50th anniversary of the United Nations in 1995 provides a special framework and point of reference for exploring the kind of world structures needed for the next century. When the United Nations Charter was drafted and signed in 1945, the world faced a particular set of problems and challenges. Now, 50 years later, there is a new nexus of military, economic, environmental, population, human rights, and health problems that were not anticipated at that time. These problems can only be dealt with through new levels of global cooperation and strengthened global systems.

Existing international institutions were shaped in the shadows of World War II and the Cold War that followed. While the war was still on, Allied powers began planning for a new world order and institutions that would focus on two main concerns: (1) the prevention of future wars, and (2) the reconstruction of war-devastated economies and international monetary relationships. The United Nations was designed to address the first; the World Bank and International Monetary Fund the second.

Those involved in drafting the UN Charter were not aware of work on an atomic bomb. Even when the final document was signed in June, 1945, those who signed it were not among the few select military, scientific, and political leaders who knew of the secret work under way on a new weapon. They did not anticipate Hiroshima and Nagasaki. Nor could they foresee the nuclear arms race and threat of nuclear proliferation that followed. Nor did they anticipate the Cold War and how it would obstruct the UN's effectiveness.

Instead of the new world order based on collective security that had been envisaged, what emerged instead was a bipolar world order – one driven by the arms race and economic and ideological conflict between the military powers aligned on either side of the Cold War divide. This division dominated and obstructed the UN Security Council and some other UN agencies. It dominated international relations. The major powers viewed all their international relations through this screen. An entire generation of national and international policy-makers was trained to think and act within this framework. They, and the institutions they created and maintained, are now ill-prepared to lead their nations or the world toward solutions to the new economic and environmental threats that have emerged.

Also, in 1945 much of the world was still colonized. Great numbers of the world's peoples were under foreign domination and not represented or consulted in the San Francisco negotiations that shaped the UN Charter. Only 51 nation-states participated in determining the principles and structures that would frame the new international organization. In the decades that followed, self-determination and democratization movements spread worldwide. More than 100 new nation-states came into existence, seeking equal representation and decision-making power in the international community.

Environmental concerns were also not on many people's minds in 1945. None of the drafters of the UN Charter or the subsequent Declaration and Covenants on Human Rights foresaw threats to the Earth's air, water, soil, rain forests, and plant and animal species on the scale we do today. They never imagined that human activities would one day threaten global climate change and a growing hole in the Earth's protective ozone layer, or that the trans-boundary shipment or dispersal of toxic and radioactive wastes would become a bone of international contention. Nor did they consider the need to protect the rights of future generations to a healthy environment. Today all these issues are before the world community, but without adequate global structures to respond effectively.

Furthermore, when the Charter was drafted, the underlying assumption was that states were the only legitimate international actors. "We the peoples" were the first words in the UN Charter, but, in fact, "the peoples" were not given a real role or voice. The centrality and ultimate authority of the nation-state was enshrined in the new Charter and other international agreements that followed. Thus, in the new community of nations there was not only a failure of democratization between the member states (some states were more equal than others), there was

also a failure of democratization or representation from below – i.e., a failure to recognize the source of sovereignty or authority in peoples.

At the same time, because states were so determined to hold on to absolute national sovereignty, they failed to delegate sufficient sovereignty or authority at the global level to make the new global institutions really effective in protecting peace and security and human rights. Consequently the UN was left relatively powerless to prevent or effectively deal with acts of aggression and mass violations of human rights.

In the last few years, this state-centric system has been increasingly challenged from both above and below. From below, people's movements and nongovernmental organizations, often acting in solidarity across state borders, are pushing for a greater voice and role in shaping the global policies and structures that affect their lives. There is a growing global civic literacy and sense of global citizenship. This new global literacy is generating demands for democratization of global institutions; demands to let "we the peoples" have a greater role in global governance. At the same time there is growing recognition – including among some heads of states – that, in an interdependent world, national sovereignty is largely an illusion.

Global environmental and economic threats pay little attention to national borders or sovereign banners. If there is to be an adequate response to these trans-boundary

continued on next page

Project Global 2000

*P*roject Global 2000 is an international partnership of organizations and individuals who are combining their expertise, networks, and influence to develop a forum and process in which all sectors of society can participate in the shaping of a more equitable, sustainable, peaceful, and inclusive world order. Global Education Associates, with associates in over 90 countries, serves as the Project's coordinating partner. Project Global 2000 is sponsored by the seventeen international partner organizations which together form its International Partnership Council:

Centre for Our Common Future
Global Education Associates
Global Forum of Spiritual and Parliamentary Leaders
    for Human Survival
International Institute for Rural Reconstruction
International Peace Research Association
Parliamentarians for Global Action
Society for International Development
United Nations Environment Programme (UNEP)
United Nations Children's Fund (UNICEF)
United Nations Educational, Scientific, and Cultural
    Organization (UNESCO)
United Nations Population Fund (UNFPA)
Vienna International Institute for the Study of the Future
World Conference on Religion and Peace
World Federalist Movement
World Federation of United Nations Associations
World Future Studies Federation
World Order Models Project

Many other networks and institutes – secular and religious – are linking through six Program Councils on Education, Health, Religion, Business, Youth and Communications. The Councils provide links with key constituencies whose expertise, networks, and action are vital for resolving today's global-scale, multi-sectoral challenges. They utilize the expertise, programs, and materials of the partners for objectives beyond the reach of organizations acting alone.

The Project has four principle objectives:

• To develop a conceptual and institutional framework for responding to the new challenges of economic and ecological interdependence;

• To develop an ongoing, coordinated global process for research, dialogue, and joint action related to developing ethically-based and effective systems of global governance;

• To produce research/policy documents as tools for analysis, education, and building a multi-sectoral movement for world order policy and systems change;

• To disseminate and use these documents through the partner networks to develop and implement collaborative strategies for achieving such change.

FOR MORE INFORMATION:

Project Global 2000, c/o Global Education Associates,
475 Riverside Drive, Suite 1848, NY, NY 10115 USA;
tel. (212) 870-3290 / fax (212) 870-2729

threats, some sovereignty must be delegated to global-level institutions to make them more effective. The question is not one of totally abandoning the principle of state sovereignty. Rather, it is one of determining how much sovereignty to invest at local, national, and global levels of governance, and for which purposes. There is a need for effective systems at all the appropriate levels where decisions have to be taken – local, national, and global.

Our generation lives in a rare moment of history, a transformative moment. The end of the Cold War, the emergence of global communications systems, the continuing pressure for democratization at all levels – from local and national to global structures – are all signs of a historic window of opportunity. This is a very open and malleable period in history. Old systems are breaking down and new ones are in process of being created.

But this malleability will not last forever. There is a very narrow margin of time to make a difference in the shape of these new systems and structures. For better or worse, new systems and structures will be developed. Once institutionalized they will be very difficult to change. Decisions are being made now that will shape the norms, policies, and systems that govern the world far into the 21st century.

The important role of religious networks

Societies, cultures, and human institutions are shaped not only by political and economic forces, but also by religious and spiritual forces. Throughout history spiritual visionaries and religious leaders have had a powerful influence on the shaping and maintaining of world views and culture. The teachings of Lao Tzu, Confucius, Buddha, Abraham, Moses, Jesus, Paul, Mohammed, and Baha'u'llah, for example, have had a far more profound and lasting effect on thought patterns and lives than have political revolutionaries.

The great world religions include members from different races, nationalities, and ethnic backgrounds. Their loyalties and identities often transcend national boundaries. They are global communities in microcosm, with shared values, beliefs, and social agendas.

Of course, this does not mean that religion always plays a positive role in human interactions. The very features that contribute to a sense of belonging for some may contribute to a sense of exclusion for others. Religious differences have often turned into divisiveness, self-righteousness, and fanaticism, contributing to conflict, hostilities, and sometimes brutality, atrocities, and war. Organized religion has also sometimes been a tool of the state, used to manipulate people's loyalties toward blind obedience and unquestioning allegiance to state power. Or it has sometimes made itself indistinguishable from the state, wielding political power for its own gains. And one does not need to be a Marxist to know that religion has sometimes been an opiate that numbed people into acceptance of hunger, poverty, and injustice and thus impotent to effect change.

But the very fact that organized religion can and has sometimes been such a powerful force in war and human destructiveness also suggests that it can play a powerful role in building and sustaining systems of global peace, human rights, social justice, and ecological balance. Just as there is ample evidence of human destructiveness perpetrated in the name of religion, so is there evidence of the creative force that religion and spirituality have sometimes been in inspiring creative solutions or energizing new directions in history. In his explorations of the rise and fall of great civilizations, the historian Arnold Toynbee found that spirituality and religion played a significant role in bridging the time/space between the fall of one civilization and the rise of another. The "creative minorities" that helped build new civilizations from the ashes of the old were often operating from a strong spiritual impulse. In contrast, civilizations that lost their spiritual core were not long sustained.

If we accept Toynbee's conclusions about the importance of spirituality and religion in the rise and fall of civilizations, then we are led to certain conclusions about the importance of spirituality in the development of any truly new world order or *global* civilization in our time. Inner spiritual growth and transformation may be as, or even more, important than external political changes in global systems. Put another way, inner, spiritual growth, and the development of more democratic, effective, and humane global systems may be inseparable parts of a holistic world order. They develop in conformity to one another and are mutually reinforcing. The nurturing of a deeper, global consciousness, and the harnessing of spiritual and moral energies for a more just and humane world order, are vital aspects of its healthy development.

The more destructive behavior of some members of organized religions needs to be distinguished from the *authentic* spiritual or religious impulse. The Latin word *religare,* from which the word for religion in many Western languages is derived, means "harmony," "to unify," "bind together," "make whole." In Eastern languages the words for religion have the same or similar meanings. In Sanskrit, for example, one of the original meanings for dharma (eternal religion) is "to bind together the whole universe."

Despite some major variations between different religions and religious experience in different historical periods and societies (e.g., belief in gods or a God is not common to all religions), there are some important similarities or commonly shared aspects of religious experience. Spirituality and religion usually include a sense of the numinous or transcendent. They have evolved from a sense that reality is greater than self or the sum total of measurable physical, economic, political, or other phenomena. Religion and spirituality have been defined as our unitive experience – i.e., the experience of "the holy" or "whole," or of the "ultimate," "sacred," and "unknowable." It has also been defined as the human effort to discover some order (cosmos) in disorder (chaos).

Some have described religion as a means by which societies interpret life and develop and reinforce codes of morality and conduct in keeping with those interpretations and the requirements of community life. It has also been described as those beliefs and practices by means of which a group designates and seeks to deal with its deepest problems of meaning, suffering, and injustice.

In these understandings of authentic religion and spirituality, then, world order is not something peripheral or outside the realm of religion, but rather at its deepest core of interest, experience, and concern.

In addition to the meanings, spiritual experience, and moral/ethical considerations religion brings to questions of world order, there is also the power of its networks and institutions. The major world religions have world wide networks of organizations, educational and medical institutions, alumni, research institutes, local communities, and social- and civic- action projects. They can and often do operate across national boundaries with greater ease than many government officials, unbound by the constraints that often tie the hands of governmental actors. They can be major actors in the development of a more peaceful, equitable, and ecologically sustainable world order. They can contribute important scholarship and professional expertise to help resolve some of the grave issues that confront humanity. Their members, programs, and institutions put them in touch with leaders and shapers of public policy. They can be important partners and co-creators in the development of a more humane and just world order.

There is a growing interest by UN agencies and secular NGOs to collaborate with religious institutions and networks to develop a relevant framework of values and leadership for global systemic change. These secular bodies recognize the valuable contributions that religious networks can play in building a viable future. For example, for some years the UN Environment Programme (UNEP) has sponsored the Environmental Sabbath (or Environmental Holy Days) with the cooperation of world religions and spiritual traditions. UNEP also welcomed the cooperation and support of religious NGOs in the process leading to the Earth Summit and in efforts to develop global environmental ethics. UNESCO has sponsored conferences on the Contributions of Religions to the Development of Cultures of Peace. UNICEF and the World Conference on Religion and Peace (WCRP) collaborated in promoting the Convention on the Rights of the Child. Since 1971, the WCRP has been convening regional and global conferences of religious leaders to cooperate in building world peace, and it recently undertook an initiative in collaboration with UN officials to explore ethical guidelines for humanitarian intervention. The Global Forum of Parliamentary and Spiritual Leaders sponsors conferences bringing together governmental and religious leaders to address global issues. And UNICEF and UNESCO are working with Global Education Associates and Project Global 2000 to link religious networks....

The Religion and World Order Program provides a process and context for religious and spiritual communities to reflect on what and how, from their tradition and experience, they can contribute to the values and systemic challenges we face today...to conceptualize and work together for the fundamental elements of a cooperative world order and a global vision that affirms the oneness of the human community and the sacredness of all life.

The Religion and World Order Program

*T*he Religion and World Order Program is an initiative of the Religion Council of Project Global 2000. The program is involving scholars, educators, and community groups from the world's major religious traditions and indigenous religions in a framework and process to work together with secular and religious non-governmental organizations and UN agencies. This link is designed to increase public discourse and concerted action for policies and systems commensurate with the problems and opportunities of today's interdependent world.

Objectives of the Program

- Create a process for religious and spiritual communities to reflect upon the contributions their traditions, scriptures and networks can make to a shared global ethic and to the creation of systems of global governance.

- Produce reflection-action documents that will spell out the above contributions and formulate proposals for world order policy and systems change.

- Link human and institutional resources with those of other religions, secular NGOs, and UN agencies in collaborative research, education, publications, leadership, networking....

Program

Working groups from different religions, spiritual traditions, and indigenous peoples are holding consultations on the contribution their respective traditions, scriptures, teachings, and networks can make to a shared global ethic and to systems of global governance that transcend national boundaries. Through a participatory process, each group will produce a reflection-action document for circulation and use by their members to 1) raise consciousness on the need to redefine security and sovereignty in the context of global interdependence, and 2) promote involvement in ecuation programs and commemorative events being planned for the United Nations' 50 anniversary in 1995.

The documents will not address the question "whether there will be a new world order," but rather, "What kind of world order? Based on what values? Guided by what ethical principles and policies? Organized according to what systems and structures? Who will shape this new world order? for whose benefits?"

At an international conference in the fall of 1995, the perspectives and proposals of the documents will be shared with scholars, policy-makers, representatives of UN agencies, and leaders in education, religion, business, health, youth, communication, and civic organizations. Participants will initiate a process to produce a multi-religious document on world order. They will develop strategies and prepare programs by which diverse religious institutions and networks can collaborate among themselves and with secular organizations and UN agencies, through the year 2000, for strengthened, democratic and equitable systems of global governance.

Guideline Questions for Project Global 2000

1. Working Toward a Shared Global Ethic

The creation of a peaceful, equitable, and sustainable future is, at its heart, as much an ethical and spiritual matter as it is a matter for economic and social policy and legal systems. In today's interdependent world, there is a need for strong ethical foundations for policies and systems at global as well as local and national levels. The new global-scale challenges that are accompanying the rapid growth of global economic and ecological interdependence require that we now move toward a shared ethic that, while respecting national, cultural, and religious differences, provides a common framework for responding to global challenges. What values and principles can your sacred texts, ethical systems, teachings, traditions, history, and lived experience contribute to the development of such a shared global ethic? Specifically, how can these values and principles address the following issues?

- **a. peace and security**
- **b. economic and social justice**
- **c. human rights**
- **d. cultural identity and integrity**
- **e. ecological well-being**

2. Working Toward Just World Systems

Many transboundary problems and forces now surpass the competencies of national institutions and policy-makers. The question before the human community is not whether there will be a new world order. Rather, it is what kind of world order? On what values will it be based? Who will be its designers and decision-makers? Will it be a fragmented order of economic, ethnic, religious, and armed conflict? Will it be controlled by the economically and militarily powerful? Or will it be a genuinely participatory order, governed by effective international law and based on equity and economic and ecological sustainability? Building upon the values and principles of your religious faith tradition, what recommendations would you make in the following areas?

a. Global civilization

Globalization has both positive and negative aspects. From the perspective of your religious values and principles, what should be the criteria for a true global civilization? For a global civic society? For global citizenship?

b. Global structures and systems

What global policies, systems, and instruments would be consistent with your values and principles? Specifically, how could the policies, systems, and instruments of your preferred world order address the above issues?

c. Local initiatives

The local and global are deeply interrelated. What "bottom-up" or local initiatives can be combined with transnational initiatives to create policies and systems capable of fulfilling your desired world order?

d. Balancing tension

The achievement of a more peaceful, equitable, and sustainable future depends upon balancing the following tensions. What insights can your religious tradition give on how to balance these areas of tension?

- individual good versus the common good
- rights versus responsibilities
- rights and needs of current versus future generations
- role of the private versus public (governance) sectors
- market forces versus government institutions
- local and national versus international sovereignties
- economic versus environmental needs
- long-term versus short-term objectives

e. Religious resources

What particular expertise, institutions, networks, and other resources can your religious community utilize to participate in the building of a just world order?

- educational systems
- research institutions
- institutions of higher learning
- media and communication networks
- publications and media materials
- future studies and modeling of alternatives
- community-based networks and programs
- professional associations

3. Collaborating with United Nations and its Specialized Agencies

a. What do you judge to be the strengths and weaknesses of the current United Nations system in relationship to our ethical concern for a just world order?

b. What recommendations would you offer to make the United Nations and its specialized and affiliated agencies more effective instruments for a just world order? (Please specify program areas and agencies.)

c. In what ways have members and organizations of your religious community been cooperating with United Nations organizations and programs?

d. In what additional ways could your religious community collaborate with the UN and its agencies to make them more effective instruments for a just world order?

4. Developing a Multi-Religious Movement

a. In what ways can your religious community incorporate world-systems thinking into educational programs for its constituencies?

b. What kind of multi-religious initiatives do you recommend for advancing effective world systems that are more just, humane, and ecologically balanced?

FOR MORE INFORMATION:

(Call to confirm prices and availability of items: 1-212-870-3290)

"Religion and World Order: Proceedings of the Symposium on Religion and Global Governance." The complete proceedings may be ordered for $6.00 if mailed in US, $7.00 outside US.

"Toward a Global Spirituality," by Patricia M. Mische ($3.00)

"Information Packet for Religion and World Order Program" ($3.00)

"Leadership Institute: Linking Religion, Education, and Health to Forge our Global Future" ($3.00)

Order from: Global Education Associates, 475 Riverside Drive, Suite 1848, New York, NY 10115

The Contribution of Religions to a Culture of Peace

UNESCO

In recent years the United Nations Educational, Scientific, and Cultural Organization (UNESCO) has taken new interest in the role of religions, churches, and spiritual traditions in promoting a culture of peace. The Programme for an April 1993 conference on this topic sponsored by UNESCO noted the roles that religions may play in conflictive situations:

> Looking at international problems, it is easy to find religious components in existing wars and conflicts. Religions are often used to legitimate the ideological, economic or political interests which are the most immediate cause of conflicts. But religions can be of great help in the creation of a culture of peace that would make it possible to prevent conflicts, defuse violence and build structures that are fairer and freer. [...]

> Religions can remind us of fundamental aspects of human dignity, of openness to others, of the real priorities in individual lives and the lives of all peoples. Religions can encourage us on the paths of generosity and cooperation. Religion is a great source for insight and ethical courage.

The following materials are excerpted from a statement distributed by UNESCO in preparation for a meeting held in Barcelona from 12 to 18 December 1994. Following the statement is a Declaration that was refined and signed by the delegates to the meeting who, while acting in their individual capacities, are also influential religious or cultural leaders. UNESCO will present the Declaration to the United Nations General Assembly and promote it as part of UNESCO's programme for 1995, the International Year of Tolerance.

In 1993 UNESCO held a first meeting on "The Contribution of Religions to the Culture of Peace"....The meeting was a great success as regards the quality of the ideas and the testimonies presented and, especially, as regards the spirit of peace in which it took place. Although there were people from highly conflictive areas like the Balkans, the Middle East, Cambodia, and Tibet, we lived days of very sincere and very fraternal communication....

In view of the success of the 1993 meeting, UNESCO has decided to hold a second meeting on the same subject with the intention of continuing the dialogue begun in Barcelona and preparing a public declaration on the contribution by religions to the culture of peace.

One of the priorities UNESCO has set itself for the coming years is to promote reflection on the cultural changes that make it possible to imagine and encourage new concepts and actions for peace. War seems more meaningless every day. In the past, wars and violence were considered natural and inevitable. Today, we know that more rational and human alternatives for resolving conflicts are available to us. But we do not yet have the ideas, beliefs, symbols, and methods we need to orient culture as whole towards peace. In many respects, finance and industry are designed by war, science is committed to developing weapons, and the media provide coverage of war and fail to explain the paths of peace. The

whole of culture needs to be reoriented and a new consensus reached on the possibility of peace, the foundations of peace and the responsibility of peace. UNESCO wants to provide the setting, the drive, and the consensus for reflections on the culture of peace. It is therefore once more inviting personalities from the religious world and from the world of culture to contribute to defining the culture of peace and above all to defining themselves publicly as builders for peace.

UNESCO is pleased that amongst other events taking place after the Barcelona meeting in 1993 was the important meeting held in Chicago by the Parliament of the World's Religions which on 4 September 1993 passed an Initial Declaration *Towards a Global Ethic,* which was signed by very many leaders of the great universal religious traditions. The Initial Declaration is an unprecedented step towards establishing a shared ethic for all religions. It is an important landmark in the process of establishing an effective and complete religious peace.

The meeting planned for December 1994 in Barcelona has modest aims. The intention is to reflect only on the question of peace and to concentrate on cultural aspects of peace and on the relationship between the culture of peace and the wisdom of the great religious traditions...

UNESCO, which is an organization of states forming a specialized agency within the United Nations, believes that the culture of peace is something which can only be attained with the cooperation of a large number of people. The great religious traditions can contribute enormously to creating the culture of peace. Other non-governmental organizations can also make a decisive contribution. The Barcelona meeting is to be a continuation of the dialogue between representative figures from institutions which must take their share of responsibility in the move towards peace.

The results of the Barcelona meeting will be collected by UNESCO in the context of the programme for the International Year of Tolerance. The United Nations General Assembly has declared 1995 the United Nations Year of Tolerance and has entrusted UNESCO with the job of coordinating the programme of events. The Barcelona meeting will be a unique opportunity for the great religious traditions to join the International Year of Tolerance and the 50th anniversary celebrations.

UNESCO's founding document includes reflections on peace as the purpose behind the United Nations and UNESCO: "Since wars are born in the minds of men, it is in the minds of men that the bastions of peace must be built."

For many human beings peace is still an impossible dream. In 1993 and 1994 the war has continued against Croatia and Bosnia, violence has been unleashed in Rwanda and many countries have suffered, publicly or in silence, the effects of intolerance, discrimination, and military occupation. Religions can always take the side of justice, nonviolence, and peace. They can do so because they love truth, are free and have a great spiritual strength. At the Barcelona meeting, at the invitation of UNESCO, they will demonstrate this publicly.

Declaration on the Role of Religion in the Promotion of a Culture of Peace

We, participants in the meeting, "The Contribution by Religions to the Culture of Peace," organized by UNESCO and the Centre UNESCO de Catalunya, which took place in Barcelona from 12 to 18 December, 1994,

Deeply concerned with the present situation of the world, such as increasing armed conflicts and violence, poverty, social injustice, and structures of oppression;

Recognizing that religion is important in human life;

DECLARE:

OUR WORLD

1. We live in a world in which isolation is no longer possible. We live in a time of unprecedented mobility of peoples and intermingling of cultures. We are all interdependent and share an inescapable responsibility for the well-being of the entire world.

2. We face a crisis which could bring about the suicide of the human species or bring us a new awakening and a new hope. We believe that peace is possible. We know that religion is not the sole remedy for all the ills of humanity, but it has an indispensable role to play in this most critical time.

3. We are aware of the world's cultural and religious diversity. Each culture represents a universe in itself and yet it is not closed. Cultures give religions their language, and religions offer ultimate meaning to each culture. Unless we recognize pluralism and respect diversity, no peace is possible. We strive for the harmony which is at the very core of peace.

4. We understand that culture is a way of seeing the world and living in it. It also means the cultivation of those values and forms of life which reflect the world-views of each culture. Therefore neither the meaning of peace nor of religion can be reduced to a single and rigid concept, just as the range of human experience cannot be conveyed by a single language.

5. For some cultures, religion is a way of life, permeating every human activity. For others it represents the highest aspirations of human existence. In still others, religions are institutions that claim to carry a message of salvation.

6. Religions have contributed to the peace of the world, but they have also led to division, hatred, and war. Religious people have too often betrayed the high ideals they themselves have preached. We feel obliged to call for sincere acts of repentance and mutual forgiveness, both personally and collectively, to one another, to humanity in general, and to Earth and all living beings.

PEACE

7. Peace implies that love, compassion, human dignity, and justice are fully preserved.

8. Peace entails that we understand that we are all interdependent and related to one another. We are all individually and collectively responsible for the common good, including the well-being of future generations.

9. Peace demands that we respect Earth and all forms of life, especially human life. Our ethical awareness requires setting limits to technology. We should direct our efforts towards eliminating consumerism and improving the quality of life.

10. Peace is a journey – a never-ending process.

COMMITMENT

11. We must be at peace with ourselves; we strive to achieve inner peace through personal reflection and spiritual growth, and to cultivate a spirituality which manifests itself in action.

12. We commit ourselves to support and strengthen the home and family as the nursery of peace.

In homes and families, communities, nations and the world:

13. We commit ourselves to resolve or transform conflicts without using violence, and to prevent them through education and the pursuit of justice.

14. We commit ourselves to work towards a reduction in the scandalous economic differences between human groups and other forms of violence and threats to peace, such as waste of resources, extreme poverty, racism, all types of terrorism, lack of caring, corruption, and crime.

15. We commit ourselves to overcome all forms of discrimination, colonialism, exploitation, and domination and to promote institutions based on shared responsibility and participation. Human rights, including religious freedom and the rights of minorities, must be respected.

16. We commit ourselves to assure a truly humane education for all. We emphasize education for peace, freedom, and human rights, and religious education to promote openness and tolerance.

17. We commit ourselves to a civil society which respects environmental and social justice. This process begins locally and continues to national and trans-national levels.

18. We commit ourselves to work towards a world without weapons and to dismantle the industry of war.

RELIGIOUS RESPONSIBILITY

19. Our communities of faith have a responsibility to encourage conduct imbued with wisdom, compassion, sharing, charity, solidarity, and love; inspiring one and all to choose the path of freedom and responsibility. Religions must be a source of helpful energy.

20. We will remain mindful that our religions must not identify themselves with political, economic, or social powers, so as to remain free to work for justice and peace. We will not forget that confessional political regimes may do serious harm to religious values as well as to society. We should distinguish fanaticism from religious zeal.

21. We will favor peace by countering the tendencies of individuals and communities to assume or even to teach that they are inherently superior to others. We recognize and praise the nonviolent peacemakers. We disown killing in the name of religion.

22. We will promote dialogue and harmony between and within religions, recognizing and respecting the search for truth and wisdom that is outside our religion. We will establish dialogue with all, striving for a sincere fellowship on our earthly pilgrimage.

APPEAL

23. Grounded in our faith, we will build a culture of peace based on nonviolence, tolerance, dialogue, mutual understanding, and justice. We call upon the institutions of our civil society, the United Nations system, governments, governmental and non-governmental organizations, corporations, and the mass media, to strengthen their commitments to peace and to listen to the cries of the victims and the dispossessed. We call upon the different religious and cultural traditions to join hands together in this effort, and to cooperate with us in spreading the message of peace.

SIGNED ——————————————————————

ADDRESS————————————————————————

To add your signature, send a signed copy of this pledge to: UNESCO, Mallorca, 285, Barcelona 08037 Spain

Setting Our Leaders Free
from the National Security Straitjacket

Gerald F. Mische

President and Co-founder, Global Education Associates, and co-author (with Pat Mische) of Toward a Human World Order

Jerry Mische argues that global economic competition has become the primary consideration among nation-states and that it dominates all international affairs. This condition requires our priority attention because, despite their intentions and best efforts, governmental and international leaders are locked into the logic of this "national security straitjacket." It constrains their options for responsive leadership even as its impact is enormously counterproductive on the many crises faced by people worldwide.

We are witnessing the birth of a new era. In this final decade of the 20th century the human community is passing through an historic transition. Unprecedented dangers and opportunities are emerging at the same time as the separate histories of diverse peoples are converging toward a common future.

What direction the future takes – breakdown or breakthrough – depends upon asking the right questions and then framing them properly within the context of global economic, governmental, and ecological interdependence.

The final five years of this century are pivotal. They offer a compelling challenge to begin a global dialogue and partnerships which can determine clear policy directions. Peoples from all countries, cultures, and sectors of society must become involved as full partners in this task, for no nation, ideology, culture, or religion has produced the final answers. The North and South, East and West, national leaders and local leaders, world religions and indigenous religions – all have something important to contribute to the shaping of a global community. The peoples of the world together must learn the essential elements of the next phase of human civilization.

We must begin by developing a framework for understanding and managing the multiple dimensions and complex relationships in this economically and ecologically interdependent world. This framework must be open and non-dogmatic, encouraging serious dialogue by individuals of widely differing orientations to join in an organized search for solutions to complex problems and strategies for cooperative action.

Underlying that framework, however, must be the recognition that present global realities call for a fundamental *redefinition of national security and sovereignty*. Traditional concepts of national security and sovereignty are based upon the possibility of autonomy, self-sufficiency, and self-determination, protected by military power. In today's interdependent world, however, this possibility no longer exists. Global economic, technological, and ecological forces are more powerful than any nation. Many intractable national problems are inextricably intertwined with these larger global forces.

A structural straitjacket

Much has been said about the "powerlessness of people." Too little attention, however, has been given to the growing powerlessness of national leaders. Yet, success in overcoming the former depends on confronting the reality of the latter.

The powerlessness of which I speak is the growing powerlessness of national political leaders and institutions to cope with rampant global economic, monetary, and ecological forces that are profoundly impacting domestic priorities. Faced with new challenges and threats to national security emerging from economic and monetary interdependence, national leaders are increasingly compelled to give priority to corporate/national goals designed to compete in today's survival-of-the-fittest global economy.

With the growth of economic and monetary interdependence, the *export market* has emerged as *a primary factor in national security*. In today's global marketplace, the highest priority for all nations has become the mobilization of their economies to produce goods for the world market, yet national monetary and fiscal policies are increasingly inadequate. We are operating without an effective institutional framework for setting collaborative policies to deal with the new global economic and monetary forces.

Economic options which would enhance the overall well-being of the mass of citizens are overlooked or postponed since they do not contribute to the corporate goals of economic and military power that are inherent in today's global arena. It is not surprising, therefore, that policies to foster family farms, diversified agriculture, small-scale business, labor-intensive industry, revitalizing urban decay, and adequate health delivery systems remain on the back burner of national policy agendas.

Even the best intentioned of national leaders are experiencing an increasing powerlessness to move responsive, environmentally sustainable, and socially just priorities to the top of national agendas. The structural logic of the present nation-state system and the fierce global competition among nations compel national leaders to give special privileges to large agribusiness interests, hi-tech and capital intensive industries, multinational conglomerates, and others capable of competing for foreign currency and markets.

Identifying this "national security straitjacket" can reduce polarization between diverse constituencies. The agendas of blacks and whites, men and women, young and old, capitalist and socialist, North and South are all constrained by the current nation-state system. All of us share a common stake in working together for policies and systems that are capable of loosening the straitjacket, because **this loosening is the precondition for a secure and sustainable future.**

This straitjacket will not simply disappear with the election of leaders who are more competent or more motivated by concern for the common good. Nor will it give way to a "better ideology," or to a feminist, humanist, or even to an authentically religious worldview that a "different kind" of woman or man might provide as head of state. Personal conversions of our leaders' or voters' hearts will not subdue it. And it won't be loosened by a "nurturing" paradigm or a "new" framework of values or a global ethic.

It is not that the above changes wouldn't make a difference. They can, and they do. But even if all of them were realized, the current nation-state system and its logic would remain, continuing to provide the dominant criteria for public policy. Without the development of systems of global governance based on the principle of subsidiarity, the national security straitjacket will continue to narrow and define the options available to national and local leaders.

Due to incomplete analysis, the diverse issue-based constituencies attribute too much of their powerlessness to their traditional "enemies." In fact, these all share a common powerlessness as victims of the present nation-state system. Strategies for more humane and effective systems of governance – designed to loosen the straitjacket – can become a common agenda of mutual self-interest.

A Birthing Process

The Chinese concept of "crisis" can help us to interpret our time with a realism that transcends both paralyzing pessimism and naive optimism. Two characters express the concept: *wei*, meaning danger, to express the possibility of breakdown; and *chi*, meaning "opportunity," to express the possibility of breakthrough.

Today's global-scale crises are not only signs of old institutions breaking down, but also a crisis of growth – birth pains of a human community struggling toward a viable and sustainable future. The birth image is apt, for the healthy delivery of our shared future is not without pain and turmoil. If the birth passage remains rigid, the new life – and that of the total human community – is endangered.

Our task, then, is not to fight against today's pain and crises, merely reacting to symptoms; that would make present structures more rigid than ever. It is rather to recognize the positive pregnancy of our times and to prepare the way for a viable human future. Our labor now is to create the consciousness and the structures of global governance capable of addressing today's global-scale crises and opportunities.

We must be open to questioning and rethinking, no matter how hard we have worked to achieve the security of analytic certainties. True leadership seeks to break out of ideological rigidities and the complacencies of cultural, religious, and academic boundaries. Today, all issues must be properly framed within the context of global interdependence; it is only out of this framework that a more just, humane and sustainable future can be born.

A window of opportunity

Leaders and people alike are being challenged to go beyond denouncing systems to participating in the development of realistic alternatives. The 50th anniversary of the United Nations and the coming millennial commemorations provide important opportunities for religious and spiritual networks to join forces with global networks of local communities, schools, universities, and their alumni. By forging ongoing partnerships with UN agencies and secular, nongovernmental organizations, these sectors can provide leadership in shaping alternatives that reflect principles of good governance.

The growing vision of our time is a vision of our common future and mutual dependence on one earth. Effective change begins in the imagination, yet has the potential of redirecting the course of history. When the limits of old, restrictive assumptions are broken by the advent of a broader, more holistic and realistic framework for perceiving our current situation, we are liberated for new initiatives. Leaders are empowered and the future is seen as open.

An earlier and more detailed version of this essay was printed in *Breakthrough*, Fall '87/Spring '88

The Causes of Peace Failure

It is now widely recognized that the present plight of civilization is, in the last analysis, due to our spiritual anarchy and our spiritual impotence. The power, which new and in the last resort destructive ideologies exert over the minds of millions of men today, has forced us to face in a new way the problem of the basic presuppositions of all common living. It is now clear that no durable international settlement can possibly be arrived at unless the nations accept certain common convictions and common standards as the basis of their own life and of their relations with each other.

All schemes for a future international order depend for their realization on this presupposition of a willingness to live together in harmony, which itself depends upon some underlying unity of spirit. It is the absence of any such basis which has brought civilization to the brink of catastrophe.

As it becomes increasingly evident that the crisis of Western civilization is in the last resort a spiritual crisis which is due to the absence of great common and compelling convictions, and that none of the ideologies which are at present in control can pretend to bring about a true integration, men everywhere are searching for a new universalism. It is rightly believed that international society has become so interdependent that it will only be able to live in a harmonious and orderly fashion if some fundamental common convictions concerning man and society are held by all nations, however different they may remain in all other respects....

The Causes of Peace Failure, 1919-1939, the report of the International Consultative Group of Geneva, which met in 1940 sponsored by the Carnegie Endowment for International Peace; published in *International Conciliation*, No. 363, October 1940

A Call to Remembrance and Renewal

Campaign 1995

1995 is a particularly momentous year for commemorations and reflection on a remarkable series of half-century anniversaries. These include the 50th anniversaries of the liberation of Auschwitz, the death of Franklin Roosevelt, the founding of the United Nations, the first use of nuclear weapons, the establishment of the Nuremberg War Crimes Tribunal, and creation of the World Bank.

Campaign 1995 was established as a project-oriented network and collaboration of individuals and organizations to help shape public consciousness and action. The document from which the following materials are excerpted was published in its *New Beginnings* newsletter (February 1994).

January 26 – Human rights

The 50th anniversary of the liberation of Auschwitz, the most dramatic example of gross violations of human rights, should mark the beginning of a new period of reflection and rededication to the goal of ending all human rights abuse. [...]

In Angola, Bosnia, Cambodia, El Salvador, Kurdistan, and elsewhere, the strategy of intentionally destroying a defined group of people based on religion, race, political views, or national origin has been brutally replicated. These actions reflect a belief that human life is not of ultimate value in the geopolitical world – that national, economic, or military interests are more important than people. We see the spiritual and moral effects of this belief in the culture of violence in our society, in the abuse of women and children, and in the rise of hate crime. [...]

April 12 & December 27 – Economic and environmental justice

The anniversaries of the death of Franklin D. Roosevelt on 12 April and of the signing of the Bretton Woods agreement on 27 December can be occasions for a rededication to the dream of "freedom from want" – social and economic justice for all. The end of the Cold War provides an opportunity to achieve a new, more equitable international distribution of economic resources, and to alter spending priorities from preparation for war to meeting human needs. [...]

New approaches to international economics are imperative. The institutions of the World Bank and the International Monetary Fund have too often been the means of widening the economic gap between the industrialized "North" and the underdeveloped "South." [...]

These economic policies should be carried out in ways that protect rather than endanger the Earth's environment.... This means integrating principles of environmental sustainability into personal consumption and into every economic, political, and social policy decision....

June 26 & October 24 – United Nations

The Charter of the United Nations, signed 26 June 1945 and entering into force on 24 October 1945, expressed the vision of a world free from the horrors of fascism and world war. "We the peoples," it began, are determined to:

- save succeeding generations from the scourge of war;
- reaffirm faith in fundamental human rights, in the dignity

and worth of the human person, in the equal rights of men and women and of nations large and small;

- establish conditions under which justice and respect for the obligations arising from treaties and other sources of international law can be maintained;
- promote social progress and better standards of life.

In the past 50 years, these noble goals have been ignored more than honored. Major powers, including the United States, have often misused the UN for their own national purposes....We must reexamine the type of international organization needed in the post-Cold-War era. [...]

July 16, August 6 & 9 – The nuclear threat and disarmament

The 50th anniversaries of the first nuclear explosions are important and obvious moments for reflection, sorrow, and rededication to removing the threat of nuclear war from human affairs. The use of nuclear weapons against the Japanese people was a starting point of the Cold War, helping to shape the past 50 years as an era of violence and armed confrontation. With the end of the Cold War, a process of denuclearization has begun that can lead to the abolition of weapons of mass destruction....[T]he movement for disarmament should become an irresistible global force. [...]

The nuclear states must fulfill their obligation under Article VI of the Non-Proliferation Treaty to "pursue negotiations in good faith...on general and complete disarmament under strict and effective international control." Disarmament of the existing nuclear powers is the condition for preventing the spread of weapons to other countries.

November 20 – International law

The anniversary of the opening of the Nuremberg War Crimes Tribunal can dramatize a new commitment to eliminating all forms of militarism, crimes against humanity, and threats to the peace. The institutions of international law must be bolstered and the law itself strengthened. The decisions of the International Court of Justice should be binding on all nations, including the major states, and the mechanisms for enforcing international law must be strengthened. [...]

1995 – A year of commitment

[...] A process of fundamental change in consciousness is possible only through serious reflection and dedicated action. Such a process, we believe, can begin in 1995 if we join together in a commitment to achieve a turning point for human survival. By endorsing this Call, we pledge ourselves to that commitment and call upon all those who share this goal to join with us to develop a new vision and a new citizens' movement to achieve it.

FOR MORE INFORMATION:

Campaign 1995 Committee
1601 Connecticut Avenue, NW, 5th Floor,
Washington, DC 20009USA; tel. 202-234-9382 / fax 202-387-7915

Or contact Fourth Freedom Forum (see Chapter 42).

The United Nations at 50

How It All Began

Provided by the Fiftieth Anniversary Secretariat, United Nations, New York, as part of an information package

Since 1945, the organization has grown and changed considerably, though not enough for some. Most observers have agreed that the commemoration is not a time for uncritical celebration, but rather for a review of the UN's strengths and successes as well as its weaknesses and failures; numerous reform movements will assist anyone looking for details. We also note the increasing influence of non-governmental organizations, including representatives of the world's religions and spiritual traditions.

Inter-Allied Declaration

Signed in London on 12 June 1941, the Inter-Allied Declaration "to work together, with other free peoples, both in war and peace" was the first of a series of steps which led to the establishment of the United Nations.

Atlantic Charter

On 14 August 1941, President Franklin Delano Roosevelt of the United States and Prime Minister Winston Churchill of the United Kingdom proposed a set of principles for international collaboration in maintaining peace and security. The document, signed during a meeting "somewhere at sea", came to be known as the Atlantic Charter.

Declaration by United Nations

On 1 January 1942, the representatives of 26 nations that were fighting against the Axis proclaimed their support for the Atlantic Charter by signing the "Declaration by United Nations". This document marked the first official use of the term "United Nations," which was suggested by President Roosevelt.

Moscow and Teheran Conferences

In a declaration signed in Moscow on 30 October 1943, the governments of the USSR, UK, US, and China called for an early establishment of an international organization to maintain peace and security. That goal was reaffirmed at the meeting of the leaders of the US, USSR, and UK at Teheran on 1 December 1943.

Dumbarton Oaks Conference

The first blueprint of the UN was prepared at a conference held at a mansion known as Dumbarton Oaks in Washington, DC. During two phases of meetings which ran from 21 September through 7 October 1944, the representatives of the USSR, UK, US, and China agreed on the aims, structure, and functioning of a world organization.

Yalta Conference

On 11 February 1945, following their meetings at Yalta, President Roosevelt, Prime Minister Churchill, and Premier Stalin declared their resolve to establish "a general international organization to maintain peace and security."

San Francisco Conference

Beginning on 25 April 1945, delegates of 50 nations met in San Francisco for the conference known officially as the United Nations Conference on International Organization. The delegates drew up the 111-article Charter which was adopted unanimously on 25 June 1945. The next day they signed it in the auditorium of the Veterans' Memorial Hall.

Background on the Founding of the United Nations

From information provided by the UN50 Committee of San Francisco, a non-partisan organization founded in 1992, comprised of leading civic organizations

*O*n April 25, 1945, with World War II winding down in Europe and Asia, and with the American public still reeling from the recent death of President Roosevelt, delegations from 50 nations met in San Francisco as part of the United Nations Conference on International Organization (UNCIO). With the end of the war in sight, their mission was to lay the foundation for a new global institution which could serve to guide the world community to a more peaceful future. Over the next two months, 282 delegates spent thousands of hours hammering out agreements that culminated in the signing of the United Nations Charter at the War Memorial's Herbst Theatre on June 26, 1945.

The role of non-governmental organizations

The efforts of the delegates were paralleled by representatives from forty-two U.S. citizens' groups (NGOs) invited by the US government to serve as consultants to the negotiators. Through involving a wide range of citizens' groups, the U.S. hoped indirectly to engage the American public's support for the proposed United Nations (UN). The government had learned a valuable lesson from its experience with the League of Nations which had suffered from widespread apathy on the part of the public. This time the UN would have the backing of the nation – not just its government.

Historical accounts of the UNCIO, however, indicate that NGO's played an even more important role of monitoring the negotiations, caucusing with delegates, and offering draft texts on critical sections of the Charter. It was due largely to their efforts that the Commission on Human Rights was created and that the Economic and Social Council was elevated to status of parity with the Security Council and the General Assembly. Among the NGOs represented were: American Association of University Women, American Federation of Labor, American Jewish Committee, Catholic Association for International Peace, Church Peace Union, Federal Council of Churches of Christ, National Catholic Welfare Conference, National Association for the Advancement of Colored People, League of Women Voters, and Rotary International.

San Francisco, then and now

When the delegates and journalists arrived in San Francisco for the conference they saw a city strained by its role as a transit point for troops and materiel moving to and from the Pacific front. In fact, things were so busy that the city, alone among the 30 under consideration as the site of the conference, neglected to send the State Department the logistical information it had requested. Nevertheless, the city was informed in February that it had been selected as the site for the UNCIO and had but two months to prepare. As host, the city had to tend to the needs of not only the delegates but the 2,500 staff, 2,600 journalists, and several hundred citizen consultants. By all accounts, the city rose to the challenge and met with efficiency and good humor all of their collective needs.

As a result of the goodwill generated by San Francisco's role as host, President Truman offered the use of the Presidio as the site for the UN's headquarters. However, the British and Soviet governments declined, citing long travel times.

The absence of an official UN presence, has not, however, inhibited the interest of Bay Area residents in international affairs and the work of the UN. San Francisco is home to a consular community that represents more than 60 nations. In addition, the Bay Area contains one of the nation's richest communities of public interest and educational institutions concerned with international affairs, including human rights, environment, and cultural exchange. All of these sectors will be invited to participate in UN50's programs.

An Overview of the UN at 50

From information provided by the Fiftieth Anniversary Secretariat in New York

"We the Peoples of the United Nations... United for a Better World"

The United Nations Fiftieth Anniversary in 1995 coincides with a turning point in history that calls for serious rethinking of the ways the international organization deals with development, peace and security. The Fiftieth Anniversary is therefore a time not only for reflection on the achievements and difficult lessons of the past, but also for charting a course for the next century.

There is much to celebrate. When the Charter of the United Nations came into force on 24 October 1945, it heralded the birth of the United Nations as a universal international organization created to maintain world peace and security and to work for social progress. Although its failures and frustrations have received widespread attention, its successes in economic and social development, decolonization, human rights, disarmament and peace-keeping have clearly made a difference in the second half of this century. A forum for all nations, the UN represents the highest aspirations of the world's peoples for a world free of war, poverty, repression and suffering. It remains a priceless inheritance.

To carry out its mandate, the UN must have basic resources. It requires not only the political and financial backing of Member States, but also needs the support and understanding of its larger constituencies – the general public, non-governmental organizations, and the business community. The Fiftieth Anniversary commemoration seeks to deepen this understanding and commitment and to inspire a new generation of UN supporters.

A year-long commemoration

The UN General Assembly established a Preparatory Committee for the 50th Anniversary chaired by Ambassador Richard Butler (Australia). The year-long program of events, including many special celebrations in San Francisco during June, will culminate with a special commemorative meeting of the General Assembly in New York, attended by world leaders, on 24 October 1995. That meeting is expected to adopt a Declaration reaffirming the principles of the UN Charter and setting guidelines for the future work of the Organization.

A UNSO Secretariat, headed by Special Adviser to the Secretary-General Gillian Martin-Sorensen, will coordinate the worldwide observances, serving as a catalyst and a clearinghouse for global projects, information, and program.

Global participation

The Anniversary provides the opportunity for the UN to reach out to broad constituencies, new and old, across national, political, and social boundaries, bridging gaps of understanding and information regarding its work. UN50-related events, projects, and studies are designed to inform and encourage debate on vital issues.

Participants include:

- Every Member State, each asked by the Secretary-General to establish a UN50 National Committee to encourage and sponsor commemorative activities.
- The UN System, the Secretariat, every UN agency, fund, regional commission, and local office, taking up the challenge to explain their work and support global and local initiatives.
- The March 1995 World Summit on Social Development in Copenhagen and the September 1995 World Conference on Women in Beijing.
- United Nations Associations, through their activities in 87 countries.
- Non-governmental organizations, vital links between the UN and their world-wide constituencies.
- Parliamentarian groups, such as the Inter-Parliamentary Union, Parliamentarians for Global Action, and the Global Committee of Parliamentarians on Population and Development.
- The business community, contributing resources, expertise, and creativity as a new partner in the effort to support the commemoration.
- The academic world, preparing conferences, debates, and symposia on the UN.
- The cultural world, celebrating with music, art, and drama.
- People in all countries, in all walks of life, in religious, civic, and other organizations, encouraged to observe this Anniversary in their own way.

Funding

Fiftieth Anniversary programs and events are not funded from regular UN budget sources. A Trust Fund for the 50th Anniversary has been created to receive donations from corporations, foundations, individuals, and governments. Many programs and events are being underwritten by governments and NGOs.

Message from Boutros Boutros-Ghali, Secretary General of the United Nations

20 October 1994

"Just in the time since I took office as Secretary-General of the United Nations, changes in world affairs of vast significance have been recognized. Everyone's life, wherever lived, is now lived in a global context. Societies which once felt able to stand alone now see themselves interlocked with others. The great human goals of peace, justice, and prosperity are now understood to require ever widening cooperative effort for their achievement. And a new array of problems of undeniable global dimensions are beyond the ability of any single country or group of states to solve.

"The Fiftieth Anniversary of the United Nations has arrived, therefore, at one of the turning points in modern history. At this moment the first words of the Charter, 'We the Peoples of the United Nations,' convey a meaning originally intended but perhaps never before fully comprehended. We – all of us – are the United Nations. Unique in its universal character as the world organization, the United Nations is not a substitute or surrogate for individual, community, national, or international action. The United Nations is now and increasingly will be what we choose to make of it. The United Nations in its second half-century will be ever more indispensable and can be ever more effective as peoples and their governments recognize and fulfill the responsibilities and opportunities that now are placed before us."

The Purposes and Principles of the United Nations

The deep-felt needs and intentions which inspired the founding of the United Nations are proclaimed in the Preamble to the Charter signed at San Francisco on the 26th day of June, 1945.

We the peoples of the United Nations determined to save succeeding generations from the scourge of war, which twice in our lifetime has brought untold sorrow to mankind, and to reaffirm faith in fundamental human rights, in the dignity and worth of the human person, in the equal rights of men and women and of nations large and small, and to establish conditions under which justice and respect for the obligations arising from treaties and other sources of international law can be maintained, and to promote social progress and better standards of life in larger freedom,

and for these ends

to practice tolerance and live together in peace with one another as good neighbours, and to unite our strength to maintain international peace and security, and to ensure, by the acceptance of principles and the institution of methods, that armed force shall not be used, save in the common interest, and to employ international machinery for the promotion of the economic and social advancement of all peoples, have resolved to combine our efforts to accomplish these aims.

Accordingly, our respective Governments, through representatives assembled in the city of San Francisco, who have exhibited their full powers found to be in good and due form, have agreed to the present Charter of the United Nations and do hereby establish an international organization to be known as the United Nations.

The purposes of the United Nations are:

1. To maintain international peace and security, and to that end: to take effective collective measures for the prevention and removal of threats to the peace, and for the suppression of acts of aggression or other breaches of the peace, and to bring about by peaceful means, and in

conformity with the principles of justice and international law, adjustment or settlement of international disputes or situations which might lead to a breach of the peace;

2. To develop friendly relations among nations based on respect for the principle of equal rights and self-determination of peoples, and to take other appropriate measures to strengthen universal peace;

3. To achieve international cooperation in solving international problems of an economic, social, cultural, or humanitarian character, and in promoting and encouraging respect for human rights and for fundamental freedoms for all without distinction as to race, sex, language, or religion; and

4. To be a centre for harmonizing the actions of nations in the attainment of these common ends.

New Roles for Non-Governmental Organizations, including Religious NGOs

Joel Beversluis

*T*he past few decades have seen a considerable increase in the number and effectiveness of non-governmental organizations affiliated with the United Nations. Although the common image of the United Nations depicts the Security Council, the General Assembly and a few high-profile events and crises, much more goes on behind the scenes in numerous agencies, in the creation of many important treaties, declarations, conferences, and in programs of action such as education, health, commerce, development and relief. It is in these diverse activities that NGOs have greatly increased their value and influence at the UN.

Background

*T*he Benchmark Survey of NGOs notes that, as they were originally conceived in the UN Charter discussions, NGOs were to be recognized only by the Economic and Social Council of the UN as important participants in considering issues before that Council. (ECOSOC still serves the function at the UN of granting "consultative status" to those who apply for it and are qualified.) In subsequent years, when large numbers of NGOs began arriving at conferences with their own agendas, and making their presence felt through counter-conferences, demonstrations and parallel events, other UN agencies and venues began to open up to their contributions.

During the '70s, special arrangements allowed some experts and individuals from leading NGOs to participate in specialized conferences and staff planning meetings. Some NGOs began providing important services such as background data, in-house news services, and even the monitoring of Member States and reporting back to intergovernmental agencies regarding compliance on matters such as human rights conventions. NGO expertise is valued by agencies such as the World Heath Organization; the Bergen conference on sustainable development employed the consensus of governments, business, labor, youth, and environmental organizations. In 1993, for the first time in its 18-year history, the United Nations Non-Governmental Liazon Service (NGLS) received explicit recognition from the UN General Assembly as well as a financial contribution from the UN's

regular budget. This move makes NGLS a jointly-financed activity of the UN system and reflects the UN's increased commitment to NGO participation in its work.

Roles and importance of the NGOs

Dr. Keith Suter has identified a number of important roles of NGOs (in *Global Change,* Albatross Books, Australia)*:*

1) NGOs investigate and identify problem areas, as an early warning system that brings data to public attention;

2) NGOs generate ideas and then advocate and promote them widely, as an important educational medium;

3) NGOs lobby governments to change their own policies and to influence the policies of other governments;

4) NGOs provide services and model behaviors unrestrained by the self-interested boundaries of national sovereignty;

5) NGOs provide citizens with opportunities for service, self-help, and the expression of personal commitments on a global scale;

6) NGOs represent people or issues which otherwise have no voice or power at national or international levels;

7) NGOs offer new methods of addressing and settling international issues.

"World order can be founded only on an unshakeable consciousness of the oneness of mankind, a spiritual truth which all the human sciences confirm. Anthropology, physiology, and psychology recognize only one human species, albeit infinitely varied in the secondary aspects of life. Recognition of this truth requires the abandonment of prejudice – prejudice of every kind – race, class, colour, creed, nation, sex, degree of material civilization, everything which enables people to consider themselves superior to others...." from *The Promise of World Peace,*
issued 1986 by The International House of Justice,
Bahá'í International Community

"We the People..."

*W*omen's NGOs and caucuses are especially credited for helping to shape the new roles and influence of all NGOs. Their effective work since the mid-70s on the International Women's Conferences (in '75, '80, and '85), the Decade for Women, the Earth Summit, and more recently at the Cairo Conference on Population and Development, as well as at numerous smaller conferences and preparatory meetings, has helped to bring a whole new power base into the United Nations. This democratic power is expressed in the service of dedicated advocates based in non-governmental organizations, representing not governments or profit-oriented groups but "we the people," whose loyalties are quite often transnational and altruistic. There are now well over ten thousand NGO's worldwide who represent concerns that cross national boundaries; some of these are affiliated with the UN.

While some of these NGO's are sponsored by business, professional, or political associations, others represent educational, disaster relief, or development organizations; still others are focused on critical global issues – human rights, environment, population, disarmament, hunger, children-at-risk, medical and health care, peace, justice, or social concerns. Within this mix, religiously-based and motivated NGOs have always been present; since the founding of the UN, they have brought their own combinations of altruism, values, world-views, and perspectives; they may also bring highly politicized or ideological agendas.

Religiously-based NGOs

*I*n the mid-'90s, several historic circumstances and developments have provided religious NGOs with new opportunities within the United Nations. They may now take advantage of the end of the Cold War and the collapse of the most powerful anti-religious state. Religious NGOs also are seeing new needs arising among global issues and are identifying new ways that religious and spiritual traditions may respond to these issues out of their traditional wisdom and values. In addition, the enviromental, population, and social summits, and the new emphases on interreligious cooperation and global ethics, are providing religions and their NGOs with a new image in the international community.

There are numerous religiously-based NGOs functioning within the UN community (some of these are annotated in the Resource Guides at the end of this *SourceBook*). They also come together in several interfaith forums. The Temple of Understanding, the World Conference on Religion and Peace, and the International Association for Religious Freedom have provided excellent interfaith leadership at the UN. NGOs such as the Brahma Kumaris, the Bahá'ís, the National Council of Churches, the Won Buddhist Association and many others have also contributed their energies and resources to many projects. Collaborative forums for religious and like-minded NGOs include the Association of Religious NGOs, the NGO Committee on Freedom of Religion or Belief, and the new Group of Reflection and the Values Caucus, formed around the desire to have an impact at the UN Summit on Social Development and beyond [see also Chapter 34].

*R*eligions and spiritual traditions have many new opportunities to be active in the international arena. They may act individually, but they also are discovering the value of interreligious cooperation in the NGO processes at the UN as well as locally and regionally. The trans-national and trans-ethnic memberships of religions and spiritual traditions, their ethical base, and their potential for providing much-needed leadership to their congregations offers them an unprecedented and historic role in good governance.

On the United Nations

"Man has reached a critical point in history, where he must turn to God to avoid the consequences of his own faulty thinking. We must pray, not a few of us, but all of us. We must pray simply, fervently, sincerely, and with increasing power as our faith grows. We must condition the world's leaders by asking God's Spirit to descend upon their hearts and minds. We must condition ourselves, each and every one, by asking God's help in living so that peace may be possible. We must pray in church, at home, on the train, while driving, on the job – and keep at it. Each of us is important now. The ability of every individual to seek divine help is a necessary link in the golden chain of harmony and peace.

"Prayer is a dynamic manifestation of love by the concerned, reaching out for God's help for man. You can help change the world by your prayers and your prayerful action."
DAG HAMMARSKJOLD,
former Secretary-General, at the dedication of the of the United Nations Prayer Room, United Nations Headquarters

"The United Nations is something that the Creator, the author of all good, at every moment cherishes. No human force will ever be able to destroy the United Nations, for the United Nations is not a mere building or a mere idea; it is not a man-made creation. The United Nations is the vision-light of the Absolute Supreme, which is slowly, steadily, and unerringly illuminating the ignorance, the night of our human life. The divine success and supreme progress of the United Nations is bound to become a reality. At his choice hour, the Absolute Supreme will ring His own victory-bell here on Earth through the loving and serving heart of the United Nations."
SRI CHINMOY,
Director of the UN Meditation Group;
printed in Robert Muller's *My Testament to the UN*

To the Secretary-General of the United Nations –
for a Permanent Center for Nonviolent Conflict Prevention and Resolution

Declaration of the 7th World Religions Conference

Proposals for change at the UN include the establishment of new commissions, centers, and services. The following request evolved at the 7th World Religions Conference, World Fellowship of Religions, held on 6 February 1994, in New Delhi, India. It has been endorsed by Archbishop Desmond Tutu, Robert Muller, His Holiness the Dalai Lama, Very Reverend James Morton, and many others. It is not only a request but also a statement that the signatories volunteer to serve at the request of the Secretariat.

*W*e, the undersigned, request of the Secretary-General of the United Nations that he create a permanent center for nonviolent conflict prevention and resolution that will utilize all available means of mediation, negotiation, conciliation, and nonviolent conflict resolution techniques known to humankind.

Considering that the cold war was characterized by a cycle of fear wherein armaments bred insecurity and insecurity bred more armaments, it is time to create a new cycle of life where trust, confidence, and nonviolent preventive diplomacy can be utilized to generate disarmament, which will in turn strengthen trust and confidence.

Considering further that the disproportionate reliance on military means of addressing conflicts is a wasteful misapplication of resources which should be used to address the suffering caused by poverty, overpopulation, consumerism, and environmental degradation,

Considering likewise that techniques to preempt violence need to be applied in a more organized and systematic fashion,

We affirm that the time has come to take hard decisions that will lead to a new era of peace.

We, the undersigned, believe these decisions are based on the Report of the Secretary-General pursuant to the statement adopted by the Summit Meeting of the Security Council on 31 January 1992, *An Agenda for Peace* (DPI/1247), where it is stated that

1) The use of preventive diplomacy needs to be seen as an "action to prevent disputes from arising between parties, to prevent existing disputes from escalating into conflicts, and to limit the spread of the latter when they occur" (*op.cit.*, art. 20).

2) "...peace in the largest sense cannot be accomplished by the United Nations system or by governments alone. Non-governmental organizations, academic institutions, parliamentarians, business and professional communities, the media, and the public at large must all be involved" (*idem*, art. 84).

We believe also that the creation of this Center for preventive diplomacy on the occasion of the forthcoming 50th Anniversary of the United Nations will enhance the "increasingly common moral perception that spans the world's nations and peoples" (*idem*, art. 15) by enhancing the activities of the United Nations, and by making a real difference in the quality of life on the planet.

Further we believe that faith-based non-governmental organizations need to be involved in a substantial manner in this Center, since so many conflicts have roots in ethnic and religious misunderstanding, and "one requirement for solutions to these problems lies in commitment to human rights with a special sensitivity to those of minorities, whether ethnic, religious, social, or linguistic" (*idem art.* 18).

We, the undersigned, therefore request of the Secretary-General that he create a permanent center for preventive diplomacy. That it be named the United Nations Center for Nonviolent Conflict Prevention and Resolution. The Center will require spiritual, moral leadership, plus full time skilled personnel.

We further request, at the earliest possible time, that the United Nations declare a Year of Nonviolent Conflict Prevention because when humankind ceases to resolve disputes through violence, truly a new era of peace and justice will dawn. This is the time and the opportunity to bring into action the deepest intentions for peace which are at the heart of humankind.

Therefore, we, the undersigned, offer the services of ourselves and institutions, within reason, to serve as mediators, negotiators, and facilitators of nonviolent conflict prevention and resolution at the call of the Secretariat. Many of us have years of extensive experience in cultivating peace and feel that now is the time to step forward and offer any skills we might have in this area.

"Let us pray in our hearts for a League of Souls and a United World. Though we may seem divided by race, creed, color, class, and political prejudices, still, as children of the one God we are able in our souls to feel brotherhood and world unity. May we work for the creation of a United World in which every nation will be a useful part, guided by God through man's enlightened conscience.

"In our hearts we can all learn to be free from hate and selfishness. Let us pray for harmony among the nations, that they march hand in hand through the gate of a fair new civilization." PARAMAHANSA YOGANANDA

Recommendations for Action by the World Community

Dr. Robert Muller

Former Assistant Secretary-General of the United Nations, author, Chancellor of the University for Peace (Emeritus)

Known for his prodigous output of ideas and visions, and for his persistent optimism, Dr. Muller has recently begun generating "2000 Ideas to the Year 2000." Working from his hillside writer's cabin near the University for Peace in Costa Rica, Dr. Muller began this project on July 10, 1994, when the world was 2000 days from the year 2000. The short list below, excerpted from two longer agendas, offers global insights, models futures-thinking, provides others with visions to act upon, and encourages us to be visionary and proactive.

1) On the environment:

- Hold the next UNCED (Earth Summit) in the year 2002
- Establish a Global Data and Optimum Design Agency where all data on the environment would be accessible, using computers to monitor the planet and suggesting optimum designs for human life and Earth preservation
- Establish a world consumers' agency
- Establish a world restoration agency
- Transform the military into peace and environmental protectors, and shift world military expenditures
- Amend economic standards and measurements to account for the deterioration and consumption of the Earth's capital

Hold the following world conferences over the next 8 years:

- World conference of environmental scientists
- World conference on garbage
- World conference on advertising, marketing, and obsolescence
- World conference on more simple, frugal living

2) On development:

- Transform the UN Fund for Population activities into a UN specialized agency on population
- Create a World Marshall Plan for the improvement of the well being of the poor countries
- Design a world plan in which the European Community takes care of the development of Africa; North America (US, Canada) takes care of Latin America; and Japan, Australia, New Zealand, take care of poor areas of Asia
- Design a proper world migration policy
- Use labor in poor countries in manufacturing, health, and geriatric services
- Initiate a UN study of errors in transferring development models from the West to poor countries
- Hold an International Labour Organization-sponsored world conference on small and medium enterprises
- proclaim an International Year of Villages and Rural Areas

3) On planetics or planetary management:

- Use the UN's 50th anniversary for an unprecedented review of where we stand in the world, where we want to go, and how to get there
- Establish a Peoples Assembly at the UN as a second body to the General Assembly

- Establish a World Group of Eminent Persons to deal with the way this planet should be governed
- Create a Commission for a Renaissance of Spirituality
- Develop more regional communities along the lines of the European Community and transform the UN into a true World Community on the same pattern

from "Framework for Preparation for the Year 2000...",
Albert Schweitzer Institute, Quinnipiac Press, 1994

4) Other visions for the near future

- By the year 2000, all Ministries of Foreign Affairs will have been transformed into Ministries of Peace and World Cooperation, and Ambassadors into Ambassadors of Peace.
- Delegates to the United Nations are elected by popular vote.
- The world community decides to tackle the fundamental, ominous question of truthful, objective information, the exercise of democracy being possible only if people are objectively informed. The UN and its agencies and world programs are major contributors to such information.
- The International Court of Justice's judgements are now enforceable and no nation can take exception. The Court is reorganized as the World Supreme Court. The UN Secretary-General is entitled to submit cases to it.
- A World Ethics Chamber determines what is ethical from the world's and humanity's point of view rather than from that of nations, sub-groups and special interest groups. A Sub-Chamber on Media Ethics receives complaints against unethical treatments by the media.
- For the year 2000, an unprecedented, hopeful, optimistic world-wide celebration of the Bimillennium takes place all over the Earth, preceded by much public and governmental preparation and excitement. Gratitude is expressed and prayers are held for having overcome one of the most dangerous and promethien periods of change on any planet in the universe. Innumerable rich materials have been published on the human journey and ascent over the last 5,000 years and on hopes and remaining challenges.

from A World Peace Plan for 2010, in First Lady of the World

5) On religious education

- Considering the importance of religions to the human future, I propose the creation of a World University of Spirituality. Students would be taught about what religions have in common and about the great moral and spiritual concepts and practices that have helped humanity throughout the ages to pursue its ascent and to believe in its destiny: hope, love, prayer, faith, meditation, forgiveness, tolerance, sanctity, and others. Such a University might also develop a universal science of spirituality, an all-encompassing strategy for the presence of spirituality in all walks of life, and an art of religious or spiritual living.

FOR MORE INFORMATION:

Albert Schweitzer Institute for the Humanities, Quinnipiac College, 515 Sherman Avenue, Hamden, CT 06514; tel. (203) 281-8926

Visioneer's International Network (and newsletter about Countdown 2000), 503-1508 West 2nd Avenue, Vancouver, B.C., Canada V6H 344

Global Governance: *Reform Movements and Alternative Visions*

Compiled by Joel Beversluis

Critiques of one or another aspect of the United Nations and proposals for its reform or replacement are fairly widespread, especially during and following the 50th anniversary of its founding. Even formerly-staunch defenders such as the United Nations Association (USA) are now becoming constructive critics and entertaining proposals for the reform and democratization of the UN.

The most serious critiques have to do with the structure which allows abuses of power by dominant nation-states such as the US or the Soviet bloc (during the Cold War years); equally distasteful to others is the power wielded by blocs of nonaligned states or those with small populations.

The Security Council takes hits from all sides, for good reason. The arrogation of power by five controlling countries in 1946 – the United States of America, France, the United Kingdom, Russia (formerly the Soviet Union), and China – gives each of them inordinate amounts of power. Particularly problematic is their veto power which can effectively block the will of all other countries in the Security Council and in the General Assembly.

At the same time, the United Nations does not now have the legislative power to establish global law backed by a world police force to deal with issues ranging from war crimes to environmental and financial matters. The General Assembly's role seems to be primarily advisory, except regarding budgetary matters. Furthermore, those who reread the UN Charter are quickly struck by the fact that "we the people" really have very little voice and no vote at all in the doings of either the General Assembly or the Security Council. Critics also note that the voting system itself does not yield effective legislation.

Proposals in response to these critiques range from doing away with the UN or bypassing it entirely, to creating a parliamentary Peoples' Assembly within its structure; others propose amendments that tinker with the Charter to create a more effective legislative process. Some proposals advocate changes in the veto procedures and/or membership on the Security Council; current controversy centers around whether to add new permanent members from among the newer global powers: Japan, Germany, India, Brazil, and so on.

Although some of the more modest reform proposals could be fairly simple to enact, it is unlikely that any of these will happen quickly because of the entrenched power and self-interested behavior of the countries sitting on the Security Council. On the other hand, some observers note that if the US were committed to substantive reform and to limiting its own veto power, it might well be able to provide the leadership needed to enact significant changes.

The organizations described below advocate numerous approaches to the reform or replacement of the United Nations, and some offer new visions of global governance. Their concerns and proposals are well worth considering, especially during this commemoration of the UN's first 50 years. It is, after all, a time for reflection and a renewed vision, not for a simplistic celebration of the status quo.

Action Coalition for Global Change (ACGC)
55 New Montgomery St., Suite 225, San Francisco, CA 94105 USA; tel. (415) 227-4880 / fax. (415) 227-4878

Promoting democratic world government and a just and peaceful world in the 21st century. Hoping to unite and synergize a movement, the Coalition is attempting to convene a series of world meetings, beginning with a pilot "United Peoples Assembly" during the UN's 50th anniversary which will simulate a globally-focused, democratically elected body that fulfills the mandate of the UN as stated in the Preamble of its Charter.

Campaign for a More Democratic United Nations
308 Cricklewood Lane, London NW2 2PX UK; tel. 081-455-5055

301 E. 45th St. 20B, New York, NY 10017 USA; tel. (212) 983-3353

Among its efforts to make the United Nations more democratically representative of local interests is the primary aim of realizing an official forum or People's Assembly within the UN system.

Center for UN Reform Education
139 East McClellan Ave, Livingston, N.J. 07039 USA; tel. (201) 994-1826

The Center and its many cooperating and participating organizations do analysis and offer materials on topics such as the reform and restructuring of the United Nations Security Council.

Center for War/Peace Studies – The Binding Triad
218 East 18th St., New York, NY 10003 USA; tel. (212) 475-1077
Richard Hudson, Executive Director

Critiques the mismanagement of the planet and its nations as well as the UN for an obsolete international political structure. The result is that the national sovereignty and self-interests of nearly 200 nation-states, disproportional voting in the General Assembly, and veto powers in the Security Council prevent the system from working out fair and practicable solutions. By making two amendments to the UN Charter, the Binding Triad would transform the world body into a limited world federal government, with sufficient authority to do the job but with a variety of checks and balances to assure that authority is not abused.

Commission on Global Governance
11 Avenue Joli-Mont, Case Postale 184, Ch-1211 Geneve 28, Switzerland; tel. (+41 22) 798-2713 / fax. (+41 22) 798-0147
(See the article on the following page.)

One World Now
P.O. Box 1145, Houston, TX 77251-1145 USA; tel. 1-800-5-Earth-5

One World Now is pressing for an empowered, transformed, and democratized United Nations. It hopes to work with existing citizens groups to inform and inspire public opinion and to press countries to deal with neglected realities.

Philadelphia II and One World
665 Munras Ave, Suite 226, P.O. Box 2566 Monterey, CA 93942 USA; tel. (408) 646-0300 / fax. 646-0398

Proposes state, national and global citizen initiatives to establish "Direct Democracy" through use of the existing Initiatives laws which enable people to make public policy and laws in partnership with their representatives. Is involved in a ratification effort, beginning at the state level in Washington.

The United Nations Association

**UNA-USA, 485 Fifth Avenue, New York, NY 10017 USA;
tel. (212) 697-3232 / fax. (212) 682-9185**

*U*NA-USA is the nation's largest foreign policy organization, building public support for constructive US leadership in a more effective United Nations. UNA-USA is a constructive critic of the UN and US policy at the UN, and is a force for change. 175 community-based chapters assist its 135-member Council of Organizations and its vigorous Washington/New York-based staff in creating a better UN.

World Constitution and Parliament Association

**1480 Hoyt St., Suite 31, Lakewood CO 80215 USA;
tel. (303) 233-3548 / fax. (303) 237-7685**

*P*romoting a democratically-elected organization to replace the United Nations. The World Constitution would mandate a world legislative Parliament and administration, with a world executive, administrative agencies, and a World Court, all to act directly and without bias in areas of global and supra-national problems, to achieve peaceful and rational solutions for the mutual benefit of all inhabitants of Earth. *A Constitution of the Federation for the Earth* has been formulated, debated, and amended in four sessions of a World Constituent Assembly beginning in 1968. A global ratification process has begun to give it the force of law; worldwide over 400 organizations with memberships over 15 million have joined the effort.

World Federalist Association

418 7th St. SE, Washington, DC 20003 USA; tel. 800-WFA-0123

*T*he World Federalist Association is an educational organization focused on restructuring and strengthening the United Nations, with a goal of peace through unity. WFA has launched the Campaign for Global Change, a plan and vision to be accomplished by the year 2010. Action projects are designed to establish an International Criminal Court, a democratic United Nations Parliamentary Assembly, mechanisms for reliable UN funding, strengthening UN peacekeeping/peace-enforcement mechanisms, and shaping a more effective Commission on Sustainable Development.

The Commission on Global Governance

"The collective power of people to shape the future is greater now than ever before, and the need to exercise it is more compelling. Mobilizing that power to make life in the twenty-first century more democratic, more secure, and more sustainable is the foremost challenge of our generation." from *OUR GLOBAL NEIGHBOURHOOD*, the report of the Commission on Global Governance

*A*mong those re-thinking global governance is the high-profile Commission on Global Governance. Recognizing the new climate in international relations, Chancellor Willy Brandt brought a group of international leaders together in 1989 to explore new, integral approaches to managing global relations. This led to the setting up of the Commission in 1992, composed of 28 men and women from around the world and from a variety of backgrounds; they were invited to evaluate the needs and structures of global governance, and to report on their conclusions during 1995. Their report:

suggests ways in which the world community might use the present confluence of circumstances to reshape global cooperative arrangements to serve the common needs of the world's people more effectively. We are convinced that it is time for the world to move on from the designs evolved in the past.... By global governance we mean the way in which we manage global affairs, how we relate to each other, how we take decisions that bear on our common future....we do not mean global government, as that would only reinforce the roles of states and governments; global governance is about putting people at the centre of world affairs...

A new world order must be organized around the notion of governance of diversity, not uniformity; of governance through democracy, not dominion; of governance at all levels within society, and not just from above. By definition, global governance implies a decentralized system built on the foundations of a common set of values.

from *OUR GLOBAL NEIGHBOURHOOD*, published by Oxford University Press; available at good bookstores worldwide

---

FOR MORE INFORMATION:

Agencies and Organizations:

United Nations, Dept. of Public Information
Rm. S-845, New York, NY 10017, USA;
tel. (212) 963-4295 / fax. (212) 963-4556

United Nations Environment Programme,
DC2-0803 United Nations, New York, NY 10017 USA;
tel. (212) 963-8093

UNICEF Geneva Office, Palais des Nations,
CH-1211 Geneva 10, Switzerland

UNICEF Headquarters, UNICEF House, 3 UN Plaza, 3 UN Plaza,
New York, NY 10017 USA (there are regional offices worldwide)

UNIFEM USA, 485 Fifth Avenue, Suite 250,
New York, NY 10017 USA; 1-800-982-9781

Books:

Basic Facts About the United Nations. This title and thousands of other books on a huge range of topics from numerous governmental and intergovernmental organizations can be obtained from:

UN Bookstore, Room GA 32, United Nations, New York, NY 10017 USA; tel. (212) 963-7680

United Nations Sales Section, 2 United Nations Plaza, Room DC2-853, Dept. 037A, New York, NY 10017; tel. (212)963-8302

United Nations Sales Office and Bookshop, CH-1211, Geneva 10, Switzerland; tel. 41(22)734-1473

For catalogs from the UN's primary distributor, contact:

UNIPUB, 4611-F Assembly Dr., Lanham, MD 20706;
tel. 800-274-4888 (US), 800-233-0504 (Canada), and 301-459-7666 (local). Since 1955 UNIPUB has grown to represent many prestigious government and intergovernmental organizations with a huge active backlist.

Planethood: The Key to Your Future, by Benjamin Ferencz and Ken Keyes, Jr., available from Love Line Books, 700 Commercial Avenue, Coos Bay, OR 97420 ($2.50)

Publications by Robert Muller are available from:
World Happiness and Cooperation,
P.O. Box 1153, Anacortes, WA 98221 USA

Earth Day, Every Day:

Analyses, Visions, and Strategies

Spiritual Dimensions of the Environmental Crisis

Dr. Daniel Gómez-Ibáñez

Executive Director (Emeritus), Council for a Parliament of the World's Religions

Dr. Gómez-Ibáñez first presented this essay at an interfaith meeting in 1990. The insights offered here have informed his work at the Parliament, with the declaration *Towards a Global Ethic,* and since then with the Peace Council.

*I*n the spirit of interreligious understanding, I wish to begin this discussion of the critical issue of environment, and its relationship to spiritual matters, with a Sanskrit invocation from the *Vedas.* I ask those of you who are not Hindus to understand that any invocation must arise from one tradition or another, and to reflect on the relevance of these words for your own tradition or to reflect on their meaning for the earth and for those of us who would restore it to health. This is a chant for peace from the *Yajur Veda.*

Om
Dyauh Shantir Antariksham Shantih
Prithivii Shantir Aapah Shantir
Oshadayah Shantih Vanaspatayah Shantir
Vishvedevaah Shantir Brahma Shantis
Sarvam Shanti Shantireva Shanti
Saa Maa Shantiredhi   *Yajur Veda* 36, 17

May there be peace in the heavens, peace in the skies
    and peace on earth.
May the waters be peaceful.
May the grasses and herbs bring peace to all creatures,
    and may the plants be at peace also.
May the beneficent beings bring us peace,
    and may the way of all creation bring peace
    throughout the world.
May all things be peaceful, and may that peace itself bring
    further peace.
May we also bring peace to all.

*T*he attention given to the environment has varied enormously over the last few decades. In 1990, however, over 100 million people observed Earth Day and in some way gave thanks for the Earth, which sustains us all. One hundred million people are about two percent of humankind – more than enough to start a revolution! Since then, newspapers and television networks of all political shades have been featuring the plight of the Earth, and this ten-year period is widely held to be the decade of the environment.

We have made some progress since 1970. The rate of growth of the Earth's population has begun to slow down, although the numbers of people added each year – nearly 90 million this year – are unprecedented and still rising. The United Nations predicts that the total world population will stabilize around the end of the 21st century at somewhere between eight and 13 billion persons.[1] The margin of error is about the same as the present population of the world: five billion persons. It is in the developing countries that population growth will be greatest and where increasing demand for energy and material goods will put enormous strains on the earth's resources of air, water, and soil. Twenty years ago, leaders in those nations often voiced the cynical attitude that the environmental concerns of the industrialized nations were yet another ploy to keep the developing regions in a state of subjugation. But today that attitude is giving way to the realization that environmental problems are indeed a threat to every country and perhaps especially threatening to the welfare of developing regions.

In wealthy countries, people now nearly unanimously say they support environmental causes. In the United States, 80 percent of those questioned in a June 1989 *New York Times*/CBS News poll agreed that protecting the environment is so important "that requirements and standards cannot be too high and continuing environmental improvements must be made regardless of cost." Forty-three percent had agreed with the statement in September 1981.[2] Laws protecting the environment have been passed in most developed countries, and in Germany the Green Party has significantly changed the political landscape, if not yet the physical landscape. Even the normally conservative and complacent business community is awakening to environmental issues. Articles about the environment appear frequently in periodicals such as *Business Week, Fortune, Forbes, The Economist* and *The Wall Street Journal.*

Despite these encouraging signs, by most measures we have failed during the last 20 years to improve the health of the planet on which we all depend. The rate of extinction of species has quickened, not slowed. At least two or three species are lost irretrievably each day. Not only are we strangling the creation's genetic diversity, but entire ecosystems are being ravaged. Deforestation and erosion are destroying the once pristine Himalayas. Deserts are spreading in Africa south of the Sahara. We are losing 20 hectares of tropical forest each minute – an area the size of Ohio every year. The rate is increasing. Eighty percent of all Amazonian deforestation has occurred in the last ten years.[3]

In industrialized regions, forests, lakes, and fields suffer increasingly from acid precipitation. There have been ominous decreases in crop and forest yields recently. Production, consumption, and dissipation of toxic chemicals have increased since 1970. We have a landfill crisis, an ocean dumping crisis, and an air quality crisis. The energy efficiency of Western economies increased during the last two decades, but after a brief slowdown around 1980, overall energy use continued to climb. Carbon emissions from fossil fuels increased worldwide by about 40 percent, 1970–1990.[4] The increase in atmospheric carbon dioxide may be causing significant global warming. We may not know enough about the earth's climate to know exactly what we are doing to it, but many scientists are deeply concerned. In my opinion, the uncertainty itself is cause for concern, and restraint is the prudent response.

And finally, as if these and other assaults on life were not enough, global spending on weapons and military activities has nearly doubled (in constant dollars) in 20 years. Each year we spend about one trillion dollars on arms which, if ever they were used, would lay waste to the entire biosphere.[5] We should be spending the money instead on healing the earth; and if we are to survive, we soon will need to do so.

These threats to creation are not just numerous or widespread, they encompass the whole ecosphere, and this emergence of the universal scale of our influence is what distinguishes our activities from those of previous generations. The natural resources we are consuming are no longer simply local, such as deposits of minerals, or tracts of forest, prairie, or marsh. They now include the global reserves of air, water, soil, and genetic material on which we all depend.

Furthermore, our environmental problems are intertwined with and in a real sense indistinguishable from the other great afflictions of the world. The divisions which wound the human community, such as racism, sexual discrimination, or xenophobic nationalism; the grotesque coexistence of affluence and poverty; the prevalence of all kinds of violence, oppression, and exploitation; and the alienation of individuals: these ills, like our environmental problems, all have common origins in the vision which increasingly has guided human affairs during the last two centuries.

In most of our daily affairs, in our prognoses for the human condition and in prescriptions for making the world a better place to live in, we accept or assume this vision. It is the vision in which material progress produces increasing happiness and well-being.

For millennia people have had faith in progress, or at least believed that progress was the birthright of humankind, but it is only relatively recently that we have come to associate progress almost exclusively with increases in *material* prosperity. When the great teachers of the world – Christ, Buddha, Mohammed, Krishna, Confucius, Lao-Tzu and others – point the way to joy and fulfillment, they are not talking about money and material goods, but today these have become the nearly universal talismans of goodness and wealth. In the Sermon on the Mount, Christ puts the issue clearly, but few have listened. "...Where your treasure is, there will your heart be also."[6]

Many individuals understand that spiritual growth brings greater freedom and more lasting happiness than material growth, but as a society we are reluctant to admit that premise in our collective, corporate, or political debates on the purposes of society or the future of the world.

A result of this vision of a purely material prosperity is that we usually use material, that is economic, criteria to allocate worldly resources. The familiar concepts of economics – calculations of costs and benefits, rent, the laws of supply and demand, rights of property (ownership), the concept of a free market – are defended in the delusion that an economy somehow operates independently of cultural or spiritual biases. On the contrary, the economy is an especially clear reflection of our spiritual or metaphysical priorities. One brief example will make this point.

Before the British colonized Nigeria, the land in that part of West Africa was not a commodity. Land was an attribute of the community or kinship group which inhabited it, but it was not property. It could not be owned (in the European sense), much less bought or sold. Land was associated with the group perhaps similarly to the way we associate last names with families. Boundaries were correspondingly fluid. In fact the idea that something so essential as land might be an object of trade was beyond the experience of many non-Western peoples.

Not understanding how the landscape mirrored West African attitudes, the British simply saw this state of affairs as primitive and as a hindrance to economic progress. So they surveyed the land, determined ownership on the basis of occupation, set up a system of cadastral records, and issued titles to parcels of land. Suddenly it became possible to own land, to buy and sell it, to use it as collateral, and to enforce rights of property against others. Thinking they had done the Nigerians a great service, the British proceeded to purchase the land for farms and plantations and to develop the colonial economy. The Nigerians reacted with bewilderment. They were dispossessed before they could understand what was happening to them. One can only imagine the social and cultural upheaval which this bit of European "progress" caused. Of course the British assumed that the money they paid Nigerians for the land was appropriate compensation. The whole process was sustained and enforced by the British legal system – another "gift" to the colonies.[7]

European settlers produced a similar effect in North America, though without resorting to the niceties of surveys and titles. Here is the response of Chief Seattle, speaking in 1855: "How can you buy or sell the sky, the warmth of the land? The idea is strange to us. If we do not own the freshness of the air and the sparkle of the water, how can you buy them?"[8]

I give this example simply to make the point that

attitudes we take for granted have enormously important consequences for the way we treat the earth and the way we treat each other. Reducing the earth's resources and creatures to the status of commodities has made it difficult to discuss or even to recognize their transcendent values – to put a "value" on diversity, or beauty, or life itself, which can somehow be compared with the "values" of the conventional transactions of the marketplace, such as building a road or a factory, or sales of automobiles, television sets, or tuna fish.

Conventional economists assume that markets are indeed able to put a price on sunsets, for example, because people willing to pay for an unobscured view will do so, forcing the factory owner to build elsewhere. But not everyone who wants to see the sunset can afford to buy the view. Further, many potential "customers" have no access to the market, hence no say in determining the sunset's "value," for the simple reason that they have not been born yet. They are the future generations for whom we ought to be holding this beautiful earth in trust. Their welfare, or the beauty they inherit, depends on our willingness to defer our own gratification for the sake of theirs. (Sadly, the marketplace simply mirrors our intentions: in fact many of us heavily discount the future. The proof is our willingness to pay very high rates of interest to be able to satisfy our desires immediately.) A few economists, like Nicholas Georgescu-Roegen, Kenneth Boulding, Herman Daly, and E. F. Schumacher have worked to construct an economics grounded in environmental realities and designed for a sustainable future, but they are as yet a small voice in the wilderness.[9]

Society's powerful, materialistic vision of progress seems to leave little room for the gentler, more loving vision which also finds a home in us. This is the vision of the heart and spirit we all share: the vision in which progress means caring for creation, for each other, for the earth and the environment we live in; building a peaceful community and world; and living harmoniously together, with fairness and justice. With such a vision we are moved by love.

But the modern, materialistic vision of progress depends on self-interest as the motivation for transactions, rather than love. So it can only be maintained by coercion – usually tacit, sometimes explicit. Coercion is violence to the spirit as well as to creation. Listen to the words of Wendell Berry, written 20 years ago:

Do we really hate the world? Are we really contemptuous of it? Have we really ignored its nature and its needs and the problems of its health? The evidence against us is everywhere. It is in our wanton and thoughtless misuse of the land and the other natural resources, in our wholesale pollution of the water and air, in strip mining, in our massive use and misuse of residual poisons in agriculture and elsewhere, in our willingness to destroy whole landscapes in the course of what we call "construction" and "progress," in the earth-destroying and population-destroying weapons we use in our wars, in the planet-destroying weapons now ready for use in the arsenals of the most powerful and violent nations of the world. It is in our hatred of races and nations. It is in our willingness to honor profit above everything except victory. It is in our willingness to spend more on war than on everything else. It is in our unappeasable restlessness, our nomadism, our anxiousness to get to another place or to "the top" or "somewhere" or to heaven or to the moon.

Our hatred of the world is most insidiously and dangerously present in the constantly widening discrepancy between our power and our needs, our means and our ends. This is because of machinery and what we call efficiency. In order to build a road we destroy several thousand acres of farmland forever, all in perfect optimism, without regret, believing that we have gained much and lost nothing. In order to build a dam, which like all human things will be temporary, we destroy a virgin stream forever, believing that we have conquered nature and added significantly to our stature. In order to burn cheap coal we destroy a mountain forever, believing, in the way of lovers of progress, that what is of immediate advantage to us must be a permanent benefit to the universe. Fighting in Vietnam in the interest, as we say and would have ourselves believe, of the Vietnamese people, we have destroyed their villages, their croplands, their forests, herded the people into concentration camps, and in every way diminished the possibility of life in that country; and the civilian casualties are vastly greater than the military. In order to protect ourselves against Russia or China, or whoever our enemy will be in ten years, we have prepared weapons the use of which will, we know, involve our own destruction and the destruction of the world as well. Great power has always been blinding to those who wield it.[10]

A great danger in this materialistic and mechanistic view of the universe is that even when we see the problems it has wrought, we often assume that the solutions are to be found only in the same material realm, perhaps because we forget to consider any other possibility. For example, in the many stories on the environment which have appeared in the business press recently, the most frequently cited reasons for our environmental ills are ignorance, inefficiency, misapplied technology, population growth, institutional inertia, and lack of political will. All these reasons are true, but they are symptoms, not the root causes, of our failure to create a friendly and sustainable world.

Similarly, most proposals for cleaning up the environment focus on technical fixes. We want more miles-per-gallon, aerosols, and refrigerants that don't destroy the ozone, more efficient homes and factories, and non-toxic pesticides. All these things will help. We have used science and technology to get us into this predicament and I think we will use science and technology to get us out.

But the greatest help and the only lasting solution to the violence we do to the world and to each other will arise from an ethic based on compassion and love rather than self-interest. Aldo Leopold's vision of a land-ethic is one expression of this truth:

In short, a land ethic changes the role of *Homo sapiens* from conqueror of the land community to plain member and citizen of it. It implies respect for his fellow-members, and also respect for the community as such.[11]

But the hour is late. The signs of our heedlessness, selfishness, and fear are all about us. This beautiful earth, mother to us all, groans beneath the blows. The trends are worrisome rather than reassuring. For the first time in many generations our children are no longer confident of being able to live in a better world. Have we reached the end of hope?

I think not. We only reach the end of hope when we abandon our claim to being whole human beings. If we believe that the future will be simply a projection of past trends, then we yield it and ourselves helplessly to the notion that our destiny has already been determined by the destructive processes we have set in motion.[12]

We cannot assume that only one possible future lies before us without being guilty of idolatry, because to do so would amount to worshipping our present technological civilization, submitting to the thralldom of the machine rather than accepting our responsibility to control it. We would be guilty of forgetting the importance of human consciousness, of divine purposes and transcendent visions which might call us to a different destiny. There are many instances when the path of history has taken an unforeseeable turn because of the passions and convictions of dreamers, heroes, and saints. We stand at such a place today and the earth calls us to recognize and create a new way forward.

Against the strength, even the apparent omnipotence, of the machine, we need to call forth a power that is greater still, the power of compassion and love. In place of self-interest let us cultivate selflessness. We must be willing to restore the primacy of the heart, and to make every intention and action an expression of kindness and love.

In all the world's religions we find the ethic of loving kindness, compassion, and relatedness. In some, this earth and all upon it are sacred because they are created by God: "The earth is the Lord's and the fulness thereof, the world and those who dwell therein..."; or because creation is a reflection of God's glory: "The heavens are telling the glory of God; and the firmament proclaims his handiwork." "O Lord, how manifold are thy works! In wisdom hast thou made them all; the Earth is full of thy creatures."[13]

All creation is part of the divine, only differentiated by our power to respond. From the Hindu *Isha Upanishad*:

The Spirit moves, and it moves not. It is far, and it is near. It is within all, and it is outside all. Who sees all beings in his own Self, and his own Self in all beings, cannot hate. To the seer, all things have truly become the Self. What delusion, what sorrow, can there be for the one who sees this unity?

The words of Black Elk, a holy man of the Oglala Sioux:[14]

My friend, I am going to tell you the story of my life, as you wish; and if it were only the story of my life I think I would not tell it; for what is one man that he should make much of his winters, even when they bend him like a heavy snow? So many other men have lived and shall live that story, to be grass upon the hills.

It is the story of all life that is holy and is good to tell, and of us two-leggeds sharing it with the four leggeds and the wings of the air and all green things; for these are children of one mother and their father is one Spirit.

And from the great vision he had when he was a boy:

...I was seeing in a sacred manner the shapes of all things in the spirit, and the shape of all shapes as they must live together like one being. And I saw that the sacred hoop of my people was one of many hoops that made one circle, wide as daylight and as starlight, and in the center grew one mighty flowering tree to shelter all the children of one mother and one father. And I saw that it was holy.

Listen again to the voice of Chief Seattle:[15]

Every part of this earth is sacred to my people. Every shining pine needle, every sandy shore, every mist in the dark woods, every clearing and humming insect is holy in the memory and experience of my people.... We are part of the earth and it is part of us. The perfumed flowers are our sisters; the deer, the horse, the great eagle, these are our brothers. The rocky crests, the juices of the meadows, the body heat of the pony, and man – all belong to the same family.... What is man without the beasts? If all the beasts were gone, men would die from a great loneliness of spirit. For whatever happens to the beasts, soon happens to man. All things are connected.

Here is a metaphor from Saint Paul: "God has arranged the body so that... each part may be equally concerned for all the others. If one part is hurt, all parts are hurt with it."[16]

Ecologists know that everything is connected to everything else. That is one of Barry Commoner's "four laws of ecology." Other scientists also are moving towards an explanation of the universe as infinitely related. The new science of chaos and the mathematics of fractal geometry draw attention to this essential unity.[17]

Let me borrow a lesson from the teachings of a Buddhist monk, Thích Nhât Hanh:[18]

If you are a poet, you will see clearly that there is a cloud floating in this sheet of paper. Without a cloud, there will be no rain; without rain, the trees cannot grow; and without trees, we cannot make paper. The cloud is essential for the paper to exist. If the cloud is not here, the sheet of paper cannot be here either. So we can say that the cloud and the paper *inter-are*. "Inter-being" is a word that is not in the dictionary yet, but if we combine the prefix "inter-" with the verb "to be," we have a new verb, *inter-be*. Without a cloud, we cannot have paper, so we can say that the cloud and the sheet of paper inter-are.

If we look into this sheet of paper even more deeply, we can see the sunshine in it. If the sunshine is not there, the forest cannot grow. In fact, nothing can grow. Even we cannot grow without sunshine. And so, we know that the sunshine is also in this sheet of paper. The paper and the sunshine *inter-are*. And if we continue to look, we can see the logger who cut the tree and brought it to the mill to be transformed into paper. And we see the wheat. We know that the logger cannot exist without his daily bread, and therefore the wheat that became his bread is also in this sheet of paper. And the logger's father and mother are in it too. When we look in this way, we see that without all of these things, this sheet of paper cannot exist.

Looking even more deeply, we can see we are in it too. This is not difficult to see, because when we look at a sheet of paper, the sheet of paper is part of our perception. Your mind is in here and mine is also. So we can say that everything is in here with this sheet of paper. You cannot point out one thing that is not here – time, space, the earth, the rain, the minerals in the soil, the sunshine, the cloud, the river, the heat. Everything coexists with this sheet of paper. That is why I think the word "inter-be" should be in the dictionary. "To be" is to inter-be. You cannot just *be* by yourself, alone. You have to inter-be with every other thing. This sheet of paper is, because everything else is.

This lesson on interdependence is at the heart of understanding. (In fact it is part of a commentary on the *Sutra* of the Heart of Wisdom.) Once you begin to see the world in this way, you are forever changed. At first you may think that seeing yourself as one with all that is might put an intolerably heavy burden on you. If everything is everything else, then everyone is responsible for everyone else too; and everyone's suffering is also our own. But this *is* the truth which sets you free, because now you know who you are and what you can do. From this heart of wisdom come compassion and loving kindness to all.

The violence we wreak on the earth is a kind of hatred done in ignorance, and it comes back to haunt us in many ways. We poison the soil, water, and air, and they in turn poison us. We build terrifying arsenals, and live in fear.

But when we live fully aware of the creation and the web of life in which we humans are but a strand, we will begin to do unto the earth as we would have done unto us. It is ignorance which drives us apart from creation.

When we accept the earth as our home and mother, and all the inhabitants as our kin, then we will be able to find the peace which now eludes us. Black Elk's prayer was, "Grandfather, Great Spirit, give me the strength to walk the soft earth, a relative to all that is!"[19]

Our new awareness brings both joy and suffering, because the new-found kinship demands new responsibility. When we accept the responsibility of seeing, we learn how to love. Let me turn to Thích Nhât Hanh again:[20]

At the beginning of each meal, I recommend that you look at your plate and silently recite, "My plate is empty now, but I know that it is going to be filled with delicious food in just a moment." While waiting to be served or to serve yourself, I suggest you breathe three

times and look at it even more deeply, "At this very moment many, many people around the world are also holding a plate, but their plate is going to be empty for a long time." Forty thousand children die each day because of the lack of food. Children alone. We can be very happy to have such wonderful food, but we also suffer because we are capable of seeing. But when we see in this way, it makes us sane, because the way in front of us is clear – the way to live so that we can make peace with ourselves and with the world. When we see the good and the bad, the wondrous and the deep suffering, we have to live in a way that we can make peace between ourselves and the world.

Seeing more clearly and the transcendence of self are the most fundamental teachings of all religions. Truly to restore the earth we must first restore ourselves. The inner and outer worlds are inseparable. They must be in harmony. Here is the prayer of a Sufi (Muslim) mystic, Ansari of Herat:[21]

Watch vigilantly the state of thine own mind.
Love of God begins in harmlessness.

Know that the Prophet built an external *kaaba*
Of clay and water,
And an inner *kaaba* in life and heart.
The outer *kaaba* was built by Abraham, the holy;
The inner is sanctified by the glory of God himself.

On the path of God
Two places of worship mark the stages,
The material temple
And the temple of the heart.
Make your best endeavor
To worship at the temple of the heart.

A heedless person cannot bring caring to the world. A fearful person cannot see clearly; a selfish person does not embrace the wholeness of all creation and an angry person does not bring peace to the world. We must ourselves be whole and healthy if we would heal the earth. Its peace begins with ours, at home, in our daily lives, in our peaceful hearts.

The healing of creation will not be accomplished by the judicious application of technology alone, but by a commitment which must be as intense as any religious faith. Our personal commitment to spiritual growth will lead us to ecologically responsible behavior, because it will make clear the interrelatedness of all beings.

In fact caring for creation is a commitment for which the religions of the world provide the essential teachings. Faced with unprecedented global environmental and social crises, the challenge to us all is to recover the meaning of those teachings for today, to renew our kinship with all creation, to restore the primacy of spiritual values and of communal and personal spiritual growth, and to rediscover the simple truths: that there is no separateness and therefore there can be no selfishness, and that compassion for all is the heart of understanding.

Let me close with a poem by Gerard Manley Hopkins, an English mystic poet of the late 19th century.

PIED BEAUTY

Glory be to God for dappled things
   For skies of couple-colour as a brindled cow;
   For rose-moles all in stipple upon trout that swim;
   Fresh-firecoal chestnut-falls; finches' wings;
   Landscape plotted and pieced–fold, fallow and plough;

And áll trádes, their gear and tackle and trim.
All things counter, original, spare, strange;
   Whatever is fickle, freckled (who knows how?)
     With swift, slow; sweet, sour; adazzle, dim;
He fathers-forth whose beauty is past change:
       Praise him.

NOTES

This essay is adapted from a lecture given on July 21, 1990, at the conference on "Spiritual Values in the Global Village," at Vivekananda Monastery, Ganges, Michigan.

1. United Nations Department of International Economic and Social Affairs, *World Demographic Estimates and Projections, 1950–2025* (New York, 1988), cited in *The Economist*, January 20, 1990.

2. *The Economist*, September 2, 1989. A poll in April 1990 by *The Wall Street Journal*/NBC News indicated that 86 percent of respondents want to protect the environment even if it means they will have to pay higher prices. (*The Wall Street Journal*, April 20, 1990.)

3. Lester Brown, *et al.*, *State of the World, 1990* (New York: Norton, 1990)

4. *Ibid.*

5. Lester Brown, *et al.*, *State of the World, 1989* (New York: Norton, 1989)

6. Matthew, 6:21

7. See Paul Bohannan, "The Impact of Money on an African Subsistence Economy," *Journal of Economic History*, XIX (1959), 491–503; and Paul Bohannan, "Africa's Land," *The Centennial Review*, IV (1960), 439–449.

8. *Chief Seattle's Testimony* (London: Pax Christi & Friends of the Earth, 1976)

9. Nicholas Georgescu-Roegen, *The Entropy Law and the Economic Process* (Cambridge: Heard University Press, 1971); E. F. Schumacher, *Small Is Beautiful* (New York: Harper, 1973); Herman Daly, ed., *Toward a Steady-state Economy* (San Francisco: Freeman, 1973); Herman Daly, *Steady-state Econonics* (San Francisco: Freeman, 1977); and Herman Daly & John Cobb, Jr., *For the Common Good* (Boston: Beacon Press, 1989).

10. Wendell Berry, "A Secular Pilgrimage," in *A Continuous Harmony* (New York: Harcourt Brace Jovanovich, 1975) pp.10–11.

11. Aldo Leopold, "The Land Ethic" in *A Sand County Almanac* (New York: Ballantine, 1970) p.240.

12. See Lewis Mumford, "Prospect," in W. L. Thomas, ed., *Man's Role in Changing the Face of the Earth* (Chicago: University of Chicago Press, 1956) pp.1141–1152.

13. From Psalms 24, 19 and 104.

14. John G. Neihardt, *Black Elk Speaks* (New York: Pocket Books, 1972), pp.1, 36.

15. *Chief Seattle's Testimony*

16. 1 Corinthians, 12:24–26. Christianity has been criticized for emphasizing separation between humans and creation and for teaching that creation is subservient and intended for humankind's use and enjoyment. See Lynn White, Jr., "The Historical Roots of Our Ecologic Crisis," *Science*, v. 155 (1967), pp.1203–1207. The first two chapters of Genesis appear to support these views, although there are also thoughtful contrary interpretations. The true picture is more complex. Attitudes towards the environment are rooted in the secular culture as well as in religion, and neither the West nor Christianity has any monopoly on environmental damage or disrespect.

The Christian mystical tradition reveals the sense of relatedness and responsibility for creation. From a sermon by Meister Eckhart: "Though we talk about human beings, we are speaking at the same time of all creatures, for Christ himself said to his disciples: 'Go forth and preach the gospel to all creatures.' God poured his being in equal measure to all creatures, to each as much as it can receive. This is a good lesson for us that we should love all creatures equally with everything which we have received from God.... So God loves all creatures equally and fills them with his being. And we should lovingly meet all creatures in the same way." (Matthew Fox, *Breakthrough: Meister Eckhart's Creation Spirituality in New Translation* [New York: Doubleday, Image Books, 1980], p.92.)

Many Christians are deeply sensitive to the tensions between Christian doctrine and a creation in urgent need of healing. See, for examples: Gerald Barney, "The Future of the Creation: The Central Challenge for Theologians," *Word & World*, v. 4 (1984), pp.422–429; William E. Gibson, *Keeping and Healing the Creation* (Louisville, KY: Presbyterian Church [USA], Eco-Justice Task Force, 1989); Thomas Beny, *The Dream of the Earth* (San Francisco: Sierra Club, 1988); Matthew Fox, *Original Blessing* (Santa Fe, NM: Bear, 1983).

17. Barry Commoner, *The Closing Circle* (New York: Knopf, 1971); see also Benoit B. Mandelbrot, *The Fractal Geometry of Nature* (New York: Freeman, 1983); James Gleick, *Chaos* (New York: Viking, 1987).

18. Thích Nhât Hanh, *The Heart of Understanding* (Berkeley, California: Parallax Press, 1988), pp.3–4. This is a commentary on the *Maha Prajñaparamita Hridaya Sutra*.

19. Neihardt, p.5.

20. Nhât Hanh, p.54.

21. Abdullah al-Ansari al-Harawi (d. 1088). This translation is by Sardar Sir Jogendra Singh, quoted in Eknath Easwaran, *God Makes the Rivers to Flow* (Petaluma, CA: Nilgiri Press, 1982), p.55.

Earth Day 25

Provided by Earth Day USA

*T*he environmental movement of 1970 was charged with the responsibility of "raising awareness about the environment." We weren't aware at that time that there even was an environment, let alone that there was a problem with it. With Earth Day 1990, people learned that the problems are so urgent that just passing pollution laws wasn't enough, and people began taking personal responsibility by beginning to change their living habits.

But now we know that the very survival of the humanity and other species is the ultimate issue, requiring that Earth Day 25 and thereafter encourage a fundamental shift in values and consciousness. The reality of this ultimatum will be a great shock to human belief structures, and therefore to our values, priorities, and commitments.

To achieve this shift in consciousness, we must reach beyond people's intellect to their hearts and souls over the next few years. In addition to the more traditional Earth Day events and activities, you are encouraged to include song, dance, ritual, etc. that reveal the pain and suffering throughout the world – both that of people and of the rest of nature – to implore each and every one of us to heed the cry, celebrate all that Life is and can become, and to raise people to a new plateau of confidence, hope, and love, thereby internalizing their dedication to a better world.

The slogan, "The time has come!" signals an urgent call to action. It's time to roll up our shirtsleeves and work harder than ever to choose the health of the planet and all life on it. If not now, when?

The Earth Covenant:
A Citizens' Treaty for Common Ecological Security

There are many ways in which religious communities can address global ethics and the systems of global governance. One accessible process and framework is this *Earth Covenant*, which resulted from an initiative by Global Education Associates in 1988. Individuals and organizations from more than 50 countries provided input; in September 1989, twenty people from nine countries met to reflect on this input and to draft the *Covenant*. By the time of the Earth Summit in Rio in 1992, more than a million people in some 100 countries had signed the *Covenant*, which was circulating in some 20 languages. By 1994 an estimated two million people had signed it, making a commitment to live ecologically responsible lives according to its four principles.

Rather than a petition to governments, the *Covenant* is a citizens' agreement and process. It recognizes that governments alone cannot assure environmental sustainability or basic human needs for present and future generations. It affirms that both individuals and civil society – especially religious networks of educational, social, and community institutions – have an important role.

The *Covenant* is now also linked with the *Earth Charter* Initiative, described on the following page. The *Covenant* has also been endorsed and publicized by the United Nations Environment Programme; its four principles are described by a UNEP official as the "best available framework" for developing an intergovernmental Earth Charter.

PREAMBLE

*W*e, the peoples of the Earth, rejoice in the beauty and wonder of the lands, skies, waters, and life in all its diversity. Earth is our home. We share it with all other living beings.

Yet we are rendering the Earth uninhabitable for the human community and for many species of life. Lands are becoming barren, skies fouled, waters poisoned. The cry of people whose land, livelihood, and health are being destroyed is heard around the world. The Earth itself is calling us to awaken.

We and all living beings depend upon the Earth and upon one another for our common existence, well-being, and development. Our common future depends upon a reexamination of our most basic assumptions about humankind's relationship to the Earth. We must develop common principles and systems to shape this future in harmony with the Earth."

Governments alone cannot secure the environment. As citizens of the world, we accept responsibility in our personal, occupational, and community lives, to protect the integrity of the Earth.

PRINCIPLES AND COMMITMENTS

*I*n covenant with each other and on behalf of the whole Earth community, we commit ourselves to the following principles and actions:

Relationship with the Earth

*A*ll life forms are sacred. Each human being is a unique and integral part of the Earth's community of life and has a special responsibility to care for life in all its diverse forms.

Therefore, we will act and live in a way that preserves the natural life processes of the Earth and respects all species and their habitats. We will work to prevent ecological degradation.

Relationship with each other

*E*ach human being has the right to a healthful environment and to access to the fruits of the Earth. Each also has a continual duty to work for the realization of these rights for present and future generations.

Therefore – concerned that every person have food, shelter, pure air, potable water, education, employment, and all that is necessary to enjoy the full measure of human rights – we will work for more equitable access to the Earth's resources.

Relationship between economic and ecological security

*S*ince human life is rooted in the natural processes of the Earth, economic development, to be sustainable, must preserve the life-support systems of the Earth.

Therefore, we will use environmentally protective technologies and promote their availability to people in all parts of the Earth. When doubtful about the consequences of economic goals and technologies on the environment, we will allow an extra margin of protection for nature.

Governance and ecological security

*T*he protection and enhancement of life on Earth demand adequate legislative, administrative, and judicial systems at appropriate local, national, regional, and international levels. In order to be effective, these systems must be empowering, participatory, and based on openness of information.

Therefore, we will work for the enactment of laws that protect the environment and promote their observance through educational, political, and legal action. We will advance policies of prevention rather than only reacting to ecological harm.

Declaring our partnership with one another and with our Earth, we give our word of honor to be faithful to the above commitments.

Signatures are being gathered by Global Education Associates. Readers are invited to make and distribute copies of this page, discuss it, sign it, encourage others to do so, and send a copy of the signed *Covenant* to: GEA, 475 Riverside Drive, Suite 1848, New York, NY 10115 USA

SIGNED:

_____

Please send _____
information to
(address): _____

_____

New Life for the Earth Charter:
An Inter-governmental Initiative

The *Earth Charter* initiative, facilitated and sponsored by the Earth Council and Green Cross International, is building upon the unfinished business of the Rio Earth Summit. The initiative is characterized by inclusiveness in the conviction that broad participation is essential to achieving consensus.

*W*hen the United Nations *Charter* was drafted in 1945, no one foresaw today's global-scale environmental threats. Hence, no provisions were made in the Charter for ecological security. Environmental damage since then, and long-range predictions of worse to come, require that we now enact an *Earth Charter* to supplement the UN *Charter*. Such a charter was a goal of the Earth Summit, but when governments settled instead on a weak, non-binding "Rio Declaration," the Summit's chief organizer, Maurice Strong, proposed that an *Earth Charter* be taken up again in conjunction with the UN's 50th Anniversary.

In April 1994, a worldwide "Earth Charter Initiative" was set in motion. Backed by a grant from the Netherlands government, two international non-governmental organizations will facilitate the process: the Earth Council, chaired by Maurice Strong, and Green Cross International, headed by Mikhail Gorbachev.

The *Earth Charter* initiative will advance in three stages:

1) A first draft will be prepared through an international process in time for the United Nations' 50th Anniversary;

2) Worldwide discussions and negotiations will lead to an advanced draft to be submitted to the UN in 1997 (when implementation of the Rio agreements will be assessed);

3) An intergovernmental process of ratification will be pursued, leading to the signing and proclamation of a binding Earth Charter by January 1 of the year 2000.

The *Earth Charter* initiative and the *Earth Covenant* process (see p. 201) are complementary. The *Charter* initiative and its timeline enhance the political relevance of the citizens' *Covenant* for ecological and economic security. Conversely, the *Covenant's* multi-sectoral movement – with its focus on governance in its fourth principle – enhances the possibility of broad public support needed if governments are to ratify a binding *Charter* by 2000. The Religion and World Order Program and other programs of Project Global 2000 (including 17 international agencies and organizations), as well as Green Cross International and the Earth Council will work in partnership to facilitate linkages between the processes.

*I*ndividuals, religious communities, and civic organizations can participate in these ways:

1) Promote the *Earth Covenant*, showing how it is linked to the *Earth Charter* initiative;

2) Give input toward a first draft of an *Earth Charter* (by Spring 1995);

3) Organize public discussions providing feedback for an advanced draft (1996-1997);

4) Promote public support for *Charter* ratification.

compiled by the Editor from information provided by Global Education Associates in *Breakthrough News* (Fall 1994) and from the Earth Council

FOR MORE INFORMATION:

Earth Council Headquarters
P.O. Box 2323-1002, San José, Costa Rica
tel. (506) 223-6410 / 223-3418 / fax. (506) 223-2197 / 223-1822
E-mail: ecouncil @igc.apc.org

Global Education Associates,
475 Riverside Drive, Suite 1848, New York, NY 10115 USA

On sustainable development:

"The dictionary distinguishes between growth and development. To grow is to increase naturally in size. To develop is to realize potentialities or to come gradually to a better state. World Bank economist Herman Daly, writing in Ecological Economics *(1990, No.2), notes that 'growth is a quantitative increase in physical scale, while development is qualitative improvement or unfolding of potentialities.' Sustainable growth is an oxymoron; sustainable development is 'much more apt' for a world that can't stand much more environmentally destructive economic growth."* DIETER T. HESSEL
from *The Egg:* An Eco-Justice Quarterly, Spring 1992, p.8

"The work of Christian relief and development... must involve spiritual transformation, setting people free from destructive attitudes, beliefs, values, and patterns of culture. The proclamation of the gospel and the making of disciples, then, is an unavoidable dimension of relief and development work – not only for eternal salvation, but also for the trans- formation of culture and economic life."

excerpted from the "Villars Statement on Relief and Development;" for the full document see *Freedom, Justice, and Hope,* edited by Marvin Olasky, Herbert Schlossberg, *et al.* (Westchester, IL: Crossway Books, 1988) p.145.

"Economic growth is part of development, but it cannot be a goal in itself; ...some [development goals] are virtually universal. These include a long and healthy life, education, access to... a decent standard of living, political freedom, guaranteed human rights, and freedom from violence."

"A national program for achieving sustainability should involve all interests and seek to identify and prevent problems before they arise...."

from *Caring for the Earth,* published by IUCN, pp. 5, 10.

Caring for the Earth: A Strategy for Sustainable Living

The first edition of the *World Conservation Strategy* was published in 1980 by the International Union for Conservation of Nature and Natural Resources (IUCN), with the United Nations Environment Programme (UNEP) and the World Wildlife Fund (WWF). An expanded and updated edition, *Caring for the Earth: A Strategy for Sustainable Living*, was published in 1991 by a partnership including the above three groups plus numerous other sponsoring and collaborating organizations. The following excerpts are from the *Summary*, which outlines the principles and concepts included in the 228-page *Strategy*.

A message to the world

*H*umanity must live within the carrying capacity of the Earth. There is no other rational option in the longer term. Unless we use the resources of the Earth sustainably and prudently, we deny people their future. We must adopt lifestyles and development paths that respect and work within nature's limits. We can do this without rejecting the many benefits that modern technology has brought, provided that technology itself works within those limits.

[...] Our new approach must meet two fundamental requirements. One is to secure a widespread and deeply-held commitment to a new ethic, the ethic for sustainable living, and to translate its principles into practice. The other is to integrate conservation and development: conservation to keep our actions within the Earth's capacity, and development to enable people everywhere to enjoy long, healthy, and fulfilling lives.

A new strategy of care

*I*n the past 20 years, the world has been deluged with reports, action plans, and other prescriptions to cure our environmental ills. International conferences, ministerial declarations, government policy documents, political manifestos, campaigns by "green" groups, and somber scientific pronouncements have all pointed in the same direction. So – what's new about *Caring for the Earth?* Two points need to be made: it is founded on an ethic of care for nature and for people; and it is a strategy of mutually reinforcing actions at individual, local, national, and international levels.

Caring for the Earth is both an analysis and a plan of action. It is intended as a broadly-oriented but practical guide to the policies we must adopt and the actions we must undertake. It is divided into three parts.

Part I defines the principles of a sustainable society and recommends 60 actions. [...]

Part II describes 62 additional actions required to apply the principles set out in Part I to the more familiar sectors of environment and policy. These are energy; business, industry and commerce; human settlements; farm and range lands; forest lands; fresh waters; and oceans and coastal areas. [Part III deals with implementation and follow-up.]

Who should use the Strategy?

*T*his *Strategy* is aimed at everybody. But its particular targets are those who will decide on the next essential steps. We address national leaders, ministers of government departments, heads of national agencies, and intergovernmental organizations. Because the powers of governments, while indispensable, are not unlimited, we also address leaders of business and industry and the great range of local, national, and international non-governmental bodies. This *Strategy* will have a chance of success only if caring and thinking people read it, understand its message, demand action – and opt for sustainable living.

We urge every reader to measure his or her personal behavior and lifestyle against these actions, and to assess the policies and practices of the citizens' groups, communities, firms and nations to which he or she belongs.

Sustainability: a question of definition

*C*aring for the Earth uses the word "sustainable" in several combinations, such as "sustainable development," "sustainable economy," "sustainable society" and "sustainable use." It is important for an understanding of the *Strategy* to know what we mean by these terms.

If an activity is sustainable, for all practical purposes it can continue forever.

When people define an activity as sustainable, however, it is on the basis of what they know at the time. There can be no long-term guarantee of sustainability, because many factors remain unknown or unpredictable. The moral we draw from this is: *be conservative in actions that could affect the environment, study the effects of such actions carefully and learn from your mistakes quickly.*

The World Commission on Environment and Development (WCED) defined "sustainable development" as "development that meets the needs of the present without compromising the ability of future generations to meet their own needs."

The term has been criticized as ambiguous and open to a wide range of interpretations, many of which are contradictory. The confusion has been caused because "sustainable development," "sustainable growth," and "sustainable use" have been used interchangeably, as if their meanings were the same. They are not. "Sustainable growth" is a contradiction in terms: nothing physical can grow indefinitely. "Sustainable use" is applicable only to renewable resources: it means using them at rates within their capacity for renewal.

"Sustainable development" is used in the *Strategy* to mean **improving the quality of human life while living within the carrying capacity of supporting ecosystems.**

A "sustainable economy" is the product of sustainable development. It maintains its natural resource base. It can continue to develop by adapting, and through improvements in knowledge, organization, technical efficiency, and wisdom.

FOR MORE INFORMATION:

IUCN, 1196 Gland, Switzerland.
Copies of the *Strategy* may be purchased from Island Press in the USA (1-800-828-1302) and in the UK from IUCN (44 223-277-894).

Environmental Sabbath/Earth Rest Day

and the United Nations Environment Programme (UNEP)

*E*stablished in 1987 by the United Nations Environment Programme and its advisory board and planning committee, the Environmental Sabbath/Earth Rest Day provides a way to meld spiritual values with environmental science. Many churches, temples, synagogues, mosques, and other institutions have adopted the first weekend in June each year as a special time to remember the needs and value of the Earth through worship and liturgy, education and personal commitment. Other organizations have built upon UNEP's resource base to develop programs of their own that extend throughout the year.

Among the publications produced for these activities is *Only One Earth,* a substantial resource guide containing scientific environmental data, action guides, and declarations from religious bodies in response to contemporary environmental deterioration. The booklet also includes selected scriptures, prayers and reflections from many of the world's religious traditions which suggest the historic wisdom of the traditions regarding the earth. (Many of these texts have been used throughout this *SourceBook* to shed light on how members of the religions may respond to environmental issues.)

In his letter addressed to religious and spiritual leaders – and to all who can use *Only One Earth* – Dr. Noel J. Brown, Director of UNEP explains:

> The need for establishing a new spiritual and ethical base for human activities on Earth has never been greater – as the deterioration of our Planetary Home makes the protection of the human environment a new global imperative.

The United Nations Environment Programme

*U*NEP is the international organization given authority to monitor and control the global environment, responding to the problems that transcend national boundaries. It is the world leader in dissemination of global environmental information. Within the United Nations, UNEP oversees the environmental work being done by all other agencies to ensure that an ecological perspective is incorporated in development projects supported by the U.N.

In addition to the Environmental Sabbath/Earth Rest Day, UNEP played a major role in the Montreal Protocol on ozone depletion; the Rio Earth Summit (UNCED) and recent developments since Rio; the Global Environmental Monitoring System offering early warning alerts on immediate and potential dangers; INFOTERRA, a global computer network; and the annual *State of the Environment.*

"All human societies are built on fragile ecological foundations. Without clean air, fresh water, productive soil and a sustaining web of life, Homo sapiens *can neither survive nor prosper. In a few short decades we are eroding those foundations beyond repair. By the year 2000, if present trends continue, one third of the world's productive land will have eroded or turned to dust. One million species may have been driven to extinction, the sharpest setback to life on earth since our remotest ancestors first appeared on the planet. And the world's climate will almost certainly change, with enormous, but incalculable consequences. In each case, human activities will be to blame."*

excerpted and adapted from the UNEP Profile in *Only One Earth* and other publications, by the Editor

The Earth Summit (UNCED)

*O*n December 22, 1989, the United Nations General Assembly called for a global meeting that would devise strategies to halt and reverse the effects of environmental degradation "in the context of increased national and international efforts to promote sustainable and environmentally sound development in all countries."

Also known as the Earth Summit, the United Nations Conference on Environment and Development was held in Rio de Janeiro, Brazil, from June 3 to 14, 1992. After two years of preparations, the 178 governments at the Conference reached agreement on three texts: Agenda 21, a comprehensive strategy for global action on sustainable development; the Rio Declaration on Environment and Development, outlining the rights and responsibilities of governments in this area; and a statement of principles to guide the sustainable management of forests worldwide.

Agenda 21

Underlying Agenda 21 is the notion that humanity has reached a defining moment in its history. We can continue our present policies which serve to deepen the economic divisions within and between countries; which increase poverty, hunger, sickness and illiteracy worldwide; and which are causing the continued deterioration of the ecosystem on which we depend for life on Earth.

Or we can change course. We can improve the living standards of those who are in need. We can better manage and protect the ecosystem and bring about a more prosperous future for us all.

"No nation can achieve this on its own," states Mr. Maurice Strong, Secretary-General of the Conference, in the preamble to Agenda 21. "Together we can – in a global partnership for sustainable development."

from the press summary of Agenda 21 and Earth Summit press releases

More details about ratification, implementation, and monitoring of the conventions are available from:

United Nations Environment Programme
DC2-803, United Nations, New York, NY 10017 USA

UNCED Information, DPI, Room S-894, United Nations, New York, NY 10017 USA; tel. (212) 963-4295 / fax. (212) 963-4556

Prayers, Scriptures, and Reflections

Most of the prayers, scriptures, and reflections below and on the next six pages were originally published in *Only One Earth* by the UNEP in 1990 (see previous page).

The Universal Prayers on this page are deliberately given "secular" language, making them useful either as they are for those who so choose, or modified for a particular congregation's use in a celebration of care and appreciation for Creation. Where a *Reader* is noted, he or she repeats the bold, italic phrases beween responses from the congregation.

Universal Prayers

A Call to Prayer

We who have lost our sense and our senses – our touch, our smell, our vision of who we are; we who frantically force and press all things, without rest for body or spirit, hurting our earth and injuring ourselves: we call a halt.

We want to rest. We need to rest and allow Earth to rest. We need to reflect and to rediscover the mystery that lives in us, that is the ground of every unique expression of life, the source of the fascination that calls all things to communion.

We declare a Sabbath, a space of quiet: for simply being and letting be; for recovering the great, forgotten truths; for learning how to live again.

A Prayer of Awareness

*T*oday we know of the energy that moves all things: the oneness of existence, the diversity and uniqueness of every moment of creation, every shape and form, the attraction, the allurement, the fascination that all things have for one another.

Humbled by our knowledge, chastened by surprising revelations, with awe and reverence we come before the mystery of life.

A Prayer of Sorrow

Reader:
We have forgotten who we are.

We have forgotten who we are.
We have alienated ourselves from
  the unfolding of the cosmos.
We have become estranged from
  the movements of the earth.
We have turned our backs on the
  cycles of life.

Reader...

We have sought only our own
  security.

We have exploited simply for
  our own ends.
We have distorted our knowledge.
We have abused our power.

Reader...

*N*ow the land is barren,
And the waters are poisoned,
And the air is polluted.

Reader...

*N*ow the forests are dying,
And the creatures are disappearing,
And the humans are despairing.

Reader...

We ask forgiveness.
We ask for the gift of remembering.
We ask for the strength to change.

Reader...

[Silence]

A Prayer of Healing

Reader:
*We join with the Earth and with
  each other*

*T*o bring new life to the land,
To restore the waters,
To refresh the air.

Reader...

*T*o renew the forests,
To care for the plants,
To protect the creatures.

Reader...

*T*o celebrate the seas,
To rejoice the sunlight,
To sing the song of the stars.

Reader...

*T*o recall our destiny.
To renew our spirits.
To reinvigorate our bodies.

Reader...

*T*o create the human community,

To promote justice and peace.
To remember our children.

Leader:
*We join together as many and
diverse expressions of one loving
mystery:
for the healing of the earth and
the renewal of all life.*

[Meditation]

A Prayer of Gratitude

Reader...
We rejoice in all life.

We live in all things.
All things live in us.

Reader...

We live by the sun.
We move with the stars.

Reader...

We eat from the earth.
We drink from the rain.
We breathe from the air.

Reader...

We share with the creatures.
We have strength through their gifts.

Reader...

We depend on the forests.
We have knowledge through their secrets.

Reader:
*We have the privilege of seeing
  and understanding.
We have the responsibility of caring.
We have the joy of celebrating.*

Leader:
We are full of the grace of creation.

We are graceful.
We are grateful.
We rejoice in all life.

Bahá'í Reflections

*W*ith respect to environment . . .

*W*e cannot segregate the human heart from the environment outside us and say that once one of these is reformed everything will be improved. Man is organic with the world. His inner life molds the environment and is itself also deeply affected by it. The one acts upon the other and every abiding change in the life of man is the result of these mutual reactions.

*N*ature is God's will and is its expression in and through the contingent world. It is a dispensation of Providence ordained by the Ordainer, the All-Wise. The earth is but one country, and mankind its citizens.

*L*ook not upon the creatures of God except with the eye of kindliness and of mercy, for Our loving providence hath pervaded all created things, and Our grace encompassed the earth and the heavens.

...it is not only their fellow human beings that the beloved of God must treat with mercy and compassion, rather must they show forth the utmost loving-kindness to every living creature.... The feelings are one and the same, whether ye inflict pain on man or on beast.

*B*lessed is the house, and the place, and the city, and the heart, and the mountain, and the refuge, and the cave, and the valley, and the land, and the sea, and the island, and the meadow where mention of God hath been made, and His praise glorified.

from Bahá'í Sacred Writings

Buddhist Prayers

The Rain Cloud

It is like a great cloud rising above the world,
Covering all things everywhere—
A gracious cloud full of moisture; lightning-flames flash and dazzle,
Voice of thunder vibrates afar, bringing joy and ease to all.
The sun's rays are veiled, and the earth is cooled;
The cloud lowers and spreads as if it might be caught and gathered;
Its rain everywhere equally descends on all sides,
Streaming and pouring unstinted, permeating the land.
On mountains, by rivers, in valleys,
In hidden recesses, there grow the plants, trees, and herbs;
Trees, both great and small, the shoots of the ripening grain,
Grape vine and sugar cane.
Fertilized are these by the rain and abundantly enriched;
The dry ground is soaked; herbs and trees flourish together.
From the one water which issued from that cloud,
Plants, trees, thickets, forests, according to need receive moisture.
All the various trees – lofty, medium, low, all according to their sizes –
Grow and develop roots, stalks, branches, leaves,
Blossoms and fruits in their brilliant colors;
Wherever the one rain reaches, all become fresh and glossy.
According as their bodies, forms, and natures are great and small,
So the enriching rain, though it is one and the same,
Yet makes each of them flourish.
In like manner also the Buddha appears here in the world
Like unto a great cloud universally covering all things;
And having appeared in the world, for the sake of living,
He discriminates and proclaims the truth in regard to all laws.
The Great Holy World—honored One among the gods and humans,
And among all living beings proclaims abroad this word:
"I am the *Tathagata**, the Most Honored among humans;
I appear in the world like this great cloud,
To pour enrichment on all parched living beings,
To free them from their misery to attain the joy of peace,
Joy of the present world and joy of *Nirvana*...
Everywhere impartially, without distinction of persons...
Ever to all beings I preach the Law equally;...
Equally I rain the Law – rain untiringly.

from the *Lotus Sutra*
*the "Thus-Gone"

Loving Kindness

May every creature abound in well-being and peace.
May every living being, weak or strong, the long and the small,
The short and the medium-sized, the mean and the great –
May every living being, seen or unseen, those dwelling far off,
Those near by, those already born, those waiting to be born –
May all attain inward peace.

Let no one deceive another. Let no one despise another in any situation.
Let no one, from antipathy or hatred, wish evil to anyone at all.
Just as a mother, with her own life, protects her only son from hurt,
So within yourself foster a limitless concern for every living creature.
Display a heart of boundless love for all the world
In all its height and depth and broad extent –
Love unrestrained, without hate or enmity.
Then as you stand or walk, sit or lie, until overcome by drowsiness,
Devote your mind entirely to this, it is known as living here the life divine.

A Call to Prayer

The earth is at the same time mother.
She is mother of all that is natural,
mother of all that is human.
She is the mother of all,
for contained in her are the seeds of all.
The earth of humankind contains all moisture,
all verdancy, all germinating power.
It is in so many ways fruitful.
All creation comes from it.
Yet it forms not only the basic raw material for mankind,
but also the substance of the incarnation of God's son.

HILDEGARD OF BINGEN

A Reflection on Our Present Plight

The high, the low, all of creation,
God gives to humankind to use.
If this privilege is misused,
God's Justice permits creation to punish humanity.

HILDEGARD OF BINGEN

A Prayer of Gratitude

Most High, all powerful, good Lord,
to you all praise, glory, and honor and all blessing;
to you alone, Most High, they belong
and no man is worthy of naming you.
Praised be you, my Lord, with all your creatures,
especially My Lord Brother Sun,
who brings day, and by whom you enlighten us;
he is beautiful, he shines with great splendor;
of you, Most High, he is the symbol.

Praised be you, my Lord,
for Sister Moon and the Stars:
in the heavens you formed them, clear,
precious and beautiful.

Praised be you, my Lord, for Brother Wind
and for the air and for the clouds,
for the azure calm and for all climes
by which you give life to your creatures.

Praised be you, my Lord, for Sister Water,
who is very useful and humble, precious and chaste.

Praised be you, my Lord, for Brother Fire,
by whom you enlighten the night:
he is beautiful and joyous, indomitable and strong.

Praised be you; my Lord,
for Sister our Mother the Earth
who nourishes us and bears us,
and produces all kinds of fruits,
with the speckled flowers and the herbs.

FRANCIS OF ASSISI,
Canticle of the Sun

The Mystery of Mankind

When I look at the heavens,
the work of thy fingers,
the moon and stars which thou has established –
what is mankind that thou art mindful of them, and the
children of mankind that thou dost care for them?

Yet thou hast made them little less than God, and dost crown
them with glory and honor.
Thou hast given them dominion over the works of thy hands;
thou has put all things under their feet.

PSALM 8:3-6

In the Day of the Lord

The wolf shall dwell with the lamb,
and the leopard shall lie down with the kid,
and the calf and the lion and the fatling together,
and a little child shall lead them.

The cow and the bear shall feed;
their young shall lie down together;
and the lion shall eat straw like the ox.

The sucking child shall play over the hold of the asp,
and the weaned child shall put his hand on the adder's den.

They shall not hurt or destroy
in all my holy mountain;
for the earth shall be full of the knowledge of the Lord
as the waters cover the sea.   ISAIAH 11:6-9

A Voice from the Earth

Enoch looked upon the earth; and he heard a voice
from the bowels thereof, saying,

"Woe, woe is me, the mother of men;
I am pained, I am weary, because of the wickedness of my
children. When shall I rest and be cleansed from the filthiness
which is gone forth out of me?
When will my Creator sanctify me, that I may rest,
and righteousness for a season abide upon my face?"

And when Enoch heard the Earth mourn, he wept,
and cried unto the Lord, saying,
"O Lord, wilt thou not have compassion upon the Earth?"

Pearl of Great Price, Moses 7:48-49,
from the scriptures of the
Church of Jesus Christ of the Latter-day Saints

Hindu Prayers

The Waters of Life

Waters, you are the ones who bring us the life force. Help us to find nourishment so that we may look upon great joy.
Let us share in the most delicious sap that you have, as if you were loving mothers.

Let us go straight to the house of the one for whom your waters give us life and give us birth. For our well-being let the goddesses be an aid to us, the water be for us to drink.
Let them cause well-being and health to flow over us.

Mistresses of all the things that are chosen, ruler over all peoples, the waters are the ones I beg for a cure.
Soma has told me that within the waters are all cures and Agni who is salutary to all.

Waters, yield your cure as an armor for my body, so that I may see the sun for a long time.
Waters, carry far away all of this that has gone bad in me either what I have done in malicious deceit or whatever lie I have sworn to.

I have sought the waters today; we have joined with their sap.
O Agni full of moisture, come and flood me with splendor.

A Prayer for Blessing

May the axe be far away from you; May the fire be far away from you; May there be rain without storm; Lord of Trees, may you be blessed; Lord of Trees, may I be blessed.

Prayer for Peace

Supreme Lord, Let there be peace in the sky and in the atmosphere, peace in the plant world and in the forests;
Let the cosmic powers be peaceful; let Brahma be peaceful;
Let there be undiluted and fulfilling peace everywhere.

ATHARVA VEDA

The Waters, Who Are Goddesses

They who have the ocean as their eldest flow out of the sea, purifying themselves, never resting.

Indra, the bull with the thunderbolt, opened a way for them;
let the waters, who are goddesses, help me here and now.

The waters of the sky or those that flow, those that are dug out or those that arise by themselves,
those pure and clear waters that seek the ocean as their goal—
let the waters, who are goddesses, help me here and now.

Those in whose midst King Varuna moves, looking down upon the truth and falsehood of people,
those pure and clear waters that drip honey—
let the waters, who are goddesses, help me here and now.

Those among whom King Varuna, and Soma, and all the gods drink in ecstasy the exhilarating nourishment,
those into whom Agni Of-all-men entered –
let the waters, who are goddesses, help me here and now.

from the RIG VEDA

The Jain Declaration on Nature

"There is nothing so small and subtle as the atom nor any element so vast as space.
Similarly, there is no quality of soul more subtle than non-violence and no virtue of spirit greater than reverence for life."

"One who neglects or disregards the existence of earth, air, fire, water, and vegetation disregards his own existence which is entwined with them."

MAHAVIRA, 500 CE

The Jain tradition which enthroned the philosophy of ecological harmony and nonviolence as its lodestar flourished for centuries side-by-side with other schools of thought in ancient India. It formed a vital part of the mainstream of ancient Indian life, contributing greatly to its philosophical, artistic, and political heritage. During certain periods of Indian history, many ruling elites as well as large sections of the population were Jains, followers of the *Jinas* (Spiritual Victors).

The ecological philosophy of Jainism, which flows from its spiritual quest, has always been central to its ethics, aesthetics, art, literature, economics, and politics. It is represented in all its glory by the 24 *Jinas* or *Tirthankaras* (Path-finders) of this era whose example and teachings have been its living legacy through the millennia.

Although the ten million Jains estimated to live in modern India constitute a tiny fraction of its population, the message and motifs of the Jain perspective, its reverence for life in all its forms, its commitment to the progress of human civilization and to the preservation of the natural environment continue to have a profound and pervasive influence on Indian life and outlook.

In the 20th century, the most vibrant and illustrious example of Jain influence was that of Mahatma Gandhi, acclaimed as the Father of the Nation. Gandhi's friend, Shrimad Rajchandra, was a Jain. The two great men corresponded until Rajchandra's death, on issues of faith and ethics. The central Jain teaching of *ahimsa* (nonviolence) was the guiding principle of Gandhi's civil disobedience in the cause of freedom and social equality. His ecological philosophy found apt expression in his observation that the greatest work of humanity could not match the smallest wonder of nature. [...]

The ancient Jain scriptural aphorism *Parasparopagraho jivanam* (all life is bound together by mutual support and interdependence) is refreshingly contemporary in its premise and perspective. It defines the scope of modern ecology while extending it further to a more spacious "home." It means that all aspects of nature belong together and are bound in a physical as well as a metaphysical relationship. Life is viewed as a gift of togetherness, accommodation, and assistance in a universe teeming with interdependent constituents.

excerpted by the Editor from
The Jain Declaration on Nature, by Dr. L. M. Singhvi

*A*nd God saw everything that He had made, and found it very good.

And He said: "This is a beautiful world that I have given you.
Take good care of it; do not ruin it."

It is said: Before the world was created,
the Holy One kept creating worlds and destroying them.
Finally He created this one, and was satisfied.
He said to Adam: "This is the last world I shall make.
I place it in your hands: hold it in trust."   *Gates of Prayer*, p. 655

Let the heaven rejoice, let the Earth be glad.
Let the sea and all it contains roar in praise.   Psalm 96

Let the sea roar, and all its creatures; the world, and its inhabitants.
Let the rivers burst into applause,
let the mountains join in acclaim with joy.
The Lord is coming to sustain the Earth.
He will sustain the Earth with kindness,
its people with graciousness.   Psalm 98

How wonderful, O Lord, are the works of Your hands!
The heavens declare Your glory,
the arch of sky displays Your handiwork.
The heavens declare the glory of God.
In Your love You have given us the power to behold the beauty of Your
world, robed all its splendor. The sun and the stars, the valleys and hills,
the rivers and lakes all disclose Your presence.
The Earth reveals God's eternal presence.
The roaring breakers of the sea tell of Your awesome might;
the beasts of the field and the birds of the air bespeak Your wondrous will.
Life comes forth by God's creative will.
In Your goodness You have made us able to hear the music of the world.
The raging of the winds, the whisperings of trees in the wood, and the
precious voices of loved ones reveal to us that You are in our midst.
A divine voice sings through all creation.   *Gates of Prayer*, p.652

Environmental responsibility

The Earth is Adonai's and the fullness thereof.   Psalm 24:1

God acquired possession of the world and apportioned it to humankind
but God always remains the Master of the world.   Rosh Hashanah 31a

All that [we] see – the heaven, the Earth, and all that fills it –
all these things are the external garments of God.

Shneur Zalman of Liadi, Tanya, chapter 42

In the hour when the Holy One created the first human being,
God took the person before all the trees of the garden of Eden,
and said to the person:
"See my works, how fine and excellent they are!
Now all that I have created, for you have I created. Think upon this,
and do not corrupt and desolate my world; for if you corrupt it,
there is no one to set it right after you."   Ecclesiastes Rabbah 7:28

The land is for our use

And God said: "Behold, I have given
you every herb-yielding seed, which is
upon the Earth, and every tree in which
is the fruit of a tree-yielding seed – to
you shall it be for food."

Genesis 1:29

God blessed them; and God said to
them: "Be fruitful and multiply, and
replenish the Earth, and subdue it; and
have dominion over the fish of the sea,
and over the fowl of the air, and over
every living thing that moves on the
Earth."   Genesis 1:28

Reforestation – reclaiming the land

One day he, Honi the circle-drawer,
was journeying on the road and he saw
a man planting a carob tree; he asked
him, "How long does it take [for this
tree] to bear fruit?" The man replied,
"Seventy years." He then further asked
him, "Are you certain that you will live
another seventy years?"
The man replied,
"I found [ready grown] carob trees in
the world; as my ancestors planted
these for me, so I too plant these for
my children."   Taanit 23a,
Rabbi Yochanan Ben Zakai

Environmental land usage

Six years shall you sow your field, and
six years shall you prune your
vineyard, and gather in the produce
thereof. But the seventh year shall be a
Sabbath of solemn rest, Sabbath unto
the Lord, you shall neither sow your
field, nor prune your vineyard."

Leviticus 25:3-4

The Holy One blessed be God said to
the children of Israel: "Sow for six
years and leave the land at rest for the
seventh year, so that you may know the
land is Mine!"   Sanhedrin 39a

Muslim Reflections and Prayer

Under Islam, everything is created by Allah (God) and therefore everything is sacred, useful and has its place in the general scheme of things and in the interest of man.

The protection of God's creation is therefore the duty of the Muslim and God will reward all who protect his creation.

God has created the skies, the earth, the sun, and the moon, the rivers and the mountains. God has created the animals and vegetables, the birds, the fish, and all that exists between the earth and sky!

The totality of the environment is God's creation and man's responsibility to protect.

The Holy *Qur'an* declares, "We have created everything from water." Hence the importance of water resources for human life. The survival of human life also depends upon agriculture and animal husbandry. Hence the Muslim obligation to be kind to animals and grateful for the availability of the rivers and the rain. Indeed, there are special prayers for rain in which Muslims express appreciation for God's bounty and beg Him to continue it by providing the faithful with rain.

The relationship of the Muslim to God is a direct and simple one. A Muslim calls upon his Creator for everything! When he is sick, he prays for God to provide him with health. If he is poor and hungry, he begs God for food and support, and so on. Hence, the permanent link between man and the environment through God and prayers to the Creator.

Islam is a religion which started in the deserts of Arabia with a universal message. Its concern for the environment is a universal concern, cutting across national, religious, and geographical barriers. Its major commandments are directed, not to the Muslims, but to the human race. Hence its call upon "people" (not the Arabs nor the Muslims) to conserve the natural resources which are God's gift to mankind.

There are many verses from the Holy *Qur'an* and *Hadith* (statements by the Prophet) urging people to be kind to the land, to the rivers, to the air and not to abuse the fertile valleys. Kindness to "those who cannot speak" (animals) is urged by the Prophet again and again.

In his letter of recommendation, the First Muslim Khalifa, Abu-Baker, ordered his troops, "Do not cut down a tree, do not abuse a river, do not harm animals, and be always kind and humane to God's creation, even to your enemies."

Muslim commitment to the sanctity of life is most pronounced during the *Hajj* to Mecca, where the pilgrims are not permitted even to kill an insect.

Under Islam, the individual is responsible for the "good" and for the "bad." *En Ahsantutn, Ahsantum le-Anfosekum wa en Asaatumfa-lahaa,* (If you do good things, you do that for yourselves, and if you do wrong things, that is for you, too!) Hence, the responsibility for the protection of the environment is an individual responsibility in the first place and a "collective" obligation of the society secondarily.

Following is a Muslim prayer for rain, called "Prayer for *Istesquaa.*"

O God! The Creator of everything!
You have said that water is
the source of all life!
   When we have needs,
You are the Giver
   When we are sick,
You give us health.
   When we have no food,
You provide us with your bounty.

And so God, presently,
we have no rain. We need water.
Our water resources are dry;
we need you to help
us with rain—
rain for our fields, our orchards
and our animals.
We need water for ablution
and general cleanliness
to prepare for worshiping You,
O Lord.

Our confidence, O Lord,
is in You and Your unlimited mercy
and compassion.

Please, Merciful God,
provide us with rain.

provided by Dr. Mohammed Mehdi, Secretary General,
National Council on Islamic Affairs

Native American Prayers and Reflections

A Call to Prayer

O Great Spirit,
Whose breath gives life to the world
   and whose voice is heard in the soft breeze,
We need your strength and wisdom –
May we walk in beauty.

May our eyes
   ever behold the red and purple sunset;
Make us wise so that we may understand
   what you have taught us.
Help us learn the lessons you have hidden
   in every leaf and rock;
Make us always ready to come to you
   with clean hands and straight eyes,
So when life fades, as the fading sunset,
   our spirits may come to you without shame.

A Prayer of Awareness

Now, Talking God,
With your feet I walk,
I walk with your limbs.
I carry forth your body,
For me your mind thinks,
Your voice speaks for me.
Beauty is before me,
Above and below me hovers the beautiful –
I am surrounded by it,
I am immersed in it.
In my youth I am aware of it,
And in old age I shall walk quietly
The beautiful trail.

The Rights of the Natural World

"There is a hue and cry for human rights –
human rights, they said, for all people.
And the indigenous people said:
   What of the rights of the natural world?
   Where is the seat for the buffalo or the eagle?
   Who is representing them here in this forum?
   Who is speaking for the waters of the earth?
   Who is speaking for the trees and the forests?
   Who is speaking for the fish – for the whales –
   for the beavers – for our children?
We said:
   Given this opportunity to speak
   in this international forum, then it is our duty
   to say that we must stand for these people,
   and the natural world and its rights;
   and also for the generations to come."

                CHIEF OREN LYONS,
   of the Onondaga Nation and the Iroquois Confederacy,
     in his account of speaking to the United Nations in Geneva

Sikh Reflections

Guru Nanak, the founder of Sikhism, very aptly said:

"Air is the vital force, water the progenitor
The vast earth the mother of all.
Day and night are nurses,
fondling all creation in their lap."

Nature is not only the source of life, beauty, and power,
but it is also an inspiration of strength
in formulation of our character.

Man is composed of five elements.
According to the Sikh Scripture, *Guru Granth Sahib*,
these five elements of nature teach us valuable lessons:

Earth teaches us:	patience, love
Air :	mobility, liberty
Fire :	warmth, courage
Sky :	equality, broadmindedness
Water :	purity, cleanliness

We have to imbibe these fine traits of nature
into our personalities for fuller, happier, and nobler lives.

For the sake of posterity, those countless generations
of unborn children to come, let us save this Earth.
Let us not misuse our privileges.
Please don't let the song of birds die.
Don't let the water babies perish.
Don't let magnificent animals become extinct.
Above all, don't let human beings die of starvation
and manmade disasters.

       Live and let live.

Taoist Reflections

Trees and animals, humans and insects,
flowers and birds:
these are active images of the subtle energies
that flow from the stars
throughout the universe.
Meeting and combining with each other
and the elements of the Earth,
they give rise to all living things.

The superior person understands this,
and understands that one's own energies play a part in it.
Understanding these things,
the superior one respects the Earth as mother,
the heavens as father,
and all living things as brothers and sisters.

Those who want to know the truth of the universe
should practice...
   reverence for all life.

This manifests as unconditional love
and respect for oneself and all other beings.

                     LAO TZU

The Gaia Hypothesis

Joel Beversluis

"Most of us sense that the Earth is more than a sphere of rock with a thin layer of air, ocean, and life covering the surface. We feel that we belong here, as if this planet were indeed our home. Long ago, the Greeks, thinking this way, gave to the Earth the name of Gaia."

James Lovelock, *The Ages of Gaia*

A new scientific paradigm and a new mythology

Despite Greek, pagan and other indigenous approaches to Earth, for many hundreds of years the intellectual crest of Western civilization has believed and acted on a clear distinction between "dead" earthly matter and the very precious and improbable forms of life. Furthermore, this scientific belief system – a major paradigm of past and present western civilization with clear ties to Judeo-Christian beliefs – has placed humanity at the pinnacle of earthly life, and perceived all else, alive or not, as arranged for the convenience of humans. This world view, as many Christians and Jews have pointed out, overlooks some of the wisdom from the biblical tradition, and certainly overlooks other religious traditions; nevertheless, this anthropomorphic view of creation, especially the view that the Earth has no intrinsic value apart from human utility, undergirds our religion, science, industry, and ethical systems.

What is remarkable now, in the midst of technological marvels utilizing those assumptions, is that this view is now undergoing a major set of challenges, both scientific and philosophical. It now seems possible that the perspectives of the "dead earth," and mechanistic evolutionary theories about the selection and survival of the fittest, are inadequate science. It also seems that the assumptions which generated these beliefs and methods have led us to the disasters that we are now courting, including widespread extinction of countless species of life.

Earth as a self-regulating organism

Many people are reevaluating both the science and some of the underlying assumptions of Western civilization. They include indigenous friends of the Earth and neo-pagans, but also biochemists, atmospheric scientists and climatologists, geologists, geophysicists, ecophilosophers, and activists, as well as advocates of spiritual and mystic traditions. The Gaia Hypothesis, presented to a once-skeptical but now-interested community of scientists by Dr. James Lovelock, is one focal point of that re-evaluation.

Lovelock is a brilliant and highly respected interdisciplinary scientist with advanced degrees and professorships in medicine, cybernetics, chemistry, marine biology, and atmospheric analysis. In his research he uses state-of-the-art equipment (some of which he invented) to analyze atmospheric, geological, and biochemical conditions. His hypothesis – that Earth functions as though it is a self-regulating organism – is currently undergoing considerable scrutiny by a large and growing body of scientists forced into interdisciplinary studies by his work and its implications.

According to Dr. Michael Cohen, an environmental educator and founder of the National Audubon Society Expedition Institute, and author of *How Nature Works*, the Gaia Hypothesis Symposium sponsored by the National Audubon Society had to turn away more than 100 prospective speakers. Held at the University of Massachusetts in 1985, the excited synthesis and research of respected scientists, philosophers, and others were recorded in conference proceedings that exceeded 1,300 pages. This major conference explored the startling question: *Is the Earth a Living Organism?*

The hypothesis suggests that over a long period, the Earth self-regulates its temperature, atmospheric gas ratios, salinity, chemistry, and geology, utilizing sunlight which it ingests as energy and converts as needed; in short, it functions like a warm-blooded plant cell. Lovelock doesn't say it *is* one, but that the earth *behaves* like a living organism. Furthermore,

> All the entities [of the Earth] interact as a whole, like organelles in a cell. Only when [the scientist] separates them or observes them individually for a short time, do they assume different properties including life and death. Long term, in congress, the entities appear to sense and communicate, thereby sustaining the optimum environment for their cell's life. (Cohen, *How Nature Works,* p. 78.)

Biologist and author Lewis Thomas *(The Lives of a Cell)* suggests that the atmosphere is the Earth cell's membrane wall as it regulates precise amounts of energy capture, storage, and release.

Life means holding out against equilibrium – banking against entropy by using membranes. The Earth has its own membrane, the atmosphere, to constrain the effects of the sun. In Lovelock's words,

> The biota – the sum of all living things, including plants, animals, and micro- organisms – not only profoundly affects the Earth's environment, but acts to maintain and enhance life on the planet. (*Gaia: A New Look at Life*)

Despite entropy

Some evidence suggests that Earth preserves a life-enhancing direction in response to circumstances, despite the laws of chemistry and of entropy. Examples include the following: Earth's many atmospheric gases do not settle into a lifeless equilibrium; oxygen levels remain a constant, life-enhancing 21% by means of the photosynthesis of countless organisms; planetary temperatures tend to remain constant, maintained not only by clouds and carbon dioxide, but by the actions of microorganisms in the oceans in an extensive inter-dependent network of geology, biology, and chemistry; the massive excess of poisonous carbon now stored (buried) in the earth in the form of oil and coal, as well as other signs of the control of disequilibrium suggest that unidentified regulating mechanisms are at work on a global scale, with the apparent purpose of the maintenance of life.

From hypothesis to mythology

There is much more to the hypothesis and its debate than I comprehend or can present in this introduction. I'm not able to confirm or critique its science, though that also has its critics. I can appreciate the hypothesis, however, as part of a new metaphor for Earth, as contributing to the story of a new relationship with it. The bottom line here is, "What difference does it make to us or to Earth's survival?"

At the simplest level, as we learn more about the processes of regulation and adaptation, we may be heartened somewhat by the possibility that we could get unexpected help from Earth as it self-regulates the biosphere. On the other hand, we are also learning how complex the interconnections are, and how serious is the damage that we are doing to those regulating mechanisms. Perhaps we will learn how to work *with* the Earth in processes it once performed autonomously. Certainly, we can better learn to anticipate new causes of damage.

We are learning that Gaia may be resilient, but we also see that we are changing nature, permanently. Increasingly, acts of nature are not "acts of God," but of humanity – or, we might say, *in-humanity*. Nature is no longer an independent and autonomous force, and it's no longer true that "everybody talks about the weather, but nobody does anything about it." We are, in fact, doing much about it; for instance, recent storms which have ripped into the Caribbean and southeastern U.S. coasts, and across Asian islands and continents, are increasing in intensity as a direct result of the oceans' warming. As the band of warm water in which such storms incubate widens and deepens, the size of the storms increases, and the power of the wind increases geometrically. It is probably not coincidence but rather human intervention which has brought us, in the last

15 years many of the most destructive tropical storms ever recorded.

Stewards or pirates?

In response to the Gaia paradigm, we may learn to see Earth-life as inherently valuable; we are coming to see ourselves as part of a whole system, not above it or separate from it; and we can, if we accept that place in it, reestablish our role as stewards of the Earth rather than as abusive, short-term tenants, owners, or profiteers.

Another impact of Lovelock's hypothesis and subsequent responses to it is that the mechanistic sciences are forced to reevaluate their methodologies of specialization and reductionism. It is becoming apparent that holistic, interdisciplinary approaches are crucial to an accurate understanding of the larger picture. Much current science and technology is revealed as inadequate when it appears that a deeper system and apparent "purpose" drive the interconnected forces of evolution, geology, and atmospheric balances.

At the level of popular culture and religion, the hypothesis will encourage appreciation for the relationship of indigenous peoples to Earth. Within Christianity, the Gaia hypothesis can revitalize the appreciation of what it has called "Natural Revelation," reinforcing its wisdom that Earth and life are created blessings and are themselves revelation from God, and that we are gardeners or stewards of Earth, at our best. Within the wider culture, the Gaian mythology and derivative Earth stories may play a role in the conversion of secular cultures to new appreciation for various forms of creation spirituality.

One unexpected consequence of the theory is the assessment – or *hope*, in the face of despair – of some that the Earth's restorative abilities will over-ride the damage we do. As Stephen Scharper notes in "The Gaia Hypothesis," the Gaia theory offers an inspiring vision of interrelatedness, but it may also diminish the human by neglecting our ability to build the world – or to destroy it."

Nature, Gaia, or God?

Many purely scientific proponents of the hypothesis, including Lovelock, resist references to any source of power or purpose outside of Earth itself, claiming that, since Earth and life-forms are the only knowable objects of our science, they also represent the proper limits of reflection. Those who are agnostic, atheist, or who insist on separating their science from metaphysics, are uncomfortable with speculative thinking about God or spiritual powers. It may well be that their science suffers rather than gains from those self-imposed blinders.

Most religious people past and present have believed that Earth-life and visible creation have origins and direction from outside of this system. From the perspective of logic, it is equally reasonable for humans to believe in transcendent sources of life and purpose as it is to believe that all the intelligent direction, interaction, and apparent self-regulation within Nature have evolved autonomously on Earth, out of primordial chaos. While the "scientific" approach claims to believe only in what it can prove, it too

---

James Lovelock participated in the first Global Forum of Spiritual and Parliamentary Leaders in Oxford, UK:

"Politicians of the West and East, the North and South, were at last able to talk of planetary problems, not just human ones. It seemed as if being forced to think of the future of our planet instead of just ourselves induced a larger form of ecumenism, one that encompassed not just the human religions but also the commonwealth of species that form the living part of the Earth itself."

reported in *Earth Conference One,*
by Anuradha Vittachi, Shambhala Publications, 1989, p. x

requires a substantial leap of faith in claiming that what it can't prove doesn't exist.

The Gaia hypothesis, along with other personal and species-wide inclinations, may help nudge science and our modern cultures back to the concept that a directive energy is functioning within Earth's systems. The witness of many religious traditions, of course, declares it – there is One (with many names and descriptions) who created and sustains Earth-life and the mediating forces which act as beneficent caretakers of the systems of this biosphere.

The locus of consciousness

*O*ne chapter of the Gaia mythology describes humans as the locus of Earth-life's upward drive to intelligent and moral consciousness. This scenario places contemporary humans in a period of testing, a window of opportunity where we can choose to match our technological powers with corresponding inner development. That choice may be our only alternative to destroying much of life and ourselves. This *story* can empower us through helping us envision that the species *Homo sapiens* is now challenged

by – take your pick – Earth-life, the crises, the Creator, and/or laws of the cosmos, to join as co-creators in this work of the renewal and care of the Earth. As in mythologies and religions, our response to the challenge can be a spiritual journey, a vision quest in which we discover our values, our calling, and the meaning of our lives within the greater meaning of the cosmos.

REFERENCES:

The Ages of Gaia: A Biography of Our Living Earth, James Lovelock. New York: Bantam Books. Originally published by W.W. Norton, 1988.

Gaia: A Way of Knowing. Political Implications of the New Biology, William Irwin Thompson. Great Barrington, MA.: Inner Traditions/Lindisfarne Press, 1987.

The Gaia Hypothesis: Implications for a Christian Political Theology of the Enviroment, Stephen B. Scharper. "Cross Currents", Summer 1994, pp. 207 - 221.

How Nature Works: Regenerating Kinship with Planet Earth, Michael Cohen, Stillpoint International, Inc., PO Box 640, Walpole, NH, USA

Microcosmos: Four Billion Years of Evolution from our Microbial Ancestors, Lynn Margulis and Dorion Sagan. NY: Summit Books, 1986.

The Universe Story: From the Primordial Flaring Forth to the Ecozoic Era; A Celebration of the Unfolding of the Cosmos, Thomas Berry and Brian Swimme. San Francisco: HarperCollins, 1992

ICCRE and the Earth Charter

The Earth Charter printed below preceded the Earth Charter Initiative described on page 202. This one lays out important ethical and spiritual principles around which legally binding structures and mechanisms could be formulated in the newer, intergovernmental Initiative.

*D*uring the past several years the International Coordinating Committee on Religion and the Earth (ICCRE) has cooperated with the World Council of Churches, the World Conference on Religion and Peace, the World Wide Fund for Nature, the South American Conference on Religion and Ecology, and other international and interfaith organizations in formulating this Earth Charter. The Charter was designed to help people live in harmony with each other and with Earth.

As a distillation of charters written around the world – in New York, Geneva, India, Africa, the Philippines, and Brazil – by members of many religious traditions, the

Earth Charter has been widcly recognized as a document of substance. It was endorsed at the Parliamentary Earth Summit in Rio and adopted at the state level in Minnesota; New Jersey will consider doing the same later this year. The Charter also contributed to the Preamble to the founding constitution of the International Green Cross.

The principles articulated in the Earth Charter are also providing the basis for an intersectoral initiative that ICCRE is launching with business, education, religion, and the arts to create actions and programs that will move us toward a more environmentally responsible society. Additionally, the Charter will be used in efforts by many organizations to lobby the United Nations for the proclamation of an Earth Charter.

Provided by Nancy Moshé

Daniel Martin, Director, ICCRE, P.O. Box 67, Greenwich, CT 06831-0767 USA; tel./fax. (914) 238-5032

The Earth Charter: *A Religious Perspective*

PREAMBLE

I am because we are.

The crisis we face today is a spiritual one:

We have forgotten who we are
We have lost our sense of wonder
We have degraded the Earth
We have exploited our fellow creatures

And we have nowhere else to go.

In our ignorance we have disrupted the balance of life. Now the air we breathe

hurts us and the water we drink poisons us.

All things are bound together:

If we lose the sweetness of the waters, we lose the life of the land.
If we lose the life of the land, we lose the majesty of the forest.
If we lose the majesty of the forest, we lose the purity of the air.
If we lose the purity of the air, we lose the creatures of the Earth.

Not just for ourselves but for our children – now and in the future.

But a new spirit is being born, and a new awareness of our place in this delicate balance. This spirit calls us to:

• a transformation of our hearts and minds
• concrete changes in our way of life
• the renewal of our religions
• the creation of a global society

Today:

We remember who we are
We reclaim our sense of wonder
We acknowledge our responsibility
We commit ourselves to the Earth

**We turn toward each other
in friendship**

We turn again together towards home.

SPIRITUAL PRINCIPLES:

INTERDEPENDENCE

The Earth is an interdependent community of life. All parts of this system are interconnected and essential to the functioning of the whole.

THE VALUE OF LIFE

Life is sacred. Each of the diverse forms of life has its own intrinsic value.

BEAUTY

Earth and all forms of life embody beauty. The beauty of the Earth is food for the human spirit. It inspires human consciousness with wonder, joy, and creativity.

HUMILITY

Human beings are not outside or above the community of life. We have not woven the web of life; we are but a strand within it. We depend on the whole for our very existence.

RESPONSIBILITIES

Human beings have a special capacity to affect the ecological balance. In awareness of the consequences of each action, we have a special responsibility to preserve life in its integrity and diversity and to avoid destruction and waste for trivial or merely utilitarian reasons.

RIGHTS

Every human being has the right to a healthy environment. We must grant this right to others: both those living today and the generations to come.

ETHICS FOR LIVING

SUSTAINABLY

Human beings must live in a way that meets the needs of the present without compromising the ability of future generations to meet their own needs.

JUSTLY

Sufficiently

In a world of great disparities between rich and poor, justice demands that every human being be able to obtain the basic needs of life.

In Participation

Justice demands universal participation in all aspects of a sustainable society through legal
and institutional structures.

In Solidarity

Sustainability with justice will only be achieved through an ethic of global solidarity, which includes the rights of future generations.

PEACEFULLY

The sacredness of life demands the practice of nonviolence; differences must be resolved by consultation rather than conflict. War and the production of weapons destroy the environment as well as human life.

SIMPLY

To establish economic justice, people in the industrialized world must learn to live more frugally. Simplicity of life fosters both inner freedom and outer sustainability.

KNOWLEDGEABLY

Environmental education and free access to information are essential for global awareness and skillful care of the Earth.

HOLISTICALLY

Human life, to be fully human, must include physical, intellectual, moral, and spiritual development within the community of all life.

PROGRAM AREAS:

Our concern for all life expresses itself not only in our prayers and in statements of principles, but in actions in our personal, professional and political lives. We, representatives of the world's religious communities, recommend action in the following program areas. We also call upon our members to develop actions around these areas, and to promote and implement them in their personal and professional lives.

LOCAL AND INDIVIDUAL LEVEL

1. Education

The promotion of environmental education as an integral and compulsory part of school curricula.

2. Health

The promotion of environmental education as a mandatory component of all health care, both in medical schools and in medical practice.

3. Food Production

The promotion of sustainable farming systems as the basis of all agricultural food production, including the preservation and integration of indigenous methods and indigenous foods.

4. Food Consumption

The promotion of food consumption that is lower on the food chain (less energy consuming), as well as food that is organically, humanely, and locally produced.

5. Energy

The promotion of sustainable patterns of energy consumption through net reduction, increased efficiency, and minimal use of fossil fuels.

6. Transport

The promotion of transport forms that are less energy consuming and less polluting.

7. Wildlife

The protection and, where necessary, the restoration of biological diversity, and the revival of the traditional peaceful coexistence between people and wild animals.

8. Family and Community

The promotion of the "extended family" or similar forms of community as the basic unit for integrated and environmentally balanced living.

9. Population

The promotion of population education toward the reduction of birth rates, and the related appreciation of economic and social factors.

10. Grassroots Movements

The promotion of grassroots movements to protect the environment from vested interests of all kinds (i.e. the Chipko Movement in India).

11. Religious Traditions

The promotion of religious traditions and practices that foster concern and responsibility for the environment, and the challenging of those that do not. This would include the protection and restoration of many of the indigenous values and practices which have a particular contribution to make in this area.

12. Regional Policies

The promotion of regional policies and legislation that would consider not only local effects, but also the impact on the rest of the world.

13. Local Government

The development of local government policies and structures for the promotion of the above programs.

INTERNATIONAL LEVEL

1. International Wealth

The redistribution of land, wealth and natural resources for the good of many. This will require a restructuring of the present economic system that would include the promotion of "quality of life indicators," rather than simply measures of quantity, and address the issue of debt and world trade agreements.

2. A Transnational Approach

The establishment of procedures and mechanisms that would permit a transnational approach to environmental issues and disputes, including standards, accountability, and enforcement.

3. Transnational Sharing

The promotion of appropriate technology exchange: new technology from the industrialized countries and indigenous technology from the poorer nations.

4. Finances

The creation of a "world fund" for the protection of the environment: money to be raised through projects like "energy taxation," an "Earth stamp," etc.

5. Transnational Corporations

The limitation of the power of transnational corporations, as well as the encouragement of their enormous ability to foster justice and sustainability.

6. Militarization

The promotion of complete disarmament, the termination of all weapon production and trade, and the ending of military technology transfer.

7. Science

The encouragement of scientists to be environmentally responsible and to use their knowledge and skill to help alleviate environmental problems.

8. Media

The promotion of mass/electronic media for the development of ecological attitudes, values, and skills.

9. Women and Children

The promotion of full and equal participation of women in all government and nongovernmental organizations, in decision-making, implementation, administration, and funding at international, national, and community levels. The protection of women and children as the most vulnerable to environmental and economic injustice.

10. Indigenous Peoples

The support of indigenous peoples in their efforts to protect their natural environments, and the recognition of the special contribution of indigenous peoples in providing vital wisdom and leadership in resisting the forces that are destroying the earth.

11. Biotechnology

Contribution to the ethical process involved in the development and application of biotechnology and genetic engineering.

12. Wilderness

The promotion of protection of remaining habitat (forests, wetlands, rivers, estuaries, etc.) through wilderness preservation and sustainable life practices.

FOR MORE INFORMATION:

The Earth Council,
P.O. Box 2323-1002, San José, Costa Rica
tel. (506) 23-3418; or
Chairman's Office: Maurice Strong,
700 University Avenue (H19A27), Toronto,
Ontario, M5G 1X6 Canada
Working to mobilize popular and political support for the Earth Charter Initiative, a legally-binding global structure.

Earth Day Energy 2000
P.O. Box 266, Amherst, NH 03031
(603) 672-5441 or 5442
A five-year program to assist communities in implementing energy efficient standards.

Earth Pledge, One World, Inc.
Cronkhite Beach Building 1055,
Sausalito, CA 94965; tel. (800) 327-8495
A powerful pledge and campaign to further empower people's commitment to the earth.

Greenpeace, 1436 U Street, N.W.,
Washington, DC 20009 USA.
This very activist and grassroots organization is known for dramatic

interventions and publicity on behalf of endangered species, from whales to humans.

The National Religious Partnership
for the Environment
1047 Amsterdam Avenue,
New York, NY 10025 USA
tel. 212-316-7441 / fax. 212-316-7547
Four faith traditions have joined in an enormous cooperative effort to provide resource materials to congregations.

Project Earthlink,
NOAA Office of Global Programs,
Suite 1225, 1100 Wayne Avenue,
Silver Spring, MD 20910
tel.(301) 427-2089 ex. 20
A massive public education program on global change created and sponsored by 13 major federal agencies and involving programs for education among formal and informal educators as well as for community environmental organizers.

Shomrei Adamah – Keepers of the Earth
5500 Wissahickon Ave #804C,
Philadelphia, PA 19144
tel. (215) 844-8150

Renewing Jewish ecological wisdom with numerous resources.

United Nations Environment Programme
Regional Office for North America:
Room DC2-803, United Nations, N.Y. 10017
tel. (212) 963-8139 / fax. (212) 963-7341

UNEP International Headquarters:
P.O. Box 30552
Nairobi, Kenya
tel. (254) (2) 333939/ 520600

Worldwatch Institute
1776 Massachusetts Ave., N.W.,
Washington, D.C. 20077-6628
tel. (202) 452-1999 / fax. (202) 296-7365
E-mail: wwpub@igc.apc.org
Annual State of the World Reports. For nearly two decades, the Worldwatch research team has gathered and published some of the most up-to-date and reliable information on the condition of our planet and species. Believing that knowledge is the key to effective action, Worldwatch has helped spur the debate and spark action on the world's most pressing environmental and development problems.

Congregations Fight Environmental Degradation

National Religious Partnership for the Environment (NRPE)

March 31, 1994 – A mysterious chemical release in the air in the Newark area has local activists organizing against mercury emissions caused by incineration and against other suspected carcinogenic pollutants in their environment. They attend hearings, sign petitions, write letters and demonstrate at the Rahway incinerator – all as members of St. John's Episcopal Church under the guidance of Rev. Joseph Parrish.

Environmental activism in the American religious community continues to spread as diverse congregations across the country become Earth stewards in their communities. Other examples of faith-based environmental activism include:

- Cajun country Catholic parishes working to protect coastal Louisiana from flooding and erosion
- A West Dallas black pastor establishing a church-based health clinic for victims of lead poisoning
- A Wisconsin interfaith organization fighting statewide environmental degradation due to gravel-pit mining
- A Savannah Christian school opening EDEN, a 227-acre schoolyard natural habitat for environmental education
- An Englewood, Colorado, church undergoing a $2 million renovation incorporating environmentally-sound practices such as solar heating and natural lighting
- A rabbi in St. Louis researching the damaging effect of river levees on their ecosystems
- Akron-based nuns offering inner-city children a hands-on educational farming experience

Major faith groups offer kits to over 50,000 congregations

*S*uch initiatives are fueling a three-year mobilization recently undertaken by the National Religious Partnership for the Environment (NRPE), a coalition of major faith groups serving more than 100 million Americans. To further encourage these local efforts, members of NRPE sent educational and action kits to 50,000 congregations on Earth Day (April 24, 1994), including every Catholic parish and reform and conservative synagogue in the country.

These kits will suggest ways for congregations to integrate environmental themes into sermons, worship and liturgy, religious education, lifestyle changes, community outreach, and legislative advocacy.

Member groups of NRPE include: the U.S. Catholic Conference, the National Council of Churches of Christ, the Evangelical Environmental Network, and the Coalition on the Environment and Jewish Life. NRPE's mission is to offer a distinctively religious response linking issues of environmental protection and social justice.

See National Religious Partnership on the Environment in Chapter 42 for information on ordering the kits from major faith groups.

An Evangelical Declaration on the Care of Creation

One significant indication of the growing environmental concern among Christians is the work of the Evangelical Environmental Network (EEN). Initiated by Evangelicals for Social Action (ESA) and World Vision, EEN is a part of the National Religious Partnership on the Environment, an interfaith environmental movement with four partners: Roman Catholic, mainline Protestant, Jewish, and evangelical Protestant. The following is adapted from a press release.

*A*fter a year of preparation, leaders representative of a wide cross-section of evangelical constituencies recently issued [early 1994] the first substantial evangelical call for environmental stewardship. By May 26, the resulting document, *An Evangelical Declaration on the Care of Creation,* had been endorsed by over two hundred evangelical leaders and organizations.

The Declaration's intent is to call evangelical Christians to greater ecological faithfulness. The document addresses the environmental "degradation" that the church has silently been complicit in, and calls Christians to both theological reflection and practical repentance. Noting that many have become convinced that environmental healing is outside the realm of the Church, the Declaration decries the tendency of Christians to let environmental activism become the realm of only the non-believer. While carefully distancing itself from the pantheistic notions of the New Age, and reaffirming the notion of a fallen creation and humanity's creatureliness, the document makes clear the biblical responsibility of every Christian to care for God's Earth. Indeed, the document affirms that the impact of the redemptive work of Christ extends to the whole of the Earth, and the reconciliation Christ offers the Christian reaches to all relationships:

> The presence of the Kingdom of God is marked not only by renewed fellowship with God, but also by renewed harmony and justice between people, and by renewed harmony and justice between people and the rest of the created world.

The authors of *An Evangelical Declaration on the Care of Creation* were gathered by the Evangelical Environmental Network (EEN), and include a distinguished group of evangelical leaders. The EEN will continue its effort to provide a biblical basis for evangelical churches to use in responding to environmental issues and challenges. In the spring of 1994, EEN distributed 20,000 environmental awareness kits to evangelical congregations across the country. These kits contain resources to help churches both provide biblical environmental education and concrete approaches to action in their communities. As well, the EEN will continue to work closely with other evangelical environmental groups, including the Green Cross and the Christian Environmental Association.

Copies of the *Declaration* may be obtained from EEN, 10 East Lancaster Avenue, 10 Lancaster Avenue, Wynnewood PA 19096-3495
tel. (610) 645-9393 / fax. (610) 645-9395

Human Rights and Religious Freedom

Faith in Human Rights: *Our Challenge in the 1990s*

Dr. Robert Traer

General Secretary of the International Association for Religious Freedom, an interreligious organization based in Oxford, England, with NGO affiliation with the United Nations

*W*e are challenged both by the events of our time and by our faith commitments to support human rights. Brutal warfare, starvation, ethnic cleansing, and religious intolerance make the struggle for human rights more necessary than ever. At the same time greater cooperation among people of different faith traditions and the support within their communities for human rights make the struggle for human rights more encouraging. Human rights are violated everywhere, but everywhere men and women of faith assert that every person has the right to human dignity.

I say "men and women of faith" are asserting human rights, because human rights are not simply a matter of law but of faith. The Universal Declaration of Human Rights, which was passed without dissenting vote by the General Assembly of the United Nations in 1948 and is the foundation of international human rights law, affirms that

> "the peoples of the United Nations have in the (UN) Charter reaffirmed their *faith in fundamental human rights,* in the dignity and worth of the human person and in the equal rights of men and women and have determined to promote social progress and better standards of life in larger freedom." *[emphasis added]*

Human Rights cannot simply be derived from legal precedents of the past, nor from empirical evidence or logic, but require a "leap of faith."

Human rights in the 20th century

*P*rior to World II, international law was the law of nations, and thus the rights of a human person were the rights granted by his or her government. This understanding of rights was supported by modern legal theory which holds that laws are simply the decisions of governments and that there is no other "higher law." Faith in this theory and system of law was shattered by the acts of Nazi Germany, for the Nazis legislated the extermination of the Jews. These Nazi laws were clearly wrong, but how were they to be condemned by a system of international law which allowed for no standards by which to judge the authority of a state?

The Nuremberg trials assessed a higher standard, and the United Nations codified this as international human rights law. Since 1948 these laws have grown to include numerous covenants (or treaties) and international mechanisms such as the UN Human Rights Commission and Subcommission. At the same time the number of nations in the UN has expanded rapidly, due to the liberation of peoples in Africa and Asia from colonial rule. The UN has become more prominent, if no less controversial, and assertions of human rights have continued to capture international attention.

In the last 45 years human rights have expanded conceptually as well. The Universal Declaration of Human Rights was dominated by notions of civil and political rights, which are most familiar to Westerners. But economic and social rights concerning employment, food, shelter, education, and health care were also affirmed. More recently, accompanying the growing strength of formerly colonized peoples in the UN, cultural and peoples' rights have been asserted. We see here a shift in emphasis from the individual to the group, from protection of the dignity of the individual from state intervention, to providing for communities the elements of life deemed necessary for human dignity through state intervention.

Agreement on the nature and scope of human rights is a matter of debate, of course, not only among political leaders and international lawyers, but also among religious leaders from a variety of cultures and traditions. As conflict between religious communities seems to be increasing in many parts of the world, support for human rights among religious leaders may prove ever more important.

Religious support for human rights

*W*hen we reflect on the historical development of human rights, we see immediately that for most of human history religious leaders resisted what we today describe as human rights. Traditionally, religious leaders have been primarily concerned with enforcing their authority and with the welfare of their community, rather than with the rights of its members, especially if recognizing these rights meant permitting dissent. Thus, religious people who now support human rights should in good conscience confess that their traditions and teachings have generally been used to deny many of these rights.

Yet, religious leaders were among the first to assert that

the UN promulgate a Declaration of Human Rights, and Christian and Jewish leaders actively lobbied the UN Commission that drafted it. The World Council of Churches provided leadership among Protestant Christian groups, and, after Vatican II, members of the Roman Catholic Church have been in the forefront of the human rights struggle in Asia, Africa, and Latin America. Jewish participants in the human rights movement are far more numerous than their small numbers in the world would lead one to expect. And more recently prominent Muslims have asserted that the Islamic tradition supports fundamental human rights.

Within the theistic traditions human rights are understood as God-given. Men and women created in the image of God are seen as having rights, because of the freedom of God. The nature of these rights is discerned from the scriptures of the particular tradition. As the word "right" rarely appears in these scriptures, notions of human rights tend to be derived from teachings about duty.

The idea that rights are part of relationships is something that all religious traditions share, although the emphasis on individual rights may vary considerably. From the religious point of view a person has a right in relation to others, in the context of relationships and mutual obligations. These duties and rights are part of the fabric of community. Communities are constituted by religious teachings, common discipline, and (from the point of view of theistic traditions) by God. Rights are thus a fundamental part of the nature of communities.

This is different from the view which dominated the drafting of the Universal Declaration of Human Rights, and the development of human rights law in the first part of the second half of the 20th century. From this other point of view, which dominates modern, Western political thought, rights are inherent in the individual, who joins together with other individuals to form communities. Thus rights are brought into society by individuals, who in theory form a "social contract" with one another in order to live together. In this perspective the community is a voluntary association, which the individual can leave or join, as he or she chooses.

These two different understandings of the nature of human rights can lead to disagreements. For example, the more individualistic perspective dominates the formulation of religious freedom in the Universal Declaration of Human Rights and the Covenant on Civil and Political Rights. In the words of the Universal Declaration, it is "freedom of thought, conscience and religion" which is protected and this includes the freedom to change one's religion or belief as well as the freedom to join with others in teaching, practicing, worshipping, and observing the religious disciplines of one's tradition. Thus freedom of religion is primarily an individual right, although it may be asserted by a group of individuals.

This understanding of the right to religious freedom reflects the Western notion of religion, as a voluntary activity of individuals who join together to practice what their individual consciences tell them is right. Because this is largely a modern, Western notion of religion, it is not surprising that more traditional religious communities are

less than enthusiastic about this emphasis on the rights of the individual believer. In their view, if rights are given by God to the community of the faithful, then individual rights are secondary, not primary. The rights of the entire community take precedence.

For example, many Muslims are loath to support the right of an individual to convert from Islam to another religion. They believe that God has constituted the Islamic community to rule in his stead. To convert from Islam is thus to reject God and those who are charged to rule for God. It is inconceivable, for many Muslims, that one can have a right to turn away from God, to err, and to go astray.

This position is not unique to Islam. Prior to the 18th century it was the view of most religious communities, at least among the theistic traditions. It was the position of the Roman Catholic Church until the latter part of this century, and it is affirmed in slightly different ways by many Christian groups today. What is neglected in such a position, of course, is the idea that God wants obedience to be freely given. Muslims who support the right of conversion quote from the Quran: "Let there be no compulsion in religion." Such a text, however, envisions the religious community more as a voluntary association of believers, rather than as a community constituted by God which must be protected from deviation by its leadership. And this view of religious community is strongly opposed by the leaders of many religious traditions.

It is not helpful to characterize a position which stresses community interests over individual interests as counter to human rights, for those who assert such a position believe they are affirming the community's right to religious freedom. The claim of the Unitarian Church in Romania may put this perspective in a more sympathetic light for many of us. The Unitarians in Romania, who are part of the Hungarian minority community, claim the right to operate confessional secondary schools in their own language, for their own people, but to have these schools supported by the state. The Romanian government asserts the right to integrate Romanian students (who are neither Hungarian nor Unitarian) into state supported schools, claiming that the right to religious freedom is protected by freedom of worship and religious education in the churches, and that the government has no obligation to support confessional schools for minority students so that they may study their religion with one another in their own language.

The International Association for Religious Freedom (IARF) has supported the Unitarians in its struggle with the Romanian state, as it is clear that integrating Romanian students into the confessional schools, which have for centuries nurtured the minority Hungarian Unitarian community, is part of the government's plan to destroy the minority Hungarian community by assimilating it into Romanian society. Denying places for the public education of young people in the Hungarian Unitarian tradition would make it much more difficult for that minority community to pass on its religious traditions and identity to its young people.

Yet, the issue is not a clear-cut one, and thus assertions of the right of religious freedom may genuinely be made by those who stress community rights as well as those who recognize only individual rights. What is needed here is communication between the two, respect for their differences, and protection within the society for minority views whatever the law may decide about the balance between the two positions.

Notwithstanding these differences, it must be stressed that support for human rights among leaders of different religious traditions is substantial. Given the history of conflict between religious communities, both in different religious traditions and within the same tradition, we might well conclude that this agreement is astonishing. Certainly it is unprecedented, as is the *faith* in human rights as expressed in the Universal Declaration of Human Rights and as affirmed by men and women of faith all around the world.

Human rights enforcement

*T*he religious communities have played and can now play a significant role in the enforcement of human rights law. This is particularly the case because of the unique nature of international law in our time. Unlike the laws of a state, international human rights law has no coercive authority to back it up. The United Nations does not have enforcement powers, except as granted by its member nations, and then only for very limited purposes.

For many, this fact suggests that human rights law is merely a legal fiction, a romantic idea, until a world government with enforcement powers is created. Others argue, however, that the enforcement of international human rights law is an experiment in nonviolent community building. Nonviolent methods for enforcing human rights laws include exposing human rights violations to public scrutiny and shame, economic and political sanctions, and forms of cooperation among community groups including religious organizations.

Religious ideals and discipline may help keep the human rights struggle nonviolent, may encourage political leaders to live up to the higher aspirations of their religious and cultural traditions, and may help build trust between minority and majority communities in a society. We see examples of this in the movement led by Gandhi in India, in the role of Christians and Jewish leaders during the civil rights movement in the United States during the 1960s, in the leadership of Christians and Muslims in fighting apartheid in South Africa, and in the martyrdom of religious leaders in the struggle for human rights all around the world.

Thus support in religious traditions not only provides a foundation for human rights, which may otherwise appear to be merely the consensus of a particular culture or a particular time, but also translates the imperatives of human rights into the moral and spiritual language of different religious and cultural traditions, allowing more people to claim these rights as their own heritage.

Our challenge now

*W*hat then is our challenge now? Often human rights issues seem beyond our control, involving governments and political forces that are hard to influence. Yet, the human rights struggle is compelling, because it affirms the fundamental human dignity of each person. This is a radical assertion and deserves our active support. It is a leap of faith to claim that each person, regardless of his or her intelligence, morality or circumstances, is a human being who deserves to be treated with respect. There is little in the history of civilization to support this claim and much to deny it. It is simply wonderful that this claim even has a hearing today.

In the IARF we support the claim to human dignity both as a legal claim under international law and as a religious claim, which has found support within many of the world's religious traditions. As an association of religious and humanist groups, the IARF does not hold to one theory of the nature of human rights, but urges members within all the religious traditions to find their own way of understanding and supporting human dignity. It acknowledges that different conclusions may be drawn within different religious communities, and that these different conclusions deserve to be taken seriously and discussed in good faith.

This is why the IARF supports interfaith activities which bring together people of different religious traditions. It seeks to discover areas of agreement and cooperation among members of diverse religious communities. Conceptual differences may not necessarily inhibit cooperation among different religious communities in support of human rights. In fact, it is the experience of the IARF that members of all the major religious traditions are able to join together in support of many fundamental human rights.

Because of its heritage as an association of minority groups, who have suffered ostracism and been oppressed, the IARF focuses on the human right of religious freedom. Moreover, as its constituency of religious and humanist groups includes a diversity of traditions, the IARF has developed a particular methodology emphasizing support for constructive community leadership. Specifically, the IARF assists religious communities, rather than taking up individual cases in the way that Amnesty International does. It seeks to help local religious leaders create the social conditions necessary for the enforcement of laws protecting religious freedom. Wherever there are cases of individual violations of religious freedom, there are religious communities that are oppressed. But in these same communities, there are religious leaders struggling to create viable alternatives to being victimized. The IARF supports the initiatives of these local leaders.

Thus, the IARF supports efforts to develop respect among the different religious and ethnic communities and the enforcement of international law in the society. It sponsors interfaith activities to develop the social understanding and consensus necessary for the protection of religious freedom. It promotes and publicizes constructive programs in divided societies, programs which bring together people of different faith and ethnic traditions.

For example, at the IARF Congress in Bangalore, India, in August 1993, Muslims, Hindus, Christians, Buddhists, members of indigenous traditions, and others talked and ate and prayed together. Muslims who had not previously been involved in interfaith dialogue invited more than 200 visitors to their College in order to share their views and to listen to those who might disagree with them (and some did, rather vociferously). Visitors went to a village of Muslims and Hindus, where the IARF has supported efforts to improve agriculture and education and to care for orphans.

As an association of religious and humanist groups, the IARF is founded on the belief that people of different faith traditions and philosophies can become friends, can share in eating and celebrating, can act in solidarity with minority religious communities which are being persecuted, and can help religious people of different traditions understand each other and cooperate together. The work of the IARF puts this belief to the test.

In the end, this all comes down to what you and I do in our own communities. All life is local. There is no global or international life, although today there is a global or international dimension to all local life. We are all affected by what is happening all over the world. But we live our lives in the world of our friends and neighbours and communities and voluntary associations and societies.

Our religious traditions are real for us in our fellowships and churches and synagogues and mosques and temples and, for some, in our interfaith activities as well. But it is here, among people we know and others we hope to know, that the human rights struggle goes on and will either be won or lost. The IARF is thus nothing other than the local activities of people like you and me, people who care enough about the whole world to care about their part of it, people who care enough about human dignity to care about the persons in their own communities, people who care enough about those yet to be born to care about what kind of neighborhood and community they will inherit.

The IARF methodology is basic to every religious tradition. It involves reaching out in friendship, getting to know others who are different, sharing by listening as well as talking, respecting differences and building on agreements, supporting constructive leadership, being compassionate, and standing by our friends when they are in trouble. Support for religious freedom is as simple, and as challenging, as that.

The NGO Committee on Freedom of Religion and Belief

*T*he United Nations has long been concerned with promoting greater religious freedom, beginning with the adoption of Article 18 of the Universal Declaration of Human Rights in 1948. Its most recent achievement was the adoption in 1981 of the Declaration on the Elimination of All Forms of Intolerance and or Discrimination Based on Religion or Belief. Among the official UN offices concerned with religious freedom is a Human Rights Committee which monitors the Covenant on Civil and Political Rights and a Special Rapporteur on Religious Intolerance who works out of the office of the Commission on Human Rights in Geneva.

The NGO Committee on Freedom of Religion and Belief is composed of representatives of many nongovernmental organizations working in the UN community. The Committee was formed in 1990-91 to seek to strengthen the effectiveness of the United Nations in the prevention of religious intolerance and discrimination and in the advancement of religious freedom. While working to enhance the effectiveness of existing UN human rights mechanisms, the Committee also continues consultations with missions and encourages the drafting and passage of a UN convention on freedom of religion and belief.

Another effort (by Project Tandem with the help of Sue Nichols, President of this NGO Committee) is a World Report on Freedom of Thought, Conscience, Religion or Belief, which will consist of reports on the situations in 65 countries. The NGO Committee and the Committee of Religious NGOs at the UN also organize the annual Day for Freedom of Religion or Belief at the UN.

This committee provides a very good example of an interfaith organization that is working for the common good, including for those with no organized voice in international forums. Its members come from more than 30 religiously diverse NGOs, including Anglicans, Baha'is, Franciscans, the Humanist and Ethical Union, the International Association for Religious Freedom, Mahavir Jains, the Women of Reform Judaism, Lutherans, Pax Christi, Presbyterians, Seventh Day Adventists and the World Conference on Religion and Peace, among many others.

Compiled by the Editor from documents provided by the Committee

FOR MORE INFORMATION:

NGO Committee on Freedom of Religion or Belief,
Sue Nichols, President, 546 East 11th Street - Apartment 4-A,
New York, NY 10009; tel. 212-687-2163 / fax 212-808-5480

See Chapter 42 on IARF and other organizations.

"...in my understanding of the challenge we face, we might be guided by Gandhi, who believed that the political campaign he led for justice and freedom would only succeed if it was grounded in community building efforts. I want to suggest that this is also true of an interfaith campaign for the realization of religious freedom. Interfaith support for religious freedom ought to include affirming international human rights standards and their enforcement, but such assertions ought not to be the sole focus of an interfaith

strategy. The law sets only minimum standards and is more effective in addressing intolerance than in creating respect. An interfaith strategy ought to seek to strengthen community life, which reduces the emotional appeal of intolerance and fosters respect for different religious and cultural traditions, because these are the conditions which make it possible to enforce religious freedom."
DR. ROBERT TRAER,
at the May 25, 1994, meeting of the NGO Committee

Universal Declaration of Human Rights

Adopted by the United Nations General Assembly, December 10, 1948.

This *Declaration,* now nearly fifty years old, remains highly relevant. It continues to be the standard for numerous international declarations and conventions on topics ranging from the rights of children and women, to religious freedom, and political, social and economic development.

The United Nations Conference on Human Rights, held in Vienna from June 14 – 25, 1993, drew more than 2,000 representatives of 171 Member States along with more than 3,000 representatives of 813 NGO's, and many others.

The conference was marked by an unusually high level of passion and clash over the universality of the principles and over the mesh of human rights, democracy, national sovereignty, and development. In addition, other issues such as torture, sexual slavery of women, and mistreatment of indigenous peoples vied for attention. Many NGO groups were frustrated by missed opportunities and by a lack of new initiatives for promoting and protecting human rights. Pierre Sane of Amnesty International summed up this critique:

> There has been no reprieve for the victims, as governments [merely] fine-tuned their official declarations.... No radically new principles have been articulated...to move... from a 'common standard of achievement' to 'an obligation under international law'.

Among the challenges that remain are: 1) identifying the political, economic and cultural world views that cause human rights violations; 2) challenging those systems that allow human rights abuses to continue even where, in principle, they are found objectionable; 3) moving to effective enforcement through international law.

Whereas recognition of the inherent dignity and of the equal and inalienable rights of all members of the human family is the foundation of freedom, justice and peace in the world,

Whereas disregard and contempt for human rights have resulted in barbarous acts which have outraged the conscience of mankind, and the advent of a world in which human beings shall enjoy freedom of speech and belief and freedom from fear and want has been proclaimed as the highest aspiration of the common people,

Whereas it is essential, if man is not to be compelled to have recourse, as a last resort, to rebellion against tyranny and oppression, that human rights should be protected by the rule of law,

Whereas it is essential to promote the development of friendly relations between nations,

Whereas the peoples of the United Nations have in the Charter reaffirmed their faith in fundamental human rights, in the dignity and worth of the human person and in the equal rights of men and women and have determined to promote social progress and better standards of life in larger freedom,

Whereas Member States have pledged themselves to achieve, in cooperation with the United Nations, the promotion of universal respect for and observance of human rights and fundamental freedoms,

Whereas a common understanding of these rights and freedoms is of the greatest importance for the full realization of this pledge,

Now, therefore, the General Assembly proclaims this **Universal Declaration of Human Rights** as a common standard of achievement for all peoples and all nations, to the end that every individual and every organ of society, keeping this Declaration constantly in mind, shall strive by teaching and education to promote respect for these rights and freedoms and by progressive measures, national and international, to secure their universal and effective recognition and observance, both among the peoples of Member States themselves and among the peoples of territories under their jurisdiction.

Article 1. All human beings are born free and equal in dignity and rights. They are endowed with reason and conscience and should act towards one another in a spirit of brotherhood.

Article 2. Everyone is entitled to all the rights and freedoms set forth in this Declaration, without distinction of any kind, such as race, colour, sex, language, religion, political or other opinion, national or social origin, property, birth, or other status.

Furthermore, no distinction shall be made on the basis of the political, jurisdictional, or international status of the country or territory to which a person belongs, whether it be independent, trust, non-selfgoverning, or under any other limitation of sovereignty.

Article 3. Everyone has the right to life, liberty and security of person.

Article 4. No one shall be held in slavery or servitude; slavery and the slave trade shall be prohibited in all forms.

Article 5. No one shall be subjected to torture or to cruel, inhuman or degrading treatment or punishment.

Article 6. Everyone has the right to recognition everywhere as a person before the law.

Article 7. All are equal before the law and are entitled without any discrimination to equal protection of the law. All are entitled to equal protection against any discrimination in violation of this Declaration and against any incitement to such discrimination.

Article 8. Everyone has the right to an effective remedy by the competent national tribunals for acts violating the fundamental rights granted him by the constitution or by law.

Article 9. No one shall be subjected to arbitrary arrest, detention, or exile.

Article 10. Everyone is entitled in full equality to a fair and public hearing by an independent and impartial tribunal, in the determination of his rights and obligations and of any criminal charge against him.

Article 11. (1) Everyone charged with a penal offence has the right to be presumed innocent until proved guilty according to law in a public trial at which he has had all the guarantees necessary for his defence.

(2) No one shall be held guilty of any penal offence on account of any act or omission which did not constitute a penal offence, under national or international law, at the time when it was committed. Nor shall a heavier penalty be imposed than was applicable at the time the penal offence was committed.

Article 12. No one shall be subjected to arbitrary interference with his privacy, family, home, or correspondence, nor to attacks upon his honour and reputation. Everyone has the right to the protection of the law against such interference or attacks.

Article 13. (1) Everyone has the right to freedom of movement and residence within the borders of each State.

(2) Everyone has the right to leave any country, including his own, and to return to his country.

Article 14. (1) Everyone has the right to seek and to enjoy in other countries asylum from persecution.

(2) This right may not be invoked in the case of prosecutions genuinely arising from non-political crimes or from acts contrary to the purposes and principles of the United Nations.

Article 15. (1) Everyone has the right to a nationality.

(2) No one shall be arbitrarily deprived of his nationality nor denied the right to change his nationality.

Article 16. (1) Men and women of full age, without any limitation due to race, nationality or religion, have the right to marry and to found a family. They are entitled to equal rights as to marriage, during marriage, and at its dissolution.

(2) Marriage shall be entered into only with the free and full consent of the intending spouses.

(3) The family is the natural and fundamental group unit of society and is entitled to protection by society and the State.

Article 17. (1) Everyone has the right to own property alone as well as in association with others.

(2) No one shall be arbitrarily deprived of his property.

Article 18. Everyone has the right to freedom of thought, conscience, and religion; this right includes freedom to change his religion or belief, and freedom, either alone or in community with others and in public or private, to manifest his religion or belief in teaching, practice, worship, and observance.

Article 19. Everyone has the right to freedom of opinion and expression; this right includes freedom to hold opinions without interference and to seek, receive, and impart information and ideas through any media and regardless of frontiers.

Article 20. (1) Everyone has the right to freedom of peaceful assembly and association.

(2) No one may be compelled to belong to an association.

Article 21. (1) Everyone has the right to take part in the government of his country, directly or through freely chosen representatives.

(2) Everyone has the right of equal access to public service in his country.

(3) The will of the people shall be the basis of the authority of government; this will shall be expressed in periodic and genuine elections which shall be by universal and equal suffrage and shall be held by secret vote or by equivalent free voting procedures.

Article 22. Everyone, as a member of society, has the right to social security and is entitled to realization, through national effort and international cooperation and in accordance with the organization and resources of each State, of the economic, social and cultural rights indispensable for his dignity and the free development of his personality.

Article 23. (1) Everyone has the right to work, to free choice of employment, to just and favourable conditions of work and to protection against unemployment.

(2) Everyone, without any discrimination, has the right to equal pay for equal work.

(3) Everyone has the right to just and favourable remuneration ensuring for himself and his family an existence worthy of human dignity, and supplemented, if necessary, by other means of social protection.

(4) Everyone has the right to form and to join trade unions for the protection of his interests.

Article 24. Everyone has the right to rest and leisure, including reasonable limitation of working hours and periodic holidays with pay.

Article 25. (1) Everyone has the right to a standard of living adequate for the health and well-being of himself and of his family, including food, clothing, housing and medical care, and necessary social services, and the right to security in the event of unemployment, sickness, disability, widowhood, old age or other lack of livelihood in circumstances beyond his control.

(2) Motherhood and childhood are entitled to special care and assistance. All children, whether born in or out of wedlock, shall enjoy the same social protection,

Article 26. (1) Everyone has the right to education. Education shall be free, at least in the elementary and fundamental stages. Elementary education shall be compulsory. Technical and professional education shall be made generally available and higher education shall be equally accessible to all on the basis of merit.

(2) Education shall be directed to the full development of the human personality and to the strengthening of respect for human rights and fundamental freedoms. It shall promote understanding, tolerance and friendship among all nations, racial or religious groups, and shall further the activities of the United Nations for the maintenance of peace,

(3) Parents have a prior right to choose the kind of education that shall be given to their children.

Article 27. (1) Everyone has the right to freely participate in the cultural life of the community, to enjoy the arts and to share in scientific advancement and its benefits.

(2) Everyone has the right to the protection of the moral and material interests resulting from any scientific, literary, or artistic production of which he is the author.

Article 28. Everyone is entitled to a social and international order in which the rights and freedoms set forth in this Declaration can be fully realized.

Article 29. (1) Everyone has duties to the community in which alone the free and full development of his personality is possible.

(2) In the exercise of his rights and freedoms, everyone shall be subject only to such limitations as are determined by law solely for the purpose of securing due recognition and respect for the rights and freedoms of others and of meeting the just requirements of morality, public order, and the general welfare in a democratic society.

(3) These rights and freedoms may in no case be exercised contrary to the purposes and principles of the United Nations.

Article 30. Nothing in this Declaration may he interpreted as implying for any State, group, or person any right to engage in any activity or to perform any act aimed at the destruction of any of the rights and freedoms set forth herein.

Hunger

Myths and Realities

Office on Global Education of Church World Service

The reality of hunger both in our own urban and rural areas as well as in the dramatic droughts and famines in other countries has brought much publicity to this problem. At the same time, there is some confusion over the causes and cures for hunger. Some private relief and government aid efforts meet with mixed reviews because, while they try to solve very real and immediate problems, they may be overlooking both the long-term causes and development needs of people who are at risk in both the short and long terms. This summary of one of the critiques – that of Food First analysts – introduces the issues and the painful extent of the problem, bringing its connections right into our kitchens and marketplaces.

MYTH ONE: There is not enough food and not enough land.

Untrue: Measured globally, there is enough to feed everyone. For example there is enough grain being produced today to provide everybody in the world with enough protein and about 3,000 calories a day, which is what the average American consumes. But the world's food supply is not evenly distributed. Those who have much accumulate more, while those who have little edge toward starvation. In most countries with widespread hunger, a few large landowners control nearly all agricultural production, sometimes with disastrous results. Much rich farmland remains unused, or one harvest is gathered per year when there could be two or three. Land is used for "cash crops" such as cotton or coffee instead of food. To the owners, land becomes an "investment" not a source of food for the people who live on it.

MYTH TWO: There are too many people to feed.

Contrary to popular belief, overpopulation is not the cause of hunger. It's usually the other way around: hunger is one of the real causes of overpopulation. The more children a poor family has the more likely some will survive to work in the fields or in the city to add to the family's small income and, later, to care for the parents in their old age. All this points to the disease that is at the root of both hunger and overpopulation: the powerlessness of people who must rely on food that is grown and distributed by wealthy people who have never felt hunger pangs, yet who determine how the land will be used, if at all and who will benefit from its fruits. High birth rates are symptoms of the failures of a social system – inadequate family income, inadequate nutrition and health care and old age security.

MYTH THREE: Growing more food will mean less hunger in poor countries.

But it doesn't seem to work that way. "More food" is what the last 30 years' War on Hunger has been about. Farming methods have been "modernized," ambitious irrigation plans carried out, "miracle" seeds, new pesticides, fertilizers, and machinery have become available. But who has come out better off? Farmers who already have land, money, and the ability to buy on credit – not the desperately poor and hungry. In Pakistan for example a farmer must have at least 12.5 acres of land to get a loan from the Bank: but this excludes over 80 percent of Pakistan's farmers! Who else benefits? Moneylenders, landlords, bureaucrats, military officers, city-based speculators, and foreign corporations – as the value of the land goes up only the rich can afford to buy the farming land. Small farmers go bankrupt or are bought out.

Human energy and imagination can be organized to turn a desert into a grain field. This can be done – we have the

---

"By the next century the population of the countries giving aid will total around 800 million; the populations of countries needing aid will reach around 5.3 billion. Thus the ratio is about 1 to 7....

"The Buddha described three kinds of hungry spirits: those with no possessions, those with few, and those with great wealth. The first group is miserable, having nothing to eat. Those in the second have little and also deserve sympathy. Those in the third, however, have great wealth and more than enough food, yet turn a deaf ear to people in dire necessity. It is believed that this last group goes to hell.

"We in the developed nations must not allow ourselves to become wealthy hungry spirits. Let each of us do as much as we can to help seven people in need."

KINZO TAKEMURA,
excerpted from an editorial in *Dharma World*, Jan./Feb. 1993

know-how. When land is in the hands of the people who live and work on it, they are more likely to be motivated to make the land more productive and distribution of food more equitable, thus benefitting all peoples.

MYTH FOUR: Hunger is a contest between rich countries and poor countries.

To many Americans the hungry world is seen as the enemy who, in Lyndon Johnson's words, "wants what we got." But hunger will never be eliminated until we recognize the poor of Bangladesh, Colombia, or Senegal as our neighbors. Rich or poor we are all part of the same global food system which is gradually coming under the control of a few huge corporations. These giant businesses grow and market food for the benefit of those people who have money, which means primarily people in North American and Europe. Poor people in the Third World market pay food prices that are determined by what people in rich countries are willing to pay. This is the direct cause of hunger in many poor countries.

On the other hand, people in rich countries are unaware that their own consumption is creating a suction force in the world food market, diverting food from meeting the needs of the very people who have grown it. In both rich and poor countries, farmers, workers, and consumers feel the impact of this system of international control, through artificial shortages of certain products, through high food prices, through poor-quality goods. Even in countries like the United States and Canada, small farmers find themselves unable to afford the machinery they need to keep their farms running well. Older people on small pensions – even in the United States and Canada – find themselves unable to afford the food they deserve.

MYTH FIVE: Hunger can be solved by redistributing the food to the hungry.

Over and over we hear that North America is the world's last remaining "bread basket." The rich world's overconsumption and wastefulness are endlessly compared with the misery of the poor. True. Adopting a simpler lifestyle helps us to understand our interrelatedness with all people, and less wastefulness is better stewardship. But neither "one less hamburger a week" nor massive food aid programs will eventually solve widespread starvation and poverty in the poorest nations.

People will only cease to be poor when they control the means of providing and/or producing food for themselves. We must face up to the real questions. Who controls the land? Who cultivates it? A few, or all who need to? What will be grown in poorer nations – strawberries to export to the tables of the well-fed in the United States or basic grains for local consumption? How can control of the land get back into the hands of the people who need it? Who influences the distribution of food? How can people be enabled to provide food for themselves?

MYTH SIX: A strong military defense provides a secure environment in which people can prosper.

But who feels secure on an empty stomach? The extraordinary investment the world makes in armaments annually (currently $900 billion) ensures that few funds are available for agricultural and economic development and shows that those who decide how a nation's money is spent are not intimately acquainted with the violence of hunger. The security of countries both great and small depends first of all on a population that has enough food, enough jobs, adequate energy, and safe, comfortable housing. When a society cannot provide these basics, all the guns and bombs in the world cannot maintain peace.

This article was compiled by staff of the Office on Global Education based on material by Frances Moore Lappé and Joseph Collins, co-authors of *Food First* and *World Hunger: Twelve Myths*

On the other hand . . .

There is clearly a link between declining agricultural capacity, caused by a variety of environmental factors, and hunger. According to the newsletter of the United Nations Development Fund, desertification and the degradation of fragile drylands is now threatening the livelihood of over 900 million people in some 100 countries. The desertification process seems to be occuring at an accelerating rate, according to the United Nations Environment Programme. Causes include overgrazing, overcropping, poor irrigation practices, and deforestation, combined with climatic variations.

The situation is particularly serious in Africa, where 66% of the continent is desert or dryland, and 73% of agricultural drylands are already degraded. Most of the world's 800 million people without adequate food live in the drylands, according to the Food and Agriculture Organization of the UN.

"When the Son of Man comes as King, and all the angels with him, he will sit on his royal throne, and all the earth's people will be gathered before him. Then he will divide them into two groups, just as a shepherd separates the sheep from the goats: he will put the sheep at his right and the goats at his left. Then the King will say to the people on his right, 'You that are blessed by my Father: come! Come and receive the kingdom which has been prepared for you ever since the creation of the world. I was hungry and you fed me, thirsty and you gave me drink; I was a stranger and you received me in your homes, naked and you clothed me; I was sick and you took care of me, in prison and you visited me.

"The righteous will then answer him, 'When, Lord, did we ever see you hungry and feed you, or thirsty and give you drink? When did we ever see you a stranger and welcome you in our homes, or naked and clothe you? When did we ever see you sick or in prison, and visit you?'

"The King will answer back, 'I tell you, indeed, whenever you did this for one of the least important of these brothers of mine, you did it for me!'"

Matthew 25.31-46, from the *New Testament*

Situation Report:
Crises in Rwanda, Haiti, the Horn of Africa, Liberia and the former Yugoslavia

US Committee for UNICEF

The following summaries depict some of the harsh facts that can overwhelm and numb us. Yet many religious and secular relief and development organizations, UN agencies such as UNICEF, and supportive governments are trying to help in each of these and numerous other cases of need. The question is not, "What can we do?" but, "What shall we do first?" The *Situation Report* that follows, from a fundraising appeal by UNICEF, indicates the extext of the need and some of the steps that must be taken.

Fall 1994

Rwanda:

The most brutal civil war in recent memory, including terrible massacres of as many as 500,000 people, has devastated this tiny African nation. More than 5 million people have fled their homes to refuge within Rwanda or in neighboring Zaire. More than 200,000 children are now unaccompanied, either orphaned or separated from their parents.

Haiti:

The situation of women and children in Haiti is by far the worst in the Western Hemisphere and has deteriorated sharply under the combined impact of political and economic instability and three years of international sanctions. Approximately 55 percent of Haitian children under five are malnourished. Lack of access to clean drinking water, limited practice of breastfeeding, and low vaccination rates combine to produce an under-five mortality rate of 133 per 1,000 live births – nearly three times higher than the regional average of 50. Diarrheal disease is responsible for approximately 40 percent of all childhood deaths. The collapse of the measles immunization program played a major role in the measles epidemic that spread through the country for 30 months, ending December 1993. The exact death toll is difficult to estimate, but in September 1993, 58 percent of all deaths in Haiti were of children under five compared to an already high 38 percent in 1991.

Drought returns to the Horn of Africa

*T*he Horn of Africa, an area encompassing Ethiopia, Eritrea, Sudan, Somalia, and Kenya, is again suffering severe drought. In addition, insects such as locusts and armyworms have devastated what few crops have grown. More than 14 million people, two thirds of whom are children and women, are threatened by desperate shortages of water and food. Given the already poor health of children in this region, the outlook is grim without emergency food, water, and medicine.

Ethiopia:

In many villages, 80 percent of the children were already malnourished at the beginning of this new famine. Less than one quarter of Ethiopia's children have safe water. Half of the children in the affected areas are suffering from typhoid, acute diarrhea, malaria, and eye and skin diseases. Thousands of children have died in the last few months.

Eritrea:

Two thirds of the 2.5 million people in this new nation are threatened by grave food shortages because a brutal combination of drought and insect plagues has devastated crops. There are an estimated 100,000 children orphaned by war. Severe water shortages are also widespread, creating dangerous risks to the health of children.

Sudan:

A decade of war between the northern and southern halves of Sudan, combined with recurrent drought, has disrupted the lives of a generation of Sudan's children. The new drought may be too much for them to survive. In some areas, 80 percent of children are already malnourished. Vitamin A deficiency and acute respiratory infections are severe problems. At least 18,000 children have been separated from their families, and thousands of others have been orphaned.

Somalia:

The northern and central areas of Somalia had absolutely no rain last spring, and 900,000 people are in need of assistance. A combination of drought and prevailing insecurity has left much of the population at risk.

Kenya:

Even Kenya, which in the past has been less vulnerable to famine than its neighbors, is suffering severely. Many areas have had three straight years of drought. More than a million people are threatened by severe shortages of food and water.

Liberia

Fighting has resumed in Liberia, where one of the most brutal wars has raged for years. Accurate reports on the number of children killed or orphaned by the violence are unavailable, but the suffering has been intense. Many children have died of diseases like pneumonia, measles, and diarrhea, which prey on children weakened by hunger and poor health. Throughout Liberia, thousands of children have been orphaned or separated from their parents. Thousands of health clinics, hospitals, water supplies, and schools have been destroyed. And still the conflict goes on.

The former Yugoslavia

The stop-and-start war in the former Yugoslavia continues to take its toll on children. Farming has been disrupted, and the delivery of food is precarious. Bombing and violence have destroyed the health care system, leaving children in danger of deadly disease. Winter is quickly approaching, and millions of children are now dependent on outside aid for emergency food, medical care, and shelter.

U.S. Committee for UNICEF
333 East 38th Street, New York, NY 10016

FOR MORE INFORMATION:

In addition to UNICEF, there are numerous religious and secular organizations that offer information about, analyses of, and responses to the problems of hunger and poverty. Additional information is provided in Chapter 42. Here are just a few of the many excellent ones:

Bread for the World

1100 Wayne Avenue, Suite 1000, Silver Spring, MD 20910
tel. (301) 608-2400 / fax. (301) 608-2401

*T*his Christian citizens' movement has shown that when Christians work together even in relatively small numbers, they can play a decisive role in shaping important national decisions on hunger, such as acceptance of the "right to food" as a public policy, establishment of a US. farmer-held grain reserve, and reforms of the food stamp and food aid programs.

Breakthrough on Hunger

World Development Productions, Inc.
153A Brattle St., Cambridge, MA 02138

*T*his organization has worked with several others, including the related Interreligious Coalition for Breakthrough on Hunger, to provide a number of curricular materials, video series, and guides for congregational use and education on development, hunger, the geopolitical contexts, economic,s and both personal and institutional transformation.

Catholic Relief Services

Global Education Office,
209 W. Fayette St., Baltimore, MD 21201; tel. (410) 625-2220

*P*rovides various resources including films and videos of a quality for use in educational settings.

Church World Service

Office on Global Education
2115 N. Charles St., Baltimore, MD 21218-5755

*T*he Office on Global Education provides a large range of resources – print and film – on hunger, development, human rights, environment and other public policy issues; many films are available on loan, and many of the publications – sheets, pamphlets, and books – provide extensive lists of other useful resources. CWS is a ministry of the National Council of the Churches of Christ in the USA.

EarthSave

706 Frederick St., Santa Cruz, CA 95062
tel. (408) 223-4069

*E*arthSave is a nonprofit environmental, educational and health organization. It publishes *Diet for a New America* by John Robbins and promotes a shift from the substantial meat consumption in our societies as a means to enable better distribution of grains to the people of the world and less environmental destruction from the impact of the meat industry.

Food First – Institute for Food and Development Policy

Executive Director, Walden Bellow
145 Ninth St., San Francisco, CA 94103-3584
tel. (415) 864-8555

*A*gain and again we read that nearly 40,000 children die each day from hunger and hunger-related causes. What should be done? Food First research reveals that famine is not usually an act of nature, but a consequence of politics. Somalia and Ethiopia are only two highly publicized examples of how hunger and poverty are caused by social inequity, political oppression, and misguided aid policies. Food First offers many publications and other resources for individuals and groups.

General Board of Global Ministries

Church St. Station, Box 5050, New York, NY 10248

Heifer Project International

P.O. Box 808, Little Rock, AR 72203

*H*PI provides animals and related assistance to families and communities to help them produce food and income on a long-term basis; it enables people to share resources that enhance the dignity of all and it educates people about the root causes of hunger and poverty and the opportunity for alleviating them in our interdependent world.

Hunger Project

1388 Sutter St., San Francisco, CA 94109
(415) 928-8700

Interfaith Hunger Appeal

475 Riverside Dr.,
Suite 1630, New YOrk, NY 10115-0079

*I*HA is a partnership of four relief and development agencies: Catholic Relief Services, Church World Service, Lutheran World Relief and the American Jewish Distribution Joint Committee. Interfaith Hunger Appeal's Office on Education fosters learning and teaching about the needs of the poor through curriculum, projects and Town Meetings; IHA also publishes a quarterly journal, *Hunger TeachNet*.

Results – Generating Political Will to End Hunger

Sam Harris, Executive Director, 236 Massachusetts Avenue, NE, Suite 300, Washington, D.C., 20002 USA
tel. (202) 543-9340 / fax. (202) 543-3228

*R*ESULTS is an international, grass roots hunger lobby creating the political will to end hunger and poverty. Results empowers people to realize that they are the key to making a difference.

Population

The International Conference on Population and Development

Earth Negotiations Bulletin (ENB)

ENB is a reporting service on international environment and development negotiations, sponsored by the International Institute for Sustainable Development

Of particular interest to readers of this book are the religious and ethical issues raised at the 1994 Conference on Population and Development (ICPD); to provide an overview of these and related elements, the Editor has excerpted portions from ENB's "Summary." The full document, though lengthy, provides very interesting reading on the background and procedures of such conferences, as well as considerable insight into the debates, objections, positions and compromises of the participants. Because this Conference, like the Rio Earth Summit in 1992 and the Human Rights Conference in 1993, addressed global issues that are linked to national and international policies and that are, at the same time, tied to the heart of religious and interreligious concerns, this chapter deserves special attention.

The following excerpts identify some of the contentious issues raised in the *Programme of Action*. The chapters in the *Programme* that received less attention are also listed below to indicate the wide – and related – range of the Conference. As with most documents that come before international conferences such as this one, the *Programme of Action* had been prepared in three Preparatory Committee meetings, beginning in March 1991. This process allowed for considerable negotiation and consultation from both govenmental and nongovernmental organizations on the structure and language of the document. Even so, many key issues were left to be resolved in Cairo: the definitions of family planning, reproductive and sexual health and rights, and safe motherhood; the reproductive and sexual needs of adolescents; the preamble and principles; and the resource requirements needed for implementation of the plan.

*I*n a city known for both its history and its burgeoning population, the International Conference on Population and Development (ICPD) met in Cairo, Egypt from 5-13 September 1994. An estimated 20,000 government delegates, UN representatives, NGOs and media representatives descended on Cairo for the nine-day Conference and the parallel NGO Forum. Although the issue of abortion proved to receive most of the media attention, Conference participants also addressed a number of important, and often controversial, issues including immigration policy, reproductive health and reproductive rights, the empowerment of women, urbanization and access to healthcare.

During the course of the Conference, delegates negotiated a sixteen-chapter *Programme of Action* that sets out a series of recommended actions on population and development, including those that lead to sustained economic growth within the context of sustainable development, protection of the integrity of the family, combatting HIV/AIDS, protecting the health of adolescents, and closing the gender gap in education. The negotiations were not easy and there were times when it appeared as though consensus would be impossible on such controversial issues as abortion, sexual and reproductive health, family reunification, and the definition of the family. Yet, by the time the last chapter was adopted and the last speech was given, thousands of weary delegates, observers, and NGOs agreed that in spite of some difficult

moments, the Conference was a success and the Programme of Action, compared with earlier documents on population and development, represents a "quantum leap."

The Programme of Action

I. The Preamble. . . . affirms the application of universally recognized human rights standards to all aspects of population programmes. The Preamble also notes that the "Programme of Action will require the establishment of common ground, with full respect for the various religious and ethical values and cultural backgrounds." [...]

II. Principles. This chapter was initially discussed in the first session of the Main Committee on Monday, 5 September 1994.... After this initial discussion in the Main Committee, the "Friends of the Chair" became the primary negotiating forum on this chapter. These often protracted negotiations continued until Monday, 12 September. The most contentious issue was the *chapeau,* which qualifies not only how the principles are to be interpreted but also provides that the implementation of the whole Programme of Action will be carried out at the national level and according to each State's laws, religious and ethical values. Part of the *chapeau* now reads:

The implementation of the recommendations in the

Progranune of Action is the sovereign right of each country, consistent with national laws and development priorities, with full respect for the various religious and ethical values and cultural backgrounds of its people, and in conformity with universally recognized human rights.

[Chapters not discussed here include:
III. Interrelationships Between Population, Sustained Economic Growth And Sustainable Development. IV. Gender Equality, Equity and Empowerment of Women. V. The Family: Its Roles, Rights, Composition and Structure. VI. Population Growth and Structure.]

VII. Reproductive Rights and Reproductive Health.

This chapter covers some of the most controversial issues to be addressed by the ICPD and brought the Holy See and certain Catholic and Islamic States head-to-head with those who advocate or do not object to sexual and reproductive health programmes, including family planning, which may include abortion and contraception. This chapter contains five sections: reproductive rights and reproductive health; farnily planning; sexually transmitted diseases and HIV prevention; human sexuality and gender relations; and adolescents.

This chapter was the subject of lengthy and often heated discussion both in the informal sessions of the Main Committee and in a working group chaired by Hernando Clavijo (Colombia). On Wednesday, 7 September, delegates discussed the former paragraph 7.1 (now 7.2), which gives the definition of reproductive rights and reproductive health. The primary issue in this paragraph was the "right" of men and women to have access to methods of "fertility regulation." A number of delegations could not accept this because fertility regulation can be interpreted to include abortion. When consulted, the WHO [World Health Organization] confirmed that according to its working definition, fertility regulation includes family planning, delayed childbearing, the use of contraception, treatment of infertility, interruption of unwanted pregnancies, and breastfeeding. The final compromise text reads:

> "Implicit in this last condition is the right of men and women to be informed and to have access to safe, effective, affordable and acceptable methods of family planning of their choice, as well as other methods of their choice for the regulation of fertility which are not against the law...."

During a lengthy debate on Saturday, 10 September, more than 70 delegates commented on the former paragraph 7.2 (now 7.3) on sexual and reproductive rights. Issues in this paragraph included ambiguities in the first sentence on the relationship between sexual and reproductive rights and human rights; the use of the term "sexual rights;" and the right of "couples and individuals" to decide freely and responsibly the number, spacing, and timing of their children, as well as the right to make decisions concerning reproduction free of discrimination, coercion and violence. Many Central American and Muslim delegates called for deletion of the reference to "individuals." ...The compromise text for this paragraph reads:

...reproductive rights embrace certain human rights that are already recognized in national laws, international human rights documents and other relevant United Nations consensus documents. These rights rest on the recognition of the basic right of all couples and individuals to decide freely and responsibly the number, spacing and timing of their children and to have the information and means to do so, and the right to attain the highest standard of sexual and reproductive health. It also includes the right of all to make decisions concerning reproduction free of discrimination, coercion and violence. [...]

VIII. Health, Morbidity and Mortality.

This chapter contains sections on: primary health care and the health-care sector; child survival and health; women's health and safe motherhood; and human immunodeficiency virus (HIV) infection and acquired immune deficiency syndrome (AIDS).

Vice-chair Nicolaas Biegman opened discussion on the most contentious issue, abortion, as referred to in paragraph 8.25 on Tuesday, 6 September. Delegates were urged to move swiftly on this issue to show the world and the media that this Conference was not about abortion, but about population and development. Nevertheless, during the course of the week, scores of delegations took the floor to comment on this paragraph. . . .

Paragraph 8.25 now reads [in part]: "In no case should abortion be promoted as a method of family planning. All Governments and relevant intergovernmental and non-governmental organizations are urged to strengthen their commitment to women's health, to deal with the health impact of unsafe abortion as a major public health concern and to reduce the recourse to abortion through expanded and improved family planning services. Prevention of unwanted pregnancies must always be given the highest priority and all attempts should be made to eliminate the need for abortion. " [...]

[Chapters in the Programme not discussed here include: *IX. Population Distribution, Urbanization and Internal Migration. X. International Migration; XI. Population and Development Information, Education and Communication; XII. Technology, Research and Development; XIII. National Action; XIV. International Cooperation; XV. Partnership with the Non-Governmental Sector; XVI. Followup.*]

A brief analysis of the ICPD

*A*s Nafis Sadik commented in her closing remarks, there are many aspects of the ICPD Programme of Action that represent a "quantum leap" for population and development policies. These include: a shift from the previous emphasis on demography and population control to sustainable development and the recognition of the need for comprehensive reproductive health care and reproductive rights; strong language on the empowerment of women; reflection of different values and religious beliefs; reaffirmation of the central role of the family; and recognition of the needs of adolescents.
    [...]

Reflection of different values and religious beliefs

Many commented that as a result of the concerns of the Vatican and certain Latin American and Islamic countries, the document now reflects different moral, ethical, religious, and cultural values that should, in the end, make it more implementable and legitimate in many countries. A key element in giving the document greater sensitivity was the agreement on the *chapeau* of Chapter II (Principles), which clearly states that the implementation of the Programme of Action will be carried out within the context of national laws and development priorities, with full respect for the various religious and ethical values and cultural backgrounds of its people, and in conformity with universally recognized human rights. This not only enabled those countries with strong religious fundamentalist communities to join the consensus, but it also undermined the claim by some protesters that the Programme of Action is yet another manifestation of Western imperialism, where the view of a select few on contraception would be imposed on the developing world.

Furthermore, this language served to neutralize some of the efforts undertaken by the Holy See, among others, to prevent consensus on certain issues, including abortion, contraception, fertility regulation, and sexual and reproductive rights. Prior to the Conference, the majority of the media attention was on the so-called "un-holy alliance" between the Vatican and the fundamentalist Islamic countries. The media hype proved to be unfounded in the end, when even the Vatican admitted that it could join the consensus on Chapter II. [...]

Missed opportunities

Although delegates agree that the Cairo Conference was a success, the Conference did not succeed in meeting all of its objectives. Several important issues, including the relationship between population and development, the relationship between population and environmental issues, patterns of production and consumption, the role of the individual, the needs of specific sectors of society, and implementation and follow-up did not receive sufficient attention. Although the Programme of Action does reference each of these issues, the protracted debate on abortion and reproductive health issues served to detract attention from these important concepts. [...]

from *Earth Negotiations Bulletin*, vol. 6 No. 39, published by the International Institute for Sustainable Development (IISD), on Wednesday, September 14, 1994. Printed with permission.

FOR MORE INFORMATION:

International Institute for Sustainable Development *(and ENB)*
161 Portage Ave, East, Sixth Floor
Winnipeg, Manitoba, CANADA   (Also see listing in Chapter 44)

Cairo Declaration on Population and Development

An Inter-Religious Statement

Inter-Religious Federation for World Peace

The Inter-Religious Federation for World Peace (IRFWP) is an international and inter-religious peace organization incorporated in New York State. Its six Presidents, sixteen Presiding Council Members, and over seven thousand religious leaders and scholars of religion are members of the world's major religious traditions. The *Introduction* below appeared in the *IRFWP Newsletter,* Vol. II, No. 2, Fall 1994, along with the Declaration, which was first issued by IRFWP in a press release on September 9, 1994.

Introduction

*D*elegates from 189 nations gathered in Cairo, Egypt, from September 5 to 14, 1994, for the United Nations-sponsored International Conference on Population and Development. This, perhaps more than any previous U.N. conference, brought to the fore a fascinating interplay of forces, both spiritual and secular, that currently inform the evolution of human affairs. The high-profile figures who emerged in this setting as those through whom these powers manifest and interact included Pope John Paul II, U.S. Vice President Albert Gore, Conference Chairwoman Nafis Sadik, Prime Ministers Brundtland of Norway and Bhutto of Pakistan, and the Sheikh Al-Azhar. These leaders communicated such diverse perspectives on the issues as Catholic, Muslim, Secular Feminist, and Secular Rationalist.

As the conference approached, leaders of the Inter-Religious Federation for World Peace (IRFWP) felt that the debate on the all-important issues of population and development had degenerated on at least two important levels:

1) By having only Catholics and Muslims identified as representing religious and spiritual concerns, the potential benefits which could come from a broad spectrum of religions was lost.

2) The decision on the part of the religious spokespeople to focus debate on concrete issues such as abortion and contraception forfeited a golden opportunity to present on the world stage a more comprehensive expression of religious and spiritual concerns *à propos* the all important considerations of family life and human development.

For these and other reasons, IRFWP Presidents and Presiding Council Members drafted the following statement. The IRFWP sought to present a position representing a broader constituency of the world's religions, and offer a more broadly defined set of religious and spiritual concerns. The document was distributed during the conference to the appropriate UN organizations and major international wire services.

The Cairo Declaration on Population and Development

*T*he United Nations Conference on Population and Development, held in Cairo from September 5 - 14, 1994, has highlighted the pressing problem of the earth's finite capacity to support the growing human population. This issue should receive paramount attention from all, parallel to the equally urgent issue of a sustainable life environment on our planet.

We note that the Conference has been controversial. At least four nations – Iraq, Lebanon, Saudi Arabia, and Sudan – with large Muslim populations, have chosen to boycott the Conference. The Vatican has used strong words to protest elements of the Conference working documents. In the Roman Catholic constituency many have expressed dissent from the official Vatican position. Thus in dealing with birth and death, sexuality, marriage and family, and human development, the Conference obviously has touched upon issues directly affecting the religious consciousness of humanity.

It is in this context that Presidents and Members of the Presiding Council of the Inter-Religious Federation for World Peace wish to make the following modest observations for the prayerful consideration of all concerned.

1. Religion – a central issue

*G*iven the importance of religion for peoples throughout the world, no serious effort to engage crucial global problems should discount the core values and wisdom represented in the world's religious traditions. The course of the deliberations of this Conference has demonstrated how unwise it is to ignore the religious perspective and to presume that a purely secular analysis and secular solutions could adequately or effectively handle this perplexing problem which involves such momentous issues as human reproduction and the regulation and planning of the family. Reason demands that religious organizations should be fully involved in discussing these problems and finding solutions.

2. Sciences as well as religions have their limits

*W*e recognize the enormous contribution made by science and technology in promoting general health, in increasing life expectancy, in reducing infant mortality, in eliminating epidemics, and in facilitating general health care. But as regards the problems of population stabilization and human development, even when all significant and relevant findings and discoveries of the physical and social sciences have been fully taken into account, the sciences cannot offer the necessary ethical elements of social policy; what ought and needs to be done is a moral judgment, which science by definition is not designed to provide. Scientific data can clarify aspects of the human situation and point to possible options in an ethical issue; but the final decision on what to do depends on the moral conscience, which is largely shaped by the religious heritage of humanity.

Religions also have their limits, and sometimes represent vested interests. But the same is true of the physical and social sciences. They too are prone to misuse and manipulation by vested interests willing to finance scientific research; military establishments and large corporations can be cited as examples.

While religions are often accused of dogmatism, it should be noted that advocates of secular causes are not entirely free from this characteristic. Ideological dogmatism in the pursuit of moral positions, passionately held, may belie claims of scientific objectivity. Religions and sciences need to cooperate in facilitating debate and public discussion of issues pertaining to human development and population stabilization.

3. Religion and education

*D*espite the quickening pace of the process of global secularization, religions still play a leading role in shaping the moral consciousness of humanity. Eighty percent of the world's people still profess one religion or another. If programs for promoting human development and stabilizing population growth are to succeed at all, the religions of the world must take a major part of the responsibility for educating and inspiring the people.

The role of governments and secular programs for sexual education and family planning should not be minimized; but neither should that role be overvalued or absolutized. A purely secular approach can have only limited effect. There are few societies which do not link sexuality, marriage, and childbirth with religion. Throughout the world marriages are performed in religious contexts precisely in order to place sexuality and childbirth in a sacred context. Societies where these biological and social practices are divorced from authentic religious norms and rites suffer grave consequences manifested in the proliferation of promiscuous behavior, the denigration of women, epidemics of sexually transmitted diseases, rising divorce, and grossly defective forms of child rearing. In technologically advanced societies, social scientific strategies for arresting such problems have been largely unsuccessful. Social policies, however well intentioned, which encourage the violation of important religious values may be counterproductive.

What needs to be reoriented is the religious and moral attitudes of people. The religions of the world have an enormous infrastructure for education. If in addition, the vast number of conscientious religious teachers in the world can be mobilized and projected by the public media, with free and frank discussion of issues relating to human development and population stabilization, the effect can be quite phenomenal.

4. Inter-religious cooperation

*A*ll religions need to learn from each other in this regard and to coordinate their efforts. If, for example,

Muslims and Roman Catholics have special convictions in matters of human reproduction, such convictions can be discussed in inter-religious gatherings; only then will their validity or questionability come clearly to light. The presence of inter-religious strife plays a large part in the advocacy of a-religious, and sometimes even anti-religious secularism. Yet in this century the world's religions have made great strides toward concord, through dialogue and discussion.

A consensus among major religious leaders can have a high positive value. The religions owe it to humanity to come together in dialogue and cooperation on this crucial issue.

5. Religion And Women

*T*he women of the world should have a major role in the debate on human development and population stabilization. No programs in this area can be conceived properly, or effectively implemented, without benefit of the unique insights and universal talents of women. In actual fact women now play a major, but often unrecognized, role in maintaining religious traditions, in the practice of religion, and in education both in the family and in society.

Many religions have tended to marginalize women from their teaching, decision-taking, and implementing structures. All religions need to reexamine their position and practice in relation to discrimination against women, and to marginalization, denigration, oppression, and abuse of women. When women are oppressed the entire social world is oppressed, the youth are impoverished, and prosperity flees. Thus all religions have responsibility to provide for women to play a leading role in decision-making and implementation of programs.

6. Abortion, family, and promiscuity

*T*he debate on the ethics of abortion of the human fetus is far from concluded. Although there is much disagreement as to whether a fetus is a person entitled to rights, few deny that an abortion is the termination of human life at some very early stage of development. While there may indeed be cases where abortion may be morally legitimate, at the very least when a mother's life is endangered, it should never be viewed simply as a morally neutral medical procedure. No strategy for solving population growth should rely on or encourage abortion as a solution. Any society which is cavalier about abortion will tend toward discounting the value of human life.

Religions of the world have a special responsibility to deepen our understanding of the moral implications of abortion, for this is an issue which calls for deeper, more informed, more enlightened attention.

Conclusion

*W*e applaud the open and straightforward debate on these issues which the Cairo Conference has freshly stimulated. The United Nations cannot on its own decide which religious views to promote, or which particular religious leaders to invite or boycott. Religions have to come forward to help the United Nations in this regard, and to discuss these questions in an ambiance of harmony, cooperation, and mutual openness. Consensus may be difficult to achieve immediately; but a consensus eliminating inconvenient positions can hardly be worthwhile, in the long run.

The Inter-Religious Federation for World Peace, 4 West 43rd Street, New York, NY 10036 USA tel. 212-869-6023 / fax 212-869-6424

Priority Statement on Population

"Because of its pervasive and detrimental impact on global ecological systems, population growth threatens to overwhelm any possible gains made in improving human conditions. Failure to curb the rate of world population growth will magnify the deterioration of the Earth's environment and natural resources and undermine economic and social progress. A humane, sustainable future depends on recognizing the common ground between population and the environment.

"Current national and international efforts to address the world's rapidly expanding population are not sufficient. A new commitment to population programs which enhance human rights and conditions is urgently needed... all nations of the world must make an effective response to the issue of population growth a leading priority for this decade." Zero Population Growth

FOR MORE INFORMATION:

The Population Institute
107 Second Street, NE, Washington, DC 20002 USA
tel. (202) 544-3300 / fax (202) 544-0068

United Nations International Conference on Population and Development, 22nd Floor, 220 East 42nd St.,
New York, NY 10017 USA; tel. (212) 297-5222

Zero Population Growth
1400 Sixteenth St. NW, Washington, DC 20036 USA
tel. (202) 332-2200

Values and Social Development

A Plea to the World Summit on Social Development

The Group of Reflection

This document represents a collective effort created through the dialogue of a multifaceted group calling itself the Group of Reflection. The Group included members of the United Nations Secretariat, scholars, NGOs and religious leaders of various traditions, participating in their individual capacities. The Group was convened in 1994 through the efforts of Father Luis M. Dolan, CP, who was, at that time, Acting Executive Director of the Temple of Understanding and is its UN Representative. Although the Summit will be held before publication of this book, the document's analysis and proposals may be debated and adapted to new policies and ongoing programs of social development for years to come. Father Dolan's introduction follows.

Introduction

*O*ne of the greatest needs people and nations face today is to discover vistas for the new civilization in the making. We are heading towards a more global, environmentally sounder, and more peaceful world. In the process, some deep questions are being asked:

What shared values can the world have?

How can these values contribute to the ongoing development of nation-states? and, more concretely,

What can international organizations do to help achieve this civilization-in-the-making?

This paper is a contribution to a more comprehensive vision of the future of the world and the role social development can play. The document is directed to four communities who have major roles in enacting this future: the religious community throughout the world; the Member States of the United Nations; the United Nations' agencies and public servants; and international NGOs. The Preamble of the document gives the elements of the new vision, and throughout the paper programs are suggested that can help achieve this development.

Presentation to UN PrepCom II

Jonathan Granoff, a member of the Group of Reflection, a lawyer, and member of the Board of Temple of Understanding, presented the *Plea* to the Second Session of the Preparatory Committee for the World Summit of Social Development, United Nations, New York, at its August 23 plenary session. Most of his remarks follow:

I thank the Chair of the Preparatory Committee and the Secretariat for the bold steps being taken with their leadership. At this critical historical juncture, it is we who must hear the cries of poverty and hunger and respond. I am struck by language in the current Draft Declaration and Programme for Action (A/Conf..166/PC/L.13). Paragraph 6 says, "We ardently call for an intellectual, aesthetic, and spiritual renewal." Paragraphs 136–140 talk about our global village and a framework of shared basic values. However, there is an absence in the document and in our deliberations of the means by which such spiritual renewal and an invigoration of values might occur.

There is, in the draft, extensive discussion regarding poverty, social integration, employment (I prefer "sustainable livelihood"), and development without any reference to greed, arrogance, or exploitation and their counterparts of compassion, humility, and service. Regardless of one's spiritual heritage, whether Buddhism, Christianity, Hinduism, Islam, Judaism, or any other, the power that has created all creation, the power that allows our hearts to beat, that gives us vision, that gives us life itself, the mysterious power that sustains us can be described in terms of compassion and love. And we are instructed to utilize these qualities in our dealings with one another. Each faith directs us toward these beautiful qualities. Yet, in the draft declaration we are calling for a spiritual renewal without reference to these qualities. [...]

Criteria

*T*he first paragraph of our paper identifies the criteria which must be used to evaluate our policies – compassion, love, tolerance, justice, peace, harmony, beauty, and unity. This is not a new idea. These criteria are embodied in all of the world's religious and ancient traditions. These are our guideposts. Addressing any form of social development requires use of the moral dimension, so let us look toward humankind's clearest ideals.

Can we be so arrogant as to think that the social-scientific methodologies which have evolved in the past few hundred years are so effective that we can discard the ancient spiritual traditions of the planet in our deliberations? *Can* we define development without reference to the paramount human qualities of love and compassion and kindness? How will we mobilize the hearts and minds of humanity to make the kinds of sacrifices necessary to address the enormity of suffering going on in the world?

Many people believe that for us to inspire and lead we must tap these roots of spiritual inspiration and experience.

Towards Deeper Values and Fuller Development: A Plea to the World Summit on Social Development

Preamble

We are persons and institutions affirming the existence of universally recognized values rooted in and arising from an immeasurable Ultimate Reality. These values include compassion, love, tolerance, justice, peace, harmony, beauty, and unity. These values are at the very core of human society and there can be no effective social development without them.

As people of faith, we emphasize the critical need to articulate and bring these universal values into action. The spiritual dimension, the deeply moral dimension, needs to be included forthrightly in United Nations documents and activities, particularly those relating to social development such as the World Summit for Social Development and the United Nations Conference on Women and Development.

These universal values are the treasury of humanity. Expressing them through service constitutes a part of the chain of giving that sustains every human individual. Institutions derive their justification from their ability to express these values.

There are organizations, institutions, and individuals focused on developing our awareness of these values. These persons and spiritual associations can be utilized to a far greater extent by the United Nations than they have been in the past. Let us no longer underestimate the rich resources of energy, programs, vision and inspiration found in the world's religions and spiritual traditions.

There is an inner dimension of human experience from which individuals derive their appreciation of these values. Let us call this dimension of the human being intrinsic goodness. Development of this dimension must never be overlooked when addressing social, cultural, and economic development. When we fail to nurture and rely on the potentials inherent in this intrinsic goodness we allow ignorance in varied forms – injustice, poverty, war, and ecological and human degradation – to survive and even thrive.[1]

The well-being of individuals, families, nations and the community of humanity depends on the development of loving and compassionate qualities. They provide the proper standard to measure human development as well as the energy necessary to manifest consistent actions leading to social justice. It is the compassion swelling up from deep within the heart of each individual, informing the leaders of each Member State of the United Nations, that must motivate us to address and even make sacrifices to eliminate poverty and the suffering caused by disenfranchisement and marginalization.

The level of human misery that exists in the world is unconscionable. Many of the developing countries are suffering from a lack of material resources and social organization that has resulted in countless deaths due to starvation and disease. The ravages of tribal and ethnic wars have driven millions of defenseless people from their homes, often into other countries where their safety and survival cannot be guaranteed.

The developed countries, although enjoying many benefits of modern technology, are suffering from a breakdown in moral values, the disintegration of the family, and a resurgence of ethnocentrism and racism. Violence and crime threaten an entire generation. A growing culture of nihilism, hopelessness, and despair threaten all possibilities of coherent social progress.

There is a critical need for spiritual perspectives that articulate universal values, that present ideals, hopes, goals, and methods to direct us beyond prejudice and selfishness. Spiritual values are the trust of the various religions and they can be utilized as a resource. Religions are agents for the collective and personal expression of universal values. Without such values individuals can become objects of commerce or production, rather than sacred subjects of experience with potential for divine expression and true exaltedness.

Attempts to achieve social development without reference to spiritual and moral values such as love and compassion will result in unhappiness, frustration, depression, isolation, social disintegration, and a high degree of suffering not related to questions of food, shelter, or clothing. We note with dismay the social fragmentation in the developed industrial states as examples of this alienation. It is a kind of starvation in the midst of plenty.

The dominant institutional framework in the world today is the nation-state. The stability of nations is the dominant institutional framework out of which United Nations activities originate. We propose an added dimension:

the expression of full humanity based on universal values with social theory and social policy manifesting these values.

Just as the United Nations Conference on Environment and Development affirmed the biological and ecological interdependence of the planet, championing the creation of new political institutions based on this awareness, so must the World Summit on Social Development, the United Nations Fiftieth Anniversary, and the Women and Development Conference affirm our spiritual interdependence, thereby providing an accurate and comprehensive context for development. This fundamentally moral foundation for social policy can no longer be ignored. We can enliven the heart and vision of humanity only if we tap its deeper roots. The world needs nothing less.

Development, in its true sense, includes physical, intellectual, moral, and spiritual dimensions; it integrates our humanity. Without moral boundaries, greed and violence are unleashed and lead to the exploitation of the weak, and poverty increases. Without intellectual and spiritual expression, social vision becomes impoverished, and cohesion fails. Moral and spiritual dialogue have been neglected in the deliberations of the international community, overshadowed by the language of technocracy, *realpolitik*, and ideology. We believe it is time to reset our course and to encourage the expression of intrinsic goodness, which is at the heart of human society, and empowers development and humanitarian activity. Spiritual and moral values, treasures at the core of human experience, supported by the religious and wisdom traditions of all peoples, need to be articulated and honored as the goals and methods for all meaningful social development.

Although the application of scientific methodology has helped humanity immensely, it is limited by the nature of those who utilize its power.

The scientific and technological worldview is capable of

reducing values to the realm of aesthetics, thereby making them optional and subject to standards of self-interest or mere practicalities. The benefits of scientific knowledge and technological application will only be achievable when founded on objective values and justified by uses always consistent with them. These values reflect the nature of Ultimate Reality. The world's religions attest to this fact.

Social policy can be guided by these values. For example, preventive diplomacy between nations and creating social integration within nations are imperative precisely because they are actions which are compassionate and lead to the elimination and prevention of suffering. Such actions must be undertaken by the international community, even in areas where conflicts will not affect the stability of other states. Failure to act when compassion dictates it places our humanity and therefore civilization itself at risk.

Science claims to be the universal language of truth. We do not deny the importance of science as a tool, but assert that there are values and qualities, such as love and compassion, which cannot be measured or even discovered by empirical scientific methodology.

Where people are denied love and compassion society produces human beings whose eyes, ears, and hearts are closed to others – dangerous creatures with intellectual and technological capacities for destruction, exploitation, and oppression without objective principles of conscience to direct them.

We must develop ethically, spiritually, and ecologically sensitive individuals who are able to form the basis of communities with the ability to direct the awesome powers that science, technology, and modern social organization provide.

We acknowledge that creation itself is a gift arising from a source beyond our full comprehension, and we accept our duty to live with a sense of the suffering of others as our own and with the birthright to develop profound joy and love in serving to help eliminate this suffering.[2] We look for institutions with this same dedicated attitude toward service and conclude that religious and value-based institutions can provide meaningful service in helping to fulfill the UN World Summit for Social Development's eleven objectives.[3]

As people of faith, we therefore call upon the United Nations, the religions and spiritual traditions of the world, the Member States, and all non-governmental organizations[4] concerned with creating a new vision for the United Nations, alleviating poverty, and enhancing social integration and productive employment, to act in the following ways:

The responsibility of the religious community

The world's religious community possesses ethical and social characteristics that can allow it to act as a constructive force in addressing issues of human survival and development. However, all too often atrocities have been committed in the name of religion. For this reason, religions need to purge themselves of all manner of definitions based on conflict with and opposition to others and to affirm with all due vigor the beautiful qualities of justice, love, peace, and compassion at the core of all religions.

In order for the global religious community to be a catalyst for change it must serve as an example by showing respect and tolerance for the grand variety of differences that the one

human family encompasses. The communities of faith must not only teach, but practice love and compassion for the entire human family, not just their own. It is through adherence to the teachings of these great faith traditions that the human family can choose to rise to its highest level. In order to eradicate the unconscionable level of human misery that exists in this era of scientific achievements, global cooperation, especially among faith communities, is necessary. Ethical progress must be made to match the technological advancements that can be used to injure life.

The international religious community should state without hesitation that the present condition of humanity is not acceptable to people who are morally conscious, that the ethical standards of the UN Member States and the religions themselves need to be raised quickly and that the coldheartedness that permits so many to live in inhuman conditions must begin to melt, such that service to others becomes a recognized universal ideal and norm.

We call upon religions as follows:

1. To contribute a spiritual vision for the World Summit on Social Development that reinvigorates the inner person: the formless aspect of the human experience, from which the beautiful qualities of love, compassion, peace, tolerance, reverence for the hallowedness of creation, and wisdom emerge;

2. To make their resources, particularly their human resources as peacemakers, available to the UN, and to strengthen religious institutions and facilities which provide social resources;

3. To articulate a vision of development that includes prayer, contemplation, meditation, compassionate selfless service, a recognition of the interdependence of creation, and the pursuit of human perfection in the areas of consciousness, purity, qualities, and morality;

4. To demonstrate the direct relationship between personal development and service as a method of self-purification and fulfillment;

5. To challenge all parliaments, business centers, academic and religious institutions, temples, and places of worship to live within the exalted qualities of compassion and integrity, such that no one should be caused injury by the actions of any of these institutions and such that they no longer can be used to rationalize violence;

6. To challenge all religious and political institutions to function based on the universal principles of loving all lives as one's own, feeling and treating the suffering of others as one's own, and to acting without the prejudice of treating those of other religions, races, ethnic groups, nations, or classes differently than one's own;

7. To offer ongoing courses on universal spiritual values in the UN, in order to support and educate the UN community – including missions, diplomats, international civil servants, and NGOs – preparing each individual for service from a more universal perspective;

8. To find creative ways of using meditation, prayer, worship and their connection to peacemaking and regional programs on social justice and conflict resolution. This will be particularly useful in instances in which different religions are in conflict without any deep understanding of the profound harmonies of their practices at their most authentic levels of devotion;

9. To seek ways of collectively expressing their deep appreciation for the sacredness of life, the dignity of all beings, the hallowedness of the delicate biosphere we call the environment, and the imperative of finding viable means for the peaceful cooperation of different ethnic and religious groups.

10. To pray for and support the World Summit for Social Development and for the work of the UN and to establish regular prayer activities that will advance universal progress toward a world without violence and inequity.

The responsibility of Member States

Member States have a special obligation "to promote social progress and better standards of life in larger freedom" and "to practice tolerance and live together in peace with one another as good neighbors."

Thus, Member States must create through laws and other measures an environment which allows and encourages all citizens of goodwill, religious communities, NGOs, and other organs of civil society, to freely contribute their ideas, blessings, and services to the improvement of social conditions and the promotion of social justice and progress.

We call upon Member States as follows:

1. To acknowledge that the religious community[5] is an important provider of social services and a unique fountain for social ethics.

2. To involve the religious community in deliberative processes and actions aimed at building up and strengthening social harmony and stability.

3. To provide the religious community with the support needed in its efforts to improve social and humanitarian conditions.

4. To build on family, educational, and cultural values nurtured by the religious community in order to achieve greater social integration and development and help build the human character such that skills for meaningful employment are more easily developed.

5. To develop the greatest tolerance possible for the variety of spiritually informed world views with particular reference to the most ancient, those of indigenous peoples whose cultural heritages and survival as distinct peoples are seriously endangered, to the detriment of all humanity.

6. To adhere with the full force of legal protection to the guarantees of freedom of religion and conscience as embodied in numerous United Nations declarations, conventions and agreements (documents) relating to human rights.[6] Rigorous and universal adherence to such documents is essential since they embody the values of tolerance, peace, and harmony.[7]

7. To create Ministries of Co-existence to diminish all modes of intolerance based on ethnic or religious differences.

Responsibility of the United Nations

The UN as a visionary institution needs to engage continually in idealistic dialogue to offer the world futuristic vision and to utilize the spiritual resources as found in the religious traditions to aid in this process.

The UN and its specialized agencies are vehicles of collective expression, agents for humanity to express its majestic ideals and qualities that affirm the intrinsic goodness of this gift of life.

The UN must set forth universal standards of value, an articulation of clear moral and ethical principles to which Member States can look for guidance. The very cohesion of States is presently threatened by brutal ethnic, religious, social, cultural, or linguistic strife.[8] Creating clear expressions of universal values can be done[9] and indeed the Secretary-General has highlighted this, referencing "an increasingly common moral perception that spans the world's nations and peoples."[10]

The United Nations World Summit for Social Development can set forth a comprehensive definition of social development which includes the physical, intellectual, moral, and spiritual dimensions of the human experience.[11] This comprehensive definition must be transnational and "put people first" and address "all aspects of development."[12] It must be universal and "common to all countries" not just "developing" countries.[13] Poverty and suffering, which are eliminated by the application of programs of compassion and justice, are common to all humanity and must be viewed as collective problems – part of an increasingly interdependent world.[14]

We call upon the United Nations as follows:

1. To utilize the great religious traditions of the world as a resource for transnational ethical values. Thus we recommend a study addressing the creation of a Council of World Spiritual Traditions and Religions to serve as an Advisory Body to the UN.

2. To explore the promulgation of programs that teach tolerance, cultural appreciation, and harmony at a profound level by creating forums for authentic inter-religious dialogue and the experiential sharing of the different methods of prayer, contemplation, and meditation. We suggest the promotion in UNITAR and amongst UN personnel and the personnel of missions, of actual retreat-like experiences of prayer and meditation. Such shared understanding will function as preventive diplomacy at the deepest level, for when there is authentic spiritual sharing, trust and confidence are easier to accomplish. Also, the UN community will begin actually to be a model of intercultural respect and tolerance to which the Member States can look for guidance.

3. To provide experiential courses on each of the religions' prayer and meditation methods. Each of the world's religions utilizes prayer and contemplation to help achieve inner peace and harmony. Such experiences lead people to a greater ability to perform inspired public service. We thus encourage the use of such methods be made explicitly available to all in the UN community in the form of offerings of on-going regular events designed to enrich multi-religious, ethnic and cultural development and understanding and for the enrichment of the personnel such that greater inspiration in documents and programs might be forthcoming from the UN.

4. To engage religious communities in service to the suffering. Charity, service, and compassion are universally recognized values in all religions and areas of social development that can be more fully utilized by the UN. Religious communities, as a world resource, have been under-utilized in this regard, and could help in coordination of resource distribution.

5. To create a true vocation of service at the heart of UN work, forums need to be created in which spiritual and moral

shared values and experiences can be expressed by UN personnel to one another.

6. To explore the establishment of a Permanent Center for Non-Violent Conflict Prevention and Resolution that will utilize all available means of mediation, negotiation, conciliation, and conflict-resolution techniques available. This center could have regional offices at which on-going multi-cultural, interreligious, and inter-ethnic dialogue could take place as a method of preventive diplomacy. It could take full advantage of the world's religions and could, in this context, be utilized to preempt cycles of misunderstanding, fear, and violence.[15] The extraordinary waste of resources for armaments and the suffering caused by their uses simply cannot be overlooked when addressing poverty. As long as resources are disproportionately diverted for violence, ending poverty will remain beyond reach.

The responsibility of NGOs

The international community recognizes the growing importance of NGOs in the adoption of policies and strategies that emphasize the need to place people at the center of development processes and to give priority to poverty alleviation, social justice, and advancement. NGOs have special experience in serving and assisting people at the grassroots level and in poor communities.

We call upon NGOs as follows:

1. To develop consultations with the WSSD Preparatory Committee and ECOSOC "to the fullest practicable extent" and to contribute spiritual vision and perspective on the issues facing the WSSD.

2. To contribute an articulation of values that emphasizes the wholeness of the human family, the sacredness of creation, and the importance of a global perspective to overcome all provincialism of race, caste, religion, and nation.

3. To express a sense of gratitude and humility, recognizing human limitation in the face of the reality that the human has not created this world nor do we fully understand its origins and mysteries.

4. To express the sacred mystery of life such that our paradigms of value do not reduce the created realm to a mere series of material objects to be selfishly exploited, but as a school to learn goodness, love, and virtue – a temporary abode in which development occurs on both the outer and inner dimensions.

5. To develop a culture of non-violence and thereby reduce the excessive waste of funds for military purposes.[16]

6. To propose methods of respecting the rights of those least capable of protecting their own rights, such as the poor, the outcasts, the disabled, the elderly, the sick, the destitute, the dying, the addicted, the prisoners, children, and the infirm.

7. To address the present crisis situations involving refugees, children, women, the disabled, the elderly and to enter into consultation with specific countries in order to create pilot programs from a spiritual perspective that can help support, inspire, and generate other socioeconomic programs.

8. To help the WSSD achieve its goals on an ongoing basis and to view the work of the UN and its agencies as potential agents of expression of the highest ideals of universal love and harmony.

9. To provide to the UN and its agencies services and resources to the extent possible for poverty alleviation and social development.

NOTES

1. Even the creation of welfare systems not utilizing these qualities often results in the proliferation of bureaucracies with cynical personnel delivering social services without personal satisfaction, engendering an experience of dependency and dehumanization by its recipients. This can be juxtaposed with the examples within numerous spiritual traditions of charitable endeavors which enrich the givers and assist the recipients to empower themselves, bringing them into the chain of giving as a blessing with the express expectation that they too will learn of compassion and offer their charity when able. Simply: one process ennobles and the other unintentionally degrades; the difference is founded on the presence or absence of spiritual qualities and universal values.

2. Many spiritual traditions view service to those who are suffering as a pre-eminent human duty, not an option, but the very defining characteristic of human social organization.

3. Noting the importance of the social component of sustainable development, General Assembly resolution 47/92 of 16 December 1992, which calls for convening the World Summit for Social Development, identifies eleven major Summit objectives:
* Place the needs of people at the center of development;
* Secure international governmental and NGO policies that promote social development and enable the active involvement of all citizens;
* Place special priority on the social development needs of the least developed countries;
* Attain an appropriate balance between economic efficiency and social justice in growth-oriented, equitable, and sustainable development environments, in accordance with nationally defined priorities;
* Address creatively the interaction between the social function of the State, market responses to social demands, and the imperative of sustainable development;
* Identify common problems of socially marginalized and disadvantaged groups and promote their social integration and attainment of equal opportunities;

* Promote legal protection, effective social welfare and education and training for all;
* Ensure effective delivery of social services to the disadvantaged;
* Mobilize resources for social development at the local, national, regional and international levels; and
* Recommend effective actions and policies for the UN system in the sphere of social development, and particularly for the Commission for Social Development.

4. By NGO we mean to include, at a minimum, all NGOs that appear in the UN Publication *Non-Governmental Organizations Associated with the Department of Public Information*, which includes organizations that are "concerned with matters dealing with international, economic, social, cultural, educational, health, scientific, technological, and related matters, and to questions of human rights (ECOSOC Res. 1296, Part I, #1). However, we seek a broader definition attempting to gain the largest possible constituency of people and organizations who seek to serve. We emphasize NGOs whose mission involves peace work in the broadest sense and, of course, NGOs addressing the three social development issues of enhancing social integration, reducing and alleviating poverty, and creating productive employment.

5. When we refer to religious community, it is meant in the broadest sense. However, we are fully cognizant that some Member States have state religions and, as stated in the Preamble, the importance of religious tolerance and pluralism cannot be overlooked, for otherwise religion can turn from a force of peace to one of conflict.

6. There is an evolving discipline of Human Rights. Its most important expression is found in the following United Nations documents:

The Charter of the United Nations makes repeated reference to human rights and fundamental freedoms. In the present context, two of them shall be quoted. The preamble states:

We the peoples of the United Nations determined ... to reaffirm faith in fundamental human rights, in the dignity and worth of the human person, in the equal rights of men and women and of nations large and small....

United Nations World Summit for Social Development

United Nations Department of Public Information

The first ever UN Summit on Social Development was held in March 1995, at Bella Centre, in Copenhagen, Denmark (during publication of this book). Among its objectives, agreed to in a Resolution by the General Assembly of the United Nations, was the intention to "address in creative ways the interaction between the social function of the state, market responses to social demands, and the imperatives of sustainable development." The WSSD attempts to shift social development issues higher up the international agenda. Ambassador Juan Somavia of Chile, Chair of the Preparatory Committee, noted that "...the end of the Cold War has produced uncertainty and instability....It is a moment of transformations, but the changes are as yet unmapped, the directions as yet uncharted." Sweden's representative at the first PrepCom noted that "We have no method of ascertaining to what extent globalization is a force for good or evil. The only certainty is that it is a force for change." (Quoted in *Go Between,* newsletter of the Non-Governmental Liason Service, February 1994.)

Why a Social Summit?

*A*lthough promising a future of accelerated social and economic progress, the end of the cold war has had a destabilizing effect on many societies in the short term. Unemployment, poverty, crime, inter-ethnic violence and civil warfare are on the rise in most parts of the world. Social and economic crises are eroding, often drastically, the substantial material progress achieved overall during the second half of the century.

Social tensions do not stay within national borders – they travel. Increasing migration and flows of refugees fuel xenophobia and racism. Crumbling political stability in one nation threatens peace and security in others.

In past decades, summit meetings have brought together world leaders to defuse political crises and find common ground on pressing problems. The World Summit for Social Development will likewise bring heads of State or Government together to address the social disintegration and world disorder that threaten global security and development. Meeting in Copenhagen in 1995, world leaders will define social development and human security priorities and agree to action at national and international levels.

The Summit furthers the commitment, made in the Charter of the United Nations, to promote "higher standards of living, full employment, and conditions of economic and social progress and development with a view to the creation of conditions of stability and well-being". Three core issues have been identified:

NOTES, continued

The purposes of the United Nations are listed in Article 1 of the Charter, of which the third paragraph reads:

> To achieve international co-operation in solving international problems of an economic, social, cultural, or humanitarian character, and in promoting and encouraging respect for human rights and for fundamental freedoms for all without distinction as to race, sex, language, or religion.

The UN Charter offers no further analysis, but from this foundation arose the Universal Declaration of Human Rights (1948), The International Covenant on Economic, Social, and Cultural Rights (1966), The International Covenant on Civil and Political Rights and The Optional Protocol thereto, providing for the right of Individual Petition (1966). These documents actually provide for an international Bill of Human Rights and include the Rights of Religious Freedom.

The UN Commission on Human Rights in 1986 mandated the Special Rapporteur on Religious Intolerance "to examine reports of incidents and governmental actions in all parts of the world which are inconsistent with the provisions of the Declaration on the Elimination of all Forms of Intolerance and of Discrimination Based on Religion or Belief" and to make remedial recommendations.

Particular reference is made to the "rights of freedom of thought, conscience and religion" found in the International Covenant on Civil and Political Rights, Articles 17 and 18 (1966), and International Convention on the Elimination of all Forms of Racial Discrimination, Article 5(d-vii).

7. The problems of marginalization will only be solved in an atmosphere of tolerance and appreciation; additionally, diversity generates a plethora of new ideas, as cultures cross-fertilize. Without adherence to these basic rights, religions themselves, which have the very real potential for fanaticism and irrationality, present dangers to the very values upon which they are actually based. This danger becomes most pronounced where a nation adopts a religion absent of guarantees of human rights for nonmembers. Where these legal protections are absent the healthy development of the spiritual dimension of the human is thwarted and states could evolve without room for religious experience. We are fully aware that there are Member States in which religion is denigrated and we ask them to rethink their attitude in light of the potential resources for moral and ethical values available in religious institutions.

8. *Agenda For Peace,* United Nations, NY, 1992, paragraph 11.

9. See "Towards a Global Ethic: An Initial Declaration," 1993, Parliament of the World's Religions.

10. Agenda for Peace, paragraph 15.

11. For a spiritual approach to world affairs, see U Thant, "How I Conceived My Role" in his memoirs, *The View from the UN*; cf. *Human Development Report 1990,* Chapter 1, p. 10 and HDR 1992, Chapter 1.

12. A/Conf.166/PC/6 Art. 4; also "The Vienna Declaration", June 1993 Art. 10.

13. Idem, Art. 8.

14. On subject of increased interdependence, *Agenda for Peace,* UN, NY, 1992.

15. This request has been initiated by a resolution taken at the 7th Conference of the World Religions, New Delhi, India, February 7, 1994, and by resolution at Programme One of the International Inter-religious Organizations Coordinating Committee, Bangalore, India, August 1994. It has been reduced to a formal petition by the interfaith organization the Temple of Understanding and has been endorsed by numerous world leaders, such as Archbishop Desmond Tutu (Archbishop of Cape Town, S.A.), Douglas Roche (fmr. Ambassador of Canada), Rev. James Dean Morton of St. John the Divine, His Holiness the Dalai Lama, Robert Muller, Juliet Hollister and many others.

16. For an excellent straightforward proposal of a five-point agenda for peace and development, see Mahbul Ul Haq's presentation in the panel "Disarmament, Peacebuilding and Global Security: Objectives for the Nineties" in *New Realities: Disarmament, Peace-Building, and Global Security,* pp. 53-57 United Nations, 1993.

No nation will be eternal, as will no body.
We must ask ourselves: have we as persons or nations
expressed intrinsic goodness during our lifespan?

- Reduction and elimination of widespread poverty;
- Productive employment and the reduction of unemployment;
- Social integration.

The Summit will tackle these issues by charting new directions for social policies. It will make a moral case for solidarity, for the integration of disadvantaged groups and for the promotion of existing UN agreements, including those concerning human rights, labour rights and social justice. The future of the UN's work in the social and economic fields will be shaped by the policies and commitments agreed to in Copenhagen in 1995.

A cycle of United Nations conferences

Social issues have been placed at the top of the international agenda by an ongoing cycle of major UN conferences, including the 1990 World Summit for Children, the 1992 Earth Summit (UN Conference on Environment and Development) and the 1993 World Conference on Human Rights. Scheduled for 1994 [were] the Global Conference on the Sustainable Development of Small Island Developing States, the World Conference on Natural Disaster Reduction and the International Conference on Population and Development. The cycle culminates in 1995 with the World Summit for Social Development and the Fourth World Conference on Women, capped by the commemoration of the United Nations Fiftieth Anniversary on 24 October 1995.

Who will participate in the Social Summit?

The two-day Summit will be held at the level of heads of State or Government. It will be preceded by five days of meetings among their personal representatives, other high-level officials, and experts. Summit consultations will also involve representatives from Governments, United Nations agencies, non-governmental organizations, intergovernmental organizations, national liberation movements recognized by the Organization of African Unity, experts, and professional associations.

The role of non-governmental organizations

The level of non-governmental organization (NGO) involvement in UN conferences has been rising since the 1992 Earth Summit. Recognizing that these organizations are key actors in advancing social development, the Summit Preparatory Committee adopted special modalities for NGO accreditation. [...]

Background

Noting the importance of the social component of sustainable development, General Assembly resolution 47/92 of 16 December 1992, which calls for convening the World Summit for Social Development, identifies eleven major Summit objectives:

- Place the needs of people at the centre of development;
- Secure international, governmental, and NGO policies that promote social development and enable the active involvement of all citizens;
- Place special priority on the social development needs of the least developed countries;
- Attain an appropriate balance between economic efficiency and social justice in growth-oriented, equitable, and sustainable development environments, in accordance with nationally defined priorities;
- Address creatively the interaction between the social function of the State, market responses to social demands, and the imperatives of sustainable development;
- Identify common problems of socially marginalized and disadvantaged groups and promote their social integration and attainment of equal opportunities;
- Promote legal protection, effective social welfare and education and training for all;
- Ensure effective delivery of social services to the disadvantaged;
- Mobilize resources for social development at the local, national, regional, and international levels;
- Recommend effective actions and policies for the UN system in the sphere of social development, and particularly for the Commission for Social Development.

[...]

DPI/1455–19696–May 1994

FOR MORE INFORMATION:

Key United Nations Documents:

Report on the World Social Situation 1993 and *World Summit for Social Development. An overview.* (See UNIPUB in Chapter 42.)

Electronic Databases:

Official United Nations documents on the Summit may be accessed on a number of electronic networks including:

Association for Progressive Communications (APC) users can access files via the access code: <.socdevdocs> conference

Internet users can access files via gopher by connecting to gopher.undp.org

International Institute for Sustainable Development
161 Portage Ave, East, Sixth Floor, Winnipeg, Manitoba
electronic mail: IISD!IISDPOST!JWAGEMAKER@iisdnet.attmail.com

Among its activities is the excellent service "Earth Negotiations Bulletin", published both in print and electronically as a complete reporting and synthesizing service about international negotiations, conferences, and proceedings of the United Nations, NGOs and governments. For electronic access to the ENB, connect to the gopher at gopher.igc.apc.org (under *Environment*)

Other resources:

NGLS (United Nations Non-Governmental Liason Service)
866 UN Plaza, A-6015, New York, NY 10017 USA
tel. (212) 963-3125 / fax. (212) 963-8712

The World Bank, External Affairs Division,
1818 H Street NW, Washington, DC 20433 USA
tel. (202) 473-1818

Also see development organizations in Chapter 42.

Weapons and Disarmament

Weapons Proliferation In the Third World:

How Many More Rwandas?

Warren Van Tongeren

Teacher (retired), relief worker and advocate for humane food and weapons policies

Rwanda – have we forgotten Rwanda, that little country tucked away in Central Africa? It is the home of the Tutsi and Hutu, whose tribal rivalry surely was exacerbated by its poverty and crowdedness, where people live at 250 to the square kilometer and women bear on average 8.2 children in their lifespan.

Little Rwanda, a country of desperately poor people, became yet another African nation which was plunged into civil war, a war of genocide which may have eliminated as many as three-fourths of the 1.1 million Tutsi people, almost all of them non-combatants. Thousands of people fleeing the advancing Tutsi RPF (Rwandan Patriotic Front) fled to Tanzania, Uganda, Burundi and Zaire. In Zaire, especially, thousands met their deaths from a wave of cholera which swept through the squalid camps. Although no one can say with certainty, more than 100,000 children were orphaned, and perhaps that number is too conservative.

I worked among thousands of these refugees in the Benaco Refugee Camp of northwestern Tanzania, where 250,000 people had crossed the Rusumo Bridge in just 24 hours. I cannot forget Rwanda and the suffering of its people. The tragedy which came to Rwanda in April of 1994 can hardly be exaggerated. Almost 3 million of Rwanda's people have fled their homeland, boosting the number of the world's refugees past the 23 million mark.

Yet the greater tragedy, perhaps, lies in the fact that this was just the latest – and perhaps the worst – of so many tragic wars in the developing world. Have we forgotten Sudan, or Angola, where wars still continue? Or Mozambique, some of whose destructive war's effects I could see from along Malawi's eastern border. Do we remember Liberia, Eritrea, Sierra Leone? But surely, few Americans will have forgotten Somalia.

The weapons connection

Upon our return to the States, one question we were never asked during our discussions of Rwanda was, "Where did these people obtain their modern weapons?" After all, little Rwanda, the "Switzerland of Africa," does not make modern weapons. Nor, to my knowledge, do any

of the other nations of Africa except South Africa, which was among several which supplied the Hutus and Tutsis. The proliferation of these sophisticated weapons of death in poor, developing nations constitutes one of the great overall tragedies of the late 20th century.

Michael T. Klare, Professor of Peace and World Security Studies at Hampshire College, recently stated it most emphatically:

The international arms community made the holocaust in Rwanda possible.

Klare knows what most people do not: that the weapons which have been supplied to most developing countries, but especially in Africa, have been used, not for security of these countries against potential enemies beyond their borders, but in power struggles, some related to the Cold War of the two superpowers, between rivals for control of their nations. A recent United Nations Development Report showed that of the 82 conflicts since 1950 which have resulted in the deaths of more than 1,000 people, 79 of these occurred within a country's borders. And most of these have been non-industrial or developing countries. The same UN report states that an African has a 33 times greater chance of dying from malnutrition than from a war with a neighboring country.

The enormity of the tragedy of the proliferation of modern weapons is most clearly evident in the growing problem of refugees, more than three-fourths of whom are women and children. In 1982, refugees numbered 12 million. By 1989, they had risen to 15 million. Our refugee population now numbers 23 million. Moreover, the number of displaced persons is 25 million, a growth which is faster than that of refugees. The UNHCR's budget of $1.4 billion is also double that of 1989 and now exceeds the budget of the UN Development Program. An August 18 article in the *Christian Science Monitor* stated that nations have increasingly reduced their budgets for refugee work and closed their borders. Ironically, some of the nations most instrumental in arming the Third World are among those now most reluctant to aid its refugee victims.

Another consequence of the proliferation of weapons in developing countries is the monumental external debt of these countries. While not all of this debt has resulted from the purchase of weapons through loans, much of it has. Between 1975-1985, for example, 45 percent of the debt incurred by developing nations resulted from the purchase of weapons. Today, at least 16 African nations struggle with Structural Adjustment Programs imposed by the World Bank and International Monetary Fund for the repayment of their debts. The poor of these countries experience considerable suffering as their governments are forced to devalue their currency, increase their food exports, and reduce their already limited budgets for health and education by 25 percent. Children in these nations die today because their countries have been sucked into the trend to modernize their armies with the latest weapons of the industrialized West. They have mortars but no medicines, and children in countries in conflict will continue to die from legs blown off by the estimated 100 million landmines presently embedded in our world.

While assessing impending famine in two areas of Tanzania in late May and early June 1994, I noted that row upon row of army barracks were under construction in an area in which villagers were digging in the almost dry river bed to obtain their drinking water, though it was then the end of the rainy season. The health centers I entered were virtually empty because they would have no medicines until the new month. In a second area, I found a hospital with only the barest of essential equipment and very limited drugs. While health facilities operated by religious and secular voluntary agencies serve the people in developing countries fairly well, I have never left a government health facility without a feeling of despair. The most serious impediment to development of a better life for Africa's poor today is the strangling debt and the militarization of their countries, which has added so much to that debt. While the need for development aid from government and non-governmental sources has never been greater, the impact of militarization in these countries continues to negate the effectiveness of this aid. It is not strange that conditions in many developing countries today are worse than they were 20 or 30 years ago.

Who profits from weapons sales?

Developing nations do not manufacture modern weapons of war. They buy them from a number of manufacturers and distributors in other nations eager to realize some of the considerable profit which this global enterprise brings. And their number is growing. The common argument is, "After all, if we don't sell them, someone else will. Besides, we have to keep our arms industries busy; it is important for the welfare of our workers and their families."

So, increasingly, not only the superpower and the former superpower but also other nations sell arms. South Africa and Egypt, for example, were among those countries supplying Rwanda. France supplied the Hutu militia in Rwanda. And increasingly, surplus weapons from the countries of the former Soviet bloc are being offered for sale to interested nations at bargain prices. In a world already filled with weapons, the competition for the lucrative markets is only increasing.

While many countries supply arms to developing countries, the only remaining superpower dominates the market. That is not surprising in light of the fact that the U.S. is the home of 9 of the 10 largest arms manufacturers

in the world. Furthermore, since 1991, the United States government has agreed to subsidize the sale of arms by underwriting promotional costs associated with weapons fairs and arms shows anywhere in the world market. Consider some of the following data reported by Robert Drinan in the September 24 issue of *America* magazine:

- The U.S. now controls 67 percent of weapons sales to underdeveloped countries.
- Over the last 30 years, the U.S. has transferred $1.3 trillion worth of military equipment to foreign nations.
- Of 48 nations in which some kind of ethnic warfare was under way in 1993, 26 had received weapons from the U.S.
- Since 1991, the U.S. has sold $43.9 billion in arms to the Mideast.
- Between 1989 and 1992 the United States sold 917 fighter jets, 4,948 military tanks, 848 helicopters, 33 warships, and 484 long-range missiles. (Few high ticket items are sold to poor nations, which rely on small arms for their forces).

That the United States government is serious about the business of weapons is evident in the expenditure in 1991 of $37 billion on the research needed to create new weapons. And, as ever more sophisticated weapons are developed and manufactured, older weapons are offered for sale. In 1991, the U.S. sold $12 billion; in 1992, $31 billion; in 1993, $35 billion.

One may well ask why the United States has become so militaristic, and why it has become a major arms supplier. A least three reasons have been suggested.

First, people in the United States have developed a militaristic mindset, as one observer has called it, a mentality of over 40 years in the making. Our perceived enemies are everywhere, trying to destroy our "way of life" and all that we cherish. Not only do we perceive ourselves as the keepers of the world's freedom, but weapons are a necessary part of guaranteeing our supremacy over a world we deem hostile.

Second, the arming of the world is a reflection of the arming of our own society, which has been wracked by ever-increasing levels of violence resulting from the unrestricted sale and use of guns. The failure to curb arms sales abroad likely reflects our own reluctance to control the proliferation of guns in our own cities. Ours is a violent society.

The third reason notes the power and influence of the military-industrial complex, whose lobbyists today preserve the huge industry which benefits so much from its military contracts and effectively maintain its preeminent place in American life.

But efforts are being made to stop the rising arms trade. *Christian Century* (May 18-25, 1994) reported that African Catholic bishops termed it "imperative" that arms sales to Africa be stopped and that a just solution to the problem of external debt be found. NBC Nightly News used several segments in examining the problem of the growing proliferation of arms and the problems which have resulted from sales of weapons. Human Rights Watch, Amnesty International and other advocacy groups are becoming increasingly vocal in opposition to the sale and export of more weapons to an already violent world. NBC reported that two-thirds of the countries receiving weapons from the

United States are designated as human rights violators by the State Department.

How does this happen? It happens because an often-apathetic Congress can oppose a sale only *after* it has been authorized by the President and can block such a sale only with a two-thirds majority vote. But there is now legislation in the Congress to curb arms sales to certain countries now receiving weapons. Rep. Cynthia McKinney (D-GA) and Senator Mark Hatfield (R-OR) have sponsored legislation which requires the President to certify that the recipient nation is not engaged in violations of internationally recognized human rights, forbids sales to military dictatorships and countries engaged in acts of aggression against their neighbors, and bans sales to nations at war. Three years ago the Congress wisely stopped the export of anti-personnel land mines, which now cause the deaths of many victims long after a conflict has ended.

It is not surprising to find Senator Hatfield leading such legislation. For many years, he has been the "dove" in the Senate, and he has spoken articulately against the militarism which gained such ascendancy in the last several decades. It was Hatfield who chided his Senate colleagues in a speech of August, 1989, in which he expressed his outrage at the weapons proliferation of the eighties. "Is there no ethical dimension," he asked, "to the definition of national security that we are passing on to the developing nations of the world, where arsenals are now as bloated as the bodies of the Third World's children?" The "Arms Trade Code of Conduct Bill" is presently in the Congress. U.S. citizens can support this legislation by writing to their senators and representative.

Over 40 years after he issued his prophetic warning, the words of the late President Dwight D. Eisenhower continue to reflect his prescience.

> Every gun that is made, every warship launched, every rocket fired, signifies, in the final sense, a theft from those who are hungry and not fed, those who are cold and not clothed. This world-in-arms is spending the sweat of its laborers, the genius of its scientists, the hope of its children.

It is a tragedy of immense proportions that the prophetic warning of this former warrior was lost upon a world which now appears unable to cope with the violence of the wars taking place. Since 1945, 40 million people in the developing world have died as a result of war.

The Christian witness

*T*he response of the Christian community in the United States to these issues follows very closely the positions of various church bodies to the Gulf war. It may be recalled that many of the mainline churches opposed the bombing and destruction of the the infrastructure of Iraq, pleading rather for negotiation, not confrontation and ultimatums. It is significant that when President Bush rejected the 11th hour plea of his pastor and the Presiding Bishop of the Episcopal Church in the U.S., the Rev. Dr. Edmund Browning, not to begin the bombing, he turned to the foremost representative of the Evangelical churches, the Rev. Dr. Billy Graham. Dr. Graham was present at the White House as the bombing began. For lack of a better paradigm, one can place most churches' support for peace and justice issues on the commonly used continuum of Left to Right.

In 1993, while my wife and I helped coordinate relief efforts in Eastern Zambia, we had opportunity to travel along the western border of Malawi. For many miles, the road we travelled was the border of Mozambique. We saw first hand, even from the border, the destruction of buildings just into Mozambique. Over a million refugees were present just inside Malawi and over a million people had already died in the war. Half of them were children. The supporters of RENAMO, the guerrilla army responsible for this extension of the cold war, included South Africa's apartheid government and numerous leaders and groups from the religious right. These same groups supported the Contras during the war in Nicaragua.

Christians from the Conservative Right can be counted on to accept, often uncritically, the military policies, huge military budgets and active projection and use of military power by their country. One will not find among them a Commission on Peace and Justice. While deeds of mercy often accompany their efforts to save souls, they resist peace and justice or war resistance efforts as "leftist," and they are immediately suspect as liberal or unorthodox. Patriotism, for the religious right, is synonymous with unquestioned support for the use of military power by the United States. Its supporters continue to suspect, if not oppose, the United Nations, and find the concept of world citizenship unpatriotic and threatening.

It is not always easy to place denominations or churches along a continuum. Activists from Roman Catholic, Episcopal, and other mainline churches often feel very much alone in their peacemaking activities and opposition to militarism. Yet there is considerably more freedom in mainline churches for opposition to obscene military budgets and for sales of weapons to the developing world. Of particular note is the consistent opposition to war and continued activism in peacemaking by the Friends (Quakers) and the Mennonite bodies. One does not need to speculate regarding the views on war and peacemaking by menbers of these groups.

In a time of resurgent nationalism, is there a commonly accepted belief which can surmount the alienation of the people of our war-ravaged world? Dr. Nicholas Wolterstorff, professor in the Yale Divinity School and longtime peace and justice activist, states that "what unites us as bearers of the Image of God is more important than what divides us as members of nations." Perhaps no other Biblical teaching is so important to the understanding that the deaths of Iraqis or Rwandese, our brothers and sisters as God's image bearers, no matter what their religion, are as tragic as the deaths of American soldiers or civilians. The belief in the image of God in all people is not the stuff out of which nationalism is nurtured.

To an increasingly violent society in a violent, suffering world, the Prince of Peace still speaks:

> Blessed are the peacemakers, for they shall be called the sons and daughters of God.

Steps to Abolish Nuclear Weapons

After discussing actions to be taken to mark the year 1995, which will be the 50th anniversary of the bombing of Hiroshima and Nagasaki as well as the expiration date of the Nuclear Non-Proliferation Treaty, the Japan Congress Against A- and H-Bombs developed the following proposal.

*T*he present Non-Proliferation Treaty cannot prevent nuclear proliferation. The present system is unequal in that the nuclear weapons of the nuclear nations are allowed, and opaque in that the control of nuclear materials and technology are in the hands of the member governments and their agent, the International Atomic Energy Association. While non-nuclear states should abandon nuclear weapons development, the nuclear states should not stage military attacks with NPT violations as an excuse. In order to overcome the weakness of the present system and establish a nuclear non-proliferation system true to its name, we must achieve the following goals in 1995:

1. Conclusion of a Comprehensive Nuclear Test Ban Treaty based on the continuation of the present nuclear testing moratorium.

2. Conclusion of a treaty banning nuclear weapons research and development through other means than nuclear testing, including missile flight testing.

3. Conclusion of an agreement to ban the production and use of nuclear weapons-usable materials (i.e., plutonium and highly enriched uranium), including those in civil programs, while placing existing materials under international control, in order to prevent the proliferation of nuclear weapons.

4. Honoring by the nuclear nations of existing and future Nuclear Free Zones.

5. Rendering of an advisory opinion by the International Court of Justice that the use and threat of use of nuclear weapons are illegal.*

6. The nuclear nations demonstration of a process of securing, by the end of the century, concrete procedures for the abolition of nuclear weapons, in fulfillment of the duty of nuclear disarmament set forth in Article VI of the NPT.

7. Guarantee of NGOs involvement in discussions aimed at realization of nuclear non-proliferation systems and their enforcement, including inspection.

8. Establishment of an inspection system for nuclear materials, nuclear weapons, and nuclear facilities of the nuclear nations in order to make the NPT more equitable.

9. International control of nuclear weapons, with the final goal being the disposal of these weapons.

10. Extension of the Nuclear Non-Proliferation Treaty in a form strengthened in the ways described above.

In order to achieve the above goals, we propose to stage an international signature campaign and to organize an international joint action. We hope that the ideas put forth here will be enriched through worldwide discussion.

Printed in "New Beginnings,"
the newsletter of Campaign 1995

"The world needs a clear, decisive, moral lead. It needs a lead that will be full of idealism, even with a touch of the romantic; it needs a lead that will help people to dream of a future full of hope and peace, and will inspire them to turn a dream into a goal. The world does not need the tired arguments of the politicians who hope for peace by bullets. Nor the discredited hopes of those who look for peacekeeping forces and justified warfare. A new generation of church leaders is emerging: they will bring a fresh approach and a new way of thinking and they will be more open to new ideas drawn from the heart of the Gospel."   ANGLICAN PACIFIST FELLOWSHIP

"I refuse to believe the cynical notion that nation after nation must spiral down a militaristic stairway into the hell of thermonuclear destruction. I believe that unarmed truth and unconditional love will have the final word in reality.... I believe that even amid today's mortar bursts and whining bullets, there is still hope for a brighter tomorrow.... I have the audacity to believe that peoples everywhere can have three meals a day for their bodies, education and culture for their minds, and dignity, equality, and freedom for their spirits."

MARTIN LUTHER KING, JR.
Nobel Prize Acceptance Speech, 1964

FOR MORE INFORMATION:

International Peace Bureau,
41 Rue de Zurich, 1201 Geneva, SWITZERLAND

Japan Congress Against A-and H-Bombs (Gensuikin)
5F Hitotsubashi-KI-BLDG, 3-17-11 Kanda-Jinbo-Cho, Chiyoda-ku, Tokyo 101, JAPAN

Lawyers' Committee on Nuclear Policy
666 Broadway, #625, New York, NY 10012 USA;
tel. (212) 674-7790 / fax. 674-6199
USA affiliate of the International Association of Lawyers Against Nuclear Arms

NGO Committee on Disarmament
777 United Nations Plaza, 3B
New York, NY 10017 USA; tel. (212) 687-5340.
Networking organization and publisher of *Disarmament Times*

Peace Action (formerly SANE/FREEZE)
1819 H Street, Suite 640,
Washington, DC USA 20006-3603 USA

* **World Court Project, c/o Lawyers' Committee,**
666 Broadway, #625, New York, NY 10012 USA

Also see Chapters 28 and 42.

A Culture of Peace

Towards a Universal Civilization with a "Heart"

Brother Wayne Teasdale

Christian monk and sannyasi *in the lineage of Dom Bede Griffiths, author, member of the Board of Monastic Interreligious Dialogue, and Trustee of the Council for a Parliament of the World's Religions*

*T*here is a longing that stirs deep within all of us, innate to the human family, found in every nation, culture, every religious tradition, in the ancient myths, in poetry, song, and historical experience. It is the inspiration behind them all—the desire for the paradisal state of life, the beatitude of the perfect society. Whether it is conceived as a garden of heavenly delights, a pure utopian state, or a more realistic process that brings transformation of society gradually over many years through a deliberate approach, the desire itself is real; it's in touch with something ultimate, something that is as mysterious as it is inviting.

In this essay I am suggesting that a universal society of a higher order than is presently the case is not only possible, but perhaps inevitable! I will try to show how the culture of peace is related to the emergence of a new civilization, what the foundation of this global society is, and what its characteristic elements are, especially the roles of nonviolence and spirituality.

Remembrances of paradise

*A*ll the myths about the original state of the human condition speak of it in terms that convey a kind of intimacy with the Divine, with Ultimate Reality and mystery. This is clear not only in the Bible, but is also true of the Hindu tradition, especially in the Bhakti school, but also, more generally, in every other school of Hindu mysticism. It is equally true of Greek mythology as it is of the experience of indigenous societies of Africa, Australia, and the Americas. It is true, in its way, of Buddhist, Jewish, and Islamic or Sufi mysticism, as it is of Taoism, Confucianism, Shintoism, and Shamanism. In all these forms there is present the faint memory of beatitude as a real experience of intimacy with the Source of Being.

As the ancient cultures became more stable and were informed by the spirit of their original revelation experiences, they evolved societies that were essentially pacific or deeply peaceful and in a state of inner harmony. This pacific quality is evident in the great pre-Vedic Harappa culture of the Indus Valley. This culture is probably the prototype[1] of the one that arose from the Aryan-Dravidian union. We still do not know the age of the Harappa-Mohenjo-Daro civilization, but the discovery of two seals with the image of a deity seated in the meditation *asana*[2] (posture), suggests a high degree of spiritual awareness coming from the practice of meditation and an attitude of contemplative interiority. It may be that the Harappans were the progenitors of the rishic seers of Indian antiquity, and perhaps were the recipients of a primordial revelation from which they learned the cosmic and social harmony that is enshrined in the Vedic notion of *rta*.[3]

Similar to the notion of *rta*, on a social and political level in Chinese history and civilization, is the Confucian ideal of *Ta-t'ung,* the "Great Society," or "Great Commonwealth"[4] It can also be translated as the "Great Unity in Common," or simply as the "Great Harmony." I prefer the latter two expressions. China knew centuries of civil peace when her empire was socially and politically cohesive, centuries in which crime and corruption were nearly nonexistent, when relationships within the family, the state, and the society were harmonious. These periods of China's golden ages, for example, the Tang dynasty (618-906 CE), were the consequence of the *Ta-t'ung,* when it prevailed.

We also marvel at the example of tolerance and enlightened government of the Buddhist emperor Ashoka, of the Maurya Empire in India, who reigned from 268–233 BCE. His example is often cited as constituting a brilliant star in the constellation of ancient rulers.

In the West, we have the seemingly perfect blueprints of Plato's *Republic* and Thomas More's *Utopia* – "seemingly perfect" because both of these attempts, though originating in spiritual wisdom, still are somewhat abstract, untried, and so, theoretical, even though they portray societies where genuine justice exists. But it was St. Augustine who, in his monumental *City of God,* his philosophy of history, describes the perfect Christian society, whose foundation is peace, as "the tranquillity of order."[5] He elaborates this order in its highest sense: "The peace of the celestial city (the City of God, Heaven) is the perfectly ordered and harmonious enjoyment of God, and of one another in God."[6] The harmonious order of human society derives from its heavenly archetype, and the basis of the latter realm is this mystical relationship with the divine Source, which is also the end for each of us.

There is also the extremely ancient Tibetan legend of

Shambhala, a mystical kingdom hidden away somewhere in or beyond the Himalayas, where a perfect utopia exists. Many of Tibetan Buddhism's secret or esoteric writings are attributed to Shambhala, including the texts associated with the Kalacakra initiation. The Dalai Lama is said to have once remarked: "If so many Kalacakra texts are supposed to have come from Shambhala, how could the country be just a fantasy?"[7]

Whether or not these legends refer to real places, however, they are found in most cultures, and we must garner their spirit, their deep spiritual truth, and apply it to our own attempts at building a new civilization. For all of these myths and treatises are inspired by an intuition that we are meant for something better.

Toward a universal society

All memories of paradise and the attempts to create it in this world again point to the possibility and, indeed, the urgency of moving toward this *something better,* this new civilization. I believe that we have a unique opportunity today to introduce the possibility of such a new global order as the child of enlightened values and wisdom. The introduction of a new universal civilization as well as its dissemination require the permanent collaboration of the world's religions. For just as there can be "no peace on Earth unless there is peace among the religions," as Hans Küng[8] has rightly observed, no advance to an enlightened global order is possible unless these same religions decide to work together.

The logic of our global life and situation with all its complexity and all the international problems we face as a planet, the fact of interdependence on all levels, and our precious and rich pluralism have brought us to this intense moment of focus in history. We are compelled and challenged to leap beyond, transcend, even outgrow our old limits, and become a *new humanity.* This new humanity receives its direction and inspiration from the discovery of our common, larger identity in what Thomas Berry, the eloquent ecological thinker calls the *Earth Community,*[9] a natural commonwealth of species united in the one planetary world, *living* in genuine harmony with one another and with the Earth itself.

In many ways, the Parliament of 1893 was a prophetic act because – just by happening – it pointed to the need for the religions to have a forum in which they can discover,

through trial and error, their common voice and acceptance of a *universal responsibility*[10] for the Earth. In the same way, the recent Parliament was a significant instrument and catalyst for a new civilization by focusing world attention upon it.

The Parliament in our time represented an historical promise, a unique opportunity to forge ahead towards a deeper sense of our identity as the *Community of Religions* within the Earth Community itself. From this profound realization – that religions constitute a larger reality of community than any one tradition standing alone – we can begin to place the stones in the edifice of the new, enlightened civilization. Along with the United Nations, the nation states, the individual religious traditions, and non-governmental and international organizations, a permanent forum for the community of the world's religions could become an essential institution in this global society and a *vehicle* for its actualization on a global scale. Thus the prophetic direction of the first Parliament can be realized in our time.

Nonviolence and the culture of peace

A culture of peace is slowly developing within the larger context of the new global civilization. This culture is unquestionably fundamental to it, one of its enduring pillars. More basic still, and essential to the growth and deep rootedness of the culture of peace and the new civilization, is the value and attitude of nonviolence. As Mahatma Gandhi, Martin Luther King and the Dalai Lama well understood, one of the most effective tools in educating for peace is teaching nonviolence.

All of us know that we must come to grips with the escalating problem of violence, both in society and in ourselves. It is especially critical that we confront it as it emanates from communities of faith in conflict. Everything would seem to depend on getting violence under control; one way to do this – a way which serves the culture of peace and brings us nearer to the universal civilization – is to make a solid commitment to nonviolence among religions, nations, groups, and persons. In committing ourselves to nonviolence in our individual intentions and actions, and, collectively, through our religious institutions, our international organizations and our governments, we are making a quantum leap forward. [See *The Seville Statement on Violence*[11] and the *Universal Declaration on Nonviolence*[12] in Chapter 27.]

Teilhard de Chardin spoke eloquently of the eventual emergence into a higher, planetary consciousness. I believe that we have arrived at the very threshold of this exciting process. We require only the radical, childlike courage and wisdom to walk through that door! In passing through this threshold we assume the responsibility of what is essentially a new commandment for us; that commandment is nonviolence.

Nonviolence is the active living out of peace and the very essence of a culture of peace. It is infinitely more effectual to *be* a concrete example of peace than merely to talk about it. Nonviolence means a sensitivity towards all life, a respect and reverence for it, without exception. Nonviolence – *ahimsa* – is rich and all-embracing as a

---

In My Dream

I see a door into another world,
and as I pass through this door
I see wonders and beauty galore.
I see love, peace and happiness.
I am amazed by all I see:
no prejudice, no lies, no hate,
only good, nothing bad or evil;
and in the instant before I awake
I see how Eden must have been.

COLLEEN MC GARGAL,
8th grade

virtue, an attitude, a habit, and a value. It is at once an active commitment to nonharming in any form, whether physical, emotional, intellectual, social, economic, political, or spiritual. It is also the disposition of gentleness, of humility, of selflessness, and yet includes moral clarity, firmness, patience, perseverance, and openness. Nonviolence is all of these and more. In its ultimate depth of reality, nonviolence is love! Thus it is necessarily not only the basis of a culture of peace – the way to teach peace in the deepest sense – but also the basis of the new universal society, the civilization of love.

The shape of the new civilization

*I*n this space I can offer only the barest of outlines of the future global society: it will require a new metaphysics, cosmology, theology, ethics, and, of course, a new way to conduct economics and politics. On the social level, in the relationship of the various religious traditions to one another, and in the interest of peace among the traditions, this planetary society will be established firmly on the insight that the community of religions is the primary religious organization of humankind.

Spirituality is the soul of this civilization, and what will animate it. For it is spirituality that unites us all on the deepest level, and each one of us has some kind of personal spirituality. As a universal tradition of wisdom and an individual process of inner development, as the unfolding and flowering in relationship to Ultimate Reality, and as the fruits of this inner process reflected in one's life, spirituality is the foundation of the new civilization's culture and vitality. The spirituality of humankind emphasizes the mystical awareness of unity as the essence of enlightenment, whether conceived or experientially understood as *Advaita, Nirvana, Dzogchen, Satori, Fana,* or the *Unitive Life.* This intense and ultimate awareness of unity is the ground of genuine solidarity in the evolving universal tradition of wisdom.

The moral[13] foundations of the new civilization include the values of love, compassion, nonviolence, empathy, respect for pluralism, justice, courage, respect for human rights, and for the rights of all species, and solidarity. The new civilization also relies upon personal commitment to universal responsibility, especially as this embraces the total Earth Community, its environmental needs and values, the guarding of justice and making peace.

The social, political, material, and economic foundations[14] of a new culture lie in the balance between the individual's rights and those of the Earth Community. The common well-being is the basis of personal well-being, but personal well-being guides the interpretation of communal welfare. Social structures exist for the person – for his or her protection and development, but equally, the person has a responsibility to the Earth Community always to consider the larger welfare of the whole, and always to live in harmony with it.[15]

A civilization with heart

*S*olutions to humankind's problems must originate in and flow from the heart, from an *inner change* of attitude and direction. Although the intellect will make its contribution, our problem is not one of understanding. We all grasp the crisis of our planet in its many facets. Our problem, rather, is one of *will:* the capacity to change before it's too late for our beloved Earth. Together, the religions have the immense *challenge* of *inspiring* this *will* to change in the human family. Building the culture of peace is a major step toward a new civilizational reality that is truly global in scope, universal in culture, and informed by our ultimate values. The culture of peace is the ambience of this new global society, this civilization with a heart.

We are all collaborators in the construction of this civilization possessed of a heart. In this great labor, the emergence of a permanent forum for the world's religions is an absolute necessity and an urgent responsibility to which, I believe, the Spirit calls us in our time of monumental transition. In view of this necessity and responsibility, the existing interfaith organizations should work together with the religions and other organizations, disciplines and institutions, to see to it that such an entity becomes a permanent reality. We must seize the initiative to make it happen.

Baby Earth

In a dream I see a small boy's heart
reaching out to the earth,
and all our troubles are being taken out
on such a small child

Who cannot understand his feelings,
who just needs
to be held and cared for.

Although the boy can see the world
and its troubles,
they cannot see him.

ANGIE DOMIENIK,
8th grade

The Beautiful God

In a dream I see a beautiful god
watching over his world.
There he is with the golden moon.
I see him put out his hand.
He touches mars and moves it a little.

I see a jaguar run and jump,
and as he jumps
the god gives him wings.
The jaguar flies away.

Then it starts to rain
warm purple rain drops on my head,

and all the animals come out
and jump.
And as they jump,
the god gives them wings.

Then the god looks at me
and gives me wings.
Then I soar through the air
with the animals.

SHYLA WALKER,
4th grade

Let us realize the historic opportunity we are being offered; the emerging forum of the world's religions will provide a place for all of us who wish to serve the Earth Community. The question comes to this: can we model in ourselves, for the sake of the world, that quality of dynamic change so indispensable to our planet? Much depends on the answer we give to this question.

NOTES

1. See Mircea Eliade, *Yoga: Immortality and Freedom, Bollingen Series* , Princeton Univ. Press, 1969, pp.353–358.

2. *Ibid.,* pp.355–356.

3. For a profound and comprehensive study of *rta*, see Jeanine Miller, *The Vision of Cosmic Order in the Vedas*, Routledge & Kegan Paul, London, 1985.

4. Dun J. Li, *The Essence of Chinese Civilization*, Von Nostrand, New York, 1967, p.109. See also K'ang Yu-wei (1858–1927), a modern Confucian thinker, especially his *Ta-t'ung shu (Book of Great Unity)*, Peking, 1956.

5. S. Augustinus, *De Civitate Dei*, bk. 19, ch. 13.

6. *Ibid.*

7. Edwin Bernbaum, *The Way to Shambhala: A Search for the Mythical Kingdom Beyond the Himalayas*, Tarcher, Los Angeles, 1989, p.27.

8. Hans Küng, "No Peace in the World without Peace among Religions, *World Faiths Insight*, New Series 21, Feb. 1989, p.14.

9. Thomas Berry, *The Dream of the Earth*, Sierra Club Books, San Francisco, 1988 *cf.* ch. 2, "The Earth Community," pp.6–12.

10. The term "universal responsibility" is the Dalai Lama's. He has been and is popularizing it. See, for instance, his, *The Global Community and the Need for Universal Responsibility*, Wisdom Pub., Boston, 1992.

11. The Seville Statement on Violence was written in 1986 by an international group of scientists for the UN, and was adopted by UNESCO in 1989. See Chapter 27 of this book and *The Seville Statement on Violence: Preparing the Ground for Peace*, ed. David Adams, UNESCO, Paris, 1991.

12. All documentation relating to the Universal Declaration on Nonviolence is with Sister Katherine Howard, OSB, Committee for the Universal Declaration, St. Benedict's Convent, St. Joseph, MN 56374-0277, USA.

13. Some beginnings have been made here by the UN and various interfaith organizations, *i.e.*, The International Association for Religious Freedom, Temple of Understanding, Anuvrat Global Organization, World Conference on Religion and Peace, Monastic Interreligious Dialogue, etc. These groups, and others, have all generated documents or statements of principles. See Marcus Braybrooke's *Stepping Stones to a Global Ethic*, SCM Press, London, 1992.

14. Two important books here are E. F. Schumacher's *Small is Beautiful: Economics as If People Mattered*, Harper & Row, San Francisco, 1973, and the less known, but significant work by Gerald and Patricia Mische, *Toward a Human World Order*, Paulist Press, 1977.

15. Mention should also be made of the role of the media, especially journalism, which must exercise a greater sense of responsibility, always keeping in mind the common good of the entire Earth Community. It cannot be a tool of special interests, nor operate in isolation from the guiding values of a universal society. The media has to become more accountable to the community through a process of self-regulation, that is, imposed on it by its own standards of enlightened journalism.

Seeking the True Meaning of Peace:
The Declaration of Human Responsibilities for Peace and Sustainable Development

From June 25 to 30, 1989, an unusual conference met in Costa Rica to explore the meaning and implications of the concept of *Peace*. Participants gained new appreciation for the very real connections between such factors as population pressures, ecological crises, development and resource use, religious teachings and spirituality, and international political activity.

In preparation for the conference, a commission of representatives from the Foreign Ministry of the Government of Costa Rica and the University for Peace carried forth an international consultation and drafted the *Declaration of Human Responsibilities for Peace and Sustainable Development*. This document (printed on following pages) identifies universally acceptable principles, based upon diverse philosophical and religious wisdom as well as recognizing the requirements of the ecological systems of the earth. The Declaration was enthusiastically considered, improved, and endorsed by most of the participants in the conference, and is now distributed by the government of Costa Rica, the University for Peace, and conference attendees as an instrument for reflection and commitment.

Noteworthy among the participants were Oscar Arias, (then) President of Costa Rica, His Holiness Tenzin Gyatso, the 14th Dalai Lama of Tibet, and Monsignor Roman Arrieta, Archbishop of San Jose; also participating were Robert Muller, Jaime Montalvo of the University for Peace, and Rodrigo Carazo, former President of Costa Rica and founder of the University for Peace.

In addition, other distinguished guests and more than 500 persons of various creeds, professional training, political orientation, and nationalities – including representatives of indigenous populations – came together to study, reflect, identify the contents of the idea of *Peace*, and take action that would have impact throughout the planet.

Since the conference, the Declaration was presented in October 1989 to the General Assembly of the United Nations and was formally adopted through a presidential decree of the government of Costa Rica as an instrument for reflection and commitment. As a statement of universal principles, the document can have many applications in forums ranging from religious and ethical studies to economics and political science.

By linking the pursuit of peace with the concepts of sustainability, personal responsibility, and interdependence, the Declaration's insights bring a holistic perspective to ecology and environmental studies, and have important implications for the development of personal and planetary resources. The values it promotes have implications for economic aid programs, as well as for international policies and cooperation. Its greatest value, however, is its focus on the universal responsibility of each individual, so it is through personal reflection and commitment that the Declaration will have its most significant impact.

FOR MORE INFORMATION:

University for Peace, P.O. Box 199-1250 Escazu, Costa Rica, CENTRAL AMERICA

Declaration of Human Responsibilities
for Peace and Sustainable Development

Preamble

Considering that both the report of the World Commission on Environment and Development[1] and the United Nations Environmental Perspective to the Year 2000 and Beyond[2] have recognized the imminent danger threatening the existence of the Earth as a result of war and environmental destruction;

Recognizing that the world has been evolving from a group of separate communities towards interdependence and the beginnings of a world community, a process reflecting global concerns, common goals, and shared ideals;

Recalling that, according to the Universal Declaration of Human Rights, recognition of the inherent dignity and of the equal and inalienable human rights of all members of the human family is the foundation of freedom, justice, and peace in the world;

Considering the aspirations of all the members of the human family to realize their potential to the maximum through the cultural, social, political, and economic development of individuals and of communities, recognized in the Declaration on the Right to Development[3] as an inalienable human right;

Recognizing the necessity of ensuring the full and equal participation of women and men in the decision-making processes relating to the promotion of peace and development;

Bearing in mind that the international community has proclaimed that people have a sacred right to peace[4] and has recommended that national and international organizations should promote peace;[5]

Observing that the international community has recognized the fundamental right of human beings to live in an environment of a quality that permits a life of dignity and well-being;[6]

Bearing in mind the challenge posed by the growing imbalances in the dynamic relationship between population, resources, and the environment;

Considering that the General Assembly has established that all human rights and fundamental freedoms are indivisible and interdependent;[7]

Aware that the attainment of those rights has been recognized as being the responsibility of individuals as well as of states;[8]

Concerned because the efforts of human society thus far have not been sufficient to achieve the full recognition of those rights;

Considering that the United Nations has emphasized that wars begin in the minds and through the actions of human beings[9] and that the threats to continuing development and the conservation of the environment arise from diverse but interrelated forms of human behavior;[10]

Bearing in mind that the General Assembly has determined that, in order to ensure the survival of natural systems and an adequate level of living for all, human activity should be reoriented towards the goals of sustainable development;[11]

Considering that the present generation, having reached a crossroads where new challenges and decisions must be faced, bears the immediate responsibility for its own development and for the survival of future generations, so that they may consciously constitute a single world, just, peaceful, and based on cooperation with nature;

Convinced, therefore, that there is an urgent need for a greater awareness of the unity of life and of the special character of each of the expressions of life, and for a more profound human sense of responsibility and a reorientation of human thoughts, feelings, and actions;

Considering that this Declaration can contribute to the achievement of this reorientation and can inspire many practical applications at the level of the individual, the family, and the community as well as at the national and international levels;

In accordance with all the foregoing considerations, the Government of Costa Rica offers the present Declaration of Human Responsibilities for Peace and Sustainable Development as an instrument for reflection and commitment.

NOTES

1. Accepted by General Assembly resolution 42/187 of 11 December 1987.

2. Adopted by General Assembly resolution 42/186 of 11 December 1987.

3. General Assembly resolution 41/128 of December 1986.

4. Declaration on the Right of Peoples to Peace, General Assembly resolution 39/11 of 12 November 1984.

5. Declaration on the Preparation of Societies for Life in Peace, General Assembly resolution 33/73 of 15 December 1978.

6. Report of the United Nations Conference on the Human Environment (the Stockholm Declaration), 16 June 1972.

7. General Assembly resolution 37/199 of 18 December 1982.

8. See World Charter for Nature: General Assembly resolution 37/7 of 28 October 1982, and resolution 38/124 of 16 December 1983.

9. Declaration on the Preparation of Societies for Life in Peace: General Assembly resolution 33/73 of 15 December 1978; Constitution of the United Nations Educational, Scientific and Cultural Organization, preamble, paragraph 1.

10. General Assembly resolutions 37/7 of 28 October 1982; 42/186 of 11 December 1987 and 42/187 of 11 December 1987.

11. General Assembly resolutions 42/186 of 11 December 1987 and 42/187 of 11 December 1987.

CHAPTER I.
Unity of the World

Article 1. Everything which exists is part of an interdependent universe. All living creatures depend on each other for their existence, well-being, and development.

Article 2. All human beings are an inseparable part of nature, on which culture and human civilization have been built.

Article 3. Life on Earth is abundant and diverse. It is sustained by the unhindered functioning of natural systems which ensure the provision of energy, air, water, and nutrients for all living creatures. Every manifestation of life on Earth is unique and essential and must therefore be respected and protected without regard to its apparent value to human beings.

CHAPTER II.
Unity of the Human Family

Article 4. All human beings are an inseparable part of the human family and depend on each other for their existence, well-being, and development. Every human being is a unique expression and manifestation of life and has a separate contribution to make to life on Earth. Each human being has fundamental and inalienable rights and freedoms, without distinction of race, color, sex, language, religion, political or other opinion, national or social origin, economic status or any other social situation.

Article 5. All human beings have the same basic needs and the same fundamental aspirations to be satisfied. All individuals have the right to development, the purpose of which is to promote attainment of the full potential of each person.

CHAPTER III.
The Alternatives Facing Mankind and Universal Responsibility

Article 6. Responsibility is an inherent aspect of any relation in which human beings are involved. This capacity to act responsibly in a conscious, independent, unique and personal manner is an inalienable creative quality of every human being. There is no limit to its scope or depth other than that established by each person for himself. The more activities human beings take on and become involved in, the more they will grow and derive strength.

Article 7. Of all living creatures, human beings have the unique capacity to decide consciously whether they are protecting or harming the quality and conditions of life on Earth. In reflecting on the fact that they belong to the natural world and occupy a special position as participants in the evolution of natural processes, people can develop, on the basis of selflessness, compassion and love, a sense of universal responsibility towards the world as an integral whole, towards the protection of nature and the promotion of the highest potential for change, with a view to creating those conditions which will enable them to achieve the highest level of spiritual and material well-being.

Article 8. At this critical time in history, the alternatives facing mankind are crucial. In directing their actions towards the attainment of progress in society, human beings have frequently forgotten the inherent role they play in the natural world and the indivisible human family, and their basic needs for a healthy life. Excessive consumption, abuse of the environment, and aggression between peoples have brought the natural processes of the Earth to a critical stage which threatens their survival. By reflecting on these issues, individuals will be capable of discerning their responsibility and thus reorienting their conduct towards peace and sustainable development.

CHAPTER IV.
Reorientation towards Peace and Sustainable Development

Article 9. Given that all forms of life are unique and essential, that all human beings have the right to development, and that both peace and violence are the product of the human mind, it is from the human mind that a sense of responsibility to act and think in a peaceful manner will develop. Through peace-oriented awareness, individuals will understand the nature of those conditions which are necessary for their well-being and development.

Article 10. Being mindful of their sense of responsibility towards the human family and the environment in which they live and to the need to think and act in a peaceful manner, human beings have the obligation to act in a way that is consistent with the observance of and respect for inherent human rights and to ensure that their consumption of resources is in keeping with the satisfaction of the basic needs of all.

Article 11. When members of the human family recognize that they are responsible to themselves and to present and future generations for the conservation of the planet, as protectors of the natural world and promoters of its continued development, they will be obliged to act in a rational manner in order to ensure sustainable life.

Article 12. Human beings have a continuing responsibility when setting up, taking part in, or representing social units, associations, and institutions, whether private or public. In addition, all such entities have a responsibility to promote peace and sustainability, and to put into practice the educational goals which are conducive to that end. These goals include the fostering of awareness of the interdependence of human beings among themselves and with nature and the universal responsibility of individuals to solve the problems which they have engendered through their attitudes and actions in a manner that is consistent with the protection of human rights and fundamental freedoms.

Let us be faithful to the privilege of our responsibility.

The National Conference

During the Persian Gulf War in 1991, the interfaith community of metropolitan Chicago recognized that, regardless of perspective, one day the war would end and that everyone had to live peacefully with his or her neighbors. The interfaith community recognized that it was in a unique position to offer guidance to the community at large on how to live together in peace and with respect when hostilities had ceased. The following texts were published in a pamphlet titled "The World House" by the National Conference of Christians and Jews (the name is now changed to National Conference) in cooperation with representatives from 12 religious traditions in order to help people from every community begin to think in terms of those values they wished to live by once the war was over.

The National Conference; used with permission

Among its various programs, the National Conference also publishes group study materials on diversity and dialogue and a full-color Interfaith Calendar. Publications and programs are designed to promote a greater understanding of the rich heritage of religious diversity in America.

FOR MORE INFORMATION:

**National Conference,
Chicago and Northern Illinois Region
360 N. Michigan Ave., Suite 1009
Chicago, IL USA**

tel. (312) 236-9272 / fax. (312) 236-0029

The World House

As the Reverend Dr. Martin Luther King, Jr., once said, we live in a "world house." The interfaith community is in a unique position to offer guidance on how we can live together in peace and respect for the diversity of our world house. NCCJ presents the thoughts and prayers of 12 different religious communities in metropolitan Chicago – each presented in its own way and in its own words.

AMERICAN INDIAN

*T*he sacred hoop of any nation is but one of many that together make the great circle of creation. In the center grows a mighty flowering tree of life sheltering all the children of one mother and one father. All life is holy.

People native to this land have long lived by the wisdom of the circle, aware that we are part of the Earth and it is part of us. To harm this Earth, precious to God – to upset the balance of the circle – is to heap contempt on its Creator. Therefore, with all our heart and mind, we must restore the balance of the Earth for our grandchildren to the seventh generation.

compiled from the wisdom of Black Elk, Chief Seattle, and many other American Indian spiritual leaders.
Anawim Center, Native American Indians of Chicago

BAHÁ'Í

*T*he primary question to be resolved is how the present world, with its entrenched pattern of conflict, can change to a world in which harmony and cooperation will prevail.

World order can be founded only on an unshakable consciousness of the oneness of mankind, a spiritual truth which all the human sciences confirm.

Acceptance of the oneness of mankind is the first fundamental prerequisite for reorganization and administration of the world as one country, the home of humankind. Universal acceptance of this spiritual principle is essential to any successful attempt to establish world peace. It should therefore be universally proclaimed, taught in schools, and constantly asserted in every nation as preparation for the organic change in the structure of society which it implies.

The Promise of World Peace, a statement by the Universal House of Justice to the Peoples of the World, October 1985.
Spiritual Assembly of Bahá'ís of Chicago

BUDDHISM

*W*e are what we think.
All that we are arises with our thoughts.
With our thoughts we make the world. . .

"Look how he abused me and beat me,
How he threw me down and robbed me."
Live with such thoughts and you live in hate.

"Look how he abused me and beat me,
How he threw me down and robbed me."
Abandon such thoughts, and live in love.

In this world
Hate never yet dispelled hate.
This the law,
Ancient and inexhaustible.

The Dhammapada,
Buddhist Council of the Midwest

ANGLICAN CHRISTIANITY

O God, you made us in your own image and redeemed us through Jesus your Son: look with compassion on the whole human family; take away the arrogance and hatred which infect our hearts; break down the walls that separate us; unite us in bonds of love; and work through our struggle and confusion to accomplish your purposes on earth; that, in your good time, all nations and races may serve you in harmony around your heavenly throne; through Jesus Christ our Lord. Amen.

Episcopal Diocese of Chicago

CATHOLIC CHRISTIANITY

'But I say to you that listen, love your enemies.' (Luke 6:27) Because Jesus' command to love our neighbor is universal, we hold that the life of each person on this globe is sacred.

Communion with God, sharing God's life, involves a mutual bonding with all on this globe. Jesus taught us to love God and one another and that the concept of neighbor is without limit. We know that we are called to be members of a new covenant of love. We have to move from our devotion to independence, through an understanding of interdependence, to a commitment to human solidarity. That challenge must find its realization in the kind of community we build among us. Love implies concern for all—especially the poor—and a continued search for those social and economic structures that permit everyone to share in a community that is a part of a redeemed creation (Rom. 8:31–33).

Economic Justice for All (#326 and #365)
National Conference of Bishops, November 18, 1986.
Catholic Archdiocese of Chicago

ORTHODOX CHRISTIANITY

*L*ord our God, it is truly just and right to the majesty of Your holiness to praise You and to offer to You our spiritual worship. We entreat You, Lord, to:

Remember us and grant us profound and lasting peace. Speak to our hearts good things concerning all people, so that through the faithful conduct of our lives we may live together peacefully and serenely. As Your children, may we come to understand that we are all brothers and sisters to one another, created in Your Image and Likeness. We call upon You, the God of Peace, to enlighten us to treat all people with the very same dignity, freedom, and respect which You will for all humans to enjoy; for You have revealed to us that dignity is the essence of life itself and from it alone do we obtain the right to call ourselves Your children.

Remember us, O Lord, and all Your people. Pour out Your rich mercy upon us. Be all things to all, You, who know each person. Receive us all into Your kingdom. Declare us to be sons and daughters of the light and of the day. Grant us Your peace and love, Lord our God, for You have given all things to us. Amen.

Greek Orthodox Diocese of Chicago

PROTESTANT CHRISTIANITY

O Thou whose love embraces every child of the world, forgive our easy labels and simple answers. As Thou hast created every living organism in complexity and beauty, give us grace to see each other as people with many needs and hopes and dreams. In some way touch us with the spirit of Jesus, whose love embraced everyone and whose sympathy knew no bounds.

In times of stress and disappointment, through every dark valley and every moment of limited vision, be Thou our stay. And when we come through those moments, stop us, O God, that we may remember on whose grace we have depended, and we may give Thee the thanks and praise.

This prayer and all prayers we are able to make because Thou hast first put the spark of divinity within us. Amen.

Church Federation of Greater Chicago

ISLAM

*I*s he who knoweth that what is revealed unto thee from thy Lord is the truth like him who is blind? But only men of understanding heed;

Such as keep the pact of Allah, and break not the covenant;

Such as unite that which Allah hath commanded should be joined (taking care of their mutual duties), and fear their Lord, and dread a woeful reckoning;

Such as persevere in seeking their Lord's countenance and are regular in prayer and spend of that which We bestow upon them secretly and openly, and overcome evil with good. Theirs will be the sequel of the (heavenly) Home,

Gardens of Eden which they enter, along with all who do right of their fathers and their helpmates and their seed. The angels enter unto them from every gate,

(Saying): Peace be unto you because ye persevered. Ah, passing sweet will be the sequel of the (heavenly) Home.

And those who break the covenant of Allah after ratifying it, and sever that which Allah hath commanded should be joined, and make mischief in the earth: theirs is the curse and theirs the ill abode.

Allah enlargeth livelihood for whom He will, straiteneth (it for whom He will); and they rejoice in the life of the world, whereas the life of the world is but brief comfort as compared with the Hereafter.

The Qur'an (13:19–26),
Muslim Community Centers of Chicago

HINDUISM

O Lord, lead us from the unreal to the Real,
Lead us from darkness to Light,
And lead us from death to Immortality.

May all be free from dangers,
May all realize what is good,

Continued on next page

May all be actuated by noble thoughts,
May all rejoice everywhere.

May all be happy,
May all be free from disease,
May all realize what is good,
May none be subject to misery.

May the wicked become virtuous,
May the virtuous attain tranquility,
May the tranquil be free from bonds,
May the freed make others free.

May good betide all people,
May the sovereign righteously rule the earth,
May all beings ever attain what is good,
May the worlds be prosperous and happy.

May the clouds pour rain in time,
May the earth be blessed with crops,
May all countries be freed from calamity,
May holy men live without fear.

May the Lord, the destroyer of sins,
The presiding Deity of all sacred works, be satisfied.
For, He being pleased, the whole universe
      becomes pleased,
He being satisfied, the whole universe feels satisfied.

Swami Yatiswarananda, Universal Prayers
Vivekananda Vedanta Society

JUDAISM

*I*n Jewish tradition, there are many deeply held values that govern a nation's conduct in war, so that the subsequent peace may be based on dignity and justice. We are told:

> "Rejoice not when your enemy falls
> and be not glad in your heart when (he) stumbles."

(Pirke Avot)

> "Who is the greatest hero?
> The one who changes an enemy into a friend."

(Avot D' Rabbi Natan)

> "How great is peace? Even in time of war,
> peace must be sought."

(Sifre Deuteronomy)

> "When besieging a city to capture it,
> one may not surround it on all four sides . . .
> (so that) anyone who wishes to flee may escape."

(Mishneh Torah)

> "Peace without truth is false."   (Mendel of Kotzk)

Chicago Board of Rabbis

SIKHISM

*S*ays Nanak:

There are many dogmas, there are many systems,
There are many spiritual revelations,
Many bonds fetter the self (mind):
But Release is attained through God's Grace;
Truth is above all these,
But even higher is life lived in Truth.
All God's creatures are noble,
None are base.
One Potter has fashioned all the pots,
One Light pervades all Creation.
Truth is revealed through Grace,
And no one can resist Grace.

Siri Rag, Ashtpadiyan, p.62

*A*dds Tegh Bahadur:

Oh saints (seekers of Truth),
real peace is achieved through God,
The virtue of studying the scriptures,
Lies in contemplating the Name.

Gauri, p.220

We all pray for peace in the world,
through peace of mind.

ZOROASTRIANISM

*I*n this worldly abode of ours,
May communication drive away mis-communication
May peace drive away anarchy
May generosity drive away selfishness
May benevolence drive away hostility
May compassionate words prevail over false protestations
May truth prevail over falsehood.

From the *Dahm Afringan* prayer.
Federation of Zoroastrian Associations of North America

Choosing Our Future

*Learning from the Past
and Looking to the 21st Century*

"Our world is in travail. It takes no special sensitivity to realize how pervasive is the stress to which the fabric of our contemporary lives is subjected. Over and over again, violence tears apart what, often, it has taken centuries to fashion.

"And yet violence is not the substance, it is the symptom. Something new is waiting to be born. We are experiencing the birth pangs of a new age, of a new hope. We are present at that sacred moment when new life is about to emerge from the womb of the past. What struggles to arise out of the past might become our shared future of mutual hearing and understanding, of mutual openness, of unprecedented willingness to acknowledge and accept others in all their differentness. The questions which address themselves to each of us are:

Will we recognize the mystery of this possibility?

Will we be open to its opportunities?

Are we willing to help it be pulled into the light of tomorrow?

Will we turn away preoccupied or cynical, or will we step forward to assist?

"These are not merely questions. They are the agenda of tomorrow, they are the exciting, irresistible invitation to each of us to abandon prejudgement and stubborn refusals to deeply hear one another. They are the program and the means to make that leap of faith with each other which will move humanity and our earth into a new era of reconciliation and hope."

RABBI HERMAN SCHAALMAN

The Next Generations

The State of the World's Children

James P. Grant

Executive Director of UNICEF

What do we know about the state of children worldwide? What is being done and what can be done to meet their needs? UNICEF has made it its business to find answers to these and other questions, to try to remedy problems where possible, and to mobilize others to do the same. Those for whom we are choosing among possible futures will some day be making the choices for succeeding generations.

*A*mid all the problems of a world bleeding from continuing wars and environmental wounds, it is nonetheless becoming clear that one of the greatest of all human aspirations is now within reach. Within a decade, it should be possible to bring to an end the age-old evils of child malnutrition, preventable disease, and widespread illiteracy.

As an indication of how close that goal might be, the financial cost can be put at about $25 billion a year. That is the UNICEF estimate of the extra resources required to put into practice today's low-cost strategies for protecting the world's children. Specifically, it is an estimate of the cost of controlling the major childhood diseases, halving the rate of child malnutrition, bringing clean water and safe sanitation to all communities, making family planning services universally available, and providing almost every child with at least a basic education.

In practice, financial resources are a necessary but not sufficient prerequisite for meeting these needs. Sustained political commitment and a great deal of managerial competence are even more important. Yet it is necessary to reduce this challenge to the denominator of dollars in order to dislodge the idea that abolishing the worst aspects of poverty is a task too vast to be attempted or too expensive to be afforded.

To put the figure of $25 billion in perspective, it is considerably less than the amount the Japanese Government has allocated this year to the building of a new highway from Tokyo to Kobe; it is two to three times as much as the cost of the tunnel soon to be opened between the United Kingdom and France; it is less than the cost of the Ataturk Dam complex now being constructed in eastern Turkey; it is a little more than Hong Kong proposes to spend on a new airport; it is about the same as the support package that the Group of Seven has agreed on in 1992 for Russia alone; and it is significantly less than Europeans will spend this year on wine or Americans on beer.

Whatever the other difficulties may be, the time has therefore come to banish in shame the notion that the world cannot afford to meet the basic needs of almost every man, woman, and child for adequate food, safe water, primary health care, family planning, and a basic education.

A ten percent effort

*I*f so much could be achieved for so many at so little cost, then the public in both industrialized and developing countries might legitimately ask why it is not being done.

In part, the answer is the predictable one: meeting the needs of the poorest and least politically influential has rarely been a priority of governments. Yet the extent of present neglect in the face of present opportunity is a scandal of which the public is largely unaware. On average, the governments of the developing world are today devoting little more than ten percent of their budgets to directly meeting the basic needs of their people. More is still being spent on military capacity and on debt servicing than on health and education.

Perhaps more surprising still, less than ten percent of all international aid for development is devoted to directly meeting these most obvious of human needs...about $4 billion a year. This is less than half as much as the aid-giving nations spend each year on sports shoes. It could therefore fairly be said that the problem today is not that overcoming the worst aspects of world poverty is too vast or too expensive a task; it is that it has not been tried. [...]

Promises on paper

*T*he importance of the Convention [on the Rights of the Child], the Summit [for Children], and the national programs of action that have been drawn up should neither be overestimated nor underestimated. At the moment they remain, for the most part, promises on paper. But when, in the mid-1980s, over 100 of the world's political leaders formally accepted the goal of 80 percent immunization by 1990, that, too, was just a promise on paper. Today it is a reality in the lives of tens of millions of families around the world.

One lesson to be learned from that achievement is that formal political commitments at the highest levels are necessary if available solutions are to be put into action *on a national scale*. But a second lesson is that such commitments will only be translated into action by the dedication of the professional services; by the mobilization of today's communications capacities; by the widespread support of politicians, press and the public; and by the reliable and sustained support of the international community. Most of the countries that succeeded in reaching the immunization goal succeeded primarily because large numbers of people and organizations at all levels of national life became seized with the idea that the goal could and should be achieved.[...]

To maintain the political momentum that has been generated, nothing less is now required than a worldwide strengthening of the basic needs movement to the point where it begins to exert the same kind of pressure as is today being brought to bear for the protection of the environment.

Such pressure will not be easy either to create or sustain. A movement to overcome the worst aspects of poverty, and particularly to protect children, has no obviously powerful constituency and no immediate vested interest to appeal to. The environmental and women's movements are, in varying degrees, becoming everyone's concern, for the obvious reason that almost everyone is directly touched by both of these issues. A movement to meet basic human needs will not succeed unless it, too, becomes everyone's concern. And to achieve that, the complex realities of common cause must also become more widely known and understood. None of the great issues that are assuming priority today – the cause of slowing population growth, the cause of achieving equality for women, the cause of environmentally sustained development, the cause of political democracy – will or can be realized unless the most basic human needs of the forgotten quarter of the earth's people are met. This cause, too, must therefore become the concern of all. [...]

Twenty percent for basics

*A*s the end of the 20th century approaches, there is therefore an accumulation of reasons for believing that ending the worst aspects of poverty is an idea whose time may finally have come.

New strategies and low-cost technologies are available. Specific goals which reflect this potential have been agreed upon. The commitment to those goals bears the signatures of more Presidents and Prime Ministers than any other document in history. The plans for achieving them have been or are being drawn up in most nations. And there is a growing acceptance of the idea that targeting some of these worst effects of poverty, particularly as they affect children, is an essential part of long-term development strategy.

In the wider world, the ground being gained by democratic systems means that the long-starved concerns of the poor may begin to put on political weight. At the same time, economic reforms may also create the kind of environment in which a new effort to meet basic human needs would have a much greater chance of success. Meanwhile, the powerful tide of demographic change is also beginning to turn.

For all of these reasons, a new potential now exists for moving towards a world in which the basic human needs of almost every man, woman, and child are met. But it is equally clear that this attempt will not gather the necessary momentum unless the political commitment is sustained and the extra resources made available.

If advantage is to be taken of the political commitments that have been made, and of the national programs of action that have been drawn up, then those extra resources must begin to become available in the next 12 months to two years.... UNICEF strongly supports the United Nations Development Programme's suggestion that at least 20 percent of government spending should be allocated to these direct methods of meeting priority human needs. If implemented, such a restructuring of government budgets would enable the developing nations as a whole to find

Don't Compromise Our Future!

"We are speaking on behalf of the young people. We are here because we have a right to be involved in these decisions.... Your pursuit of diplomatic compromises is compromising our future!

"We have a right to demand a safe future for ourselves and all generations to come. What is required is a fundamental change in attitudes, values and lifestyles, particularly in the developed nations. We insist that... you make decisions which reflect intergenerational equity and a concern for the environment. Remember that we will inherit the consequences of your decisions. We will not sign the Montreal Protocol – you will. You will not bear the brunt of ozone depletion – we will. We demand that you think in the long term.... Have the courage to put aside your short-term national concerns and act in the interests of our common well-being. Will you protect our future?"

SUSANNAH BEGG, 17, of Australia, at the June 1990 meeting in London where nations agreed to phase out production of the chemicals that destroy Earth's protective ozone layer. Printed in *Our Children Their Earth*, UNEP, p.23

Rediscovering Justice

*Y*outh is often described by developmental psychologists as the "Age of Discovery." From their late teens through their twenties, young people discover who they are, their identities, their spiritual and religious commitments, their careers, and their potential for marriage and family. For many youth, this is also the age of discovering a refined moral framework, a sense of justice that will serve as a guide for a lifetime. In this [interfaith conference] we will challenge 200 selected youth, culturally and religiously diverse, from around the world, to develop a personal moral framework and a concrete action plan to address the following questions:

How can their own spiritual resources and the spiritual resources of the world's religions be tapped for global justice?

How can the UN model of dialogue and partnership among nations challenge youth and the world's religions to a new mutuality in addressing issues of war, peace, and equity? ecological justice? poverty, race and ethnicity?

from materials about *Rediscovering Justice: Awakening World Faiths to Address World Issues,* an Interfaith Conference for Youth on the 50th Anniversary of the United Nations, June 22-25, 1995, at the University of San Francisco, co-sponsored by Grace Cathedral and the Christopher Columbus Foundation. Call (415) 666-6848 or fax (415) 666-2772 about related resource information.

several times the $25 billion a year that is needed to achieve the agreed goals. [...]

In the decade ahead, a clear opportunity exists to make the breakthrough against what might be called the last great obscenity – the needless malnutrition, disease, and illiteracy that still casts a shadow over the lives and the futures of the poorest quarter of the world's children.

It is almost unthinkable that that opportunity to reach these basic social goals should be missed because the political commitment is lacking or because the developing world and the donor nations cannot, together, find an extra $25 billion a year.

... It is time that challenge replace excuse. If today's obvious and affordable steps are not taken to protect the lives and the health and the normal growth of many millions of young children, then this will have less to do with the lack of economic capacity than with the fact that the children concerned are almost exclusively the sons and daughters of the poor—of those who lack not only purchasing power but also political influence and media attention. And if the resources are not to be made available, if the overcoming of the worst aspects of poverty, malnutrition, illiteracy, and disease is not to be achieved in the years ahead, then let it now be clear that this is not because it is not a possibility but because it is not a priority.

Conclusion

*I*n 1992, many specific tragedies have again assaulted the very idea of childhood in such places as Somalia and the former Yugoslavia. The response to these tragedies, wherever they occur, is a major part of the work of UNICEF and is addressed in many other UNICEF publications and statements during the course of the year.

But for more than ten years, the *State of the World's Children* report has concentrated on issues which profoundly affect far larger numbers of children but which do not constitute the kind of news event which qualifies for the world's attention. This is a tragedy which does not happen in any one particular place or time; it happens quietly in poor communities throughout the developing world. It is therefore not news, and so it slips from the

public eye and from the political agenda. But it is nonetheless a tragedy far greater in scale than even the greatest of the emergencies which so often command the world's, and UNICEF's, concern. No famine, no flood, no earthquake, no war has ever claimed the lives of 250,000 children in a single week. Yet malnutrition and disease claim that number of child victims *every week*. And for every one of those children who dies, many more live on with such ill health and poor growth that they will never grow to the physical and mental potential with which they were born.

When little or nothing could be done about this larger-scale tragedy, then neglect was perhaps understandable. But slowly, quietly, and without the world taking very much notice, we have arrived at the point where this tragedy is no longer necessary. It is therefore no longer acceptable in a world with any claim on civilization. The time has therefore come for a new age of concern.

Political and economic change in the world is beginning to create the conditions which, however difficult, offer new hope for overcoming the worst aspects of world poverty, particularly as they affect the world's children. The cost of providing health and education services in the developing world remains relatively low, and the gradual stabilization in the numbers of infants being born means that further investments in basic services can now begin to increase the proportion of the population served. Meanwhile, the technologies and strategies for controlling malnutrition, disease, and illiteracy have been tried and tested and now stand waiting to go into action on the same scale as the problems they can so largely solve.

The convergence of all of these different forces means it is now possible to achieve one of the greatest goals that humanity could ever set for itself – the goal of adequate food, clean water, safe sanitation, primary health care, family planning, and basic education, for virtually every man, woman, and child on earth.

In 1990, this new potential for specific action against these worst aspects of poverty was formulated into a set of basic social goals which accurately reflect that potential and which have been formally accepted by the great majority of the world's political leaders. A start has been made, in many nations, towards keeping the promise of those goals.

We therefore stand on the edge of a new era of concern for the silent and invisible tragedy that poverty inflicts on today's children and on tomorrow's world. Whether the world will enter decisively into that new age depends on the pressure that is brought to bear by politicians, press, public and professional services in all nations. And among the readers of this report, there is hardly any individual or organization that could not now become involved.

Excerpted from the official Summary of the 1993 report, issued by James P. Grant, the Executive Director of UNICEF. For the full text of the 1993 *State of the World's Children,* contact any UNICEF office or write to the Division of Information, UNICEF House, 3 UN Plaza, New York, NY 10017 USA. The report is also published by Oxford University Press.

Spirit

The spirit is still here
somewhere in the sky,
somewhere in the trees.
But who knows where?
No one you see.

Does Nature? Does the wind?
Do the trees? All we know
is the spirit is somewhere
in there.

JESSICA DENNIS,
7th grade

The World's Religions for the World's Children

Prior to the World Summit for Children, held at the United Nations in September 1990, a Conference on The World's Religions for the World's Children was held in Princeton, New Jersey. Organized by the United Nations Children's Fund (UNICEF) and by the World Conference on Religion and Peace, it was attended by 150 people from 40 countries drawn from 12 major religions. The participants agreed that there is still time to reclaim the future for our children and succeeding generations. And they said that "despite differences in our traditions, our practices, our beliefs, and despite our inadequacies" they would work together to influence their nation's political leaders and their own religious communities so that children's basic needs will be given priority. To this end they issued the following Declaration and an action plan with specific goals.

Princeton, New Jersey, July 25–27, 1990

Conscious of the plight of vast numbers of children throughout the world, we representatives of 12 religions from 40 countries participating in the World's Religions for the World's Children conference, meeting in Princeton, New Jersey, USA, July 25–27, 1990, speak with common voice. We commend the United Nations for its efforts in creating and adopting the Convention on the Rights of the Child. We urge its ratification and adherence in practice by all governments. We commend those government leaders who have recognized the urgency and priority of addressing the needs and rights of children. Cognizant of the efforts of earlier generations represented by the 1924 League of Nations Geneva Declaration on the Rights of the Child, and the United Nations 1959 Declaration on the Rights of the Child, we are aware of the difficulty of moving from the statement of rights to their realization. Our common voice resounds despite differences in our traditions, our practices, our beliefs, and despite our inadequacies. Our religious traditions summon us to regard the child as more than a legal entity. The sacredness of life compels us to be a voice of conscience. We speak hereby to heads of state and government, to the United Nations, to our religious communities and to all, throughout the world, who have held a child in love, with joy for its life, with tears for its pain.

Recognizing the rights of the child

The Convention on the Rights of the Child, which acknowledges the rights of the world's children to survival, protection and development, is rooted in the Universal Declaration of Human Rights which recognizes the inherent dignity and the equal and inalienable rights of all members of the human family. We recognize that, lamentably, such rights are not universally respected or legally guaranteed, nor are they always accepted as moral obligations.

As religious men and women, however, we dare to assert that the state of childhood, with its attendant vulnerability, dependence and potential, founds a principle that the human community must give children's basic needs priority over competing claims—and a "first call"—upon the human and material resources of our societies. Such a principle needs to be both recognized and accepted as a guide for relevant actions in human communities.

Society's responsibility to children

The survival, protection and development of children is the responsibility of the whole world community. However, for countless girls and boys there is no survival, no protection, no chance for development. Societies are morally bound to address the obscene conditions which result in the death of 14 million children during every year, two thirds from preventable causes, and the other conditions of abject poverty that result in wasted bodies, stunted physical development or permanent handicaps. Existing health care knowledge and technology, promptly and persistently applied, have the potential to make dramatic improvements in child survival and health with relatively moderate financial costs. Such possibilities underscore our obligations. To fail to make such efforts for the well-being of children is morally unconscionable.

Societies are also bound to rectify the gross injustices and violations which children suffer, such as child abuse, sexual and labor exploitation, homelessness, victimization due to war, and the tragic consequences of family disintegration, cultural genocide, social deprivations stemming from intolerance based upon race, sex, age, or religion, to name but a few. Addressing these issues will require fundamental structural change.

Societies are obliged to confront the broad constellation of human forces and failures which affect children. The social and international order necessary for the full realization of children's rights does not exist. Our interdependent political and economic systems can be restructured and refined to provide children their basic needs. The world has the resources to provide the basic needs of children. Wars, in which children are increasingly the victims and even the targets of violence, need not be the inevitable expression of human conflict. Our readiness to resolve conflict through violent means can be changed. Development cannot succeed under the illusion that our resources are inexhaustible or uniformly self-renewing. While our air, water, and soil are polluted, we still have the chance to reverse the most devastating trends of environmental degradation. What will we bequeath to our children? The dangerous forces that impact upon children jeopardize the full realization of freedom, justice, and peace.

The grim realities we confront demand our outrage because they exist; they demand our repentance because they have been silently tolerated or even justified; they demand our response because all can be addressed, some of them quite readily.

Responsibilities of governments and international organizations

We religious women and men gathered in Princeton urge governments and relevant international organizations to fulfill their responsibilities to children through at least the following:

- To sign, ratify, fully implement, and monitor compliance with the Convention on the Rights of the Child.
- To undertake those actions which would have a dramatic impact upon child survival at very low cost.
- To take vigorous and immediate action to rectify the myriad obscene injustices which children suffer, such as abuse from exploitation.
- To take the steps necessary, in each country, to achieve the goals for children and development in the 1990s, as defined by the international community.
- To utilize peaceful means of conflict resolution in order to protect children from the ravages of war.
- To create new, or adjust existing, political and economic structures that can provide access to and distribution – for all – of both the natural resources and the products of human labor, including information, so that the claims of justice may be met.
- To undertake the bold steps known to be necessary and to develop new steps to protect and reclaim the environment as the heritage for our children and succeeding generations' development.
- To allocate adequate funds to undergird the global programs addressing health, education, and development.
- To ensure full participation of NGOs in the implementation of appropriate actions.
- To provide basic education for all children.
- To reduce the burden of debt that robs a nation's children of their rightful heritage.
- To support the family, help keep it intact, and provide the resources and services for the adequate care and protection of its children.
- To provide resources and develop programs for the survival, health and education of women, the bearers and primary caregivers of children.
- To ensure the participation of women in the entire range of social governance and decision-making.
- To take steps to ensure that children actually receive a first call on society's resources.

Religious and spiritual responsibilities

*O*ur consciences as religious men and women, including those of us bearing governmental and other forms of social responsibility, will not allow us to evade the responsibilities of our religious traditions. We therefore call upon religious women and men and institutions:

- To order our own priorities so as to reaffirm our central claims about the sacredness of life.
- To examine any of our own traditional practices that may violate the deeper spirit of our faiths and indeed the sacredness of human life.
- To provide resources for families, from single parent to extended in size, so that they can fulfill their roles in spiritual formation and education.
- To protect and support parents in their rights and responsibilities as the primary religious educators.
- To undertake actions to promote the well-being, education, and leadership roles of female children and their right to equal treatment with male children.
- To engage in services of nurture, mercy, education, and advocacy, and to exemplify before the world the possibilities for compassion and care.
- To cooperate with all agencies of society, including other religious bodies, that have as their purpose the well-being of the children in our societies.
- To advocate the ratification and implementation of the Convention on the Rights of the Child in our respective countries and communities.
- To work for the protection of the unborn in accord with the teachings of our respective religious traditions.
- To establish independent systems to monitor the state of children's rights.
- To coordinate with other religions in the removal of religious and other forms of prejudice and conflict in all contexts.
- To re-order our communities' resources in accord with the principle of the right of children to a first call on those resources.

*P*olitical will is necessary to create the social and international climate in which survival, protection and development can be achieved. We call on governments and the international community to manifest that will.

Spiritual will is necessary to establish a shared ethos in which children can flourish in freedom, justice and peace. We call on all spiritual and religious peoples and institutions to manifest that will.

Hold Hands

Hold hands until dawn.
Hold hands until the bell rings.
Hold hands until the stars come out.
Be friends, hold hands.

Until the sun is high, hold hands.
Holding hands makes you feel
warm and safe.
Hold hands forever.

ZOE WARD, *3rd grade*

My Poem for the World

I wish the world could be free
and have no illegal things.
I wish I could just close my eyes
and have heaven float
and God could have the power
 to release
the men who are not free.

I wish we could go wherever
we wanted to on a cloud.

I wish we could help everyone.

God, if we fall,
catch us, lift us up
to where we belong.

MARY MC LAUGHLIN,
3rd grade

Listen to the Children

Therese Becker

Poet, teacher, photographer, journalist, and advocate for the creative process

Most of the poems by children that are scattered throughout this book were written by students of Therese Becker, who is compiling a book of children's poems and descriptions of the exercises she uses to evoke them, titled *When a Child Sings*.

I began working with children through the Michigan Council for the Arts Creative Writers in the Schools program in the spring of 1986, and I've been learning from them ever since. I read everything they write as a result of the exercises that I put them through and I am continually stunned at the deep wisdom that emerges when they listen to themselves.

I've never forgotten a statement made by Oakland University Professor Margaret Kurzman: "If you don't become who you are, then what you might have contributed to the world will never have a chance to be." I instantly knew it was true. Everything I do in a classroom is directed toward fostering self-trust which produces self-esteem. I also encourage journal writing (the more you write, the more you can write) and reading and writing as twins in the writing process.

I've worked with grades K through 12 and with children who are labeled "learning disabled," "average," "the smart students," "the trouble makers," and the "gifted and talented;" I've found that every group has its own barriers to overcome, but when the writing is finished, you can't tell one group's work from another.

Learning to trust the self seems, at first, quite simple, but it is more difficult than one might imagine. Almost everything in our society encourages us to believe that our answers lie somewhere outside of ourselves instead of within. The poet Rainer Maria Rilke said, "What is happening in your innermost self is worthy of your entire love," and that love is real power, the bricks in the path to freedom.

One of my most successful exercises is having students take a trip inside their hand. When they do this with their imagination, anything can become something else. Recently, a ninth grade girl wrote in her hand exercise, "When I look into my hand, I see nothing but an empty space where my soul used to sit." She then went on to tell about the criticism she's received for being different. It was an incomplete piece, so I encouraged her towards exploration by asking questions evoked by the original piece of writing. Should she fight for her soul, and is that something that artists and writers had to do if they were to pursue their art in any true way? I also asked her if "different" was really less or was it more. I believe it's more, and we must encourage and honor our differences if the planet and species is going to survive.

Listening to children has taken me right to the heart of their spiritual and moral struggles. Although I can encounter a great deal of violence in their work, it has restored my faith in the human race, rather than destroyed it. The bottom line in every school I visit is that our children want to love the earth and each other, and they particularly yearn to become who they are. As Gandhi said, "If we are to attain real peace in this world, we will have to begin with the children." Listen to the children and applaud.

"We can easily forgive a child who is afraid of the dark;
the real tragedy is when men are afraid of the light." PLATO

"You have to ask children and birds how cherries and strawberries taste." GOETHE

"Our children are living messages that we send into a world we'll never see." anonymous

To My Students

You danced on the page,
reinvented yourselves,
opened the ancient doors
and bright birds of every color
flew out to greet me.

You showed me how well you hear
the earth's music,
the music in yourselves
and each other.

You will be with me always
an invisible necklace
of water and light—
a distant song in my ear.

Remember, the journey
is everything;
the key is trust:
the world is waiting
for you to name it
and you will.

THERESE BECKER

Previously published in
Louisville Review, Spring 1990

The Wild Man's Heart

It is the same dream.
It is the wild man's heart, prancing.
It is the wild wings of a flying eagle.

They will dance—
the wild man and his heart:
prancing on, and on.
It is love.

BILL THIRY,
7th grade

Asking the Stars

I was sneaking around,
asking the stars: "may I,
may I behold you?"
"You may far child, you may."

"Who are you might I ask?"
And they answered, "The moons,
the moons, yes, the moons."

And then they said to me:
"And you are a true genesis
in your own way, a type of god,
not a big god, but a god."

ROBERT JONES,
7th grade

Peace

As you enter the wild depths
Phantoms below,
You notice the whale's call,
As if wanting help
Or maybe telling us
We should live in peace.

God must have made them
    for a purpose.
Maybe they are the peacemakers.
Their voices are mysterious
like a fog horn on the misty dock.

There's so much violence
In the world,
So much chaos,
So much terror.
If we are to survive
This imperfect world,
We must listen
Listen to the peace.

GABRIEL MYLIN,
6th grade

The Meadow's Shadow

The morning starts up
and I arise,
Traveling wherever
the sun goes,
Bringing new sights
to my eyes.
Over the dry grasses
and over the rustling creek,
I travel the prairie
until the sunset
makes me meek.

GABRIEL MYLIN,
6th grade

Children's Sabbaths Reach Thousands of Congregations

*T*he Children's Defense Fund (CDF), in cooperation with several presbyteries, synods, the Presbyterian Child Advocacy Network, the Child Advocacy Project of the Presbyterian Church (USA), and over 140 denominational and interfaith groups, coordinated the third annual nationwide observance of Children's Sabbaths on October 14-16, 1994.

The National Observance of Children's Sabbaths grew out of individual denominational movements for children, coalescing this concern in a united moral witness. CDF distributed more than 30,000 Children's Sabbath Kits in 1993 in response to requests from clergy, lay persons, and organizations.

In 1994 more than 40,000 kits were ordered from over 150 denominations and religious groups. Many thousands of congregations and schools held Children's Sabbaths, and dozens of interfaith groups held services, reflecting both the depth and the potential of the religious community's commitment to children.

The theme of the 1994 National Observance of Children's Sabbaths was "Cease Fire: Stopping the Gun War Against Children," emphasizing the urgent need to protect children from violence. We hope congregations will help to create safe havens and positive alternatives for children in their own communities.

In 1995 the Sabbath will be observed on October 20-22; its focus will be on combating child poverty. Organizing Kits will be available during the summer in versions for Protestant, Catholic, African-American Protestant, African-American Catholic, and Jewish congregations. The Kits include sermon/homily resources, prayers, liturgies, bulletin inserts, adult education materials, children's activity materials, and more.

What is the National Observance of Children's Sabbaths?

*T*he National Observance of Children's Sabbaths seeks to lift a united voice of concern for children by exploring the faith-based imperative to speak out on behalf of the vulnerable, and encouraging a commitment to help children and families through prayer, education, service, and advocacy.

Beginning with Shabbat services on Friday and concluding with church services on Sunday, congregations nationwide will hold special worship services, education programs, and related activities on how people of faith can respond to children's needs. Most Children's Sabbaths are held in individual congregations, but some congregations join community-wide interfaith efforts.

Why is CDF coordinating the observance?

*T*he Children's Defense Fund (CDF) is a nonprofit, nonpartisan organization that exists to provide a strong and effective voice for the children of our nation who cannot vote, lobby, or speak out for themselves. Our goal is to educate the nation about the needs of children and encourage preventive investment in children before they get sick, drop out of school, suffer family breakdown, or get into trouble.

Since 1981 CDF has worked with the religious community to mobilize congregations across the United States to engage in direct service, public education, community outreach, and advocacy. To obtain more information or to order an Organizing Kit (for $3.00 each), write to CDF, indicating the version you'd like to receive.

Children's Sabbath, c/o Children's Defense Fund,
25 E. Street, N.W., Washington, DC 20001 USA
tel. (202) 662-3589

PART FOUR: CHOOSING OUR FUTURE

Growing Up
in Earthly Danger

Dr. Noel J. Brown

Director, United Nations Environment Programme,
Regional Office for North America

The article which follows introduces the Spring 1991 Environmental Sabbath/Earth Rest Day Guide, *Our Children Their Earth: Playing for Keeps.*

*E*nvironmental degradation is killing our children.

Children are the first victims of environmental destruction – as we have seen in the aftermath of the Gulf War – because their growing bodies and minds are more vulnerable to malnutrition and a contaminated environment.

Our children's access to the fresh food and water that a healthy environment provides depends on us as parents, guardians and governments. Children have no other recourse. The have nothing to do with the causes of environmental devastation – "They do not vote, they have no political or financial power, they cannot challenge our decisions," says *Our Common Future*, the influential report on sustainable development – yet they are the first to suffer.

Today, the earth tries to support nearly two billion children under the age of five, and of them 1.5 billion live in developing countries. These hundreds of millions of children mean even larger populations for decades to come. Most will struggle to survive in countries with minimal financial resources that can be allocated for their needs and for protection of the natural resources on which their lives are based.

This year, 14 million children under the age of five will die from common, mostly preventable diseases and malnutrition – unless we act now to protect them and the environments in which they live. Many of these deaths are from "environmental" causes – unsafe water, air pollutants, and hazardous chemicals. Others are caused by the "environments of poverty." Environment is not the cause; the causes are environmental mismanagement and development that destroys earth's resource base.

The natural resources we have today are the basis for future development; so are today's children. Both tend to be undervalued by decisionmakers because "they are difficult to quantify in economic terms." And, as we see once again, in times of economic hardship, budgets for children's welfare and environmental protection are the first to be cut, everywhere.

Yet in these tough times, it is the children in many countries who are taking the lead, who are filled with hope and a belief that morality and practicality can be combined. Given a chance, they have boundless energy and open, ethical minds. They can be powerful forces for positive change in many fields, and especially in environmental protection where, as you will see in these pages, so many young people already are proving their commitment and potential leadership.

This guide [*Our Children Their Earth*] is dedicated to them and to children of all ages. It is designed as a practical and moral road map to the Environmental Sabbath, to be used in conjunction with the UNEP Sabbath booklet, *Only One Earth.*

In recent years the United Nations has given children and their environment international priority. Now it is up to us to shine a moral spotlight on what the UN has done by mobilizing our faith communities. Only we can infuse these legal and ethical texts with spiritual energy, so that they have force and vitality for the future of our earth – its children.

In a Dream I had a Wolf Come to Me

In a dream I had a wolf come to me
and say how he's tired
of his followers being killed.
He said they need space
to run around and space
from humans, space
from pollution, space
from construction.

We are free spirits
and cannot be tamed
or kept in captivity.

The wolf gave
one giant howl to the full moon.
And left me to just a memory
of his black fur
and his great thought.

Brett Johnson,
7th grade

Mindwalking

When I am mindwalking,
exploring my inner garden,
there is so much peace within me.
Touching. Holding. Smelling.
The flowers of Happiness, Joy and Love
grow and prosper in my garden.

Insects live here too.
They fly from flower to flower
picking up more wisdom and laughter
with every stop.
These insects fly on giving
happy messages to others,
telling them of everything good
and happy, and sometimes sad.

Miracles can happen here.
They are ideas, memories,
all of which come out of a doorway,
and are released so all may hear
and experience them.

The ideas and everything else
that tumble out,
fly around like doves
who want to tell others
about what they have to tell.

LISA BROWN,
8th grade

Our Children, Their Earth

"If a child is to keep alive his inborn sense of wonder... he needs the companionship of at least one adult who can share it, rediscovering with him the joy, excitement and mystery of the world we live in."

RACHEL CARSON,
from *The Sense of Wonder*

"Those who have the humility of a child may find a key to reverence for, and kinship with, all life."

J. ALLEN BOONE,
from *The Language of Science*

"When I bring you colored toys, my child, I understand why there is such a play of colors on clouds, on water, and why flowers are painted in tints."

RABINDRANATH TAGORE,
Nobel Laureate, India

"The world was not left to us by our parents, it was lent to us by our children."

AFRICAN PROVERB

The Environmental Sabbath/Earth Rest Day was established in 1987 by the United Nations Environment Programme (UNEP). Its advisory board and planning committee established this annual focus as a way to meld spiritual values with environmental science. Among its publications is *Only One Earth* which contains scientific data, declarations and texts from religious bodies, and relevant scriptures from many of the world's religions. Many churches, temples, synagogues, mosques, and other institutions have adopted the first weekend in June as a special time to remember the needs and value of the earth through worship and liturgy, education and personal commitment. Other organizations have built upon UNEP's resource base to develop programs of their own that extend throughout the year.

In July 1990, the United Nations gathered religious leaders from 12 faiths and 40 nations to enlist their help in easing children's suffering worldwide. The UN has developed laws guaranteeing children's rights and protecting them and the environments they are born into, for both are dying at terrifyingly rapid rates. UNEP and UNICEF supported these UN initiatives with a variety of programs.

In Spring of 1991, the Environmental Sabbath/Earth Rest Day focused on children and the environment, and produced the resource guide *Our Children Their Earth,* from which the following scriptures are drawn.

Adapted from the Spring 1991 Environmental Sabbath/
Earth Rest Day Newsletter

United Nations Environment Programme
Regional Office for North America
DC2-0803, United Nations
New York, NY 10017 USA

"We have reached a point in human evolution when we must ask ourselves some very fundamental questions regarding the meaning of life and evolution itself. If we assume that all we have learned, all that is happening, all we are trying to do makes little sense, then there is no hope and the human species might as well destroy itself and disappear.

If, on the contrary, we assume that some cosmic force or law or God or Creator in the universe has put in the human species certain objectives, functions, expectations and destinations, then it is our duty to ascertain on a contemporary scale what these objectives are."

ROBERT MULLER,
"A World Core Curriculum,"
from *Essays on Education*

Scriptures and Reflections on Children and the Earth

Bahá'í

O God! Educate these children. These children are the plants of Thine orchard, the flowers of Thy meadow, the roses of Thy garden. Let Thy rain fall upon them; let the Sun of Reality shine upon them with Thy love. Let Thy breeze refresh them in order that they may be trained, grow and develop, and appear in the utmost beauty. Thou art the Giver. Thou art the Compassionate.

ABDU'L-BAHÁ,
Bahá'í Prayers, p.35

Train your children from their earliest days to be infinitely tender and loving to animals. If an animal be sick, let the children try to heal it; if it be hungry, let them feed it; if thirsty, let them quench its thirst; if weary, let them see that it rests.

From the writings of ABDU'L-BAHÁ,
No. 130. p.158

Buddhist

It's time for elders to listen to the child's voice. You see, in the child's mind there is no demarcation of different nations, no demarcation of different social systems of ideology. Children know in their minds that all children are the same, all human beings are the same. So, from that viewpoint, their minds are more unbiased. When people get older, though, they start to say, "our nation," "our religion," "our system." Once that demarcation occurs, then people don't bother much about what happens to others. It's easier to introduce social responsibility into a child's mind.

His Holiness the XIVth Dalai Lama,
TENZIN GYATSO, in *My Tibet*,
written with Galen Rowell

Christian

One generation passeth away, and another generation cometh: but the earth abideth forever.

ECCLESIASTES 1:4

They brought young children to Christ, that he should touch them: and his disciples rebuked those that brought them. But when Jesus saw it, he was much displeased, and said unto them, "Allow the little children to come unto me, and forbid them not: for of such is the kingdom of God. Verily I say unto you, whosoever shall not receive the kingdom of God as a little child, he shall not enter therein."
And he took them in his arms, put his hands upon them, and blessed them.

MARK 10:13–16

Hindu

The Hindu mind is singularly dominated by one paramount conception: the divinity of life. Regarding the creation of the universe, Hindu tradition, based on the experience of illumined mystics, asserts with deep conviction that God is the supreme creator of every thing and every being.... [We] Hindus give God a favored place in our homes as mother, friend, child, even husband or sweetheart. God, being the most beloved object of life, must find a place in our family life. He must be dear and near to us. This ideal of the sweet God, lovable God, playmate God, child God has been admirably illustrated in Hinduism in the personality of Sri Krishna. So, every child can be looked upon by anyone as a baby God, and spiritual life can be quickened in this manner.

SWAMI TATHAGATANANDA,
Vendanta Society, New York

Let us declare our determination to halt the present slide towards destruction, to rediscover the ancient tradition of reverence for all life and, even at this hour, to reverse the suicidal course upon which we have embarked. Let us recall the ancient Hindu dictum: "The earth is my mother, and we are all her children."

DR. KARAN SINGH
at the World Wide Fund for Nature gathering
of religious leaders, Assisi, Italy

Jewish

Just as you found trees which others had planted when you entered the land, so you should plant for your children. No one should say, "I am old. How many more years will I live? Why should I be troubled for the sake of others?" Just as he found trees, he should add more by planting even if he is old.

MIDRASH TANCHUMA,
Kedoshim 8

A person's life is sustained by trees. Plant them for the sake of your children.

From SEDER TU BISHEYAT,
the Festival of Trees,
Central Conference of American Rabbis

Muslim

The Prophet [Mohammed] was very concerned about wasting and polluting water. Even when we were very young, our mothers taught us that whoever soils the river, on the day of judgment that person is going to be given the responsibility of cleaning the river. So we were really learning about preserving the purity of water from childhood.

SHEIKH AHMAD KUFTARO,
Grand Mufti of Syria, in *Shared Vision*, 1990

Native American

We are taught to plant our feet carefully on Mother Earth because the faces of all future generations are looking up from it.

OREN LYONS,
Chief Joagquisho of the Haudenosaunee
(Iroquois) Confederation

Teach your children what we have taught our children, that the earth is our mother. Whatever befalls the earth, befalls the children of the earth. If we spit upon the ground, we spit upon ourselves. This we know. The earth does not belong to us; we belong to the earth. One thing we know, which the white man may one day discover, our God is the same God. You may think now that you own Him as you wish to own our land, but you cannot. He is the God of all people, and His compassion is equal for all. This earth is precious to God, and to harm the earth is to heap contempt on its Creator.... So love it as we have loved it. Care for it as we have cared for it. And with all your mind, with all your heart, preserve it for your children, and love it... as God loves us all.

CHIEF SEATTLE
of the Squamish, *circa* 1855

Sikh

For the sake of posterity, those countless generations of unborn children to come, let us save this Earth. Let us not misuse our privileges. Please don't let the song of birds die. Don't let the water babies perish. Don't let magnificent animals become extinct. Above all, don't let human beings die of starvation and man-made disasters.

From the World Wide Fund
for Nature gathering of religious leaders
at Assisi, Italy

The Convention on the Rights of the Child

Children are especially vulnerable to rights violations. Each day nearly 35,000 children die from lack of food, shelter, or primary health care. About 30 million children live in the world's streets, and another 20 million have been displaced, physically disabled, or otherwise traumatized by armed conflict.

The United Nations Convention on The Rights of the Child is an international treaty establishing an international legal framework for the civil, social, economic and political rights of children. Unanimously adopted by the UN General Assembly on November 20, 1989, as of February 1993, 129 countries have ratified the Convention so far. Drafted over a ten-year period by the 43 nations that are members of the United Nations Human Rights Commission, the Convention is the most comprehensive international expression of children's rights. By gathering them into a single legal instrument, the Convention represents an unprecedented international consensus.

The Convention commits all ratifying nations to recognize that children have special needs and encourages all governments to establish standards for their survival, protection, and development. *Survival* means the right to food, shelter, and essential health care. *Protection* includes sheltering children from abuse and from involvement in war, and gives them the right to a name and nationality. *Development* guarantees the right to a basic education and provides special care for handicapped children.

The preamble recalls the basic principles of the United Nations Charter and specific provisions of relevant human rights treaties such as the Universal Declaration of Human Rights. It reaffirms the fact that children, because of their vulnerability, need special care and protection, and it places special emphasis on the primary caring responsibility of the family and extended family.

The Convention also reaffirms the need for legal and other protection of the child before and after birth, the importance of respect for the cultural values of the child's community, and the vital role of international cooperation in securing children's rights. It also includes provisions never before recognized in an international treaty, requiring countries to:

- do everything possible to ensure child survival;
- pursue "full implementation" of the child's right to the highest level of health possible by working to provide primary health care, to educate mothers and families about breast feeding and family planning, and to abolish harmful practices such as the preferential treatment of male children; and
- work toward achieving universal primary education, and take measures to reduce drop-out rates and encourage regular school attendance.

The World Summit for Children

Nearly one year later, in September 1990, a unique summit meeting was held at the United Nations in an extraordinary effort to address the problems of the world's children. With 72 heads of state and government, the World Summit for Children was the biggest gathering of national leaders in the history of humankind up to that time. It also was the first time that leaders from around the globe had met for a single, common purpose – to give children priority on governmental agendas in the 1990s.

The World Summit's goals were to:

- draw attention to major problems affecting children – debt, war, and other hostilities, environmental deterioration, drugs, and AIDS;
- give children "first call" on society's resources;
- accelerate implementation and monitoring of the Convention on the Rights of the Child; and
- encourage people and their governments to "do the doable" – mass, low-cost, available means of action.

Excerpted and adapted by the Editor from *Our Children Their Earth*, pp. 21-22, from the UNICEF *Backgrounder*, and from the Convention on the Rights of the Child.

For the complete text, contact:
UNICEF, 777 United Nations Plaza,
New York, NY 10017 USA; tel. (212) 687-2163

When I Look into My Hand

I see rivers, streams,
and oceans with little islands
and trees on them: Lonely
and confusing, mystifying
and dangerous.

In the oceans the whales
and dolphins swim freely,
but then man comes.

In the rivers fish swim gracefully,
but then man comes
and pollutes in the water.

In streams the water
glistens and sparkles,
but then man comes.

MELISSA ROLAN, *8th grade*

My Hand

is extended into space,
but it is not a hand—
it is a colony:
prosperous, magnificent.
Spectacularly structured
tunnels rise above.

Where do they lead?
To another star?
To my own room?
They are the tunnels
of imagination,
of power.

ALINA CLARK,
8th grade

My Home

The palm of my hand
is the house of feelings.
I live in the commonest path
which is the longest
which is my joy.

The shortcut is my anger.
I barely ever take that path.
Then over the bridge
I travel and feel lonely.

I'll travel to the hills
and feel loved:
then I'll go home.

ELIZABETH FREEMAN,
6th grade

Religious Education –
Including Environment, Peace, and Values

Environmental education

There are strong parallels between the study of religious education and environmental education. The principal motivation for both is first hand experience. In simplest terms, one could be said to be the study of *Who am I?* and the other to be of *What am I doing?*

…To understand the problems of population, pollution, and conservation, the study of religious and other cultural life is vital. Probably the most valuable product of this study for the student is the accumulation of tolerance, understanding, concern, and commitment to change the nature of society and its exploitation of resources.

ROBIN NORBURY,
"Environmental Education," in *A Dictionary of Religious Education,* edited by John M. Sutcliffe. SCM Press, Ltd., in Association with The Christian Education Movement, London

Environmental studies

The religious and moral dimension of environmental studies is fundamental for three principal reasons.

1. All religions, including humanism and scientific rationalism, imply a view of the relation of man to nature, the content of which affects the way the environment is treated.

2. Policy decisions themselves involve evaluations of nature and the environment which may properly be considered moral.

3. Environmental problems of pollution, the conservation of resources, the preservation of nature itself, the growth of population globally and locally, and of migration and aggregation into burgeoning urban complexes, cannot be set apart from social and economic questions which have an undisputed moral dimension.

R.P. Moss, "Environmental Studies," in
A Dictionary of Religious Education,
edited by John M. Sutcliffe, p.124

"Each second we live in a new and unique moment of the universe, a moment that never was before and will never be again. And, what do we teach our children in school? We teach them that two and two make four, and that Paris is the capital of France.

When will we also teach them what they are?

We should say to each of them: 'Do you know what you are? You are a marvel. You are unique. In all the world there is no other child exactly like you. And look at your body. What a wonder it is. Your legs, your arms, your cunning fingers, the way you move!

You may become a Shakespeare, a Michelangelo, a Beethoven. You have the capacity for anything. Yes, you are a marvel.' "

PABLO CASALS

The Shield Within

I carry an inner shield
that no one can see
unless I let them –
it's woven from time,
a snow-capped mountain, the sun,
a star and a whale.

My snow-capped mountain: knowledge
true, stupendous, towering
ready to explode!
It is burning with the desire to be more
to learn more.
Quietly, gently, the snow calms
this anxiety rushing.

My sun – no ordinary sun,
but one of great importance
shedding rays of love and spirituality
penetrating
the souls of all creatures
of all beings.

Me, a star, an artist.
My star brings on a wonderful calm.

My whale to me
is a mysterious marvel,
a giant soul
filled with wisdom beyond
a conscious reach.

ALINA CLARK,
8th grade

The Right Hand

I am holding
a beautiful planet.
I feel the warmth
from her soil,
the breeze
from her sky,
and her soft flowing
plasma; two moons
peer out of her surface
splitting the soil
in new directions:
blood flows around her,
in rivers so deep,
while I, the right
hand, help to hold her
in place, for if I let go
she would perish.

BRIAN URBANOWICZ,
11th grade

Peace studies

Peace Studies has become a viable teaching prospect for two reasons:

1. It fits into the pattern of topic studies that emerged in the era of expansion and experiment as an alternative to the subject-based approach and

2. The intensity of political confrontation coupled with rapid development of weapons technology in the nuclear, electronic, chemical and biological fields has produced a new level of consciousness about the urgency that permeates issues of peace and conflict.

At the same time it is ironic that it is this very sense of urgency that makes Peace Studies a controversial item in schools and colleges since it can be used as a cover for manipulation by devotees of any part of the political spectrum. Total academic integrity that demonstrably seeks to equip pupils with the capacity to analyze both existing and potential alternative values in the topic are a teacher's only defense when such accusations fly.

Peace Studies cannot be soundly built on a revulsion from War/Conflict Studies. The topic is as inexorably bound to these as Feminist Studies are to the doctrine of man. Indeed, analysis of conflict helps to define aspects of Peace Studies from inner mental conflict of the individual, through family tensions to neighborhood animosities, on through class and ethnic antipathies to terrorism and to conflicting interests and ideologies at the international level. Each level of conflict has a corresponding "peace with distinctive features that deserve close study. In each case there is also the recurring issue of whether one is talking of containing conflict as a form or peace or is reserving the word "peace" for a genuine resolution and removal of conflict.

RE [Religious Education] may relate to Peace Studies in two ways.

1. Peace Studies may be included as a topic within an RE syllabus, considering the relationship of religion to society and the various belief systems as they interpret the human situation. The need for and capacity of religious groups to challenge society is important although often lost within the context of state or civic religions.

2. RE can make a contribution to a Peace Studies program. An important stage in this is to overcome common misconceptions and even prejudices about the involvement of religion in war and its causes throughout history. It is profitable in contrast to consider religious resources for peace. In both approaches to the relationship of RE and Peace Studies the contribution of major religious figures to the cause of peace will play a significant part.

James Green, "Peace Studies,"
in *A Dictionary of Religious Education*,
edited by John M. Sutcliffe, p.254

Values education

Values Education is an inescapable part of any educational system, though it may not always be openly acknowledged as such. Its presence may be observed in anthropological accounts of young people growing up in primal societies, e.g., Samoa or the early colonial period in Africa, through to the sophisticated system of modern states, e.g. France, China, USA, or USSR. Primal and sophisticated alike have a common expectation that young people will take their place as responsible adults to their own benefit and that of their community....

Aims. There are three aims that mark off polarities in Values Education [VE]:

1. to produce conformity to existing values;

2. to produce dedication to radical change;

3. to foster a capacity for critical appraisal of both existing and potential values.

Historically one is unlikely to find a pure example of any of these so they are best used as *types* or markers by which to review and assess one's own work in VE. One has to keep in mind that the capacity for critical appraisal needs to be applied to alternative as well as existing values for it is not difficult to show that radical change is often demanded on the basis of views which their exponents cannot or do not critically examine. Indeed today's radical critics have often become tomorrow's tyrants enforcing a new conformity.

Where all adults are able to take part in the political process and even more where there is a variety of culture and interest-groups in one society, the most appropriate aim is to maximize the capacity for critical appraisal of all existing and alternative values and to enable openness to the existing and alternative values that survive such appraisal.

James Green, "Values Education,"
in *A Dictionary of Religious Education*,
edited by John M. Sutcliffe, p.356

"Global education or education for global justice is a process which helps people understand the conditions of hunger, poverty, and oppression, and why these conditions exist and persist. Global education arouses and nurtures in individuals a commitment to envision and actively promote a more just, sustainable, and participatory earth community."

from *Make a World of Difference*,
published by the Office on Global
Education of the Church World Service

FOR MORE INFORMATION:

ON VIOLENCE:

Helping Teens Stop Violence, by Allen Creighton and Paul Kivel, Hunter House Publishers (1990) $11.95

War Resisters League's Youth Peace Task Force, Jesse Heiwa, 339 Lafayette St., New York, NY 10012 tel. (212) 228-0450 / fax (212) 228-6193 / E-mail. wri@igc.apc.org.

ORGANIZATIONS AND RESOURCE CENTERS: See Chapter 42
EDUCATION AND MULTI-RELIGIOUS EDUCTION: See Chapter 43

Women are Speaking Out

Finally – Choosing Our Future As Women

Rev. Marchiene Vroon Rienstra

Author, minister (Reformed Church of America), and counselor

*F*or the first time in recorded human history, women who are adherents of the world's religions are claiming the right and power, in a whole new way, to choose their faith and their future for themselves. This empowerment has two contexts – within their separate religious communities and in the emerging globalization of the women's movement.

No longer can it be said that this movement is primarily a white, middle-class, Euro-American women's movement. It has become a world-wide phenomenon, transcending national, cultural, racial, and economic boundaries. It defies definition and dismissal as simply feminist. In fact, the movement is in such ferment, charged with such energy, so fast-growing, and filled with such variety, that it is itself only beginning to come to a kind of self-understanding and clarity about its goals.

Fortunately, at this point in history, certain common ground is emerging in this women's movement in the context of the community of the world's religions. One piece of that common ground is the ever clearer understanding of the ways in which all of the major religions of the world have been, to a greater or lesser degree, patriarchal, and therefore limiting of women's gifts and roles in the religious community and society as a whole. As women scholars representing the major religions of the world have had increasing opportunity to meet in global religious forums, they have compared notes and found that in spite of their many differences, there are certain striking similarities in their experience and observation. The Preface to *The Spiral Path* sums it up in eloquent words:

Women have been given steps to spirituality by the same patriarchal groups that have given them their place in society, in politics, in the arts, in the work place. Her spirituality was developed for her alongside her subjugation and invalidation. Masculine values have been taught as the norm in spirituality…. Women have so internalized these concepts that they themselves guided young women in those same male norms…. The resultant pain of women throughout the ages, the loss of the gifts in spiritual literature and service that they might have given humankind, can only be mourned. But after

our mourning, we must begin again the process of discovery. There is much to discover. (p. ix)

As women have discovered the specific ways in which their experience and views have not been taken into account in the scriptures, theology, worship, and customs of their various religious traditions, they have begun to review those traditions with a view to recovering what is life-giving in them for women. Gifted women like Islamic scholar Riffat Hassan, Buddhist scholar Rita Gross, Hindu scholar Lina Gupta, Jewish scholar Judith Plaskow, and Christian scholar Phyllis Tribble have found neglected elements in their respective traditions which can be recovered and reinterpreted to establish claims for a just and equal treatment of women in the world's religions. Even more, their studies are helping to lay the foundation for transforming the world's religions into traditions that are respectful of and hospitable to the special wisdom and gifts women can contribute to the future of religious life around the globe.

An important element of such studies is the asking of hard questions which serve to arouse the kind of creative dissonance out of which real learning arises. These questions are often painful for both women and men, and they can shake the very foundations of the faiths to which they are addressed, for they go the the root of the religious systems which express these faiths.

Ursula King, editor of *Women in the World's Religions*, summarizes these dissonance-creating questions:

Looking at the past, one can ask: what do the sacred scriptures, the theological and spiritual writings of the religions of the world, teach about women? How far do the different religions draw on feminine symbols in speaking about ultimate reality, about the nature and experience of the spirit? To what extent do women take part in ritual and religious practises, choose to follow the religious life, or hold positions of authority in particular religions? Most important, what is the religious experience of women? Why has it been so little reflected in the official theological literature whereas it has contributed so much to the wealth of mystical and spiritual writings in different religions? Perhaps the central question today is how far women are still hindered or, alternatively, encouraged in giving full expression to their religious experience. Contemporary feminists often sharply criticize traditional religions and explore the meaning of religion for women in a new way. Although this challenge has barely been met by the official religious leaders of the world, in each tradition women and men are beginning to reflect on its meaning. (p. vii)

Along with such questions come discoveries that are the result of the consciousness raised by such questions. In the past, this sort of consciousness was rare among the adherents of the world's religions. But in our age, for the first time, believers of various faiths are beginning to realize that sexual differentiation has been taken for granted without being critically reflected upon by both men and women in positions of authority in past human history. The critical reflection now necessary highlights gender differences in religious experience and expression, but also seeks eventually to embrace them in a new, more meaningful unity. This new unity requires religious symbol-systems, action, and organization which fully reflect the experience and wisdom of both women and men in equal measure.

For example, Friday M. Mbon has this to say about the role of women in African traditional religions.

While educated African women in the towns and cities today can sing, 'What men can do, women can also do,' in the areas of political, educational, and scientific achievements, the uneducated women in African villages could sing the same slogan in areas of African traditional religious life. Yet if they dare sing such a slogan, the menfolk may mistake it as a song of equality between them and the women and therefore a threat to their supposed divinely sanctioned superiority over the womenfolk. (p.10, *Women in the World's Religions*)

Anne Bancroft has this to say about women in Buddhism.

It is interesting to speculate on the extent of fear which women seemed then and still seem to engender in men. They are regarded as not only personal but universal obstacles, preventing the spiritual progress of humankind and even filling the Buddha with fear that they would bring about the fall of the Sangha. Denise Carmody takes the view that early conservative Buddhism linked desire and productive becoming with samsara, the realm of change and endless redistribution of the life-force. Since samsara was the enemy and the trap, so too was femaleness. Thus, women took on symbolic force as epitomizing karmic bonds. (p.86, *Women in the World's Religions*)

Lina Gupta critiques the Hindu tradition, and brilliantly reshapes the understanding of the goddess Kali in Hinduism to envision a new order of mutuality and equality between women and men.

Scripturally, both the husband and the wife are considered to be reflections of the divine nature. Therefore, any hierarchical order negates the very premise on which it appears to be based. Manu used the symbols of duality found in the principles of Siva and Sakti to support a hierarchical and patriarchal system in which women's understanding and experience of their own power have been severely restrained. In doing so, he violated the very spirit of those symbols. The more the patriarchal mind recognized the force of the creative power present in the divine female, the more it created an environment for the feminine to be restricted and restrained.... The patriarchal reading neglects the source of both subject and object, the One unmanifested Brahman who is neither a subject nor an object, male nor female. Both subject and object in reality are the same. Union transcends sexual differences and the individual ego. Kali illustrates this.... As we listen to the various stories of the goddess Kali we see them take shape into a definite pattern of experience.... By reviewing these stories over and over again, understanding them in their most liberating sense, and reappropriating from them those elements which are most powerful as resources for the liberation of both men and women – taken as authentic and genuinely spiritual those aspects that promote our over-all welfare – we can eliminate the unessential details and the patriarchal distortions and finally identify the sources and patterns of our oppressed past and present. It is this pattern that finally reveals the way we are now, and what we could possibly become. It shows the ways in which the images and the stories of Kali can be liberating and empowering to all through exposing an essence that goes beyond male and female, beauty and ugliness, life and death, and all forms of alienation and separation. (p. 35-37, passim, *After Patriarchy*)

Lina Gupta's words reveal the essential method and approach being taken by women scholars and leaders in all of the world's great religions. The women writers mentioned above, and others too numerous to mention, are challenging traditional religious teachings and practices. A veritable torrent of books and papers are carrying this flood-tide of new questions and ideas into the minds and hearts of men and women the world over. At heart, they challenge the dualistic thought patterns about men and women which were the matrix of and became enshrined in the great historical religions, whether one looks at their scriptures, teachings, worship, rites, or institutions. Not only do they probe just how far women's experience has been taken into account in the world's religious traditions; they also ask how far traditional religious teachings can still speak to women and men today whose consciousness has been changed, and who find the old patriarchal assumptions incredible.

So far, as many women scholars and leaders are noting, the loss of the plausibility of much traditional religious doctrine and worship has escaped the attention of many male religious authorities, who are inexcusably ignorant of the wider issues being raised by the women's movement, and often do not wish to take its critique of religion seriously. This situation contains within it the serious possibility of crisis for the world's religions as the women's movement grows in power and credibility, winning men as well as women to a point of view which poses a profound challenge to the religious status quo all over the world.

The societal changes brought about by the ongoing processes of Westernization and globalization simply make the challenge all the greater as more and more women the world over exercise leadership in more and more fields previously closed to them. "Nothing is as powerful as an idea whose time has come," goes an old saying. Indeed. And the power of the idea that women may and must choose their future also in terms of how they will participate in the world's religious communities is one that is growing daily. News magazines and religious periodicals carry constant accounts of the changes taking place as more and more women and men refuse to believe that women must take an inferior place. Women are in the forefront now of the ecological, peace, and inter-faith movements which value the inter-connection of all people and things, and seek a global order which makes the survival and flourishing of this fragile planet a priority. The very violence of certain reactions to all of this by fundamentalist wings of various religious communities only serves to reinforce the power of this turn in the tide of human history. The world community of religions really has no choice but to accept the challenge of this historic movement in which women are choosing their own future in terms of their faith commitments.

The world's religions contain within them a rich deposit of hard-won wisdom which is universal and life-giving for men and women the world over. Though it is buried under patriarchal layers of interpretation and custom, it is crucially important to preserve this treasure-trove of wisdom. If women and men in increasing numbers desert their faith traditions because they cannot find in them the spiritual resources they need for a flourishing spirituality that equally honors the gifts and wisdom of women and men, then those faith traditions will gradually weaken and perhaps even fade away, be it ever so slowly. That would be a great loss to the human race, which is in desperate need of the accumulated wisdom of the world's religions. If there is to be a future worth choosing for any of us, a recovery of religious wisdom and a transformation of the religious traditions in which wisdom is imbedded – making them equally hospitable to women and men – are urgent necessities. For too long, the human race and the world's religions have flown with only one wing fully outspread. When women's wings are added to men's, what a glorious flight of the Spirit there will be!

Books quoted in this article and useful for further study:

After Patriarchy, edited by Paul M. Cooey, William R. Eakin, and J.B. McDaniel *(Faith meets Faith: An Orbis Series in Interreligious Dialogue)* published by Orbis Books, Maryknoll, NY, 1991.
Women in the World's Religions, edited by Ursula King (God: the Contemporary Discussion Series) published by Paragon House, NY, 1987.
The Spiral Path, edited by Theresa King O'Brien *(Essays and Interviews on Women's Spirituality)* published by YES International Publishers, St. Paul, MN. 1988.

"There are, however, many [women] who have difficulty in tuning in to these thoughts and spiritual problems, because the daily struggle for life and survival, against death in all its varied forms, demands all the energy they can get. […]

"Among them, and even right in their vanguard, are women like Domitilla de Chungara from the tin mines of Bolivia. She organized a hunger strike in the midst of starvation, in order to obtain better living conditions. Or Rigoberta Menchu from Guatemala who has experienced how her people are being destroyed, and rises up against it. Among them are also the women of the Plaza de Mayo in Argentina, who each Thursday for years now have been marching up and down in silent protest in front of the government palace in Buenos Aires, in order to obtain information about their disappeared children. And the Philippino nuns who are demonstrating their concern for the young prostitutes, and exposing the scandal of the human slave trade. Or the Babushkas in Russia who are keeping the church alive. The women in the peace movements and the anti-apartheid movements everywhere: they get to grips with these issues through practical action, for, whatever the question about God-father or mother-goddess may be, the surest way of finding an answer lies in looking at the faces of the women, men, and children who have been entrusted to us, and in whom God, as woman, man or child, meets us and waits for our response."

BARBEL VON WARTENBERG-POTTER
We Will Not Hang our Harps on the Willows,
World Council of Churches, RISK series, p.52

Religious Women's Commitment to Healing the World Community

Ven. Chung Ok Lee

Head Minister of the Won Buddhist United Nations Office, a religious nongovernmental organization in New York

Chung Ok Lee is also Vice-President of the Association of Religious NGOs at the UN, and serves on many committees, including the new Values Caucus. The author presented the following speech to the 6th Assembly of the World Conference on Religion and Peace, held in Rome and Riva del Garda, Italy on November 3-9, 1994; the conference theme was *Healing the World: Religions for Peace*.

*W*e are living in a time of global transition. The world is becoming increasingly interconnected and interdependent, resulting in greater participation of minority groups.

Healing our own people first

*T*raditionally, women in many cultures were taught that subordination and endurance were womanly virtues for which they should strive. These "virtues" are still extolled in many societies. Women are thus subtly persuaded to be silent. Our inner silence, however, can be a positive force, a healing power. In my life, contemplative silence and the silence of compassionate listening are very positive. Silence in meditation can be the power that heals the wounds inflicted by the pressures to be silent. Silence is the power that leads to the discovery of the Divine within, the Buddha Nature in every one of us. Through silent meditation, we discover ourselves and learn to use our own wisdom, our own Truth, and our own inner strength. I have learned to channel my silence to overcome many challenges and difficulties such as sexism, racism, and religious discrimination. Through silent meditation, I gained the self-awareness that I have an unlimited capacity within myself that is far more powerful than any external difficulties.

I was born in a small village in Korea. I remember vividly the day I first encountered gender discrimination. In Korea, it is customary to maintain a genealogy, a family lineage book. Once every few years, names of the new family members are added. However, to my surprise and chagrin, although my brothers' names were listed, neither my name nor my sister's name were. As females we simply did not exist. In Korean genealogy, females only exist when they become subordinate members of their husbands' households.

My second vivid encounter with gender inequality occurred when I was denied the opportunity of higher education beyond the ninth grade, by my father. My father explained his stance by voicing the common Korean consensus that "modern education spoils women, especially when they are young girls." With the aid of my more enlightened schoolteachers, however, I moved to a city to continue my education.

From this very young age, I have asked simple questions: who am I? how and where do I stand, as a female, in our patriarchal society? It has been a long journey to find some of the answers and my journey of self-discovery is still continuing.

Through much intense inner struggle in seeking these answers, I have found a strong spirituality, the awakening of the Divine within, the Buddha Nature within myself. Spirituality helps me to see meaning in my life and in my place in the world and in the Ultimate Reality. It is an arduous journey well worth undertaking to come to terms with the Buddha nature within. This journey, however, is not meant to be a solitary one. We should use the wisdom we acquire to illuminate the way for others so that we can all travel this path together, as One.

As religious women, we have an obligation to nurture ourselves and other women, so we can be ourselves. We do not have to become men to have an equal partnership. At the same time, we have to heal our own people, helping all women and men to become more enlightened. Only through this approach can we find the journey home to our True Selves. Along the way, we will lift, nourish, and foster families and societies.

Healing religion itself

*R*eligion can provide vision for humanity and can and should act as a constructive force to create a peaceful global village where harmony is the norm. However, religious views in the past were evolved and written by men with dominant perspectives. Our understanding of life is distorted, because these explanations have been written by only one half of the human race. Only through the full inclusion of women's views and experiences of life and spirituality will we gain a fuller understanding of human behavior, development, and religious experience.

We must work together, therefore, to create a more unified social structure where men and women have an equal voice. For this change to transpire, women must establish first their own identities as individuals. Thus, we as religious women must renew our commitment to nurturing ourselves in order to attain enlightenment for the benefit of all human beings. We cannot even begin to hope for a more equal societal structure unless we are willing to make the same change in our own religious tradition. Many intelligent women turn away from religion, however, because they think religion cannot heal women's wounds and cannot change patriarchal hierarchy.

Despite these fears, I can assure you that women and men can share a balanced measure of opportunity and power for the benefit of all. An example is readily evident in the Won Buddhist community, where a distinctive women's movement can be observed. Won Buddhism was founded by the Great Master So-Tae-San in Korea in 1916. So-Tae-San emphasized that women ought to explore their full potential as complete persons equal to men.[1] Based on

PART FOUR: CHOOSING OUR FUTURE

his great enlightenment and wisdom, So-Tae-San established a relationship of mutual respect between men and women, educating women as religious leaders. Following So-Tae-San's example, Won Buddhists have been practicing this theory of equality in and out of our community. Won Buddhism has recognized women ministers as equally capable and eminent leaders in the religious order. It has provided equal opportunity for men and women to grow and develop as distinguished leaders. They, in return, have met and overcome daunting social and political challenges to expand and contribute their learning to the spread of Won Buddhism's teachings.

As with the first generation of female Won Buddhists, religious women today face many obstacles throughout the world. As religious women, however, we must remember that we are concerned not only in our own spirituality but also with the dissemination of our wisdom. It is certainly obvious, then, that a change in our thoughts, perceptions, and values is required to bring about a truly equal relationship. Before we heal the world, we must heal religion itself and our own people first, so that we may grow spiritually strong enough to open ourselves to cooperation and peaceful co-existence. As religious men and women, we must provide a model for the rest of the world. We must embrace this religious calling and this noble goal to assist others in discovering our unlimited capacities, in order to heal the world more effectively.

Healing the world

As Diana Eck described so eloquently in her Pluralism Project, we are living in an increasingly inter-cultural, inter-religious, and international world. It is imperative that we learn to cooperate and coexist peacefully, respecting each other's beliefs and value systems while remaining true to our own.

The idea of cooperation and coexistence is nothing new. Buddhists believe in Co-Dependence of Origination, which means the interconnectedness and interdependency of all creation. In Won Buddhism, this is known as the Graces, to emphasize further the importance of interdependency, essential to the functioning of the whole. In this view, the true self has a sense of unity and connectedness with all of creation in its living and non-living manifestations.

We must encourage others to see that the sacredness of life demands the practice of nonviolence. All forms of life embody beauty and thus inspire human consciousness with wonder, joy, and creativity. The shared responsibility of all religions is to enrich the quality of life for all human beings and also for non-human beings.

Nowadays, people question the moral and spiritual aspects of global issues and concerns.

The most prominent role of the United Nations has been its active involvement in promoting world peace through political means. The results, however, have been slow in coming. Against this backdrop, there has been a recent upsurge of support for the active involvement of spiritual leaders. The second Secretary-General of the UN, Dag Hammarskjold stated, near the end of his term:

> I see no hope for permanent world peace. We have

tried and failed miserably. Unless the world has a spiritual rebirth, civilization is doomed.[2]

This message should alert us to the urgent need for action.

Religious representatives at the United Nations are in a unique position to bring together the spiritual and moral values in their religious traditions with global issues in order to create a positive change. Spiritual values are inherent in the UN Charter and these values are becoming increasingly applicable. For example, the draft Programme of Action for the Summit for Social Development states:

> We, Heads of States and Government, are committed to an intellectual, spiritual, and ethical vision for social development based on human dignity, equality, respect, mutual responsibility, and cooperation.[3]

At this momentous time in human history, the spiritual leaders and the United Nations must embark on a mission of world peace. Now is the time to translate our talking into action. In this age of overwhelming material and technological advancement, we face the very real risk of a receding tide of spirituality, We must seize this opportunity to turn the tide toward spirituality. We simply have to work together to incorporate spirituality into our daily lives and endeavors. Our wonderful heritage of spirituality must not be lost in the rush of modern material and technological advancement.

In the upcoming millennium, religious leaders must fulfill our calling to unify the human race into one human family. To begin to accomplish this seemingly impossible task, we, as religious leaders, must first set an example of a united front among ourselves, before we can provide the moral and spiritual guidance for others to do likewise.

Suggestions for future action

1. Community of Religions Working toward the United Religions Organization

I urge the World Conference on Religion and Peace to become a vital force and to play a prominent role in establishing a strong United Religions organization (under this or some other name) analogous to the United Nations, through earnest cooperation with people of all faiths and international interfaith organizations. Often the intolerance of political striving leads to hideous violence in the world. But we must remind ourselves that religion is not immune from this same temptation, for almost every persisting international conflict is intensified by religious intolerance. It thus is imperative to establish a permanent world religious organization in order to provide such a forum for spiritual and moral leadership.

2. Religion's role in the World Summit For Social Development

I call upon the world religions to provide the spiritual and moral framework for the Social Summit so that a global and spiritual perspective will be emphasized in addressing issues of poverty, social integration, the role of women, employment, and social justice. In order for all humankind to live in peace and prosperity, we need a global spiritual philosophy grounded on the principle of Mutual Benefit.

By providing the right nurturing environment for the Social Summit, the community of religions can become a beacon of spiritual light for the Summit and for the entire world. This legacy of peace and hope is a debt that we owe to the future, to the past, and to ourselves.

3. Religious women and the Fourth World Conference on Women

I encourage the world's religious women to take an active role in the UN Fourth World Conference on Women and to address issues of gender equality from a spiritual perspective. We should invite religious men and women from all religious traditions to participate and engage in constructive dialogue to forge a viable path to an equal partnership in all aspects of life.

4. Religious Communities and the Fiftieth Anniversary of the United Nations

I urge religious communities to participate in the fiftieth Anniversary of the UN. The world religions can cooperate with all religious NGOs on a major inter-religious service on October 22, 1995, to celebrate the UN's accomplishments of the past half century and to provide an inspirational and spiritual vision for the next century. I wish to emphasize that this interfaith service for the United Nations must not remain merely a symbolic gesture. It must be a beacon, a positive guiding light for the world, especially in those strife-torn areas so desperately in need of spiritual guidance and hope.

In conjunction with this anniversary service, religious communities might organize an interfaith conference. We should seize this opportune moment to unite religious leaders with a spiritual vision and hope for the future of the Earth community.

As "Co-Workers in one Work Place," we each have our own individual roles to play. We have, however, a universal responsibility to build a House of Truth, to create a home based on love and justice. As many of you know, Buddhists believe in rebirth. Through global and interreligious cooperation imbued with spirituality, we will build a better world together, you and I. Indeed, I look forward with joy and enthusiasm to returning and sharing a better home and a happier house in my next life with you, my family – one family in one house.

REFERENCES

1. So-Tae-San. *The Scripture of Won Buddhism.* (Pal Khn Chon Trans. Iri, Korea: Won Kwang University Publication, 1991), 20-22.

2. Robert Muller. *My Testament to the United Nations: A Contribution to the 50th Anniversary of the United Nations 1995.* (Washington: World Happiness and Cooperation, 1992), 175.

3. The United Nations. "Outcome of the World Summit for Social Development: Draft Declaration and Draft Programme of Action," (A/CONF.166/PC/L. 18, August 31, 1994), 4.

Mestiza Legacy

The ships have left the harbour,
    the ghosts remain.
Whips, leather long ago,
    crafted now in silence
and absent looks.

The ships have left the harbour,
    the ghosts remain.
The child looks to her mother for
strength;
    Mother has no time.

    Mother is cleaning
    always cleaning,

    with water,
    with spit,
    with blood;

cleaning,
always cleaning.

    This is a ceremony
    which is no ceremony;

    it is meaning without healing,
    it is death without joy,

it is life without sorrow,
it is dance without spirit;

    it is only clean.

The ships have left the harbour,
    the ghosts remain.

The child looks to her father for love,
    he is hunting, always hunting;

    with hands
    with feet
    his body
    exposed

to the elements.

The hunter tangled in the net he
never saw,
wounded by the bullet
he cannot find,
choked by the tears
that will not come
he hunts.

There is no time for love;
a liquid fire dance burns.

This is a dance
which is no dance.

    It is meaning without healing,
    it is death without joy,
    it is life without sorrow,
    it is dance without spirit;

it is only ceremony.

The ships have left the harbour,
    the ghosts remain.

The child looks to herself for healing,
finds meaning in
dances, ceremonies.

She finds no life,
she finds no death.

She must go to the harbour
where the ghosts remain.

MAGDALENA GÓMEZ,
poet, performance artist, arts educator

International Conferences and Conventions

United Nations Department of Public Information

Fourth World Conference on Women: Action for Equality, Development and Peace

Beijing, China, on September 4-15, 1995

Why another Conference on Women?

- To review and appraise the advancement of women since 1985 in terms of the objectives of the Nairobi Forward-looking Strategies for the Advancement of Women to the Year 2000.
- To mobilize women and men at both the policymaking and grassroots levels to achieve those objectives.
- To adopt a "Platform for Action," concentrating on some of the key issues identified as representing a fundamental obstacle to the advancement of the majority of women in the world. It will include elements relative to awareness-raising, decisionmaking, literacy, poverty, health, violence, national machinery, refugees, and technology.
- To determine the priorities to be followed in 1996-2001 for implementation of the strategies within the United Nations system.

Who will participate?

The Conference has been convened by the United Nations General Assembly, with the United Nations Commission on the Status of Women serving as the Preparatory Committee. This intergovernmental body, representing 45 United Nations Member States, meets annually to formulate guidelines on actions to improve women's status in the economic, political, social, cultural and educational fields.

Gertrude Mongella (United Republic of Tanzania) is Secretary-General of the Conference. Her office and the Conference secretariat, which is responsible for organizing the Conference and preparing its documents, are located at United Nations Headquarters in New York.

Conference participants and observers will include: governments; organizations of the United Nations system; intergovernmental organizations; national liberation movements recognized by the Organization of African Unity; non-governmental organizations; experts and professional associations.

Prior conferences on women

There have already been three world conferences on women. The first conference, held during International Women's Year in Mexico City, 1975, led to the United Nations' General Assembly declaring the Decade for Women (1976-85). At the second conference, held in Copenhagen in 1980, participants adopted a Programme of Action for the Second Half of the United Nations Decade for Women. The third conference, which took place in Nairobi, 1985, at the end of the decade, adopted the "Nairobi Forward-looking Strategies for the Advance of Women to the Year 2000." The strategies provide a framework for action at the national, regional, and international levels to promote greater equality and opportunity for women. They are based on the three objectives of the United Nations Decade for Women – equality, development, and peace.

Compiled by the editor from the UN/DPI Fact Sheet of September 1993

International conventions

On 18 December 1979, "The Convention of the Elimination of All Forms of Discrimination Against Women" was adopted by the United Nations General Assembly. It entered into force as an international treaty on 3 September 1981 after the twentieth country had ratified it. By the tenth anniversary of the Convention in 1989, almost 100 nations have agreed to be bound by its provisions. The Convention was the result of work by the United Nations Commission on the Status of Women, a body established in 1946 to monitor the situation of women and to promote women's rights. The Commission's work has been instrumental in bringing to light all the areas in which women are denied equality with men. These efforts for the advancement of women have resulted in several declarations and conventions, of which the "Convention of the Elimination of All Forms of Discrimination Against Women" is the central and most comprehensive document.

from the Introduction to the "Convention on the Elimination of All Forms of Discrimination against Women"

Stronger focus on human rights

[...] One of the major achievements of the past 10 years has been the support by a growing number of countries for the Convention.... First adopted in 1979, it has now [1993] been accepted by 126 countries. However, many of those countries have placed reservations on key provisions that they view as conflicting with their religious or cultural practices, especially with regard to marriage and family law – an area notorious for discrimination against women.

Women's human rights have also gained increasing recognition in recent years as the focus of women activists has expanded from economic development and equality to encompass more immediate and personal threats against women's well-being. Violence against women, for example, was not even mentioned in the 1979 Convention because it was not generally recognized as a human rights problem. Now, however, it is receiving urgent attention, in part because the Nairobi "Forward-looking Strategies" helped people to see the close connection between violence at the personal and international levels. Today, many "women's rights watch" organizations are energetically engaged in getting women's human rights onto the international agenda.

Women's non-governmental organizations attending the 1993 World Conference on Human Rights in Vienna aggressively lobbied delegates to include references to women's human rights in the Vienna Declaration and Programme of Action. They helped draft the Declaration on Violence Against Women, which was expected to be adopted by the United Nations General Assembly. This ground-breaking document is the first universal legal instrument aimed specifically at combating violence against women and putting that abuse on the map of international human rights legislation.

At Vienna, women's groups were widely viewed as the best organized and most influential in official proceedings. Through that Conference, as through the United Nations Conference on Environment in Rio de Janeiro and the three previous world conferences on women, women have learned they can have an impact – not only on policies in their own countries, but also on international legislation....

"We have to recognize that there is no women's agenda as such," exhorts Ms. Mongella, Secretary-General of the 1995 Fourth World Conference on Women. "There is just one national, one global agenda. But women will put different emphases and different priorities on the issues based on where they come from and where they want to go. The result is that societies will be different, but built equally on the visions of men and women."

Excerpted and compiled from *Conference to Set Women's Agenda into Next Century*, published by the United Nations, DPI/1424 – December 1993.

The Conference on Population and Development

Continuing their strong and collaborative presence at the International Conference on Population and Development (ICPD), more than 3,000 women gathered at the Cairo NGO Women's Caucus meetings. Reports indicate that once again women were highly organized and effective, that their leaders were forthright and courageous. Many women were also upset by the publicity given to the abortion and family planning controversies, claiming that the ICPD was not about abortion or even about population growth in the southern hemisphere; these women claimed that more significant development issues had been marginalized or deliberately overlooked by Northern and some southern governments, and by single-focus population and aid agencies.

Some women pointed out numerous problems that should have been but were not addressed, including: the effects on development of the unequal and unjust world economic order; the destructive effects of debt rescheduling and structural adjustment policies on familes of the South; the dumping of dangerous contraceptive technologies; the question of unsustainable consumption and lifestyles in the North.

Compiled by the editor from news reports and from the conference icpd.general on PeaceNet.

Liberation Stories

Bärbel von Wartenberg-Potter

From her position in the World Council of Churches, where she could observe women of numerous religions and races, Bärbel von Wartenberg-Potter gained special insights into their lives and the challenges they face. In the essay that follows, the author interprets a biblical story about Jesus in a way that demonstrates his special support for all women.

This loving and global portrait of women's struggles and of their victories presents examples of how women of many traditions are perceiving and reshaping religious experience through the lenses of real lives, needs, and issues.

During my ecumenical wandering-year, women have shared many stories with me, and many images and circumstances of women's lives are in my mind's eye. I have retained them in my heart and in my head. Many of them, of course, I have been able to keep alive through the unerring eye of my camera. Now that all these pictures are as it were spread out before me, they combine to explain our women's story, brimful of fear, distortion, crying needs, brutality, and failure. Yet at the same time there are stories and pictures of liberation, healing, acceptance, walking-tall, courage, determination, joy at being alive, the will to live, sisterhood. Something has happened there, giving rise to a movement, a movement in the direction of becoming free.

Because I read the Christian tradition with feminine eyes nowadays, I recognize in our own women's story (as many women have done before me) the biblical story of the healing of the crippled woman. And so I put all the pieces of my discovery of the women's world together until those

many stories, alongside the biblical story, become one complete story, or picture, in which all of us feature somewhere, as those who are crippled, healing, made whole, giving thanks.

"One Sabbath Jesus was teaching in a synagogue and there was a woman there possessed by a spirit that had crippled her for 18 years. She was bent double and quite unable to stand up straight" (Luke 13:10–13).

For centuries, we women have been possessed by a spirit that used to cripple us. Throughout history it fed itself on the privilege of male interpretation and culture. It thrived on life's harsh constraints humiliatingly inflicted especially on women. We ourselves also fed it with our internalized weakness and lack of self-worth, with the talents we decided not to make available, with the sacrifices made (though not of our own free will), with the magic cloak that makes our real self invisible. We did not count, we just faded into the dark of history, in childbirth, kitchens, and sitting rooms. The evil spirit of female weakness caused us to be bowed down and bent double.

And so I see before my eyes:

- The women in Thailand – knee-deep in water, they are planting rice, bent double all their life to produce a little food, so that they may survive, they and the children, so that they need not flee to the big city.
- The mother in Soweto, bent double with grief over her child, shot down. She had brought it into the world hoping for better times.

- The women in industry at the assembly lines of the multinationals, their backs bent over the small components they have to assemble, and which give no meaning to their lives as women.
- The women behind the veils of a piously prescribed chastity, their eyes with shame averted in the face of curiosity. That is how it has always been and always will be, say the Mullahs. And those without any veils at all, on naked display in Manila, vulnerable and exposed before lustful stares – and not just stares. Money will buy anything.
- The mother with four children, looking for shelter in a sewer, as long as it does not rain. A few rags protect her, that is all; until the next rain.
- The woman refugee, with bag and baggage – the husband happens to be on the wrong side in the war. Her meager possessions – a cooking pot, a blanket – dwindling as she flees, and the unknown country will bring yet more humiliations.
- The woman giving birth on the pavement in an Indian city, worn out, her puny baby in a plastic bag in the midst of dust and stench. Who is going to bother about them?
- The water-carriers – from miles away they are hauling the precious liquid in jars on both shoulders – to do the laundry for strangers. Maybe there will be some left for their own washing.
- The desperate one, her hands covering her face. Her husband has gone away to the city, leaving her without saying good-bye, without any promises. The burden of field work, looking after the animals, the children, now lies on her shoulders alone. He ran away out of desperation, leaving her alone with no way out.
- The seamstresses, row upon row of them, sewing luxurious dresses for a pittance. Hardly a word is spoken, though there would be so much to say; the whirring of the sewing machines is the only sound to be heard, so much sweat for the beauty of other women in Europe and America adorning themselves without giving it a second thought. Where are they, the sisters?
- The bearers of heavy baskets full of sand and stones – they are staggering under them day in and day out, for a few measly rupees, with the supervisor behind them. To satisfy his lust, he will not hesitate to pick one out – any quiet corner will do.
- The black maid in the white lady's house in Capetown, where she washes and cleans, makes children who are strangers laugh, bowed down with yearning for love and human closeness. Her own children back in the homeland are starving.
- The old woman, rummaging through stinking rubbish, looking for anything of value, anything edible, perhaps, that she might pull out of the muck. What is left of human worth? How can one retain one's self-respect – after that?
- The woman living in fear of her husband's beatings. He is unemployed and spends his last cent on drink at his local. When he comes home, he shouts, and beats her, and forces his daughter into bed with him. And she has to stand there and watch, biting her fingers till they bleed, sobbing, "O my God!"
- Those who are hiding – horror just outside the door, they are listening for the soldier's footsteps, for the plunging of bayonets into the front door, for steps and shouts. Hiding will be no good; defenseless, they will be slashed open.
- The forgotten one, Camille Claudel, lover and source of inspiration of the great master Rodin, the giant. Her sculptures are beautiful, majestic, playful, as good as his. Together they created many things over the years. He remained famous, she died in misery, her work long ignored, until recently.

That is how I see her in my mind's eye – with her fear of the future, of being alone, of being deserted, with the fear that drains the marrow from her bones, turning her into a mere shadow of herself. No God, no Goddess looks upon her. Woman, who are you, so bent double and unable to stand up straight?

"When Jesus saw her he called her and said:
'You are rid of your trouble.' Then he laid his hands on her."

*S*omething flows across, a wave of love and power, recognition and becoming whole, healing for body and soul. Someone has seen her, at long last. Her eyes encounter a human face. She stands up straight, a daughter of God, put at the same level with her whole-maker, with the others!

Where God is at work through the hand of the sister, the brother, where we help each other, lovingly touch each other, desolateness fades away and we raise each other up.

Those scenes, too, I see before my eyes:

- In front of me there is a picture of Chinese women workers, putting arms around each other during the afternoon break. It gives strength for the next round of work and living.
- Unforgettable is for me the scene in a beauty salon of the psychiatric clinic in Havana: a disturbed patient with tousled head makes another one beautiful – painting her fingernails red, giving her a magnificent hair-do, so that she can carry herself with beauty into the darkness of insanity.
- Or the woman doctor in the bush, injection needle against the child's skin, fighting against fever, blindness – life-giving touch.
- Or the women's refuge in a West German city, where the telephones keep ringing and cries for help meet with a response: a bed, protection, safe accommodation and counseling for the next steps.
- A woman and a man – for a little while the outside world is forgotten, touching, only you and I, before life invades and separates again.
- Together the African women pound the yam roots to pulp, in a rhythmic one-after-another, full of community, in a common bond against hunger.

"Then at once she straightened up and began to praise God."

*S*he stands up straight and needs someone whom she can thank. We women are today standing up straight and are beginning to live, to think, to act. The Spirit that used to cripple us is withdrawing, has left us. The pictures I see before me also include these:

- The rebellious nuns of America, who will no longer allow themselves to be pushed around by regulations decreed from "the very top," because they have changed from being minors into thinking human beings who cannot go back again. They are acting on their own responsibility, in the light of their own faith.
- The peace women in England, taking root in the face of missile bases, their feminine determination making those in command unsure of themselves. They are standing upright.

- Women who break bread and share the cup with each other, though often still in secret. Since Jesus raised us up, who can possibly stop us? What is holiest of all, given into women's hands.
- The babushka sneaking into church, kneeling before the priest and secretly bringing her grandchild for baptism. The laughter of her gold teeth lighting up her pious face, she is the truly indestructible woman, who has been walking tall and upright for decades. One day the priests will at last bow down in homage to her and her faithfulness. She has time and can wait.
- The women of Kenya, planting trees against the desert and against hunger, united with each other as "women of the world for development and the environment." They just make simple beginnings: planting, tending future forests, the life of generations yet to come. However much their work makes them bend down, they are walking tall.
- The women who will no longer accept what male language, male symbols, a purely male religion would want to dictate to them. They are discovering the secret roots of female piety and bring to light a new language of the faith in a frightened church.
- Women working at conveyor belts are organizing themselves, walking out of the places that used to cripple them, speaking of their self-worth, their wages.
- Women against the bank, words against gold. Has anyone ever seen such a thing? How they are carrying placards, the women for South Africa, calling for a boycott, and depositing the golden calf outside the bank, where it belongs.
- Mothers in the Pacific: after nuclear tests they have given birth to jelly-fish babies, a formless bag, breathing. Now they are shouting it from the rooftops: *you spoilers of our seas, our fish, our beaches, our children! Test your bombs in Paris, store them in Washington, bury your nuclear waste in Tokyo, if it is so safe!*
- The African mother, her baby on her arm, addressing 3,000 church people from all over the world, speaks to the glory of God of giving birth, of blood and sweat, of life as a gift entrusted to us by God. She will send her daughter into the future walking tall.
- The old Indian woman, surrounded by women who had come from far to hear her share the age-old wisdom of her people, who are historically on the side of the losers. She addresses those listening to her as daughters and granddaughters, and her voice trembles, but she walks upright and praises Mother Earth.
- My own mother, an old woman, 76 years young, who once a week gets together with two of her daughters – also grey already – to teach them to play the guitar, in order that the human race will not forget how to sing....

*T*he history of all these women will have to be written afresh, by all of them together, arising out of their experience. It must become part of the history of our human race, in which future generations will be able to recognize the courage and faith of their fore-mothers and -fathers, and be guided by them so that they may go on living and working. Today we are looking for the point of contact in the story of the women. We will never again allow the biblical stories and all other liberation stories to be taken away from us.

Many women and men draw inspiration and strength from a song from the early days of the women's movement. The first to raise the demand for "Bread and Roses" were women workers, when they began to resist the imposition of harsh working conditions and through this simple formulation held on to a great goal for the human family. Again and again it is the simple things that are the goals for which to work, to struggle, to love, to pray, to argue, and to sing. And where women become free, where they are being liberated from meaningless and crippling slavery, the whole of humanity will become more free.

from Chapter 7 of *We Will Not Hang Our Harps on the Willows,*
pp. 79–85

FOR MORE INFORMATION:

The Center for Women, the Earth, the Divine
114 Rising Ridge Road, Ridgefield, CT 06877 USA
tel. (203) 438-3867 / fax (203) 431-4345
Explores parallels between the imaging and treatment of women and of the Earth, and how our images of the Divine relate to these parallels.

Center of Concern, 3700 13th St., N.E., Washington DC 20017 USA
tel. 202 635-2757 / fax 832-9494 *(See Ch. 42)*

Department of Public Information,
United Nations, Room S-1040, New York, NY 10017 USA
tel. (212) 963-6555 / fax (212) 963-4556

Division for the Advancement of Women,
Room DC2-1220, United Nations, New York, NY 10017, USA,
tel. (212) 963-5086 / fax (212) 963-3463

Institute for Development Training
P.O. Box 2522, Chapel Hill, NC 27515-2522; tel. (919) 967-0563
IDT's mission is to improve the health of women, especially in developing countries. It works with international ecumenical church networks and has established health-related training programs in 27 countries in Africa, Asia, the Middle East, Latin America, and the Caribbean. Offers a video and discussion guide.

Interfaith Hunger Appeal,
475 Riverside Dr., Suite 1630, New York, NY 10115-0079 USA
IHA's Office on Education publishes a journal, *Hunger TeachNet,* dedicated to the growing curricular needs in development issues, and particularly gender, justice, and development.

UNIFEM USA, 485 Fifth Avenue, Suite 250, New York, NY 10017 USA; tel. 1-800-982-9781
The United Nations Development Fund for Women helps women living in poverty to help themselves by providing labor-saving technology, training, and access to credit.

Women and World Development Series: Nine titles on women provide students, activists, and educators with the most recent information and debate on world development issues. Published by Zed Books and the U/NGO Group on Women and Development. Themes include economics, health, environment, disability, refugees, literacy, family, human rights, and work.

Women's History Network (and National Women's History Project)
7738 Bell Road, Windsor, CA 95492; tel. (707) 838-6000

The World's Women: Trends and Statistics; the 1994 World Survey on the Role of Women in Development. Published by the UN (See addresses in Chapter 29).

Science and Religion

Common Ground and Common Challenges

The Convergence of Science, Religion, and Values

Erika Erdmann

Library research assistant for neuroscientist and Nobel laureate R. W. Sperry for nine years, and co-author, with David Stover, of Beyond a World Divided *(Shambhala, 1991), which examines the contributions of Roger Sperry to bridging of the chasms between facts and values, science and religion*

This article, excerpted by the author from a larger paper submitted to the Parliament and to the Commission on Global Governance, begins to demonstrate how neuro-scientists and other scientists are taking seriously the impact of values and consciousness in all human endeavors, and the increasing need for interdisciplinary research and integration.

*H*umanity's attempts to progress toward a more humane future are blocked by two mutually exclusive world views. One segment of our population pursues facts at the expense of values, while another sector is preoccupied with values at the expense of facts. These two worlds, the world of science and the world of religion, are separated by a deep, harmful, and unnecessary chasm which has lasted too long. [...]

If the founders of the world's religions were with us now, they would implore us to benefit from new facts, new knowledge, and new insights as well as from wisdom and teachings of the religions. They would ask us to break down the walls into which we imprisoned their words and to free the spirit from which they were spoken—the spirit of true concern for the fate of humanity in the universe.

This is indeed being attempted by the work of the Institute on Religion in an Age of Science (IRAS), in Chicago, which combines great thinkers from both science and religion.*

Reading the article "Bridging Science and Values: A Unifying View of Mind and Brain" by Roger W. Sperry was a revelation to me. Here a neuroscientist of world renown, a Nobel laureate, merged intuition, vision, values, poetic expression, scientific expertise, and original thinking into a majestic whole.

As a neuroscientist, Sperry provoked his contemporaries through his conviction that "mind moves matter in the brain," not as an outside agent, but as an emergent with new and superior powers. Before he revolted against the neglect of consciousness in science, subjective experience had generally been considered by scientists as an ineffective byproduct of physico-chemical activity in neurons (with harmful results for a meaningful life). Sperry elevated its importance to that of a leading agent. Only ten

years after he had written his pathbreaking papers on the subject in the late sixties, the entire field of behavioral science was turned around. Consciousness, previously considered a subject unsuitable for scientific attention, became a predominant target of research. [...]

That religion should adjust to science has been demanded by other pioneers. Sperry for his part demands that science must also be changed. Instead of concentrating on the smallest possible building blocks in nature alone, and recreating from them a meaningless and purposeless world, Sperry draws attention to the essential role that the concept of "emergence" plays in reality.

Emergence occurs whenever two or more entities in combination create a new entity with new laws and properties formerly nonexistent in the universe. Thus, when subatomic particles combine into atoms, when atoms combine into molecules, when molecules combine into more complex structures, each time new creations occur with formerly nonexistent effects on the world.

Sperry calls these new effects and their role in our world "downward causation." Downward causation becomes significant through the gradual emergence of life, of consciousness, of purpose, of values, and the enormous power exerted by all these new phenomena, which disappear when reduced to their previous components. They are, however, quite real when seen as wholes; they are part of our world, and an increasingly important part of reality. Scientific logic cannot explain them away.

Values have thus become part of a new world view, combining science and religion. They have become the most powerful factors of our world. As Sperry states in this quotation which has become a classic:

Human values, viewed in an objective, scientific perspective, stand out as the most strategically powerful causal control force now shaping world events. More than any other causal system with which science now concerns itself, it is variables in human value systems that will determine the future.   ROGER SPERRY,
in Bridging Science and Values, *p.8*

* A worldwide organization founded in 1954.

FOR MORE INFORMATION:

The Chicago Center for Religion and Science, founded in 1988, is dedicated to relating religious traditions and the best of scientific knowledge. Contact them at:
CCRS/LST, 1100 East 55th St., Chicago, IL 60615-5199 USA

World Scientists' Warning to Humanity

Union of Concerned Scientists

A non-profit partnership organization of leading scientists and committed citizens which addresses the most serious environmental and security threats facing humanity. UCS conducts studies, promotes education of both the general public and world leaders, and seeks to influence public policy.

This comprehensive statement has been endorsed by over 1,680 members or fellows of national or international science academies, including 104 Nobel laureates. The signers include a substantial number of the senior officers from organizations such as the Third World Academy of Sciences, the Brazilian Academy of Sciences, the Royal Society of London, the Chinese Academy of Sciences, the Pontifical Academy of Sciences, and others. They come from 71 countries, including all of the 19 largest economic powers, all of the 12 most populous nations, 12 countries in Africa, 14 in Asia, 19 in Europe and 12 in Latin America. The document specifically appeals to the religions to assist all humanity in responding suitably to the needs presented.

Introduction

Human beings and the natural world are on a collision course. Human activities inflict harsh and often irreversible damage on the environment and on critical resources. If not checked, many of our current practices put at serious risk the future that we wish for human society and the plant and animal kingdoms, and may so alter the living world that it will be unable to sustain life in the manner that we know. Fundamental changes are urgent if we are to avoid the collision our present course will bring about.

The environment

The environment is suffering critical stress:

The atmosphere

Stratospheric ozone depletion threatens us with enhanced ultraviolet radiation at the earth's surface, which can be damaging or lethal to many life forms. Air pollution near ground level, and acid precipitation, are already causing widespread injury to humans, forests, and crops.

Water resources

Heedless exploitation of depletable ground water supplies endangers food production and other essential human systems. Heavy demands on the world's surface waters have resulted in serious shortages in some 80 countries, containing 40 percent of the world's population. Pollution of rivers, lakes, and ground water further limits the supply.

Oceans

Destructive pressure on the oceans is severe, particularly in the coastal regions which produce most of the world's food fish. The total marine catch is now at or above the estimated maximum sustainable yield. Some fisheries have already shown signs of collapse. Rivers carrying heaven burdens of eroded soil into the seas also carry industrial, municipal, agricultural, and livestock waste – some of it toxic.

Soil

Loss of soil productivity, which is causing extensive land abandonment, is a widespread byproduct of current practices in agriculture and animal husbandry. Since 1945, 11 percent of the earth's vegetated surface has been degraded – an area larger than India and China combined – and per capita food production in many parts of the world is decreasing.

Forests

Tropical rain forests, as well as tropical and temperate dry forests, are being destroyed rapidly. At present rates, some critical forest types will be gone in a few years, and most of the tropical rain forest will be gone before the end of the next century. With them will go large numbers of plant and animal species.

Living species

The irreversible loss of species, which by 2100 may reach one third of all species now living, is especially serious. We are losing the potential they hold for providing medicinal and other benefits, and the contribution that genetic diversity of life forms gives to the robustness of the world's biological systems and to the astonishing beauty of the earth itself.

Much of this damage is irreversible on a scale of centuries, or permanent. Increasing levels of gases in the atmosphere from human activities, including carbon dioxide released from fossil fuel burning and from deforestation, may alter climate on a global scale. Predictions of global warming are still uncertain with projected effects ranging from tolerable to very severe – but the potential risks are very great.

Our massive tampering with the world's interdependent web of life – coupled with the environmental damage inflicted by deforestation, species loss and climate change – could trigger widespread adverse effects, including unpredictable collapses of critical biological systems whose interactions and dynamics we only imperfectly understand.

Uncertainty over the extent of these effects cannot excuse complacency or delay in facing the threats.

Population

The earth is finite. Its ability to absorb wastes and destructive effluent is finite. Its abililty to provide food and energy is finite. Its ability to provide for growing numbers of people is finite. And we are fast approaching many of earth's limits. Current economic practices which damage the environment, in both developed and underdeveloped nations, cannot be continued without the risk that vital global systems will be damaged beyond repair.

Pressures resulting from unrestrained population growth put demands on the natural world that can overwhelm any efforts to achieve a sustainable future. If we are to halt the destruction of our environment, we must accept limits to that growth. A World Bank estimate indicates that world population will not stabilize at less than 12.4 billion, while the United Nations concludes that the eventual total could reach 14 billion, nearly tripling today's 5.4 billion. But, even at this moment, one person in five lives in absolute poverty without enough to eat, and one in ten suffers serious malnutrition.

No more than one or a few decades remain before the chance to avert the threats we now confront will be lost and the prospects for humanity immeasurably diminished.

WARNING:

We the undersigned, senior members of the world's scientific community, hereby warn all humanity of what lies ahead. A great change in our stewardship of the earth and the life on it is required if vast human misery is to be avoided and our global home on this planet is not to be irretrievably mutilated.

What we must do

Five inextricably linked areas must be addressed simultaneously:

1. **We must bring environmentally damaging activities under control to restore and protect the integrity of the earth's systems we depend on.**

We must, for example, move away from fossil fuels to more benign, inexhaustible energy sources to cut greenhouse gas emissions and the pollution of our air and water. Priority must be given to the development of energy resources matched to third world needs – small-scale and relatively easy to implement.

We must halt deforestation, injury to and loss of agricultural land, and the loss of plants, animals and marine species.

2. **We must manage resources crucial to human welfare more effectively.**

We must give high priority to efficient use of energy, water, and other materials, including expansion of conservation and recycling.

3. **We must stabilize population. This will be possible only if all nations recognize that it requires improved social and economic conditions and the adoption of effective, voluntary family planning.**

4. **We must reduce and eventually eliminate poverty.**

5. **We must insure sexual equality, and guarantee women control over their own reproductive decisions.**

The developed nations are the largest polluters in the world today. They must greatly reduce their overconsumption, if we are to reduce pressures on resources and the global environment. The developed nations have the obligation to provide aid and support to developing nations, because only the developed nations have the financial resources and the technical skills for these tasks.

Acting on this recognition is not altruism, but enlightened self-interest: whether industrialized or not, we all have but one lifeboat. No nation can escape from injury when global biological systems are damaged. No nation can escape from conflicts over increasingly scarce resources. In addition, environmental and economic instabilities will cause mass migrations with incalculable consequences for developed and undeveloped nations alike.

Developing nations must realize that environmental damage is one of the gravest threats they face, and that attempts to blunt it will be overwhelmed if their populations go unchecked. The greatest peril is to become trapped in spirals of environmental decline, poverty, and unrest, leading to social, economic, and environmental collapse.

Success in this global endeavor will require a great reduction in violence and war. Resources now devoted to the preparation and conduct of war – amounting to over $1 trillion annually – will be badly needed in the new tasks and should be diverted to the new challenges.

A new ethic is required – a new attitude towards discharging our responsibility for caring for ourselves and for the earth. We must recognize the earth's limited capacity to provide for us. We must recognize its fragility. We must no longer allow it to be ravaged. This ethic must motivate a great movement, convincing reluctant leaders and reluctant governments and reluctant peoples themselves to effect the needed changes.

The scientists issuing this warning hope that our message will reach and affect people everywhere. We need the help of many.

We require the help of the world community of scientists – natural, social, economic, political;

We require the help of the world's business and industrial leaders;

We require the help of the world's religious leaders; and

We require the help of the world's peoples.

We call on all to join us in this task.

Preserving and Cherishing the Earth
A Joint Appeal in Religion and Science

An Open Letter to the Religious Community from the Scientific Community

January 1990

The Earth is the birthplace of our species and, as far as we know, our only home. When our numbers were small and our technology feeble, we were powerless to influence the environment of our world. But today, suddenly, almost without anyone's noticing, our numbers have become immense and our technology has achieved vast, even awesome, powers. Intentionally or inadvertently, we are now able to make devastating changes in the global environment – an environment to which we and all other beings with which we share the Earth are meticulously and exquisitely adapted.

We are now threatened by self-inflicted, swiftly moving environmental alterations about whose long-term biological and ecological consequences we are still painfully ignorant: depletion of the protective ozone layer; a global warming unprecedented in the last 150 millennia; the obliteration of an acre of forest every second; the rapid-fire extinction of species; and the prospect of a global nuclear war which would put at risk most of the population of the Earth. There may well be other such dangers of which we are still unaware. Individually and cumulatively, they represent a trap being set for the human species, a trap we are setting for ourselves. However principled and lofty (or naive and shortsighted) the justifications may have been for the activities that brought forth these dangers, separately and taken together they now imperil our species and many others. We are close to committing – many would argue we are already committing – what in religious language is sometimes called "Crimes against Creation."

By their very nature these assaults on the environment were not caused by any one political group or any one generation. Intrinsically, they are transnational, transgenerational and transideological. So are all conceivable solutions. To escape these traps requires a perspective that embraces the peoples of the planet and all the generations yet to come.

Problems of such magnitude, and solutions demanding so broad a perspective, must be recognized from the outset as having a religious as well as a scientific dimension. Mindful of our common responsibility, we scientists – many of us long engaged in combatting the environmental crisis – urgently appeal to the world religious community to commit, in word and deed, and as boldly as is required, to preserving the environment of the Earth.

Some of the short-term mitigations of these dangers – such as greater energy efficiency, rapid banning of chloro-fluorocarbons, or modest reductions in nuclear arsenals – are comparatively easy and at some level are already underway. But other, more far-reaching, long-term, and effective

approaches will encounter widespread inertia, denial, and resistance. In this category are conversion from fossil fuels to a nonpolluting energy economy, a continuing swift reversal of the nuclear arms race and a voluntary halt to world population growth – without which many other approaches to preserve the environment will be nullified.

As with issues of peace, human rights, and social justice, religious institutions can be a strong force here, too, in encouraging national and international initiatives in both the private and public sectors, and in the diverse worlds of commerce, education, culture, and mass communications.

The environmental crisis requires radical changes not only in public policy, but also in individual behavior. The historical record makes clear that religious teaching, example, and leadership are able to influence personal conduct and commitment powerfully.

As scientists, many of us have had profound experiences of awe and reverence before the universe. We understand that what is regarded as sacred is more likely to be treated with care and respect. Our planetary home should be so regarded. Efforts to safeguard and cherish the environment need to be infused with a vision of the sacred. At the same time, a much wider and deeper understanding of science and technology is needed. If we do not understand the problem, it is unlikely we will be able to fix it. Thus, there is a vital role for both religion and science.

We know that the well-being of our planetary environment is already a source of profound concern in your councils and congregations. We hope this appeal will encourage a spirit of common cause and joint action to help preserve the Earth.

"The Open Letter to the Religious Community from the Scientific Community" was signed by:

Carl Sagan, *Cornell University, Ithaca, NY*
Richard L. Garwin
  IBM Corp., Yorktown Heights, NY
Hans A. Bethe, *Cornell University, Ithaca, NY*
Elise Boulding
  University of Colorado, Boulder, CO
M. I. Budyko
  State Hydrological Institute, Leningrad
S. Chandrasekhar
  University of Chicago, Chicago, IL
Paul J. Crutzen
  Max Planck Institute for Chemistry, Mainz, West Germany
Margaret B. Davis
  University of Minnesota, Minneapolis, MN
Freeman J. Dyson
  Institute for Advanced Study, Princeton, NJ
Gyorgi S. Golitsyn
  Academy of Sciences of the U.S.S.R. Moscow, U.S.S.R.
Stephen Jay Gould
  Harvard University, Cambridge, MA
James E. Hansen
  NASA Goddard Inst. for Space Studies, NY
Mohammed Kassas
  University of Cairo, Cairo, Egypt
Henry W. Kendall
  Union of Concerned Scientists, Cambridge, MA

Motoo Kimura
  National Institute of Genetics, Mishima, Japan
Thomas Malone
  St. Joseph College, West Hartford, CT
Lynn Margulis
  University of Massachusetts, Amherst, MA
Peter Raven
  Missouri Botanical Garden, St. Louis, MO
Roger Revelle
  University of California, San Diego La Jolla, CA
Walter Orr Roberts, *National Center for Atmospheric Research, Boulder, CO*
Abdus Salam, *International Centre for Theoretical Physics, Trieste, Italy*
Stephen H. Schneider, *National Center for Atmospheric Research, Boulder, CO*
Nans Suess
  University of California, San Diego La Jolla, CA
O. B. Toon
  NASA Ames Research Center, Moffett Field, CA
Richard P. Turco
  University of California, Los Angeles, CA
Yevgeniy P. Velikhov
  Academy of Sciences of the U.S.S.R. Moscow, U.S.S.R.
Carl Friedrich von Weizsacker
  Max Planck Institute, Starnberg, West Germany
Sir Frederick Warmer
  Essex University, Colchester, United Kingdom

Victor F. Weisskopf
  Massachusetts Institute of Technology Cambridge, MA
Jerome B. Wiesner
  Massachusetts Institute of Technology Cambridge, MA
Robert R. Wilson
  Cornell University, Ithaca, NY
Alexey V. Yablokov
  Academy of Sciences of the U.S.S.R. Moscow, U.S.S.R.

(Affiliations for identification purposes only.)

from the Office of Joint Appeal in Religion & Science (now named The National Religious Parnership)

FOR MORE INFORMATION:

National Religious Partnership for the Environment,
1047 Amsterdam Avenue
New York, NY 10025 USA;
tel. (212) 316-7441

Also see addresses on p. 322 for the Union of Concerned Scientists and for ordering NRPE Program Kits.

The Seville Statement on Violence

Stating that peace is possible because war is not a biological necessity, this document was written by an international team of scientists in 1986 for the United Nations-sponsored International Year of Peace. Based on scientific evidence and endorsed by scientific and professional organizations around the world, the statement was adopted by UNESCO in 1989.

Believing that it is our responsibility to address from our particular disciplines the most dangerous and destructive activities of our species, violence and war; recognizing that science is a human cultural product which cannot be definitive or all encompassing; and gratefully acknowledging the support of the authorities of Seville and representatives of the Spanish UNESCO, we, the undersigned scholars from around the world and from relevant sciences, have met and arrived at the following statement on violence. In it we challenge a number of alleged biological findings that have been used, even by some in our disciplines, to justify violence and war. Because the alleged findings have contributed to an atmosphere of pessimism in our time, we submit that the open, considered rejection of these misstatements can contribute significantly to the International Year of Peace.

Misuse of scientific theories and data to justify violence and war is not new but has been made since the advent of modern science. For example, the theory of evolution has been used to justify not only war, but also genocide, colonialism, and the suppression of the weak.

We state our position in the form of five propositions. We are aware that there are many other issues about violence and war that could be fruitfully addressed from the standpoint of our disciplines, but we restrict ourselves here to what we consider a most important first step.

1) It is scientifically incorrect to say that we have inherited a tendency to make war from our animal ancestors. Although fighting occurs widely throughout animal species, only a few cases of destructive intra-species fighting between organized groups have ever been recorded among naturally living species, and none of these involve the use of tools designed to be weapons. Normal predatory feeding upon other species cannot be equated with intra-species violence. Warfare is a particularly human phenomenon and does not occur in other animals.

The fact that warfare has changed so radically over time indicates that it is a product of culture. Its biological connection is primarily through language which makes possible the coordination of groups, the transmission of technology, and the use of tools. War is biologically possible, but it is not inevitable, as evidenced by its variation in occurrence and nature over time and space. There are cultures which have not engaged in war for centuries, and there are cultures which have engaged in war frequently at some times and not at others.

2) It is scientifically incorrect to say that war or any other violent behavior is genetically programmed into our human nature. While genes are involved at all levels of nervous system function, they provide a developmental potential that can be actualized only in conjuction with the ecological and social environment. While individuals vary in their predispositions to be affected by their experience, it is the interaction between their genetic endowment and conditions of nurturance that determines their personalities. Except for rare pathologies, the genes do not produce individuals necessarily predisposed to violence. Neither do they determine the opposite. While genes are co-involved in establishing our behavioral capacities, they do not by themselves specify the outcome.

3) It is scientifically incorrect to say that in the course of human evolution there has been a selection for aggressive behavior more than for other kinds of behavior. In all well-studied species, status within the group is achieved by the ability to cooperate and to fulfill social functions relevant to the structure of that group. *Dominance* involves social bondings and affiliations; it is not simply a matter of the possession and use of superior physical power, although it does involve aggressive behaviors. Where genetic selection for aggressive behavior has been artificially instituted in animals, it has rapidly succeeded in producing hyper-aggressive individuals. This indicates that aggression was not maximally selected under natural conditions. When such experientially-created hyper-aggressive animals are present in a social group, they either disrupt its social structure or are driven out. Violence is neither in our evolutionary legacy nor in our genes.

4) It is scientifically incorrect to say that humans have a *violent brain*. While we do have the neural apparatus to act violently, it is not automatically activated by internal or external stimuli. Like higher primates and unlike other animals, our higher neural processes filter such stimuli before they can be acted upon. How we act is shaped by how we have been conditioned and socialized. There is nothing in our neural physiology that compels us to react violently.

5) It is scientifically incorrect to say that war is caused by *instinct* or any single motivation. The emergence of modern warfare has been a journey from the primacy of emotional and motivational factors, sometimes called *instincts*, to the primacy of cognitive factors. Modern war involves institutional use of personal characteristics such as obedience, suggestibility, and idealism, social skills such as language, and rational considerations such as cost-calculation, planning, and information processing. The technology of modern war has exaggerated traits associated with violence both in the training of actual combatants and in the preparation of support for a war in the general population. As a result of this exaggeration, such traits are often mistaken to be the causes rather than the consequences of the process.

We conclude that biology does not condemn humanity to war, and that humanity can be freed from the bondage of biological pessimism and empowered with confidence to take on the transformative tasks needed in this International Year of Peace and in the years to come. Although these tasks are mainly institutional and collective, they also rest upon the consciousness of individual participants for whom pessimism and optimism are crucial factors. Just as *wars begin in the minds of men*, peace also begins in our minds. The same species that invented war is capable of inventing peace. The responsibility lies with each of us.

SIGNERS

David Adams, *Psychology*
S.A. Barnett, *Ethology*
N.P. Bechtereva, *Neurophysiology*
Bonnie Frank Carter, *Psychology*
José M. Rodríguez Delgado, *Neurophysiology*
José Lewis Díaz, *Ethology*
Andrzej Eliasz, *Individual Differences Psychology*
Santiago Genovés, *Biological Anthropology*
Benson E. Ginsburg, *Behavior Genetics*

Jo Groebel, *Social Psychology*
Samir-Kumar Ghosh, *Sociology*
Robert Hinde, *Animal Behavior*
Richard E. Leakey, *Physical Anthropology*
Taha H. Malasi, *Psychiatry*
J. Martin Ramírez, *Psychobiology*
Federico Mayor Zaragoza, *Biochemistry*
Diana L. Mendoza, *Ethology*
Ashis Nandy, *Political Psychology*
John Paul Scott, *Animal Behavior*
Rita Wahlstrom, *Psychology*

The New Consciousness

Dom Bede Griffiths

Catholic Christian monk, philosopher and author who established a monastic community in India in 1955, to "find the other half of my soul"

Bede Griffiths also discovered new insights into the intuitive and mystical aspects of consciousness; his gift to us is his harmonizations of the religious and mystical with the scientific, of the East with the West, of the past with the future. This article, expressing Bede Griffith's prophetic vision, is his acceptance speech for the John Harriott Memorial Award. Dictated in Shantivanam Ashram in Tamil Nadu, India, this is his last article written and published during his lifetime. It was first printed in *The Tablet* (of London) on January 16, 1993.

*W*e are entering a new age. The European civilization which we have known for the past 2,000 years is giving way to a global civilization, which will no longer be centered in Europe but will have its focus more in Asia, Africa, and South America. Christianity will no longer be a separate religion but will be seen in the context of the religious traditions of humankind as a whole.

As we enter this new civilization, the meeting-place of East and West, and of the nations of the world, will be science. The changes in contemporary Western science have provided a new outlook on life for humanity as a whole. The central point is the new understanding of the universe which is no longer perceived as consisting of solid bodies moving in space and time but rather, according to quantum theory, as a field of energy pervaded by consciousness. Western scientists, for the first time, have seriously faced the fact that if they want to understand the universe, they have to understand their own consciousness. A leader in this development was David Bohm, for he was one of the first scientists to take seriously the place of consciousness in scientific understanding.

The new understanding of science and consciousness provides, as it were, a platform on which religions can meet. We are beginning to see that we can now interpret the religious traditions, particularly the myths and symbols of all the scriptures, within the context of a world where science and consciousness interrelate.

In this new global civilization, Christianity, as I understand it, will be seen in relation to Hinduism, Buddhism, Taoism, Sufism, and the primordial religious traditions – the Australian, the Native American, the African, and so on. A new consciousness is emerging, moving beyond the rational mind with its awareness of separate entities and its dualistic approach. We are beginning to discover the unitive consciousness which goes beyond dualistic awareness.

David Bohm speaks, as a theoretical physicist, of unity and interconnectedness in what he calls the implicate order, prior to the world of separate entities which is our normal experience. The implicate order is constantly unfolding, giving rise to the explicate order of particular forms and structures. This is where the new scientific understanding of the universe meets with the non-dualist traditions of Hinduism, Buddhism, and so on. As we move beyond the present religious forms and structures we begin to see that, behind and beyond their diversity, there is an underlying unity. All the religions are expressing symbolically something which cannot be expressed in rational terms.

Any attempt to express fully that which is beyond expression is bound to fail. The new *Catechism of the Catholic Church* attempts to put the content of the Catholic faith into rational discursive terms. The aim is illusory because the *content* of the Catholic faith, in common with that of the other great religious traditions, transcends all rational, discursive thought. When he had finished his great theological work, the *Summa Theologica*, St. Thomas Aquinas realized that all he had written was as straw in comparison to his mystical experience. He was fully aware that no image or concept is remotely adequate to the fullness of the faith.

Within Christianity the focus will be on the mystery of faith, which Jesus called the mystery of the Kingdom of God and St. Paul called the mystery of Christ. A mystery cannot be expressed rationally or logically, but it can be symbolized. All scientific theories and all religious doctrines are in fact symbolic structures. In each religion the symbolic structures work by opening the human mind to the transcendent Reality, to the truth. The symbolic structures within the religions each have their unique value but all have limitations because they are socially and culturally conditioned.

The unique value of Christianity is its profoundly historic structure. That to me is a key point. Christ is not an *avatara*. The Incarnation is a unique historic event and Jesus a unique historic person. In gathering all things, all of humanity, and all matter, into one in himself, he transforms the world, bringing the cosmos, its matter and its processes, back to its source in the transcendent Reality whom he called *Abba*, Father. This is unique. At the same time, one of the main limitations of institutional Christianity is its exclusivism, which stems from its cultural background in ancient Judaism. This exclusivism particularly will have to be transcended as we move more and more deeply into the mystery of Christ. We are in a position now to be open to all the religious traditions of the world, being aware of their limitations but also, most importantly, realizing their unity in the depth-dimension which underlies them all; and that, of course, is the mystical dimension.

Many people today are discovering the mystical dimension in religion. In Christianity, once we get beyond the doctrinal systems, we have a long tradition of mystical wisdom beginning with St. John and St. Paul, going through Clement of Alexandria, Origen and the Greek Fathers, and on to St. Augustine; and later St. Thomas Aquinas and Meister Eckhart. And now we can relate that to the traditions of Tibetan Buddhism, Hinduism, and the other great religions.

The Christian Gospel as originally proclaimed was: "Repent, for the kingdom of heaven is at hand." At that time the old structures were breaking down and the kingdom of God was emerging. The Apocalypse would put it, "I saw a new heaven and a new earth. The old heaven and the old earth had passed away. And a Voice said, 'Behold, I make all things new.'" That is always happening.

I think that is exactly where we are today: the breakdown of the old civilization and of the whole order which we knew, and, within that, the rebirth of meaning, penetrated by a new consciousness. Science today recognizes that all order comes out of chaos. When the old structures break down and the traditional forms begin to disintegrate, precisely then in the chaos, a new form, a new structure, a new order of being and consciousness emerges.

The old is always dying and the new is emerging, and that which is new socially and culturally transforms the old. This is really an apocalyptic age. Within this context we can take the forms of Christian symbolism, but we can also take forms like the coming of the Buddha Maitreya or the last *avatara* of Kali. Every religion looks forward to a time when the end will come and the new birth will take place. So in a very wonderful way we are at the birth of a new age and a new consciousness.

"I have felt it myself. The glitter of nuclear weapons. It is irresistible if you come to them as a scientist. To feel it's there in your hands – to release the energy that fuels the stars. To let it do your bidding. To perform these miracles – to lift a million tons of rock into the sky. It is something that gives people an illusion of illimitable power and it is, in some ways, responsible for all our troubles, I would say – this what you might call technical arrogance that overcomes people when they see what they can do with their minds."

from the Transcript of *The Day After Trinity:
J. Robert Oppenheimer and the Atomic Bomb,*
Kent, OH: PTV Publications, 1981, p. 30

"To a large extent, the future lies before us like a vast wilderness of unexplored reality. The God who created and sustained the evolving universe through eons of progress and development has not placed our generation at the tag end of the creative process. God has placed us at a new beginning. We are here for the future."

SIR JOHN TEMPLETON

Voices of Dispossessed and Indigenous Peoples

Indigenous Peoples in the Modern World

"In many ways, the contemporary state of indigenous peoples mirrors the future of us all if we continue to treat the Earth and its peoples as we have treated them."
JULIAN BURGER

For the next several pages extensive excerpts have been reprinted from *The Gaia Atlas of First Peoples: A Future for the Indigenous World,* by Julian Burger with campaigning groups and native peoples worldwide. Rearranged by the Editor, the quotations highlight the views of indigenous spokespersons; their voices are accompanied by Julian Burger's commentary.

*T*his book [*The Gaia Atlas*] is written in the belief that individuals can contribute to greater justice for indigenous peoples. Part, although not all, of the blame for the destruction of indigenous communities can be laid at the door of the rich. Governments, banks, and companies have often pursued policies and backed regimes that are unfavorable to indigenous peoples, mainly to supply market demand. It is the consumer's hands on the chain saw. But ordinary people are not powerless. We may each have a small voice, but when harmonized with others, we can make powerful institutions listen. (p.10)

Facing threats to their survival

*N*othing has been so destructive to indigenous peoples as what we call progress. Mines, dams, roads, colonization schemes, plantations, cattle ranches, and other expressions of "economic development" have forced indigenous peoples from lands they have occupied for centuries and severely damaged local environments. Deforestation, desertification, and degradation of fragile, marginal lands first affect indigenous peoples, the traditional inhabitants. (p.75)

In the long hundred years since the white man came, I have seen my freedom disappear like the salmon going mysteriously out to sea. The white man's strange customs which I could not understand, pressed down on me until I could no longer breathe. And when I fought to protect my land and home, I was called a 'savage.' When I neither understood nor welcomed the white man's way of life, I was called lazy. When I tried to lead my people, I was stripped of my authority.

CHIEF DAN GEORGE, Vancouver

In Australia, a country designated by the white pioneers as *terra nullius* (or, uninhabited), there were some 500 distinct peoples with different languages and well-defined territories. A century later, the population had been reduced to one-fifth.

The colonizers came with a sword in one hand and a Bible in the other, "to bring light to those in darkness, and also to get rich," as the soldier-chronicler Bernal Diaz del Castillo put it. Impervious to the highly developed spiritual awareness of the people, they sought to convert them – often on pain of death – to an alien religion. (p.76)

We understand that many of these racialist attitudes are subconscious and not premeditated, but nevertheless they reflect how deeply dominant ideology has penetrated society.
MAPUCHE INDIAN

We do not wish to destroy your religion, or take it from you. We only want to enjoy our own.

RED JACKET, Iroquois

The white man's advanced technological capacity has occurred as a result of his lack of regard for the spiritual path and for the way of all living things. The white man's desire for material possessions and power has blinded him to the pain he has caused Mother Earth by his quest for what he calls natural resources.

THOMAS BANYACYA,
Hopi village leader

Let me ask you this – why are there only eight inches of topsoil left in America, when there once were some 18 inches at the time of the Declaration of Independence in 1776? Where goes our sacred Earth?   HOBART KEITH,
Oglala Sioux

When forest is cleared for settlement, agriculture, grazing, mining, dams, logging, or to supply fuel, there are three interrelated repercussions. Indigenous peoples lose their land and their role as forest managers; the land is over-exploited and given little chance to recover; and uncontrolled forest fires release carbon dioxide, causing the "greenhouse effect" and adding to climate problems. (p.90)

Attitudes of the first people

*A*ccording to indigenous law, humankind can never be more than a trustee of the land, with a collective responsibility to preserve it. The predominant Western worldview is that nature must be studied, dissected, and mastered, and progress measured by the ability to extract secrets and wealth from the Earth. The First World has dominated the Earth to enrich itself in many cases. First peoples do not consider the land as merely an economic resource. Their ancestral lands are literally the source of life, and their distinct ways of life are developed and defined in relationship to the environment around them. First peoples are people of the land... all first people know the extent of their lands, and they know how the land, water, and other resources need to be shared. They understand only too well that to harm the land is to destroy ourselves, since we are all part of the same organism. They sense, too, that the Earth will survive long after human beings. (p.23)

At first I thought I was fighting to save rubber trees, then I thought I was fighting to save the Amazon rain forest. Now I realize I am fighting for humanity.

CHICO MENDEZ

I am trying to save the knowledge that the forests and this planet are alive, to give it back to you who have lost the understanding.   PAULINHO PAIAKAN,
a leader of the Kayapo of Brazil

Indigenous science

*I*n many parts of the world indigenous societies classify soils, climate, plant and animal species and recognize their special characteristics.... The Hanunoo people of the Philippines, for example, distinguish 1,600 plant species in their forest, 400 more than scientists working in the same area.... Nearly 75 percent of 121 plant-derived prescription drugs used worldwide were discovered following leads from indigenous medicine. Globally, indigenous peoples use 3,000 different species of plants to control fertility alone. The Kallaywayas, wandering healers of Bolivia, make use of 600 medicinal herbs; traditional healers in Southeast Asia may employ as many as 6,500 plants for drugs.... (p.32)

Militarization

*M*ost of our contemporary conflicts directly affect indigenous peoples. The superpowers see their homelands as "empty territory" – testing grounds for nuclear and chemical weapons. Newly independent states wanting to establish their borders and develop their economies incorporate tribal territories as part of their nation-building efforts. Sometimes indigenous territories have been invaded and occupied for strategic and economic reasons. And when conflicts break out the superpowers are often involved.

Of the 120 or more wars in the world today, 72 percent are conflicts between central state governments and a distinct nation of peoples living within its borders. (p.108)

Costs to indigenous peoples from militarization

- Almost all nuclear tests have taken place on indigenous lands and waters.... The radiation released during nuclear testing damages the environment, contaminates the staple foods of indigenous people, and increases the risk [and incidence] of birth defects, miscarriages, sterility, cancer and other diseases.

- The USA, Britain and France have exploded over 215 nuclear bombs in the South Pacific... After the atomic explosions on the Polynesian island of Bikini in the 1950s, 70 out of 1,093 people died of cancer in three years.

- Global military expenditure equals the total debt of the developing countries.

- Since the military annexation of Tibet, a Buddhist state with a central belief in nonviolence, by China, there are now well over 100,000 Tibetan refugees.

- Over one million people have been displaced because of violence in Guatemala.   Costs identified
on pp.110-112

Alternative visions and the future

Now we shall not rest until we have regained our rightful place. We shall tell our young people what we know. We shall send them to the corners of the earth to learn more. They shall lead us.   Declaration of the
Five County Cherokees

*I*ndigenous peoples are not passive victims. Nor have they ever been. In the past they resisted colonialism through negotiation, political protest, civil disobedience, or force of arms. Sometimes they succeeded, sometimes they won partial guarantees of their territory, and sometimes they were overwhelmed by numbers and superior military technology. But the resistance has not stopped. Today's movement is part of this continuing process, and the struggle to survive as a people is as urgent as ever.

Today's indigenous peoples are adopting modern and creative political techniques – using the media, joining forces, and gaining support from the wider community. Recently, indigenous peoples have scored some important victories. (p.136)

There are over 1,000 indigenous organizations worldwide – most of them established in the last 20 years. The forces of change – political, social, economic, and global – have lent impetus to this new movement.... New international laws, too, offer a legal and moral framework for indigenous peoples. The right to self-determination is now enshrined in two covenants of the United Nations. And there are international laws on genocide and racial discrimination. (p.138)

We define our rights in terms of self-determination. We are not looking to dismember your States and you know it. But we do insist on the right to control our territory, our resources, the organization of our societies, our own decision-making institutions, and the maintenance of our own cultures and ways of life.

GEOFF CLARKE, National Coalition of Aboriginal
Organizations of Australia, addressing the
International Labour Organization, 1988

Our nations have a natural and rightful place within the family of Nations of the World. Our political, legal, social, and economic systems developed in accordance with the laws of the creator since time immemorial and continue to this day. Union of British Columbia Chiefs to UN Working Group on Indigenous Populations, 1987

We hereby demand yet again recognition of our humanity and our land rights. Hear us, White Australia, we are the spirit of the land. Our name is humanity. Our aims are self-determination and justice. We will not be defeated. We are our history, we are our culture, we are our land. We are now. Declaration of the People of Musgrave Park, Australia, 1982

Global voices of indigenous peoples

We are on the one hand the most oppressed people on the globe. On the other hand, we are the hope for the future of the planet. The peoples that surround us now are beginning to experience in the 20th century that there are limitations to the kinds of economic organization that define their societies. JOHN MOHAWK, Haudenosaunee writer

*I*ndigenous peoples are one of the most persistent voices of conscience, alerting humankind to the dangers of environmental destruction. And as the world searches for alternative strategies to deal with global problems, it is turning more and more to indigenous peoples. Much of their respect for nature, their methods of resource management, social organization, values, and culture are finding echoes in the writing of scientists, philosophers, politicians, and thinkers. (p.166)

We see it like this: it is as if we are all in a canoe traveling through time. If someone begins to make a fire in their part of the canoe, and another begins to pour water inside the canoe, or another begins to piss in the canoe, it will affect us all. And it is the responsibility of each person in the canoe to ensure that it is not destroyed. Our planet is like one big canoe traveling through time. AILTON KRENAK, Brazilian Union of Indian Nations (UNI)

We need to start educating the West. . . teaching them some social alternatives which place priority on humankind – not profits, not political power, not bombs, but on humanity. JOHN MOHAWK

The concept of development in a developing country is not necessarily the same as that understood by one belonging to a "developed" country. In a developing country the idea of development is closely linked with the wish for freedom – freedom to run one's own affairs the way one knows and believes, based on familiar traditions and ways of life. Freedom is in fact development, whether material progress and wealth are realized to the extent expected or not.

FRANCIS BUGOTU, Solomon Islands

It seems to us that from the earliest times, man's natural state was to be free as our grandfathers told us, and we believe that freedom is inherent to life. We recognize this principle as the key to peace, respect for one another and the understanding of the natural law that prevails over all the universe. Adherence to this law is the only salvation of our future on the planet, Mother Earth. CHIEF OREN LYONS, Onondaga

Excerpted with permission from *The Gaia Atlas of First Peoples*, by Julian Burger with indigenous peoples worldwide

The Old Way Culture

In a despondent mood on a warm grey afternoon, I asked Talks With Loons if the Old Way is forever gone from this land, if the few aged Healers and Grandmothers are the last vestiges of a way of life in its death-throes. I didn't know whether she'd answer directly, as her way was more often that of subtle Raven. For a few long minutes she became absorbed in reflection, during which she directed me with her eyes to observe the prairie about us. Then her gaze lost its focus as it seemed to flow into and dwell within the panorama before us, and she spoke:

"Is there still life in the Rocks,
does Father Sun still visit the dawn,
does the She-Swallow diving at our heads
in defense of her young on the limb above
still Walk the Path?

"The Old Way was not born with our species
and it will not be buried with our species.
As we sit here, the Grasses in the fullness of their bloom
whisper teachings that were secret to us yesterday.
As long as the Grass shall grow,
as long as the Rocks are here to speak,
the Old Way survives."

TAMARACK SONG, from *Journey to the Ancestral Self*, published by Station Hill Press. Tamarack Song is founder of the Teaching Drum Outdoor School in Three Lakes, WI, USA. She Who Talks with Loons was (most likely) Canadian Cree-Ojibway-Metis.

Fugitive Peoples Find a Voice

Rev. Richard Leucke

Director of Studies, Community Renewal Society in Chicago, Illinois

Choosing our future wisely requires insight into the problems of the past and present. Humanity's mistakes are clearly evident in their impact on those who have been forceably separated from their cultures and lands. Whatever the causes – ranging from colonialism and ecological disasters to wars and cultural/religious conflict – the Parliament of the World's Religions recognized these matters as among the most significant issues of our time.

Because the news media grabbed onto some of the conflict expressed when these issues were aired at the Parliament, giving the whole event an inaccurate aura, this article and the next provide a factual corrective; more importantly, the authors introduce important dimensions of the issue, including the dignity and persistence of those whose voices speak for all of the dispossessed among us.

Even as fugitives or disempowered minorities, these peoples carry with them insight, tradition, and culture. Those of us in dominant cultures can learn much about ourselves – our hospitality to strangers and the ways our choices, governments, and businesses participate in disenfranchising people in other countries. These are lessons the community of religions needs to learn and teach if we claim compassion as our ideal and are guided by a global ethic.

---

*T*he flight of displaced peoples within and across national borders had increased sevenfold in the previous fifteen years. In many instances, religions were being used to justify or intensify inter-group conflicts, though in some places religious people were working to moderate disputes. It was with a sense of this growing worldwide phenomenon that program planners for the Parliament designated a three-hour assembly in which to hear from the peoples most affected; there was also a sense of risk.

A full year before the Parliament convened, members of refugee communities responded to a call from Community Renewal Society, an association related to the United Church of Christ which for more than a century had cooperated with newcomer communities in Chicago. There was no need to send overseas for the first "voices" – refugees from every continent had found their way to Chicago as to other large cities. People from ten African countries chose to confer with one another before joining with people from other continents.

The first larger exploratory gathering raised sensitive questions and reached some noteworthy decisions. The group rejected the designation "voices from the margins" (which appeared on early program grids) in favor of another proposed term, "voices of the dispossessed." Among many forms of dispossession, they would begin with what seemed most basic: loss of lived-in land, which could mean (in addition to hunger and slaughter) a loss of identity and community, of place names and children's names, of work which had proved sufficient for previous generations, of rites of passage, of healing practices and, not least, of religious places, holy objects, and sacred texts. While some of those present referred to unemployment or lack of access to services like medical care, most preferred to speak of what had been taken from them rather than of what was not now being given to them.

Would the Parliament be able to do anything about this? The questioners were at first taken aback by the idea that the world meeting would lack formal institutional power, that the most to be expected was some kind of communication or influence. Why should they participate in what seemed an impractical exercise? As often as this question was raised, first answers were rejected. They would not appear in an assembly to seek pity or to ask for charity. They would not accept a role as victims or merely express resignation. More acceptable reasons came to expression in the very first meeting, and these were repeated in many subsequent communications.

Though refugees had lost everything, they could nevertheless say and show to the world assembly that they were still alive and that they were here – *in spite of*. A Parliament that was trying to build bridges *between* world religions might then also give attention to a growing split *within* religious bodies between rich and poor. In making a positive affirmation of faith and spirit, the world's outcasts would be claiming a proper place in this meeting of world religions. They would be expressing a spirituality which was based, to be sure, in their traditional or name religions, but which was also an "alternate spirituality," one of utter dependence on God and of critical independence from failing institutions – a spirituality that is needed to transform religions and societies.

They might also be able to enter their experience into the deliberations of the Parliament on issues of the earth, development, education, health, the future of communities and of world cities. Some who described this possibility later expressed disappointment that no chair was set for anyone from this group in the councils for the Global Ethic.

Agreement on a format for the assembly took much longer. Some overview would need to be given in order to convey the worldwide extent of this problem – but this should not reduce tragic personal and social devastation to statistics. A media-competent member from São Paulo offered to prepare a slide show with voice-over, to which all participants could contribute sights and sounds from their own settings and for which additional materials could be procured from the United Nations High Commissioner for Refugees. The Bahá'ís – whose member described persecution in other homelands – made production facilities available in the media center of their national temple in Wilmette, Illinois.

Specific human stories would need to be told in this assembly without this becoming overly verbal and repetitive. Speakers were encouraged to accompany their stories with instruments, songs, or dances that were actually being used for this purpose by their people. Selection was made of ten storytellers, with hopes of adding two more: one from the Bosnian Muslims and one from the Serbian Orthodox who would describe how they kept faith amid the bitter warfare of their peoples – but misgivings in this instance proved insurmountable.

Since the "voices" differed in detail, their messages would have to be summarized and formulated in a challenge to the Parliament. Among names proposed from every continent, the choice fell to Waldemar Boff of Brazil, a former Franciscan who had formed Serviço de Educaçao e Organização Popular in Petrópolis, Rio de Janeiro.

Finally, if people in the audience were to be more than passive observers, some opportunity should be provided for their engagement and response. Memoranda were sent to participating leaders or teachers of the various religions asking for their distinctive answers to four general questions:

1. Does your tradition include a refugee or flight story among its founding narratives?

2. Does it include a teaching concerning the importance of land?

3. Does it have something to say about the spiritual importance of welcoming strangers?

4. Does it envision a divine future or an ideal society in which families, peoples, nations and tongues will be more diversified or more mixed?

*I*n her opening remarks to the assembly, Yvonne Delk of Community Renewal Society suggested that everyone present should be asking these questions. She repeated that the purpose of this assembly was not to raise political differences – there would be no opportunity and no attempt to tell "both sides." The point was, rather, to face a growing worldwide social reality in which religions were clearly implicated, and to do so in the terms of those who were most manifestly affected. Some testimonies would include cultural expressions, but these were by no means to be viewed as folkloric entertainment.

The Haitians entered with a Creole song composed by a priest of Fermathe and a statement by the bishop of Jérémie. "Voices" followed from African America, Liberia, Ghana, Ethiopia, and South Africa. ("How did we survive?" the South African concluded. "– By faith!") Stories were told from Tibet, from Kashmir, and from fishing communities in India that were losing not only their land but their waters. (Some were losing centuries-old villages and sacred stones beneath the waters of a controversial new dam.) During the Kashmiri presentation, a strong objection was raised from the floor against

"politicizing" a meeting of religions. When this protest rose again during the presentation of a Punjabi Sikh, Parliament leaders moved to close the assembly. Audience engagement had begun sooner than anyone planned – some people were expressing protest, others were clasping one another and chanting a song of hope.

The assembly did not hear an 11th-century universal hymn by a Sikh chorus, nor the story of an Afghan refugee who was to include the condition of women in her own and other countries, nor the narrative of a Guatemalan refugee who now conducted Mayan studies in Costa Rica and who had trained Guatemalan youth in Chicago as sacred dancers, nor did the audience hear the summarizing challenger. These now joined the previous presenters, singers, and dancers who were moving in a circle to Menominee-Patowatomi drums, a circle which enlarged to enfold the audience.

The program chair of the Parliament explained on the evening news that "the real world had intervened" in the Parliament of the World's Religions. The " dispossessed" presented a statement of their hopes for the next Parliament to the executive director, who said the best response would be an end to all dispossession during the intervening years. The Guatemalans, who professed no surprise at what had taken place (they had been "silenced for 500 years"), burned sage incense to invoke courage and read the group statement from the stage of a subsequent assembly.

The "dispossessed" also convened five noonday conversations in the nearby Chicago Cultural Center to continue their conversation with one another and include congregation, neighborhood, and civic leaders of the city. The Tibetans, Latin Americans, Haitians, Africans, and people from India took turns initiating these discussions. The India panel reflected the interreligious conflict between Hindus, Muslims, Sikhs, and Christians which had erupted in the assembly. The priest-organizer of fish workers described a struggle on three India coasts in which members of all these religious groups successfully cooperate.

In a post-Parliament meeting, the Chicago "voices" viewed their film once again and reviewed their experience. They noted that a primary purpose of the Parliament was being accomplished in their own new communications with one another. They repeated the only words of Waldemar Boff to the Parliament, which were pronounced in a blessing on the 21st century from the bandshell during the closing assembly. The blessing began:

"In the name of the living and loving God of all religions, in the name of the two-thirds of humankind who live in dispossession...."

Voices of the Dispossessed

David Nelson

Music producer and member of the Vedanta Society of Southern California

David Nelson wrote the essay which follows as part of his privately-published *Notes and Reflections on the Parliament of the World's Religions, 1993*.

*T*he Monday morning plenary of the Parliament turned out to be a dramatic high point. It was one of the few events deemed newsworthy by the press, though for all the wrong reasons.

The plenary "Voices of the Dispossessed" belongs to 18.9 million international refugees [the number has increased dramatically since 1993], to an equal number who are displaced within their own national borders, and to countless others who suffer dispossession in subtler forms of discrimination and human rights abuses. The organizers felt that these issues, plaguing every continent, had to be faced early in the Parliament. They planned this plenary session around experiences of loss but also to identify affirmations of the spirit that have given the victimized around the world the strength to survive.

The opening prayer by Charles Nolley, Director of Media Production of the National Assembly of Bahá'ís, preceded a filmed presentation by Luis Valenzuela of Brazil and Lourdes Sylvia of Cuba. The film portrayed how today 500 million people go hungry. Many have a short life-expectancy. To 1.5 billion of the world's citizens no medical care is available. Unemployment, poverty, and the lack of water and life's other basic necessities are rife. One out of every 135 people on Earth has been uprooted by persecution, and most of these are women and children. Dispossession is not the natural human condition but the product of processes that create extreme wealth and extreme poverty. Dispossession destroys the sense of human community, it destroys sacred places, and it creates the human degradation of homelessness.

Policies of border control leave the causes of flight unanswered, and thus far humanitarian efforts have proven inadequate. They can also serve as a smokescreen, creating the illusion that we are doing something. Dropping parcels of food from 10,000 feet does not stop genocide. Finally, the film asserted that all life is sacred, and any act against life is an act against God.

Personal stories and testimonies formed the substance of this plenary session, which diverged considerably from the printed schedule owing not just to changes beforehand but to unforeseen events.

From the main entrance of the conjoined State and Grand Ballrooms, Haitians made their way in procession toward the stage, singing and dancing. Watching them pass close by, I thought, these people have borne such suffering, yet with what dignity and humanity they come here to share something of their lives. Bishop Willie Romelus from the Diocese of Jérémie spoke with an interpreter.

Before the fall of the Duvalier dictatorship he had been a voice for the voiceless, and after the ouster of President Aristide he became the only one of Haiti's twelve Roman Catholic bishops to denounce the campaign of terror.

I come to say that Haitian people are tired of injustices. Together let us find a way to peace. In Haiti there is no freedom of speech, thought, or movement. Haitians chose a leader but were dispossessed of that choice. Supporters of the exiled president are still beaten and jailed, even for possessing a photo of him, although there is now an agreement for his return. There is also spiritual dispossession. One is not free to worship as one chooses, and there are no safe refuges. Beaten people are hunted down even in hospitals.

Ladjamaya, a Bahá'í actress and dramatist from Colorado, speaks to and from the heart on issues of peace and racial harmony. She asked,

Is there strength enough in democracy? Virtue enough in our civilization? Strength enough in religion to bring justice to the Americas? Our civilization has produced magnificent results, but American civilization lacks two things: simple justice and a humanity that lets us all look at each other as brothers.

Those words were not her own but came from a speech made in 1875, when racism ruled the South. One hundred eighteen years later, those words reflect the hypocrisy and injustice of present-day America. From the beginning the United States embraced a contradictory set of values. Alongside the highest principles there was slavery, and it took a Civil War to abolish that. Still, its evil consequences linger on in the nation's continuing neglect of the ravages of racism. Racism is the most pressing issue confronting America today; it affects the hearts of black and white Americans, and both races must strive for unity. We need close association and fellowship.

Ghulam Nabi Fai of Kashmir started his address with the statistics that Kashmir is larger in population than 114 sovereign nations and larger in land area than 87. His implication was that Kashmir should be independent. "When we lose our homeland, we lose more than real estate. We lose tradition, memories, family. We cannot recreate a homeland in a refugee camp. Occupying forces destroy beliefs, sacred books, and sacred sites." With the partition of India and Pakistan in 1947, Kashmir was forcibly occupied by the Indian government, 1.5 million refugees were created, families were divided, and a culture was destroyed. Ghulam Nabi Fai was now speaking in exile, cut off from his family....

At this point disturbances erupted. There was shouting all around, and I couldn't understand much. For the most part I wrote furiously in my notebook, but toward the front a Hindu in *gerua* was standing and shouting, all the while waving his right arm accusingly. "Point of order, Mr. Chairman!" he said. Calls came from the audience to remove the speaker. Some were protesting what they felt to be a politicization of the Parliament. But in India is it possible to disentangle the volatile mix of religion and politics?

The moderator took charge, reaffirming the Parliament's commitment to giving a voice to the dispossessed, and enthusiastic applause concurred. Before long, order returned, and Thomas M. Johnson from Liberia began a litany of the political events in Monrovia that led to his persecution. He had been arrested, beaten, and tortured as a rebel in the civil war. He was imprisoned with more than two hundred others in a small room without hygienic facilities. The daily meal was rice and oil, served in the small sort of bowl used in latex tapping, and the rice was half stones. The prisoners slept on a concrete floor. On 25 July the warring factions signed a peace treaty, which a newly formed interim government, in an about-face, decided to reject. Relief trucks with food were turned back, and 300 people starved to death. Once the most stable nation on the African continent, Liberia today lies in ruins, while its religions, Christian and non-Christian, work for peace.

"Bismillahi rakhman i rahim," intoned the black speaker, thus identifying himself as a Muslim. Resplendent in an ivory-colored silk robe and a gold crown that conjured up visions of the patriarchs of antiquity, Sheikh Ahmed Tijani Ben Omar of Ghana chanted in Arabic, then in English, and launched into a high-minded exhortation. His impassioned manner reminded me of an African-American gospel preacher, and there was power in his utterances.

> Suspicions of each other are great sins. Throw away negative attitudes. You call yourselves Christian, Jew, Hindu, Muslim, but God says "I made you all from a single man and woman, and I made you to look different, with different languages. I made you tall, short, fat, clumsy, pale, dark..." All look beautiful to the creator! Who am I to find fault with you if God is pleased with your deeds? This Parliament should be a truthful Parliament. It is not a crime to be a Christian, a Jew, a Hindu, or a Buddhist. If you trust in God, treat all believers equally. I am a Muslim. I believe in Moses [so] I am a Jew. I believe in Jesus Christ [so] I am a Christian. I believe in the prophet Muhammad; I am a Muslim.

My heart swelled with respect for this man, and I thought what a lesson this was. A follower of Islam had laid aside his own tale of dispossession and exhorted us as brothers and sisters to seek that which is best within us all. I reflected and regretted that fundamentalism has poisoned some of the faithful, and by extension our perception of the Islamic world. And fundamentalism, that scourge of our time, is a virus to which no religion is immune.

Father Thomas Kocherry related the experiences of fishermen in southern India. In the global market where all members fight for a share of the profits, anything without monetary value is rejected. Since India is becoming a part of that market, traditional ways of life are under threat. In cooperation with the West, the Indian government has put Western technology in direct competition with traditional fishing methods, and if that were not harmful enough, mechanization is also depleting the stocks of fish. Other forms of development are causing deforestation and water pollution and together with the construction of dams are further diminishing the fishermen's livelihood. With the arrival of more and more American companies the situation spirals ever downward. In India's coastal states a growing resistance movement has begun to win concessions from the government even as new threats appear. Japanese machines are replacing the women netmakers. Opposition to a nuclear power plant led to arrests. Now there is an emerging alliance throughout India of various dispossessed groups against the development measures of the government.

Norbu Samphell had come to Chicago the previous January with 92 Tibetans. He recalled in vivid detail his family's difficult escape over the snowy mountains and his 30-year stay in India, a nation of wonderful kindnesses, like no other in the world. Tibet, he urged, needs to gain independence.

The session's moderator interrupted to say that God's greatest gift is the power of speech. That same speech can unleash terrible forces and threaten our unity. This impromptu message came at the request of a consultation group, including the Parliament's board of trustees, that had met downstairs immediately following the controversy. There, Sikh, Jain, Hindu, Muslim, Buddhist, Zoroastrian, and Christian leaders expressed their wish to see the purpose of the Parliament reaffirmed. At one time each of them had suffered at the hands of another, but they came together here in harmony to encourage all by moderate speech to find ways to unity. Applause signaled the audience's approval.

Molefe Tsele from Soweto represents one of 5 million black families whose land was stolen by the white government. The experience of relocation, misery, and death energized him in the struggle against apartheid, and he participated in the 1976 uprising. Three times he was imprisoned and tortured, but, he noted, that is nothing compared to the pain and suffering of millions today.

The accounts of human misery had become all too familiar by now, and Hayelom Ayele added an almost predictable picture of cruelty in his native Ethiopia. Two million have fled the country, and 1.5 million are dead of famine or were killed by the communist junta.

When Gurmit Singh Aulakh from Punjab came to the podium wearing the characteristic Sikh turban, this one bright orange, I feared that discord might flare up again. He began with a simple statement of facts. The 1947 Partition had separated the Sikhs from the birthplace of their Guru Nanak. They had tried to make the best of their diminished Punjabi homeland, but they were only 2% of the population and were discriminated against. A brief history brought us up to the storming and desecration by Indian military forces of the Golden Temple at Amritsar, the holiest shrine. Thirty other temples were also attacked. Twenty thousand Sikhs were tortured or killed, and their scriptures were burned. Later thousands were killed with government compliance, he said, in anti-Sikh pogroms. (He failed to mention that in retaliation Sikhs assassinated the prime minister, Indira Gandhi.) The cycle of violence continues. The death toll has reached 100,000 while 70,000 more languish in prisons without charges or trial. He began to speak about rape and torture, and that is when protest erupted again.

That same Hindu whom I described earlier was on his feet again, hollering with upraised arm. This time one of the security guards tried to calm him down. Shouting was erupting all over the room, and this time it was worse than before. As tension mounted, the lights came on to full brightness, and the waiting speakers were ushered off the platform. Protesters leapt to their feet. One was an Indian woman just three seats to my right. People around tried to quiet her but to no avail. From just behind and all around, Sikhs chanted, "Let him speak! Let him speak!" Daniel Gómez-Ibáñez joined the lone Gurmit Singh Aulakh, who remained at the podium, and other Parliament organizers came to the stage. They seemed mired in indecision. Confusion reigned throughout the room.

I noticed the television cameras on the balconies and to the left and the right of the platform and wondered if this would make the news. When the presenter left the platform, dismay rang out from the audience, and Sikh voices called, "Let him speak! This is not fair! This is a democracy! These are human rights!" Daniel announced that the session would proceed.

Then, amid the welter of voices, I detected the strains of "We Shall Overcome," first quietly then swelling in numbers and volume. Hands joined everywhere, and we stood up and sang, clasped hands held high in solidarity. It was hard to sing through all the tears, but sing I did, and before long the atmosphere in the room was transformed.

Much time had been lost, and the last presentations had to be postponed. We did not hear from Sharifa Sharif of Afghanistan, David Hernandez of the Chicago homeless, Juanita Baltzibal and the sacred dancers who had come with her from Guatemala. Nor did we hear from Waldemar Boff, of Petrópolis, Sao Paulo, Brazil, who was to summarize the "voices" and formulate their questions and challenge to the Parliament.

Instead, Jennie Joe, a Navajo, spoke on behalf of all the indigenous peoples of the Americas who have suffered dispossession and genocide for 500 years. White men justified the taking of land from those people whom they deemed "without religion." She remembered in her youth greeting the rising sun with corn meal and praying for all mankind. "That is spirituality. Our religion does not believe in divine retribution." She spoke of the healing ceremonies being the most misunderstood aspect of her religion, because they are the most visible. Bad thoughts can bring illness; everything is interrelated. She recalled how Indian youths were forced into boarding schools and taught that their beliefs were heathen and valueless, how they were taught to be ashamed of their backgrounds, their families, and those closest to them. Native Americans have had to fight hard to regain their religion. They have had to go through the white man's courts. And Native Americans were excluded from the first Parliament in 1893. "[Now] it is encouraging," she concluded, "that you recognize that we *do* have a religion."

Onstage, led by four Native Americans resplendent in feathers, a circle formed of speakers and dancers from every continent. The drumming enticed more and more people to take part, and the dancers came down from the stage and merged with that larger humanity. Around the ballroom, people also joined hands and danced in a line that stretched up the aisles and circled the room's periphery. With everyone placed in it and sharing the dance, the circle was a symbol of reconciliation on behalf of humanity.

Burdened with notebook and *chaddar*, I felt constrained from joining the line. Instead I joined friends from the Vedanta Society of New York, who stood nearby. We shared our thoughts on what had been an extraordinary morning. When the drumming stopped, the moderator asked us all to embrace the next person. "Well, fellow Vedantist!" I laughed, hugging one. Another, spotting a blue-turbaned Sikh not far away, ran to embrace him. I think we all left that room better for having been there.

"If the white man wants to live in peace with the Indian he can live in peace. Treat all men alike. Give them all the same law. Give them all an even chance to live and grow. The earth is the mother of all people, and all people should have equal rights upon it. You might as well expect the rivers to run backward as that any man who was born free should be contented, penned up and denied liberty to go where he pleases.

"We ask to be recognized as men. We ask that the same law shall work alike on all men. Let me be a free man – free to travel, fee to stop, free to work, free to trade, free to choose my own teachers, free to follow the religion of my fathers, free to think and talk and act for myself – and I will obey every law."

CHIEF JOSEPH, 1879

The Declaration of the Sacred Earth Gathering

This Declaration was created for and supported by the many indigenous, religious, political, and NGO leaders who participated in the Sacred Earth Gathering held for two days preceding the Earth Summit (UNCED) in 1992. They had come to Rio from throughout the world to be a witness for spiritual perspectives on ecological issues and decision-making midst the highly politicized atmosphere of this United Nations summit conference. The presence and contribution of the indigenous leaders at the Summit was strongly supported by Maurice Strong, Secretary General of UNCED. The Gathering was co-sponsored by the Manitou Foundation in cooperation with the Organization for Industrial, Spiritual and Cultural Advancement, a Japanese-based NGO, and was organized and chaired by Hanne Strong, President of the Manitou Foundation. The Gathering was followed by the Wisdom Keepers Convocation, which met from June 1-14 at a secluded location near Rio. A sacred fire, drumbeat, and prayers from many indigenous and religious traditions continued 24 hours a day for the duration of the Summit, seeking to bring enlightenment to its meetings and decisions.

Rio de Janeiro, 1992

The planet earth is in peril as never before. With arrogance and presumption, humankind has disobeyed the laws of the Creator which are manifest in the divine natural order.

The crisis is global. It transcends all national, religious, cultural, social, political, and economic boundaries. The ecological crisis is a symptom of the spiritual crisis of the human being, arising from ignorance [greed, lack of caring, and human weakness]*. The responsibility of each human being today is to choose between the forces of darkness and the force of light. We must therefore transform our attitudes and values, and adopt a renewed respect for the superior law of Divine Nature.**

Nature does not depend on human beings and their technology. It is human beings who depend on Nature for survival. Individuals and governments need to evolve "Earth Ethics" with a deeply spiritual orientation or the earth will be cleansed [of all destructive forces].

We believe that the universe is sacred because all is one. We believe in the sanctity and the integrity of all life and life forms. We affirm the principles of peace and nonviolence in governing human behavior towards one another and all life.

We view ecological disruption as violent intervention into the web of life. Genetic engineering threatens the very fabric of life. We urge governments, scientists, and industry to refrain from rushing blindly into genetic manipulation.

We call upon all political leaders to keep a spiritual perspective when making decisions. All leaders must recognize the consequences of their actions for the coming generations.

We call upon our educators to motivate the people towards harmony with nature and peaceful coexistence with all living beings. Our youth and children must be prepared to assume their responsibilities as citizens of tomorrow's world.

We call upon our brothers and sisters around the world to recognize and curtail the impulses of greed, consumerism, and disregard of natural laws. Our survival depends on developing the virtues of simple living and sufficiency, love and compassion with wisdom.

We stress the importance of respecting all spiritual and cultural traditions. We stand for preservation of the habitats and lifestyle of indigenous people and urge restraint from disrupting their communion with nature.

The World Community must act speedily with vision and resolution to preserve the Earth, nature, and humanity from disaster. The time to act is now. Now or never.

*Brackets indicate that consensus was not reached on this wording.
**Alternative reading: "the superior law of the Divine manifest in nature and the created order."

"We are reminded by the Declaration of the Sacred Earth Gathering, which met here last weekend, that the changes in behavior and direction called for here must be rooted in our deepest spiritual, moral, and ethical values. We must reinstate in our lives the ethic of love and respect for the Earth, which traditional peoples have retained as central to their values systems. This must be accompanied by a revitalization of the values common to all of our principal religious and philosophical traditions. Caring, sharing, co-operation with and love of each other must no longer be seen as pious ideals, divorced from reality, but rather as the indispensable basis for the new realities on which our survival and well-being must be premised."

MAURICE STRONG,
Secretary-General of the United Nations Conference on Environment and Development, in his opening remarks, June 3, 1992

What Do We Do Now?

A Response to Those Who Despair About the State of the World

Dr. Willis W. Harman

Director of the Institute of Noetic Sciences, Sausalito, California, and professor (emeritus) of Engineering–Social Systems at Stanford University

*A*nyone who is sanguine about the global future probably doesn't understand. The problems of a progressively degraded environment, ravaged resources, uncontrolled man-made climate change, chronic hunger and poverty, persistent ethnic and religious conflicts, ever-increasing militarization of societies, and systemic maldistribution of wealth and opportunity seem sufficiently overwhelming, and the political responses so pathetic, that despair seems a reasonable response.

It is important to remind ourselves of the creative response which can be found at the core of the esoteric understanding in any one of the world's religious traditions. But first we need to make explicit a number of principles.

Six principles for creative action

1. Each of us can discover within ourselves a *deep sense of purpose;* the deepest yearning of each of us is to make sense of our lives, to know that our lives have meaning. The ultimate learning is that we are spiritual beings in a spiritual universe, that ultimate cause is not to be found in the physical world but in spirit, and that meaning comes through contributing creatively to the whole.

2. The *present world order is not sustainable in the long term.* The world has become unmanageable; fundamental change is required, at the level of the most basic underlying assumptions. We are all reluctant to realize this fact. But like the first step of the "12-step" programs for addiction, we can make no advance without this recognition.

3. Part of our collective confusion comes from the fact that *the scientific worldview which is at the heart of the modern world order, and is taught throughout the modern world from kindergarten to university, explicitly denies the validity of the discovery described in the first principle.*

4. *We intuitively know what are the characteristics of a sustainable and glorious society.* We know what is required at a family and community level, and we only have to extend that to the whole world. This sounds simplistic; the goal *is* simple – it's just getting there that is not.

5. *Each of us can discover our particular role.* There is a place in the system where we uniquely fit, a place where our unique gifts and the demands of the situation fit together perfectly. We may find that place partly through following intuition; partly through trying things and seeing what "wants to happen"; partly by watching for "meaningful coincidences."

6. *Each of us can say "yes" to that role.* There is a new pattern of understanding and valuing which is emerging from the various social movements and deliberations of recent decades. That "new paradigm"– which draws on the perennial wisdom of the world's spiritual traditions – affirms that all things are parts of a single, ultimately spiritual whole, and that each of us, as a part of that whole, has access to an "inner knowing" which can guide us to ultimately meaningful action.

continued on next page

Who will tell us what to do?

Thich Nhàt Hanh

*T*he [Vietnamese] boat people said that every time their small boats were caught in storms, they knew their lives were in danger. But if one person on the boat could keep calm and not panic, that was a great help for everyone. People would listen to him or her and keep serene, and there was a chance for the boat to survive the danger. Our Earth is like a small boat. Compared with the rest of the cosmos, it is a small boat indeed, and it is in danger of sinking. We need such a person to inspire us with calm confidence, to tell us what to do. Who is that person?

The Mahayana Buddhist sutras tell us that you are that person. If you are yourself, if you are your best, then you are that person. Only with such a person – calm, lucid, aware – will our situation improve.

I wish you good luck. Please be yourself. Please be that person.

from "Please Call Me by My True Names," in *The Path of Compassion,* edited by Fred Eppsteiner, Buddhist Peace Fellowship

The Practice of Meditation

K.G. von Durckheim

*T*he aim of practice [meditation] is not to develop an attitude which allows the man to acquire a state of harmony and peace wherein nothing can ever trouble him. On the contrary, practice should teach him to let himself be assaulted, perturbed, moved, insulted, broken, and battered. That is to say, it should enable him to dare to let go his futile hankering after harmony, surcease from pain, and a comfortable life, in order that he may discover in doing battle with the forces which oppose him, that which awaits him beyond the world of opposites. The first necessity is that we should have the courage to face life, and to encounter all that is most perilous in the world. When this is possible, meditation itself becomes the means by which we accept and welcome the demons which arise from the unconscious (a practice very different from the practice of concentration on some object as a protection). Only if we venture repeatedly through zones of annihilation can our contact with Divine Being, which is beyond annihilation, become firm and stable. The more a man learns wholeheartedly to confront the world that threatens him with isolation, the more are the depths of the ground of Being revealed, and the possibilities of new life and Becoming opened.

from The Way of Transformation

Elements of a personal program

*H*ow can one play one's part in all this? The following three elements comprise an effective personal program:

1. *Personal transformation (inner work).* Many guides to inner transformation are available; ultimately one has to work with what feels intuitively right. *Intention* is the key requirement for discovering within oneself the inner wisdom and deep sense of purpose that will lead to making an effective contribution. The right way will appear. It may be within an established religious tradition, or it may not – or it may be for a time one and later on the other. It will probably involve a meditative discipline, prayer or yoga. It may or may not be with a personal spiritual teacher.

2. *Local action (outer work).* Whole-system transformation involves the transformation of all parts of the system; we can contribute anywhere. Wherever we are in the system is a good place to start – our families, our jobs, our communities. All creative action is with a small group, locally – although the effects may ripple out worldwide. Taking action is essential: it provides "grounding" through which we receive feedback. Action leads to experience, and "all experience is feedback." The guidance of deep intuition as it develops in our inner work, together with feedback from our outer work, will direct us toward discovering our particular role – the place in this whole-system evolution where we uniquely fit.

3. *Global re-perception (inner work).* Modern society, like all societies that have ever existed, rests on some set of basic assumptions about who we are, what kind of universe we are in, and how we relate to one another and to the whole. The present world order is not long-term sustainable because its worldview is not accurate. But we have complicity in that order because we "buy into" the underlying belief system. It is not comfortable to discover that the experienced reality we come to through deep inner work is not that of the materialistic scientific worldview. The re-perception of a sustainable worldview reveals neither the manipulative rationality that passes for knowledge nor the prevailing ethic of acquisitive materialism, and it does not lead to the conventional belief system of economic rationality. Yet it is necessary to come to this realization if we are to clear the path to our own intuitive wisdom and make a meaningful contribution to the whole. There is no resolution of our global dilemmas short of changing these collective beliefs, beginning with ourselves.

FOR MORE INFORMATION:

Institute of Noetic Sciences
475 Gate Five Rd., Suite 300, Sausalito, CA 94965 USA.
IONS was founded in 1973 by Dr. Edgar Mitchell, Apollo 14 astronaut, to support research and educational programs that expand humankind's understanding of the nature and potential of consciousness and of the mind-body link.

Make Love Your Aim

Paul, the Apostle

"If I speak in the tongues of men
and of angels,
but have not love,
I am a noisy gong
or a clanging cymbal.
And if I have prophetic powers,
and understand all mysteries
and all knowledge,
and if I have all faith

so as to remove mountains,
but have not love,
I am nothing....

"Love is patient and kind;
love is not jealous or boastful;
it is not arrogant or rude.
Love does not insist on its own way;
it is not irritable or resentful;
it does not rejoice at wrong,
but rejoices in the right.

"Love bears all things,
believes all things,
hopes all things,
endures all things.

"Love never ends....
So faith, hope, and love abide,
these three;
but the greatest of these is love.
Make love your aim."

1 CORINTHIANS 13

Planetary Therapy
Twelve Steps of Ecological Spirituality

Albert LaChance

Author, therapist, poet, and environmentalist; founder, with his wife, of the Greenspirit Center in New Hampshire

The materials below are excerpted from *Greenspirit: Twelve Steps in Ecological Spirituality,* by Albert LaChance, Foreword by Thomas Berry. The book is a detailed description of a 12-step process of cultural therapy. These excerpts are from the Preface and Introduction.

"The industrial world is a kind of entrancement, a pathology. It's addictive. We become addicted to automobiles. It's paralyzing, because once we're totally caught up in it, we think we can't do anything about it. We have a type of religious commitment to the industrial world." THOMAS BERRY, in *Earth Conference One* by Anuradha Vittachi (Shambhala Books, 1989)

*T*here is only one problem: everything! We like to talk about the ecological problem, the nuclear problem, the drug problem, the family problem, the violence problem, the alcohol problem, the species extinction problem, and so on as though each of these were separate and distinct pathologies, each unrelated to the other. There's really only one problem. It's the way we live. The Earth has only one problem. It's the way we live. We suffer from a deep, cultural pathology.

Industrial culture has a bad chemical dependency problem. Internally, within our bodies, we call it the drug and alcohol epidemic. Externally, outside our bodies, it's the pollution problem—the two faces of one problem, a toxic human on a toxic planet. . . . We need to move into recovery *as cultures. We need to de-toxify the planet! Greenspirit* is that final stage of recovery. *Greenspirit* is a cultural therapy and therefore a planetary therapy.

The twelve steps of ecological spirituality

1) We admit that we are powerless over an addicted society, that our lives and all of life have become degraded.

2) We come to acknowledge the existence of an Originating Mystery accomplishing the evolution of the universe. We accept that, if allowed, this Originating Mystery will reveal to each of us our natural relationship to self, to others, to other species, to the Earth and to the Universe.

3) We decide to surrender our lives and our wills to this Originating Mystery, whatever we choose to name it.

4) We examine ourselves, listing all our attitudes and actions that damage the created order, thereby stopping or impeding the emergence of this Originating Mystery.

5) We acknowledge to ourselves, to that Originating Mystery, and to another person, the specifics of our illusory thinking, attitudes, and behavior.

6) We become entirely willing to have all habits of illusion removed from our thoughts, our attitudes, and our behavior.

7) In humility, we request that this Originating Mystery remove all our habits of illusory thought, attitude, and behavior.

8) We make a list of all persons, all other species, and all the life systems of the planet we have harmed, and we become ready to do everything in our power to heal them all.

9) We make a strenuous effort to heal all phases of the created order – human, animal, or planetary – injured by our illusory thinking, attitudes, or action.

10) We continue on a daily basis to go on examining our thinking and our actions as to whether they foster or impede the emergence of life. Where they impede this emergence, we admit it and become willing to be changed.

11) We continue through physical-mental-spiritual disciplines to change ourselves so as to improve our own ability to foster the emergence and health of the whole created order.

12) Having experienced a reawakening to self, to humanity, to all species, to the planet, and to the universe, we try to spread this awareness to others and to practice these disciplines in all phases of our lives.

FOR MORE INFORMATION:

Greenspirit is available from Element, Inc., 42 Broadway, Rockport, MA 01966 USA; and in the UK from Element Books Limited.

The author may be reached at:
Greenspirit, 53 Larch St., Manchester, NH 03102 USA

"The massive overconsumption by the middle and upper classes is merely a symptom of a deeper disease. That disease is materialism in its truest sense." JEREMY RIFKIN, in *The Emerging Order* (written with Ted Howard)

"The disintegration of our culture has forced many to seek various escapes into unreality. However, all unreal states – be they addictions, daytime television, over-work, or any of the other ways in which we escape – have this in common: they prevent access to creative energies. This loss of creative energy is the single greatest energy crisis we face these days." ALBERT LACHANCE, from "The Architecture of the Soul," a manuscript in preparation

A Declaration of Independence – from Overconsumption

Vicki Robin

President of the New Road Map Foundation, author, and a frequent speaker on fiscal and resource frugality

This statement is a revision by the author of an address she gave at the United Nations on April 6, 1994.

We are all consumers. Every human takes sustenance from and returns waste to the environment. But overconsumption means taking more than we can productively use – or more than the environment can sustainably provide. Overconsumption has become our way of life in the United States. We put our faith in "more," but it's never enough; we report being no happier now than we were in 1957, when cars were fewer, houses smaller and microwaves, VCRs, and personal computers did not even exist. Worse yet, our lifestyle, which threatens our social fabric and the very web of life on which we depend, has become the envy of much of the world.

As Robert Muller, retired Assistant Secretary-General of the United Nations, says, "The single most important contribution any of us can make to the planet is a return to frugality."

Overconsumption is a mounting catastrophe

Quantity as well as type of consumption defines the individual's impact on the environment. With population rising and expectations for more, better and different stuff increasing, humanity is taxing the earth's life-sustaining systems, its "carrying capacity." Each overconsumer is responsible; we must face this catastrophe in the making.

Overconsumption is a catastrophe for ourselves:

- **Declining quality of life.** Our habit of overconsumption enslaves many of us to longer hours at tedious or morally questionable jobs. We say we value relationships over possessions, yet our behavior says the opposite. As we spend less time with our families and communities, we end up with more crime, violence, and teen suicides.

Overconsumption is a catastrophe for our countries:

- **Economic weakness.** Our habit of overconsumption has led the USA into debt, bankruptcy, and the lowest savings rate in the industrialized world. We don't have money to invest in infrastructure, in education, in the future.
- **Personal excess encourages institutional abuses.** The more-is-better mentality allows us to tolerate wars over oil, and corporate practices that are wasteful, polluting, and unethical. We can't say "no" to Nintendos for our children or new gadgets for ourselves, so how can we expect our government to say "no" to deficit spending or CEO's to say "no" to exorbitant salaries?

Overconsumption is a catastrophe for humanity:

- **Modeling an unattainable and unsustainable lifestyle to the global community.** The earth cannot support everyone in the manner to which Americans have become accustomed. We must find a way to limit our excess and maintain or increase our quality of life while providing the world's people with our best knowledge and technologies so that they too can enjoy sustainable livelihoods and lifestyles.

Overconsumption is a catastrophe for the earth:

- **Environmental destruction.** Overconsumption accelerates species extinction, water and air pollution, global warming, and accumulation of toxic waste and garbage.
- **Resource depletion.** Overconsumption means we're using renewable resources faster than nature can restore them! Twenty percent of the groundwater we use each year is not restored. One million acres of cropland are lost to erosion annually. Ninety percent of our northwestern old-growth forests is gone.

We can change!
Strategies for ending overconsumption

Break the silence

We must begin to talk about our consumption and challenge the conspiracy of silence. We can't solve a problem we won't acknowledge. Challenge yourself. Challenge others. Risk being uncomfortable. Risk offending others. Ask:

- Should we be able to buy whatever we can afford, no matter what the effect on others or the earth?
- Should we allow credit cards to lure us into excessive debt?
- When is personal consumption a matter of public concern?
- Who or what will set limits for us, if we won't do it ourselves?
- Does overconsumption really make us happy?

At the 1992 Earth Summit the United States refused to talk about consumption, saying that a country such as ours could not tell its citizens what kind of lifestyles and consumption patterns to have. By the 1994 Cairo Population Conference, the United States at least acknowledged the need to reduce our consumption. The door is opening. Speak out. And keep speaking.

Reframe the game

Saving money – "creating a nest egg," "saving for a rainy day," "recession-proofing your life," ensuring a decent retirement income independent of shaky pensions or social security – benefits you, the economy, and the planet. By getting out of debt, saving money and building financial security, you consume less. By living life at a slower pace, you consume less.

Frugality isn't deprivation. Deprivation is pouring your time and talent into your job while ignoring your health and your loved ones. Poverty is wanting more than you have. Wealth is having more than you want. So make overconsumption sound dull-witted and frugality smart. (It's easy, because it's true.)

Debunk the myths

Myth: "*Standard of living* equals quality of life." Once we have enough for survival and comforts, quality of life suffers when we continue to focus on quantity of stuff. Studies show that good relationships, meaningful work and restorative leisure are core components of quality of life.

Myth: *Overconsumption is natural.* No, it isn't! It began in this century as a deliberate strategy on the part of business, media, and government to educate people to want what they don't need in order to increase markets for American products. Overconsumption is selling your life and mortgaging your future so the economy can grow. Now *that's* unnatural.

Myth: *The US (or any) economy is dependent upon overconsumption.* Respected economic observers like Lester Thurow of M.I.T., Charles Schultze of the Brookings Institute, and Alfred E. Kahn of Cornell all assert that economic health in the 90's depends on consuming less and saving more.

Myth: *Government programs, revolutionary business practices, or new technologies will take care of it.* Green taxes! Renewable energy! Fuel-efficient cars! Clean industry! Better living through chemistry! All are valuable – but, even all together, they are not sufficient. Creating a sustainable future requires a new way of thinking. We must reexamine our desires, transform our perceptions and develop a new ethic. Only then can the larger systems with which we operate be transformed.

Myth: *One person can't make a difference.* There is no "they." There is only us, a society of individuals making personal and collective choices. Legislators, CEOs and consumers are all people who can change their minds and thus change the world, no matter what they did yesterday. Lowering consumption happens one transaction at a time.

Educate about overconsumption

Every conversation is an opportunity. Share your ideas and success stories with friends, neighbors, and colleagues; write about them in your letters. Discuss and debate. Put together a study circle. Talk to the media. Show the link between overconsumption and environmental and social issues. Begin to notice all the ways that others can benefit from what you have learned.

Live a sustainable lifestyle yourself

Each of us has the mandate to consume in moderation. Ask yourself now and every day, "How much is enough?"

A call to action

*T*he shift away from excess and back to balance is on. "Voluntary Simplicity" is one of the top 10 trends in the 90's, according to the Trends Research Institute in Rhinebeck, NY. Books on getting out of debt, saving money, and working less are hot. Churches are exploring stewardship, not dominion. Foundations are funding projects to explore the issue of consumption and activate solutions. People are taking back their lives.

The can-do American character has faced challenges before. When science showed us the dangers of being couch potatoes, of smoking, of too much fat, we responded with lifestyle changes. The mandate to reduce consumption can energize our country in a similar fashion, this time in a fiscal fitness campaign. Let's transform the American way of life and pave the way to a sustainable future.

Tools for Personal Change

Beyond the what and why of overconsumption, people need the "how to." Based on 25 years of experience in living and educating about low-consumption, high-fulfillment lifestyles, Joe Dominguez and Vicki Robin wrote the best-selling book *Your Money or Your Life*. Among the other resources available from The New Road Map Foundation's is the popular booklet, *All-Consuming Passion: Waking Up from the American Dream*.

Both books and other information are available from:
New Road Map Foundation, PO Box 15981, Seattle, WA 98115 USA

Overconsumption is a Justice Issue

Dom Helder Camara

*A*n enormous effort will be needed to create awareness in the marginalized masses, both in the developed and the underdeveloped countries, to prepare them to fight their way out of their sub-human situation, and also prepare them not simply to become as bourgeois and as selfish as those whom today they condemn.

An enormous effort is also needed to create awareness in those who are privileged, both in rich countries where there are poor groups which they allow to remain, and where there is neo-colonialism which they support whether they realize it or not, and in under-developed countries where the privileged create and profit from internal colonialism. It is very difficult to create awareness in the privileged. The teacher must have great virtue, be kind but truthful, gentle but firm.

But if the effort is not made the scandal will continue and the rich will go on getting richer and the poor poorer. The spiral of violence will get worse, injustice will increase, the resistance of the oppressed or the young in the name of the oppressed will continue and repression will become more and more brutal.

When will governments and the privileged understand that there can be no true peace until justice has been established?

from *The Desert is Fertile*, pp. 47–48, Orbis (out of print).

How May I Help?

Nonviolent Social Change in the Gandhian Tradition

Dr. Guy de Mallac

Director of the Center for Nonviolence, founder of The Ways of Peace and Service and the United Peace Network, author, and professor (emeritus) at the University of California – Irvine

*A*s we know from previous essays in this *SourceBook*, the people of this planet face major global issues. One temptation for any individual is to be overwhelmed by their magnitude, so overwhelmed that one does nothing. . . which is very much against authentic spiritual endeavor, and very much against the Gandhian spirit.

The correct view is that every step (however minor) counts. Every step matters – every step that I take, trying to be of service, to be of help. Every such step contributes to fulfilling the purpose of my life. Albert Schweitzer wrote that, "The purpose of life is to serve and to show compassion and the will to help others." A key statement on the Volunteer Commitment Card of the Alabama Christian Movement for Human Rights in 1960 translates that attitude or principle into a suggested practice: "Seek to perform regular service for others and for the world."

Let us now see what Nonviolence can contribute toward finding concrete ways in which one can help.

1. Nonviolence – another name for loving, dynamic outreach

*F*ollowing in the footsteps of his mentor Leo Tolstoy, Mahatma Gandhi believed there are two global forces at work in the world: (1) the Law of Love, and (2) the Law of Violence or Aggression. He felt that love is stronger and can prevail, given our best efforts.

For those who feel that the word "love" has been unduly cheapened, we might substitute synonyms for it: "nonviolence" (although, like the Sanskrit word "*a*-himsa," *non*-violence is a negative formulation, conveying: *not* hurting, or the failure to do violence). Or, with Carl Rogers we might talk of "unconditional positive regard." Again, we might say, "loving, dynamic outreach."

Whatever term we use, we must realize the existence in ourselves and others of a positive force based on warmth, understanding, love, cooperation. Attuned to that force within ourselves, we reach out and turn on that force in others. This force, which reaches out to meet the other, promotes sharing and cooperation, and thus resolves conflicts. Generally speaking, love has been defined as having the following four characteristic attitudes toward the loved one(s): care, responsibility, respect, and knowledge (Erich Fromm, *The Art of Loving*).

In usual practice, we tend to love in a restricted way within a set of circles: most strongly, our spouse and/or close family; then other relatives, and friends; and finally perhaps members of affinity groups or associations, and fellow countrypeople. To *universalize* love, we should reach out to all within these concentric circles as sincerely and efficiently as possible.

There are several stages in dynamic outreach: first, develop acquaintance with the member or members of the "other" group, with those who are first seen as "different" from me; then, cultivate greater awareness of those "others" as worthy of respect, as unique, as close to me; demonstrate greater sensitivity, respect, and acceptance; and, finally, work toward joint goals together.

If we fail to reach out in that way, but rather insist on viewing the others as radically or forever "different" from us, then the crystallized feeling of difference or estrangement leads to such ills as racism, ethnocentrism, or triumphalism; these can give rise to enmity and, in time, generate conflict and war.

Concrete suggestions for implementing nonviolence:

1) *Practice the law of love:* Love all humans as brothers and sisters, with respect, promoting universal acceptance and *familyhood*. Challenge all discriminations and prejudices. Promote the dignity of human beings regardless of age, sex, race, or creed. Practice strategic nonviolence as part of an active struggle: denounce injustice.

2) *Alongside reasonable concern for self, work and serve for the welfare of all.* Practice the Golden Rule. "I can never be what I ought to be until you are what you ought to be." (Martin Luther King)

3) *Practice thoughtful attentiveness and creative listening to the other's side.* In dealing with an opponent, search actively for common/mutual interests; on the basis of these interests, build projects to encourage the development of increasing mutual trust.

4) *Respect other societies, cultures, races and the heritage of each.* Conduct intercultural, interreligious, interethnic, interclass, and intergender exchange and interaction. Support human freedom and dignity at home by endorsing civil liberties; not granting such liberties is also a form of violence. Persistently denounce and oppose injustice.

5) *Work for reduction in military budgets.* Actively pursue alternatives to military intervention. Support human freedom and dignity by ending foreign military interventions; military interference in another country's internal affairs is usually a form of violence.

6) *Instead of supporting narrow, parochial approaches, develop broader horizons – pluralize and globalize issues.*

7) *Foster togetherness, unity, harmony.* When two or more individuals come together to achieve that aim, the Godhead is with them.

2. Nonviolent economics

*A*wareness of the need for nonviolent economics comes with an awareness of what Mahatma Gandhi called "the wide gulf separating the few rich from the hungry millions." If a few decades ago he was warning us that this gap was significant, how much more concerned should we not be today, knowing that this gap *has been widening markedly?* Gandhi saw a direct, causal relationship between:

a) the extreme of considerable wealth and idleness, and

b) the extreme of considerable poverty and crushing labor.

We need a fuller awareness of what poverty really means: its lack of access to work and basic amenities; the biological damage it causes; the heavy restrictions and waste of human potential that it brings about. We can each develop a fuller awareness of the meaning of the *absolute poverty* which is the lot of close to one billion human beings. We need to become better acquainted with the mechanisms which stop many rich individuals from even perceiving the gap between rich and poor.

Concrete suggestions for implementing nonviolent economics:

(1) *Our caring for others should lead us to insist on nothing short of full economic justice* – leaving behind traditional "charity" and handouts.

(2) Gandhi and Tolstoy urge us all *to do some necessary manual work,* to commune with all those who are condemned to especially alienating and harsh forms of manual work.

(3) *Practice frugality and a simple lifestyle.* Over the last two decades more than a dozen stimulating books have discussed intentional simplicity as part of strategies to achieve fairer distribution of available resources.

(4) *Give all a chance to work.* Especially, give the right to work to the weak, the poor, and the disenfranchised so that they might achieve greater autonomy and self-sufficiency.

(5) *Learn to share, to give, to practice generosity* on a daily basis. Share resources, including land. In third world countries there is a crying need for land reform to make land available to the landless, who often are landless as a result of documented injustice. Establish a fairer and saner balance of resources, and view ourselves merely as stewards or trustees, to whom resources have been entrusted for a broader purpose, transcending the individual.

(6) *Implement appropriate or intermediate technology* as defined in E. F. Schumacher's landmark book *Small Is Beautiful.*

(7) *To whatever extent is feasible, practice local or regional self-sufficiency;* support local agriculture and manufacture; practice economic and political decentralization.

(8) *Nurture the environment:* practice right ecology.

(9) *Stop designing and manufacturing weapons.* Achieve economic conversion of military jobs to *jobs with peace!*

(10) *Support cooperative approaches* to work and economic problems. Gandhi's plea was to avoid and denounce the practices of exploitive capitalism.

3. Nonviolent communication

*T*o combat violent communication (which often is synonymous with oppression) and the lack of communication, foster the more complete and effective nonviolent, cooperative communication.

Concrete suggestions for implementing nonviolent communication:

(1) Let our attitude toward the person we are communicating with be one of *Love* (care + respect + responsibility + knowledge) as opposed to an attitude of domination.

(2) Let our attitudes toward the other party be ones of *flexibility*: tolerance, humility and openness to other viewpoints – as opposed to arrogance.

(3) Let us practice *trust* in the other: regard for the other, patience toward the other, and assuming the other's goodwill – as opposed to scorn for the other and disbelief in the other's potential and goodwill.

(4) Let me have a reasonably open and *questioning* attitude toward my ideas and positions, and be prepared to view them in a new light on occasion – as opposed to a closed and dogmatic mentality.

(5) Let us be prepared to engage in a two-way process of *sharing* information, facts, ideas, opinions – as opposed to a close-minded attitude.

(6) In the process of dialoguing, let us systematically *listen* to the other party or parties and be prepared to express differences as well as commonalities. Let us consider signing up for workshops in Listening Skills and undergoing training in that area. (Mostly, we are very poor listeners).

(7) Let us engage in authentic *dialogue* which, according to the definition of that term, implies a two-way flow.

(8) Practice *cooperation* as part of the process of communication and dialogue. This supposes a willingness to view issues and problems in a more general perspective, and to pluralize or globalize the issues.

(9) Practice *consultation,* which is the process whereby we seek information, opinions, advice, or guidance from others.

10) If the above approaches have not been attempted or have not worked and we are in a situation of exacerbated conflict, practice the various skills and approaches relevant to *conflict-solving/conflict-resolution*: negotiation, mediation, arbitration, reconciliation.

War is the ultimate breakdown in communication, and is the ultimate evil which the process of communication seeks to avoid.

4. Nonviolent government/politics (including international politics)

*R*easonable participation in the governmental process is a basis of the Gandhian doctrine of nonviolence; civic awareness and involvement in activities are viewed as being as important as a prayer or religious duty or act.

We must train ourselves to examine the institutions we have created. If a governing body or road repair service does not achieve what our best judgment and our moral selves want it to achieve, we must reconsider why we as citizens created such a service.

Gandhi has warned us that "the State represents violence in a concentrated and organized form." We must therefore always be on the lookout for the violence which the State and its agencies are perpetrating, claiming it is done *in our name.* It is a mistake to assume that the judiciary or the military or the government stands for justice or peace; our duty as citizens is to make sure they come closer to that ideal.

Concrete suggestions for implementing nonviolent government:

(1) Participate by making sure that through representation of our opinions, through our votes and actions, government agencies achieve their original purpose—the administration of a required service in accordance with our aims and values.

(2) Decentralize: go back to human scale.

(3) Inter-relate through adequate communication with other groups within a nation or among nations or continents.

(4) Build a society that provides for basic human needs (such as adequate housing, health, education, jobs in humane working conditions, and a safe environment). Change social structures which exploit the poor.

(5) Democratize: respect the rights and opinions of all groups, and especially of minorities.

(6) Ensure that the laws are *just.* If a given law is not just, convey our wish to have it repealed; as needed, get involved in actions to achieve that end.

(7) Democratize the international world order. Democratize relations among nations.

(8) Pluralize issues: view them in the light of the concerns of *all* parties involved; in a domestic context, this means all the groups involved; in the international context, all the nation-states involved.

5. *Nonviolent education*

Concrete suggestions for implementing nonviolent education:

(1) Develop education for peace and nonviolence, education in nonviolent communication, in mutual understanding and cooperation. This should be the basis for curriculum and the framework within which all educational subjects fit.

(2) Have the students/learners learn from work and learn from life. Encourage full and responsible (not just token) involvement in various crafts and in various other forms of work (such as agriculture). All should do some necessary manual work.

(3) Work on self-improvement, on achieving knowledge and mastery of self, on educating the individual character, and on development of truthfulness and fearlessness. This naturally leads to spiritual training.

(4) Self-sufficiency is to be developed on the basis of students' ability to learn from life, and to cope with a variety of manual tasks. Self-sufficiency is the ability to adapt to tomorrow's knowledge and context, after aspects of today's knowledge become obsolete. Educate for tomorrow's context.

(5) Develop the crucial dimension of outreach. Learn to intuit or discover the needs of others, to meet such needs, and to do committed volunteer service for the welfare of all.

FOR MORE INFORMATION:

Guy de Mallac
Center for Nonviolence
P.O. Box 1058, San Jacinto, CA 92581-1058

A Dual Awakening Process

Dr. Ahangamage T. Ariyaratne

*T*he word *sarvodaya* was coined by Mahatma Gandhi to describe a new social order, which he envisioned as being very different from the capitalist and communist systems prevalent at that time. Literally it means "the welfare of all." With my Buddhist outlook, when I came across the word *sarvodaya* I interpreted it as "the awakening of all." . . . I cannot awaken myself unless I help awaken others. Others cannot awaken unless I do. So it is an interconnected and interdependent dual process of awakening oneself and society that we have chosen in the *Sarvodaya* [organization, of which he is Director] . . . . Lord Buddha's admonition to us was [to serve]

by helping those who suffer physically
to overcome physical suffering,
those who are in fear to overcome fear,

those who suffer mentally to overcome mental suffering,
Be of service to all living beings.

This is *sarvodaya* in the most profound sense. Transcending all man-made barriers of caste, race, religion, nationality, and other ways of separating human beings, *Sarvodaya* serves all. *Sarvodaya* works to remove the causes of human physical suffering, anxiety, and fear. Working for interreligious and interracial harmony, eradicating poverty and empowering the poor, promoting peace by religious education and spiritual development programs, engaging in every kind of peace-making process, taking nonviolent action against human rights violations and other forms of injustice, are all part of the *Sarvodaya* portfolio of activities.

excerpted from his acceptance speech
for the Ninth Niwano Peace Prize,
printed in *Dharma World,* July/August 1992

The Family of Abraham

Dom Helder Camara

Archbishop of Recifé, Brazil, author, advocate for peace, justice and the human rights of the poor

*J*ews, Muslims and Christians know the story of the father of believers... Did Abraham receive great gifts? He gave a faithful return, the best he could. He served. [...] If you feel in you the desire to use the qualities you have, if you think selfishness is narrow and choking, if you hunger for truth, justice, and love, you can and should go with us. [...]

The violence of the truth

*I*n underdeveloped countries the Abrahamic minorities must try to find out what is involved in a sub-human situation. "Sub-human" is an explosive word. Take it in detail.

- Find out about housing. Do the places where some people live deserve to be called houses?... Look at the water, drains, electricity, the floor, the roof.
- Investigate clothing, food, health, work, transport, leisure. You should ask the right questions.
- With work, for example, does it pay a living wage sufficient to support a family; is employment guaranteed or are there frequent redundancies (layoffs)? Are trade unions

encouraged, tolerated, interfered with, forbidden? What are the apprenticeship conditions? the sanitary conditions? holidays? retirement provisions? Are the laws on social conditions kept? Are human beings treated with respect?

This sort of inquiry could of course arouse suspicion, and that could have unpleasant consequences. But it is necessary to find out what the real situation is in conditions of internal colonialism. What other way is there of becoming convinced and convincing others of the huge gap between those who suffer from an almost feudal situation in which the masses have no voice and no hope? Such information would not aim at inciting anger and rebellion but at providing a solid argument for the necessity to change the structures. [...]

Its aim is to supply liberating moral pressure. For many, this in itself is dangerous and subversive. But one day it will be understood that this violence of the peaceful is greatly preferable to the explosion of armed violence.... Choosing the way of moral pressure is not choosing the easy way out. We are replacing the force of arms by moral force, the violence of the truth. We must believe that love can strengthen the courage of these Abrahamic minorities who want justice but who refuse to answer violence with violence. [...]

excerpted from The Desert is Fertile,
pp. 8, 9, 54–57

Appeal Regarding the AIDS Crisis

Ma Jaya Sati Bhagavati

Founder of the Kashi Ashram in Roseland, Florida, and well-known for her work with those who are sick with AIDS, prostitutes and others outcast or ignored by society

The HIV/AIDS crisis is as intractable as any of the issues that transcend old borders. Its victims suffer from both the illnesses and as a result of social discrimination and fear. With this appeal, made to the Parliament of the World's Religions and to us all, Ma remains an outspoken advocate for suitable responses from religious and spiritual communities.

*O*f the crises facing humanity today, AIDS is the most pressing. Its potential for severely disrupting societies everywhere is frightening to comprehend. Its devastating impact is being felt but frequently not acknowledged because of the fear and prejudice associated with it. The healing must begin with the religious and spiritual leaders, we who have come together to engage in dialogue. But our lofty words will not heal the pain of those who suffer. There is no cure for AIDS and may not be one for many years, so we must be with those infected with the virus, feeding them, holding them, hugging them, loving them – people of every age, race, and culture, and at every stage of the disease. Let us pray together as we keep our hands busy touching the brows of the dying and honoring the

dead. Let us put our pious words into simple deeds. Let us remember that the person lying in bed with death right overhead doesn't have a fixed religion, but does have a fixed spirituality. We need to be there, forgetting differences, remembering the oneness of love and compassion.

What greater unity could we, the religious and spiritual leaders, show the world than to come together united in fighting this disease, physically and spiritually, gathering the resources of all paths of God? Let us make the lives of those with AIDS, those who live courageously in the face of death, a time of strength, empowerment, and love. Let them know the security they crave, and let them feel the love they so often cannot find. [...]

*H*ow can the world's religions help? Let those who call themselves religious forget religion and remember only God. The religious mind must be set aside for a moment and the spiritual heart remembered. Let us roll up our sleeves, embracing those who are dying before they have lived, serving those who too often are led to believe that God has turned his back on them. My God, my Christ, never walks away from pain and hurt. Let us fulfill our role and set an example for those who look to us for guidance and Spirit.

Decide to Network

Robert Muller

*U*se every letter you write
Every conversation you have
Every meeting you attend
To express your fundamental beliefs and
dreams.
Affirm to others the vision of the world
you want
Network through thought
Network through action
Network through love
Network through spirit.
You are the center of a network
You are a free, immensely powerful
source of life
       and goodness.
Affirm it
Spread it
Radiate it
Think day and night about it
And you will see a miracle happen:
       the greatness of your own life.
In a world of big powers, media,
and monopolies,
But of five billion individuals
Networking is a new freedom
The new democracy
A new form of happiness.

*"The Christian is not to become a
Hindu or a Buddhist, nor a Hindu or
a Buddhist to become a Christian.
But each must assimilate the spirit
of the others and yet preserve his
individuality and grow according to
his own law of growth..."*
                        VIVEKANANDA

Envisioning a World without Religious Violence

The Reverend Eileen Corbière

Presbyterian minister and Executive Director of the Religious Peace Project

*A*lbert Einstein wrote that, *"The significant problems we face cannot be solved at the same level of thinking we used when we created them."*

*T*he way we see the problem of religious violence *may be* the problem. Even our most creative, audacious thinking is bound by invisible constraints. We pray and strategize within a context in which violence is a given. We expect it. Thus, even potentially viable solutions are inadequate to deliver on our commitment to move beyond religious violence as they, too, arise within the current paradigm.

A viable program of personal and global change must begin by confronting the facts about religious violence. We must gain a clear understanding of its occurrences, of the sad irony of "religious violence," in which difference is perceived as a source of danger and fear, and of its costs: the terrible human toll, the environmental degradation and the financial waste.

Then we must gather ourselves together and boldly step into a place of not knowing, beyond our certainty, beyond the well-wrought solutions with which we are comfortable. In that uncertainty, we can begin deliberately to envision a world, a possible future, in which violent response to differentness becomes an anomaly found only in history books. Together we will invent a way of speaking which alters the direction of the present and aims it at the future. Standing in the future, as it were, we will speak that future in this moment.

This potent expression brings to life that which is spoken, calling both speaker and listener into effective action and partnership. It is a radical departure from the language of wishes, hopes, or opinions, as heartfelt or reasoned as they may be. This stand-taking includes and enhances the spiritual resources with which we are familiar.

A final step is to explore the unique access to the Divine or Ultimate which is granted by different religions. We inquire into their possible value for our own journeys. Still grounded in our own faith tradition, yet having shifted our relationship to other faiths from threat to value, we will ask of the religions questions such as:

Can another religious tradition speak to my own experience, even if I do not practice that path and have no intention to do so?

Do other religions address such basic questions as "What is worth living and dying for?" in a way which can actually make a difference to me?

Can spiritual paths other than my own even contribute to the strength and depth of my chosen religion?

In a world which is safe and free from even a thought of potential violence, spiritual exploration is not only a possibility, but a joyous, natural, human expression.

The Religious Peace Project

*D*edicated to a bold promise for global peace and an end to religious violence, The Religious Peace Project is an organization and strategy for accomplishing the end of bloodshed which is justified, excused, or motivated by religious concerns.

FOR MORE INFORMATION:

The Reverend Eileen Corbière, Executive Director
The Religious Peace Project, 151 Butternut Hollow, Acton, MA 01718 USA

Towards the Dialogue of Love

Dr. Robert L. Fastiggi

Associate Professor of Religious Studies, St. Edward's University, Austin, Texas

The story is told of a young Capuchin friar who had consulted the great French Islamicist Louis Massignon about how to overcome his negative feelings towards Islam. The scholar provided the friar with two thoughts to ponder. The first was from Augustine, *Amor dat novos oculos,"* ("Love gives new eyes"); the second was from John of the Cross: "Where there is no love put love, and you will find love Himself." These two thoughts helped to transform the young friar into an Islamic scholar capable of finding in a religion he once feared "the reflection of the infinite goodness of God" (see Giulio Basetti-Sani, *The Koran in the Light of Christ,* p. 18).

This story serves as an example of the central role of love in authentic interreligious dialogue. The new eyes given by love enable us to see people of other religious as brothers and sisters engaged in a common search for wisdom and truth. Without love there is the danger of demonizing those of other faiths – of seeing them as competitors and enemies rather than as fellow human beings who share a common humanity and common human questions. In reflecting on the meaning of the 1993 Parliament of the World's Religions, one question continuously comes to my mind: "Is it possible for people of many religions, of many races, and of many languages to truly love one another?" It is a deceptively simple question – for in the answer lies the destiny of our planet.

The amazing truth is that love is possible in spite of the differences of belief and practice that exist among the religions. These differences are real and will not go away. We should not attempt to ignore them and pretend that all religions are homogeneous, for they are not. However, the people who practice these religions do share a common language of love and compassion. For in every continent people have learned the language of love – whether from the arms of a mother or the gentle wisdom of a grandfather or the companionship of a friend. It should come as no surprise to learn of the beautiful words for love and compassion that emerge from the different traditions – from the *karuna* of the Bodhissatva to the *hesed* of YHWH; from the *agape* taught by Jesus to *Allah Ar-Rahman, Ar-Rahim* – there is a common recognition that compassion, mercy, and loving-kindness are the qualities we most wish to imitate as humans reaching towards transcendence.

As we near the end of this century, we must look for ways of growing in love. One way is that of collaborative work. When people of different religions work on common projects for better healthcare and family life, for cleaner air and safer cities, for more just laws and structures of peace, then the common humanity of fellow workers is perceived and loved. Another way is through study of different religions – but not a study that simply looks for patterns and archetypes – but a study that seeks to penetrate the heart of each tradition with empathy and a true desire to understand (insofar as is possible) how the world is seen from within the vision of that tradition. And, finally, we learn to love, as John of the Cross tells us, by putting love where there is no love, be being loving even when others are not loving, by seeking to understand even when others do not understand.

The dialogue of love is the first step needed for what has been envisioned as "the civilization of love." The shadows of war and fratricidal killing still hang like gloomy clouds over the sky of a world which is taking its first steps in learning to love. However, if love is the starting point for the survival of our planet, then all will be in vain if the various religions which preach love, compassion, and mercy fail in the exercise of these virtues. If religious people cannot learn to love each other, what are we to expect from non-religious people?

"Amor dat novos oculos" ("Love gives new eyes"). Let us love so we may have new eyes – eyes that see into the hearts of our brothers and sisters with love, and eyes that can see in the future a civilization of love.

Forms of Interreligious Dialogue

There are many ways we can participate in responding to the needs for interreligious understanding and cooperation. In the excerpt which follows, Marcus Braybrooke describes six forms of dialogue identified by Professor Diana Eck. The description distinguishes among several important aspects of the process of creating a community of religions.

The first [form] is **parliamentary-style dialogue.** [Diana Eck] traces this back to the 1893 World's Parliament of Religions and sees it carried forward by the international interfaith organizations, although... their way of working is now very different from the approach of the World's Parliament.

Secondly, there is **institutional dialogue,** such as the regular meetings between representatives of the Vatican and the International Jewish Committee for Inter-religious Consultation.

Thirdly, there is **theological dialogue,** which takes seriously the questions and challenges posed by people of other faiths.

Fourthly, **dialogue in community or the dialogue of life** is the search for good relationships in ordinary life.

Fifthly, **spiritual dialogue** is the attempt to learn from other traditions of prayer and meditation.

Lastly, there is **inner dialogue,** which is "that conversation that goes on within ourselves in any other form of dialogue."

from *A Pilgrimage of Hope* (p. 310).
Diana Eck's article is "What Do We Mean by Dialogue?"
in *Current Dialogue*, WCC, 1987

Concerning Acts of Initiative and Creation

*U*ntil one is committed,
there is hesitancy,
the chance to draw back,
always ineffectivenes

Concerning acts of initiative (and creation)
there is one elementary truth
the ignorance of which kills countless ideas
and splendid plans:
     that the moment one definitely commits oneself
     then Providence moves too.

All sorts of things occur to help one
that would never otherwise have occurred.

A whole stream of events issues from the decision,
raising in one's favor all manner
of unforseen incidents and meetings
and material assistance
which no one could have dreamt
would come one's way.

Whatever you can do,
or dream you can, begin it.
Boldness has genius, power, and magic in it.
Begin it now.

                        GOETHE

Resource Guides

Chapter 42: Service Organizations and Resource Centers

Chapter 43: Print, Audio and Video Resources

Chapter 44: The Global Brain

Service Organizations and Resource Centers

The organizations described below offer noteworthy programs and provide important resources congruent with the themes of this *SourceBook*. In addition, their stories document some of the history of religious engagement with critical issues, examples of inter-religious cooperation, and the emergence of a sense of community among religions. The articles, in most cases, have been excerpted or adapted from promotional and descriptive materials provided by the organizations themselves. Thus the articles are offered without critical evaluation, as a service to readers. The Editor is responsible for the selection and presentation of these material in this abbreviated format. The absence of fine organizations from these listings does not imply judgement against them, but reflects limits of access, scope and space. (Those who feel an important program is missing from this book are invited to send suitable information to the Editor for possible inclusion in a future edition.) Many other fine groups are listed elsewhere throughout this book (see also the Index of Organizations).

Albert Einstein Institution

Gene Sharp, Senior Scholar-in-Residence
50 Church St., Cambridge, MA 02138 USA;
tel. (617) 876-0311 / fax (617) 876-0837

The Albert Einstein Institution supports and conducts research, policy studies, and education concerning the nature and potential of nonviolent sanctions, in comparison to violent ones, for solving the problems of aggression, dictatorship, genocide, and oppression. The Institution is committed to the defense of democratic freedoms and institutions and to the reduction of political violence through the use of nonviolent sanctions. It is dedicated to examining how freedom, justice, and peace can be achieved without sacrificing one to the other. Just as the study of military strategy has yielded a more refined understanding of warfare, the strategic study of nonviolent sanctions can potentially yield a more refined understanding of their capacity and requirements for success.

The immediate goals of the Institution are to understand the dynamics of non-violent sanctions in conflicts, to explore their policy potential, and to communicate this through books, pamphlets, mongraphs, translations, conferences, and other forms of public communication and education.

Albert Schweizer Institute for the Humanities

515 Sherman Avenue, Hamden, CT 06514
USA; tel. (302) 281-8926

The ASIH is a non-profit, non-partisan, non-governmental organization affiliated with the United Nations. The Institute's mission is to perpetuate Albert Schweitzer's philosophy of reverence for life by promoting the physical, spiritual and educational well-being of humanity within a balanced environment. Concerns range across areas of health care, environment, theology and ethics, human rights, music and arts, animal issues, and peace issues.

Programs include a lecture series, publications, workshops, awards, courses, and international symposia. ASIH has global development, humanitarian relief, and medical programs, as well as academic expeditions. Schweitzer/Quinnipiac Press publishes proceedings of lectures and workshops, studies on Schweitzer's life, and an independent scholarly journal.

The American Indian Institute & the Traditional Circle of Indian Elders and Youth

A.I.I., P.O. Box 1388, Bozeman, MT 59715
USA; tel. (406) 587-1002

The relationship between the American Indian Institute and the Traditional Circle of Indian Elders and Youth is the result of creative interaction between traditional leaders of Indian nations from the Four Directions and American Indian Institute personnel. The resulting coalition based upon trust is unprecedented in cross-cultural relationships.

The coalition is expressed in Indian imagery as a "two-circle" concept. The American Indian Institute and the Traditional Circle of Indian Elders and Youth work together as equal but independent partners committed to common goals. In the history of North American cross-culture relationships this non-hierarchical organizational structure is unique in both function and spirit.

The Traditional Circle of Indian Elders and Youth is a spiritual circle open to all Indian people. Its purpose is to nurture a grassroots renewal of traditional values and lifeways among Native peoples, to ensure the continuity of Native wisdom and to bring that wisdom to bear upon the threats to land and life that are increasing with each passing day. The Circle is a repository of indigenous wisdom and values, and the Circle gatherings and projects represent a means of reinforcing and strengthening that wisdom within the participating delegations and extending it through them to grassroots communities as well as across cultures.

The official support group and administrative agency for the Traditional Circle of Indian Elders and Youth is the American Indian Institute, which is the heart of the non-Indian Circle. Its connection with the Circle is in its support function, and in shared ideals and commitments. Each is separate but there is a spiritual binding force which is stronger than written documents and signed agreements. The relationship embodies freedom and the ideals of the Iroquois Confederacy two-row wampum: support and cooperation but no interference.

The support of the Institute to the Circle is given freely. Neither partner has a self-serving agenda. The goal is the welfare of traditional Native people first and the welfare of all people through the joint effort of the two partners; neither side will dishonor that goal.

An important function of the Institute is to provide administrative support. For example, each year the Circle holds an international Council lasting six or seven days, in a different location each year. The staff of the Institute, in cooperation with the Indian host community, makes all arrangements including notification of participants and dissemination of the communiqués issued to report on the deliberations of the Elders. The same services apply to the Youth and Elder education programs, and to domestic intercultural programs as well as cross-cultural dialogue in international conferences such as the Global Forum.

Another responsibility of the American Indian Institute is to assist the Elders Circle in projecting the traditional voice across cultures on Indian terms. The Traditional Circle of Indian Elders and Youth continues to be a beacon of hope for Native people specifically, and for all people generally.

The organizational structure which has brought this about is the result of a conviction that the challenges of our day need fresh thinking and new human resources organized in innovative ways. It also results from a conviction that the ancient wellspring of indigenous wisdom, overlooked by the larger society through 500 years of coexistence, has new relevance for a new era.

ROBERT STAFFANSON,
Executive Director

Amnesty International / USA
322 Eighth Ave., New York, NY 1001 USA

AI works to help free prisoners of conscience, to ensure fair and prompt trials for all political prisoners, and to end torture, "disappearances" and executions – judicial and extrajudicial. Because of its experience, networks and international access, Amnesty has the capability of conducting research and exposing the human rights abuses of every nation, no matter how secretive and closed. Although its goal is to assure universal human rights for all people, AI finds human rights abuses escalating all over the world today. Its Urgent Action Networks, comprised of student and religious groups, and other concerned individuals, continue to publicize and communicate by mail with perpetrators of abuses. The record indicates that exposure can effect changes in the treatment of individuals and in public policies.

Anuvrat Global Organization
S. L. Gandhi, International Secretary, Anuvrat Global Organization, B-94, Saraswati Marg Bajaj Nagar, Jaipur-302015 India tel/fax 91-141-510118

Vishva Shanti Nilayam (Global Peace Palace) Post Box 28, Rajsamand 313326 India

Also known as Anuvrat Vishva Bharati in Hindi, with its widely publicized acronym, ANUVIBHA, this nonprofit socio-cultural organization is dedicated to peace and nonviolent action. It seeks to popularize the Anuvrat Movement, which attempts to cultivate self-discipline among the people by persuading them to commit themselves to the observance of small vows (Anuvrats) embedded in ahimsa or nonviolence. Anu means 'small' and Vrat means 'a vow.' It

seeks to rejuvenate moral and spiritual values through individual commitment to certain basic human values – the degeneration of which are at the root of the violence, hatred, religious fundamentalism and conflict that mark the world today.

The Anuvrat Movement, launched by His Holiness Acharya Tulsi in 1949, has inspired millions of people to practice purity and self-discipline in personal life. The ultimate aim of the movement is to create a nonviolent socio-political world order with the help of a worldwide network of self-transformed people.

Founded in 1983 mainly to carry the message of Anuvrat beyond the frontiers of India, ANUVIBHA has steadily grown in size and stature. It has created a worldwide network of thousands of people in many countries who believe that all conflicts should be resolved through nonviolent actions. One of its aims is to extend support to the UN and its agencies in their endeavor to achieve world peace. ANUVIBHA organized the first international conference on peace and nonviolent action at Ladnun in December 1988. The theme was "unifying the forces of peace and nonviolence." The Ladnun Declaration has been hailed as a practical action plan for the eradication of violence from this beautiful planet; it was followed by a symposium and camps orienting people to nonviolence. Anuvrats propagated by the Movement include:

- I will not kill any innocent creature.
- I will neither attack anybody nor support aggression and will endeavor to bring about world peace and disarmament.
- I will not take part in violent agitations or in any destructive activities.
- I will believe in human unity, and will not discriminate on the basis of caste, color, etc.
- I will practice religious tolerance.
- I will observe rectitude in my dealings with other people.
- I will try to develop a pure tenor of life and control over senses.
- I will not resort to unethical practices in elections.
- I will not use intoxicants like alcohol, hemp, heroin, etc.
- I will lead a life free from addictions.
- I will do my best to refrain from such acts as are likely to cause pollution and harm the environment.

Association of Professors and Researchers in Religious Education
**Executive Secretary, APRRE
10 Phillips Street, Medway, MA 02053 USA**

APPRE welcomes colleagues from all faith

traditions into membership and provides them with a number of services:

- Co-publication of *Religious Education*, the quarterly Journal of the Religious Education Association and the Association of Professors and Researchers in Religious Education
- Task Force Groups related to: Adult Education, Electronic Technology, Evaluation, History of Religious Education, Multicultural and Multiethnic Religious Education, Ethnography as Methodology, and Gender
- An annual meeting of APRRE, and a directory of Association membership
- the quarterly *Bulletin* of the Council of Societies for the Study of Religion

The Association on American Indian Affairs
245 Fifth Avenue, Suite 1801, New York, NY 10016-8728 USA; tel. (212) 689-8720

The Association on American Indian Affairs (AAIA) celebrated its 70th year in 1994. AAIA is the oldest Native American advocacy organization and has played a fundamental role in improving and enhancing the lives of Native Americans. The Association is active in many fields involving the freedoms and rights of tribes and their members. AATA supports tribes in their pursuit of basic human rights by providing assistance in several ways:

Religious freedom

As a founding member of the American Indian Religious Freedom Coalition, AAIA is at the forefront of advocating religious freedom. The Coalition is composed of tribes and tribal advocacy groups, and has worked to get U.S. Senate Bill S-1021 to the hearing stage. This bill, The Native American Religious Freedom Act, ensures that "it shall be U.S. policy to protect the inherent right of Native Americans to exercise their traditional religion. This includes access to religious sites, use and possession of sacred objects, and freedom to worship through ceremonial rites."

Federal recognition

AAIA is actively petitioning the Bureau of Indian Affairs on behalf of "forgotten" tribes. Many tribes are not Federally recognized and the government has denied their existence because they had never signed treaties. To date, AAIA has assisted over 22 tribes in gaining Federal Acknowledgement to secure fundamental health care, hunting and fishing rights, grants and loans, and to stimulate socio-economic development.

Repatriation

AAIA continues to lead the fight for

reburial of funerary remains and the repatriation of sacred objects. The Association has helped several tribes in recovering ancestral remains and sacred objects from museum warehouses. The tribes are then re-dressing these skeletal remains in traditional clothing and giving them the burial that they properly deserve.

Indian child welfare

Another major accomplishment of AAIA is the Indian Child Welfare Act. Passed in 1979, this Act ensures that children taken from their parents in times of crisis (poverty, neglect, or abuse) be placed in homes of responsible Indian relatives or other tribal members so that, while safe, the child's culture and identity remains intact.

Scholarships

AAIA has also awarded thousands of scholarships to promising Native Americans. By encouraging and promoting academic accomplishment, the Association is sending hope through generations of Native Americans. AAIA assists several types of students, from those just-out-of-high school to displaced homemakers wanting a better life for themselves and those who depend on them.

AAIA has many accomplishments, but much work remains to be done. Programs are designed to empower tribes, guarantee rights, and allow Native Americans to rejoice in their heritage and spirituality.

Auroville

605 101, Tamil Nadu INDIA
tel. + 041-386-2268

Planned as an international experimental township, Auroville was inspired by the evolutionary vision of Sri Aurobindo and founded by Mirra Alfassa, known in India as the Mother.

Auroville was inaugurated on February 28, 1968, in a ceremony attended by representatives from 124 nations and all the states of India. The community has been endorsed by three resolutions of the UNESCO General Assembly and recognized as an international trust by a unique parliamentary act of the Indian government. Auroville welcomes people from all parts of the world to live together and explore cultural, educational, scientific, spiritual, and other pursuits in accordance with the Auroville Charter.

Auroville is located on the southeast coast of India in the state of Tamil Nadu, 100 miles south of Madras and just north of the city of Pondicherry. The Auroville site, previously eroded and barren, is a flat plateau 150 feet above sea level. There are now about 50 different settlements spread out over 2,600 acres within a 20-square-mile circle that is substantially restored and

reforested. Auroville's population currently numbers more than 700 people from 25 different countries. In the immediate vicinity are a dozen Tamil villages with a total population of 20,000.

The Matrimandir is both the physical and spiritual center of Auroville. Matrimandir, in Sanskrit, means Temple of the Divine Mother. Its inner chamber is meant to be a place for silence and concentration, void of sectarian ritual – a place for finding one's true being and consciousness. Physically, Matrimandir is a 100-foot high elliptical sphere resting on four pillars, and surrounded by a network of 12 gardens and a lake. Built with the support of people from all over the world, Matrimandir stands as an example of human unity in diversity – a unity essential for our planet's survival.

The whole of Auroville is seen as an experiment: a field of educational research, a campus for applied learning. Schools and academic studies began in 1970. Perhaps the most pressing task for the first settlers in Auroville was to discover and implement methods of regenerating the eroded land. Over the past two decades, Aurovillians have developed sustainable and effective techniques. Since energy is in short supply, expensive and often harmful to the environment, Aurovillians have also explored ways of generating nonpolluting, renewable, and affordable energy and technologies appropriate to local conditions.

Striving to become a self-sufficient community, Auroville has established many other basic services over the years for its own residents and development, for visitors, and for the neighboring Tamil villages. At present there are over 50 income-earning production units, including handicrafts, construction and architecture, printing, biogas-converter and windmill manufacturing, fish farming, and cheese-making. Aurelec manufactures PC-compatible computers and provides training and employment for thousands of local villagers.

FOR MORE INFORMATION:

Institute for Evolutionary Research
1621 Freeway Dr., Mount Vernon, WA 98273 USA; (write for addresses for books in languages other than English)

Sri Aurobindo Association
2288 Fulton St., #310,
Berkeley, CA 94704 USA

Au Sable Institute of Environmental Studies

7526 Sunset Trail N.E., Mancelona, MI 49659 USA; tel. (616) 587-8686

Outreach Office: **Dr. Calvin B. DeWitt, 731 State St., Madison, WI 53703 USA**

Au Sable Institute is a Christian

environmental stewardship institute whose mission is to bring healing and wholeness to the biosphere and to Creation. Au Sable offers programs and courses of study for college students, evangelical Christian colleges, and the broader world community.

In a setting of northern lower Michigan forests, wetlands, lakes, and wild rivers, students at Au Sable take college courses, gain field experience, and develop practical tools for environmental stewardship. In recognition of the need for certified professionals at the baccalaureate level, the Institute grants certificates for environmental analysts, land resources analysts, water resources analysts, and naturalists, under license of the State of Michigan Department of Education.

Persons taking Institute courses or working for a certificate remain students at their home college, university or seminary. Most students enroll through participating colleges that retain control of admitting students to Institute courses and programs, including collection of tuition and fees.

Brahma Kumaris World Spiritual University

An international organization with over 3,000 branches in sixty-five countries, the Brahma Kumaris World Spiritual University (BKWSU) works at all levels of society seeking to help bring about positive change in the world. It offers a range of educational programs in moral and spiritual values aimed at building a greater awareness of the worth and dignity of the human person. The curriculum is based on the recognition of the intrinsic goodness and spirituality of every human being. Education in spiritual principles is combined with development of latent qualities and the awakening of dormant personal power. It teaches a practical method of meditation which enables individuals to achieve peace of mind, develop their full potential and interact with others in a constructive and fulfilling way.

As a large non-governmental organization in consultative status with the United Nations Economic and Social Council and UNICEF, the BKWSU has coordinated and participated in numerous UN activities. It has supported programs on human rights, the environment, youth, development, women, health, drug and substance abuse, child welfare, disarmament, and other humanitarian issues. In addition, the Brahma Kumaris have also organized two major international projects. The first project, in 1966, entitled "Million Minutes of Peace," was dedicated to the UN International Year of Peace and reached the people of 88 countries. For this work the Secretary-

General of the UN awarded the Brahma Kumaris six national and one international Peace Messenger Awards. The second project, entitled "Global Cooperation for a Better World," was launched from the United Nations in New York and the Houses of Parliament in London in 1988. This international Peace Messenger initiative had the support of over 400 companies worldwide and involved tens of thousands of people.

Sharing Our Values for a Better World

For the 50th Anniversary of the United Nations, BKWSU has created and is coordinating an international project focusing on the tenet in the Preamble to the UN Charter, "To reaffirm the dignity and worth of the human person." Sharing Our Values for a Better World will involve all 3,000 Centres in public programs to:

- Raise awareness of the existence of higher-order values as spiritual qualities inherent within the individual regardless of political, economic, social, cultural or ethnic background;

- Create a safe environment for individuals to explore and express these spiritual values individually and collectively;

- Offer specific self-development and self-management methods and techniques which can be used to revive and strengthen spiritual values within the individual;

- Increase awareness of the value of self-development, undertaken individually and collectively, as a contribution to a better world.

The twelve values around which the project's activities will be organized are: respect, tolerance, honesty, cooperation, humility, love, responsibility, unity, freedom, simplicity, happiness, and peace. In its work during the last fifty years the Brahma Kumaris have made clear their belief that values cannot be imposed and instead have sought to stimulate individuals toward a greater awareness of higher values latent within themselves. The ethos of all SVBW activities will be a combination of celebration, education, sharing, and practical application of the above values.

Participants in the University's activities come from all backgrounds and ages and no pre-qualification for attendance is required. While the University's world headquarters are in Mt. Abu, India, many of its activities outside India are coordinated from Global Cooperation House, in London, with the assistance of a worldwide network of regional offices.

**Global Cooperation House
65 Pound Lane, London, NW102H UK
tel. 081 459 1400 / fax 081 451 6480**

**Global Harmony House, 46 S. Middle Neck Road, Great Neck, New York, NY 11021 USA
tel. 516 773 0971 / fax 516 773 0976**

Global Museum for a Better World,

**Maua Close off Parklands Road, Westlands, P.O. Box 12349, Nairobi, KENYA
tel. 254 2 743572 / fax 254 2 743885**

**Brahma Kumaris World Spiritual University, 78 Alt Street, Ashfield NSW 2131, Sydney, AUSTRALIA;
tel. 61 2 716 7066 / fax 61 2 716 7795**

**Brahma Kumaris World Spiritual University, International Headquarters
P.O. Box 2, Mount Abu 307501, Rajasthan, INDIA; tel. 91 2974 3348 / fax 91 2974 3352**

Bread for the World

**1100 Wayne Avenue, Suite 1000, Silver Spring, MD 20910 USA;
tel. (301) 608-2400 / fax (301) 608-2401**

For twenty years one of the most effective anti-hunger organizations in the United States has been mobilizing Christians and others to learn about hunger and to lobby their elected officials to change policies – particularly the harmful or ineffective government policies that help to cause hunger. David Beckmann, president of the Bread for the World Institute, says that policies can affect hungry people on a scale that dwarfs the impact of private assistance, both in the U.S. and worldwide.

BFTW Institute has published many books, educational guides, and reports, including *Causes of Hunger:* the *BFW Leader's Guide; Putting Children First; Transforming the Politics of Hunger;* and *Bread for the World,* by Arthur Simon, the award-winning book which has initiated thousands into hunger activism (for only US$3.00 + $3 S&H); the Institute also offers many resources for use by churches, schools and families, action notes and a newsletter.

Buddhist Peace Fellowships

Box 368, Lismore, NSW 2480, Australia

ACFOD, GPO Box 2930, Bangkok, 10501, Thailand

c/o Aleda Erskine, 16 Upper Park Road, London NW3, UK

P.O. Box 4650, Berkeley, CA 94704 USA

Grounded in the beliefs and practices of Buddhism regarding nonviolence and compassionate relationship with all, Buddhist Peace Fellowships in many countries have publications and provide leadership in social, political, and environmental activities. The offices listed above are affiliates of the International Fellowship of Reconciliation; since there are other fellowships as well, contact the offices listed above for more information.

Campaign 1995

1601 Connecticut Avenue, NW, 5th Floor,

**Washington, DC 20009 USA;
tel. 202-234-9382**

Campaign 1995 was established as an informal, project-oriented network of individuals and organizations to encourage the peace and human rights communities to shape public consciousness and action. It will publicize activities and encourage cooperation among various organizations that are planning events for the 1995 commemoration of half-century anniversaries. These include the ending of World War II, the atomic bombing of Hiroshima and Nagasaki, the signing of the U.N. Charter, the liberation of Auschwitz, the death of Franklin Roosevelt, the establishment of the Nuremberg War Crimes Tribunal, creation of the World Bank and International Monetary Fund, and others. To do this publicizing, "New Beginnings" newsletter is published by the Campaign 1995 Committee of the Fourth Freedom Forum (see the "Call for Remembrance..." in Chapter 28).

In addition to publicizing others' activities, [at least] two specific projects have developed from these discussions: One is to engage the religious community in calling for the abolition of nuclear weapons. The second project is the Peoples' Assembly toward a weapons-free world, held at the time of the Nuclear Proliferation Treaty review conference in April 1995.

Canadian Ecumencial Action

**David Spence, Managing Editor, 33 Arrowwood Place, Port Moody, British Columbia, CANADA V3H 4J1
tel.&fax (604) 469-1164**

CEA is publisher of the Multifaith Calendar whose 1995 theme is Celebrating Spiritual Principles in International Affairs and, particularly, the fiftieth anniversary of the United Nations. This beautiful and large full-color calendar, published annually with varying contents, provides fairly detailed information about the world's religions, their particular calendars, holidays, and festivals. The 1995 calendar also depicts art, sculptures, and photographs from the UN, peace parks, and religious centers worldwide. (In the US order from Multifaith Resources.)

Celebrating the Spirit – at UN50 in San Francisco

Rev. Aaron Zerah, 520 14th Ave., Santa Cruz, CA 95062 USA; tel. (408) 479-9484; *or*

Rt. Rev. David Ponedel, Church of Divine Man, 2018 Allston Way, Berkeley, CA 94704 USA; tel. (510) 848-2361

Inspired by the 1993 Parliament, the Board of Directors of Celebrating the Spirit, an interfaith organization, is promoting *Towards a Global Ethic*. It seeks to implement the principles of this transforming document by creating a forum for discussion, workshops, a conference for sharing our world faiths, and a city-wide celebration of shared Spirit.

A two-day conference titled "Celebrating the Spirit: Towards a Global Ethic" on June 20 and 21, 1995, and related activities including worship services throughout the month will participate in the "Nine Weeks for the World" between Earth Day 25 and the United Nations' 50th anniversary.

Center for Nonviolence
Guy de Mallac
PO Box 1058, San Jacinto, CA 92581-1058

The Center for Nonviolence is devoted to an investigation of the principles of peace, nonviolence and social service inherited from Leo Tolstoy, Mahatma Gandhi, Martin Luther King, Jr. and others. It publishes and distributes information on the implementation of these principles, and fosters the ethics of love and nonviolence.

Guy de Mallac's primary interests are in spreading this message and encouraging peace education. He maintains contacts with those in Western and Third World countries concerned with implementing strategies of nonviolent social change (see his article in Chapter 41).

Center of Concern – Women Connecting
3700 13th St., N.E.,
Washington DC 20017 USA;
tel. (202) 635-2757 / fax (202) 832-9494

As women concerned about our children, our cities, our economy, and our environment, we need to understand how our local problems are part of the larger world picture. CoC encourages women to join with other women to create effective local and global solutions, to connect for change. Because our voices are stronger when we speak together, the upcoming United Nations Fourth World Conference on Women, 1995, in Beijing, China, offers women in local communities the opportunity to unite and be heard by world leaders. The CoC has developed a variety of opportunities to engage in the global women's movement through participation in the UN Conference, whether at home or in attendance at Beijing in '95.

Women connecting through workshops and global leadership seminars
The Women Connecting workshop materials and educational seminars provide ways for participants to connect with the UN Fourth World Conference on Women from their local base. Through guided discussions and group activities, participants identify their local concerns, explore how these are linked to the concerns of women around the world, and develop strategies for action. Scholarships for the seminars and the Beijing trip are being sought to ensure that younger women and grassroots women from diverse communities can participate.

Rethinking Bretton Woods
Center of Concern also provides educational resources promoting justice, peace and Catholic social teaching. In the context of the 50th anniversary of the World Bank and IMF, and questions about their ability to promote equitable, participatory and sustainable development, CoC has released the report *Rethinking Bretton Woods*; the report promotes a vision of global development that is a multidimensional, people-centered process ($5.95 plus $1.50 for S&H).

Children's Defense Fund – and the Children's Sabbath
Marion Wright Edelmen, President,
25 E. St. N.W., Washington, DC 20001 USA;
tel. (202) 662-3589

CDF is a nonprofit organization that seeks to provide a strong and effective voice for children who cannot vote, lobby, or speak out for themselves. We pay particular attention to the needs of poor, minority, and disabled children. Our goal is to educate the nation about the needs of children and encourage preventive investment in children before they get sick, drop out of school, suffer family breakdown, or get into trouble.

Among our most visible programs is the National Observance of Children's Sabbaths, held each October in thousands of congregations of many faiths and races. (See Chapter 37 for more information and about the several faith and culture-based versions of Organizing Kits.) Other programs include Annual Conferences, networking, and lobbying.

Church World Service – and the Office on Global Education
475 Riverside Dr., New York, NY
10115-0050 USA; tel. (212) 870-2257

CWS, founded in 1946, is a ministry of the Church World Service and Witness Unit of the National Council of the Churches of Christ in the USA. It is the cooperative agency of 32 Protestant, Anglican, and Orthodox communions working in partnership to meet human needs and foster self-reliance in more than 70 countries through programs of social and economic development, emergency response, and service to refugees.

In the United States CWS resettles refugees, assists communities in responding to disasters, promotes fair and environmentally sound U.S. policies, provides educational resources, and offers opportunities for communities to join a people-to-people network.

Each year, through CROP Walks, people across the United States join hands and hearts to help neighbors help themselves, both globally and locally. CROP Walks provide opportunities for communities to return up to 25% of the funds they raise to share with local hunger programs. For more information on specific programs, consult the following:

- CROP Walk, publications and curriculum materials, videos, calendars:
  CWS, P.O. Box 968, Elkhart, IN 46515
  tel. (219) 264-3102
- Resources and curriculum for global education, environment, hunger, *Children at Risk, Children Hungering for Justice*, and others are available from:
  Office on Global Education, 2115 N. Charles St., Baltimore, MD, 21218-5755
  tel. (410) 727-6106 (or from Elkhart).
- Many publications, including *Affective Approaches to Global Education*, are available from:
  Friendship Press Distribution Office, P.O. Box 37844, Cincinatti, OH 45222-0844
- Many CWS publications include useful bibliographies and resource listings.

Circle Sanctuary (Circle)
Circle, PO Box 219, Mt. Horeb, WI 53572
USA; tel. (608) 924-2216 / fax (608) 924-5961

Circle Sanctuary, also known as Circle, is an international nature spirituality resource center and shamanic Wiccan church. It is headquartered on a 200-acre sacred nature preserve near Mt. Horeb in the forested hills of southwestern Wisconsin. Founded in 1974 and incorporated as a nonprofit religious organization in 1978, Circle's ministry includes networking, publishing, academic research, counseling, spiritual healing, education, sponsoring gatherings, nature preservation, religious freedom activism, interfaith and multicultural dialogue, and other work. Circle operates Circle Network, an information exchange and contact service which links thousands of individuals, groups, networks, centers, and other groups of Wiccans, Pagans, and other nature religions folk throughout the United States and more than fifty other countries. Contemporary Paganism's oldest and largest Wiccan/ Pagan network, Circle publishes a variety of periodicals, resource directories and a quarterly newsjournal.

Seasonal festivals, rites of passage, moon circles, nature meditations, workshops, and other activities are held at Circle Sanctuary land and in other locations throughout the year and are open to those affiliated with the Circle network and their guests. Some events are also open to the general public and media. Circle also plays a leading role in public education and religious freedom endeavors. A packet with more information about Circle and its services is available upon request.

Citizens Network for Sustainable Development

73 Spring St., Suite 206, New York, NY 10012 USA; tel. (212) 431-3922 / fax (212) 431-4427 E-mail: cca@IGC.APC.ORG

The Citizens Network links over 400 constituency-based organizations and roughly 600 other members. Its work includes representing its members' concerns to the UN, and encouraging NGOs to develop collaborative approaches to UN and US policies.

City of God

RD 1, Box 319, New Vrindaban, WV 26041 USA; tel. (304) 895-9370

The City of God is not only a place in West Virginia but a concept of a special place. Instead of being a center for businesss and economic development, the City of God is reserved for worshipping the Supreme in beautiful ways. It is also an interfaith city where people of all religious traditions can live, work, and worship in proximity to one another. It is a city of diverse spiritual communities; a city of mosques, temples, synagogues and churches; a city of prayers and chants, music and dance.

In West Virginia, the New Vrindaban City of God was founded by Swami Bhaktipada in 1969, inspired by Srila Prabhupadha, founder of the Krishna movement in North America. It was understood as continuing the teachings of Lord Caitanya in 16th-century India and Srila Bhaktivinode Thakur, who pioneered the distribution of spiritual consciousness to the English-speaking world. He wrote, "Pure, unalloyed love of God is the actual eternal religion of the spirit soul. Thus, in spite of the distinctions among religious systems, we should recognize as genuine any religious process whose goal is the realization of pure love of God. It is useless to quarrel over superficial differences. If the goal of a process is pure, then the system is fully auspicious."

New Vrindaban City of God established its independence from the International Society for Krishna Consciousness (Hare Krishna movement) and, in 1987, formed the "League of Devotees," embracing religious pluralism and the concept of the interfaith City of God. The League now has centers in New York City and Tallahassee, Florida, as well as two centers in Australia.

Consortium on Peace Research, Education, and Development

George Mason University, Fairfax, VA 22030-4444 USA; tel. (703) 993-3639

COPRED is committed to changing the conditions that give rise to poverty and innercity rebellions; eliminating ignorance, bigotry, intolerance, and hate crimes; finding nonviolent alternatives in regional conflicts and wars; transforming the mass media into a force for peace; halting injustices toward Native Peoples; strengthening global security through grassroots citizens' peace initiatives and regional security arrangements; and restructuring unjust global economic institutions and systems.

COPRED sponsors workshops, trainings, symposia, and publications.

Council for a Parliament of the World's Religions

PO Box 1630 Chicago, IL 60690-1630 USA; tel. (312) 629-2990; fax: (312) 629-2991

See Chapters 21, 22, and 23 for descriptions of the organization, the Parliament, and ongoing activities.

Council of Societies for the Study of Religion

Valparaiso Univ., Valparaiso IN 46383-6493

CSSR is a federation of learned societies in religion interested in enhancing coordination of the field as a whole; it seeks to initiate, coordinate, and implement projects to strengthen and advance scholarship and teaching and to support the activities of constituent societies and of their executive offices and officers. CSSR publishes a quarterly *Bulletin* and a scholarly journal

Covenant of the Goddess

P.O. Box 1226, Berkeley, CA 94701 USA

The Covenant of the Goddess is one of the largest and oldest Wiccan religious organizations, with members in North America, Europe, and Australia. Wicca, also known as the Old Religion or Witchcraft, is the most popular expression of the religious movement known as Neo-Paganism or Goddess worship. Its practitioners are reviving the practices of the ancient, pre-Christian Earth religion of Europe and adapting them to modern life.

In the 1970's there was a marked rise of interest in Wicca throughout the world, reflecting a growing feminist awareness and global concern for the environment. In the spring of 1975, a number of Wiccan elders from diverse traditions, all sharing the idea of forming a religious organization for all

practitioners of Witchcraft, gathered to draft a covenant among themselves. These representatives also drafted bylaws to administer this new organization, now known as Covenant of the Goddess, which was incorporated as a nonprofit religious organization on October 31, 1975.

The Covenant is an umbrella organization of cooperating autonomous Wiccan congregations with the power to confer credentials on its qualified clergy. The Covenant is non-hierarchical and governed by consensus. Two-thirds of its clergy are women. The Covenant holds an annual national conference open to the Wiccan community, as well as regional conferences, and publishes a newsletter. In recent years, the Covenant has taken part in spiritual and educational conferences, interfaith outreach, large public rituals, environmental activism, community projects and social action, as well as efforts to correct negative stereotypes and promote accurate media portrayal. Member congregations have also prosecuted cases in which they have secured Constitutional rights of freedom of religion, assembly and speech. Its clergy perform legal marriages (*handfastings),* preside at funerals and other rituals of life-transition, teach and provide counseling.

The Covenant's participation in the 1993 Parliament of the World's Religions continued its efforts to restore the respect due to a venerable but misunderstood religious tradition, enhance the status of women, protect and preserve the Earth through public dissemination of its wisdom and traditions, and participate in dialogue as a contributing member of the world's community of faiths.

Cultural Information Service – Values and Visions, a Resource Companion for Spiritual Journeys

P.O. Box 786, Madison Square Station, New York, NY 10159 USA; tel. 1-800-929-4857

Values and Visions is the bi-monthly membership magazine of CIS. It seeks the spiritual dimensions of contemporary life as they are reflected in today's fiction and nonfiction books, films, videos, TV programs, and spoken-word audiocassettes. The magazine's reviews describe the best and latest resources which are expressive of the quest for meaning and purpose, wholeness and healing, commitment and community, contemplation and social activism. CIS serves those with open heart and mind, an active imagination, appreciation for the sacred, and a willingness to share with others the stories of their lives.

Earth Council

P.O. Box 2323-1002, San José, Costa Rica

tel. (506) 223 6410 / 223 3418
fax (506) 255 2197 / 233 1822

The Earth Council was established in September 1992 following the Rio Earth Summit. Its Chairman, Maurice Strong, was also Chair of the Summit. The Council's mission is to support followup to the agreements reached at the Summit and to empower people in building a more sustainable future. Activities include:

- monitoring and reporting on people's perceptions, independent initiatives, and progress by national governments and other actors in achieving various aspects of sustainable development;
- facilitating initiatives (such as the Earth Charter Initiative) that empower civil institutions and supporting national and community networks for sustainable development;
- building bridges of awareness, understanding and information among the various components of civil society and between them and policymakers.

Environmental Sabbath/
Earth Rest Day

c/o United Nations Environment Programme, DC1-803, UN, New York, NY 10017 USA

Established in 1987 by UNEP and its advisory committees, including religious nongovernmental organizations affiliated with the UN, the Earth Rest Day provides a way to meld spiritual values with environmental science. Many churches, temples, synagogues, mosques, and other religious bodies have adopted the first weekend in June as a time for special commemoration, education, and personal commitment, often utilizing resources provided or recommended by the UNEP, including the materials provided in its annual Environmental Sabbath/Earth Rest Day publications. (See Chapter 30.) UNEP is the international organization given authority to monitor the environment; it also attempts to ensure that work done by other agencies of the United Nations incorporates an ecological perspective.

In 1994 UNEP published *Ethics and Agenda 21: Moral Implications of a Global Consensus*, edited by Noel J. Brown and Pierre Quiblier ($9.95 +S&H, pb, 187 pages). Seventeen essays assess the ethical implications of the document of the Earth Summit, review social, economic, scientific, and technological perspectives, and present five religious or spiritual perspectives on environmental issues.

Faith and Values Channel –
ACTS/VISN Network

74 Trinity Place, 9th Floor, New York, NY 10006 USA; tel. (212) 964-1663 ex. 106

This 24-hour-a-day cable television channel serves 8,000 communities in the US and over 20 million homes on more than 1,300 local cable systems. The channel is programmed by two networks – the Vision Interfaith Satellite Network (VISN), which provides two-thirds of the daily programming, and the American Christian Television System (ACTS). The channel brings together over sixty national Catholic, Protestant, Jewish, Evangelical, and Eastern Orthodox faith groups; it allows no maligning of any faith group, no on-air fundraising, and no proselytizing. Programming includes documentaries, dramas, worship, call-in talk shows, music and children's fare. *A VISN Special Report: The Parliament of the World's Religions* offered interviews with participants and excerpts from speeches; this 30-minute broadcast surveys the Parliament's context, goals and issues, including perspectives from Christians on how to relate to persons of other faiths. To add this programming to your community, contact cable system managers who try to respond to requests of potential subscribers.

For more information, call 1-800-841-8476

Fellowship of Reconciliation

Box 271, Nyack, NY 10960 USA;
tel. (914) 358-4601

FOR is composed of men and women who recognize the essential unity of all humanity and have joined together to explore the power of love and truth for resolving human conflict. While it has always been vigorous in its opposition to war, the Fellowship has insisted equally that this effort must be based on a commitment to the achieving of a peaceful world community, with full dignity and freedom for every human being.

The Fellowship seeks the company of those of whatever faith who wish to confront human differences with nonviolent, compassionate, and reconciling love. The FOR began as a movement of protest against war, with its origins in the ethic of love as found in Jesus Christ. While many of its members today are Christian, the participation of others is nourished in the Jewish faith and community, with its prophetic emphases on universalism, justice, and love. The FOR was also deeply affected by Gandhi and the freedom struggle in India, with its roots in the ancient teachings of Hinduism. And the powerful pacifist movement in Vietnam

brought to FOR still another tradition of nonviolence, that derived from Buddhism.

Although members do not bind themselves to any exact form of words,

- They identify with those of every nation, race and religion who are the victims of injustice and exploitation, and seek to develop resources of active nonviolent intervention with which to help rescue them from such circumstances;
- They work to abolish war and to create a community of concern transcending national boundaries and selfish interests; they refuse to participate in any war, or to give any sanction they can withhold from physical, moral, psychological, or financial preparation for war.
- They strive to build a social order that will utilize the resources of human ingenuity and wisdom for the benefit of all, and in which no individual or group will be exploited or oppressed for the profit or pleasure of others;
- They advocate methods of dealing with offenders against society that will be founded on understanding and forgiveness, and that will seek to redeem and rehabilitate the offender rather than impose punishment;
- They seek to avoid contention in dealing with controversy, and to maintain the spirit of self-giving love.

The Fellowship was founded in 1914 when an English Quaker and a German Lutheran pastor pledged to remain friends and continue to work for peace, even though their countries were at war. The following year the FOR was established in the United States. FOR groups have subsequently been organized in 27 countries. (See IFOR, below.)

Food First – Institute for Food
and Development Policy

Executive Director, Walden Bellow
145 Ninth St., San Francisco, CA 94103-3584
USA; tel. (415) 864-8555

Again and again we read that nearly 40,000 children die each day from hunger and hunger-related causes. What should be done? Food First was founded by Frances Moore Lappé and Joseph Collins to empower citizens. Their research and educational materials reveal how anti-democratic institutions and belief systems sustain hunger and environmental deterioration, and that famine is usually a consequence of politics.

Food First traces the cause of hunger and poverty to social inequity, political oppression, and misguided aid policies. Food First's analysis demonstrates that US and World Bank aid programs create *more* hunger and poverty among their Third World recipients. In September 1991, FF foretold the problem which was to come in

Somalia; yet it firmly believes that together we can turn this appalling injustice around.

Food First believes the only strategy of development that can end hunger and poverty is one that is participatory, equitable, and sustainable. To this end, FF is working with various organizations in the Third World in an urgent effort to promote democratic development. Members help to:

- Expose political causes of hunger.
- Promote agrarian reform.
- Educate people on the toxic effects of chemical-intensive agriculture and the unpredictable consequences of bio-technological farming.
- Stop mega-dam projects that threaten the environment and communities in India, Indonesia, Senegal, and China.
- Combat the destructive impact of World Bank export-oriented strategies in Asia.
- Assist grassroots organizations in Third World countries in developing a program of democratic involvement.

Food First also offers books, a newsletter, action alerts, tours, and other resources.

Foundation for Global Community

222 High Street, Palo Alto, CA 94301 USA; tel. (415) 328-7756

Foundation for Global Community is a nonprofit, educational movement whose mission is to discover, live and communicate what is needed to build a world that functions for all life. Its services include international mediation teams, a bimonthly newsmagazine in English (*Timeline*) and Spanish (*Sucesos*), conferences and workshops.

Fourth Freedom Forum

Dr. David Cortwright, Director, 803 North Main St., Goshen, IN 46526 USA; tel. (219) 534-3402

Founded in 1982, the Forum advocates freedom from fear of mass destructive weapons and aggression. It stimulates informed public discussion of international security issues, emphasizing the use of economic power instead of military power. The Forum publishes a newsletter, "Inforum" and sponsors conferences and symposia.

The Forum is also a primary organizer of the Campaign 1995 Committee, which publicizes activities and encourages cooperation among various organizations for the 1995 commemoration of half-century anniversaries (see Chapter 28).

Freedom, Justice, and Peace Society

Mr. James S. Mulholland, Jr., President,

150 Werimus Lane, Hillsdale, NJ 07642-1223; tel. (201) 664-2148 / fax (201) 664-2261

Every year, invitations are mailed to religious leaders throughout the world asking them to participate in a "World Day of Prayer for Human Rights" in their locality to thank God for the human rights we enjoy and to pray for the restoration of human rights to those currently denied them. This event coincides with the anniversary of the United Nations Universal Declaration of Human Rights. In 1994, participation included 954 religious leaders representing 100 million members. The Society is also organizing a 1995 worldwide computer conference of religious leaders on the need for a United Nations Convention on Freedom of Religion or Belief.

Global Education Associates

475 Riverside Drive, Suite 1848 New York, NY 10115 USA; tel. 212 870-3290 / fax 212 870-2729

Global Education Associates was formed in 1973 by Gerald and Patricia Mische in response to their experiences with and analysis of development programs in Central America, Africa, and worldwide. They had concluded that the assumption on which most international development was based – i.e., that nations are sovereign – was now a fiction. Expanding circles of economic and monetary interdependence were giving birth to an increasingly integrated global economy that paid little heed to national borders or claims of sovereignty. Thus, rather than working from a "globalist" perspective, conforming with international relations theory, GEA's concerns were ultimately for decentralization and the viable sovereignty of the local community.

Beginning with this grassroots-based analysis, GEA has grown into an international association of individuals and affiliates in over 90 countries working to empower people to understand and respond constructively to the crises and opportunities of today's interdependent world. Toward this end, the associates sponsor educational programs, conduct research and leadership seminars, publish materials, offer consulting services, and facilitate networking at local, national, and international levels.

Highlights from 20 years:

Over 2,500 workshops, institutes, and symposia have been conducted by staff and core associates around the world.

A 17-part television series was produced by CBS based on co-founders Jerry and Pat Mische's book, *Toward a Human World Order.*

Publications and projects

GEA's newsletter, *Breakthrough,* and the *Whole Earth Papers,* a series of essays, have been acclaimed worldwide as being among the best material available on global interdependence and world order issues. Graduate-level institutes on these subjects have been conducted by staff and core associates at more than 20 universities around the world. More than 300 monographs, articles, and books have been written by GEA staff and core associates on world order issues, ecological security, and global spirituality,

Project Global 2000 is a major partnership of 17 agencies and organizations on questions of global governance. Religion and World Order is one of the programs of the Religion Council of Project Global 2000. (See Chapter 28.)

The Earth Covenant has been signed by over 2 million people as is providing popular support for the Earth Charter Initiative, which aims to have a legally-binding Charter ratified by all nations in the UN by the year 2000. (See Chapter 30.)

GEA affiliate organizations include: International Institute of Concern for Public Health, Toronto; Philippine Council for Peace and Global Education, Manila; Genesis Farm and Environmental Center, New Jersey; Upper Midwest GEA, St. Paul, Minnesota; Michaela Farm, Oldenburg, Indiana. Global Education Associates is also a co-publisher of this *SourceBook.*

Global Exchange – People to People Ties

2017 Mission Street, #303, San Francisco, CA 94110 USA; tel. (415) 255-7296 / fax (415) 255-7498 / E-mail: globalexch@igc.org

Formed in 1988 to help build people-to-people ties between caring citizens in North America and people struggling for peace and justice abroad, Global Exchange has four key program areas which share the common goal of building international awareness and mobilizing people to create peace, social justice, and democracy.

Reality Tours bring North Americans to the third world to learn from local people about community-initiated development; Public Education campaigns present alternative news and analysis about global issues through a public radio show, newsletters, special publications, and speaking tours; the Fair Trade Program and Third World Craft Stores provide artists and crafts people in over thirty countries with markets and livable wages. In recent years these programs have also focused on the plight of Haiti's poverty-stricken citizens and environmental degradation.

The Global Forum of Spiritual and Parliamentary Leaders on Human Survival

304 East 45th St., 4th Floor, New York, NY 10017 USA;
tel. 212 953-7947 / fax 212 557-2061

In October 1985, while the United Nations was celebrating its 40th anniversary, a core group of religious and political leaders met for the first time in a village north of New York City. Ten spiritual leaders, two each from five major religions, and eight elected officials from parliaments on five continents came to Tarrytown to explore the possibility of a dialogue that intermingled their perspectives.

The politicians were members of the Global Committee of Parliamentarians on Population and Development. The spiritual leaders were invited by the Temple of Understanding, an organization devoted to building understanding among the different religions. The lawmakers tended toward practical solutions while the spiritual leaders emphasized morality and ethics.

From their differing viewpoints new possibilities emerged. In the end, the religious and political leaders decided that their dialogue had become so meaningful that it must be continued and expanded. They called upon colleagues worldwide to join them in a conference on global survival.

The Oxford and Moscow forums

The first Global Survival Conference in April 1988 drew nearly 200 spiritual and legislative leaders to the historic university city of Oxford, England, for five days. Among the participants were cabinet members, speakers of parliaments, Mother Teresa, the Dalai Lama, the Archbishop of Canterbury, High Priest of Togo's Sacred Forest, Cardinal Koenig of Vienna, and Native American Chief Oren Lyons. They conferred with experts, including astronomer Carl Sagan, Soviet scientist Evguenij Velikhov, Gaia scientist James Lovelock, Kenyan environmentalist Wangari Maathai, and Cosmonaut Valentina Tereshkova. *Earth Conference One: Sharing a Vision for Our Planet,* by Anuradha Vittachi (Shambhala), provides an eloquent description of this meeting.

A second meeting of the Global Forum was hosted in the (former) Soviet Union in January 1990 by a unique alliance of scientists, faith communities, the first freely elected Supreme Soviet, and the International Foundation for the Survival and Development of Humanity. More than 1,000 spiritual and parliamentary leaders, scientists, artists, journalists, businessmen and young people from 83 countries came to the Moscow forum. Mikhail Gorbachev, now head of Green Cross International,

hailed it as "a major step toward the ecological consciousness of humanity."

National Forums have also been held in Indonesia, the Phillipines, and Japan.

The Parliamentary Earth Summit

Co-sponsored by the National Congress of Brazil and the Global Forum, the Parliamentary Earth Summit gathered in Rio de Janiero during the first weekend of the UNCED Earth Summit in June 1992. Parliamentarians from more than 100 countries met with extraordinary leaders from many different fields of endeavor.

Value change for global survival

Another general assembly was held in Kyoto, Japan from April 17–23, 1993. Through the Global Forum process of dialogue and interaction, leaders are given the opportunity to influence each other and to extend their spiritual and political influence for peaceful, positive change.

Gray Panthers Peace Committee

Ruth Anna Brown and Ralph Odom
1065 Toedtli Drive, Boulder, CO 80303 USA

As a contribution to the 50th anniversary of the United Nations, the Gray Panthers, an NGO with representation at the UN, held a "People's Summit for Peace" in Costa Rica, December 4-11, 1993, in cooperation with the University for Peace. A number of proposals for peace, for the UN and for the United States were brainstormed by the Conference. These include appreciation to the Parliament of the World's Religions for producing a model Declaration of a Global Ethics and for contributing toward much-needed cooperation and peaceful co-existence among the religions of the planet. The 40,000 members of the Gray Panthers are invited to contribute further proposals; their work is offered to other NGOs and peoples' organizations as an example of what the people can and should exhort their leaders to do.

Graymoor Ecumenical & Interreligious Institute

475 Riverside Dr., Suite 1960, New York, NY 10115-1999 USA; tel. (212) 870-2330

This ministry of the Franciscan Friars of the Atonement is an information and service organization serving primarily, but not exclusively, the Roman Catholic Church in the United States in its mission of Christian unity and interreligious dialogue. The Institute employs several means to accomplish this goal:

- the specialization desks of the Institute
- the Week of Prayer for Christian Unity
- the publications "Ecumenical Trends" and "At-One-Ment"

- membership in and collaboration with national and local ecumenical and interreligious organizations and agencies
- cooperation with individuals engaged in ecumenical and interreligious work.

Over the years the Graymoor Ecumenical & Interreligious Institute has sponsored and cosponsored meetings, colloquia, and workshops in areas of ecumenical and interreligious dialogue. These have been as diverse as colloquia between African-American and Hispanic Pentecostal scholars; Christians, Muslims and Jews; state Councils of Churches; and interfaith training workshops for Christian leaders. Some of these discussions have appeared as "The Graymoor Papers" in the *Journal of Ecumenical Studies.*

Recent structural changes include the introduction of specialization desks serving specific areas of concern within the ecumenical and interreligious movements:

- African-American Churches
- Evangelical and Free Churches
- Lutheran, Anglican, Roman Catholic Affairs
- Interreligious Dialogue
- Social Ecumenism.

Heifer Project International

P.O. Box 808, Little Rock, AR 72203 USA

HPI is an interfaith organization which welcomes participation from all who are concerned about hunger and support HPI's approach to ending hunger. Begun more than 40 years ago, HPI has developed an innovative process which: 1) provides animals and related assistance to families and communities to help them produce food and income on a long-term basis; 2) enables people to share resources by passing on the offspring of the donated animals to others within the community, a step that enhances the dignity of all; and 3) educates people about the root causes of hunger and poverty and the opportunities for alleviating them in our interdependent world.

HPI raises, receives, and transports donated animals, does research and education, and maintains followup with recipient communities worldwide.

Human Rights Watch

485 Fifth Avenue, New York, NY 10017 USA

HRW is working in more than 60 countries to extend human rights and principles into several crucial fronts – on arms and weapons distribution, in prisons and cases of torture, free expression, and womens' rights, including the right not to be enslaved into prostitution.

The enslavement and manipulation of women into prostitution against their will remains a serious and, up till now, mostly overlooked problem. It is significantly due to the work of women in the human rights organizations that the abuses of women in particular were addressed at the United Nation Conference on Human Rights (1993) and in exposés ever since. The systematic rape of women, as in Bosnia, is now being regarded as an act of war and is under consideration for designation as a "crime against humanity."

Institute of Cultural Affairs – USA and International

4750 North Sheridan Rd., Chicago, IL 60640 USA; tel .(312) 769-1144

rue Amedee Lynen, 8, B-1030 Brussels, Belgium; tel. (32-2) 219-0087

ICA International is a private, non-sectarian organization with 31 affiliate organizations and numerous field offices throughout the world. Having evolved out of the Ecumenical Institute which began in Chicago in the mid-50's, many of the members and staff are faith-based, but clearly also pluralist in outlook.

Concerned with the human factor in world development, ICA acts as a catalyst for positive change in communities, organizations, and individuals throughout the world. ICA's highly participatory techniques for strategic planning and problem-solving foster creative thinking, consensus-based decision making, and teamwork. Its methods also create clear goals, broaden perspectives, open lines of communication, and motivate people to adapt to change while honoring the cultures and diversity of all involved.

At the heart of ICA's work is the belief that long-term, sustainable development happens only when people grasp the significance of their own lives in the larger scheme of things – when they actively participate in the the changes taking place around them instead of merely being targets of that change.

Indian Institute for Human Research and Development

947, Poonamalee High Road (Opp. Dasaprakash), Madras - 600 084 S. India; tel. +91 44 6421326 / fax +91 44 5322065

Founded as a voluntary institution for peaceful human co-existence, the IIHRD is a non-governmental organization that administers grass roots programs for the welfare of children, women, and families. It is coordinating approximately 65 other NGOs and their programs in different parts of India. Their motto is "Love and sharing unites mankind."

Institute for Interreligious Studies (Interreligiose Arbeitsstelle)

Dr. Reinhard Kirste and Dr. Udo Tworuschka, Am Hardtkopf 17, P.O. Box 1201, D-58766, Nachrodt, Germany

The Interreligiose Arbeitsstelle is an association of educators, theologians, teachers, economists, and others who want to promote interfaith dialogue through encounters and publications. The Institute believes that these encounters must be accompanied by observation, analysis, and careful evaluation, undergirded by theological, historical, and educational research into the character and purposes of dialogue, absolute claims, and missions.

Publications in the series *Religions in Dialogue,* and in the *Iserlohner Con-Texte* series of theoretical and contextual approaches to pluralism and education, and a special library for inter-religious studies and research, help to increase and spread the study of literature in this field. While many of the materials are published in German, the essay "Interreligious Dialogue and Religious Pluralism in Germany," by Reinhard Kirste, was published in English in the journal *World Faiths Encounter* in 1994.

The Institute also arranges conferences such as the one in September 1995 titled: Changes of Values and Religious Revolutions in Europe.

The Interfaith Alliance

1511 K. Street, NW, Suite 738, Washington DC 20005 USA; tel. (202) 639-6370

Statement of Principle

The Interfaith Alliance is a coalition of concerned religious leaders and other citizens who have joined together to articulate and promote the unifying principles of all faiths – compassion, tolerance, and justice. In a world plagued by strife, fear, and hatred, we affirm the values of respect and community against the politics of division. We reject efforts to pit groups of people against each other for personal or political gain. We consider it our moral obligation to promote understanding and participation. We will work to inform and unite citizens, to reinvigorate public discourse, and to hold our leaders accountable for their words and deeds. We enthusiastically welcome all people of good will to join in our effort to affirm these ideals.

America was founded on the premise that its citizens would participate in the debate over our nation's direction. Today, with so many crucial issues on the agenda, public debate plays an even greater role. The religious community has always been an important voice in that dialogue. The

Interfaith Alliance has been created to ensure that this proud tradition continues.

The challenge: the radical right

Radical right-wing extremists have declared a holy war in America, promoting an agenda based on hate and intolerance. They are preying on Americans' very real concerns about their families and communities in an attempt to impose one narrow set of beliefs on an entire nation. Organizations such as the Christian Coalition, the Oregon Citizen's Alliance, and the Traditional Values Coalition have adopted a broad strategy that is succeeding in state after state. Religious extremism is increasingly being used to attack politicians, pull textbooks out of classrooms, cut back on school breakfast programs and promote discrimination.

This movement has polarized the political debate, choking off discussion with its harsh and unyielding rhetoric. Claiming to be the only religious voice in the debate, the radical right attempts to silence its critics with charges of religious bigotry. At stake is the fundamental ideal of America as a haven of religious liberty and tolerance, where individuals have an uncompromised right to their own beliefs.

The response: The Interfaith Alliance

This is a time when we must work harder to bring our families and communities together, not drive them apart. We must look to religious diversity as a source of strength, not a weakness. Thousands of religious and other leaders are eager to speak out against these messages of division, yet they have had no platform from which to make their voices heard.

The Interfaith Alliance has a three-part strategy:

- Public dialogue: it will work to restore civility and common sense to the public debate, attempting to make its voice heard in the national forum.
- Public Education: in states targeted by the radical right the Alliance will work to educate voters about the far right's activities, positions and affiliations. Working closely with other national and state organizations, it will coordinate grassroots and other educational activities.
- National clearinghouse: it will serve as a national clearinghouse for religious, grassroots and political citizens looking for ways to respond to the radical right.

The Interfaith Alliance Board of Directors consists of a diverse group of religious leaders. The Board, recognizing that this issue extends to all aspects of public policy, is also developing a bipartisan advisory group that will draw from labor, business, grassroots activists, elected officials, and other concerned citizens.

Interfaith Hunger Appeal

**475 Riverside Dr., Suite 1630,
New York, NY 10115-0079 USA;
tel. (212) 870-2035 / fax (212) 870-2040**

IHA is a partnership of four relief and development agencies: Catholic Relief Services, Church World Service, Lutheran World Relief, and the American Jewish Distribution Joint Committee. Interfaith Hunger Appeal's Office on Education fosters learning and teaching about the needs of the poor through research, grants, projects and institutes designed to enhance curriculum development at the undergraduate levels. It also publishes a quarterly journal, *Hunger TeachNet,* dedicated to the growing curricular needs in development and world hunger issues. The 1993 issues were dedicated particularly to questions of gender and justice in development.

Interfaith Impact for Justice and Peace

**110 Maryland Avenue, N.E.,
Washington, DC 20077-0620 USA;
tel. (202) 543-2800 / fax (202) 547-8107**

Interfaith Impact is a united voice for the religious community. Protestant, Jewish, Catholic, and Muslim organizations and individuals work to make their voices heard on Capitol Hill. Interfaith Impact brings grassroots leaders to Washington to help coordinate local and Washington-based advocacy efforts, helping organizations become effective advocates for change. Twenty state Impact offices help to coordinate these efforts.

Thousands of individuals and organizations receive information to turn their values into votes. The voices of many organizations are needed in Washington to speak to the issues we address:

- Winning rights for women and families
- Improving civil, human, and voting rights
- Promoting international peace
- Fighting poverty
- Working for a more just economic policy
- Protecting and preserving the environment
- Assuring health care for everyone

Affiliate organizations receive background information on issues, the quarterly magazine, and coordinated mailings and action alerts to notify members when their representatives need to hear about timely issues. Through Interfaith Impact, members of Congress and their staffs are informed on a wide range of issues to improve the quality of life for millions of people.

Inter Faith Network for the United Kingdom

**5-7 Tavistock Place, London WC1H 9SS, UK;
tel. 0171-388 0008 / fax 0171-387-7968**

The IFNUK is a national body linking nearly 70 organizations with interest in good relations between British faith communities. Affiliated organizations include representative bodies from the faith communities themselves as well as from national interfaith organizations, local interfaith groups, and educational and academic bodies. The Network acts as a central information and contact point, provides a national forum for discussion of key issues, fosters local initiatives, and organizes meetings and seminars on topics such as religious identity and the law.

In addition to publishing and distributing its code, "Building Good Relations with People of Different Faiths and Beliefs (printed in Chapter 26), IFNUK has recently published *Religions in the UK: A Multi-Faith Directory* in conjunction with the University of Derby's Religious Resource and Research Centre. Seven other publications address the subjects of mission and dialogue, toleration and integrity, law and blasphemy, and respect for religious identity in a multi-faith society.

Interfaith Volunteer Caregivers

**National Federation of Interfaith Caregivers
368 Broadway, Suite 103, P.O. Box 1939,
Kingston, NY 12401 USA;
tel. (914) 331-1358 / fax (914) 331-4177**

IVC projects bring groups of congregations together to develop projects that recruit, train, and mobilize volunteers to provide in-home assistance to those in need. More than 400 IVC projects are now in operation in 45 states.

A typical project will be a coalition of 30 or more congregations including most mainline Protestant, Catholic, and Jewish denominations as well as Baha'i, Buddhist, Mennonite, secular groups, and traditional Native American religions in some areas. It will have a corps of 300 trained volunteers, serving 700 people each with services that include transportation, friendly visits, personal care, light housekeeping, chores services, and respite care.

International Association for Religious Freedom

**2 Market Street, Oxford OX1 3EF, UK;
tel. 44-1865-202-744 / fax 44-1865-202-746
E-mail: iarf@iicentre.demon.co.uk**

**or, in the United States, addressed to:
IARF, 777 United Nations Plaza,
New York, NY 10017 USA;
tel. 212-867-9255 / fax 212-867-9245
E-mail: iarfna@nywork2.undp.org**

The International Association for Religious Freedom is the oldest global interreligious organization and the only one with corporate memberships by constituent religious communities. For more than 90 years the IARF has worked for multicultural understanding, justice and peace, and religious freedom.

Religious communities from Europe, America, Asia, and Africa contribute to the spiritual breadth of the IARF. Members include Buddhist, Christian, Hindu, Jewish, Muslim, Shinto, Sikh, Unitarian, and Universalist groups, as well as tribal communities. IARF members differ in many ways, but are united by a commitment to religious liberty and liberating religious practice.

Our roots are deep and diverse. The Unitarian churches in Romania date back to the 16th century Protestant reformation. The Tsubaki Grand Shrine in Japan is served by the 96th generation of its priests. The largest IARF member group, the lay Buddhist movement Rissho Kosei-kai, was founded only a generation ago but grounds its teachings in the ancient *Lotus Sutra*. The Ramakrishna Mission Lokasiksha Parishad is widely recognized in modern India for its leadership in community service and religious reform.

The IARF brings together people from different cultures and countries, from national denominations and local congregations, from village communities and metropolitan churches, from academic institutions and religious communities. Its individual members are young and old, female and male. Its member groups come from east and west, from north and south.

IARF encompasses 70 member groups in 25 countries which seek to expand its spiritual horizon, giving IARF a worldwide identity and moral involvement in response to the global issues of our time. The IARF world community is based on personal sharing to foster openness, understanding, compassion, service, and solidarity. In cooperation with local IARF groups, the Social Service Network has some 50 projects such as emergency relief, cooperative development projects and neighborhood women's centers.

Congresses were most recently held in India (1993), Germany (1990), United States (1987), and Japan (1984). In 1995 the IARF will hold regional meetings in the Philippines, India, Taiwan, Germany, and the United States to address subthemes of the 29th IARF Triennial Congress, which will be held at Won Kwang University in Iri City, Korea in 1996. The theme will be "Responsibility, Cooperation, Spirituality: Challenging our Religious Communities."

IARF:

- publishes a magazine, *IARF World*.

- is interreligious, intercultural and interracial in composition and vision;
- is recognized as an NGO, accredited in category II at the UN in New York and Geneva, at UNESCO in Paris, and at UNICEF;
- has a seven-person office at the UN in New York; members chair the NGO committees on religious freedom in New York and Geneva;
- works with religious communities and secular organizations committed to openness and free religious inquiry, human dignity and mutual acceptance, social responsibility and service;
- is guided by the Spirit of truth, which transcends time and place, and yet is revealed in and through the spiritual and moral traditions of the world.

International Council of Christians and Jews

Werlestrasse 2, 6148 Heppenheim, Federal Republic of Germany
tel.(+49) 6252 5041 / fax (+49) 6252 68331

The ICCJ is the umbrella organization of 23 national Jewish-Christian dialogue organizations worldwide, with many more local affiliates. Envisaged to deal with relations between Christians and Jews, its activities now increasingly engage Islam, in view of growing Islamic populations in Europe and North America, as well as because of the situation in the Middle East.

Through its methods, principles, colloquia, consultations, Women's and Young Leadership sections, ICCJ also serves as a model for wider interfaith relations. Publications include *The Last Word*, the magazine of the Young Leadership Section, and *ICCJ News*, as well as occasional papers.

Created in Germany at the house where the great Jewish thinker Martin Buber lived, the ICCJ also creates a wide local outreach with international flavor. (See also the National Conference.)

International Fellowship of Reconciliation

Spoorstradt 38, 1815 BK Alkmaar, The Netherlands
tel. 31-72-123014 / fax 31-72-123014

Founded in 1914 in England and later in Germany by Christians who believed there must be a nonviolent alternative to war, the IFOR is composed of women and men who recognize the essential unity of all creation. They have joined together to explore the power of love and truth for resolving human conflict. They act out of their own religious tradition, with an absolute respect for every human life and with a deep faith in the power of self-giving love to heal, forgive, repair, and overcome

injustice without violence and hatred, and restore community. They seek support from each other, linked as members of a large family, beyond national borders and religious convictions.

IFOR encourages the integration of a spiritual dimension into the lives of its members. At the same time, IFOR works to extend the boundaries of community and to affirm its diversity of religious traditions as it seeks the resolution of conflict by the united efforts of people of many faiths. IFOR has branches, affiliates, chapters, or fieldworkers in over 50 countries.

International Interfaith Centre

2 Market St., Oxford OX1 3EF UK
tel. 44 (0)865 202 745 / fax 44 (0)865 202 746

The dream becomes reality

For over one hundred years, since the World's Parliament of Religions held in Chicago in 1893, some men and women have dreamed that people of different faiths could in friendship seek deeper understanding of the Eternal Mystery and work together for human welfare and to protect the environment. There are now many interfaith groups across the world, some local, some national, some international. At the same time, more universities and colleges have developed courses for the study of religions. These efforts, however, lack coordination.

To fill this need, a centre to support the developing interfaith movement and the study of religions has now been established. Rev. Marcus Braybrooke, now Chair of the World Congress of Faiths (WCF), first suggested such a centre to the WCF Executive in 1988. Dr. Robert Traer, General Secretary of the International Association for Religious Freedom (IARF), proposed a similar idea to the IARF Council in March 1991. Similar visions have been shared by members of the Temple of Understanding (ToU) and the World Conference on Religion and Peace.

In September 1992 a Working Committee was established to develop a detailed plan for a Centre at Oxford to be:

- *An education centre* to promote research into ways of developing interreligious understanding, mutual respect, and cooperation; to relate the academic study of religions to interfaith activity; to promote research into teaching methods and to encourage the production of educational materials.
- *A coordinating centre* to facilitate cooperation between people and groups actively engaged in interreligious work and to be a source of information about interfaith activities worldwide.
- *A support centre* to strengthen personal

contact between those engaged in interfaith work and the study of religions.

- *A spiritual centre* to provide opportunities for deep understanding of prayer, worship, and meditation in the world's religions.

The Centre was launched on 6 December 1993 at Westminster College, Oxford, which is a founding institution along with IARF and WCF. Since then the programme of the Centre has begun to be implemented and coordinators have been engaged – including Mrs. Celia Storey, who worked to plan, administer and staff the 1993 Centennial Celebrations in Bangalore, India. An Advisory Committee and International Consultants have been appointed. A lecture is planned as are events designed to share worship and fellowship with academic and religious institutions in and around Oxford. International seminars are also being held, and a Newsletter is available upon request.

IIC has also published *Visions of an Interfaith Future*, edited by Celia and David Storey, which contains the proceedings of the Sarva-Dharma-Sammelana Conference in 1993. (Available from the IIC at the address above.)

Discussions are under way to select an architect for the Centre and a site at Westminster College. In essence, the Centre aims to help curb religious extremism and ensure that the spiritual and moral heritage of the world's religions is available to all who work to build a just and peaceful world, who struggle to end poverty and the abuse of human rights, and who seek to preserve the environment.

Inter-Religio

c/o Brian Lawless, Christian Study Centre on Chinese Religion and Culture, 6/F Kiu Kin Mansion, 566 Nathan Road, Kowloon, Hong Kong; tel. (852) 770-3310 / fax (852) 782-6869

This network of Christian organizations for interreligious encounter links institutions in Hong Kong, Indonesia, Japan, Korea, Malaysia, Philippines, Taiwan, and Thailand. Its substantial newsletter is published twice annually, carrying news about members of the network, program and conference reports, and theoretical essays.

Inter-Religious Federation for World Peace

4 West 43rd St., Fifth Floor, New York, NY 10036 USA; tel. (212) 869-6023

The IRFWP was founded by the Reverend Sun Myung Moon at the second Assembly of the World's Religions, held in San Francisco, August 1990, following 23 years of investment in ecumenical and interfaith work on the part of Reverend Moon.

Fourteen of these years transpired on the world-wide level from New York-based headquarters. The active database of associates who have been sponsored to attend international interfaith gatherings is approximately 7,000 religious leaders, scholars and youth leaders. As well as individual membership, institutional membership enables religious bodies, organizations, and groups to affiliate with the Federation. A network of regional and national chapters is being expanded.

The IRFWP, like the organizations upon which it is modeled, is guided by prominent leaders from all major world religions. Presently the IRFWP consists of six presidents, a secretary general, a four-person executive committee, a 16-person presiding council, and a significantly larger advisory board. Among these approximately 60 core leaders of the Federation, four are Unificationists. IRFWP's program areas include peace initiatives, global cooperation, inter-religious dialogue and service, education, research and publications.

The *IRFWP Newsletter* is published twice each year; the journal *Dialogue and Alliance* is published by a sister organization, the International Religious Foundation, which also sponsored publication of *World Scripture: A Comparative Anthology of Sacred Texts*, edited by Andrew Wilson and published by Paragon House *(see details in Chapter 43).*

In 1985 the predecessor and current partner of the IRFWP, the International Religious Foundation (IRF), hosted the first Assembly of the World's Religions, an international gathering of over 800 religious leaders and scholars, in McAffee, New Jersey. This inaugurated an orientation toward 1993 with the commitment to hold the first three Assemblies quadrennially – the second in 1989, and the third in 1993 – fortified by extensive interfaith activities and programs in the intervening years. At Ammerdown in 1986, IRF offered to work collaboratively with major extant interfaith organizations, but this proposal was rejected, requiring the IRF and the IRFWP to prepare independently for 1993.

From February 1–7, 1993 the IRFWP hosted the Delhi Congress, the first major event to commemorate the 1893 Chicago Parliament. Over 600 participants heard talks by Dr. Ninian Smart, Huston Smith, Raimundo Pannikkar, IRFWP presidents Metropolitan Paulos Mar Gregorios and Sri Swami Chidananda of the Divine Life Society, IRFWP presiding council member Baba Virsa Singh, and many others.

Although the dates for the Congress had been established over a year earlier, tragic circumstances allowed the Congress to answer the desperate prayers of a nation

shredded by violence in the name of religion. Just the week before the Delhi Congress, militants had torn down the Babri Masjid in Ayodhya leading to violence and resulting in death and tragic internal division. For this reason government officials at the highest levels attended the conference, seeking throughout the event guidelines for the restoration of peace.

The IRFWP sponsored its second Congress in Seoul, Korea, from April 28–May 2, 1994. The theme was "The Reality of Evil and the Response of the World's Religions." Participants from religions and cultures throughout the world explored not only the ways in which we might better understand the foundations and manifestations of evil, but also how our traditions offer guidance for overcoming evil. *(See also Chapter 27.)*

The 1995 Congress in Seoul on August 20–27 has the theme, "Realizing the Ideal: The Responsibility of the World's Religions." As with its other Congresses, one of the goals is to draw from the individual and collective wisdom of scholars and religious leaders the resources for bringing practical solutions to global problems.   Material for this article by Dr. Frank Kaufmann, Exec. Director of IRFWP

The Islamic Society of North America – ISNA

P.O. Box 38, Plainfield, IN 46168 USA; tel. (317)839-8157

ISNA is an outgrowth of the Muslim Student's Association of US and Canada. The original MSA so successfully tapped the Islamic consciousness of Muslims in North America that by 1982-83 it blossomed into a new organization, ISNA.

The main objective of ISNA is to advance the cause of Islam and Muslims in North America. It seeks to foster unity and brotherhood among Muslims and to raise their Islamic consciousness as a people enjoying the right and forbidding wrong, to convey the Islamic message to non-Muslims, and to promote friendly relations between them and Muslims.

ISNA also supports constituent professional associations and the Islamic Teaching Center, and provides a range of services to individuals and Muslim communities. These include a speakers' bureau, film loans, schooling workshops, a library assistance program, conference facilities, a housing cooperative, a credit union, shahadah and marriage certification, and a *Zakah* fund for helping the needy, orphans, and others. ISNA also provides many resources, including Islamic correspondence courses, information for prison bureaucracies, distribution of Islamic dawah literature, American Trust

Publications, the Islamic Book Service, the Audio-Visual Center, electronic data processing, and it serves as trustee for many Islamic centers. In addition several conferences and publications are available.

IUCN – The World Conservation Union

1400 16th St., NW, Washington, DC 20036 USA; tel. (202) 787-5454 / fax (202) 797-5461

rue de Mauverney, 28, CH 1196 Gland, Switzerland

IUCN, in collaboration with the United Nations Environment Programme and the World Wide Fund for Nature and others, has produced both a "Summary" and the extensive publication, *Caring for the Earth: A Strategy for Sustainable Living.* In its "Message to the World," an introduction to the *Strategy,* the authors note that: "...our new approach must meet two fundamental requirements. One is to secure a wide-spread and deeply-held commitment to a new ethic, the ethic for sustainable living, and to translate its principles into practice. The other is to integrate conservation and development: conservation to keep our actions within the Earth's capacity, and development to enable people everywhere to enjoy long, healthy and fulfilling lives." (See also Chapter 30.)

Caring for the Earth may be purchased from Island Press, Box 7, Covelo, CA 95428 USA; tel. 1-800-828-1302 (US only); from outside the US: 1-707-983-6432

Jewish-Arab Dialogue in Europe
25 Elliot Square, London, NW3 3SU, UK

JADE works to promote Jewish-Arab dialogue in Europe through a network committed to the exchange and distribution of information aimed at futhering the peace process in the Middle-East. Numerous activities are sponsored within both Jewish and Arab (particularly Palestinian) communities and among European supporters of peace in the Middle East. The JADE *Journal* provides useful examples of active dialogue and cooperation, as well as reporting on European initiatives. The issue for January 1993, for example, reports on dialogue centers in Israel. Ulpan Akiva is a residential study centre where groups of Jews, Christians and Muslims live together, learning each other's languages. Oasis of Peace (Neve Shalom/Wahat al Salam) is a cooperative village and School of Peace whose community is made up of an equal number of Palestinians and Israelis. The October 1994 journal contains numerous reflections on the PLO-Israel peace accord. JADE members groups exists in Brussels,

Paris, Geneva, Milan, Rome, Amsterdam, London, Vienna, Frankfurt, and Barcelona.

Lucis Trust – the Arcane School, World Goodwill and Triangles

International:
**Suite 54, 3 Whitehall Court,
London SW1A 2EF, UK**

North America:
**The Beacon,
120 Wall St., 24th Fl.
New York, NY 10005 USA**

Europe:
**1 Rue de Varembé (3e)
Case Postale 31, 1211 Geneva 20, Switzerland**

South America:
Casilla de Correó No. 23, Sucursal 2(3) (C.P. 1402), Buenos Aires, Argentina

Lucis Trust is an educational charity working for right human relations. Activities include support of the Arcane School, the Lucis Publishing Companies, World Goodwill, Triangles, Lucis Trust Libraries, and Lucis Productions.

Through Lucis Press it distributes the works of Alice A. Bailey and other publications, including *The Beacon,* a magazine of esoteric philosophy presenting the principles of the Ageless Wisdom as a contemporary way of life, and a *Newsletter.*

The Arcane School was created by Alice Bailey in 1923 as a training school for adults in meditation techniques and the development of spiritual potential. The school is conducted by correspondence through the headquarters listed above.

Triangles was founded in 1937 as a spiritual service activity for men and women of goodwill who believe in the power of thought and prayer. Working in groups of three, they establish a worldwide network of light and goodwill.

World Goodwill, established in 1932, works to establish right human relations through the practical application of the principle of goodwill. Actions consist of publications, a study course, cooperation with the United Nations and its specialized agencies, and world service forums.

Members believe that: "...the world has a spiritual destiny and that behind evolution there is an abiding purpose – what may be called the Plan of God. Everyone who responds to spiritual need can co-operate in fulfilling this divine Plan, which works out through humanity. We are responsible for understanding it, and for doing what we can through our daily living to express its meaning and significance." (See also Chapter 15.)

Kashi Ashram

11155 Roseland Rd., Unit 10, Sebastian, FL 32958 USA; tel. (407) 589-1403

At Kashi Ashram, established in 1976, Eastern and Western spiritual traditions come together, guided by the interfaith teachings of Ma Jaya Bhagavati.

Ma describes the *ashram*, which means a spiritual community, as a place where "anyone can come who wants to find the spirit of God or any religion, a place without prejudice or bigotry." Inspired by Hinduism, Christianity, Judaism, and Buddhism, Ma teaches that all paths followed with a pure heart lead to the God within. At Kashi, each person's preferred way of seeking and worshiping is respected. Temples representing different faiths are located around the pond at the center of the ashram.

Widely recognized for her work with those facing death and for her teaching on care-giving, Ma and her students feed, touch, counsel, and hold people who otherwise might be forgotten; these include abused children, the elderly, and those who have been affected by AIDS. For many years Ma has encouraged those in the HIV/AIDS community and their loved ones to live life with fullness and passion. (See related article in Chapter 42.)

MADRE – A National Friendship Organization

**121 West 27th St., Rm. 301,
New York, NY 10001 USA;
tel. (212)627-0444 / fax (212) 675-3704**

MADRE is a woman-to-woman, people-to-people connection. MADRE links the problems women and children face every day with the challenges women and children in other parts of the world face as a result of US policies. Founded in 1983, we are a multi-cultural, cross-class network, firm in our commitment to peace, justice, and human rights.

The founders of MADRE were inspired to action by Nicaraguan women who invited us into their hearts and shared with us their faith that the US women, if they knew what was happening, would make the Contra war stop. Through MADRE, women in the US worked with women in Nicaragua to ensure that such basic needs as day care and health care were satisfied. At the same time, we build bridges of cooperation and dreams made of real stuff like milk, medicines, diapers, ambulances, darkrooms, legal services, play areas. And we built understanding and the informed action that can come of understanding.

Today MADRE has projects in Nicaragua, El Salvador, Guatemala, the Caribbean, the Middle East, and the USA. On the local, national, and international levels we support women who are working to improve the conditions of their everyday lives and to guarantee their rights. Though founded, staffed, and led by women,

MADRE's membership includes women, men and children. One of the building blocks of MADRE is our sister relationships with women's organizations in the countries where we work. We learn from each other as we plan ways to support projects for women and their families. We struggle with issues of disempowerment, lack of access and prejudice. Different communities and different cultures define the issues and approaches which will work for them. Our partnerships are built on mutual respect and encouragement.

Manitou Foundation

**Hanne M. Strong, President
P.O. Box 118, Crestone, CO 81131 USA**

The Manitou Foundation is responding to the degradation of Earth's natural systems and the impact of human population by encouraging and supporting programs which demonstrate sustainable living, and which manifest concrete examples of cultural, economic, and spiritual ways of life which do not tax the earth. These include solar villages, spiritual communities, sustainable agriculture, seed banks and alternative education.

Because the global mobilization needed to ensure any kind of future has to be *massive,* the Manitou Foundation put a lot of time, energy and resources into the Earth Summit and the Sacred Earth Gathering in Rio de Janiero. It is also supporting other programs whose role is to attune large numbers of humanity to their proper relationship to the Earth – a relationship of non-separation, love, and respect that also extends to the Creator.

The priority in Crestone continues to be to facilitate the establishment of a major ecumenical community in North America. It will demonstrate that amidst the diversity and richness of one another's faiths we may express our genuine humaness and embrace and respect one another's differences. Therefore, the Manitou Foundation continues to build a community of representatives of major religious traditions of unbroken lineages from around the world. In addition to the traditions located at the Baca in Crestone already, representatives from the Sufi Order and the Nyingma sect of Tibetan Buddhism are in the process of establishing retreat centers here. The community also anticipates representation from Jewish, Taoist, Greek Orthodox, Zoroastrian, and other traditions.

Millennium Institute

**1611 North Kent St., Suite 204
Arlington, VA 22209-2135 USA;
tel. (703) 841-0048 / fax (703) 841-0050**

The Millennial Moment

Building on a decade of accomplishments, the Millennium Institute is forming a worldwide coalition to harness the emotional energy of the upcoming period for the lasting benefit of all humankind. It is focusing the emotional energy of the new millennim toward a sustainable future for earth by means of a three-year Millennial Moment Celebration, to be held 1999 – 2001. The strategy includes taking time to reflect on our accomplishments, take stock of where we are, and reflect on where we must go to achieve sustainable development. Threshold "rituals" and gifts are encouraged, and projects will attempt to involve everyone in renewing the institutions and governmental structures needed to maintain the momentum of change.

What shall we do?

A non-profit organization founded in 1983, the Institute also promotes long-term thinking, sustainable development models and frameworks for action among a worldwide network of individuals and organizations. Formerly the Institute for 21st Century Studies, the Millennium Institute created the book *Global 2000 Revisited: What Shall We Do? The Critical Issues of the 21st Century*, which was prepared for the Parliament of the World's Religions (for details, see Chapter 22, "The Role of the Faith Traditions"). Its authors, Gerald O. Barney, Jane Blewett and Kristen R. Barney, also prepared the forceful and moving plenary session on the Critical Issues for the Parliament.

The book is available for $20.00 fromthe Institute and from CoNexus Press, PO Box 6902, Grand Rapids, MI 49516 USA.

Monastic Interreligious Dialogue
104 Chapel Lane, St. Joseph, MN 56374 USA

Formerly known as the North American Board for East–West Dialogue, Monastic Interreligious Dialogue is a Roman Catholic organization that grew out of the call by the Second Vatican Council for Christians to seek contacts with representatives of other traditions. This Council urged discussions, dialogical relationships and collaboration with members of other religious traditions. Before the end of the Council, Vatican II established the Secretariat for Non-Christian Religions, with Cardinal Pignedoli as its first president, to facilitate its mandate on interreligious dialogue and collaboration.

Cardinal Pignedoli approached the Benedictine Order and asked if monastics could assume some responsibility in the area of establishing and promoting dialogue with the religions of Asia, notably with representatives of Hinduism,

Buddhism, and Zen. Cardinal Pignedoli's insight was that dialogue between East and West could be carried out on a deep level through the encounter of monks and nuns, since they share the monastic dimension.

Established initially as the North American Board for East-West Dialogue, the Board changed its name to Monastic Interreligious Dialogue in December 1991 in recognition of the broader mission of dialogue, which also embraces Islam and Judaism. MID comes under the authority of the Abbot Primate in Rome, and the Pontifical Council for Interreligious Dialogue at the Vatican, the new designation for the Secretariat for Non-Christian Religions. MID now has about 70 contact persons, one from each monastery/convent in the United States and Canada, who serve as the links between the various monastic houses and MID. MID also produces a publication called the *Bulletin,* through which MID maintains its network of several thousand supporters around the world.

Since its inception, MID has pursued the work of interreligious dialogue and collaboration through conferences, workshops, videos, books, seminars, exchanges, and lecture series. MID continues exploring contacts with Hindus, Sufis, and Jews in formal and informal gatherings. One of the most fascinating and successful programs is the Intermonastic Dialogue Exchange with the Tibetans. Thomas Merton had opened up encounters with the Dalai Lama and Tibetan Buddhist monasticism in his fateful trip to India in 1968. The Dalai Lama has remarked that he never realized that Christians were spiritual until he met Merton. Much has happened since that first encounter, and both traditions are becoming more aware of the spiritual treasures residing in each other.   Adapted from an article by Brother Wayne Teasdale

---

Multifaith Resources – A Resource Center
PO Box 128, Wofford Heights, CA 93285 USA; tel./fax (619) 376-4691

Year by year throughout North America, in both Canada and the United States, there is increasing cultural and religious diversity. The rich tapestry of traditions which are encountering each other in our open societies presents opportunities to learn about and cooperate with people who are different from ourselves. This requires that religion and culture be taken seriously throughout the society – in schools along with places of work and service. It also means that people of diverse traditions need to respect and cooperate with each other. Churches and other religious institutions can help provide leadership in

this direction. Multifaith Resources provides helpful aids to persons of many traditions who are working to respond to a variety of human needs while promoting and enhancing interfaith understanding and cooperation.

Multifaith Resources is the name given to an educational ministry organized and conducted by the Rev. Dr. Charles R. White – ordained by the Presbyterian Church (USA) in 1968. While clearly based on Christian principles, our goal is to respect the integrity of other religious traditions. We encourage and support expression of thoughts and actions which are consistent with the highest values found in each of the world's religions.

Multifaith Resources publishes and/or distributes practical resources which aid in multi-cultural and multi-religious understanding and cooperation. Among the supplies available are multifaith religious education materials published by the Christian Education Movement, located in England; videos on world religions from the Hartley Film Foundation and others; the *Multifaith Information Manual* for Chaplains, the Multifaith Calendar published by Canadian Ecumenical Action in Vancouver, B.C.; and other materials such as annotated bibliographies.

Multifaith Resources also works to locate and provide almost any resource which may be needed in interfaith situations; conducts workshops which help to equip teachers, chaplains, administrators, pastors, and others to provide leadership in the pluralistic society; consults with a variety of groups and organizations who are seeking to become more inclusive in their understanding and practices; fulfills subscriptions to the journal *World Faiths Encounter;* and offers a full-color catalog describing all of the available resources (for $3, which is refundable upon purchase).

Muslim Youth of North America – MYNA at Work
MYNA Continental Office, P.O. Box 38, Plainfield, IN 46168 USA; tel. (317) 839-8158

MYNA Canadian Office, P.O. Box 160 Station P, Toronto, Ontario M5S -2S7 Canada; tel. (416) 977-2057

Realizing that the Muslim Ummah (community) was losing many of its youth due to the pressures and temptations of un-Muslim environments, and wanting to establish our own environment, concerned young Muslim youth united to form an organization to deal with these challenges.

MYNA began with programs sponsored by the Islamic Society of North America, at conferences and conventions, and was founded in 1985 as a continental organization.

Its goals are to:

1) Strengthen the faith and practice of Muslim youth, allowing them to develop an Islamic identity;

2) Help Muslim youth and communities plan and carry out educational training and spiritual, recreational, and charitable Islamic youth activities;

3) Develop Islamic leadership for the future; and

4) Establish a positive and healthy image of Islam in North America.

Membership is open to all Muslim youth of junior or senior high school age, and older youth are encouraged to become advisors and counselors. Members receive "The New Dawn" and other provisions. Programs include the Field Youth Leadership Program, the Continental Leadership Training Conferences, the Annual MYNA Associates Meetings, Summer Continental Conferences, and recreational camps. MYNA is also developing a Writers' Guild, a supportive parents organization, and a worker manual. Participation, planning, and emphasis remains strongly focused at the local level.

NGO Committee on Disarmament

777 United Nations Plaza, 3B, New York, NY 10017 USA; tel. (212) 687-5340

Serving a network of several hundred national and international organizations and NGOs concerned with proliferation and disarmament of both nuclear and conventional weapons, this NGO committee provides information to and about the UN Disarmament Commission, the non-proliferation review preparatory conferences and treaty (up for renewal in March 1995), the UN Register of Conventional Arms, and other security and arms-reduction proposals and programs. It also assists with consultations between UN departments and NGOs, including the sometimes thousands of representatives who attend special conferences.

The NGO Committee on Disarmament is a private voluntary organization whose information and educational programs reach a global audience. It is associated with the Conference of NGOs in Consultative Status with the UN Economic and Social Council. Members of its Board of Directors come from diverse organizations such as the American Jewish Committee, Economists Against the Arms Race, Gray Panthers, League of Women Voters, Science for Peace, Risho Kosei-kai, Voice of Women–Canada, World Conference on Religion and Peace, and the World YWCA, among others. Individuals and groups may subscribe to *Disarmament Times* ($15 in North Am. or $20 elsewhere) or contribute at the address above.

NGO Committee on Freedom of Religion or Belief

546 East 11th St.- Apartment 4-A, New York, NY 10009 USA; tel. (212) 687-2163 / fax (212) 808-5480

The United Nations has long been concerned with promoting greater religious freedom, beginning with the adoption of Article 18 of the Universal Declaration of Human Rights in 1948. Its most recent achievement was the adoption in 1981 of the Declaration on the Elimination of All Forms of Intolerance and of Discrimination Based on Religion or Belief.

This Committee, composed of representatives of non-governmental organizations working in the UN system, was formed in 1990-91 to seek to strengthen the effectiveness of the UN in the prevention of religious intolerance and discrimination and the advancement of religious freedom, and to encourage the drafting and passage of a convention on freedom of religion and belief. The Committee began by working to enhance existing UN human rights mechanisms.

The National Conference

Suite 1100, 71 Fifth Ave., New York, N.Y. 10003 USA; tel. (212) 206-0006 / fax (212) 255-6177

The National Conference, founded in 1927, is a human relations organization dedicated to fighting bias, bigotry, and racism in America. Although its name was recently abbreviated from The National Conference of Christians and Jews, the National Conference has long promoted understanding and respect among all races, religions, and cultures through advocacy, conflict resolution and education.

Programs include a nationwide survey of ethnic, racial, and religious groups, building bridges with public education, leadership education in schools and communities, workplace education, and interfaith education through community and scholars' trialogues. The work is sustained by hundreds of professional staff members and more than 8,000 volunteers from all walks of life, whose dedication, expertise and deep roots in the communities they serve constitute our most important asset in the continuing struggle against bias, bigotry and racism in America.

The national office in the United States has sixty-one regional chapters, for whom it points the way in the search for our finest social and cultural values. (Addresses outside the U.S. can be gotten from the office of the International Conference of Christians and Jews, listed earlier).

The National Council of Churches of Christ in the USA

Office of Interfaith Relations, 475 Riverside Dr., Room 868, New York, NY 10115-0050 USA; tel. Jay Rock: (212)870-2560; Bert F. Breiner: (212) 870-2156

The NCC is a national expression of the movement for Christian unity in the United States. The NCC's 32 member communions, including Protestant, Orthodox, and Anglican church bodies, work together on a wide range of activities that serve people throughout the world. More than 42 million US Christians belong to churches that hold NCC membership.

The Office of Interfaith Relations

This Office exists primarily to serve its member churches. In addition, however, we seek to be of service to other groups, organizations and individuals looking for information about or involvement in interfaith relations. Our goal is always to make the churches more aware of the challenges of living in an increasingly pluralist society and to help provide them and others with appropriate resources to meet those challenges.

We provide three broad categories of service: consultancy, resources and networking.

Consultancy: The staff is available for consultation by church and quasi-governmental organizations, by the press and by individuals. These are usually requests for information about interfaith relations in the United States or for more specific information about particular faith communities. We work closely with ecumenical and interfaith agencies and organizations and often help local groups to arrange conferences and programs.

Resources: Some resources relating to interfaith relations are available directly from the Office. These are publications of the Office or publications done in cooperation with other groups. We also recommend resources that are readily available from other organizations. We are hoping to expand this dimension of the Office and to encourage different groups and organizations to keep us aware of resources that they have available. We are glad to share any information or ideas we have with you.

Networking: Putting people in touch with each other is an important aspect of the work of the Office of Interfaith Relations. We will help to find dialogue partners or speakers, or, if we ourselves do not know an appropriate contact, we can probably put you in touch with someone who does. Representatives from member communions of the NCCC and other denominational bodies work together on interreligious concerns through the National Council of Churches' Working Group on Interfaith Relations. Working Group members meet regularly to study interfaith issues, to cooperate in building relationships between the churches and people of other faiths, and to provide resources promoting dialogue and study. With its partners of other faiths, the Working Group explores common concerns and commitments, and nurtures interfaith action. It also focuses on theological issues that arise among Christians in response to other religions and to today's increasing religious pluralism.

Interfaith work throughout the NCCC

The Working Group on Interfaith Relations maintains close ties with the Ecumenical Networks Working Group and with the Faith and Order Working Group of the NCCC. The Interfaith Relations Office also consults with, and from time to time represents, the General Secretary in regard to relations with other faith communities. Since interfaith affairs often have international dimensions, we maintain consultation with the overseas offices and other staff of Church World Service. We are also developing close ties with NCCC staff and committees doing work in the areas of Christian education, education for mission, and racial and social justice.

Relationships Outside the NCCC

The Working Group works in cooperation with the Office of Interreligious Affairs of the World Council of Churches and maintains a liaison relationship with the Committee for Ecumenical ard Interreligious Affairs of the National Conference of Catholic Bishops.

The National Religious Partnership for the Environment

1047 Amsterdam Avenue, New York, NY 10025 USA; tel. 212-316-7441 / fax 212-316-7547

The National Religious Partnership for the Environment is comprised of four major faith groups and denominations representing over 100 million people. In July 1993, these groups – the US Catholic Conference, the National Council of Churches of Christ, the Coalition on the Environment and Jewish Life, and the Evangelical Environment Network – initiatied a three-year, $5-million mobilization on behalf of environmental integrity and justice.

The National Religious Partnership for the Environment (NRPE) began to take form in response to an "Open Letter to the Religious Community" issued in January 1990 by 34 internationally prominent scientists (printed in Chapter 39).

Struck by that initiative, several hundred religious leaders of all major faiths from all five continents responded,

This invitation to collaboration marks a unique moment and opportunity in the relationship of science and religion. We are eager to explore as soon as possible concrete, specific forms of action.

On June 2 and 3, 1991, a small group of religious leaders convened for scientific briefings, conversations with members of Congress, and consideration of future initiatives. At the end of the gathering, measuring sentiments within their respective denominations, they concluded,

We believe a consensus now exists, at the highest level of leadership across a significant spectrum of religious traditions, that the cause of environmental integrity and justice must occupy a position of utmost priority for people of faith.

This led to an extraordinary array of programming in the American religious community. In July 1991, the Episcopal Church agreed upon and funded its first program on environment and sustainable development. Bishops of the US Catholic Conference approved their first pastoral statement on environment in November of 1991. Also that autumn, the National Council of Churches of Christ established an office on environmental and economic justice, and the United Church of Christ hosted an environmental summit for people of color. In March 1992, over 100 senior leaders from all four branches of Jewish life met and set priorities for a communal environmental program. And in April 1991, World Vision USA hosted a major environmental conference for evangelical Christian leaders.

Fresh from this year of heightened activity, representatives of major denominations brought word of the religious community's growing commitment and partnership with the scientific community to the US Congress.

About the Mission to Washington

In May 1992, 75 religious leaders and 50 Nobel laureate and other scientists convened in Washington, DC, to hear scientific updates on global environmental conditions and reports on activities within their respective communities. They met to seek common ground and vision in response to global environmental challenges and to plan strategies together for action by their respective communities. The Mission to Washington was a unique, perhaps unprecedented, gathering of eminent representatives from a diverse world of religion, science, and government, working in close consultation. At its

conclusion, the senior religious leaders formally established the National Religious Partnership for the Environment, funds were committed, and the program commenced in late September 1993.

The Partnership's initiatives have included, among others, the annual distribution of environmental kits to 53,000 congregations (including every Catholic parish in the US); major consultations on issues of environmental justice and international development; conferences for leaders of the historic African-American churches and Orthodox Christian churches; development of seminary and religious education curricula; theological scholarship and major public policy campaigns. In addition, NRPE activities have included: a teleconference to hundreds of Catholic parishes across the country, an evangelical environmental theological declaration (see Chapter 30), and several meetings with Vice President Al Gore.

The Partnership has a central communications office in New York which seeks to document the activities of the religious community and to help active congregations work with one another. Its 1992 publication, the *Directory of Environmental Activities and Resources in the North American Religious Community*, began to build such a network. The Partnership urges interested congregations to contact the office to join this growing network. This process is evidence of how local, individual action can lead to strengthened resolve and commitment at the highest level.

The NRPE has a scientific staff director headquartered at the Union of Concerned Scientists office in Boston, and each member group – Catholic, Jewish, Protestant (NCC) and Evangelical – has created its own attractive and elaborate Education/Action Kit. Each Partnership coordinator distributes these kits to its congregations for their uses in religious education programs, worship, and building maintenance.

NRPE Program Contacts and Kit-ordering Information

For further information on the Catholic kit or program, please contact:
Maureen Gross, Associate, Environmental Justice Program, US Catholic Conference, 3211 Fourth Avenue, NE, Washington, DC 20017 USA; tel. 202-541-3160

For further information on the Jewish kit or program, please contact:
Mark Jacobs, Project Coordinator, Coalition on the Environment and Jewish Life, 443 Park Avenue South, 11th Flr, New York, NY 10016 USA; tel. 212-684-6950

For further information on the Protestant program, please contact:
Dr. N. Jean Sindab,

Program Director, Economic and Environmental Justice and Hunger Concerns, National Council of Churches of Christ 475 Riverside Drive, New York, NY 10115

To order an NCC kit, contact your denominational office:

American Baptist Churches: Owen Owens, 215-768-2410

Christian Church (Disciples of Christ): A. Garnett Day, 317-353-1491

Church of the Brethren: Shantilal Bhagat, 708-742-5100

Episcopal Church: Ethan Flad, 212-922-5222

ELCA: Job Ebenezer, 312-380-2708

Presbyterian Church (USA): Bill Somplatsky-Jarman, 502-569-5809

Reformed Church in America: John Paarlberg, 212-870-3020

United Church of Christ: Don Clark, 201-667-0079

United Methodist Church: Jaydee Hanson, 202-488-5650

National Council of Churches: Jean Sindab, 212-870-2385

For other orders, contact: FaithQuest: 800-441-3712

For further information on the Evangelical kit or program, please contact: Rev. Stan LeQuire, Program Coordinator Evangelical Environmental Network 10 East Lancaster Avenue, Wynnewood, PA, 19096 USA; tel. 610-645-9392

For information on the Science Program, please contact: Dr. Charles Puccia, NRPE Science Director, Union of Concerned Scientists, 26 Church Street, Cambridge, MA 02238 USA; tel. 617-547-5552

NETWORK – A National Catholic Social Justice Lobby

801 Pennsylvania Avenue, SE, Suite 460, Washington, DC, 20003-2167 USA; tel. (202) 547-5556

"The whole reason for the existence of public authorities is for the realization of the common good."

John XXIII, *Pacem in Terris*, #54

NETWORK was founded in 1971 by 47 women religious. It is a nonprofit membership organization of lay and religious women and men who put their faith into action by lobbying in Washington. NETWORK's political lobbying goals are securing just access to economic resources, reordering federal budget priorities, and transforming global relationships.

In the September/October 1994 issue of its newsletter, *Connection*, Sister Amata Miller describes Vatican II's perception, in *Gaudium at Spes*, that the common good is "the sum of those conditions of social life which allows social groups and their

individual members relatively thorough and ready access to their own fulfillment." Sr. Amata continues:

The test of a good society is how well it treats the most vulnerable of its people, and votes must be cast not on the basis of self-interest but for the sake of the good of all.

In addition to lobbying, NETWORK provides a range of resources and services in pamphlets, books, study guides and kits, videos and workshops.

The New Road Map Foundation

PO Box 15981, Seattle, WA 98115 USA; tel. (206) 527-0437

New Road Map Foundation is an all-volunteer, nonprofit educational and charitable organization concerned with the role of personal responsibility and personal initiative in effecting positive global changes. We see the empowered, responsible, and engaged individual, working volunarily for the common good, as the key to the creation of a humane, sustainable culture. We also recognize that cultures, like individuals, can be self-reflective and capable of a change of mind and heart. Our educational programs therefore support the evolution of culture as well as the empowerment of individuals.

Recognizing that economic issues and our relationship with money are central to both personal and planetary well-being, we have focused much of our work in the arena of finances and sustainable lifestyles. Based on 25 years of experience in living and educating about low-consumption, high-fulfillment lifestyles, Joe Dominguez and Vicki Robin wrote the best-selling book *Your Money or Your Life*. Among their other resources is the popular booklet, *All-Consuming Passion: Waking Up from the American Dream*. Both are available from the Foundation, as is the audiocassette-workbook course by Joe Dominguez, *Transforming Your Relationship with Money and Achieving Financial Independence*. These resources all address the problem of overconsumption and offer practical toolkits for lifestyle change. (See the article in Chapter 41 and the Directory, "Network to Reduce Overconsumption," in Chapter 43.)

The North American Conference on Christianity and Ecology

PO Box 40011, St. Paul MN 55104 USA; tel. 612-698-0349

NACCE is an ecumenical, voluntary organization established in 1986 to unite the many strands of Christian tradition in the work of healing the damaged Earth, out of a common concern and love for creation.

NACCE's mission is:

• To encourage churches and faith communities to become centers of creation awareness and to teach reverence for God's creation.

• To challenge individuals and congregations to engage their lives on behalf of creation through celebration, reflection, and action.

• To facilitate the formation of regional, faith-based earthkeeping ministries through conferences, consultations, and workshops.

• To link earthkeeping ministries in an empowering network around North America.

• To cooperate with all people of good will in the common effort to heal the Earth.

NACCE sponsors conferences throughout North America and in other countries, has a resource center, initiates local faith and ecology groups, publishes a newsletter, and offers resources for education and action.

North American Coalition on Religion and Ecology

Dr. Donald B. Conroy, 5 Thomas Circle, NW, Washington, DC 20005 USA; tel. 202 462-2591 / fax 202 462-6534

NACRE is an ecumenical/interfaith environmental education organization, headquartered in Washington, DC, designed to help the North American religious community enter into the environmental movement in the 1990s with more informed understanding of the environmental crisis and a dynamic sense of ecological mission, as well as to assist the wider society to understand the essential ethics and value-dimensions of the environmental movement. The vision of NACRE is summed up in the phrase "Caring for Creation."

NACRE helps to envision a society which truly cares for the natural environment (creation). NACRE encourages people to visualize a world that is both sustainable and regenerative. To accomplish this on practical and theoretical levels, NACRE calls for an ongoing ECO-3 "trialogue," one in which religion (ecumenism), science (ecology), and society (economics) clarify and agree on values for a new global ethic which promotes sustainability at all levels of responsibility through private citizens, corporations, and governments.

NACRE strives to communicate its "Caring for Creation" vision by developing practical resource materials for environmental education, by organizing conferences that communicate to leaders and the public and by developing new uses of media for interactive ecological collaboration. Now, after almost 10 years of development, NACRE is launching the dynamic five-step "Caring for Creation Initiative." Using this initiative the local congregation can address the five major dimensions of Earth Stewardship Ministry and begin Eco-Ministry through clearly defined Action Steps – Discovery, Exploration, Commitment, Empowerment, and Eco-Action.

Additional Resources from NACRE

- *Eco-Letter:* Members receive NACRE's quarterly newsletter plus special reports
- *Race to Save the Planet:* Viewer's Guide and Facilitator's Resource Guide
- *World Religions and Ecology Series,* published by World Wide Fund for Nature and Cassell Publishers. Approximately 120 pp. each, the five volumes address Christianity, Judaism, Islam, Hinduism, and Buddhism; available for $10 each or $45 for the set.

The Consortium on Religion and Ecology-International is an intercontinental network established by NACRE and SACRE (South American Conference on Religion and Ecology) in 1991.

North American Interfaith Network

Ms. Elizabeth Espersen, Executive Co-Chair
P.O. Box 1770, Dallas, TX 75221 USA;
tel. (214) 969-1977

The Network is a non-profit association with a membership of nearly 80 interfaith organizations and agencies throughout the United States and Canada. NAIN builds communication and mutual understanding among its members, and with the offices of religious or denominational institutions pertaining to interreligious relations in North America.

NAIN affirms humanity's diverse and historic spiritual resources, bringing these to bear on contemporary global, national, regional, and local issues. Without infringing on the efforts of existing organizations, NAIN facilitates the *networking* possibilities of organizations large and small, and provides a coalition model for cooperative interaction based on serving the needs and promoting the aspirations of all member groups.

NAIN traces its history through many converging lines, names, and efforts over the past 25 years. The Network was born in the late 1980s, and began by developing a directory of interfaith groups. Increased membership merited Directory revision in 1990. It has fostered two major interfaith conferences in accord with its purpose of building communication, and held its first full membership meeting in Berkeley in 1992. As a co-sponsor of the Parliament of the World's Religions, NAIN hosted

workshops on interfaith networking, communication, and understanding and is now helping as a liason from the Parliament to its membership. During the summer of 1994 NAIN held a very productive meeting near Toronto, which greatly improved the networking between US and Canadian members.

The *NAIN Newsletter* is published three times each year and is available now to individuals as well as to member organizations, providing useful information about other organizations, conferences, events, resources, procedures and issues. Members are invited to provide articles or announcements to the *Newsletter.* Membership is growing in productive ways in both the United States and Canada as interfaith activities become more widely respected and visible. Organizations devoted to interfaith work or that have staff members who are responsible for interreligious relations need to be linked for better communication. The *Newsletter* and resource information is available from:

Dr. Charles White
PO Box 128, Wofford Heights, CA 93285
USA; tel./fax 619 376-4691

One World Inc. – The Earth Pledge Program

Cronkhite Beach Bldg. 1055,
Sausalito, CA, 94965 USA; tel.(415) 331-1942

The Pledge:
I pledge to protect the Earth
and to respect the web of life upon it,
and to honor the dignity of every
member of our global family.
One planet, one people, one world,
in harmony.
With peace, justice, and freedom for all.

First introduced at Stanford University on Earth Day in 1990, the pledge has now been refined and spread to other settings. Since 1993, One World Inc. has been the managing sponsor of the Earth Pledge and has developed a comprehensive program including school and university outreach, celebrity involvement, a board of advisors, musical events, speaking engagements, and the program listed below. The purpose of the Earth Pledge Program is to spread the message of environmental awareness and global cooperation to the widest possible audience with sufficient repetitiveness that it becomes integral to our thinking and way of life. Thus it is our goal to increase the level of commitment especially amongst young people to protect and preserve the Earth. The Earth Pledge Program has three main components.

1. The Earth Steward Program, part of a comprehensive effort to create a worldwide network of one million Earth Stewards by the 50th anniversary of the UN in 1995.

2. The Schools Program: Children are asked to recite the Pledge at the beginning of the school day, as a complement to the Pledge of Allegiance to the Flag.

3. The Messenger Program provides a way for individuals, environmental groups, peace groups, or religious organizations to help spread the message of environmental awareness and global cooperation.

Ontario Multifaith Council on Spiritual and Religious Care

35 McCaul Street, Suite 305
Toronto, Ontario M5T 1V7 Canada;
tel. (416) 326-6858 / fax (416) 326-6867

The Province of Ontario is one of the most faith diverse areas in the world. It is also unique in both its policies and structures for support of spiritual and religious care. Government and faith groups collaborate in the provision of spiritual and religious care programs to people in community residential facilities and institutions.

The Province's first institutional chaplains were appointed in the late 1940's. In 1972 the Ontario Provincial Interfaith Committee on Chaplaincy was established. This partnership between the government and faith groups was re-affirmed in 1992 with the Memorandum of Agreement which saw the OPIFCC succeeded by the Ontario Multifaith Council on Spiritual and Religious Care. It is now a vital link in the government's development of community-based residential and treatment facilities, enabling people with special needs to remain in communities of their choice.

Chaplaincy Services Ontario supports over 200 chaplains offering spiritual and religious care in hospitals, homes for the aged, children's treatment centres, psychiatric centres, nursing homes, facilities for people with developmental handicaps, group homes and correctional facilities for young offenders and adults. These chaplains coordinate and support the involvement, worship and efforts of hundreds of faith community leaders and over ten thousand volunteers.

Principles of chaplaincy care:
- Spirituality is at the core of being human.
- Religion is the individual's expression of spirituality through worship, practice, and relationships within a faith group.
- The government and faith groups are responsible for the provision of spiritual and religious care.
- Faith communities are responsible for providing religious care.
- Individual needs for spiritual and religious care should be assessed and therapeutically supported in any facility or programme.
- There are established standards of quality for the provision of spiritual and religious

care in government-funded facilities and programmes.

- Chaplains are professional caregivers responsible for the assessment of clients' spiritual and religious needs, the coordination and support of faith community services, the interpretation of religious rights and practices, and the process for determination of ethical issues.

The Coordinators of Chaplaincy Services Ontario provide direct support to chaplains, programmes of training and community development, support of faith community initiatives and support for the Provincial Multifaith Council and Regional Multifaith Committees. Chaplaincy Services Ontario has coordinators at eight regional offices throughout Ontario. Among the resources offered are the recently revised and published *Multifaith Information Manual,* which provides a unique reference guide for chaplains and others working in care situations for diverse populations. Each of the chapters on 31 faith traditions includes important details about the nature of the religion, basic beliefs, rituals, practices and beliefs regarding death and health care, holy days and festivals, dietary requirements, symbols and much more.

Order from the address above in Canada (call re: cost); within the USA, order from: Multifaith Resources, PO Box 128, Wofford Heights, CA 93285 USA. $21.95, includes S&H. Large format paperback, 132 pages.

Pathways to Peace

Avon Mattison, President
P.O. Box 1057, Larkspur, CA 94977USA
tel. (415) 461-0500 / fax (415) 925-0330

Envisioned in 1945 and active in research and consulting since the '60s, the mission of Pathways to Peace is:

- To expand the comprehension and expression of peace and peace-building practices at all levels;
- To build cooperation by uniting and enhancing the strengths of existing organizations and programs;
- To contribute to the evolving role of the UN and to citizens' participation in the International Day of Peace (World Peace Day; the UN General Assembly supports this effort with one minute of silence on each third Tuesday in September).

The mission is accomplished through projects such as the Children's World Peace Festival, Evenings with Peace Leaders, and Peace-Building through Business. Collaborative projects with other organizations include the World Summit on Children, the People's Assembly of the Action Coalition for Global Change, the Interfaith Youth Conference, and the Rights of the Child Caucus. Pathways for Peace was granted "Peace Messenger Initiative" status by UN Secretary-General Perez de Cuellar, and has consultative status with with several UN agencies.

Pathways to Peace also coordinates the "We the People's Initiative," a multi-cultural and inter-generational movement among organizations worldwide.

Pax Christi International and USA

348 East Tenth Street, Erie, PA 16503-1110 USA; tel. (814) 453-4955

Pax Christi was founded in France in 1945 to promote reconciliation between French and German Catholics after the destructive violence of World War II. It is now a growing international movement speaking from twenty-two countries on four continents. It has Consultative Status as an NGO at the United Nations.

Pax Christi strives to create a world that reflects the Peace of Christ by exploring, articulating, and witnessing to the call of Christian nonviolence. This work begins in personal life and extends to communities of reflection and action to transform structures of society. Pax Christi rejects war, preparations for war, and every form of violence and domination. It advocates primacy of conscience, economic and social justice, and respect for creation.

Pax Christi USA, a section of Pax Christi International, commits itself to peace education and, with the help of its 100 bishop members, 370 local groups, 430 religious community sponsors, and 12,000 members and 150 affiliated parishes, promotes the gospel imperative of peacemaking as a priority in the Catholic Church in the United States. The Youth Forum enables young people to explore and practice peacemaking in actions that identify and address critical social issues. Pax Christi USA also provides a wide selection of books on nonviolence and peacemaking, cards, posters, and pamphlets, and other resources for study and action. Through the efforts of all its members and in cooperation with other groups, Pax Christi USA works toward a more peaceful, just, and sustainable world.

Peace Action

(formerly SANE/FREEZE)

1819 H Street, Suite 640, Washington, DC 20006-3603 USA

Peace Action is one of the oldest and largest grassroots peace organizations in the country. You may know us by our former name, SANE/FREEZE – an organization created seven years ago by the merger of SANE and the Nuclear Freeze Campaign. SANE was founded in 1957 by Eleanor Roosevelt, Linus Pauling, Eric Fromm, and others concerned about the growing threat of nuclear weapons. Dr. Martin Luther King, Albert Schweitzer, and Dr. Benjamin Spock were also early SANE supporters. SANE led the "ban the bomb" efforts in the 1950s and 1960s – and later became an early leader of nationwide opposition to the Vietnam war. In the 1980s SANE worked to stop US intervention in El Salvador and Nicaragua. In 1987 SANE merged with the Nuclear Weapons Freeze Campaign to build a citizens' movement against the Reagan Administration's nuclear weapons buildup and the bloated military budget.

Today we seek to build a movement embracing all cultures, races, and nations. We believe that the primary purpose of the United Nations – " to save succeeding generations from the scourge of war" – is undermined by the proliferation of conventional and nuclear weapons. Peace Action opposes the international transfer of nuclear materials and technology which can make nuclear weapons. Peace Action already helped win a two-year moratorium on nuclear weapons testing and we're working to turn it into a permanent, comprehensive ban on all nuclear weapons tests anywhere in the world. The centerpiece of this work in 1995 will be an international citizen's assembly that will occur during the United Nations conference on the Non-Proliferation Treaty in April 1995 in New York City.

We're also working with a broad coalition of US peace, social justice, and religious groups to pressure Congress to make deep cuts in the military budget – and deliver the long-overdue "peace dividend" to meet human needs. Within the US, Peace Action has a network of 150 regional chapters with more than 50,000 members in all 50 states. This network of grassroots activists can stand up to the power and money of the arms trade – if we can build massive citizen support.

Peace Action is working with lawmakers and citizens around the country to build widespread public pressure to pass the "Arms Trade Code of Conduct" Bill to stop American arms sales to governments which use weapons against their own citizens and their neighbors. The proliferation of weapons large and small stimulates violence and wastes money and human resources which should instead be used for meeting basic human rights and needs.

Currently there are very few restrictions on arms sales. Foreign governments place a request to purchase weapons and the President authorizes their sale and transfer. Congress can oppose a sale only after it has been authorized by the President – and even then Congressional objection can be vetoed. Congress needs a two-thirds majority to block an arms sale, which is almost impossible – given the power and influence of the weapons manufacturers and their lobbyists in Washington.

US arms sales policies cause tremendous suffering and destruction around the world. The "Arms Trade Code of Conduct" Bill would forbid U.S. arms sales to undemocratic nations, military dictatorships, countries engaging in acts of aggression, and governments that violate the human rights of their own citizens. Peace Action is organizing Congressional and citizen support for this Bill.

The Pluralism Project: World Religions in America

Diana L. Eck, Project Director, Harvard University, Phillips Brooks House, Cambridge, MA 02138 USA; tel. (617) 495-5781 / fax (617) 496-5798

The Pluralism Project is a three-year research project, funded by Lilly Endowment Inc., which engages students in studying the new religious diversity of the United States. We are exploring particularly the communities and religious traditions of Asia and the Middle East that have become woven into the religious fabric of the United States in the past twenty-five years.

The information gathered will be presented on an innovative interactive CD-ROM. This full-color, interactive database will present the database of over 1,500 Buddhist temples, 1,100 mosques and Islamic centers, more than 400 Hindu temples, over 100 Jain temples, over 100 Sikh gurudwaras and centers, and dozens of religious centers of the Zoroastrian, Bahá'í, and Afro-Caribbean traditions. It will also incorporate moving and still color images, text, and stereo CD-quality sound. The geographically organized tool also introduces the history and questions of American cultural and religious "pluralism." It is scheduled for distribution in January 1996 on both Macintosh and IBM Windows-compatible CD-ROM.

Prison Fellowship

P.O. Box 17500, Washington, DC 20041-0500

Based within evangelical Christianity, Prison Fellowship works in the US and internationally to help prisoners break with the cycle of crime. The Fellowship also advocates humanitarian treatment of prisoners, supports victims' rights and reform of sentencing laws. Prison Fellowship and its international affiliates now have a staff of over 280 who coordinate the efforts of nearly 50,000 volunteers in 800 state and federal prisons and in more than 50 other nations.

Charles Colson, founder, received the Templeton Prize for Progress in Religion at ceremonies during the Parliament of the World's Religions. The prize affirmed his

dedicated work of pioneering, creating, and organizing this humanitarian and religiously-based service organization.

Project Earthlink

NOAA Office of Global Programs, Suite 1225 1100 Wayne Avenue, Silver Spring, MD 20910 USA; tel. (301) 427-2089 ex. 20

The North American Oceanic and Atmospheric Administration (NOAA) is one of thirteen US agencies that, along with business, grass-roots and national environmental groups, educators, labor and other leaders are gathering in an unprecedented partnership.

This long-term Global Change Education Program is offered in conjunction with the 25th anniversary of Earth Day and ongoing efforts. Project Earthlink's motto is "Linking people with the planet." It hopes to establish global-change education, increase understanding of change and sustainable development, lead to informed environmental choices, empower young people, and generate voluntary action through all sectors of society.

Religious Education Association

409 Prospect St. New Haven, CT 0651 USA

The REA brings together people involved in all aspects of religious education for dialogue across denominations and faith traditions. Founded in 1903, the REA has a long history of concern and activity regarding the theory and practice of religious education, religion and public education, adult faith development, and interreligious dialogue. Membership benefits include a professional journal titled *Religious Education,* a newsletter, conferences, and networking.

Religion in American Life

Dr. Nicholas B. van Dyck, President, 2 Queenston Place, Room 200, Princeton, NJ 08540 USA; tel. (609) 921-3639

RIAL is an interfaith, non-profit agency that works to get more US citizens to become active members of religious congregations. Research shows that members of congregations are far more generous in support of charities and as volunteers than are non-members. Hence, RIAL contributes to the spiritual well-being of individuals and the public interest.

Services include a person-to-person program of outreach to the religiously unaffiliated. The Invite a Friend project involves denominations and dioceses with 63 million members. Worship directories in hotels throughout the US encourage travelers and newcomers to attend churches, synagogues or mosques of their

choice. Cooperative advertising campaigns also encourage attendance and participation. The 56 religious groups currently members of RIAL account for 92,000 congregations, or 84 percent of all religiously affiliated people in the US within Protestant, Catholic, Jewish, Muslim, and other traditions.

RESULTS – Generating Political Will to End Hunger

Sam Harris, Executive Director, 236 Massachusetts Ave. NE, Suite 300, Washington, DC, 20002 USA; tel. (202) 543-9340 / fax (202) 543-3228

RESULTS is an international, grassroots hunger lobby creating the political will to end hunger and poverty. Results empowers people to realize that they are the key to making a difference.

Each and every day around the world, some 70,000 parents bury children who have died from *preventable* disease and malnutrition. People living in poverty often have no voice and few advocates. RESULTS is committed to being their partners and advocates.

In nearly 100 cities in the US and in 30 cities in seven other countries, RESULTS volunteers are educating people in their communities, encouraging local media to cover hunger and poverty issues, and communicating with their representatives. We strengthen our relationships with our elected officials so that government will act to provide basic needs to all the world's children, and opportunities for families to lift themselves out of poverty.

Since 1985, volunteers have been effective in campaigns such as in a squabble between the US and OPEC which jeopardized the International Fund for Agricultural Devlopment (IFAD) and its work with small farmers and the landless poor. RESULTS volunteers generated 46 editorials plus letters to the editor and letters and calls to officials, lobbying hard for IFAD. The President of IFAD credited the resulting consensus as "very much related to the efforts of RESULTS." In 1993, RESULTS groups in seven countries initiated a letter to presidents of the three regional development banks – African, Inter-American, and Asian – urging them to commit a greater proportion of their resources to poverty reduction and, in particular, to increased lending for primary health care and basic education. Nearly 1,000 parliamentarians signed the letter.

A recent publication by Sam Harris, *Reclaiming Our Democracy: Healing the Break Between People and Government,* serves as an introduction to the organization's strategies and values and to the context of need in which it operates.

Ribbon International

c/o Monica Willard, 3 Harbor Ct., Centerport, NY 11721 USA; tel. (516) 754-1008

Creating panels for use in large ribbons is an excellent creative expression of values and concerns. Children, families, religious and civic organizations have all been used in the past to share a message: some emphasize the importance of caring for one another; others show the importance of protecting the environment. Ribbons may reflect regional, religious, or cultural values. The original ribbons were made to express the hope for world peace and the deep concerns generated by the threat of nuclear weapons. Ribbons can also be used in commemorations of the UN's 50 anniversary or in parades on holidays.

Ribbons are study cloth panels measuring 36" x 18", with ties on the four corners. Ribbons also honor diversity while celebrating unity. To have panels exhibited with the International Collection, contact the address above.

The Rio de Janeiro Interfaith Network

Av. Rio Branco, 125 / 13 Andar, Centro, Rio de Janeiro, Brazil 20040-006
tel. 55-21-232-8213 / fax 55-21-205-8035

See Chapter 26 for a full description of this network, which was founded in conjunction with the Earth Summit in 1992, and which has since then moved forward with a full program of cooperative responses to ethical and social issues.

Risho Kosei-kai

Interfaith Relations and Affairs Section, 2-11-1 Wada, Suginami-ku, Tokyo 166 Japan; tel. (03)3380-5185 / fax (03)3381-9792

Founded in 1938 by Rev. Nikkyo Niwano, Risho Kosei-kai's membership is now 6.7 million with 239 branches throughout Japan and 6 branches overseas. As a lay Buddhist organization, Risho Kosei-kai is based on principles set forth in the Lotus Sutra, which is regarded as the comprehensive teaching of the Lord Shakyamuni Buddha, and is therefore one of the most important scriptures of Mahayana Buddhism. Through their religious interactions and unity of belief, its members strive to perfect themselves and realize a peaceful world.

Rev. Nikkyo Niwano, laureate of the Templeton Prize for Progress in Religion in 1979, has been very active in interfaith activities. He is now an honorary president of the World Conference on Religion and Peace and also of the International Association for Religious Freedom. In 1991, Rev. Nichiko Niwano, the eldest son

of Rev. Nikkyo Niwano, succeeded him as President of Risho Kosei-kai.

Two of the many programs supported by members of Risho Kosei-kai are the Fund for Peace and the Donate-One-Meal Campaign. These provide development, hunger relief, social welfare, peace-making and environmental funds or services to people, projects and organizations in need of assistance. The Donate-One-Meal Campaign is also intended to remind members

"...that we enjoy an excess of food and luxury while large numbers of others are starving; each time we forego a meal and donate its cost, we try in a small way to understand the pain of our needy brethren and pray for their happiness and peace" (from a booklet on the Fund For Peace).

Risho Kosei-kai's periodical, *Dharma World – for living Buddhism and Interreligious Dialogue* – is available anywhere in the world for $22.00 per year.

School Sisters of Notre Dame

Via della Stazione Aurlia, 95, 00165 Rome, Italy

Our congregation collaborates with the UN in its efforts to bring about justice and peace in the global community. We are especially concerned about: human rights, non-violent conflict resolution, education, elimination of all forms of discrimination, refugees, eradication of hunger, ethical models of development, environment, the rights of women and children and the right of self-determination for all people.

In 33 countries our diverse ministries bring us in touch with persons of all ages and of different races and creeds. Wherever we minister, we have a special preference for women, children and the poor. We also participate in world conferences and their Prep Coms, including the World Summit on Social Development and the Fourth World Conference on Women.

Science of Spirituality

4 S. 175 Naperville Rd, Naperville, IL USA; tel. (800) 222-2207, (708) 955-1200 / fax (708) 955-1205

Kirpal Ashram, 2 Canal Road, Vijay Nagar, Delhi 110009 India; tel. + 722 2244

Science of Spirituality – Sawan Kirpal Ruhani Mission is dedicated to spirituality, peace, and service to humanity. With headquarters in Delhi, India, and 800 centers in forty countries, it offers people all over the world an opportunity to find peace, joy, and spiritual fulfillment. Sant Rajinder Singh Ji Maharaj, the spiritual head of Science of Spirituality, teaches a simple and natural method of meditation

leading to peace which begins with the individual and spreads to the global level. This meditation technique was taught by Hazur Baba Sawan Singh Ji Maharaj (1858-1948), Sant Kirpal Singh Ji Maharaj (1894-1974), and Sant Darshan Singh Ji Maharaj (1921-1989), and a line of spiritual teachers preceding them. It provides a means whereby people of all ages, religions, and nationalities can integrate meditation into their lives. This practice has been referred to as Surat Shabd Yoga, Sant Mat, or meditation on the inner Light and Sound. Along with the study of meditation, practitioners learn how to develop noble human values that will transform and enrich their lives, enabling them to make positive contributions to the world. The goals of Science of Spirituality are to teach individuals how to:

- Develop to their fullest potential: physically, mentally, and spiritually;
- Achieve inner peace through meditation;
- Bring about outer peace in the world;
- Serve the needs of society physically, intellectually, and spiritually.

People of all faiths and backgrounds are welcome, as spirituality is taught as a science. SK publications in Naperville, Illinois, offers books, audio and video tapes, and other literature to assist inquirers in understanding the goals and teachings and in practicing the methods.

Shomrei Adamah – Keepers of the Earth, Renewing Jewish Ecological Wisdom

5500 Wissahickon Ave #804C, Philadelphia, PA 19144 USA; tel. (215) 844-8150

The mission of Shomrei Adamah/Keepers of the Earth is to inspire environmental awareness and practice among Jews by unlocking the treasure of ancient Jewish ecological wisdom. Shomrei Adamah serves its members – rabbis, educators, students, environmentalists, youth, seminaries, and a network of affiliates with authentic traditional sources, curricula, publications, wilderness experiences, music, a newsletter (*Voices of the Trees*), and "green synagogue" suggestions. Books include *Let the Earth Teach You Torah* and *A Garden of Choice Fruit*.

Why a Jewish environmental organization?

Judaism embodies a 3,000-year-old environmental ethic and a viable practice of stewardship. Unfortunately, that environmental wisdom has been dormant for several generations. Shomrei Adamah revives, invigorates, and extends the Jewish system of ecological thought, ethics, spirit, and practice, and involves the Jewish community in environmental affairs.

There is a spiritual need for Shomrei

Adamah's unique approach, which integrates thought, emotion, spirit, and action. Shomrei Adamah also strengthens and makes meaningful the work and commitment of Jewish environmentalists.

Society for Human Development and the Human Economy Center

P.O. Box 28, West Swanzey, NY 03469-0028

The Society is a worldwide network of thoughtful people developing creative new approaches to many different economic issues and practices. A recent issue of the newsletter, *Human Economy: Economics as if People Mattered* asked the question: "Given that there are some 20,000 Ph.D. economists currently on the planet, why is it that almost all of them pay serious attention to only two possible ways of organizing economic activity: free market capitalism, or socialism?

Society for International Development

International Secretariat, Palazzo Civila del Lavoro, 0144 Rome, Italy

The Society for International Development (SID) was established in 1957 as an association for people interested in international economic, political, and social development. SID has over 10,000 members in independent forums or chapters throughout 132 countries. Each is advocating local, regional, national, and international cooperation on development-related issues. SID is also a partner in Project Global 2000, organized by Global Education Associates.

SID has a three-fold purpose: to encourage the building of a sense of community at all levels and of all people in development; to promote international dialogue, understanding, and cooperation for social and economic development; and to advance the science, processes, and art of sustainable development.

To achieve these goals, SID conducts programs and conferences on current issues in the field of international development. The most recent, "People's Rights and Security: Sustainable Development Strategies for the 21st Century," centered on the need to alleviate poverty and promote social justice or a human-centered development. Human rights, secure employment, the role of women, youth development, and improving global governance systems are on the new program agenda.

Soka Gakkai International – Value Creating Education Society

SGI-USA, 525 Wilshire Boulevard,

Santa Monica, CA 90401-1427 USA; tel. 310 451-8811

Soka Gakkai was founded in Japan in 1930 by Tsunesaburo Makiguchi and Josei Toda in order to promote humanistic education based on the Buddhism of Nichiren Daishonin. In 1943, they and other leaders were brutally imprisoned as "thought criminals" for refusing to accept the precepts of state Shintoism, which was used to buttress the war efforts. After the war, the surviving leadership revived the organization and expanded its mission toward the whole of society. By the late 50's, the organization had grown to 750,000 households. Since then, Soka Gakkai's membership has grown in Japan to approximately 8 million member families; the Soka Gakkai Iinternational (SGI) membership is now approximately 1.26 million in 115 countries and regions outside Japan, and is one of the world' most rapidly expanding religious movements.

Consistent with the teachings of Shakyamuni Buddha and the exposition of the Lotus Sutra by Nichiren Daishonin, Soka Gakkai and SGI programs now encompass all aspects of life, and are particularly active in peace, environmental, educational, and cultural programs. A few examples of the peace work follow:

- SGI and its president, Daisaku Ideda have made concerted efforts to strengthen the UN and increase its effectiveness;
- SG and SGI have been registered NGOs since 1981 with various UN institutions;
- Asian and African refugees have been recipients of relief funds since 1973; and
- Antiwar and antinuclear weapons campaigns sponsored by SGI include the collection of ten million signatures in support of the total eradication of nuclear weapons, in 1975.

These and many other activities and proposals have given SGI a high profile in world affairs.

Photography, art, music, dance, philosophy, and education are also emphasized as means to the expression and appreciation of humanity's Buddha nature. Based on the conviction that human issues such as peace, the environment, and ethics can best be addressed through advances in human spirituality, SGI and the many centers worldwide, its educational and political programs, and its institutes continue to expand the networks of knowledge and to broaden the scope of their activities. For instance, SGI-USA is performing a major musical titled "Arise Like a Phoenix: A Celebration of Fifty Years of the United Nations" during San Francisco's UN50 commemorations during the summer of 1995. The *Seikyo Shimbun*, the daily newspaper of Soka Gakkai with a circulation of 5.5 million, reports on

activities to promote peace, culture, and education based on the spirit of Buddhism. More than forty other publications promote SGI activities and insights worldwide.

Sri Chinmoy Centres International

Sri Chinmoy Centres International 84-43 164th St., Jamaica, NY 11432 USA; tel. (718) 291-7406

Sri Chinmoy Centres is an international non-profit organization, dedicated to the twin goals of inner growth and service to the world around us. Our approach is integral, combining body, mind, and spirit in the pursuit of humanity's highest aspirations. We are ecumenical in the widest sense of the term, embracing people of all faiths and nationalities. In so doing we celebrate the spiritual ideal that what unites humanity is far greater than that which divides us. Founded in 1964 by philosopher, teacher, artist and author Sri Chinmoy, we have grown to over 125 centers with membership of several thousand in more than 35 countries.

With a dedication to selfless service, we sponsor inspirational events in the fields of art, music, poetry, sports and meditative disciplines. In all of our activities we consistently strive to uphold the principle that world transformation begins with each individual, and that the most enduring satisfaction comes from self-knowledge, self-giving, and self-transcendence.

Besides meditating for several hours a day and guiding his Centres, Sri Chinmoy conducts meditations twice a week for UN delegates and staff in New York.

The Temple of Understanding – a Global Interfaith Association

The Cathedral of St. John, 1047 Amsterdam Avenue, New York, NY 10025 USA

The Temple of Understanding was founded in 1960 to address the urgent need of our time for dialogue and understanding among the religions of the world. It began through the inspiration of Juliet Hollister, with the support of a distinguished group of "Founding Friends," including Eleanor Roosevelt, Pope John XXIII, Secretary-General U Thant, Dr. Albert Schweitzer, Anwar el-Sadat, Jawaharlal Nehru, Dr. Sarvepalli Radhakrishnan, Sir Zafrulla Khan, Fr. Thomas Merton, H.E.S. Zalman Shazar, and the Dalai Lama of Tibet.

Initially, a series of Spiritual Summit Conferences was developed through which a network of world spiritual leaders emerged. These took place in Calcutta (1968), Geneva (1970), Harvard University (1971), Princeton University (1971), Cornell University (1974), the United

Nations (1975), and the Cathedral of St. John the Divine (1984).

In 1988 the Temple of Understanding co-founded the Global Forum of Spiritual and Parliamentary Leaders for Human Survival, and was also instrumental in helping to found the North American Interfaith Network.

The Temple of Understanding is also affiliated as an NGO with UN agencies. It maintains a strong commitment to the integrity of each religion/faith tradition, and believes that each can better remain true to itself by respecting the truths in other traditions, and by cooperating to confront the great challenges of building a viable future for the world's peoples.

Current programs

The Group of Reflection. A number of UN-connected people from different religions and geographical areas meet to reflect together on how to incorporate spiritual values into the UN documents and conferences. We have produced one paper, "Toward Deeper Values and Fuller Development" (printed in Chapter 34) which will be presented during the Summit. We are also working on a paper indicating what religions can contribute to the solution of three core issues discussed at the Summit: a) mitigate and reduce poverty, b) increase employment, and c) foster social integration.

UN 50th Anniversary: We have been asked to organize an Inter-Religious Prayer Service for Heads of State on 22 October, 1995. We are preparing this service with the Office of the UN 50th Anniversary.

Education

The 50th Anniversary of the dropping of the Atomic Bomb is the occasion for a worldwide project of *Concerts and Prayer for Peace.* The Cathedral of St. John and ToU are collaborating to design the interfaith message for a world audience and to communicate and help gather audiences for the Concerts/Prayer series. The Temple of Understanding is working with academic institutions such as New York University, Harvard University, and Boston University to develop conferences and community-based educational programs, in order to promote greater understanding of religious diversity. ToU has also been coordinating a program of monthly lectures given by leaders of different faiths at Trinity School in New York City. The Temple also serves as a resource for the growing emphasis on teaching about religious pluralism in public and private schools, currently distributing free films to schools and libraries, courtesy of Hartley Film Foundation.

Of particular relevance is a program given by the Temple of Understanding Student Chapter at the University of Maryland, USA, where the students have organized an international conference on conflict resolution.

Among other recent educational programs are the following:

a) New Delhi, India: on the occasion of the 7th World Religions Conference of the World Fellowship of Religions in February 1994, we organized and directed the First Inter-religious Retreat on Prayer, Meditation, and Non-Violence.

b) New York: in July 1994, on the occasion of the Convocation on World Religions, commemorating the centenary of the founding of the Vedanta Society by Swami Vivekananda, and continuing the spirit of the centenary of the first World Parliament of Religions in Chicago, we organized a two-day conference on the role religions can play to help peace and nonviolence in cities today, with a special accent on the religions of India and the Indian population in American cities.

Media Projects and Publications

In production is an ongoing series of television programs illustrating multi-religious perspectives on current issues. Videotapes are available (see Chapter 43).

A newsletter with a circulation of over 2,000 is normally sent out three times a year. While the Temple of Understanding has produced a number of books throughout its history, most recently it has published two editions of the *North American Interfaith Directory,* and in 1993 the *Global Interfaith Directory* (US$15.00).

Regional Activities

Our India chapter is very active. To obtain information on its work, contact Dr. Agjoy Bagchi at 15, Institutional Area, Lodhi Road, New Delhi, India 11003. For information on our United Kingdom chapter, also very active, contact Jenny Rose, 18 Fairlawn Mansions, New Cross Road, London SE145PN, UK. In 1993 our Guatemala representatives helped us set up a very interesting meeting with the 1992 Nobel Peace Prize winner Rigoberta Menchu. Our Argentina group organized an inter-religious Consultation that took place in Buenos Aires in November 1993.

The Templeton Prize for Progress in Religion
P.O. Box N7776, Nassau, The Bahamas

Awarded annually by Sir John Templeton through an esteeemed committee of international and inter-religious judges, this very large prize honors a person whose efforts, while humanitarian, are primarily spiritual, as well as pioneering, and with wide-ranging effects. The award encourages the concept that resources and manpower are needed for progress in spiritual knowledge. The influence of the award is enhanced by the diversity of its recipients, who are deliberately chosen from different races, sexes, professions and religions. Past recipients include Dr. Kyung-Chik Han, Rt. Hon. Lord Jakobovits, Dr. Inamullah Khan, Billy Graham, Alexander Solzhenitsyn, Dame Cecily Saunders, Rev. Nikkyo Niwano, and Mother Teresa.

T.O.U.C.H. – The Organization for Universal Communal Harmony
243 Palisade Ave, Dobbs Ferry, NY 10522

TOUCH'S mission is to foster harmony among people of all religious, ethnic, caste, and racial backgrounds in India and other countries of the South Asian subcontinent through peaceful and humanistic endeavors and through the establishment of institutes and organizational networks in the region and in other parts of the world.

TOUCH'S objectives include:

- Establish an interfaith, inter communal, grassroots-level participatory organization.
- Establish a think tank of recognized religious leaders, academicians, journalists, social workers, personalities, community leaders, and others committed to secular, harmonious and humanistic philosophy.
- Develop interfaith and intercommunal educational programs, and inter- communal and inter caste participation at public, community and religious events.
- Disseminate information through multiple communication channels.

UNIFEM – The United Nations Development Fund for Women
UNIFEM USA, 485 Fifth Avenue, Suite 250, New York, NY 10017 USA; tel. 1-800-982-9781

UNIFEM helps women living in poverty in developing countries to help themselves by providing labor-saving technology, crucial training, and access to credit. UNIFEM also assists refugee women and children – who are 80% of the world's refugees. These investments contribute toward the well-being of her family, community, and country. When UNIFEM assists 250,000 women, 1,000,000 children benefit.

UNIFEM is also a major player in the preparations for the Fourth International Women's Conference in Beijing, in September 1995, and in ongoing programs for women's and family rights and development.

Union of International Associations
rue Washington 40, B-1050 Brussels, Belgium; tel. (32 2)640 18 08 / fax (32 2)646 05 25

Founded in Brussels in 1907, the UIA is an independent, non-governmental, non-profit and a-political body. Its programmes are oriented toward the international associations whose actions they are designed to facilitate, whether through special studies or through new uses of information. Its work contributed to the creation of the League of Nations and the International Institute of Intellectual Cooperation (the precedessor of UNESCO).

Aims:

- Facilitate the evolution of the activities of the worldwide network of non-profit organizations, especially non-governmental or voluntary associations.
- Promote understanding of how international bodies represent valid interests in every field of human activity or belief, whether scientific, religious, artistic, educational, trade, or labour.
- Enable these initiatives to develop and counterbalance each other creatively, in response to world problems, by collecting information on international bodies and their interrelationships.
- Make such information available to all who may benefit from this network.
- Experiment with meaningful and action-oriented ways of presenting information as a catalyst for the emergence of more appropriate organizations.
- Promote research on the legal, administrative and other problems common to these international associations, especially in their contacts with governmental bodies.

UIA also publishes the *Yearbook of International Organizations* and maintains contact with over 1,000 inter-governmental bodies and over 13,000 international non-governmental organizations. Note also the *Encyclopedia of World Problems and Human Potential, 1991* (see Chapter 43).

United Nations Environment Programme

International Headquarters
P.O. Box 30552 Nairobi, Kenya
tel.(254) (2) 333939/520600

Regional Office for North America
Room DC2-803, United Nations,
N.Y. 10017 USA;
tel. (212) 963-8138 / fax (212) 963-7341

See *Chapters 30 and 37 for details.*

United States Agency for International Development

320 Twenty-First St., N.W.,
Washington, DC 20523 USA
tel. (202) 647-9620 / fax (202) 647-1770
Internet Address: gopher:info.usaid.gov

USAID plays many roles in US policy,

foreign aid, and in international development and relief efforts. General areas of concern include: broad-based economic growth, stabilizing population growth, protecting the environment, promoting democracy, humanitarian and disaster assistance, regional/country focuses, and procurement and business opportunities. Controversies arise regarding many of these areas depending on one's analysis of the political and economic agendas attached to the money distributed.

USAID cooperates with private voluntary and religious organizations (PVOs), by providing grants, coordinating activities, and sharing resources in the work of development. Although PVOs have been engaged in humanitarian work overseas for more than a century, recent decades have seen a rapid upswing in activities and a clearer focus on long-term development.

Unity and Diversity World Council

5521 Grosvenor Blvd. Suite 22,
Los Angeles, CA 90066-6915 USA;
tel. (310) 577-1968

UDC is a worldwide membership organization, a coordinating body of individuals, groups, and networks that affirm our unity based on the dynamic integration of our diversity.

> Being of common sacred origin, we hereby declare our interdependence; for we, the people, shall kindle the torch of hope, link hands over space and time, and fulfill our interdependence through action. (from the UDC Declaration of Interdependence)

Formed in 1965 and voted into being by the General Assembly of the United Nations, UDC seeks to help establish and sustain a global civilization based on all races, cultures, and religions working to create a new framework for a caring society. The "Unity and Diversity" concept is the central principle of democracy. Now, in this 30th anniversary year of UDC, the world has become ready for the expansion of this idea into most parts of the globe. A pluralistic basis for society can now be established for a global civilization.

UDC offers a bookstore, monthly gatherings, special programs, convergences and a World Festival in conjuction with the 50th anniversary of the UN, seminars and trainings. UDC publishes *Spectrum*, a quarterly magazine, a newsletter, a world directory and books that support the UDC vision; one of these is *Unity-and-Diversity Spiritual Celebration: A Guide for Small Groups or Interfaith Celebrations*. Other, specialized affiliates pursue ongoing facets of UDC's framework for unity.

University for Peace

P.O. Box 199 - 1250, Escazu', Costa Rica;
tel. 506 249-1072 / fax 506-249-1929

The University for Peace is an International Institution located close to Ciudad Colón, some 25 kilometers west of San José, on an area of 350 hectares, including 250 of undisturbed forest. Its creation was approved by the XXXVth General Assembly of the United Nations on December 5, 1980 "...with the purpose of contributing to the promotion of peace through education and diffusion of knowledge and in accordance with the principles of the Charter of the United Nations and the Universal Declaration of Human Rights."

The University engages in such fields as irenology, education for peace, human rights, communications for peace and conflict resolution, among others. The discipline of natural resources and quality of life was also programmed with the aim of studying and teaching the management of natural resources as they affect scenarios of conflict, and can directly or indirectly promote peaceful relations between individuals and countries.

In addition to its ongoing classes, the UPeace has co-sponsored many regional initiatives and international conferences, including, in 1989, "Seeking the True Meaning of Peace," with keynote speakers Dr. Oscar Arias S., Nobel Peace Prize winner in 1987, and H.H. Tenzin Gyatso, the 14th Dalai Lama of Tibet. Among the conference's products was the "Declaration of Human Responsibilities for Peace and Sustainable Development" (printed in Chapter 36).

Dr. Robert Muller is Chancellor (Emeritus) of the UPeace and an avid proponent of its goals and vision. The University's enrollment capacity is now over 700 students, most in graduate-level programs. UPeace operating expenses do not come directly from the United Nations but must be granted by supporting countries, foundations, and individuals.

The Urantia Foundation

533 Diversey Parkway, Chicago, IL 60614
USA; tel. (312) 525-3319

The Urantia Foundation publishes *The Urantia Book*, name for planet Earth as it is known throughout the cosmos according to this revelation, which came from higher beings about fifty years ago. The book includes a complex and astounding description of the creation and evolution of the universes; it also provides philosophy, history, and narrative, including details about Jesus' life, travels, and teachings not included in the Bible.

Related societies of readers and students of the book see their task as being:

> ... a living community of the higher way of truth, beauty, and goodness which the searchers of humanity may discover. In the present phase of activity as guardians of the Urantia Revelation, serving mainly in the capacity of study groups and engaging in discriminating personal evangelism, [readers] should endeavor to become the leaven which will eventually transform the religious institutions of the world. Our present goal is not to start a new religion or to organize another religious body designed to replace our present religious organizations.

Meredith J. Sprunger, in a printed version of his speech titled Our Task.

Readers of the *Urantia Book* see themselves as a brotherhood whose true loyalty and dedication is to the Universal Father, and to Him alone. The *Urantia Book* and brotherhood are both seen as means to bringing others closer to God.

The Values Caucus – at the UN
431 East 57th St., New York, NY 10022 USA; tel. (212) 750-2773 / fax (212) 750-2774

Members of the newly formed Values Caucus began meeting following the Social Development Prep Com in August 1994, where the Group of Reflection had presented its paper on incorporating universal religious values into the declaration and policies to be enacted at the Social Summit (Copenhagen, March 1995).

Many interested NGOs attended these gatherings to offer their ideas on developing a strong and effective caucus. The group's long-term goal is to establish a strong, collaborative partnership of NGOs to form an ongoing Values Caucus. When established, members of this Caucus would actively engage their own organizations and would link with like-minded UN missions, agencies, the Secretariat, and others who share a common vision.

The Caucus encourages groups to become members who believe that underlying all events in the world are a set of spoken or unspoken values and principles; members believe that it is crucial to make these values explicit if we are to understand events, know which policies and actions we can develop and support, and learn what ways of relating with others lead to personal, group, and world solidarity. The Caucus hopes that representatives from professional, business, peace, women's, children's, human rights, environmental, social, religious, and other groups will find a home within it as we

approach world concerns from the perspective of values in action.

VISION/TV – Canada's New Faith Network
315 Queen Street East, Toronto, Ontario M5A 1S7, Canada; tel. (416) 368-3194 / (416) 368-9774

VISION/TV was born in 1988 as the culmination of years of effort by people who saw the promise and potential of a new kind of television – television for the spirit. The vision was to do programming that looked at life in terms of ethics and values and that provided access to the power of TV for Canada's many religious and cultural communities. Today the dream is a reality in five-and-a-half million Canadian homes, 21 hours a day.

Handling issues that conventional networks won't touch, VISION TV offers television that enlightens as it entertains, yet provides room for all kinds of perspectives. In addition to the approximately half of the programming that is a mixture of top-quality drama, documentary, music, and human affairs, *Mosaic* offers air time to established religious and cultural groups; over 40 religious and cultural communities have provided programming. Commercials are limited to six minutes per hour, and on-air solicitation of funds, when it occurs, is limited to 90 seconds per half-hour.

Among the documentaries for sale on videotape are candid interviews with world-faith leaders, filmed at the Parliament of the World's Religions. This 26-part series, produced in conjunction with PBS, offers viewers insights into spiritual perspectives on some of the most difficult issues of the day (see listing in Chapter 43).

Witness for Peace – Making Injustice Visible
2201 P St. NW, Rm. 109, Washington, DC 20037 USA; tel. (202) 797-1160 / fax (202) 797-1164

Since 1983, delegations of Witness for Peace have been placing themselves in situations of combat or social violence to act as peacemakers, witnesses to injustice, and non-violent "bodyguards" of targeted individuals. Religiously-motivated members have also brought information from these situations, particularly in Central America and the Caribbean, back to congregations, to the media and to members of legislative bodies, hoping to enact changes in policy.

Women and Spirituality
Co-facilitators:
Pat Kenoyer, SL

3 Haven Plaza (4H), New York, NY 10009 USA; tel./fax 212 473-4904

**Alayne Brown, Ph.D.
1 Washington Sq. Vlg. (PHE), New York, NY 10012 USA; tel. 212 777-6614**

Women and Spirituality is a working group of the New York NGO Committee on the Status of Women, preparing for active participation in the UN Fourth International Conference on the Status of Women in Beijing, China, from August 30 to September 8, 1995. The focus of W&S is on the importance of spiritual values – grounded in self-respect and dignity, and a humanistic concern for all life – as essential to world peace and an equitable society. Our approach is visionary as well as critical. Priorities include: support of equal access for women to leadership positions in religious institutions; recognition of indigenous and alternative traditions that honor the Sacred Feminine aspect of Divinity; and disavowal of all forms of human rights violations made in the name of religion, especially against women.

Our working group consists of an ever-growing and diverse group of women from around the globe: Africa, Asia, Europe, South America, as well as North America. Our goal is to bring women's spirituality to its rightful place in the international setting as well as in our daily lives and to empower women to provide leadership for a just, safe and healthy world.

Women's International League for Peace and Freedom
1213 Race St., Philadelphia, PA 19107-1691 USA; tel. (215) 563-7110 / fax (215) 864-2022

WILPF was founded in 1915 during World War I, with Jane Addams as its first president; international membership now empowers women to work together in over 34 countries and 110 US communities. WILPF members are supported by an international office in Geneva and at the UN in New York and Geneva. Throughout its history its purpose has been to work for those political, economic, social and psychological conditions throughout the world which can assure peace, freedom, and justice for all.

WILPF has long believed that peace requires dedication to nonviolent means of conflict resolution and the building of institutions for world development and community. WILPF believes that to achieve freedom and justice in our country and peaceful relations with other countries we must build a non-exploitive society. As our Third International Congress of 1921 stated, we must "transform the economic system in the direction of social justice."

WILPF supports a strong role for the UN as an organization working for world peace and disarmament, world development, and human rights. WILPF offers educational materials on these issues, on the transfer of resources from militarism to human needs, and on ending all forms of violence: rape, battering, poverty, exploitation, intervention, and war. Legislative alerts are available as are subscriptions to WILPF's quarterly (in English), *Pax et Libertas*.

World Conference on Religion and Peace

777 United Nations Plaza
New York, NY 10017 USA;
tel. (212) 687-2163 / fax (212) 983-0566

Introduction

The World Conference on Religion and Peace (WCRP) is an international multi-religious organization dedicated to reaffirming religions' moral commitments to peace and to translating their shared concerns into practical, effective action. WCRP is based upon respect for religious differences as well as the conviction that religious persons and groups can cooperate with great value on shared commitments for peace with justice.

On local, national, regional, and global levels, WCRP convenes meetings and assemblies to promote dialogue on the peace-promoting teachings of religions. This dialogue, in turn, provides a basis for commitments to common actions in eight program areas: (1) Children and Youth, (2) Conflict Resolution, (3) Disarmament, (4) Economic and Social Development, (5) Environmental Protection, (6) Human Rights, (7) Peace Education, and (8) Refugees and Displaced Persons.

The significance of multireligious cooperation for peacemaking

What roles do the world's religions have in offering guidance and helping to ameliorate strife in the modern world? Skeptics would point out that historically, and currently, religious differences often have been a component cause of conflict and warfare. While acknowledging this fact, the members of WCRP believe the world's religions can be highly constructive forces in promoting peace.

The world's religious communities possess both moral and social characteristics which equip them in unique ways to cooperate and participate in efforts designed to promote peace.

First, religions found ethical visions. They provide their adherents with forms of ethical discourse about the ultimate meaning and value of reality. These ethical visions can summon those who believe in them into powerful forms of committed action.

Second, religions possess remarkable social characteristics. Religions exist

everywhere in the world; they reach into every village and town; and they are often organized at national and international levels. Taken together, the world's religious groups make up a vast network with unique capacities for communication and mobilization.

Both the moral and social characteristics of religious communities provide them with exceptional possibilities to function as powerful "agents for change" in the pursuit of peace.

Today, however, the constructive roles of individual religions for peacemaking can be strengthened greatly by cooperation among religions. Multireligious efforts can be both substantively and symbolically more powerful than the efforts of a single religious group. Moreover, cooperation among religious groups can serve to promote religious tolerance in circumstances where religious people, tragically and all too often, contribute to conflicts. These realizations led to the formation of WCRP and continue to guide its development.

As a forum for the world's religious leaders and believers, WCRP provides a potent base for a variety of peace initiatives which can address the needs and concerns of individuals, groups, governing bodies, and international organizations.

Origins

The organization was formed in 1970 as a consolidation of separate movements in Japan, the United States, and India. Interest in Japan began with a National Religious Conference for International Peace, convened in 1931. Following World War II and the nuclear bombing of Hiroshima and Nagasaki, cooperation grew among senior Japanese religious leaders on peace issues.

In the United States, senior religious leaders began gathering around the issues of cooperation for peace with justice in 1962. A National Inter-Religious Conference on Peace was convened in Washington, DC, in 1966. A delegation of US religious leaders in 1967 undertook an exploratory mission to ascertain interest by religious groups abroad in forming a multireligious world conference on peace. They visited Geneva, Rome, Istanbul, Jerusalem, New Delhi, Saigon, and Kyoto.

In 1968, religious leaders from India formed a joint US/Indian committee to sponsor a symposium on peace coincident with the centenary of Mahatma Gandhi's birth. Indian political leaders also participated in the event.

The Japanese, United States,' and Indian interests converged at a meeting in Istanbul during 1969 where the decision was made to convene an international gathering of religious leaders at Kyoto in 1970: the First Assembly of the World Conference on

Religion and Peace. World Assemblies have since been held in Louvain, Belgium (1974); Princeton, USA (1979); Nairobi, Kenya (1984); and Melbourne, Australia (1989). The most recent Assembly was held in Riva del Garda, Italy, in 1994 when participants agreed to begin a process of evaluation of the contents and implications of a global ethic.

Organization and development

WCRP has its international headquarters at the United Nations Plaza in New York City. Additional international offices are maintained in Geneva, Melbourne and Tokyo. WCRP is recognized as an NGO having consultative status with the Economic and Social Council of the UN. That role enables WCRP to function as a multireligious resource and advisor for various commissions and conferences.

WCRP members have formed three regional conferences – in Asia, Africa and Europe – and 26 national chapters in the following countries: Australia, Austria, Bangladesh, Belgium, Canada, Croatia, France, Germany, India, Indonesia, Italy, Japan, Kenya, Democratic People's Republic of Korea, Republic of Korea, Nepal, Netherlands, New Zealand, Pakistan, Philippines, Singapore, South Africa, Sri Lanka, Thailand, the UK/Ireland, and the USA.

Leaders and other believers of the following religions regularly participate as members in WCRP: Bahá'í, Buddhism, Christianity, Confucianism, Hinduism, Islam, Jainism, Judaism, Shintoism, Sikhism, Taoism, traditional indigenous cultures of Africa, the Americas, Asia, Australia and Oceania, and Zoroastrianism.

The growing WCRP network fosters activities relevant to global, regional, national, and local concerns by providing a channel for disseminating constituents' concerns throughout the world and generating support for them.

WCRP welcomes both religious organizations and individuals for membership. Contact the New York office for the names and addresses of WCRP chapters worldwide, and for more information. (See also Chapter 26.)

Asian Conference on Religion and Peace

One of the strong regional chapters of WCRP is based in Seoul, Korea. The Peace Education Center and WCRP/Japan Committee commemorated the Year of Interreligious Understanding and Cooperation with a lecture by Marcus Braybrooke, the translation of his book *Pilgrimage of Hope,* and seminars on interreligious cooperation within and outside of Korea. Since only a few Koreans were able to participate in the centennial events at Bangalore and Chicago, these events boosted interest in interreligious dialogue throughout Korea and Japan.

In Korea, especially in the South, Buddhism and Christianity, along with several indigenous religions, are very prosperous, but they are often in a rivalry relationship rather than a friendly one. The Korean Conference on Religion and Peace is the most active interfaith organization in Korea, and they, in cooperation with the Peace Education Center, have begun a major interfaith project in regard to environmental issues, including the joint "Declaration of Environmental Ethics" by six major religions in Korea.

SUNGGON KIM, Peace Education Center, Seoul, Korea (founded in 1986 by the Asian Conference on Religion and Peace)

World Congress of Faiths
2 Market St., Oxford, OX1 3EF, UK;
tel. +0865 202-751/ fax +0865 202-746

WCF aims to bring people of different faith-commitments together in mutual respect and trust in order to promote better understanding between religious communities and to further dialogue between people of different convictions about religious truth and practice. Among its recent past activities have been the arrangement of conferences, cooperation with other interfaith organizations in the commemoration of the 1993 as the Year of Interreligious Understanding, and preparations for the Sarva-Dharma-Sammelana interfaith conference held in Bangalore in August 1993.

WCF is also one of three founding institutions of the International Interfaith Centre (IIC) in Oxford (along with the International Association for Religious Freedom and Westminster College). Among WCF's publications is *Interfaith Cooperation*, written by the Rev. Marcus Braybrooke and reprinted in Chapter 26.

WCF also publishes the journal *World Faiths Encounter*, dealing with the new questions of living in a multi-faith society. *World Faiths Encounter* covers the fascinating issues which arise from the meeting between faith-communities in the contemporary world. Edited by Alan Race (UK) and Professor Seshagiri Rao (USA), it is available internationally. (In the U.S.A, order from Multifaith Resources.)

World Council of Churches – Office on Inter-religious Relations
P.O.Box 2100, 1211 Geneva 2, Switzerland
tel. 022-791-6111 / fax 022-791-0361

The WCC grew out of the Christian ecumenical movement in the early decades of this century which had culminated in the first General Assembly of the WCC in

1948. Based in Switzerland, its member churches now come from more than 100 countries worldwide.

The question "What is the WCC?" has many answers. One found in "Basis for the World Council of Churches" says that it is

> a fellowship of churches which confess the Lord Jesus Christ as God and Saviour according to the Scriptures and therefore seek to fulfill together their common calling to the glory of the one God, Father, Son and Holy Spirit.

from *Introducing the World Council of Churches*, by Marlin VanElderen.

Other answers note the WCC's response to suffering people in disaster relief and assistance; some answers focus on the theological and doctrinal explorations of Christian unity and diversity; another response focuses on the WCC's analysis of injustice (political, social, gender and ecological) as the root of much suffering, and on its work for justice, peace and reconciliation. In addition, the WCC's global constituency requires it to come to a better understanding of the relationships between members of different faiths who live alongside one another.

The dialogue concern in the WCC

Within the modern ecumenical movement, the early World Mission Conferences spent considerable time attempting to define the right attitude of the church to other religious traditions. One result of this endeavor was a study initiated on "The Word of God and Men of Other Faiths." Out of this study arose the conviction that the WCC should further explore and develop the concept of "dialogue" as the primary mode of relating to people of other faith traditions. Thus the Central Committee of the WCC, meeting in Addis Ababa in 1971, enabled the creation of a new sub-unit, "Dialogue with People of Living Faiths and Ideologies" within the Unit on Faith and Witness.

The work of the sub-unit

The primary function of the sub-unit was to build relationships between Christians and peoples of different religious traditions, enabling meetings between peoples of different faiths at national, regional, and international levels. Many Christians seek guidance in relating to and understanding people of other faiths. Often there is the request to show how a dialogical relationship could be supported from a biblical and Christian theological perspective. An important publication in this respect was the study guide, *My Neighbour's Faith – and Mine* (1986) which seeks to raise awareness among Christians of religious plurality, and calls for a new approach to other living traditions.

One way in which the sub-unit has

helped the process of animating dialogue is by developing *Guidelines on Dialogue* (1979), supplemented by *Ecumenical Considerations on Jewish-Christian Dialogue* (1983) and *Ecumenical Considerations on Christian-Muslim Relations* (1992).

The mandate of the Office on Inter-religious Relations includes:

- Relationship with peoples and organizations of other religious traditions.
- Relationship with international interfaith organizations.
- Enabling the churches in their relationship to people of other faiths.
- Monitoring developments in inter-religious relationships at different levels and dealing with specific issues such as use of religion in conflict situations, the problems of religious minority communities, etc.
- Dealing with concrete situations of conflict where religion plays a role.

A substantial publications program supports the WCC's outreach; magazines, journals, catalogs, books and other information may be obtained from Geneva as well as from WCC regional offices, including the following:

Christian Literature Society, Post Box 501, Madras 600 003, India

Methodist Publishing House, P.O. Box 708, Cape Town 8001, South Africa

US Office of the WCC, 475 Riverside Dr., Room 915, New York, NY 10115-0050 USA

World Fellowship of Religions – 7th World Religions Conference
Sawan Kirpal Ruhani Mission, Kirpal Ashram, Kirpal Marg, Vijay Nagar, Delhi 110009, India
tel. 7222244

Science of Spirituality, 4 S. Naperville, Rd., Naperville, IL 60563 USA;
tel. (708) 955-1200 / fax (708) 955-1205

For decades, conferences have been held to promote peace and unity. Sant Rajinder Singh, president of the World Fellowship of Religions and head of Science of Spirituality, began a new chapter in the movement towards peace and unity by hosting a dialogue of religious and spiritual leaders as the opening of the Seventh World Religions Conference. This historic conference, held February 1 - 7, 1994, at Kirpal Ashram, Delhi, India, shed light on a new dimension in the quest for peace. Among the attendees were hundreds of dignitaries from many religions, spiritual paths, and civic and social groups.

The Conference began with a mammoth peace march through the streets of Delhi to the Red Fort, where more than 100,000 people from thirty countries joined the inaugural event. At the end of the program, all the leaders stood on stage and led the assembly in a meditation for world peace in the hope that such moments of common prayer and meditation would lay the groundwork for a golden age of peace for the upcoming millennium.

The Spiritual Dialogue on "Meditation, Prayer, and Nonviolence" during the first two days of the conference explored in large and small group sessions how meditation, prayer, and nonviolence can lead to world peace and unity. Each of the participants shared his or her own methods of prayer and meditation in the hope that a new era of tolerance for all religions and spiritual paths would begin. Each not only spoke of peace, but developed practical action plans to take back to his or her congregation or assembly.

World Interfaith Education Association

P.O. Box 7384 Station "D", Victoria, B.C., V9B 5B7, Canada; tel./fax (604) 360-1259

WIFEA (formerly World Interfaith Colleges Association) is part of a global network of societies working together for interfaith education. Parallel organizations exist in India, Japan, the Philippines, Singapore, Tanzania, and the UK. Goals include:

- To promote inter-faith education throughout Canada – in schools, in faith communities, and among the public-at-large;
- To initiate interfaith education projects across Canada, bringing together people of different faiths, in a spirit of dialogue and social justice;
- To explore spiritual values and learn about each other's faith in order to increase mutual respect and understanding;
- To help establish and support global inter-faith educational initiatives and projects in cooperation with other national and international organizations.
- To emphasize local community service and sound development principles and strategies in all activities, as an example of inter-faith cooperation in education.

Activities include conferences for educators, inter-faith camps for young and old of different faiths, seminars to encourage dialogue on particular themes and topics, interfaith colleges for young people of many faiths to come together, and to form interfaith education societies. Resources include providing consultants on interfaith education, networking and bibliographies and other materials relating to inter-faith education.

World Network of Religious Futurists

3 Victoria Terrace, Ealing Green, London W5 5QS, UK

William A. Heins (Editor, *Global Visions*), P.O. Box 998, Eau Claire, WI 54702, USA

The World Network of Religious Futurists is an international, interfaith association for the scientific and religious study of the future of religions in the service of the present and future humanity, locally and globally. Its major objectives are:

- To study theory and method in futurism itself from the religious and/or ethical viewpoints assumed in the world's religions;
- To encourage the world's religious leaders to engage in dialogue with religious futurists;
- To develop, as an independent theological, religious, and scientific discipline the scholarly field of religious futures studies

in such way as to facilitate contributions to humanity by religions;

- To support every kind of healthy religious creativity in the service of humanity;
- To stimulate inter-religious dialogue and collaboration in the service of humanity;
- To encourage regional and national networks of religious futurists.

Goals include developing a world network of futurists, publishing a newsletter, encouraging and sponsoring conferences, and exploring the possibilities of a permanent organization, which might be designated the United Religions Organization (see Chapter 24).

World Peace Prayer Society

800 Third Avenue, 37th Floor, New York, NY 10022-7604 USA

Knöbelstrasse 4a, D-80538 Munich, Germany

The WPPS is a non-profit, member-supported, non-denominational organization, founded in 1955 in Japan. The Society is dedicated to raising peace consciousness by spreading the prayer and affirmation, "May peace prevail on Earth." (This peace message is printed on stickers, cards, posters, T-shirts and key chains, available from the Society.) Membership is comprised of individuals on the grassroots level who are sincerely interested in the concept of global citizenship and bringing peace to our planet. The Society sponsors World Peace Prayer Ceremonies, the Peace Pole Project, the Peace Message booklet campaign, the Peace Pals project (for young people) and the Peace Music initiative. The Society became affiliated with the United Nations as an NGO in 1990.

MAY PEACE PREVAIL ON EARTH

The Prayer for World Peace elevates the thought waves of oneself and others by wishing for the peace of humanity, which is the same as the thought of Universal Love. If you fling all of your thoughts into the simple words, 'May Peace Prevail on Earth,' you and the world will be purified. If you keep living your life anew from this prayer, before you know it your selfish desires for self-preservation will diminish. You will find yourself wishing for the happiness of mankind, with a deep feeling of humanitarian love welling up from within. Gradually, the individual's character will be approaching wholeness, and the person's lifestyle will strike a harmonious note – which is the greatest thing an individual can do for world peace.

from "Universal Love," by Masahisa Goi,
founder, World Peace Prayer Society, in *The Global Link Newsletter*

Print, Audio, and Video Resources:

Archives, Tapes, Bibliographies, Books, Directories, Educational Resources, Periodicals, and Videos

The annotated listings below identify a selection of resources on religions of the world, the Parliament, interreligious contact, organizations, and critical issues of our time. Some of the materials are useful for individual study, while others are designed for groups – adult or children – in educational settings or for group interaction. The list is not exhaustive; a few annotated bibliographies included can, however, direct the inquiring reader to additional resources, and most of the publications listed below have their own bibliographical references. (Note: a few annotations were derived from promotional materials; annotations do not necessarily imply endorsement by the Editor.)

New approaches to studying and practicing religions

The study of the world's religions became a wide-ranging discipline in the mid- to late-19th century, particularly in Europe; it got an added boost from the 1893 World Parliament of Religions as well as by increased travel, immigration, and communications worldwide. Since then, anthropological, religious, and philosophical studies as well as personal quests have ensured the availability of comprehensive information about religions for many years.

One significant development of recent years is that while early study of the world's religions was done mostly by Europeans and North Americans who studied and wrote about other religions and cultures – as allegedly *objective* outsiders – several recent publications, including this *SourceBook,* have taken the approach that information about religions can be most accurately and empathetically presented by scholars who are also practitioners of the religion presented. This approach presents the beliefs and experience of believing persons within specific cultures and contexts. Supporting it is the development of publishing and information centers *within* the specific traditions themselves.

Reflecting the growing practice and ideals of interfaith dialogue, this approach focuses on the perceptions and practices to ensure empathetic understanding of – and relationships with – real people, who are in one sense or another our neighbors. While face-to-face encounters would likely be most productive in terms of forming new relationships and attitudes, books and other materials are attempting to synthesize this approach; electronic media, video and audio sources offer compelling new tools.

The interfaith movement

The worldwide interfaith movement can be traced to many of the same circumstances which helped spread the study of religions. Although the current wave of interest in interfaith studies and dialogue took longer to develop, this movement has been increasingly active during the past few decades. It is propelled not only by pluralism and the globalization of communications and travel, but also by the recognition of increasingly urgent critical issues – personal, social, political, economic, and ecological – which now require improved relationships with other peoples and cultures. This new emphasis has widened our understandings of the practice of religions and of contact between them, and it has led to a new focus on the ethical dimensions of belief and culture.

A groundswell of interactions among members of the religions, combined with the extraordinary challenges of our time, have also provided direction and impetus to interreligious contact. New motivations and programs have led to an exciting and sometimes overwhelming diversity of organizations and resource materials. Nevertheless, these also demonstrate a considerable amount of common concern, a refreshing idealism, and a revitalized commitment to identifying and understanding the religious and spiritual components in all aspects of life.

ARCHIVES OF THE PARLIAMENT

Documents and records from the Parliament of the World's Religions are gathered and indexed at DePaul University Library, 2350 North Kenmore Avenue, Chicago, IL 60614 USA. The archives hold official documents, correspondence, and notes of meetings, plus media releases, several thousand news clippings, audio- and videotapes, and memorabilia from the board and staff, cosponsors, committees, participants, the media and others. Contributions are still being accepted.

AUDIO TAPES FROM THE PARLIAMENT

Recordings are available of several hundred major speeches, presentations, and workshops from the Parliament, by a wide range of scholars, clerics, and other leaders from the world's religions, on numerous topics. Brochure and tapes are available from:

Teach 'em,
160 East Illinois St.,
Chicago, IL 60611 USA;
tel. (312) 467-0424

BOOKS, BOOKLETS AND BIBLIOGRAPHIES on RELIGIONS, INTERRELIGIOUS CONTACT and CRITICAL ISSUES of OUR TIME

Contemporary Religions: A World Guide

Ed. by Ian Harris, Stuart Mews, Paul Morris and John Sheperd. A complete resource on all faiths and all significant branches of religions around the world. Published by Longman, 1993. Available in North America from Gale. $175.00

A Core Bibliography on Global Issues Related to Environment, Resources, Population, and Sustainable Development

By Walter Corson.

Global Tomorrow Coalition, 1325 G. Street, NW, Suite 915, Washington DC, 20005-3104 USA. $5.

Cosmic Beginnings and Human Ends: Where Science and Religion Meet

Edited by Clifford Matthews and Roy Abraham Varghese. Initially presented at the Symposium on Science and Religion held in conjunction with the Parliament, these essays by leading scientists, philosophers, and educators from diverse religious orientations are thematically linked around the proposal that the story of the universe is the primary place where the religions of the world can meet each other with a common point of reference. Other essays explore mysteries of the origin of the cosmos and their implications for human striving – where the religions and sciences can meet. Published 1994 by Open Court Press; pb. $17.95; cl. $41.95.

The Dawn of Religious Pluralism: Voices from the World's Parliament of Religions, 1893

Edited and Introduced by Richard Hughes Seager; with Ronald R. Kidd, and with a Foreword by Diana L. Eck. This volume contains a selection of 60 representative addresses given to the Parliament of 1893. Contributions include speeches by Protestant mainstream ministers, African-Americans, Roman Catholics, Orthodox Christians, Jews, Muslims, Buddhists, Hindus, and representatives of other Asian religions. Also included are various "points of contact and contention," in which religious leaders attempted to analyze or reach out to their counterparts in other traditions. Published 1993 in Association with The Council for a Parliament of the World's Religions by Open Court Publ. Co., LaSalle, IL 61301. pb. $28.95; cloth, $59.95.

Encyclopedia of World Problems and Human Potential, 3rd edition

Published by the Union of International Associations. A comprehensive source of information on recognized world problems, their interconnections, and the human resources available to analyze and ultimately to respond to them. It is innovative in that considerable effort has been devoted to identifying and juxtaposing the many conflicting perceptions and priorities which constitute the dynamic reality of world society. The

information is derived from the United Nations and other intergovernmental agencies, as well as from the many international nongovernmental bodies documented in the *Yearbook of International Organizations*. (1991, 2 vols, 2140 pages. 598 DM / US$450./ BF19.100)

Publications may be ordered from:

Union of International Associations, rue Washington 40, B-1050 Brussels, Belgium; tel. (32 2) 640 18 08 / fax (32 2) 646 05 25

Bowker/ Saur, 121 Chanlon Road, New Providence NJ 07974, USA. tel. (1-212) 982-1302 / fax (1-212) 908 771-7725;

K G Saur Veria , Postfach 71 10 09, D-81373 München 70, Germany. tel. (49 89) 76902 230 / fax (49 89) 76902 250

Encyclopedia of American Religions: Religious Creeds

A companion to Gordon Melton's *Encyclopedia of American Religions*, this volume presents 464 creeds, confessions, statements of faith, summaries of belief, and articles of religion associated with the many branches of Christian, Jewish, Islamic, Hindu, and other religions practiced in America. Edited by J. Gordon Melton, published 1994, $140.00, available from Gale; also available on diskette and mag-tape.

Global 2000 Revisited: What Shall We Do?

By Dr. Gerald O. Barney, Jane Blewett, and Kristen R. Barney of the Millenium Institute. Prepared and published by the Institute for the Parliament of the World's Religions, this report is an update of the Global 2000 report which Dr. Barney directed for Jimmy Carter's administration. Specifically addressed to the religions, the book "...is an invitation to reflect deeply on the critical issues we face today: threats to the global environment; divisions within the human community, such as racism, interreligious hatred, sexual discrimination, and xenophobic nationalism; extremes of affluence and poverty; and the prevalence of violence, oppression, and exploitation of all kinds." large paperback, $20. (The official *Summary of Global 2000 Revisited* is also available for $8.) Order from:

Public Interest Publications, PO Box 229, Arlington, VA 22210 USA. tel. (800) 537-9359 in the US, Canada and Mexico, or (703) 243-2252 elsewhere

A Global Ethic: The Declaration of the Parliament of the World's Religions

Commentaries by Hans Küng and Karl-Josef Kushel. This introduction

presents the complete text of the *Declaration* as it was signed (provisionally, as a work in progress), and describes the process of consultations with numerous religious scholars, the drafting process, and the nature of this minimum ethic based on a "common set of core values" derived from the ancient wisdom and teachings of the world's religions. The *Declaration* has appeared in the following editions and translations: *American:* Continuum, New York ($9.95); *English:* SCM Press, London; *Italian:* Rizzoli, Milano; *Spanish:* Trotta, Madrid; *Finnish:* Arator, Helsinki; and *French:* Du Cerf, Paris. Additional translations are expected into Chinese, Japanese and Turkish.

Note: A new book of responses to "Towards a Global Ethic" by thirty-five world-known persons, edited by Hans Küng and Karl-Josef Kuschel, will appear in the fall of 1995 in conjunction with the fiftieth anniversary of the United Nations.

Global Responsibility: In Search of a New World Ethic

By Hans Küng. Presents a compelling argument that this world needs at least a minimum of shared ethical principles on which we can all agree if we are to survive in this time of new opportunities and dangers. "Our society does not need a uniform religion or a uniform ideology, but it does need some binding norms, values, ideals and goals." Kung addresses members of the world faiths in particular but also non-believers in this preliminary study to his work of drafting the Global Ethic for the Parliament. Published 1991 for North America by:

The Crossroad Publishing Co. 370 Lexington Avenue, New York, NY 10017 USA. $18.95.

Interfaith Dialogue: An Annotated Bibliography

Compiled by John H. Berthrong in response to the large number of people who are asking for guidance on the increasingly large number of books and periodicals devoted to inter-religious understanding and cooperation. The project is useful for religious leaders, teachers in public and private schools, employers and others who are confronted with both the opportunities and challenges of growing cultural and religious diversity. Published by and available from:

Multifaith Resources, P.O. Box 128, Wofford Heights, CA 93285-0128 USA. $4.25.

International Sacred Literature Trust

Established in 1989 and launched by HRH Prince Philip at the United Nations Building, the Trust creates a single imprint for the publication in English of the world's spiritual heritage. The Trust invites cultural and religious communities to select their own scholars and writers to produce new, authoritative, and literary translations of their sacred texts. First volumes include classics of mystical and Eastern Judaism, songs of the Indian saints, key texts of the Jain and Zoroastrian faiths, a favorite book of the Buddhists of Tibet, the most widely read Taoist book in China, dreamings from elders of the Australian desert, and the first English translation of the Bible by the Greek Orthodox Church. Global distribution began in 1994 by HarperCollins in a joint imprint with ISLT.

ISLT, 23 Darley Avenue, Manchester M20 8ZD UK. tel./fax 061 445 2523

Multifaith Information Manual

Compiled and published by the Ontario Multifaith Council on Spiritual and Religious Care. This volume is particularly useful for staff of hospitals, prisons, schools, and other instititutions where the religious and spiritual needs of a diverse population must be considered and met. It is an important reference work for chaplains, spiritual/religious caregivers, multifaith services coordinators, teachers, students, and multifaith organizations. All contents – basic beliefs of the religions, practices regarding death and illness, rituals, holy days and festivals, dietary requirements, symbols, and much more – were created and authorized by the faith traditions described.

In Canada order directly from:

Ontario Multifaith Council, 35 McCaul St., 2nd Floor, Suite 200, Toronto, Ontario M5T 1V7, CANADA. $33.95 (+ 15% tax, + $3 S&H)

Available in the USA from:

Multifaith Resources, PO Box 128, Wofford Heights, CA 93285 USA. $23.95 postpaid.

A Museum of Faiths: Histories and Legacies of the 1893 World's Parliament of Religions

Edited by Eric J. Ziolkowski. Reassesses the meaning and significance of the 1893 Parliament and its impact on the development of the academic study of religion. Contents include an extensive introduction, six papers on comparative religion from the Parliament's original proceedings, two early appraisals of the event's signficance for world religious history and the comparative study of religion, and eight essays reassessing the Parliament's impact on interfaith dialogue and comparative religion. Published 1993 by Scholars Press of the American Academy of Religion, Atlanta, GA. pb. $29.95; cl. $44.95.

Our Religions

Edited by Arvind Sharma. This book is the first detailed and extensive introduction to the seven major world religions by preeminent scholars from each tradition. Authors include Sharma on Hinduism, Masao Abe on Buddhism, Tu Wei-ming on Confucianism, Liu Xiaogan on Taoism, Jacob Neusner on Judaism, Harvey Cox on Christianity, and Seyyed Hossein Nasr on Islam. Published by Harper SanFrancisco in conjunction with the 1993 Parliament. 536 pp., cb: US$30.

Pilgrimage of Hope: 100 Years of the Interfaith Movement

By Rev. Marcus Braybrooke. Details the history of interfaith organizations, events, and trends, as well as the people and historical contexts which helped shape the movement since the 1893 Parliament. This volume was published in anticipation of 1993, the Year of International, Interreligious Cooperation and Understanding. Written by an Anglican clergyman with wide interfaith experience, and one who is respected worldwide for his leadership in organizations and activities, this volume widens the focus of study well beyond North American experience to the global arena. Braybrooke is also editor of Stepping Stones to a Global Ethic, which introduces and reprints signficant declarations and documents which helped shape the movement toward a global ethic. Both volumes are published in the US by Crossroad and by SCM in the UK.

Praying Their Faith: An Insight into Six World Religions through the Prayers of their Members

Edited by Colin Johnson, published by CEM, Derby, England; available in North America from Multifaith Resources. Contains eighty prayers with notes setting each into its context in the tradition. $13

Religious Traditions of the World

Edited by H. Byron Earhart. Described as a journey through Africa, North America, Mesoamerica, Judaism, Christianity, Islam, Hinduism, Buddhism, China, and Japan, this large volume gathers the ten books earlier edited by Earhart into a newly edited, combined edition. Providing an introduction to the comparative study of religion, its instructional enhancements include illustrations, diagrams and maps, chronologies, study questions, cross-references, glossaries, selected reading lists, and a general index. Published 1993 by Harper SanFrancisco. 1224 pp., cb. $39.00

Resources for Buddhist-Christian Encounter: An Annotated Bibliography.

Prepared by the Educational Resources Committee of the Society for Buddhist-Christian Studies. Available from:

Multifaith Resources, PO Box 128, Wofford Heights, CA 93285-0128 USA. $4.25.

State of the World Annual Reports

For nearly two decades, the Worldwatch research team has gathered and published the most up-to-date and reliable information on the condition of our planet and species. Believing that knowledge is the key to effective action, Worldwatch has helped spur the debate and spark action on the world's most pressing environmental and development problems.

The Worldwatch team was among the first to clue people in on the dangers of global warming, water shortages, soil erosion, and the ecological disasters in Eastern Europe. Worldwatch also helped redefine security, warning that threats to our future are more likely to be environmental that military.

In addition to the annual State of the World series, Worldwatch publishes a library of Papers, How Much is Enough? The Consumer Society and the Future of the Earth, Vital Signs 1994: The Trends that are Shaping Our Future, and Saving the Planet: How to Shape an Environmentally Sustainable Global Economy, as well as books on population and energy.

With readership in the millions in 27 different languages, State of the World 1995 is the planet's most widely-used analysis of environment and public policy. ($11.95 + $3 s&h; pb.)

Worldwatch Institute, 1776 Massachusetts Ave., N.W., Washington, DC 20077-6628 USA

A Study Guide for Interreligious Cooperation and Understanding

By Rev. Marcus Braybrooke. Developed for use by discussion groups. Drawing from his more extensive survey, Pilgrimage of Hope, Braybrooke describes the growth of four international interfaith organizations and the changing direction in the movement from theological discourse toward interfaith cooperation and a global ethic. (Reprinted in Chapter 26 of the SourceBook.)

Towards a Global Ethic (An Initial Declaration)

This is the document prepared for the 1993 Parliament and then discussed and signed, provisionally, by most participants in the Assembly of Religious and Spiritual Leaders. Printed and discussed in Chapter 23 of this *SourceBook*, the document is also available from the Council for a Parliament of the World's Religions and in Hans Küng's *A Global Ethic*. The document provides an excellent forum for discussing the claim that a minimum ethic already exists which can help define the conditions for – and guide us to – a more peaceful, just and sustainable world.

TRANET – A Bi-Monthly Digest

TRANET is a transnational network and publication of, by, and for people who are participating in transformation – people who are changing the world by changing their own lives; people who are adopting appropriate technologies and lifestyles. TRANET believes that grassroots, people-to-people networks can ameliorate the evils of nation-states and perform many of the functions needed to create a world of peace and equity. This bi-monthly digest lists resources, describes conferences and organizations, notes publications and offers a calendar of related events.

BOX 567, Rangeley, ME 04970 USA; tel. (207) 864-2252; e-mail: tranet@igc.org

Visions of an Interfaith Future

Edited by Celia and David Storey. Contains the proceedings of the Sarva-Dharma-Sammelana Conference held in Bangalore, India, in 1993. This meeting was the Centennial Commemoration of the 1893 Parliament arranged by four international interfaith organizations – International Association for Religious Freedom, Temple of Understanding, World Conference on Religion and Peace, and the World Congress of Faiths.

International Interfaith Centre, 2 Market St., Oxford OX1 3EF, UK. US$25.

UNIPUB – A Publications Distribution Company for the UN

UNIPUB represents many prestigious government and intergovernmental organizations with an active backlist of many thousands of titles. Several catalogs and a computerized searching capability identify books and monographs dealing with topics related to UN activities.

Among the titles found in a search on religious subjects were several studies dealing with new religious movements and social change, others dealing with religious and ethnic challenges to democracy, and some on religious education and observance in schools.

4611-F Assembly Dr., Lanham, MD 20706 tel. 800-274-4888 (US); 800-233-0504 (Canada); 301-459-7666 (local)

WCRP: A History of the World Conference on Religion and Peace

By Homer A. Jack, with Forewords by Dana McLean Greeley and Nikkyo Niwano. Afterword by Archbishop Angelo Fernandes. (Includes illustrations.) Founded in 1969 at Istanbul, Turkey, WCRP has been a unique and fully representative interreligious body, dedicated to the cause of world peace. In addition to its detailed description of the formation, assemblies, initiatives and relationships of WCRP, the book presents the vision of Homer A. Jack, a veteran activist who was prominent in directing the focus of the interfaith movement toward issues of peace and justice. Published 1993.

WCRP, 777 United Nations Plaza, New York, NY 10017

World Religions in America

Edited by Jacob Neusner. Designed as an introductory textbook with study questions, this volume has also attempted to portray the character of religion throughout the world through the facts of religions in North America, where so many of those religions are represented. The contributors include an array of knowledgeable scholars who describe religious history and practice and also present insights about how religion affects personal life and society. Westminster/John Knox Press. pb.: US$12.99; cb. $22.00.

World Scripture: A Comparative Anthology of Sacred Texts

A Project of the International Religious Foundation, edited by Andrew Wilson, Foreword by Dr. Ninian Smart. Utilizing the labor of more than forty scholars and religious leaders from every faith, this extensive anthology is a topical journey through the sacred writings of the world's great religions, including ancient, recent, and contemporary religions and spiritual traditions. Comparing religious beliefs on similar themes demonstrates the existence of a vast sphere of spiritual common ground despite the diversity of religious practices and beliefs.

IRF Publications Dept., 4 West 43 St., New York, NY 10036. US$39.95 plus $3S&H

The World's Wisdom: Sacred Texts of the World's Religions

Edited by Philip Novak, Foreword by Huston Smith. Texts are arranged by categories with subheads and brief introductions. Published by Harper SanFrancisco, 1994. cb. $22.00.

DIRECTORIES

Note: Directories generally have at least four characteristics in common: 1) they slowly (sometimes quickly) become obsolete due to movement of people and organizations; 2) they are usually not comprehensive even at the time of publication; 3) nevertheless, they're all we've got at the moment, so we're grateful for them; and 4) we anticipate publication of up-to-date editions.

A Canadian Interfaith Directory

Compiled by M. Darrol Bryant and Doris Jakobsh in 1993. Lists more than 50 Canadian interfaith groups.

Dr. M. Darrol Bryant, Renison College, Waterloo, Ontario, N2L3G4, Canada.

A Directory of Environmental Activities and Resources in the North American Religious Community

Published summer 1992 as a Project of the Joint Appeal by Religion and Science for the Environment, now named the National Religious Partnership on the Environment. An extensive listing of ideas, resources, congregations, publications, networks, and national organizations that are contributing to understanding and action on environmental concerns.

Kutztown Publishing Company, Inc., PO BOx 346, Kutztown, PA 19530 USA. pb. large format, 172 pages, US $12.95 (plus $1.95 S&H).

Global Interfaith Directory, 1993

Lists and annotates organizations engaged in interfaith work, to help people to locate and communicate with each other, and to acknowledge the growth of interfaith activities; organized by denomination, nationally, and worldwide. ($15.00)

The Temple of Understanding, 1047 Amsterdam Avenue, New York, NY 10025

Guide to Careers, Internships, and Graduate Education in Peace Studies

Compiled by the Five College Program in Peace and World Security Studies.

Michael Clare, Director PAWSS Publications, Amherst, MA 01002

Network to Reduce Over-consumption: A Directory of Organizations and Leaders

Published in 1994, this handy guide lists and describes 160 active organizations and/or people who are part of a loose network whose goal is to reduce overconsumption, particularly in the developed nations, if we are to reduce pressures on resources and the global environment. Some call it a movement toward sustainable or ecological lifestyles, or a return to frugality, or simple living. Compiled by and available from:

New Road Map Foundation, P.O. Box 15981, Seattle, WA 98115 USA. US$10, postpaid.

Religions in the UK

Britain is now home to many different religious communities and traditions. The University of Derby's Religious Resource and Research Centre and the Inter Faith Network of the UK have produced this comprehensive and unified guide to Britain's major religious communities, their organizations and places of worship, as well as advice on how to make contact, guidance on visiting places of worship, and information on interfaith organizations, consultations, and initiatives.

Religious Resource and Research Center, University of Derby, Mickleover, Derby DE3 5GX,UK. £25 postpaid, pay to Univ. of Derby.

Who is Who in Service to the Earth

Second Edition 1993, edited by Hans Keller. Provides many "Visions of a Positive Future," plus very extensive listings of people, projects, and organizations, organized under each of those categories and by key word. The first edition has 530 pages, large format, and is full of detailed information. Databases for this directory and the related one, below, are also available on TogetherNet (see Chapter 44) and are more up to date than the books, which are published by:

VisionLink Education Foundation, 130 Biodome Dr., Waynesville, NC 28786 USA. $30. (plus $2. S&H)

Who is Who at the Earth Summit

Editor, categories, publisher and price same as above. Lists nearly all registrants at the 1992 Rio Earth Summit and Global Forum, including many NGOs, other organizations, and interested citizens.

RESOURCES FOR MULTI-RELIGIOUS EDUCATION
(Especially Elementary and Secondary)

Appreciating Differences: A Resource Manual

The first in a series designed to provide materials and exercises to help people become more aware of and more sensitive to their attitudes and beliefs about differences as well as the commonalities we share. In addition to overviews and instructions for each exercise, the manual includes assessment sheets, bibliographies, questions for discussion, and other resources. Appropriate for upper grades, high schools, college-age, and adult groups. (Spiral bound, large format, US$10.00)

Available from the National Conference Institute for Human Relations, 360 North Michigan Ave, Suite 1009, Chicago, IL 60601-3803 USA; tel. (312) 236-9272

Beliefs and Values Series

A set of four multi-religious education resource books for students and teachers, published by Christian Education Movement. Despite the focus implied in its name, CEM publishes excellent materials for religious education which, in the UK, includes education about the world's religions from a pluralistic perspective. Titles include:

- Caring Beliefs – Valued People; concerning relationships.
- Green Beliefs – Valued World; the environment.
- Consumer Beliefs – Valued Riches; wealth, work, leisure, and the spiritual.
- Human Beliefs – Personal Values; self, addiction, prejudice and disablement.

In addition, CEM's *British Journal of Religious Education* reports on various approaches used in European countries.

Christian Education Movement, Royal Building, Victoria St. Derby DE1 1GW, U.K.

CEM's curriculum materials are available in North America through **Multifaith Resources, PO Box 128, Wofford Heights, CA 93285-0128; tel./fax (619) 376-4691**

Facts on File

A world religions series which may be used with grades 5 through 12. Each volume treats the history, literature, beliefs, and practices of a major faith tradition.

460 Park Ave., S, New York, NY 10016 USA; tel. 800-322-8755

The Mysteries Sourcebook

Developed by Shelly Kessler and the Mysteries faculty of the Human Development Dept. of Crossroads School. A compendium of essays, curricula, and sample lesson plans (secondary level) which immerse the reader in the philosophy and methodology of the Mysteries program.

Crossroads School, 1714 21st St., Santa Monica, CA 90404

The Pluralism Project: World Religions in America

The Pluralism Project engages college students in studying the religious diversity of the US. The information gathered will be presented on an innovative interactive CD-ROM scheduled for distribution in January 1996 on both Macintosh and IBM Windows-compatible CD-ROM. (See also Pluralism Project in Chapter 42.)

Diana L. Eck, Project Director, Harvard University, Phillips Brooks House, Cambridge, MA 02138 USA; tel. (617) 495-5781 / fax. (617) 496-5798

Religion in Human Culture

Described by *Teaching Tolerance* as "the most comprehensive program available on world religions for secondary teachers," this flexible curriculum was developed by teachers and includes six units in a multi-media program ($320). Includes student readers, teacher guides, filmstrips, and blackline masters.

Curriculum Development Center, St. Louis Park Public Schools, Minneapolis, MN 55426 USA; tel. (612) 925-4300

Religion in the Curriculum

Religion in the Curriculum is a booklet reviewing issues surrounding the study of religions in public schools. See also, *Religion in American History: What to Teach and How.*

Association for Supervision and Curriculum, 1250 N. Pitt St., Alexandria, VA 22314 tel. (703) 549-9110

Religious Liberty Education Resources

Provides a substantial catalog of resources from many organizations, all providing information for teaching *about* religion and religious liberty in the schools. Categories include: Guidelines and Policies, Materials and Lessons, and Suggested Background Reading.

Americans United Research Foundation, 900 Silver Spring Avenue, Silver Spring, MD 20910-9807 USA; tel. (301) 588-2282 / fax (301) 495-9173

The Shap Working Party on World Religions in Education

The Shap Working Party on World Religions in Education is a group of people who are actively interested in all stages of education. Founded in 1969 at the Shap Wells Hotel, Cumbria, UK, it now has connections worldwide.

The Shap World Religions approach places the emphasis upon understanding the nature of religious beliefs and practices, and the importance which these have in the lives of believers. It is concerned with understanding what it means to be a Christian or Muslim, for example, in terms of beliefs, practices, values, and how each sees the world – what it means to take a religious commitment seriously. The case for a broad-based study of beliefs and values is grounded in the education which all children deserve, one which cherishes those aspects of life which make us human. Through such an education, children are enabled to understand their place in their community in local, national, and global terms, and to discover and aspire to reaching their full human potential in a mature democracy.

The annual Shap Journal, *World Religions in Education*, and the *Calendar of Religious Festivals* are two principal publications. Themes of journal issues include: Women in Religion (1988); Humankind and the Environment (1989); Religion and Story (1990/91); Religious Education and the Creative Arts (1991/92); Religion and Truth (1992/93). The most recent Shap book is:

Teaching World Religions

By Clive Erricker, with Alan Brown, Mary Hayward, Dilip Kadodwala, and Paul Williams (Heinemann, 1993). This handbook offers distinctive approaches to world religions in the classroom and an exploration of world views; includes detailed resource lists. The Shap Working Party produces other books as well. Details may be obtained from:

Alan Brown, The RE Centre, 23 Kensington Square, London W8 5HN UK; tel: 071 937 4241

For further information about the information services, contact:

Owen Cole, Shap Publicity Officer, WSIHE, College Lane, Chichester PO 19 4PE UK; tel. 0243 781 455

Teaching Tolerance

This excellent magazine for educators is published by the Southern Poverty Law Center. Among its regular features are lists of recommended resources. The Spring

1994 issue addressed the questions of religions and multi-religious education in the public schools of the USA.

Teaching Tolerance, 400 Washington Ave., Montgomery, AL 36104 fax. (205) 264-3121

World Interfaith Education Association

WIFEA (formerly World Interfaith Colleges Association) is part of a global network of societies working together for interfaith eduction. Presently, parallel organizations exist in India, Japan, the Philippines, Singapore, Tanzania, and the United Kingdom.

Marks McAvity, P.O. Box 7384 Station "D", Victoria, B.C. Canada V9B 5B7 tel./fax. (604) 360-1259

World Religions and Ecology

This series from Cassell, produced in association with the World Wildlife Fund, addresses the issues of the environment in the context of the five major religions. Each book examines the traditions and teachings relating to ecology, the lifestyles of the different faiths and their positive and negative effects on the environment, and the response of each religion to the current ecological crisis. Available from:

Schools Dept., Cassel plc, FREEPOST SW1 412, London WC2N 5BR, UK

Also available in North America from NACRE (see Ch. 42).

PERIODICALS ON ECUMENISM AND INTERFAITH DIALOGUE

Following is a partial list of publications that report on aspects of interfaith dialogue.

*Areopagus: A Living Encounter with Today's Religions,
Tao Feng Shang Christian Center
P.O. Box 33 Shantin, Hong Kong

Buddhist-Christian Studies
Society for Buddhist-Christian Studies
University of Hawaii
2840 Kolowalu St., Honolulu, HI 96822

Bulletin of the Pontifical Council for Inter-religious Dialogue,
Via Dell Erba I, Vatican City, Italy 00120

Ching Feng: A Journal on Christianity and Chinese Religion and Culture
6-F Kiu Kin Mansion, 566 Nathan Road
Kowloon, Hong Kong

Current Dialogue
Office on Inter-Religious Relations
World Council of Churches
150 Route de Ferney, P.O. Box 2100
CH1211 Geneva 2, Switzerland

Dialogue, Ecumenical Institute,
490/5 Havelock Road, Colombo - 6, Sri Lanka

Dialogue and Alliance
International Religious Foundation, Inc.
4 West 43rd Street, New York, NY 10036

Discernment: A Christian Journal of Inter-Religious Encounter
Churches' Commission for Britain and Ireland
Theology Office, Westminster College
Oxford, OX2 9AT, UK

The Ecumenical Review, Publications Office
World Council of Churches
150 Route de Ferney, P.O. Box 1200
CH-1211 Geneva 2, Switzerland

Japanese Religions
Christian Council of Japan,
Kordsumd - Shimotochiuri
Komikyo-ky, Kyoto-shi 602 Japan

Journal of Ecumenical Studies
Temple University 022-38
Philadelphia, PA 19122

The Journal of Religious Pluralism
Faculty of Religious Studies
McGill University, 3520 University St.
Montreal, Quebec H3A 2B2, Canada

Monastic Interreligious Dialogue Bulletin
North American Board for East-West Dialogue
Abbey of Gethsemani 3642 Monks Road
Trappist, KY 40051-6102

*Newsletter of the North American Interfaith Network, P.O. Box 128
Wofford Heights, CA 93285-0128

*World Faiths Encounter
2 Market St., Oxford, OX1 3EF, UK

*US residents are invited to subscribe to asterisked publications through:

**Multifaith Resources, P.O. Box 128
Wofford Heights, CA 93285
tel./fax (619) 376-4691**

This list is from *Interfaith Dialogue: An Annotated Bibliography*, compiled by John Berthrong, (available from Multifaith Resources – above)

VIDEO TAPES and some sources for videos

From Church World Services Film Library

Films for free loan or purchase from the relief, development, and refugee assistance arm of the 32 Christian denominational members of the National Council of Churches of Christ in the USA. Well over 100 audio-visual media reinforce educational efforts with children, teens, and adults, regarding hunger and development, poverty and economics, environment, faith in action, lifestyle choices, human rights, war and peacemaking. For more information, contact:

Church World Service, P.O. Box 968, Elkhart, IN 46515 USA; tel. (219) 264-3102 or 1-800-456-1310.

Faith in the First Person

This is a fine series of interviews of visionaries, religious leaders from many traditions, and Nobel and Templeton prize winners who were interviewed at the Parliament of the World's Religions. The Dalai Lama, Robert Muller, Charles Colson, Al Huang, Martin Marty, Rabbi Irving Greenburg, Robert C. Henderson, and Hans Küng are among the 26 world-faith leaders featured in one-on-one interviews hosted by Bettina Gray. The series was produced by Michael Tobias in conjuction with PBS for cable stations VISION TV (Canada) and the Faith and Values Channel (VISN/ACTS), with the support of the Presbyterian Church (USA) and the North American Interfaith Network.

The series can be purchased in its entirety or individually. Each program is approximately 25 minutes in length; the cost for one program on VHS is $44.00 (Canadian), which includes shipping, handling, and taxes.

Call (416) 368-3194 ex. 552. Discounts are available for multiple tape purchases.

From Hartley Film Foundation, Videos on World Religions

Many narrated by Huston Smith.
The Art of Meditation;
Hinduism and the Song of God;
Buddhism: The Path to Enlightenment;
Buddhism Comes to America;
Christian Mysticism and the Monastic Life;
The Way to Baba;
The Best of Alan Watts.
US$39.95 each.

**Multifaith Resources,
P.O. Box 128,
Wofford Heights, CA 93285-0128 USA.**

How to Find God: Mystics Explore the Path to God

Produced by Dr. Kirk Laman with Majestic Film & Video. This video addresses questions about the mystical and religious encounters that some people have with God. The footage provides personal and in-depth interviews that Dr. Laman held during the Parliament with Brother Wayne Teasdale, a Roman Catholic monk; Sister Jayanti, a nun from the Brahma Kumari World Spiritual University; Reverend Robert Thompson, a Baptist minister; Brother Anandamoy from the Self-Realization Fellowship; and Ma Bhagavati, a former Jewish housewife who now works with AIDS patients. 55 minutes; US$19.95 from:

Mosaic, Inc. 2801 N. Woodward, Suite LL120, Royal Oak, MI 48073 USA

The Interfaith Message of the Parliament of the World's Religions.

Directed and produced by Andre Porto. This video presents a fine montage of the speakers and topics, the music, symbols and dance, and the diverse participants at the Parliament; it also includes a dramatic reading of part of the declaration *Towards a Global Ethic* and other dramatic clips from the closing plenary session of the Parliament. It describes these as "all ways to find the common spiritual heart." US$25.

Also produced by Andre Porto is:
One Day for the Earth: World Religions at UNCED

Depicts the 12-hour interfaith vigil held in conjunction with the Global Forum at the United Nations Conference on Environment and Development Summit in Rio de Janeiro in 1992. Includes the context, the vigil, performances, interfaith meetings in tents, and presentations by religious leaders. Also includes the more recent Interfaith Vigil for Ethics in Government and the growing movement by the Rio Interfaith Network to eradicate hunger in Brazil. Created by Instituto de Estudos da Religiao in Brazil, produced by Andre Porto. US$25. Both documentaries are available from:

**InnerSong, 4095 Jackdaw St.,
San Diego, CA 92103 USA**

Live, The Dalai Lama in Chicago

Features the keynote speech to an audience of 30,000 in Grant Park, at the dramatic, public conclusion to the Parliament of the World's Religions.

Includes montages of the diverse and enthusiastic audience and chants by Tibetan monks. Available (for $20 plus $4.95 S/H) from:

Lioness Films, 1535 W. Estes Ave., 3rd Fl., Chicago, IL 60626 USA

Peace Like a River: The 1993 Parliament of the World's Religions

Shown nationwide on PBS, this remarkable film captures and dramatizes the Parliament's focus on the critical issues. Using both short and long excerpts from speeches and interviews, combined with clips highlighting contemporary political, ecological and social issues, this 55-minute video is also an excellent introduction to the interaction of religions with global issues. The video cassette was created by and is available (for $25 plus $5 S/H) from:

The Chicago Sunday Evening Club, 200 N. Michigan Ave, Suite 403, Chicago, IL 60601 tel. (312) 236-4483

From Temple of Understanding:

A series of television programs featuring multi-religious perspectives on current issues through interviews with outstanding religious leaders.

1. When Bad Things Happen to Good People; 2.Racial and Religious Violence; 3. Muslims, Jews, and Christians in the Middle East; 4. Religion and the Environment; 5.A Buddhist In Today's World; 6. A Profile of the Temple of Understanding; 7. Dream of the Earth; 8.Pilgrimage of Hope; 9. The Cathedral in a Multi-Faith World; 10. Judaism and Interfaith Dialogue; 11.Transition to a Global Society; 12. Global Responsibility; 13.Visions of Perfect Worlds; 14. The Art of Being Human.

T.o.U., c/o Cathedral of St. John the Divine, 1047 Amsterdam Avenue, New York, NY 10025 USA

Voices from the 1993 Parliament

Two 30-minute videos feature an introductory montage of music, chants, dances, and excerpts from featured speakers, interspersed among interviews with participants and leaders at the Parliament and interpretations of the living legacy of the centennial meeting. Produced and hosted for ABC-TV by Lydia Talbot. Parts I and II can be bought separately for $20 each, or together for $35 (VHS, postpaid) .

Greater Chicago Broadcast Ministries, 112 East Chestnut St., Chicago, IL 60611 USA

The Global Brain

Interfaith Networking on the Information Superhighway

Bruce Schuman

Creator of the on-line conference, The Bridge Across Consciousness, Schuman proposes that a mind-boggling variety of interreligious work and dialogue can now be done through Internet and the electronic resources available to its users.

*T*he explosive growth of the Internet, the world's largest computer network, offers unprecedented opportunities for the global interfaith community. Today, from any computer terminal in the world that is linked to this single "network of networks," it is possible to connect instantly with thousands of other computers, hundreds of thousands of essays, articles, and discussions, and many millions of other networkers. With estimates as high as 30 million users on the Internet, and new and astonishing technologies appearing every day, it is not only fascinating and increasingly exciting to join the global community of cyberspace pioneers, but it is becoming easier and considerably less expensive.

Through the RAIN computing network here in Santa Barbara, California, a community project put together by a local coalition of friends and businesses, I am now able to directly access a bottomless array of information resources, institutions, and people, all at high speed and extremely low cost. RAIN charges individual members only $10 per month for unlimited Internet connectivity. The result is that I am today limited only by my own personal capacity to handle and process information effectively.

My approach to "the net" has been largely through e-mail; since early 1993, I have operated a mailing list called The Bridge Across Consciousness (BRIDGE-L), a discussion forum for interfaith dialogue and the problems of religious knowledge. Such mailing lists are operated through a central computer which receives messages from individual subscribers, then broadcasts them to all subscribers. Across the Internet, there are literally thousands of such mailing lists, on every conceivable subject.

Cyberspace resources for the global electric mystic

*T*here are lists that cater to every facet of religion, and to every interest. There are lists for every sort and brand of religion, and every denomination. There are lists for scholars, and lists for believers, and lists for people who are both. Today, there is a growing community of religionists around the world who are convinced that the process of dialogue with "the other" is an essential aspect of the search for spiritual truth, and that the medium of Internet telecommunications is a forum for dialogue, par excellence.

For me, the most exciting new area is the "World Wide Web," or WWW, an emerging Internet technology that permits the instantaneous "hypertext" linkage of any system

anywhere on the Internet that is connected to the Web. By building a simple HTTP "Home Page," essentially a directory and an interface, I can create an archive that anyone on the Internet can instantly access and download. I can also create direct connections through my Home Page to files in any other system on the Internet which operates on this same protocol. Michael Strangelove, author of the well-known *Electric Mystic's Guide to the Internet,* describes the Internet as "one giant hard drive." The HTTP protocols of WWW make this vision a practical and instant reality. By building a network of connections with friends and correspondents, cyberspace pioneers are jointly creating a vast library of files and articles and projects, all interconnected through a single framework and instantly accessible, just as if they were stored on their own personal computers.

Through The Bridge Across Consciousness, we are joining this HTTP/WWW revolution, and have just completed the initial phase of our new ORIGIN web-server archive, which now contains the complete text of the 914-page *World Scripture: A Comparative Anthology of Sacred Texts*, edited by Andrew Wilson. Organized in terms of 164 themes, and emphasizing what the world's religions have in common, we see this book as a possible foundation for a 21st century global electronic ecumenism. To this archive we are adding a wide variety of linked articles and projects relating to interreligious affairs, universal religion, world theology, etc.

Another new project is the development of "The Internet Interfaith Consortium" which is a loosely associated group of networks, list owners, technologists, writers and archivists who are working together to coordinate and organize interfaith resources on the Internet. We are promoting dialogues, building new networks, gathering resources about the world's religions, and organizing them.

At the First Spiritual Summit Conference sponsored by the Temple of Understanding, Thomas Merton said, "We are already one, but imagine that we are not. What we have to recover is our original unity." Through the Bridge Across Consciousness mailing list and many other on-line media, there is coming together a growing group of visionaries, pioneers, and cybernaut explorers who are following a similar vision of Oneness. There is no doubt that the process of interfaith dialogue and reconciliation can be subtle and complex, and can involve the highest sort of philosophic sophistication. But at a basic level, the global interfaith community can be best understood as a group of friends who come together simply because they like each other and because they all just happen to be living on the same small planet.

The global electronic networks today can accommodate every religious interest, and every sort of project and design.

Network builders like myself are reaching out across the world, working to build a single integrated web that preserves both unity and diversity, in a sustainable context of Godliness and true goodness. And every day, we are employing new tools and making new friends. We invite you to join us as we seek to weave into oneness this "electronic antankharana."

For further information, contact the author by e-mail at origin@rain.org, or at PO Box 23346, Santa Barbara, CA 93121

A Guide to Selected Electronic and Internet Resources

The Association for Progressive Communications

The computer networks that make up the APC are a coalition of independent, non-governmental and mostly non-profit systems cooperating to provide networking and information-sharing tools worldwide. Sixteen inter-linked computer networks participate in the APC, including systems in the US, Brazil, Australia, Mexico, Slovenia, Russia, Ukraine, Nicaragua, the United Kingdom, and Canada. More than 30,000 NGOs, research institutes, UN agencies, and several governments are users of the APC nodes and regularly exchange information. Most users of the APC networks can connect to an APC host by making a local telephone call. For more information on the networks and how you can connect to one near you, send a message to apc-info @apc.org and an APC brochure will be sent automatically to your e-mailbox, or call ECONET at + 1 415 442 0220.

The Bridge Across Consciousness

Bruce Schuman is listowner of The Bridge Across Consciousness (BRIDGE-L) and a co-listowner of INTERREL

PO Box 23346, Santa Barbara, CA 93121 (origin@rain.org).

The Bridge Across Consciousness (BRIDGE-L) is an international electronic discussion forum for interreligious and ecumenical dialog, and the development of universal religious science. It operates over telephone lines through modem-linked microcomputers, from any place in the world that is connected to the Internet, the world's largest and fastest-growing computer network.

BRIDGE-L is operated as a mailing list, controlled through "Listserv" software, running on the "VM" computer system at U.C. Santa Barbara. This software receives written messages sent to BRIDGE-L, and distributes them to all members of the mailing list, doing this in a matter of minutes. In this way, all members of the list can conduct an ongoing discussion forum, from wherever they are in the world. The BRIDGE-L discussion group focuses on matters related to philosophical epistemology and intuitive analysis of the meaning of religious experience.

In addition to this outreach program, BRIDGE's online file archive, "The Online Cathedral," provides the complete text of the 914-page International Religious Foundation's *World Scripture: A Comparative Anthology of Sacred Texts.* Developed through the cooperation of 40 international scholars, *World Scripture* contains over 4,000 scriptural passages, from 268 sacred texts and 55 oral traditions, and is arranged around 165 themes. *A SourceBook for Earth's Community of Religions* will most likely be installed into the ORIGIN site on WWW, along with many other online dialogues, papers, and other resources. Look for http://rain.org/~origin/csb.html

Selected mailing lists

Compiled by Bruce Schuman

For anyone with access to a computer and modem, who wishes to participate, international interreligious dialogue can easily be established and maintained, 24 hours a day, through the Internet using forums such as BRIDGE-L or any of numerous other existing online discussion lists, some of which are listed below along with research and academic lists. The format of the listings below is:

NAME OF LIST, description, address to subscribe, subscription command:

- BRIDGE-L The Bridge Across Consciousness LISTSERV@UCSBVM.UCSB.EDU SUB BRIDGE-L Your Name
- ALEXANDRIA Western Esoteric Traditions majordomo@world.std.com Subscribe Alexandria
- DIFTX-L Dialogue of Different Christianities LISTSERV@YALEVM.CIS.YALE.EDU SUB DIFTX-L Your Name
- WISDOM-L The Wisdom Society MAJORDOMO@RAIN.ORG SUBSCRIBE WISDOM-L
- INTERREL Interreligious Dialogue Consortium (See more, below) LISTSERV@VM.TEMPLE.EDU SUB INTERREL Your Name
- ISTHMUS Roundtable Workgroup on Interfaith Dialogue LISTSERV@YALEVM.CIT.YALE.EDU SUB ISTHMUS Your Name (private list)
- HERMETICA Gnosticism, Western

Esotericism Hermes_owner@cofc.edu Private, apply by personal e-mail application
- MERTON-L Research on the Contemplative Life LISTSERV@BYRD.MU.WVNET.EDU SUB MERTON-L Your Name
- THEOSCI Science and Theology MXSERV@ALPHA.AUGUSTANA.EDU SUBSCRIBE THEOSCI Your name
- ECOTHEOL Ecological Theology MAILBASE@UK.AC.MAILBASE SUBSCRIBE ECOTHEOL Your Name

There are numerous other resources available as well as aids to finding them and assistance for doing such tasks as using the WorldWideWeb to locate files on remote systems. Here are a few places to start:

- The ORIGIN hypertext, linked archive address on WWW is http://rain.org/~origin. It contains _World Scripture_ and many other projects, connects to hundreds of resources through the "Bridge Mirror."
- *The Electric Mystic's Guide to the Internet,* by Michael Strangelove
- "Shortlist of Discussion Forums for Theologians", by Michael Fraser at gopher://delphi.dur.ac.uk/11/Academic/PT/Theology/Computing/Lists. It can also be retrieved via email (100K) by sending the following message to mailbase@mailbase.ac.uk: *send religion-all shortlist.txt.*

Finally, the November 1994 issue of Religious Studies News published by the American Academy of Religion (available in most seminary, college, or university libraries) includes an extensive article describing some of the procedures and listing useful tools and resources for researchers, students, and scholars.

ECUNET – Supporting Christian communities of faith via computer

What's available on ECUNET?

- ABNET, American Baptist Churches
- BRSNET, Black Religious Studies
- CIRCUITWRITER NETWORK, United Meth.
- COBWEB, Church of the Brethren
- DISCIPLENET, Christian Church, Disciples
- FISHNET, Catholics
- LUTHERLINK, ELCA
- MENNOLINK, Mennonites
- NAESNET, Ecumenical Staff
- NCC LINK, National Council of Churches
- PRESBYNET, Presbyterian Church (USA)
- QUAKERNET, Friends
- QUEST INTERNATIONAL, Anglican/Episc.
- UCCHRISTNET, United Church of Christ

- UCHUG, United Church of Canada; and others

ECUNET is home to thousands of conversations ("meetings") on a myriad of subjects that support ordained, lay, and denominational staff ministries, worship resources, youth ministry, music ministry, Bible study. New meetings open constantly as a timely response to religious, political, and social issues of the moment. The network also allows any user to create a meeting on any topic at any time, public or private, to share your questions and ideas, and get feedback and support. To take more advantage of ECUNET'S convenience, you can use Internet's "electronic mail" gateway to correspond with individuals or to send and receive files of almost any size.

Some of the meetings and services:

- NCC CWS DISASTER BULLETINS: Immediate access to Church World Service updates on disasters worldwide. Check it regularly to keep yourself, your congregation, youth group, and others informed and to find out what you can do to help global neighbors.
- DENOMINATIONAL NEWS
- REVIEWS: Reviews of current religious books, produced by Pilgrim Press and the Graduate Theological Union Bookstore in Berkeley, California. Reviews of the spiritual dimensions in current books, movies, TV programs, and spoken-word audios, prepared by *Values and Visions* magazine.
- SERMONSHOP & LECTIONARY: Weekly Bible, exegetical notes, themes, illustrations, and entire sermons.
- TIMELY DISCUSSIONS: Conversations on almost any subject – health care, AIDS, local and national elections, church policy feminist perspectives and much more.

Equipment needed:

A computer, preferably one with the flexible storage space of a hard disk, and a printer so that you can print ECUNET notes you want to save or distribute.

A modem allows your computer to transmit through the phone system. We recommend at least a 2,400 baud modem, but any speed from 300 to 14,400 bps will work. If you're using an MS-DOS (IBM compatible) machine, we recommend Convene software for your communications. It is an easy-to-use software package written expressly to work with the ECUNET system. ECUNET has negotiated a special price for this software package – $50.00. To order a trial copy, write Convene International at 591 Redwood Highway, Suite 2355, Mill Valley, CA 94941. You may also reach them by phone at (415) 380-0510, or by fax at (415) 380-0505. Alternatively, your denomination may provide a less expensive means of obtaining Convene. If you are using a Macintosh, various communication software packages work well, including Microphone 11 or

Termworks. Contact Online Service Company, at 1-800-733-2863, for more information.

GO NEWAGE – a "Virtual Family"

*SYSOP 76702,1766. Or write to GO NEW AGE, 7363 Arbol Dr., NE, Rockford, MI 49341

"Welcome to the dawning of of a New Age on Compuserve!" is the message greeting new users of this New Age Forum which draws a wide range of users, from New Thought Christians to free-spirited Techno Pagans. Discussion groups on all aspects of beliefs and practices, on-line rituals, theories of science and religions, questions and answers, data libraries, real-time conferences such as the Virtual Bar and Grille, and interviews are some of the resources available through this energetic community.

GO NEWAGE is found via Compuserve (Information Services, 5000 Arlington Centre Bovd, Columbus OH; call (614) 457-8600 for a free, introductory offer).

International Institute for Sustainable Development –

161 Portage Ave, East, Sixth Floor, Winnipeg, Manitoba e-mail:IISD!IISDPOST!JWAGEMAKER @iisdnet.attmail.com

Among its activities is the excellent service "Earth Negotiations Bulletin" (ENB), published both in print and electronically as a complete reporting and synthesizing service about international negotiations, conferences, and proceedings of the United Nations, NGOs and governments.

To access the "Earth Negotiations Bulletin," connect to the gopher at gopher.igc.apc.org (under *Environment* select from the 10 volumes). The ENB has also set up a World Wide Web Mosaic server on the Internet called *Linkages: A Multimedia Resource for Environment and Development Policy Makers*. To access the IISD WWW server you will need a direct Internet connection and either Mosaic or Linx software, and should point your WWW browser to: http://iisd.ca/linkages/

The United Nations Development Programme (UNDP) has placed issues of the ENB on its gopher, together with a variety of other relevant information. Access the UNDP gopher by connecting to: gopher.undp.org For all Commission on Sustainable Development materials, look under "ECOSOC" in the main menu.

Internet Interfaith Consortium

Bruce Schuman (origin@rain.org, facilitator, the Internet Interfaith Consortium)

The Internet Interfaith Consortium is a

loosely organized general association of friends and acquaintances, working together to promote an improved quality of dialogue on intercultural issues across the Internet. We are an ad hoc association of on-line networkers, list-owners, system developers, writers, poets, scholars, academics, and caring human beings interested in spirituality, the search for truth, and the spiritual welfare of humanity.

There are no by-laws, no rules, no structures, nothing to agree to – except the general proposition that cooperative communication on intercultural issues is useful and illuminating, and ought to be promoted wherever possible.

Members of this organization share no common religion, no common spiritual or ethical or moral agenda, no one single approach to philosophy, politics, networking, or spirituality. Instead, what is shared is a general sense of respect for "the other", with whom we desire to be friends and from whom we desire to learn, and a general instinct that by working cooperatively we can build a substantial pool of philosophic, spiritual, and scientific insights that can assist both individuals and entire cultures as we undergo the cultural transitions of our time. You are invited to join the IIC; let us know of your interest, and perhaps join one of our mailing lists if you can.

To join the IIC mailing list:

The IIC mailing list is operated as a "topic" on the BITNET-type INTERREL@vm.temple.edu mailing list. To subscribe to INTERREL, send the command (one line message with no subject):
SUB INTERREL Your Name (inserting your name) to LISTSERV@vm.temple.edu

This command subscribes you to all messages sent to INTERREL with no defined "topic". To join the IIC mailing list exclusively, add a second line to your subscription command so that it takes the form:
SUB INTERREL Your Name (insert your name) SET INTERREL TOPICS = IIC (subscribes you to IIC exclusively)
or in the second line:
SET INTERREL TOPICS = ALL (subscribes you to all INTERREL topics). To download a complete explanation of the use of "topics" on INTERREL, send the command:
GET INTERREL TOPICS INTERREL

Internet Interfaith Consortium Founding Members:

- Dr. Len Swidler, Listowner INTERREL@ and VATICAN2@vm.temple.edu
- Dr. Gary Mann, Listowner THEOLOGOS@ and THEOSCI@alpha.augustana.edu
- Dr. Ermel Stepp, Listowner MERTON-L@byrd.mu.wvnet.edu
- Dr. Andrew Wilsm, Editor *WORLD SCRIPTURE*

- Dr. "Zos Imos," Listowner HERMETICA
- Dr. Ingrid Shafer, Professor of Philosophy and Religion, USAO
- Dr. T. Matthew Ciolek, Listowner TAOISM-L@coombs.anu.edu.au
- Ramon Sender Barayan, Host, WELL.sf.ca.us Spirituality Conference
- Antony Dugdale, Listowner DIFTX-L@ and ISTHMUS@yalevm.cis.yale.edu
- Bruce Schuman, Listowner BRIDGE-L@@ucsbvm.ucsb.edu IIC web-site: http://rain.org/~origin/iic.html World Scripture_ Web-site: http://rain.org/~origin/ws.html

Jainism Information on E-mail, Internet, and by fax

Provided by Mahesh Varia and Pravin Shah of the JAIN BBS, Federation of Jaina, Jain Study Center of North Carolina, 401 Farmstead Drive, Cary, NC 27511. Contacts: Pravin Shah, 919-469-0956, Chair and Editor; Kanlesh Shah, 919-571-1077, System Manager; Parul Shah, 919-933-1907, E-Mail Bulletin.

There have been several exciting developments in the services offered by the JAIN BBS that makes it easy to receive information directly on your computer or by fax, via modem. E-mail bulletin service and Internet connections have also been established. Both services are available without charge. A fax subscription is also offered at a nominal cost.

Information on Jainism is now available directly on personal computers through the e-mail service. E-mail bulletins feature articles on the many facets of Jainism such as the life of Lord Mahavira, interpretation of the Namokar Mantra, introduction to Jain philosophy, and a tribute to the remarkable contributions of Sushil Muni. There are no subscription charges, but e-mail access is required; Bulletins are sent about every 2-3 weeks and will be discussing both introductory and in-depth topics on Jainism. It is hoped that the e-mail network can develop into a discussion group.

JAIN BBS database has also been installed in the Sunsite computer databases at the University of North Carolina at Chapel Hill. The JAIN BBS has been available since 1993 using a modem connection to 919-469-0207.

For Internet information: varia@med.unc.edu

For E-mail Bulletins: pshah@gibbs.oit.unc.edu

Journal of Buddhist Ethics

A new peer-reviewed electronic serial was made available to scholars of Buddhism and Buddhist ethics via the Internet in July 1994. For more information contact the editors at: jbe-ed@psu.edu

To subscribe, send a E-mail message to: listserv@psuvm (Bitnet) *or* listserv@psu.edu (Internet).

Leave the "subject" field blank. The body of the message should contain the following: sub jbe-1 (your full name).

TogetherNet – and the Together Foundation for Global Unity

130 South Willard St., Burlington, VT 05401 USA; tel. (802) 862-2030, fax (802) 862-1890, or e-mail: todd_tyrrell@together.org

TogetherNet is a user-friendly computer network that puts you in touch with people, projects, and organizations working in service to the Earth and its inhabitants. It enables you to easily exchange electronic mail with other TogetherNet subscribers as well as any of the millions of individuals connected to other systems on the global Internet. Resources from the world's information highways are compiled and posted on TogetherNet for use by not-for-profit programs and socially responsible businesses.

What do I need to access it?

TogetherNet is accessible to virtually any computer with a modem or direct Internet access. Each TogetherNet subscriber is presented with an easy-to-use, yet technologically sophisticated graphic-user interface for the Macintosh or Microsoft Windows operating systems. The graphical software enables subscribers to navigate the system through a simple point-and-click method whether accessing via modem or TCP/IP from the Internet. TogetherNet also has a menu-driven interface for subscribers accessing via any standard modem communications software or via telnet from the Internet.

Keeping up with the United Nations

TogetherNet works with the United Nations and other partners to provide timely and important UN information. The Together Foundation has a strong commitment to Agenda 21 and the Charter of the UN, so the Net works to compile, organize, and disseminate information related the UN's agencies and departments, and to provide comprehensive information about the UN process to UN constituents. TogetherNet provides access to communications services, technical support, trainings, and information services to the UN Secretariat staff located in New York and Geneva.

"TogetherNet gives us access to our own documents in a way that is easy and time-saving. TogetherNet frees us up to spend less time searching for information and more time actually using it in our responsibilities at the United Nations. In other words, it changes the ratios between search time and use time."

DR. NOEL BROWN, UNEP

What can I do with TogetherNet?

TogetherNet provides subscribers with vast information resources plus advanced search features to locate easily and quickly the information you require. TogetherNet is also an advanced yet easy-to-use communications tool. The system enables subscribers to create their own electronic mailing lists for distributing documents or news flashes efficiently, and provides powerful conferencing features which allow subscribers to share their knowledge with millions of others around the world on subjects such as political and human rights, global warming, socially responsible business, and environmental education.

What if I need help?

TogetherNet employs a full-time customer and technical support staff. A toll-free support number is available for TogetherNet subscribers between 9am and 5pm EST, Monday through Friday. There is also an online "TogetherNet Feedback" forum for questions from subscribers, which is monitored by support staff from Monday through Friday.

What else can you offer?

Private conferences and online database services are available to groups and organizations for additional charges based upon their size. Organizational consulting and training services are also available. Please contact TogetherNet for more information.

fees?

- Sign-up and software fee: $15.00
  Monthly account fee: $10.00
  Annual student account fee: $50.00
- Communications fees:
  800 number access – 1200-19200 baud, $8.00/hr
  SprintNet X.25 access – 1200-9600 baud, variable*

TogetherNet's 800 number is available in the United States and Caribbean US Territories to credit card customers and qualified commercial accounts only. Charges will be billed in six second increments. There are no communications fees billed by TogetherNet for access via telnet or TCP/EP over the Internet, or for access via direct dial to Burlington, VT; New York; Geneva, Switzerland; or Caracas, Venezuela. Communications fees for direct dial subscribers will be billed to you by your local or long distance service provider.

Moving through the CoNexus

Joel Beversluis

Action and Prayer

Righteous action among the people saves prayer from becoming an escape into self-satisfied piety.

Prayer saves righteous action among the people from self-righteousness.

Righteous action saves prayer from the hypocrisy among the pious which the children of this world will never fail to spot.

Prayer saves righteous action from the fanatical ideologizing through which those who are committed to change become bad representatives of their own commitment.

Righteous action saves prayer from pessimism. Prayer saves righteous action from resignation.

Action keeps prayer in the realm of reality; prayer keeps action within the realm of truth.
EBERHARD BETHGE,
Am gegebenen Ort

It is not difficult to hear God's call today in the world about us. It *is* difficult to do more than offer an emotional response, sorrow and regret. It is even more difficult to give up our comfort, break with old habits, let ourselves be moved by grace and change our life, be converted.

Prayer:

What is the point of your presence
if our lives do not alter?

Change our lives,
shatter our complacency.
Make your word flesh of our flesh,
blood of our blood,
and our life's purpose.
Take away the quietness of
a clear conscience.
Press us uncomfortably.
For only thus that other peace
is made, your peace.
DOM HELDER CAMARA,
The Desert is Fertile, pp.17 and 19

*T*his book offers numerous resources for our consideration and use – the perceptions and beliefs of the world's religions and spiritual traditions, insights into a global ethic, visions of a community of religions, strategies for good governance, the wisdom of indigenous voices, the dreams of children, the needs of future generations, and the hopeful programs of hundreds of service organizations. Taken together, these begin to reveal the glistening web that connects us to each other and to critical global concerns.

This *SourceBook* also presents evidence of the interconnectedness between the challenges we face and our underlying values and practices. Yet, when we map the connections from situations of crisis back into our homes and communities, this knowledge can cause us pain and frustration. We tend to assume that *our* society is basically generous and principled, that *our* values and *our* tribal and religious identifications are righteous.

The evidence, however, suggests that there is a chasm between our personal beliefs and the impact of our collective actions on the larger world. For example, we continue to buy bananas and coffee despite evidence that they are generally grown on plantations stolen from indigenous pcoplcs, that their production dumps toxic chemicals on the earth and into the water table, that the laborers who produce them work at unsustainable wages, have no land on which to grow basic foods, and, if they organize or protest, are persecuted by militia trained in the interests of "national security."

This book has also highlighted some of the questions that now are challenging traditional assumptions. Who is my neighbor? What are my personal responsibilities to the community? to the future? The answers to these venerable religious questions now have planetary implications. The desire for community, once expressed in tribal, national and religious allegiances, now encounters the global village. It is no small matter to become a community of religions or to pledge allegiance to the community of the Earth.

Other assumptions are also under assault. We can no longer pretend –

- that the creation and consumption of products is unqualified *progress;*
- that *the good life* we've worked for grants us the right to pursue and defend short-term interests at the expense of long-term values;
- that *other* people, religions, corporations, and governments must change, first.

We are learning how our lifestyles have been built on the intersections of business, national power, consumer demand and inadequate values. These intersections connect us to the world's problems and bring those issues into our homes and into our religious and civic communities.

Truth or consequences

*H*ow do we respond to challenges like these views of reality that diverge from the world we thought we knew? The issues seem to make unreasonable demands on us. It's certainly tempting to re-warm the American Dream, to retreat to comfort and entertainment, to beat the dangers back around the corner and out of sight, and to place our hopes in technology. However, old ways of thinking and technological fixes can't save us from ourselves. We need new models, new ways of perceiving the meaning of life.

Although it can be painful, we can begin to cut loose from dying assumptions, from inappropriate attachments, and from being overwhelmed by the issues. We can begin to live in ways that demonstrate that we do respect each other and honor the Earth, but to do that we must learn from traditions of meaning and spirituality far wiser than the toxic worldviews that inform modern cultures. We must find an alternative to our pursuit of industrial and commercial luxury – what Thomas Berry calls our "cultural pathology" – because too much of humanity is enticed to imitate us and because our lifestyles are neither sustainable nor ethical.

This liberation won't come cheap. We'll have to make commitments to specific values and concrete tasks. We'll need to nurture hope, act boldly, and watch for signs of grace. As we deal with failure – our own and that of others – and are tempted by apathy, we must trust in our commitments and in gradual but persistent transformations.

The CoNexus – ecology, governance, spirituality, and action

Along with the challenges, helpful concepts of ecology, governance, and spirituality are also swirling around us. Offering new approaches to the expression of our spiritual impulses, these transformative perceptions can illuminate our paths through the nexus of crises and opportunities. We can also derive hope from seeing that many others are already on this journey and that they, too, are attempting an appropriate analysis and response:

- Those who've worked on single-focus issues such as the environment are learning that most problems and solutions are tied to other issues.
- Religious leaders are connecting ecology, justice, peace, and spirituality.
- Workers are learning how their job losses are related to exploitation of fellow workers elsewhere.
- Neighborhood leaders describe how enormous military budgets affect homelessness, local investments, health care, and education.
- Hungry people and those who advocate for them realize that corporate profits and national policies also cause starvation.
- Freedom-loving people are experiencing the power of nonviolence.

Truth and reverence will carry us through

When we have seen the connections and want to begin to move through the nexus, we can do as Gandhi proposed: invite the truth-force to work in us. It requires a process of action and reflection, a series of steps that moves us toward personal and collective truths – if we don't short-change it. We must test all the spirits, including the "emerging global consciousness," to distinguish the highest spiritual values from fashion, personalities, and deception. The following insights may be used as a wholistic perceptual matrix to guide such an inquiry:

- *All the world's affairs are rooted in ecology:* human life, governance, culture, commerce, and religious institutions are all interconnected with the Earth.
- *All our choices are grounded in a spirituality:* our values and actions reflect the meanings we choose for our lives; our personal spirituality is revealed in our relationships with other life, the Earth, the cosmos, and the creative One.
- *Most of our actions are inevitably making political choices: this is where global governance begins;* we're always voting with our time or energy or money, even when we're apathetic or following cultural patterns.
- *There is no separate, neutral, or higher ground where religions and spiritual traditions may stand;* they either help or hinder the process of transformation.

Finally, *reverence and appreciation* for the beauty of the Earth, the interconnectedness of the cosmos, and the mysteries of the Source, provide the key perceptions and the strongest foundation for new ways of living. These qualities, combined with our responsiveness to the global matrix, point us through the nexus, toward what we seek.

On that sacred journey, we become *the CoNexus* – what we already are.

Toward a Global Spirituality

Dr. Patricia Mische

Authentic spirituality is awakening awareness and conscious attunement to the sacred source of life. At the deepest part of every and all being is the sacred. Spirituality is the process of ordering our life in intimate communion with this sacred center and source. Spirituality is not static. It is not a finished state we ever finally achieve and then hold onto. It is a process. It is a sacred journey.

...In a certain sense we each make this journey alone. No one else can make it for us. But in another sense we make this journey together, in communion with others. The whole planet with all its life forms and billions of people – indeed the whole cosmos – is on a collective journey. This is true in a physical sense as we hurtle through space. This is also true in a spiritual sense. There is a sacred source at our collective center from which all our separate journeys originate and in which we all find life and direction.

There is a flow between this collective Earth journey and our personal journeys. They cannot be separated....

True spirituality – the authentic religious journey – can never be an escape from life's problems. God, the sacred center at the source of all authentic spiritual journeys, must be met in the midst of life, not in escape from life. Today we live in a global age – an age of planetary exploration and communications and new global interdependencies. Our spiritual journey – our search for life in God – must be worked out now in a global context, in the midst of global crises and global community. Our spirituality must be a global spirituality.

from *Toward a Global Spirituality,*
a booklet published by Global Education Associates

Scriptures, Reflections and Prayers

A CHRISTIAN PROMISE

In the tender compassion of our God,
the dawn from heaven will break
upon us, to shine upon those who live
in darkness, under the shadow of death,
and to guide our feet into the way
of peace.

from the SONG OF ZECHARIAH;
Luke 1:78 & 79

A TAOIST TEACHING

I have three precious things which
I hold fast and prize. The first is
gentleness; the second is frugality;
the third is humility, which keeps me
from putting myself before others.
Be gentle, and you can be bold;
be frugal, and you can be liberal; avoid
putting yourself before others, and you
can become a leader of men. Gentleness
brings victory to him who attacks,
and safety to him who defends.
Those whom Heaven would save,
it fences round with gentleness.
The greatest conquerors are those who
overcome their enemies without strife.

LAO TSE

A MUSLIM SCRIPTURE

There is no kind of beast on earth,
nor fowl which flieth with its wings,
but the same is a people like unto you.
Unto their Lord shall they return....
God is the light of the heavens
and of the earth.

Hast thou not seen how all in the
heavens and in the earth uttereth the
praise of God?
The very birds as they spread their
wings? Every creature knoweth its
prayer and its praise.

THE QUR'AN

A BUDDHIST REFLECTION

Now under the loving kindness and
care of the Buddha, each believer of
religion in the world transcends the
differences of religion, race and
nationality, discards small differences
and unites in oneness to discuss
sincerely how to annihilate strife from
the earth, how to reconstruct a world
without arms, and how to build the
welfare and peace of mankind, so that
never-ending light and happiness can be
obtained for the world of the future.

May the Lord Buddha give His
loving kindness and blessing to us for
the realization of our prayers.

from "BUDDHIST PRAYERS"
in *Religion for Peace*, 1973, WCRP

A HINDU PRAYER

May the winds, the oceans,
the herbs, the nights and days,
the mother earth,
the father heaven,
all vegetation, the sun,
be all sweet to us.

Let us follow the path of goodness
for all times, like the sun and the moon
moving eternally in the sky.
Let us be charitable to one
another. Let us not kill or be
violent with one another.
Let us know and appreciate the points of
view of others. And let us unite.
May the God who is friendly,
benevolent, all-encompassing,
measurer of everything,
the sovereign, the lord of speech,
may He shower His blessings on us....
Oh Lord, remove my indiscretion
and arrogance; control my mind.
Put an end to the snare of endless
desires. Broaden the sphere of
compassion and help me to cross the
ocean of existence.

from "HINDU PRAYERS"
in *Religion for Peace*, 1973, WCRP

A JEWISH TEACHING

In that hour when the Egyptians
died in the Red Sea,
the ministers wished to sing the song of
praise before the Holy One,
but he rebuked them saying:

"My handiwork is drowning
in the sea; would you utter a song
before me in honor of that?"

from the *SANHEDRIN*

PEACE PRAYER

Adorable Presence!
Thou who art within and without,
above and below and all around;
Thou Who art interpenetrating
the very cells of our being –

Thou who art the Eye of our eyes,
the Ear of our ears,
the Heart of our hearts,
the Mind of our minds,
the Breath of our breaths,
the Life of our lives,
and the Soul of our souls.
Bless us Dear God,
to be aware of Thy Presence
Now and Here.
This is all that we ask of Thee:

May all be aware of Thy Presence in
the East and the West,
and the North and the South.
May Peace and Goodwill abide
among individuals as well as among
communities and nations.
This is our Earnest Prayer.
May Peace be unto All.
Om Shanti!   Peace!   Shalom!

SWAMI OMKAR,
offered by the Mission of Peace
Shanti Ashram, India, for the
1993 PARLIAMENT OF THE
WORLD'S RELIGIONS

ISLAMIC PRAYER

Oh God,
You are Peace.
From You comes Peace,
To You returns Peace.
Revive us with a salutation of Peace,
and lead us to your abode of Peace.

a saying from THE PROPHET,
used in daily prayer by Muslims

A JAIN (UNIVERSAL) PRAYER FOR PEACE

Lead me from Death to Life,
    from Falsehood to Truth.
Lead me from Despair to Hope,
    From Fear to Trust.
Lead me from Hate to Love,
    from War to Peace.
Let Peace fill our Heart,
    our World, our Universe.

               SATISH KUMAR

A SIKH PRAYER

May the kingdom of justice prevail!
May the believers be united in love!
May the hearts of the believers
be humble, high their wisdom,
and may they be guided in their
wisdom by the Lord.
O Khalsa, say "Wahiguru,
    Glory be to God!"
Entrust unto the Lord what thou
wishest to be accomplished.
The Lord will bring all matters
to fulfilment:
Know this as truth
evidenced by Himself.

               from "Sikh Prayers"
          in *Religion for Peace,* 1973, WCRP

A SHINTO PRAYER

O Most High, help to bring thy Light
into the darkened conditions of the
world! Be gracious to us thy humble
servants and bless us with illumination
as to that which is Divinely relevant to
the fulfilment of thy will!

    O Most High, inspire thy servants
throughout the world to further efforts
towards leading back thy children who
are led astray to the right way, and to
live and act on the faith of what has
been taught by the great founders of
the religions!

    Bless all spiritual leaders with thy
power and enable them to give help,
joy, comfort and reassurance to those
suffering, to whom they minister!

             from "Shinto Prayers"
       in *Religions for Peace,* 1973, WCRP

A CHRISTIAN PRAYER

Lord,
Make me an instrument of thy peace.

    Where there is hatred,
        Let me sow love.
    Where there is injury,
        Pardon.
    Where there is doubt,
        Faith.
    Where there is despair,
        Hope.
    Where there is darkness,
        Light.
    Where there is sadness,
        Joy.
O Divine Master,
Grant that I may not so much seek
    To be consoled,
    As to console;

Not so much to be understood,
    As to understand;
Not so much to be loved,
    As to love.
For it is in giving
    That we receive.
It is in pardoning
    That we are pardoned.
It is in dying
    That we awaken
    To eternal life.

          ST. FRANCIS OF ASSISI
               (1182–1226)

A NATIVE AMERICAN PRAYER

Let us know peace.
For as long as the moon shall rise,
For as long as the rivers shall flow,
For as long as the sun will shine,
For as long as the grass shall grow,
Let us know peace.

         A CHEYENNE INDIAN

A BAHÁ'Í TEACHING

When love is realized and the ideal
spiritual bonds unite the hearts of men,
the whole human race will be uplifted,
the world will continually grow more
spiritual and radiant, and the happiness
and tranquillity of mankind be
immeasurably increased. Warfare and
strife will be uprooted, disagreement
and dissension pass away, and
Universal Peace unite the nations and
peoples of the world. All mankind will
dwell together as one family, blend as
the waves of one sea, shine as stars of
one firmament, and appear as fruits of
the same tree.

    This is the happiness and felicity of
humankind. This is the illumination
of man, the glory eternal and life
everlasting; this is the divine bestowal.

               'ABDU'L-BAHA,
    The Promulgation of Universal Peace

A ZOROASTRIAN PRAYER

With bended knees,
with hands outstretched,
do I yearn for the effective expression
of the holy spirit working within me:
For this love and understanding,
truth and justice;
for wisdom to know the apparent from
the real that I might alleviate the
sufferings of men on earth. . . .

God is love, understanding,
wisdom and virtue.
Let us love one another,
let us practice mercy and forgiveness,
let us have peace,
born of fellow-feeling. . . .
Let my joy be of altruistic living,
of doing good to others.
Happiness is unto him
from who happiness proceeds
to any other human being.

RESPONSE:

We will practice what we profess.

            from the Avesta prayer
         in "Zoroastrian Prayers,"
      in *Religion for Peace,* 1973, WCRP

**PRAYER
FOR THE SACRED COMMUNITY**

O Blessed Source,
    eternal Lord of creation,
    sustainer of all worlds,
    you embrace the whole cosmos within yourself,
    for everything exists in you.
Let your winds come and breathe your everlasting Spirit in us.
Let us inhale your divine Spirit and be inspired.
Enlighten us in your truth.
Pour your grace into our hearts.
Wipe away our sin and all negativity.
Transform us into your Love,
    and let us radiate that Love to all others.
Inflame us with your unending life.
Dissolve our limited way of being.
Elevate us into your divine Life.
Give us your capacity to share that Life with everyone.
Shape us in your wisdom.
Grant us your joy and laughter.
Let us become that divine wisdom, sensitivity,
    laughter and joy for all beings.
Let us realize fully that we are members of that Sacred Community
    with all humankind, with other species,
    with nature and the entire cosmos.
Grant us a heart that can embrace them all in you.
Let us be in communion with you forever in the bliss of that Love:
    the Love that sustains all
    and transforms all
    into your Divine Radiance.

BROTHER WAYNE TEASDALE

Subject, Author, and Title Index

Nancy Freedom, A.S.I.

NOTES:
Please see the second index, on page 366, for organizations and resource centers annotated in Part Five and listed throughout the text.

Asian personal names may not be inverted since the family name comes first in many countries. If in doubt about which part of an Asian name to look under, please try both parts.

Honorific titles (Swami, Rev., Dom, Sri, Ven., Roshi, His Holiness, etc.) are omitted except where needed for clarification or if the person is widely known under title (e.g.Paul, St., or Paul VI, Pope; Dalai Lama, The).

There may be minimal variations in headings owing to inconsistencies and imprecision in nomenclature between the various contributions.

UN agencies are usually listed under UN by subject, not name, and UN documents are usually listed by title under UN.

budgets for children's welfare and environmental protection, vulnerability of, 261
Bugotu, Francis, 286
bureaucracy, 51
bureaucratism, avoiding, 155
Burger, Julian, 284
Burgess, Hayden, 37
burial remains on public display, 169
business, instrumental logic of, 28

Cairo Declaration on Population and Development, an Inter-religious statement, 230-2
Calvin, John, 22
Calvinism, 22, 23
Camara, Helder, 109, 175, 297, 301, 348
Cambodia, 16, 185
Campaign 1995, 185, 309
capitalism, 26
caring, lack of, as a threat to peace, 182
Caring for the Earth: A Strategy for Sustainable Living, 203
Carson, Rachel, 262
Casals, Pablo, 265
cash crops, 224
caste system, condemnation of, 74
Catechism of the Catholic Church, 282
Catholic Christian statement, 251
Catholic Church, 21
causality, 15
Ceric, Mustafa, 57
Ch'an. SEE Zen
challenges facing humanity, 11-12, 25, 42-3
    Theosophical view of, 83
    Zoroastrian view of, 92
challenges facing humanity, response to
    Baha'i, 12
    Christian, 25-6
    Hindu, 43-4
    Maitreya, 84
    Sikh, 74
    Zoroastrian view of, 92
challenges facing Japanese and Shinto, 71
challenge to support human rights, 218-21
change, four principles of, 32
Chang Tzu, 99
chanting, 89
    names of God, 47
chaos, order coming out of, 283
chaos and creativity, 97
character building, 236
Charge of the Goddess, The, 89
charity, 60
    religious, freedom to do, 168
    toward unfortunates, 68, 147
Charleston, Steve, 30
chastity, 63, 73, 127
chauvinism, sexual, 50
chemical dependency as drugs and pollution, 295
Chi Kung, 85, 86
child abuse, 135-6, 185
childbirth
    consequences of secular context, 231
    sacred context, 231
child deaths, 226, 256, 257, 261, 264

Children's Appeal: Don't Compromise Our Future, 255
Children's Defense Fund, voice for children who can't speak for themselves, 260, 310
children's ecology and poetry, 98-101, 245-6, 258-61, 264-5
children's rights, monitoring, 258
children's sabbaths, 260
children, 254-266
    basic education for all, 258
    basic needs, 254, 257, 258
    best interests of, guiding religious matters, 168
    cooperation of all agencies for well-being of, 258
    development, right to, 257
    female, equal treatment with male children, 258
    governments' and organizations' responsibilities to, 257
    health, 229, 257
    homeless, 264
    injustices and intolerance toward, 257, 258
    listening to, 259
    orphaned, 226
    powerful forces for positive change, 261
    powerless politically and financially, 255, 261
    preventive investment in, 260
    protecting from religious discrimination, 168
    protection, right to, 257
    recognizing rights of, 257
    religious and spiritual responsibilities toward, 258
    rights of, 254, 264
    right to social protection regardless of wedlock, 223
    right to special care and assistance, 223
    society's responsibility to, 257
    state of the world's, 254-6
    survival, right to, 257
    survival and health, 229
        dramatic, inexpensive improvements possible with health care, 257
    traumatized by war, 264
    unaccompanied, 226
    under five years old, statistics, 261
    vulnerability to malnutrition and contamination, 261
    vulnerability to rights violations, 264
    world summit for. SEE UN World Summit for Children
    SEE ALSO poor children
Children and the Earth, scriptures and reflections on, 262-3
Chinmoy, Shri, 190, 328
cholera, 240
Choosing our Future as Women, 267-9
chosen, 124
chosen people, 56
Christ, mystery of, 282, 283
Christ, as Sun Myung Moon, 87
Christian creeds, 19-20, 21, 22, 23
Christianity, 19-31
    contemporary world, 25-8
    denominations, 21-4
    ethical guidance in, 26-7
    exclusivism, 283
    historic structure, 283

origins and beliefs, 19-20
types of, 21-4
will no longer be a separate religion, 282, 283
Christianization in Africa, 163
Christian Peacemaker Teams, 173
Christian prayers, 207, 351
Christians
    conservative Right, militarism, 242
    environmental studies, 308
    interfaith relations, 20
    mainline churches peacemaking activism, 242
    statistics, 20
    weapons sale and war attitudes, 242
Christian Science, 24
Christian scriptures, 25, 29, 207, 262, 274, 275, 350
Christification of the Earth, 80
Chu Hsi, 35
Chung, Douglas K., 33-35, 85-6
Church of God and Saints of Christ, 30
Church of Jesus Christ of the Latter-Day Saints, 23, 24
Church of the Living God, 30
Church World Service, Office on Global Education, 224-5, 310
circle, symbology of, 30, 306
citizens' peace movements, 172, 174, 309. SEE disarmament
citizenship, global, 51, 177, 180
citizen well-being postponed or ignored, 183
citizen witnesses, 172
City of God, 47, 311
civic awareness and involvement, 299-300
civic literacy, global, 177
civic society, global, 180
civilization
    contemporary breakdown of old, 283
    doomed without spiritual rebirth, 271
    global, 99, 178, 180
    industrial-urban-technological, 166
    new, values of, 246
    new vision of, based on love and compassion, 171
    universal, 244
    with heart, 246
civilizations, spiritual core of, 178
civil liberties, 50
Civil Rights Movement, 29
civil rights struggle, nonviolent army for, 173
clarification of commonalities and differences, 120
Clarke, Geoff, 285
Clark, Francis, 108, 140
class antagonisms, 50
cleansing, ethnic, 134
clothing, right to, 223
Cobb, John, 28
co-creation, 96
co-creation with the Divine of Earth's future, 117
Co-Dependence of Origination, 271
Coffin, William Sloane, 144
coldheartedness, 235
Cold War, 176
    end of, 178, 185
    destabilizing effect, 238

collision course, humans and the natural world, 278
colonialism, 36, 176-7
    elimination of, 168, 182
    internal, 297, 301
    SEE ALSO Western imperialism
commercialism, 135
commitment, 304
common convictions, fundamental, needed for peace, 184
communalism, 24
communication, nonviolent, suggestions for implementing, 299
communications, religious, right to maintain, 169
communications systems, global, 51, 178
communion, 166
community, 56
    duties to, 223
    Earth, 7, 17-18
    and family concerns central, 163
    and morals, 93
    renewal of, 26
community building as grounding for campaigns for justice and freedom, 221
community life, strengthening to foster respect, 221
community of religions, 1, 5, 6, 93-174, 166, 246, 347. SEE ALSO sacred community
comparative religion, 82
comparing our ideals with our dialogue partner's ideals, not her practice, 157, 158
compassion, 62, 63, 233, 234, 235
    basis for new vision of civilization, 171
    developing for sufferers, 135
    failure to act when it dictates, 235
    and reason in politics, 175
competition, 99
    international, for foreign currency and markets, 183
    linear, 27
computer documentation for interfaith dialogue, 142
conception of life, religion fundamental to one's, 168
Concerning Acts of Initiative and Creation, 304
concourse, global, foci for, 105
concourse of religions, global, 104-6
CoNexus, 5-6, 119, 346
Conference on the World's Religions for the World's Children, 257
confessional political regimes, 182
confidential message-carrying between warring factions, 144
conflict prevention and resolution, 182, 237
conflict resolution, 12, 31, 58, 59, 85, 86
    peaceful, 134, 171, 258
    use by governments, 172
conflicts
    sanctified by religion, 172
    wholistic nature of, 172
Confucian Analects, 34
Confucianism, 33-5
    basic principles, 33-5

integration with Buddhism and Taoism, 35
Confucian texts, 33-34
Confucius, 33-4, 35, 99
connections, life-enhancing or deadly, 5-6
conscience, 147, 222, 235
right to freedom of, 223
Conscious Evolution: A Meta-Religio for the 21st Century, 79-81
consciousness, 78, 277
individual change of, needed to change the Earth, 136
the new, 282-3
reflexive, 96, 97
spatial mode of, 96
transformation of, individual and global, 136
unitive, going beyond dualistic awareness, 282
consensus among religions, 124
consensus eliminating inconvenient positions, 232
consequences of actions and omissions, 136
conservatism and organized religion, 124
conservatives, interfaith context hospitable to needed, 123
consideration and respect, mutual, instead of competition, 135
consubstantiation, 21
Consultation on the Environment and Jewish Life, 69
consumerism, 31, 146, 292
eliminating, 182, 323
consumption
lowering, 297
personal, matter of public concern, 296
principles of personal, integrating into policy, 185
of resources, 249
consumption floors and ceilings, 27
contemplation. SEE meditation
contempt for Creator by harming the Earth, 250
contingent genesis, 14
contraception, 229, 230
contradictions, integrating, 166
controversies, suitable solutions being found for, 136
Convention of the Elimination of All Forms of Discrimination Against Women, The, international treaty, 273
convergence of religions, 109
Convergence of Science, Religion and Values, 277
conversion of the heart, 136
conversion to another religion
as rejecting God, 219
right of, 219
convictions held in common, 132
cooperation, 37-8, 298
across ideological borders, 51
global, 235
Islamic imperative, 57
and peaceful co-existence, 271
cooperative action, strategies for, 182
cooperative planning for resource use, 51
cooptation, 163
co-prosperity, 71

Coptic Churches, 21
Corbiere, Eileen, 302
corporate
commitments to peace, 182
fascism, 166
power goals, 183
practices, unethical, tolerating, 296
corruption, 134, 182
cosmology, new, 79, 80
cosmology of religions, 95-8
Costa Rica, 247, 248
Council for a Parliament of the World's Religions. SEE CPWR
courage, 181, 294
courtesy and respect, interfaith, 157
covenant, God/humans, extended to science and politics, 141
covenant ethics, 25-6
Co-Workers in one Work Place, 272
CPWR
Ad-hoc international advisory committee, 22
approval of Toward a Global Ethic, 127-8
broadening base, 123
funding and infrastructure, 122-3
history, 125
key staff and trustees, 116
periodic parliaments and assemblies, 122
Projects 2000, with Millennium Institute, 122
proposed religious conflict resolution program, 122
regional chapters, 122
resources on, 335-7
restructuring, 121-2
United Religions Organization feasibility study, 122
Craft, the. SEE Wicca
creation
caring for, 69
for multiplication of love, 19
a sacred gift, 235
Creation-Centered Spirituality, 90, 213
creative action, 293-4
creative dissonance, 267
creative energy, 295
creative response at core of religions, 293
credit card debt, excessive, 296
Creme, Benjamin, 84
crime, 182
Crimes against Creation, 280
crimes against humanity, 185
criminality, exalting, 164
crisis, Chinese concept of, 184
critical issues, entangled, 125
critical issues and religion, encounter of, 125
Croatia, 181
crop choice, 225
cropland, 296
cross, the, symbology of, 26-7
cross-cultural worship, 30
cruel, inhuman or degrading treatment, freedom from, 222
Cultivating Stillness: A Taoist Manual for Transforming Body and Mind, 86
cultural expressions, 287, 288
cultural genocide. SEE genocide
cultural life, common, right to participate in, 223

culture
disintegration of, 295
as language of religions, 182
orienting as a whole towards peace, 181
Culture and Development, World Commission on, 1995, 2
Culture of Peace, 244-52
Contribution of Religions to a, 181-2
Contribution of Religions to a, 1993 UNESCO meeting, 181, 1994, Barcelona, 181-2
Declaration on the Role of Religion in the Promotion of a, 182
culture of peace, mass cooperation required, 181
cultures, intermingling of, 182
Curott, Phyllis W., 88
currency devaluation, 241
cycles, destructive and creative, 85

Dahm Afringan prayer, 252
Daily Word, 24
Dalai Lama, The, 16, 126, 171, 262
dancing, 9, 86
dancing and drinking parties, Muslim aversion to, 60
Daniels, David D., 29-30
Darby, John Nelson, 23
death, fear of, 38
death-squad targets, protection for, 173
debt, from loans to buy weapons, 240-1
debt crisis, second and third worlds, 134
debt relief, 26
debt and bankruptcy from overconsumption, 296
Decade for Women, 190
decentralization, 300
Declaration of a Global Ethic. SEE Towards a Global Ethic
Declaration of Human Responsibilities for Peace and Sustainable Development, 247-9
Declaration of Independence, 80
decolonization, 3
dedicated service. SEE selfless service
Deegale, Mahinda, 17-18
defenseless, the, respecting the rights of, 237
deforestation, 278
old-growth forests, 296
of Tibet, 171
deism, 48
Della Mirandello, Ficino and Pico, 80
demagogues, 110, 124
de Mallac, Guy, 298-300
democratization, failure of, 177
denouncing systems, beyond, 184
denuclearization, 185
depersonalization, 43
deprivation, 296
descendants, endless advance of, 70
desertification, causes of, 225
Desert is Fertile, 175, 301, 348
despair about state of world, 293-4
destiny, human and Earth, 118

detachment and simplicity, 146
development, 201-4, 233-8, 247-9, 311-12, 315, 328-30. SEE ALSO sustainable development
destructive, 261
development goals, universal, 202
Dhammapada, 250
dialogue, 107-8
in community, 303
forms and levels of, 107
not debate, 158
partners significantly identified with community being discussed, 158
religious, 182
willingness for, 100
dialogue organization, local
forming, 156
goals, 157
ideas for groups and programs, 156-7
Dictionary of Religious Education, 265-6
die and kill for religion, willingness to, 124
differences
accepting without convergence, 104
encouraging and honoring our, 259
religious, enriching, or cause of conflict, 149
dignity. SEE ALSO respect
dignity
individual, 49
rights indispensable for, 223
dignity and equality inherent in humans, 167, 222
dilemma, spiritual, 5
diplomacy
failures of, 172
preventive, 191
directions, four sacred, 30
disability, right to security in, 223
disagreement, points of, no assumptions about in dialogue, 159
disarmament, 130, 134, 182, 185, 240-3, 309, 313, 320
nuclear, duty of, 243
discovering what unites us, 109
discrimination
challenging, 298
elimination of all, 50
religious, affront to human dignity, 168
religious, eliminating, 167
disease, overcoming possible but may not be a priority, 256
disease as unreal, 24
diseases, children's, 226, 227
disenfranchisement, 287-8
dispensationalism, 23
displaced persons and peoples, 240, 287-8
dispossessed, the, 120
statement of their hopes for next Parliament, 288
voices of the, 284-92
disputed territory, 3
distasteful views, need for openness to others holding, 123
diversity, 182, 250
of indigenous peoples, 36
within a religious tradition, 89
Divine Edict of Amaterasu Omikami to Her Grandson, 70

A SOURCEBOOK FOR EARTH'S COMMUNITY OF RELIGIONS

extinction decisions, 117
extremes of wealth and poverty.
  SEE economic disparity
extremism, 107, 110
  growth in, 155

fair pay for dignified existence for
  self and family, right to, 223
fair public hearing by
  independent impartial tribunal,
  right to, 222
faith
  deepened by learning about
    others, 153
  with integrity, 157
  mystery of, 282
  as opening to Ultimate Reality,
    148
  reinterpreting, 25
faith traditions, role of the, 117-8
families, spiritual formation and
  education in, 258
Family, International Year of the,
  1994, 2
family
  all life as, 86
  central role of, 229
  Confucian regulation of, 34
  fragmentation, 164
  human, 175
    unity of, 249
  integrity of, 43
  moral education in, 164
  as nursery of peace, 182
  one, "in one house", 272
  protection by society and state,
    right to, 223
  religious life, parents' right to
    organize, 168
  responsible action in, 135
  strengthening, 182
  support, 258
familyhood, 298
family life, 136
Family of Abraham, 301
family planning, 44, 164, 229
  voluntary, 279
family prayer, 164
family unity, 11
famine, 226
fanaticism, 142
  distinguished from zeal, 182
  growth in, 155
fanaticism and intolerance,
  religious representatives
  preaching, 135
fanatics, pitying, 165
farmers, small, 225
fascism, corporate, 166
fasting, 60
fatalism, 54
fear, right to be free from, 222
feminine as Divine, 88
fertility regulation, 229, 230
festivals, Muslim, 55
feudalism, 301
Ficca, Dirk, 122
field and ground undivided
  unifying, 41
financial leaders, national,
  inexperienced at hunger, 225
fire, 91, 92
First, Second and Third Worlds,
  36
first peoples, 36-9
  attitudes of, 284-5
first peoples, texts, 37-9

first peoples. SEE ALSO
  indigenous peoples
Five County Cherokees
  Declaration, 285
Five Elements, 85
food, 224-7, 312-13
  right to, 223
  distribution uneven, 224-5, 227
  enough to feed everyone, 224
  exports, 241
  shortages, 226, 312
food corporations, giant, 225
Food First, 224-5, 312-13
food prices, poor Third World
  people unable to pay, 225
forces, new global economic and
  monetary, collaborative policies
  for, 183
forgiveness, 182
fossil fuels, conversion from, 280
founding a family, right of, 223
Four Noble Truths, 15
Fourth World, 36
Fox, Selena, 90
fragility of Earth and humans, 99
Francis of Assisi, St., 146, 351
Fravashi, 92
Free Churches, 22-3
Free Church of Brethren, 23
free movement worldwide, 12
free thought, 48
free will, 19, 23, 52, 81, 82
French, William, 27
Friends, Society of. SEE Quakers
frugality, 26, 296
fugitive peoples, voice of, 287-8
fundamentalisms, as response to
  pluralism and turmoil, 120
Fundamentalist Christian
  Churches, independent, 23
fundamentalist reactions to
  women in the forefront, 269
future, the, 283
  alternatives humans are
    considering for Earth, 117
  choosing our, 253
  common, vision of, 184
  secure and sustainable,
    preconditions for, 183
  viable human, 27, 184
Futurists, World Network of
  Religious, 334

Gaia: A New Look at Life, 212
Gaia and God, 27-8
Gaia Atlas of First Peoples: A
  Future for the Indigenous World,
  36, 38, 284-6
Gaia Hypothesis, 80, 212-4
Gaia myth, 212-4
Gandhi, 30, 146, 173, 298, 299,
  300
Gardner, Gerald, 89
Gathas of the Prophet, 91, 92
Gautama, Siddartha. SEE Buddha,
  The
gender differences, in religious
  experience and expression, 268
gender equality, 74, 279
  spiritual perspective on, 272
gender relations, 32, 229, 248
genders, partnership and
  submission between, 31
genetic engineering, 117, 130,
  292
genocide, 185
  by Christians of Pagans, 90
  cultural, 171

of Jews, 68
  of Kurds, 185
  of Muslims, 57
  of Tutsi people, 240
  SEE ALSO names of countries,
    such as Angola, Bosnia,
    Cambodia, El Salvador,
    Guatemala, Nicaragua, etc.
geography, sacred, 41
George, Dan, 284
Ghosananda, Maha, 129
Gilgamesh, 79
gleaning, 26
Global 2000 Revisited: What
  Shall We Do? excerpts, 117-8
global citizenship, 177, 180
Global CoNexus, The, 5-6
global consciousness, 3, 6, 349
global economy, 183
Global Education, 266
Global Education Associates, 176,
  183-4, 201, 313
  Earth Covenant, 201-2, 313
  Project Global 2000, 176-80, 313
  Religion and World Order
    Program, 176-80
global ethic, 124-38
  common, commitment to, 136
  shared, working toward, 180
  SEE Towards a Global Ethic
global forces, 183
Global Forum on Human
  Survival, 110, 151
global governance, reforms and
  alternative visions, 176-80, 193
Global Governance, Report of the
  Independent Commission on,
  1995, 2, 194
globalizing and pluralizing issues,
  298
Global Peace Service, 173, 174
global re-perception (inner work),
  294
Global Responsibility, 125
global scale crises and
  opportunities, 184
global society, 246
global spirituality
  essential elements of, 145-7
  toward a, 349
  SEE ALSO universal spirituality
global structures and systems, 180
global unity, 248
global village, statistics, 94
glossolalia (speaking in tongues),
  22
goal of human existence, 67
goals, four-fold, 41, 43
God's justice, 30
God's love, 30
God (Allah), 56-7
God. SEE ALSO Yahweh
God
  as ancestor, 9
  Buddhists having no concept of,
    17
  commandments, 66
  connection with world, 28
  existence of, 23
  as husband to earth, 9
  image of in persons, 30, 242
  incarnations of, 41
  as intelligence, 77
  love for all humanity, 68
  manifestations of, 42
  as Mother and/or Father, 40
  nature of, 19
  oneness of, 10

as parent, 9
  personal, 40
  references to in documents, 126
  as a relational being, 9
  supra-personal, 40
  ubiquitous, 2
  as Ultimate reality, 148
  universality of, 67
Goddess, The, 88
Goddess Spirituality, 90
God Is Dead theologies, 49
God-Love, 19
God-realization, spiritual paths to,
  41
Goethe, 304
Golden Rule, the, 104, 133
Golden Words of a Sufi Sheikh, 61
Gomez, Magdalena, 272
Gomez-Ibanez, Daniel, 124-130,
  143-4, 195-200
good, triumph over evil, 91, 92
good governance, religions and,
  176-85
good life, the, 49, 348
goodness, intrinsic, 234, 236, 238
Gospel, The, 31
governance, 176-185
  and ecological security, 201
government
  authority of, based on will of the
    people, 223
  opposition to religion, 149
  right to take part in one's
    country's, 223
government spending, 20 percent
  for basic human needs, 255
government/politics, nonviolent,
  suggestions for implementing,
  299-300
Graces, The, 271
Grand Rapids Interfaith Dialogue
  Association, 156-7
Granoff, Jonathan, 233
Grant, James P., 254-6
Grant, Joseph, 169
grassroots interfaith groups, 120
gratitude, 147, 148
Great Invocation, The, 77
Great Learning, The, 33
Great Mother, 89
greed, 134, 135, 166, 292
Green, James, 266
Greenspirit, 295
Gregorios, Paulos Mar, 104-6,
  165-6
Griffiths, Bede, 282-3
Grosso, Michael, 79
Group of Reflection, 233-7
Growing Up in Earthly Danger,
  261
Guatemala, oppression of
  indigenous population in, 147
Gulf War, 174, 242
gun control, US opposition to, 241
Gupta, Lina, 268
Guru Granth Sahib, 72-4
Gurus, 41, 45, 72
Gyatso, Tenzin. SEE Dalai Lama

hair, cutting, 73
Haiti, 226
  peacemaker teams in, 173-4
Hammarskjold, Dag, 3, 190, 271
happiness, 49
Hare Krishna Movement, 47
Harman, Willis W., 293-4
harmful religious practices or

A SOURCEBOOK FOR EARTH'S COMMUNITY OF RELIGIONS

human, value of, 185
as local, 221
long-term welfare of, 38
purpose in, 46, 298
purpose in. SEE ALSO meaning in human life
respect for all forms, 182
reverence for, 86
right to live, 222
sacredness of, traditional practices violating, 258
sacredness of all, 41, 88, 93
special character of each expression of, 248
stages, 41, 43
sustainable, ensuring, 249
unity of, 248
valuable, 59
life forms, all dependent on each other, 248
lifestyles, deteriorating quality of, 43
Limits to Growth, The, 94
limits, who or what will set, 296
Lion Dance, 86
listening, creative, 298
listening, profound, 100
liturgy, universe as primary, 97
liturgy based on cosmic transformations is needed, 97
livelihood, freedom from insecurity in lack of, 223
liveliness in religion, 9
living and dying for, what is worth, 302
living species, 278
living together justly and sustainably, 125
local action (outer work), 294
local and regional problem resolution, greater effectiveness of, 119
local initiatives, 180
longevity and health, 85
loss of lands and waters, 288
love, 11, 12, 233, 234, 235
as aim, 294
basis for new vision of civilization, 171
characteristic attitudes, 298
Christian, 29-30
civilization of, 303
as concern for all, 251
cultivation of, 49
dialogue of, 303
divine, 19
for fellow humans, 25
growing in by studying different religions, 303
growing in through collaborative work, 303
in interreligious dialogue, 303
law of, 298
as nonviolence, 246
practicing law of, 298
putting it where there is no love, 303
as real power, 259
responsibe action in, 135
stronger than violence, 298
unconditional, 243
universal, expressed thru UN, 237
universalizing, 298
love and compassion, 147, 303
Love and Devotion, Path of, 41
Lovelock, James, 80, 212-4
lowliness, 75

Luther, Martin, 21-2
anti-semitism and achievements, 170
Lutheran Church, 21
Lutheran-Jewish cooperation, 170
Lutherans and Judaism, new possibility, 170
Lutheran World Federation, 170
lying
artists and writers, 135
commandment against, 127
in mass media, 135
Lyons, Oren, 286

magic, 89
Mahavira, 63, 99
Mahayana Buddhism, 15-16
mailing lists, Internet, 355
Maitreya, the World Teacher, 77, 84
major weapons supplier, US, reasons for, 241
male interpretation and culture, privilege of, 274
malnutrition, 226
overcoming possible but may not be a priority, 256
Malraux, Andre, 3
manifest one's religion, right to, 168, 223
mantras, 40, 65
Mapuche Indian, 284
marriage, 136
forced, freedom from, 223
marriage and family law, discriminatory against women, 273
marrying as an adult, right of, unlimited by race, nationality or religion, 223
Mary, 19
masculine values as the norm, 267
mass media. SEE media
materialism, 24
breeding greed, 134
as disease, 295
mindless western, 38
reeducation from, 164
renunciation of, 130
material progress, erosion of, 238, 241
Matthiessen, Peter, 37
Mbon, Friday M., 268
McCloud, Aminah B., 60
McKinney, Cynthia, 242
Meadows, Donella H., 94
meaning, rebirth of penetrated by a new consciousness, 283
meaning in human existence, 25, 105, 270
media
breaking down exclusivist attitudes, 99
commitments to peace, 182
ignoring citizens' peace movements, 172
religions influencing, 164
mediation, conflict, 143, 313
medical care, right to, 223
medicine people, proper training of, 39
medicine person, 90
meditation, 73, 82, 235, 270
Path of, 41
practice of, 294
Theravadan or Tibetan, 18
Melasquez, Inti, 37
Mendez, Chico, 285

Mennonites, 23
peacemaking activism, 242
Merton, Thomas, 1, 356
Messiah, the, 23, 77, 87
Mestiza Legacy, 272
Metaman: the Merging of Humans and Machines into a Global Super-organism, 80-1
metaphysical traditions, 19th century, 24
Methodist (Wesleyan) churches, 22
Methodist Episcopal Church, 22
Metropolitan Assembly of Religious, Spiritual and Civic Leaders, 115-6
Metropolitan Interreligious Initiative (Chicago), 122
middle way, The, 14
militarism, 185
militaristic mindset, US, 241
militarization, costs to indigenous people, 285
military alliances, 175
military budgets, 51, 106, 237, 279, 298
military-industrial lobbyists, US, 241
military intervention, pursuing alternatives to, 298
military occupation, 181
millennium, preparing for next, 2-4
Millennium Institute, 117, 319-20
Miller, William, 23
mind and brain, 277
Ministries of Co-existence, creation of state, 236
minorities
contributions of, 59
protection and support for, 134
minority groups, greater participation of, 270
Mir Sada peace team effort in Bosnia, 174
Mische, Gerald F., 183-4
Mische, Patricia, 176-9, 349
misery, human, spirituality and religions alleviating, 139
misery, unconscionable level of, 234, 235
missionary journeys to the West, eastern religions, 119
mobility of peoples, 182
moderation and modesty, 135
modern problems and longstanding religious rules, 163
Mohawk, John, 286
molecular biology, 80
Monastic Interreligious Dialogue, 171, 320
monasticism, 24
monetary relationships, reconstruction of, 176
Mongella, Gertrude, 273, 274
Monophysites, 21
monotheism, 54, 72, 91
Moon, Hak Ja Han, 87
Moon, Sun Myung, 87
moon phases, 88
Moorish Science Temple, 30
Moorish Zionist Temple, 30
moral capacity, 145
moral equality, 50
moral pressure, 301
moral values, source of, 49
Moravian Church, 22

mosque at Ayodhya, destruction by Kar Sevak Hindus, 165, 166
Mother, Divine, God as the, 44
Mother, The, Mirra Alfassa, writings of, 78
mother, the Earth as, 30
motherhood, safe, 229
mothers, right to special care and assistance, 233
movement and residence in state, freedom of, 223
Moving through the CoNexus, 348-9
Muhaiyaddeen, M.R. Bawa, 61
Muhammad, the Prophet, 52, 53
Muller, Robert, 2-4, 139-40, 192, 263, 302
multi-religious movement. SEE interfaith movement
Musgrave Park, Australia, Declaration of People of, 286
Muslim
dress, 60
fundamentalists, 55
prayer, 210, 350
reflections, 210, 263
revivalist or reform movements, 55
scriptures, 52, 53, 56-7, 251, 350
texts, 53-4, 61
SEE ALSO Islamic
Muslim Minority Affairs, Institute of, 58
Muslims, 52, 53, 320
African American, 60
enacting religious obligations in American society, 60
Mutual Acceptance, Declaration of by the Community of Religions, 166
mutual benefit, 271
mutuality in dialogue, 158
mutual understanding, commitment to, 136
Myers, Norman, 95
mystical religion, discovery of, 283
mystical wisdom, tradition of, 283
mysticism, 282
in Buddhism, 35
Iranian, 79
Muslim, 55
women's writings, 267
mystics, 283
mystics or contemplatives, universal order of, 147
myths, 36
Babylonian, 79
Gaia, 212-4
Hindu, 43
hunger, 224-5
Japanese, 70
overconsumption, 297
refugee or flight, 288
utopian, 244-5
myths and symbols, interpretation of, 282

Nagarjuna, 15
Nairobi Forward-looking strategies for the Advancement of Women to the Year 2000, 273
Nanak, Guru, 72, 74
nanotechnology, 80
nationalism, 26, 50, 99, 106
in founding UN, 177
resurgence of, 242
nationality

spiritual dimension, missing, 3-4
spiritual dimension, need to be included forthrightly in UN documents and activities, 234
spiritual dialogue, 303
spiritual duty of religions, 4
spirituality, 38
   alternate, 287
   incorporating into daily lives, 271
   through practical action, 269
   relation to actual life, 145
   risk of receding tide of, 271
   transformative, 145, 347
   universal, 101
   world's affairs and our choices grounded in, 349
spiritual leaders' forum, 143
spiritual and moral values as goals and methods for social development, 234
spiritual philosophies, 76-84
spiritual practice
   disciplined, examples, 148
   importance of, 147
   and self-knowledge, 146
spiritual priorities and economics, 196
spiritual renewal, 133, 233
Spiritual Summit Conference, First, 356
Spiritual Traditions and Religions, Council of World, recommended UN Advisory Body, 236
spiritual visionaries, influence on world views and culture, 178
Spretnack, Charlene, 121
stable population growth, religions responsible for educating about, 231
Staffanson, Robert, 38
Stalin, Josef, 80
standard of living, 297, 348
standard of living for health and well-being, right to, 223
standards of behavior of religions worldwide, 127
Star Goddess, 89
Stassen, Harold, 139
State of the Environment, annual, 204
State of the World's Children, 1993, 254-6
State of the World in 2013, 139
statistics, global village, 94
STDs. SEE sexually transmitted diseases
stealing, vow against, 63
stealing, commandment against, 127
Steiner, Rudolf, 76
Stepping Stones to a Global Ethic, 125-6
stewardship, 69, 213
   great change in, required, 279
Stock, Gregory, 80-1
straightforwardness in interfaith conduct, 157
strangers. SEE hospitality
Strategy for Sustainable Living, 203
Strong, Maurice, 37, 202, 204, 312
Structural Adjustment Programs, 241
Study Guide for Interreligious Cooperation and Understanding, 149-55

Reflection and Discussion Questions, 150, 151-2, 153, 154, 155
sub-human living conditions in underdeveloped countries, 30
submission between genders, 31
subsidized weapons sales, 241
Sudan, 226
suffering, 15
   caused by perceived separation from ultimate reality, 148
   a collective problem, 236
   reality of, 164
sufficiency, 27
suffrage, right to universal and equal, 223
Sufi prayer, 199
Sufism, 55-6
Sufi texts, 61
suicide, 50
Sulkin, Howard, 121-2
Summa Theologica, 282
Sunnis, 55
supercomputers, 141
superiority, assumptions of inherent, 182
supernatural, evidence for existence of lacking, 49
survival
   human, 248
   human, global peace needed for, 134
   of nothing unless humans will it, 117
   of other life forms relative to human needs/wants, 118
survival skills, 100
sustainability
   culture of, toward, 175-85
   defined, 203
   intuitive knowledge of, 293
sustainable development, 37, 229, 248, 311-12, 315, 328-30
   not sustainable growth, 202
sustainable ecology, 27-8
sustainable economic and social life, 100
sustainable environments, 69, 136
sustainable future
   creating a, 297
   in global interdependence framework, 184
   partners toward a, 37
Sutcliffe, John M., 265-6
Suzuki, Shunryu, 17
Swedenborg, 24, 81
Swedish Evangelical churches, 22
Swidler, Leonard, 158-60
symbology, Hindu, 41
symbols, religious, relativity of, 109
symbols of Sikhs, wearing, 73
Symposium on Religion and Global Governance, 1994, 176
syncretism, 108, 151, 160
Syrian Churches, 21

TV, interfaith, 312, 331
Tai Chi, 86
Talmud, 67
tantras, 16
Tanzania, 240, 241
Tao (truth), 33, 34, 35, 85, 86
Taoism, 85-6
   integration with Buddhism and Confucianism, 35
Taoist reflections, 211
Taoist scripture, 86

Tao Te Ching, 85
teachers, animals and Earth as, 69
Teasdale, Wayne, 6, 99, 145-7, 166, 244-7, 350
technical arrogance, 283
technocracy, 234
technology, 48, 79
   consequences of use, 51
   prisoner of corporations and defense interests, 106
   setting limits to, 182
   SEE ALSO science
Tecumseh, 38
Teilhard de Chardin, Pierre, 80
Temple of Understanding, 328-9
   Spiritual Summit Conference VI, 147
Templeton, John, 283, 329
Templeton Prize, 326, 329
tension, areas of, 180
terrorism, 171, 182
thankfulness, to Creator, 38
thanks, duty to give, 147
theft for survival, 134
theological literature, official, little by or about women, 267
theological traditions, Christian, 27-8
Theosophical poetry and texts, 82-3
Theosophy, 82-3
Theotokos Project, 81
Theravada Buddhism, 16
Thich Nhat Hanh, 198-9
Thomas Aquinas, St., 282
thought, conscience and religion, right to freedom of, 168, 223
thoughts creating self and world, 250
Tibet, 16
   Resolution on, 171
Tibetan People, violation of their human rights, 171
Tiger, Buffaloe, 37
time
   cyclical (nonlinear), 97
   cyclical, 72
tolerance, commitment to, 135
torture, 134, 222
Towards a Global Ethic, 18, 101, 120, 181
   anthropocentrism in, 129
   coming from interreligious dialogue, 138
   context, 124
   critiques of, 129-30
   discussion focus and self-analysis standard, 120
   distribution, 122
   equal partnership between women and men in, 129
   explicitly interreligious consensus, 120
   future revisions, 130
   how drafted, 127
   how to read, 138
   no changes allowed at Parliament except title, 129
   nonviolence in, 129-30
   preliminary consensus, 138
   proclamation of existing agreements, 138
   recommendations, 136
   representing nothing new, 128
   as rules for living, 127
   silent on bio- and medical ethics, 130
   test for, 138

translations of, 138
   useful to non-religious persons, 120
   vagueness of term "sexual immorality" in, 129
Towards a Global Ethic (An Initial Declaration), text, 131-6.
   for all people whether religious or not, 131, 133, 136
   basis for global ethic in religious teachings, 131, 132
   condemnations and problems listed, 131, 132
   declarations, 131
   global ethic not an ideology or unified religion, 133
   initial signers, 137
   learnings, 132
   minimal consensus confirmed, 132
   principles, 132-6
   UN Universal Declaration of Human Rights confirmed and deepened, 132
Towards Deeper Values and Fuller Development: A Plea to the World Summit on Social Development, 234-7
Toynbee, Arnold, 178
Traditional Elders Circle, 39
Traer, Robert, 218-21
trance, 89
Transcendentalism, 23
transportation, worldwide, 51
transubstantiation, 21
trinitheism, 24
Trinity, 23, 24, 80
   Hindu, 41
trouble of community, sharing, 67
True Parents, 87
trust, 106
   building, on areas of agreement in dialogue, 159
trust, self, 259
truth
   multifaceted nature of, 63
   unarmed, 243
truthfulness, commitment to, 135
truthfulness and humaneness essential for justice, 135
truthful speech and actions, 63, 127

ultimate mystery, experience of, 148
Ultimate Reality
   nature of, 235
   one's place in, 270
   unlimited, ground of infinite potentiality and actualiztion, 148
ummah, 58-9
UN (United Nations)
   21st Century, Agenda for the, 1992, 2
   50th anniversary, 1995, 2, 121, 122, 139, 140, 186-94
   observance, 187-8
   religious communities and, 272, 309-10
   advantage of First World nations, in 174
   agencies, collaboration with religious institutions and networks, examples, 179
   charity and service projects, engaging religious communities in, 236
   Charter, 167, 168, 176, 218,

war
    alternatives to, 181
    ceremonial, 38
    civil, 240
    death statistic, 242
    incompatible with religion, 171
    from infringement of human
        rights, 167
    neither instinct nor any single
        motivation a cause of, 281
    killing children, 226
    making, not an inherited
        tendency, 281
    meaningless, 181
    obsolete, 51
    over oil, tolerating, 296
    prevention of, 176
    religions, contributions to, 182
    religious, 105, 124, 142, 162
    total, no concept in Islam, 59
    totally unacceptable, 171
    warning to humanity, scientists',
        278-9
    wastefulness, 225
Watch Tower, 23
water, 278
    groundwater depletion, 296
    loss of lands and waters, 288
    shortages, 226
wealth
    defined, 296
    equitable distribution of, 38, 51
    prestige from giving away, 38
wealthy food growers and
    distributors who have never felt
    hunger, 224
weapons, 85-6, 240-3
    arguments for selling, 241
    bought by developing countries
        for internal power struggles, 240
    leading supplier to developing
        countries, 241
    modern, proliferation in poor,
        developing nations, 240
    nations selling, 241
    of mass destruction, abolition of,
        185
    sales, US, pending legislation to
        curb, 242
    sales, US, statistics, 241
    sales profits, 241
    security without, 106
    trade, rising, efforts to stop, 241
    SEE ALSO disarmament
Weapons Proliferation in the
    Third World: How Many More
    Rwandas? 240-2
weather, 213
welfare of all, 300
    serving , 298
welfare of others, 74
welfare state, ideal, 34
We Shall Overcome, 291
Wesley, John, 22
Western Catholic. SEE Catholic
Western Christianity and
    civilization
    former aggression of, 105

organizing without dominating
    now, 105
Western imperialism, 230
what to do now, 293-303
what you wish done to yourself,
    do to others, 133
When a Child Sings, 259
White Hole in Time, 80
whole, the, larger welfare of, 246
whole-maker, 275
wholeness, potential present in
    everyone, 148
wholeness of religious and
    spiritual experience, 119
wholism, 3, 17, 30, 184, 277, 294
Wicca, 88-90, 311
Wiccan Spirituality, 90
Wiccan texts, 89
widowhood, right to security in,
    223
will to change, challenge of
    inspiring, 246
wisdom
    of world's religious and spiritual
        traditions, 6
    perfect, 14, 15
    theological tradition, 27
    worth of, the, 66-9
Witch, 90
Witchcraft. SEE Wicca
Witness for Peace, 172, 173,
woman abuse, 185
woman and man, dualism about
    in historical religions, 268
women's movement
    possibility of serious crisis for
        world's religions, 268
    worldwide, 267, 268
women's rights watch
    organizations, 273
women
    as minors, 275
    choosing how to participate in
        religious communities, 269
    choosing their future, 267-9
    discrimination, Korea, 270
    domination of, reordering, 27
    emancipation of, 11
    empowerment in religious
        communities, 267, 310
    empowerment of, 229
    Fourth World Conference on,
        1995, 2, 190
    governance and decision
        making, 258, 331
    health, 229
    helping each other, examples,
        275
    higher education, 270
    history of, 276
    individual identities, 270
    Jesus' identification with, 29
    life-affirming activities,
        examples, 275-6
    NGOs and caucuses, 190, 331
    obstacles to advancement of, 273
    oppression of, 232, 319
        examples, 274-5

women, continued
    reinterpreting neglected religious
        elements, 267
    religions marginalizing, 232
    religious leaders, 232
    religious scholars, 267
    reproductive decisions, control
        over their, 279
    self-assertion, examples, 275-6
    solving their own problems, 46
    supporting to help children, 258
    UN international conferences
        and conventions, 269, 273-6
    violence against, 273
    worldwide personal
        experiences, 274-6
women speaking out, 267-76
Won Buddhist community,
    gender equality in, 270-1
wonder, 49, 262
Wong, Eva, 86
Worlds's Religions for the
    World's Children. Declaration,
    257-8
work and just working conditions,
    right to, 223
working hours, right to reasonable
    limitation on, 223
working less, 297
World's Parliament of Religions,
    1893, 2, 24, 46, 57
    attendees and faiths represented,
        150
    beginning of interfaith
        movement, 150
    centennial observations, 108
    history, 124
    responses to, 102-3
World Bank and International
    Monetary Fund, 185, 241
world community, 50-1
World Conference on Religion
    and Peace, 71, 152, 270, 332
World Congress of Faiths, 51,
    149, 333
World Council of Religions. SEE
    URO
World Day of Prayer for Peace,
    109, 313, 334
world federal system, 12, 50
World House, The, 250-2
world law, 50-1
world order, 176-80
    bipolar, 176
    holistic, 178
    not sustainable long term, 293
    and religion, 176-9
    a religious concern, 179
World Peace Conference, 1999, 2
world religions, permanent forum
    for, 246-7
World Religions Conference, 7th,
    Declaration of, 191
World Scientists' Warning to
    Humanity, 278-9
World Scripture: A Comparative
    Anthology of Sacred Texts, 355
world structures needed for next
    century, 176-7

World Teacher, 77
World Trade Organization, birth
    of, 1995, 2
world, unmanageable, 293
world views
    of each culture, 182
    tolerance of all spiritually
        informed, 236
World Wide Church of God, 23
WorldWideWeb, 355
WSSD (World Summit on Social
    Development), 139, 233-9
    A Plea to the, 233-7
    core issues, 238-9
    Draft Programme of Action, 271
    major objectives, 239
    participants, 239
    reasons for, 238-9
    religion's role in, 271-2

Yahweh, 23, 170
Yang and Yin, 33, 34, 85
Year of Interreligious
    Understanding and Cooperation,
    1993, 109, 121, 123, 149, 155
Yellow Emperor, Huang-Ti, 85
Yin and Yang, 33, 34, 85
yoga, 45
    eight limbs of, 45
    five approaches, 45
    in preventive medicine, 44
    scriptures, 45
Yoga in the West, 45
Yogananda, Paramahansa, 47, 191
Yoga-Sutras, 45
Yoruba chant, 9
Young, Brigham, 24
youth
    interfaith meetings, 154, 255
    questioning religion, 154
youth learning
    justice and moral framework, 255
    multi-religious education, 339-40
    positive sexuality, 136
    truthfulness, 135

Yugoslavia, former, 172, 227

Zaire, 226, 240
Zarathushtra (Zoroaster), 91
Zen, 17, 33, 35
Zero Population Growth, 232
Zoroaster, 79, 91, 99
Zoroastrianism, 91-2
    contemporary, 92
    contributions to western
        thought, 92
Zoroastrian prayers, 91, 92, 252,
    351
Zoroastrian thought, interchange
    with Judaeo-Christian thought, 92
Zulu traditional religion of
    Southern Africa, 8

Index of Service Organizations and Resource Centers

A SOURCEBOOK   3 4711 00093 1966   GIONS